The Golden Peaches of Samarkand

The Golden Peaches

University of California Press

# of Samarkand

A STUDY OF T'ANG EXOTICS

by Edward H. Schafer

Berkeley   Los Angeles   London

Dedicated to the memory of *Berthold Laufer*

University of California Press
Berkeley and Los Angeles, California

University of California Press Ltd.
London, England

©1963 by The Regents of the University of California
Library of Congress Catalog Card Number: 63-8922

First Paperback Printing 1985
ISBN 0-520-05462-8

Designed by Theo Jung

Printed in the United States of America

08   07   06   05   04   03   02   01
11   10   9   8   7   6   5   4   3

The paper used in this publication meets the minimum
requirements of ANSI/NISO Z39.48-1992 (R 1997)
(*Permanence of Paper*). ∞

Preface

IN THE FIRST chapter of this book there is much that is not my own. I have relied heavily on the work of American, European, Chinese, and Japanese students of T'ang civilization. In later chapters the reader will find rather more of my original labors, though I have tried to conceal most of the impedimenta of scholarship and criticism in the notes at the end of the book. Even in the later chapters, however, I stand on many learned shoulders. I am most grateful for the assistance of my colleagues, living and dead, in these necessary acrobatics, but above all to the peerless Berthold Laufer, to whom this book is unavoidably dedicated.

Much of the work which produced this book was made possible by a research grant from the American Council of Learned Societies, and I am most grateful to them. Particular thanks are due Dr. Joseph Needham, who generously allowed me to use his library of books and articles on the history of science and technology at Gonville and Caius College, Cambridge.

Translations of poetry are my own, unless otherwise stated; Mr. Arthur Waley is the second most common contributor. The epigraphs to chapters i and ii are from the Revised Standard Version of the Bible.

E. H. S.

Berkeley, California
February, 1962

Acknowledgments

Quotations: Verses from Arthur Waley's poems, "The Prisoner" and "The People of Tao-chou," which appeared in *170 Chinese Poems* and in *Translations from the Chinese,* are quoted with the permission of George Allen & Unwin, Ltd., and of Alfred A. Knopf, Inc., respectively. The poem "Foreign Fashions," given in its entirety, is reproduced with the kind permission of Mr. Arthur Waley.

Plates: Plates II, III, IX, and X are reproduced with the permission of the Joint Administration of National Palace and Central Museums, Taichung; V, VII, VIII, XI, XIII, and XIV, with the permission of the Trustees of the British Museum; IV and VI, with the kind permission of Irene Vongehr Vincent, from her book *The Sacred Oasis* (Chicago: University of Chicago Press, 1953); plate XII, most kindly supplied by Dr. Richard E. Fuller, President and Director of the Seattle Art Museum; XV, from Cheng Chen-to, *Wei-ta-ti i-shu ch'uan-t'ung t'u-lu* (Shanghai, 1951–1952); XVI, with the permission of the India Office Library. All art objects shown are of the T'ang period.

The decorations at the beginning of each chapter were redrawn from T'ang textile and ceramic designs and other pictorial elements.

Contents

Contents

List of Plates

Dates at Which Chinese Dynasties Began

ca.	1500 B.C.	SHANG
ca.	1000	CHOU
	221	CH'IN
	206	HAN
A.D.	220	Three Kingdoms
	265	CHIN (TSIN)
	317	Northern and Southern Dynasties
	589	SUI
	618	T'ANG
	907	Five Dynasties (North)
		Ten Kingdoms (South)
	960	SUNG
		LIAO (Khitan) and CHIN (KIN) (Jurchen) in North
	1260	YÜAN (Mongol)
	1368	MING
	1644	CH'ING (Manchu)

Year of Accession of the Rulers of T'ang

You cannot think what figs
My teeth have met in,
What melons icy-cold
Piled on a dish of gold
Too huge for me to hold,
What peaches with a velvet nap,
Pellucid grapes without one seed . . .
       —Christina Rossetti, *Goblin Market*

Introduction

THE CHARM of exotic goods is potent in our own times. Any American magazine will provide dozens of examples: perfume from France—"the love fragrance"; shoes from Belgium—". . . shoe artisans for over three hundred years"; automobiles from Sweden—"symbol of superb Swedish engineering and craftsmanship"; sherry from Spain—". . . tastes exactly the same as in Queen Victoria's reign"; recorders from Switzerland—". . . made of the choicest Swiss pear, maple, cherry"; gin from England—"a closely guarded recipe and age-old skill . . ."; teak flooring from Siam— "quality untouched by time"; after-shave lotion from the Virgin Islands—". . . captures the cool, cool freshness of true West Indian limes in handsome, native-wrought packages"; macadamia nuts from Hawaii—". . . all the fabled richness of the Islands." Not to mention Scotch whisky, German cameras, Danish silverware, Italian sandals, Indian madras, Indonesian pepper, Chinese damasks, and Mexican tequila. We may want these magical wares because we do not have anything like them at home or because someone has persuaded us that they are better than our home-grown goods, or, most of all, because they come to us from enchanted lands, whose images are divorced in our minds from the assumed "realities" of practical diplomacy, trade balances, and war. Their real life is in the bright world of the imagination, where we take our true holidays.

This book's title, *The Golden Peaches of Samarkand,* was chosen because it suggests simultaneously the Golden Apples of the Hesperides, the Peaches of Immortality placed by Chinese tradition in the distant West, James Elroy Flecker's *Golden Journey to Samarkand,* and Frederick Delius' music for the "Golden Road to Samarkand" in Flecker's play *Hassan.* Despite these allusions to myth and music, the golden peaches actually existed. Twice in the seventh century, the kingdom of Samarkand sent formal gifts of fancy yellow peaches to the Chinese court. "They were as large as goose eggs, and as their color was like gold they were also called 'The Golden Peaches.' "[1] Some specimens of the trees which bore this royal fruit were brought by the ambassadorial caravan all the way across the deserts of Serindia, and transplanted into the palace orchards in Ch'ang-an. But what kind of fruit they may have been, and how they may have tasted, cannot now be guessed. They are made glamorous by mystery, and symbolize all the exotic things longed for and the unknown things hoped for by the people of the T'ang empire.

How T'ang China contributed her arts and manners to her neighbors of the medieval Far East, especially to Japan, Korea, Turkestan, Tibet, and Annam, is a rather well-known story. To mention the arts of xylography, city planning, costume design, and versification is only to hint at the magnitude of the cultural debt which these peripheral countries owed to T'ang. We are also familiar with the material goods sought by foreigners in China or taken abroad by the Chinese themselves: luxuries like silk textiles, wine, ceramics, metalwork, and medicines, as well as such minor dainties as peaches, honey, and pine nuts,[2] and, of course, the instruments of civilization, great books and fine paintings.[3]

China also played the role of cultural go-between, transmitting the arts of the countries of the West to those of the East, through such agents as the Buddhist Tao-hsüan, who went to Japan in 735 with the returning ambassador Tajihino Mabito Hironari, accompanied by an Indian brahman, a Cham musician, and a Persian physician.[4] The contributions to T'ang culture itself which were made by these aliens who thronged the great Chinese cities have been the subject of much study. The influence of Indian religion and astronomy, of Persian textile patterns and metalcraft, of Tocharian music and dancing, of Turkish costume and custom, are only a small part of a stupendous total.

The *material* imports of T'ang are not so well known, and it is these which form the subject matter of this book. The horses, leather goods, furs, and weapons of the North, the ivory, rare woods, drugs, and aromatics of the South, the textiles, gem stones, industrial minerals, and dancing girls of the West[5]—the Chinese of T'ang, especially those of the eighth century, developed an appetite for such things as these and could afford to pay for them.

Even with this emphasis the book will not provide any useful statistics on medieval trade nor propose any fascinating theory about the tribute system. It is intended as a humanistic essay, however material its subject matter. There is no paradox or mystery in finding what is most human through what is most corporal and palpable. "The past," wrote Proust (in Scott Moncrieff's translation) in his "Overture" to *Swann's Way,* "is hidden somewhere outside the realm, beyond the reach of intellect, in some material object (in the sensation which that material object will give us) which we do not suspect." A cockatoo from Celebes, a puppy from Samarkand, a strange book from Magadha, a strong drug from Champapura—each took hold of the Chinese imagination in a different way, altered the pattern of T'ang life, and was ultimately embodied in a poem, an edict, a short story, or a memorial to the throne. In some one of these literary forms the exotic object found a new and extended life and became, in time, even after its physical death, a kind of ideal image. It achieved a Platonic reality that it had lacked when it first arrived at the frontiers of China destitute of mental clothing, having lost on the way most of what it had once possessed in its native land. So, whatever it may have exemplified in the Sunda Isles, the cockatoo became a visible symbol of wisdom, the puppy gladdened childish hearts in stories and pictures, the sutra astonished students seeing its abominable script for the first time, and the medicine gave a new flavor to the wine in which it was mixed, and became an ingredient in the drink of a connoisseur.

It is for the same reason that this book is named *The Golden Peaches of Samarkand*. Though they once had some kind of "real" existence, these fruits have become partly enigmatic entities, whose only true life is literary and metaphorical. In short, they belong to the mental world even more than to the physical world.

In the remarks which follow, I have tried to explain conceptions and names which are important in the book but may not be obvious to the nonspecialist.

Poetry

In translations of poems and fragments of poems, I have preferred to err on the side of faithfulness to the language of the original, even at the risk of obscurity when trying to preserve strange images, rather than to use paraphrase for the sake of poetic grace or a familiar image.

Old Pronunciations

In giving the medieval names of non-Chinese persons, places, and things, I have usually used a hypothetical but reliable reconstruction based on the work of Bernhard Karlgren, even though the diacritics and phonetic symbols make awkward reading—but sometimes I have arbitrarily simplified them. These reconstructions are prefixed by an asterisk. It is important to remember that a *-t* at the end of a syllable in medieval Chinese often represented a foreign *-r* or *-l*, and hence "myrrh" is **muət*. The conventional "Mandarin" pronunciation (that is, standard modern Chinese) used by many writers gives little or no idea of the phonetic shape of these old loan words. To follow this unfortunate custom would be like calling C. Julius Caesar "C. J. Czar." For instance, the Old Cambodian name for a pre-Cambodian nation on the Gulf of Siam is *Bnam*, "Mountain," since the kings of that country were conceived to be godlike beings reigning on the summit of the holy world-mountain.[6] Thus the modern "Pnom" of Pnom-Penh. In T'ang times this name was transcribed as **B'iu-nâm*, but we will hardly recognize it in Modern Chinese *Fu-nan*.

Archaeology

The names "Tun-huang" and "Shōsōin" appear frequently in these pages. They are the chief repositories of T'ang artifacts. Tun-huang is a frontier town in Kansu Province, officially called Sha-*chou* in T'ang times, where a hidden library was discovered early in this century. Large numbers of medieval manuscripts and scroll paintings were taken from this treasure to the British Museum by Sir Aurel Stein, and to the Bibliothèque Nationale by Professor Paul Pelliot, where they may now be studied. The Shōsōin is a medieval storehouse attached to the temple called Tōdaiji in Nara, near Kyoto, Japan. It contains rich objects of every sort from all over Asia, but especially, it seems, from T'ang China. Some Japanese scholars regard them, or some of them, as native products; in any case, they are usually congruent with known T'ang work, and at worst can be styled "pseudo-T'ang."

"Ancient" and "Medieval"

In reference to China, "medieval" here refers to approximately the same time interval as it does in Europe; "ancient" is almost synonymous with "classical" in my usage, denoting especially the Han dynasty, along with the last part of the Chou. "Archaic" refers to Shang and early Chou. Unfortunately, the traditions of Chinese philology require that "Ancient Chinese" refer to the pronunciation of T'ang and what I call "medieval China," and "Archaic Chinese" to the language of what I call "ancient China" or "classical China." *Muət*, "myrrh," is "Ancient Chinese," as we in the profession say, but it is a *medieval* form, used in T'ang. I have tried to avoid these linguistic expressions.

Hsüan Tsung

If we disregard the "tone" of *Hsüan,* two T'ang monarchs had this posthumous title, by which they are known in history. By far the better known of the two had a long and famous reign in the eighth century. He is also sometimes called Ming Huang ("Luminous Illustrious"). Both he and his "Precious Consort," the Lady Yang (Kuei-fei) are frequently mentioned in this book. The other Hsüan Tsung enjoys much less fame, though he was a good ruler in difficult times in the ninth century. To distinguish him, I have given his title as Hsüan[1] Tsung.

Rokhshan

The traditional but very real villain of the age of Hsüan Tsung is now generally known by the "Mandarin" transcription of his name, which was not Chinese. This modernized form is "An Lu-shan." I shall always call him Rokhshan, following the reconstruction of his true name by Professor E. G. Pulleyblank. He was "Rokhshan" to his contemporaries; our "Roxana," of Persian origin, is a closely related name.

Hu Barbarians

In T'ang times, persons and goods from many foreign countries were styled *hu.* In ancient times, this epithet had been applied mostly to China's Northern neighbors, but in medieval times, including T'ang, it applied chiefly to Westerners, and especially to Iranians, though sometimes also to Indians, Arabs, and Romans. A Sanskrit equivalent was *sulï*, from *Šūliķa*, in turn from **Suyδiķ* "Sogdian" broadened to "Iranian." [7] I have often translated it badly as "Western" or "Westerner."

Man *Barbarians*

Man was a name for non-Chinese peoples on the southern frontier of T'ang and also of aboriginal enclaves in Chinese territory. It was also given to certain specific Indochinese tribes, now difficult to identify.

Lingnan

The great southern province of Lingnan corresponded fairly exactly to the modern provinces of Kwangtung and Kwangsi. I use the name freely.

Annam

Annam meant "Secured South" or "Pacified South," a rather imperialistic term given to a T'ang "protectorate" in Tongking, or Northern Vietnam, immediately south of Lingnan and north of Champa.

Chinrap

The Cambodian nation which absorbed Bnam (Fu-nan) was named Chen-la (in modern "Mandarin" pronunciation), whose etymology was ingeniously explained by Professor Pelliot as *Chinrap, "The Chinese Vanquished," like the modern town Siemreap, "The Siamese Vanquished." [8]

Qočo

The great T'ang garrison at Turfan was officially styled Hsi-*chou,* "Island of the West," and to many peoples it was Činančkänt, the "City of the Chinese." [9] The Chinese themselves called it Kao-ch'ang, which became Qočo locally. I have generally used the last of these forms.

Serindia

The immense area between T'ang and Transoxania is variously known as "Chinese Turkestan," "Eastern Turkestan," "Tarim Basin," "Central Asia," and "Sinkiang." I call it "Serindia," using the name given it by Sir Aurel Stein.

Rome

The men of T'ang knew something of the Eastern Roman empire, which they called by a corrupt version of "Rome," derived from some Oriental tongue in a form like "Hrom." I have used this, and sometimes "Rūm," and sometimes "Rome." The modern pronunciation of the old transcription is "Fu-lin." This is so different from the T'ang version that I have not used it at all, despite the sanction of custom.

Chou

The T'ang empire was divided into practical administrative units called *chou,* much like our counties. *Chou* means "land bounded by water," hence "island," "continent." An important myth told how the hero Yü drained the flood waters from the Chinese lands and marked out the nine primitive *chou,* raised places on which men could live. These were the first counties. The word *chou* continued to be used in this way for areas of varying size for many centuries. We might translate it "island-province," or even just "island"; this will not surprise an Englishman, for whom the "Isle of Ely" is comparable to "Essex County" and "Cambridgeshire." "Île de France" is also comparable. But I have usually given such forms as Ch'u-*chou* and Lung-*chou* instead of "Isle of Ch'u" and "Isle of Lung."

Szu

Traditionally, the first Buddhist establishment in China, in Han times, was housed in a government office building, called a *szu.* Therefore all Buddhist monasteries and religious foundations ("temples," if we understand this word to include many buildings, galleries, and gardens in a large complex) were called "offices." I have translated *szu* as "office" or "temple-office" or "office-temple." Some government offices were still called *szu* in T'ang.

Plants

Identifications of plants in this book are based primarily on the following works: G. A. Stuart, *Chinese Materia Medica: Vegetable Kingdom* (1911); B. E. Read, *Chinese Medicinal Plants from the Pen Ts'ao Kang Mu A.D. 1596* (1936); and I. H. Burkhill, *A Dictionary of the Economic Products of the Malay Peninsula* (1935).

6

Your riches, your wares, your merchandise,
Your mariners and your pilots . . .
When your wares came from the seas,
You satisfied many peoples;
With your abundant wealth and merchandise
You enriched the kings of the earth.

Ezekiel 27:27–33

1=The Glory of T'ang

HISTORICAL MATTERS

THE TALE is of the T'ang empire, ruled by dynasts of the Li family, famous throughout Asia in the Middle Ages, and still famous retrospectively in the Far East. Let us look at it hurriedly. The three centuries of the empire's formal existence were not all alike: we must distinguish them somehow, and fashion a chronological skeleton on which to hang the flesh of our story, acknowledging readily that the framework is arbitrary, taking too much account of what is radically changed, and too little of what remains the same, or is changed only subtly. Fortunately, since we care chiefly about commerce and the arts, we can make easy divisions, roughly according to century. These fit the facts not too badly.

The seventh century was the century of conquest and settlement. First the Li family subverted the Chinese state of Sui and destroyed equally ambitious rivals, then subjugated the Eastern Turks in what is now Mongolia, the kingdoms of Koguryŏ and Paekche in what are now Manchuria and Korea, and finally the Western Turks, suzerains of the ancient city-states of Serindia, that is, of Chinese Turkestan.[1] Chinese garrisons in these regions made possible the steady flow of their men and goods onto the sacred soil. For the most part it was a century of low prices and of economic stabilization, made possible by the distribution of plots of farm land to the peasants and by the institution of a firm new tax system, the famous triple system of grain tax paid by each adult male, family tax in silk cloth or in linen woven by the women of the household (with a portion of silk floss or hemp), and *corvée*, a period of service at public works, again by the men of the family.[2] It was an age of movement, when settlers migrated in great numbers into what are now central and south China, as lands of new opportunity and possible fortune—but also to escape conscription, floods, and barbarian invasions in these underdeveloped areas.[3] It was an age of social change, in which the new provincial gentlemen from the south were established in positions of political power *via* the official examination system, at the expense of the old aristocracy of the north with its traditional ties to Turkish culture. This revolution reached its climax with the reign of the Empress Wu and her transitory empire of Chou in the last decades of the seventh century.[4] It was an age when Indian culture made great inroads, when Buddhist philosophy, accompanied by the Indian arts of astronomy, mathematics, medicine, and philology, permeated the higher levels of Chinese life. It was an age, finally, when a taste for all sorts of foreign luxuries and wonders began to spread from the court outward among city dwellers generally.

The eighth century includes the "Fullness of T'ang" of the literary critics (Tu Fu, Li Po, and Wang Wei), extending until about 765, and also most of "Middle T'ang," a period of slow recovery from many disasters, running until the second decade of the ninth century, and culminating in a real revival of literature (Han Yü, Po Chü-i, and Liu Tsung-yüan).[5] Great changes took place after mid-century, and truly the century can be divided into equal halves, the first climactic and magnificent, the second convalescent and eccentric. The first of these halves, the "Fullness of T'ang," corresponds to the glorious reign of Hsüan Tsung, a long epoch of wealth, safety, and low prices, when "there was no costly thing in the Subcelestial Realm," [6] when one could ". . . visit Ching or Hsiang in the South, go to T'ai-yüan or Fan-yang in the North, or go to Szu-ch'uan or Liang-fu in the West, and everywhere there were shops and emporiums for supplying merchant travelers. Though they should go as far as several thousand *li*, they need not carry even an inch-long blade." [7] Mules and horses were available to travelers on these secure roads,[8] and an intricate system of canals devised to provide water transport for tax silks from the mouth of the Yangtze River to the capital was now so improved that it could also be used to bring luxury goods from foreign countries.[9] Fine highways and waterways fostered overseas trade, but so did a change in the taste of the young sovereign Hsüan Tsung, who, at the beginning of his reign had an immense pile of precious metals, stones, and fabrics burned on the palace grounds to signalize his contempt for such expensive trifles. But a few years later, seduced by the tales of wealth from abroad accumulating in Canton, the emperor began to relish expensive imports, and to watch jealously over the condition of foreign trade.[10] The old natural economy, under which pieces of taffeta were the normal measure of value and could be used for the purchase of anything from a camel to an acre of

8

land,[11] creaked and finally gave way, in 731, to an officially recognized money economy, the result of unprecedented prosperity, especially at commercial centers like Yang-*chou* and Canton.[12] Cash was the oil of commerce, and its acceptance was a boon to the rising merchant class. It was inevitable that the tax system of the seventh century should be superseded: in 780 the new "Double Tax" reform went into effect, replacing the taxes in kind and labor with a semiannual tax payable in cash. This change too was in response to the developing money economy, and the merchant class was vastly encouraged by it.[13] The new world of finance represented not only the heyday of businessmen and entrepreneurs but also the collapse of the independent farmers, and the disappearance of the little fields granted them at the foundation of the dynasty. Therefore, beyond its midpoint, the century was an age of landless men and hapless tenants replacing free farmers and set against wealthy landowners and great manors. This was the result of war, the *corvée,* and the weight of taxes.[14]

The reign of Hsüan Tsung had been a time of triumph for the new literary class, exemplified by the phenomenal career of the statesman Chang Chiu-ling, a native of the tropical south, an enemy of soldiers and aristocratic politicians, a friend of southerners and merchants. But in the same reign came the final triumph of the privileged classes, with the dictatorship of Li Lin-fu, supported by the monarch's hopes for a strong administration.[15] On his death, the dictator's client, Rokhshan "the Bright," [16] encouraged by families of "pure" Chinese blood in Hopei, set himself against a new upstart government, and led his veterans from the northeastern frontier into the valley of the Yellow River, and the loot of the two capitals.[17] So the second half of the century was also an age of decline and death, and enormous reduction of population.[18] It was a century too of change on the frontiers: warriors of the new state of Nan-chao (later Yünnan Province) straddled the direct western route to Burma and India, and would not give up their independence. The Uighur Turks rose to power on the northwestern frontier in mid-century as haughty friends and rivals of the Chinese. In Manchuria the burgeoning race of Khitans (not a great menace for two centuries to come) sapped the strength of the Chinese garrisons. The Tibetans harassed the trade routes to the West, until put down by the great general Kao Hsien-chih, of Korean origin. But in 751 this hero saw his armies in turn dissolve under the onslaughts of the Abbāsid hosts by the Talas River. Then the Muslims took control in Central Asia, and indeed they began to appear in every quarter: Arab troops aided the government in the suppression of Rokhshan the Bright, and (contrariwise) Arab pirates were involved in the sack of Canton a few years later.[19] It was a century of tolerated foreign faiths, when Buddhists of every sort, Nestorians of Syrian origin, and Manichaeans of Uighur nationality performed their mysteries and chanted their prayers in their own holy places, protected by the government within the cities of China.

The cultural and economic resurrection following the harrying of the north by the well-beloved Rokhshan lasted into the first two decades of the ninth century. That century begins, for our purposes, about 820, and ends with the obliteration of the dynasty in 917. The period of deflation following the promulgation of the Double Tax law was followed by an era of gradually rising prices, beginning in the third decade of this unhappy century. Natural calamities, such as droughts and plagues of locusts, along with disasters of human origin, led to a scarcity of essential goods and costly imports alike, and to universal suffering.[20] Most fatal of the human disasters of this century was the rebellion of Huang Ch'ao, who ravaged the whole country in the seventies and eighties, but was especially calamitous in his massacre of the foreign merchants in Canton in 879, thus doing serious injury to trade and cutting off the revenues derived from it.[21] It was an age of shrinking Chinese authority among erstwhile tributary and client states, and of the appearance of new rivals, such as the men of Nan-chao, invaders now of the ancient Chinese protectorate in Vietnam,[22] and the Kirghiz, conquerors of the powerful and sophisticated Uighurs. The decline of the Uighurs left their religion, Manichaeism, defenseless in China, and in 845 it suffered with Buddhism during the great persecution of foreign faiths, aimed at the secularization of the clerical classes for tax purposes, and at the conversion of a multitude of holy bronze images into copper coins.[23] These economic motives could only be effective in a generation of fear and attendant xenophobia.[24] It was also a century when the power of the state was fatally weakened by centrifugal forces. The headquarters of great provincial warlords became royal courts in miniature, and finally, in the tenth century, the house of Li and its great state of T'ang disappeared.

FOREIGNERS IN T'ANG

Into this wonderful land, during these three kaleidoscopic centuries, came the natives of almost every nation of Asia, some curious, some ambitious, some mercenary, some because they were obliged to come. But the three most important kinds of visitors were the envoys, the clerics, and the merchants, representing the great interests of politicis, religion, and commerce. Greatest among the envoys was Pērōz, son of King Yazdgard III and scion of the Sāsānids, a poor client of the Chinese sovereign in the seventh century.[25] But there were many lesser emissaries, like him soliciting favors to the advantage of the dynasties, rising or declining, which they represented. There were Indian Buddhists in abundance, but also Persian priests of varying faith: the Magus for whom the Mazdean temple in Ch'ang-an was rebuilt in 631; the Nestorian honored by the erection of a church in 638; the Manichaean who proposed his outlandish doctrines to the court in 694.[26] Turkish princelings pondered the ways of gem dealers from Oman; Japanese pilgrims stared in wonder at Sogdian caravaneers. Indeed, hardly any imaginable combination of nationality and profession was absent. All these travelers brought exotic wares into China, either as sovereign gifts or as salable goods, or simply as appendages to their persons. In return, some found glory there, as the Sogdian merchant who was designated Protector of Annam.[27] Some found riches, as the Jewish merchant of Oman who brought back a vase of black porcelain, gold-lidded, in it ". . . a golden fish, with ruby eyes, garnished with musk of the finest quality. The contents of the vase was worth fifty thousand *dinars.*"[28] Some came, possibly more humbly, in search of wisdom, as did the aristocratic Tibetan youths sent by their fathers for reliable interpretations of the Chinese classics.[29]

Ships and Sea Routes

There were two ways to China: overland by caravan, overseas by argosy. Great ships plied the Indian Ocean and the China Seas, carrying eager Westerners to the glittering Orient. In the north, the art and trade of navigation was chiefly in the hands of the Koreans, especially after the destruction of the kingdoms of Paekche and Koguryŏ by Silla during the 660's. Then ambassadors, priests, and merchants from the victorious state, and refugees from the vanquished nations too, came in quantity.[30] The Korean vessels usually coasted around the northern edge of the Yellow Sea, and made port on the Shantung Peninsula. This was also the normal route of ships from Japan, setting sail from Hizen, at least until the end of the seventh century, when Japan and Silla became enemies.[31] In the eighth century the Japanese were forced to come across the open sea from Nagasaki, avoiding Silla, heading for the mouth of the Huai or of the Yangtze River or even for Hang-*chou* Bay.[32] But in the ninth century, to avoid these voyages, which had proved exceedingly dangerous, Japanese pilgrims and emissaries preferred to take better navigated Korean ships and come via Shantung to the mouth of the Huai, or even to risk Chinese ships, which made land further south in Chekiang and Fukien, instead of at Yang-*chou.*[33] Though the ships of Silla dominated these waters, merchant vessels of the Manchurian state of P'o-hai, culturally dependent on T'ang, also navigated them,[34] and there were government inns for the accommodation of the ambassadors of P'o-hai, as well as those of Silla, at Teng-*chou* in Shantung.[35] But the Koreans were in the majority; indeed, they formed a significant alien group on Chinese soil, living in large wards in the towns of Ch'u-*chou* and Lien-shui, on the system of canals between the Yangtze and the Yellow rivers, enjoying, like other foreigners, some extraterritorial rights.[36]

But most of China's overseas trade was through the South China Sea and the Indian Ocean, and it was governed by the periodic shifts of the monsoon. Ships outbound from Canton sailed before the northeast monsoon, leaving in late autumn or winter.[37] The northeast monsoon was also the wind of departure from the great ports of the Persian Gulf, thousands of miles to the west of China, and even before the merchant vessels were leaving Canton, the ships of Islam were under way: if they left Basra or Sīrāf in September or October, they would be out of the Persian Gulf in time for the fair monsoon of winter to carry them across the Indian Ocean, and could expect to catch the stormy southwest monsoon in June to carry them northward from Malaya across the South China Sea to their destinations in south China. The rule, both east and west, was "southward in winter, northward in summer." [38]

From the seventh to the ninth century, the Indian Ocean was a safe and rich ocean, thronged with ships of every nationality. The Arabian Sea was protected by the power of Islam, and after the Abbāsid capital was moved from Damascus to Baghdad at the head of the Persian Gulf, the eastern trade flourished greatly.[39] Basra, an Arab city, was the port nearest to Baghdad, but it could not be reached by the largest ships. Below Basra, at the head of the Gulf, was Ubullah, an old port of the Persian Empire. But richest of all was Sīrāf, on the Persian side of the Gulf, below Shīrāz. This town owed all its prosperity to the Eastern trade, and it dominated the Gulf until destroyed by an earthquake in 977.[40] Its inhabitants were Persians in the main, but there were also Arab pearl divers, and merchant adventurers who came from Mesopotamia or from Oman to take ship for India and China.[41] The decline of Sīrāf was a disaster for the trade with the Far East, already reduced by the sack of Basra and Ubullah by revolted African slaves in the 870's.[42]

From these ports, then, the ships of many nations set sail, manned by Persian-speaking crews—for Persian was the *lingua franca* of the Southern Seas, as Sogdian was the *lingua franca* of the roads of Central Asia.[43] They stopped at Muscat in Oman, on the way out into the Indian Ocean; maybe they risked the coastal ports of Sind, haunted by pirates, or else proceeded directly to Malabar,[44] and thence to Ceylon, also called "Lion Country" and "Island of Rubies," where they purchased gems.[45] From here the route was eastward to the Nicobars, where they bartered, perhaps, with naked savages in canoes for coconuts or ambergris. Then they made land on the Malay Peninsula, in Kedah it is thought, whence they cruised the Strait of Malacca toward the lands of gold, Suvarnabhūmi, the fabulous Indies. Finally they turned north, impelled by the moist monsoon of summer, to trade for silk damasks in Hanoi or Canton, or even farther north.[46]

The sea-going merchantmen which thronged the ports of China in T'ang times were called by the Chinese, who were astonished at their size, "Argosies of the South Seas," "Argosies of the Western Regions," "Argosies of the *Man*-Barbarians," "Malayan Argosies," "Singhalese Argosies," "Brahman Argosies," and especially "Persian Argosies." [47] But it is by no means certain that *Chinese* vessels of this age made the long and hazardous voyage to Sīrāf. The great ocean-going ships of China appear some centuries later, in Sung, Yüan, and early Ming.[48] But in T'ang times, Chinese travelers to the West shipped in foreign bottoms. When the Arab writers of the ninth and tenth centuries tell of "Chinese vessels in the harbors of the Persian Gulf, they mean "ships engaged in the China trade," as when we speak of "China clippers" and "East Indiamen"; the cinnamon and sandalwood of Indonesia were called "Chinese" by the Arabs and Persians because they were brought from lands near China, or possibly in Chinese vessels.[49] Similarly, the "Persian Argosies" of the Chinese books must often have been only "ships engaged in trade with the Persian Gulf," often with Malay or Tamil crews.[50]

Chinese sources say that the largest ships engaged in this rich trade came from Ceylon. They were 200 feet long, and carried six or seven hundred men. Many of them towed lifeboats, and were equipped with homing pigeons.[51] The dhows built in the Persian Gulf were smaller, lateen-rigged, with their hulls built carvel-fashion, that is, with the planks set edge to edge,[52] not nailed but sewed with coir, and water-proofed with whale oil, or with the Chinese brea which sets like black lacquer.[53]

CARAVANS AND LAND ROUTES

The wealth of the Oriental nations was brought by land too, from the North and East, from the Northwest, and from the Southwest, in carriage or on camel, by horse or by ass. The products of the peoples of Manchuria and Korea came through the forests and plains of Liao-yang, where Tungusic and proto-Mongolic tribes lived, and down the coast of the Gulf of P'o-hai to the critical spot where the Great Wall ends at a narrow passage between mountains and sea. Here was a township named "Black Dragon" (Lu lung), and a stream named Yü, which has disappeared since T'ang times; and here were a Chinese frontier fortress and a customs station.[54]

The great silk roads, leading in the end to Samarkand, Persia, and Syria, went out from the northwestern frontier of China, along the edge of the Gobi Desert. Beyond the Jade Gate there were alternative roads, none of them attractive. The caravan route could sometimes be identified by the skeletons of men and pack animals. Such was the terrible road direct from Tun-huang to Turfan, which crossed the White Dragon Dunes, part of the salt crust left by the ancient lake Lop-nor. This absolute desert was also haunted by goblins, so that caravan leaders preferred to take the road through I-wu (Hami),[55] so reaching Turfan by a northerly detour.[56] From Turfan the traveler could go westward through the lands of the Western Turks, north of the Mountains of Heaven, or cut southwestward, south of those mountains, and proceed through Kucha and the other oasis cities of Chinese Turkestan. Then there was the parallel road from Tun-huang, the Southern Road, along the northern edge of the mysterious K'un-lun Mountains, and so through Khotan to the Pamirs.[57] These roads were passable only because of the peculiar virtues of the Bactrian camel, which could sniff out subterranean springs for thirsty merchants, and also predict deadly sandstorms:

When such a wind is about to arrive, only the old camels have advance knowledge of it, and they immediately stand snarling together, and bury their mouths in the sand. The men always take this as a sign, and they too immediately cover their noses and mouths by wrapping them in felt. This wind moves swiftly, and passes in a moment, and is gone, but if they did not so protect themselves, they would be in danger of sudden death.[58]

Another overland trade route, very old, but little used in pre-T'ang times, passed from Szechwan, through what is now Yünnan Province, split into two roads through the frightful chasms of the upper Irrawaddy in Burma, and led thence into Bengal. Yünnan was then a region of barbarians, whom the T'ang government tried in vain to subdue. The efforts to reopen this ancient route to Burma were finally frustrated by the rise of the new state of Nan-chao in the eighth century, friendlier to the border-raiding Tibetans than to the Chinese. But after Nan-chao had invaded Tongking in 863, the Chinese were finally able to break its military power. By then the foreign trade of China was declining, so that what was won could be little used. One of these Burma roads passed near the amber mines of Myitkyina, not far from the locality where, in modern times, the popular jadeite of kingfisher hue was mined. This too was sent back over the old route through Yünnan to the lapidaries of Peking.[59]

Finally, Buddhist pilgrims sometimes took the circuitous and difficult route through Tibet to India, usually descending by way of Nepal.[60]

FOREIGN SETTLEMENTS IN T'ANG

Let us now look at the cities and towns of China where foreigners congregated, and at the roads they traveled when moving about within the country. We shall begin in the south. Before T'ang, seafarers coming up the South China Sea usually made port in Tongking, in the vicinity of modern Hanoi. But after the T'ang settlement the merchants of Arabia and the Indies pointed their argosies at Canton or even further north.[61] At this time Chiao-*chou* was the seat of the Chinese protectorate over the betel-chewing Annamese in Tongking, and its port was Lung-pien.[62] Though the overseas trade of Chiao-*chou* fell off with the rise of Canton in the seventh century, it never became entirely extinct. It even increased somewhat after the middle of the eighth century, and during the final decades of that century, because of the exactions of rapacious officials and agents in Canton, foreign traders preferred to go to Chiao-*chou*.[63]

But of all the cities of the south, and of all the towns where foreign merchants congregated, none was more prosperous than the great port of Canton, the Khanfu of the Arabs, the "China" of the Indians.[64] Canton was then a frontier town, on the edge of a tropical wilderness populated by savages and wild beasts, and plagued with unpleasant diseases, but handsomely set among lichees, oranges, bananas, and banyans. During the reigns of the T'ang emperors it became a truly Chinese city, even though a large part of its population of 200,000 was "barbarian." [65] It was a wealthy city, but a flimsy one: its triple wall surrounded a crowded mass of thatch-roofed wooden houses, which were repeatedly swept by disastrous fires, until, in 806, an intelligent governor ordered the people to make themselves roofs of tile.[66] In the estuary before this colorful and insubstantial town were ". . . the argosies of the Brahmans, the Persians, and the Malays, their number beyond reckoning, all laden with aromatics, drugs, and rare and precious things, their cargoes heaped like hills." [67] In exchange for their fragrant tropical woods and their almost legendary medicines, these dark outlanders sought bales of silk, boxes of chinaware, and slaves. They enriched the Chinese businessmen who were willing to give up the comforts of the north for the profits of the south, and made possible the high state of the governor of the town and province, ". . . who carries six yaktails, with an army for each yaktail, and who in his majesty and dignity is not to be distinguished from the Son of Heaven." [68]

Many of these visitors settled in the foreign quarter of Canton, which by imperial sanction was set aside south of the river for the convenience of the many persons of diverse race and nationality who chose to remain in Canton to do business or to wait for favorable winds. They were ruled by a specially designated elder, and enjoyed some extraterritorial privileges.[69] Here citizens of the civilized nations, such as the Arabs and Singhalese, rubbed elbows with less cultured merchants, such as the "White *Man*-barbarians and the Red *Man*-barbarians." [70] Here the orthodox, such as the Indian Buddhists in their own monasteries, whose pools were adorned with perfumed blue lotuses,[71] were to be found close to the heterodox, such as the Shī'ah Muslims, who had fled persecution in Khurāsān to erect their own mosque in the Far East.[72] Here, in short, foreigners of every complexion, and Chinese of every province, summoned by the noon drum, thronged the great market, plotted in the warehouses, and haggled in the shops, and each day were dispersed by the sunset drum to return to their respective quarters or, on some occasions, to chaffer loudly in their outlandish accents in the night markets.[73]

This thriving town had a mottled history, spotted with murders, pirate raids, and the depredations of corrupt officials. Such evils tended to be self-perpetuating, since one gave rise to another. For instance, in an otherwise placid century, the captain of a Malayan cargo vessel murdered the governor Lu Yüan-jui, who had taken advantage of his position to plunder him. This was in 684. The central government appointed a virtuous man to succeed the wretch,[74] but in the years which followed many other silk-robed exiles from the gay life of the capital repaid themselves fully for their discomfort at the expense of the luckless merchants. It was precisely for the purpose of bringing some order and discipline to Canton, and to ensure that the court got its luxuries and the government its income, that, early in the eighth century, the important and sometimes lucrative post of "Commissioner for Commercial Argosies," a kind of customs officer in that difficult city, was established.[75] This was done partly at the instance of the plundered foreigners who had addressed complaints to the throne.[76] But the agents of the city's misfortunes were not always Chinese: in 758 it was raided by a horde of Arabs and Persians, who expelled the governor, looted the warehouses, burned dwellings, and departed by sea, perhaps to a pirate haven on the island of Hainan.[77] This disaster made the city negligible as a port for half a century, and foreign vessels went instead to Hanoi.[78]

Another difficulty which plagued this jeweled frontier town was the practice, which developed during the second half of the eighth century, of appointing eunuchs from the imperial palace to the crucial post of "Commissioner for Commercial Argosies," a custom which led to the evil then euphemistically called "palace markets," that is, interference in trade by these haughty palatines.[79] In 763, one of the gorgeous rascals went so far as to rebel against the throne. The eunuch's insurrection was quelled only with great difficulty. Meanwhile trade had come to a virtual standstill. The poet Tu Fu remarked in two poems the discontinuance of the flow of luxury wares northward from Canton at this time: "about the luminous pearls of the South Seas, it has long been quiet," [80] and "recently the provision of a live rhino, or even of kingfisher feathers, has been rare." [81] Even an honest governor like Li Mien— who ruled the port for three years beginning in 769 without mulcting the hapless foreigners, so that the amount of overseas trade increased tenfold under his administration [82]—could not prevent lesser officials from looting.[83] Small-scale robberies multiplied a thousand times, with an occasional great robber clothed in the robes of office—like Wang O, who, in the last years of the eighth century, collected a private as well as a public tax, and sent endless boxes of ivory and pearls to his family in the north, so that his own resources surpassed those of the public treasury.[84] These chronic and acute diseases led to the diversion of some of the city's commerce to Chiao-*chou* in the south, and some to Hai-yang, the port of Ch'ao-*chou*, further north.[85] But somehow the city and its prosperity could not be permanently destroyed: there were governors of rectitude and intelligence in the early decades of the ninth century,[86] and things went fairly well until, in the final quarter of the century, the death throes of the dynasty began. In 879 the prince of rebels, Huang Ch'ao, sacked the city, slaughtered the foreign traders, destroyed the mulberry groves which fed the silkworms, producers of the nation's chief export, and so brought about the great decline of Canton's wealth and prestige, which, despite a brief rejuvenation at the end of the century, she never completely recovered.[87] Under the Sung empire, the argosies from the South China Sea began more and more to turn to the ports of Fukien and Chekiang, and although Canton remained important, her monopoly was broken forever.

An Indian monk or a Javanese ambassador or a Cham merchant who wished to journey northward from Canton to the fabulous capital of China or to some other great city had a choice of two ways to cross the mountain barrier to the north. One possibility was to travel due north on the Chen River, now called "North River," until he reached Shao-*chou,* whence he turned to the northeast, crossed the "Mountain Pass of the Plum Trees," [88] and descended into the valley of the Kan River, by which he could easily proceed through what is now Kiangsi Province, through Hung-*chou,* where many Persians were to be found,[89] and on to the Long River, the great Yangtze, and so arrive at the commercial city of Yang-*chou,* or elsewhere in the heart of China. The way over the pass could not accommodate the greatly increased trade and traffic of early T'ang, but the great minister Chang Chiu-ling, himself a southern parvenu with bourgeois sympathies, had a great new road built through the pass as a stimulus to overseas trade and the development of Canton city. This great work was achieved in 716.[90]

The other possibility, less used though very old, was to take a northwesterly course up the Kuei ("Cassia") River, through the eastern part of modern Kwangsi Province, and follow it to its source at an altitude of less than a thousand feet. Here is also the source of the great river Hsiang, which carried the traveler northward through T'an-*chou* (Ch'ang-sha) in Hunan Province, and on into the watery low-lands of central China. At its source, the Hsiang is called the Li River, and it is actually connected with the source of the Kuei by an ancient canal, no longer identifiable as such by T'ang times, so that the sources of the northward- and southward-flowing rivers are now identical. It was therefore possible for small boats to travel continuously from Canton to the great waterways of central and north China, and even all the way to the capital.[91]

Both of these routes are referred to in a couplet by the ninth-century poet Li Ch'ün-yü:

> Once we were moored on the Cassia River—
>   there was rain by the deep bank;
> And again, there, at the Plum Pass—
>   our homeward course was blocked.[92]

But whichever route he took, the traveler could proceed with ease through the great lakes south of the Yangtze, propelled by sail or by oar or by sweep or even, from the late eighth century, by paddle wheel, toward his destination,[93] which usually was the magnificent city of Yang-*chou.*

Yang-*chou* was the jewel of China in the eighth century; a man might hope to crown his life by dying there.[94] The city owed its wealth and beauty to its location at the junction of the Yangtze River, which drained all central China, with the Grand Canal (called by the Chinese "River of Transport"), which carried the produce of the whole world to the great cities of the north. Therefore the imperial agent in charge of the national salt monopoly, a very lordly personage, had his headquarters there, and the merchants of Asia congregated there, at the hub of the great network of T'ang waterways, where all goods brought by Chinese and foreign vessels were transshipped to northbound canalboats.[95] The citizens of the city were made rich by its focal position in the distribution of salt (which everyone needed), of tea (which by now had become popular in the north), of precious stones, aromatics, and drugs brought up from Canton, and of costly damasks and tapestries brought down the Yangtze from Szechwan.[96] Moreover, Yang-*chou* was a banking center and a gold market, where the financier was as important as the merchant. In short, it was a bustling, bourgeois city, where money flowed easily.[97] Yang-*chou* was also an industrial town, famous for its beautiful metalwork, especially its bronze mirrors, for its felt hats, in the mode among the young men of Ch'ang-an, for its silk fabrics and embroideries and fine ramie linens, for its refined sugar, made here since the seventh century by a process brought from Magadha, for boatbuilding, and for excellent cabinetwork.[98] Yang-*chou* was a gay city, a city of well-dressed people, a city where the best entertainment was always available, a city of parks and gardens, a very Venice, traversed by waterways, where the boats outnumbered the carriages.[99] It was a city of moonlight and lanterns, a city of song and dance, a city of courtesans. "Yang is first and I is second," went the epigram, placing the reputed elegance and bright frivolity of Ch'eng-tu in Szechwan, along with its solid prosperity, in an inferior position.[100]

It was inevitable that foreign merchants should establish their shops here.[101] We know that their numbers were considerable, for the hordes of the rebel T'ien Shen-kung killed several thousand Arabian and Persian businessmen when they looted the city in 760.[102] Despite this disaster, the city retained its riches and splendor until the last decades of the ninth century, when it was laid waste by such rival captains as Pi Shih-to and Sun Ju, jackals following the trail of the great tiger, Huang Ch'ao. Its glory was partly restored by the new kingdom of Wu, arisen from the ruins of T'ang at the beginning of the tenth century, but it was destroyed again in mid-century by the northern kingdom of Chou, when the latter invaded Wu's successor state, Southern T'ang.[103] The scene of desolation presented by Yang-*chou* in early Sung times was aggravated by the policy of the emperors of the new dynasty, who encouraged the development of trade, transportation, and finance in the village of Yang-tzu, later called Chen-*chou,* which was nearer the Long River, and directed the transfer of industries elsewhere.[104] Hung Mai, writing in the twelfth century, expressed astonishment at the enthusiasm for Yang-*chou* which had been displayed by the poets of the eighth and ninth centuries. In his own day the place could only "sour one's nostrils." [105]

The greatness of Yang-*chou* and of the Grand Canal alike were the work of the emperors of Sui, but their true flowering came in the eighth century. With the phenomenal increase in population and material wealth in that era, the farmlands of the Yellow River watershed could no longer provide for the two capitals and the other northern cities, so that cereals had to be imported from the Yangtze region. These new demands put an unforseen strain on the old canal system. A remedy was found in 734: granaries were built along the route from Yang-*chou* to Ch'ang-an at critical points where grain might be properly stored whenever the system could not provide for its transfer beyond such a point. This prevented delays and stoppages, and rot and pilfering, and permitted the transshipment of rice and millet at leisure to vessels of appropriate size. In this way a steady flow northward was assured. Unanticipated, or at least not openly advocated, were the burdens imposed on the boats and waterways of the new relay system by the transfer of increasing quantities of luxury goods from the far South: [106] ivory, tortoise shell, and sandalwood were heaped into lighters originally designed to receive bags of grain.

The traveler then, as well as the barge captain, unaware of these grave economic problems, could leave Yang-*chou* (unless he preferred to travel by horse or carriage) and proceed north- and westward up the "River of Transport," marveling at the great flocks of ducks and geese which whirred up around his boat.[107] He would pass the barges of the salt bureau, glittering like snow in the sunlight, and stop perhaps at the thriving towns of Sui-yang and Ch'en-liu, both of which had considerable foreign settlements, especially of Persians, and at Pien-*chou* (K'ai-feng), which also had its temple to the Sacred Fire,[108] a city of more than half a million inhabitants, but whose glory as a metropolis was still in the future. Finally, the traveler came to the Eastern Capital, the ancient city of Lo-yang.

Foreigners who visited China, or settled there, tended to congregate in the vigorous commercial cities of the south, like Canton and Yang-*chou*. But they also came together in the venerable cities of the north, the centers of political power, the homes of the nobility, where a great bibliophile or a great soldier counted for more than a successful merchant. Of the two great capitals, Lo-yang was the second in rank, and it was the second city of the empire in population, having more than a million inhabitants.[109] It had its holy traditions of a thousand years, was not second in pride even to Ch'ang-an, and was endowed with a spiritual atmosphere somewhat milder and more elegant than its western rival. It was the "Godly Metropolis" [110] of the Empress Wu, well on its way to becoming what it became in the eleventh century, the proudest and most beautiful city of China. It had palaces and parks and throngs of officials. It was noted for its fine fruits and flowers, its patterned damasks and fine silk crepes, and its ceramic wares of all kinds.[111] It had a great market place, the Southern Market, occupying two blocks (*fang*), with a hundred and twenty bazaars, or streets given over to the sale of a single type of ware, and thousands of individual shops and warehouses.[112] For the aliens there on business, there were the usual temples to alien gods, among them three shrines to the Sacred Fire, attesting to the presence of a Persian colony.[113]

In 743 an artificial lake, a transshipment pool, was built east of Ch'ang-an, the Western Capital. In that year, the fascinated northerner, accustomed to speaking the proverb "Boats in the south, horses in the north," could see the boats of every part of the empire gathered on this pool, loaded with the tax goods and local tribute destined for the palace: scarlet felt saddle covers from the north, vermilion bitter tangerines from the south, pink silk-fringed druggets from the east, crimson alum from the west. These goods were transferred to lighters, whose crews were specially garbed in bamboo rain hats, sleeved smocks, and straw shoes, in the fashion of the boatmen of the Yangtze.[114] This was the terminus of a continuous waterway from Canton to the greatest city of the age.

With almost two million taxable residents, Ch'ang-an was ten times as populous as Canton at the other end of this long net of rivers and canals. The capital's foreign population was proportionally large.[115] This international element had a rather different cast from that of the southern port. It was chiefly made up of men from the North and West: Turks, Uighurs, Tocharians, and Sogdians, in contrast to the Chams, Khmers, Javanese, and Singhalese who crowded into Canton. In both places, however, there were many Arabs, Persians, and Hindus. The Iranian population must have been most important. The T'ang government even had an office "of the Sārthavāk" (literally, "of the Caravan Leader") to watch over their interests.[116]

Ch'ang-an had two great markets, the Eastern and the Western, each with scores of bazaars. The Eastern Market was the less crowded of the two, and quieter and richer, being situated near the mansions of the nobles and officials; the Western was noisier, more vulgar and violent (malefactors were punished there), and more exotic. Each bazaar, with its unique kind of merchandise, was surrounded by warehouses, and each had a headman (*hang t'ou*). Each was required by law to display a sign naming its specialty. Proceeding through the Western Market, where most of the foreign merchants displayed their wares, one might see in succession the butchers' bazaar, the ironmongers' bazaar, the clothing bazaar, the bazaar of saddlers, the silk bazaar, and the bazaar of the druggists.[117] After the middle of the eighth century, the tea merchants were particularly popular. The new vogue for tea drinking was not restricted to the Chinese: it is reported that Uighur visitors to the capital, before doing anything else, spurred their horses to the shops of the dealers in tea.[118] Prominent in the Western Market, among the foreign tradesmen, were the fellow-country-men of these tea enthusiasts, the Uighur usurers, to whom numberless debt-ridden Chinese businessmen and young Chinese wastrels pledged land, furniture, slaves, and even sacred relics, as security for ready cash. These moneylenders began to be regarded as a plague in the early decades of the ninth century, when prices were rising steadily and everyone was in debt. Indeed, the arrogance of these Turks was limitless: one of them was imprisoned for stabbing a merchant in broad daylight, and was rescued by his chief, without any Chinese inquiry into the event.[119] Popular feeling against them mounted until finally, in the year 836, all private intercourse with the "various colored peoples" was prohibited.[120] The insufferable haughtiness of the Uighurs was an important factor in the outburst of xenophobia in mid-century, and the persecution of foreign religions.

But a citizen could console himself in a hundred ways, and accumulate more debts in so doing. He might, for instance, attend any of a great variety of fetes, dances, and dramatic spectacles at the wealthy Buddhist temples scattered about the city. Among these would be novel entertainments originally devised in the Buddhist nations of India and Turkestan, at once alluring and edifying.[121] Or the citizen might, if lonely, find a different kind of consolation among the whores of the P'ing-k'ang Quarter, between the Eastern Market and the imperial palace. Here he could find famous courtesans, skilled in music, dancing, and flattery, and could expect to enjoy her favors for the night by paying about 1,600 cash to her "stepmother."[122] A young aristocrat, enjoying his father's reputation, or a young scholar seeking success in the examinations as the only road to public office, could easily fall in love with one of these charmers. If he had some literary talent he surrounded her with an aura of glamour in his poems and stories.[123] Less expensive but more exotic were the pleasures of the taverns in a zone extending along the east edge of the city, southward from the "Gate of Spring Brightness," a good place to entertain a friend departing on a trip to Lo-yang and the east. Here an enterprising taverner could better his income by employing an exotically handsome Western girl, a Tocharian or a Sogdian say, to serve rare wines in cups of amber or agate, and to increase sales by means of sweet singing and seductive dancing to the accompaniment of the flutes of Western boys—and especially by means of friendly manners: "a Western houri beckons with her white hand, inviting the stranger to intoxicate himself with a golden beaker."[124] These compliant green-eyed beauties, some golden-haired, confounded the poets, and left their mark on literature. Consider the words of Li Po:

> The zither plays "The Green Paulownias at Dragon Gate,"
> The lovely wine, in its pot of jade, is as clear as the sky.
> As I press against the strings, and brush across the studs, I'll drink with you, milord;
> "Vermilion will seem to be prase-green" when our faces begin to redden.
> That Western houri with features like a flower—
> She stands by the wine-warmer, and laughs with the breath of spring
> Laughs with the breath of spring,
> Dances in a dress of gauze!
> "Will you be going somewhere, milord, *now,* before you are drunk?"[125]

Let us leave Ch'ang-an on this pleasant note, and consider briefly the remaining Chinese towns where foreigners were wont to come together. Foreign merchants could, of course, be found anywhere where profits might tempt them. You might find them looking for taffetas in the rich, high valleys of Szechwan, or in the moist lowlands about Tung-t'ing Lake.[126] But of all the regions unconnected with the major cities by water, that in which aliens tended most to settle was the corridor of the caravans, leading westward into Turkestan. Here along the margin of the Gobi were Chinese towns, spaced at regular intervals, and equipped with caravanserais. Iranian fire worshipers and musicians were to be found in all of them, and all were of doubtful allegiance: one year the Chinese mandarins were in residence, quoting the sages and counseling virtue; the next year the Turks rode in, waving their bows; often Tibetan princes were their lords. Typical of these multilingual outposts was the old town of Liang-*chou,* once subject to the Hsiung-nu and their pastoral successors. Here the regal warlord Ko-shu Han held sway for a time, entertaining fortunate guests with lion pantomimes, saber dances, and the thoughtful attentions of red-lipped cupbearers.[127] In the eighth century, Liang-*chou* had more than a hundred thousand permanent residents, reputed to be of hard and unyielding temperament, since they lived under the influence of the White Tiger and Sign of Metal.[128] Some of these citizens were Chinese, but many were of Indian extraction, surnamed in the Chinese fashion, according to their ethnic origin, *Shindu,* and many could trace their origin to the nations bordering the Oxus and Jaxartes.[129] Here were prime grazing lands for horses, especially along a river which still retained its archaic Mongolian name of Tümigen, meaning "bone marrow" in the Hsien-pi language. It was so named for the fertility of the lands thereabout.[130] Here also were produced fine damasks, mats, and wild horse hides, not to mention an excellent headache remedy.[131] This Liang-*chou* was a true melting pot, a kind of homely symbol of the exotic to the Chinese, as Hawaii is to the American of the twentieth century. The hybrid music of Liang-*chou,* at once foreign and familiar, since it was not entirely either, was in fashion in the early Middle Ages of the Far East.

TREATMENT OF FOREIGNERS

Chinese attitudes and policies toward foreigners were not simple. Even at the height of the vogue for the exotic, the best course for an alien was to adopt Chinese manners and habits of thought, as indeed many did. Sometimes, however, the government made it impossible to do this. For instance, an edict of 779 compelled Uighurs resident in the capital, of whom there were then about a thousand, to wear their native costume, and forbade them to "lure" Chinese women into becoming their wives and concubines, or to pass themselves off as Chinese in any way at all.[132] This law may have been the outcome of popular resentment against Uighur usurers, but other such laws may have had no other basis than the zeal of a pious magistrate to protect the purity of Chinese custom, as when Lu Chün, who became governor of Canton in 836, found foreigners and Chinese living together unsegregated, and intermarrying freely. He forced them to separate, forbade further marriages between them, and even prohibited aliens from owning land and houses. Lu Chün regarded himself as a man of upright principles, engaged in policing a dissolute port: he was, in short, a kind of ethnic puritan.[133]

Such Chinese stereotypes as the rich (and therefore enviable) Persian,[134] the black (and therefore ugly) Malay, and the naked (and therefore immoral) Cham belong to the world of vulgar images, and played little part in official policies. And even popular attitudes were ambiguous, to say the least. The same young poets who languished over the pretty Iranian waitresses in the metropolitan wineshops laughed at the little puppets representing drunken Westerners, with their peaked caps, blue eyes, and high noses, with which they played in houses of prostitution—when the ridiculous puppet fell over, the guest at whom it pointed had to empty his cup.[135] The eighth was a century when Central Asiatic harpers and dancers were enormously popular in Chinese cities, but it was also the century of the massacre of thousands of harmless (but wealthy) Persian and Arab traders in Yang-*chou*. In the ninth century, when exotic things were not so easily and cheaply come by, exotic literature, full of romantic reminiscence, became popular. It is curious that this period, when tales about benevolent millionaires from the Far West were being told everywhere,[136] was also an age of suspicion and persecution of foreigners. In this same age of ambivalent attitudes, it was possible for foreigners to rise to high position in the government, especially if they allied themselves with the new gentry, which had been created by the examination system, against the hereditary aristocrats; we have, for instance, the example of an Arab who gained distinction with the degree of "Advanced Gentleman" (*chin shih*) in the middle of the ninth century. Many factors were at work, separating the mental image of the "ideal" foreigner from the real one: rising prices, accompanied by resentment against wealthy merchants, and weakening political authority, which allowed foreigners to raid the Chinese soil.[137] Distrust or hatred of foreigners was, in short, not at all incompatible with a love of exotic things. This love was realistic in the fine new days of the seventh and eighth centuries, and embalmed in the literature of the ninth and tenth centuries. Then it recalled the fine old days, when foreigners universally recognized the superiority of Chinese arms and Chinese arts, and when the ordinary Chinese citizen might expect to enjoy the rare goods of distant places. Just so, in our times, a former German soldier might regret the days when he could drink freely of French wines without admitting the equality of the French, or a former English civil servant remember wistfully the treasures of barbaric India under the Empire. Foreign luxuries were too good for foreigners.

There was also something ambiguous about Chinese attitudes toward commerce. Trade was never free from political entanglements. The more necessary the goods were to the general welfare, or the more desirable they were to the upper classes, the more likely it was that the state would take a part in their distribution. Traditional government monopolies on domestic goods, such as those on salt, iron, metal currency, and sometimes on wine and other products of universal consumption, were models for the control of luxury goods from abroad. The new office of "Commissioner for Commercial Argosies," created at Canton in the eighth century, had the ancient office of "Commissioner for Salt and Iron" as its ideal and prototype. Its incumbent bought up such imports as the government desired to control (especially those in demand by the court and by groups favored by the court), prevented smuggling, and followed the pattern of an old-style internal monopoly.[138] This attitude had the corollaries that commerce should be entangled with diplomacy and that the gifts of foreign nations to the imperial court, consisting often of great quantities of costly goods and regarded as tokens of submission to the universal authority of the Son of Heaven, should be, in fact, an important part of international trade.[139] To say that "tributary nations" were compelled to offer tribute, is only part of the story. Foreign nations, both those which trembled close at hand and those whose distance made them truly independent of T'ang, sent their goods out of sheer self-interest, and received desirable "gifts" from the Chinese for their trouble.[140] There were certainly drawbacks for the foreign merchant in this system. He was hardly a free agent: he was expected to present certain of his wares formally at the imperial capital, or else to hand them into a government warehouse at the port of entry. If he attempted private enterprise, he was likely to invite official interference or even disaster. A local mandarin was more likely to go too far in the strict interpretation of the government's restraints than to risk his neck by being too liberal.[141] Even those goods which the alien was permitted to sell freely to the public [142] had to be sold in one of the great markets, closely supervised by government agents. To make matters worse, it was precisely those goods which the outlander most desired to take back to his own country which were most jealously watched by the mandarins, lest the government lose its share of the profit. We may judge the nature of these goods from an edict of 714 forbidding the export or the sale to foreigners of tapestries, damasks, gauzes, crepes, embroideries, and other fancy silks, or of yaktails, pearls, gold, or iron.[143] Contrariwise, there were erratic government restrictions on the import and sale to Chinese of items conceived to be frivolous and detrimental to the national morals, though these might prove to be the most profitable wares in the merchant's cargo. Indeed, even the sale of counterfeits of luxury goods and adulterated substances, though it made the importer liable to a prison sentence,[144] was, if undetected, a profitable industry, as was discovered by an unlucky Persian priest in Canton, who specialized in manufacturing exotic "rarities" for the sophisticated imperial court.[145] But if he were wise, and knew what could be imported and what could be exported, and under what conditions, even an honest mechant could do very well for himself, as the thousands of foreign merchants on Chinese soil attest. But even the wisest had other hazards to contend with: he was likely, if the local magistrates were not too attentive to the moral principles expected of a Chinese official, to be despoiled of a considerable part of his goods in the name of "customs duty." Even if the inspector at the customs barrier were a person of integrity, the requirements of the government were likely to be excessive. An Arab geographer reports that his compatriots were obliged to surrender one-third of their cargo into the imperial warehouses on arrival in China.[146] But nothing was permanent and predictable. Last year's caprice was next year's policy. From time to time relief came in the form of a fiat from the court which made the merchant's condition more bearable and his hope for great profit more reasonable. Such a one was the edict handed down by Wen Tsung in 834, on the occasion of the sovereign's recovery from an illness. This mandate amnestied various classes of criminals, and at the same time expressly extended the imperial protection to strangers from overseas engaged in commerce in Kwangtung, Fukien, and Yang-*chou,* instructing the local magistrates to allow them to trade freely without intolerable tax burdens, since they had placed themselves under the monarch's loving care.[147]

But the foreigner resident in China had other problems. He faced social and economic disabilities unconnected with commerce. If he were unlucky enough to die in China, his goods were sealed and, unless a wife or heir could readily be found, were confiscated by the state.[148] The search for an inheritor could not have extended very far. Moreover, if an alien took a Chinese wife or concubine, he was required to remain in China; in no case could he take a Chinese woman back to his homeland with him. This was ordered in a decree of 628, particularly designed to protect Chinese women from temporary marriages with the envoys of foreign countries and with members of their suites, who required casual comforts while away from home.[149] *CHINESE WIFE* The rule did not, of course, apply to the gift of a royal princess to a nomadic chieftain. The lady would be sent off to the steppes without a murmur if the good will of her future husband was important to Chinese policy. Such a one was the lady sent to marry the Khan of the Uighurs in the heyday of their power early in the ninth century, in exchange (as it were) for the gifts presented by the envoy sent to fetch her away: camlets, brocades, sable furs, girdles of jade, a thousand horses, and fifty camels.[150] Whether in obedience to the decree, or by free choice, we read of many foreigners of the eighth century who had lived in Ch'ang-an more than forty years, all of them with wives and children.[151] Moreover, as we have noticed, the foreigner was liable to arbitrary segregation laws, which were only partly mitigated by other laws allowing foreign colonies in Chinese cities to elect their own headmen and to settle litigation between members of the colony according to the laws and customs of their native country.[152]

TRIBUTE

Once an ordinary merchant had obtained official permission to trade in the Chinese markets, he took up quarters among his compatriots and went about his business. But an envoy, representing a foreign government, even though he might be primarily interested in commerce or at least in a profitable exchange of lordly gifts, had yet to face the vexatious splendors which awaited all representatives of tribute nations. His nation was bound to be tributary, of course, though the envoy might wink at the deception when closeted with his boon companions. Some cases were exceptional: one cannot guess what token tribute was brought, or what symbols of submission were offered to the Chinese emperor by the fugitive Sāsānid Prince Pērōz, last scion of his house, when he came to Ch'ang-an to seek the protection and assistance of T'ai Tsung against the victorious Arabs.[153] But the average ambassador was an ordinary politician, or a close relative of a king, or a distinguished priest, or perhaps a rich merchant, and ordinarily he made no difficulties about submission. A very distant country interested in encouraging trade might, rather than send its own ambassador, request representation by the envoys of a friendly neighbor. As a case in point, the kingdom of Bali sent an emissary with samples of its native products in the suite of a Cham embassy to the Chinese court in 630.[154]

To gain his rightful privileges when he arrived at the Chinese capital, the envoy needed official credentials. When a foreign potentate sought the favor or protection of T'ang, he would send a petition asking for a golden girdle and a robe of state in many colors, or for a Chinese mandarin to act as his resident adviser, or for a copy of one of the Chinese classics, or for all these things. But most of all he required the gift of a handsome wallet in which his ambassador might carry his official token.[155] This token had the form of a fish of bronze, or rather, of half of such a fish. To each country that maintained regular diplomatic relations with T'ang were assigned twelve such bifurcated fishes, each numbered in sequence, and each inscribed with the name of the nation to which it was allotted. The "male" halves remained in the Chinese palace; the "female" halves were sent to the "tributary" country. An ambassador sent to China had in his brocaded wallet the fish talisman whose number was the number of the month in which he would arrive in Ch'ang-an. If this matched the corresponding piece in the capital, he was accorded those rights and benefits to which he was entitled by nationality.[156] These prerogatives were by no means the same for all envoys. Their food allotments, for instance, were proportional to the distance of their homelands from China. Therefore the representatives of India, Persia, and Arabia were given rations for six months; the envoys from Cambodia, Sumatra, and Java had four-month rations; and the envoys from Champa, whose borders were coterminous with China, got only three.[157] Nor did the agents of great powers yield precedence easily: when, on June 11, 758, the ambassadors of the Uighurs and of the Abbāsid Caliphate arrived simultaneously with "tribute" at the Chinese court, they fought with each other for priority at the palace gate. A special decree from the throne was required to determine the protocol for the occasion: both embassies were allowed to enter at the same time, through gates to right and left.[158]

On first arriving at the capital, the embassy was put up for a while at one of the hostels situated at each of the four major gates of the city, facing the cardinal directions.[159] From this time on, the ambassador's activities were directed by officials of the Hung-lu Office,[160] which was responsible both for the funerals of members of the imperial family and for the reception and entertainment of foreign guests.[161] This important office, quite aside from its basic responsibilities, served also as a clearinghouse of information about foreign countries which was of great value to the nation, especially to the strategists of the army. A special agent of the Department of Arms was sent to interview the envoy immediately upon his arrival. He was interrogated about the geography and customs of his native country, and a map was constructed from the information supplied.[162] The great geographer Chia Tan was head of this office for a period in the second half of the eighth century. It is said that his remarkable knowledge of world geography was derived from personal interviews with visiting diplomats.[163]

The greatest day of the ambassador's period of sojourn in China was the day of his reception by the emperor. On this occasion, everything was calculated to impress the foreigner with the majestic state and awesome power of the ruler of T'ang. If the ambassador was of sufficiently high rank to attend the great reception for tributary princes held on the day of the winter solstice, he found himself face to face with twelve ranks of guards arrayed before the hall of audience. There were swordsmen, halberdiers, lancers, and archers, each group wearing splendid capes of a distinctive color, and each with its appropriate banner—a pennon of parrot or peacock feathers, or a flag embroidered with the image of a wild ass or a leopard, or another symbol of valor. Even a lesser envoy saw before him the household guards, on duty at all audiences. These were divided into five troops, of which four wore scarlet shirts and caps decorated with the tail feathers of the Manchurian snow pheasant, and the fifth wore tabards of scarlet taffeta, embroidered with the figures of wild horses. All carried staves and wore swords at their belts.[164] Dazzled by this spectacle, the foreign delegation approached, and after suitable prostrations had its gifts displayed in front of the audience hall. The chief envoy then approached the throne, and, following advice given in whispers by the Chinese official[165] who attended him, bowed toward the sovereign and said, "Your bulwark-vassal so-and-so, of such-and-such a nation, presumes to offer up these oblations from its soil."[166] The emperor continued to sit in stately silence, but the Officer of Protocol accepted the gifts in his name, and received from the ambassador other presents for distribution among his assistants.[167] In return, the tributary king and his ambassador were awarded nominal but resounding titles in the T'ang administration, in accordance with the doctrine that they were vassals of the Son of Heaven, and rich gifts were awarded them as "salary."[168] Thus, when the king of Śrībhoja[169] sent tokens of tribute to Hsüan Tsung, the monarch handed down a patent of recognition, stating, ". . . and it is fitting that there should be a robe-of-state conferred on him, and that he should be awarded, from afar, [the title of] Great Army Leader of the Militant Guards of the Left, and that we should bestow on him a purple caftan and a belt inlaid with gold."[170] After accepting these honors in the name of his lord, the envoy was shown the way out. Now he could expect a more relaxing reward for his labors, as a Japanese ambassador did in the early part of the eighth century:

The Japanese Nation, though far away beyond the seas, has sent its envoys to our levee. Now since they have traversed the glaucous waves, and have also made us presents of articles from their quarter, it is fitting that these envoys, Mabito Makumon and the others, should assemble for a feast at the [Office of] Documents of the Penetralia on the sixteenth day of the present month.[171]

EXOTIC TASTE

Such was the manner of receiving the men who brought the delightful rarities which the aristocrats and their imitators desired. The Chinese taste for the exotic permeated every social class and every part of daily life: Iranian, Indian, and Turkish figures and decorations appeared on every kind of household object. The vogue for foreign clothes, foreign food, and foreign music was especially prevalent in the eighth century,[172] but no part of the T'ang era was free from it. Some individuals, like the poet Yüan Chen, who wrote at the end of the eighth century, lamented these innovations:

> Ever since the Western horsemen began raising smut and dust,
> Fur and fleece, rank and rancid, have filled Hsien and Lo.
> Women make themselves Western matrons by the study of Western makeup;
> Entertainers present Western tunes, in their devotion to Western music.[173]

Hsien and Lo are the two capitals Ch'ang-an (under the nominal guise of its vanished precursor Hsien-yang) and Lo-yang, where these fashions were epidemic.

Some Chinese, at any rate, knew the language of the Turks.[174] There was a Turkish-Chinese dictionary available for serious students,[175] and some Chinese poems of T'ang show the influence of Turkish folksongs in their prosody.[176] Many devoted Buddhists learned some Sanskrit. But the extent of such learning, as also of the study of other foreign languages, such as Korean, Tocharian, Tibetan, or Cham, we do not know.

Fashions in the two capitals tended to follow Turkish and East Iranian modes of dress. In T'ang times, men and women alike wore "barbarian" hats when they went abroad, especially when on horseback. In the early part of the seventh century aristocratic ladies favored a hat and veil combination, a kind of burnoose called a *mi-li*. This mantle enveloped the face and most of the body, and helped a haughty lady to preserve her anonymity and to avoid the curious stares of the vulgar.[177] But modesty suffered a decline after the middle of the century, when the long veil was abandoned for a "curtain hat," [178] a broad-brimmed hat with a hood which fell only to the shoulders, and which might even reveal the face. This hat, originally designed to protect the head on long dusty journeys, was worn both by men and by women, but attracted unfavorable notice to women especially. An edict of 671 attempted to outlaw these brazen-faced equestriennes, who should have traveled in decently covered carriages, but it was ignored, and by the early part of the eighth century women were riding about the city streets wearing Turkish caps, or even bare-headed, and dressed in men's riding clothes and boots.[179] Other exotic fashions of mid-T'ang were leopard-skin hats, worn by men, tight sleeves and fitted bodices in the Iranian styles, worn by women along with pleated skirts and long stoles draped around the neck, and even hair-styles and makeup of "un-Chinese" character. Court ladies of the eighth century wore "Uighur chignons." [180] The zeal of colonials for the pure customs of the father-land, however, inspired the people of Tun-huang in the ninth century to retain Chinese dress under Tibetan rule, when citizens of towns like Liang-*chou* (notoriously prone to exoticism) freely adopted outlandish dress and manners.[181]

Enthusiasm for Turkish customs enabled some aristocrats to endure the discomfort of living in a tent, even in the midst of the city. The poet Po Chü-i erected two Turkish tents of sky-blue felt in his courtyard, and entertained guests in them, proud to demonstrate how they furnished protection from the winter wind.[182] The most eminent of such urban tent-dwellers was the unhappy prince Li Ch'eng-ch'ien, son of the great T'ai Tsung, who imitated the Turks in everything: he preferred to speak Turkish rather than Chinese, and erected a complete Turkish camp on the palace grounds, where, dressed like a Khan of the Turks, he sat in front of his tent under the wolf's-head ensign, attended by slaves in Turkish dress, and sliced himself gobbets of boiled mutton with his sword.[183]

Though the prince surely had his imitators, it is likely that this barbaric dish had only a limited number of votaries. But other food of foreign parentage was widely admired. Of these the most popular were little "foreign" cakes of various kinds, especially a steamed variety sprinkled with sesame seeds, and cakes fried in oil.[184] The art of making these had been introduced from the West, and, though enjoyed by native and foreigner alike, they were ordinarily prepared and sold by Westerners. A popular tale of the age tells of such a cake seller, visited by a young man returning from his mistress' house before dawn, and waiting for the sound of the morning drum to announce that the gate of the quarter was open:

> When he came to the gate of the neighborhood, the bar of the gate had not yet been released. Beside the gate was the dwelling of a Westerner who sold cakes, and he was just setting out his lamps, and kindling his brazier. Cheng-tzu sat down under his curtain to rest, and to wait for the drum.[185]

At the other extreme were the elegant viands prepared for the tables of the rich and respectable. Some of these were made with expensive imported ingredients, but may not have been made according to foreign recipes. Especially popular were aromatic and spicy dishes, such as the "cakelets with grated aromatics, worth a thousand in gold." [186] But some were obviously made according to a foreign formula, as the "Brahman" wheat-paste, "light and high," which was steamed in baskets.[187]

Exotic influences on costume, dwellings, diet, and other aspects of everyday life were paralleled by exoticism in the arts. The foreigners who crowded into T'ang

China were pictured by painters and poets alike. There are, of course, exotic artists in every age, since a man may be by temperament out of step with the popular and persuasive cultural trends of his own time. But exoticism flourishes most in eras of new or renewed contact with strange peoples. Therefore it is especially connected with imperialistic conquest and with commercial expansion. The typical exotic artist glorifies his country, and at the same time exposes his guilty conscience, burdened with oppression or exploitation abroad, by glamorizing the oppressed and exploited. The images of Moors and Saracens in the paintings of Gozzoli and Bellini, like those of Algerians and Tahitians in the paintings of Delacroix and Gauguin, are equally symptomatic of an expansive and imperious civilization. They had their counterparts in T'ang. Indeed, even religious exoticism, such as that centered around representations of the Magi in Renaissance art, had its analogue in the idealized arhats, with Indian visages, visible in the Buddhist art of the Far East.

Some medieval critics did not recognize exotic pictures as a special category of painting. The eminent Kuo Jo-hsü, for instance, writing of ninth- and tenth-century art from the vantage point of the eleventh century, classified old paintings under such rubrics as "glimpses of virtue," "heroism," "representations of scenery," and "popular manners and customs," but had no special pigeonhole for pictures of foreigners and their appurtenances, even though he occasionally discussed exotic themes, such as the proper manner of representing deities of Indian origin. Thus, when painting Indra, ". . . one should display a stern and imposing demeanor . . ." [188]

On the other hand, the anonymous author of the *Hsüan ho hua p'u,* a catalogue of the paintings in the collection of Hui Tsung, imperial Sung connoisseur of the twelfth century, has left us a short essay about paintings showing foreigners. [189] He includes among his examples of distinguished depicters of barbarians of T'ang the painters Hu Kuei and his son, Hu Ch'ien, many of whose works still survived in Sung times. These men were famous for hunting scenes set in remote countries, and for exotic horses, camels, and falcons. [190] Our unknown cataloguer states that the true value of such pictures is that they illustrate the inferiority of barbarian culture as compared with the Chinese. Such didactic chauvinism was certainly much more common in Sung than in early T'ang. In T'ang the characteristic feeling provoked by a painting of a foreign subject was condescending pride; in Sung it was apprehensive arrogance. We may be sure in any case that most Sung art collectors, as well as most T'ang art lovers, took the greatest pleasure in these paintings for their style and color, whatever their opinions about the value of the subject matter may have been.

Despite the rarity of generalizations about exoticism and other fashions in critical writings, we can easily create simple pictures of trends and modes in art by synthesizing the critics' statements about the themes best treated by individual artists. If we do this, we find that the great century for the exotic in T'ang painting was the seventh, when the military might of the T'ang emperors was at its apex, and when overawed barbarians thronged to the T'ang court. Victorious pride made these outlanders seem fit subjects for approved paintings. In contrast, we shall see presently that the great age for the exotic in T'ang literature was the ninth century, an age of reminiscence. Most eminent of the painters of outlandish themes was Yen Li-te, brother of the equally famous Yen Li-pen who had the honor of depicting the martial visage of T'ai Tsung himself. It is said that no painter of exotic subjects of his own or earlier times could touch him.[191] In 629, the scholar Yen Shih-ku introduced a native of the remote mountains of what is now Kweichow Province to the court. "His cap was made of black bearskin, with a gold fillet across the forehead; his outer garments were of fur, and he wore leather leggings and shoes." Shih-ku referred sententiously to appropriate examples from antiquity, and then said, "Today the myriad realms to which the Imperial virtue has extended come to court in their garments of grass and feather ornaments, to meet together in the barbarians' guest quarters. Truly this is a [sight] which might be represented in pictorial form, to exhibit to posterity the far reaching extent of that virtue." Accordingly Yen Li-te was commissioned to paint the flattering scene.[192]

Pictures of foreign countries were once hardly to be distinguished from strategic maps, and were based on the same kind of interrogation. Still, in T'ang times, the practical and aesthetic purposes and results were undoubtedly kept distinct. In 643, Yen Li-pen was commissioned to paint typical scenes of the nations that sent submissive emissaries to the court of T'ai Tsung. Among his productions were two paintings of the "Western Regions."[193] Chou Fang and Chang Hsüan, both of them otherwise famous as painters of women[194] and both active in the late eighth century, more than a century after the Li brothers, made representations of the incredible nation of Prom, or Hrom, or Rome (modern Fu-lin), that is, of some part of the Byzantine realm. We cannot now imagine the character of these scenes, though they would be incomparable treasures if they had survived.[195] Even the great Wang Wei did a landscape from some "Strange Realm," now unidentifiable.[196]

It was usual to picture the inhabitants of such distant places in their native costumes, with their curious features emphasized. Of all representations of foreigners, most of those that we can date with certainty as the works of T'ang craftsmen are the little terra-cotta figurines, among which we can find the images of Uighurs with high hats and haughty manners, Arabs (it may be) with black brows and hawklike noses, and persons with curly hair and toothy grins who, whatever their ethnic type, show the influence of Hellenistic taste.[197] But although exotic peoples were a favorite subject of the great painters as well as of the potters of T'ang, few of the painted images survive. We do not have Yen Li-pen's pictures of tribute bearers bending before the emperor of China, presenting, perhaps, a kingly lion.[198] We can no longer see the mounted barbarian archers, depicted by Li Chien and his son Li Chung-ho,[199] nor "The King of Korea Making a Ritual Circumambulation with Incense,"[200] painted by Chang Nan-pen, nor Chou Fang's picture of "A Woman of India,"[201] nor Chang Hsüan's picture of "A Japanese Equestrienne."[202] But we can see men of several Central Asiatic nations, with strange faces, unusual hats, and exotic hair-cuts in the frescoes at Tun-huang.[203] The soldier, government clerk, or weary pilgrim passing through one of the oasis cities of Serindia would have seen even stranger beings on the walls of the temples he visited under the protection of the local Chinese garrison: Buddhas in Hellenistic vestment, laics of the purest Iranian type, and nude women straight out of the fervent Indian epics.[204]

Almost equally attractive during those exciting years were the wild beasts of strange lands, especially those sent with missions as gifts to the Chinese court, and also domestic animals, in particular those admired and desired by the Chinese—the famous hawks, hounds, and horses.[205]

Finally, the artists of T'ang loved to show the gods and saints of foreign lands, above all those of the lands where Buddhism thrived: emaciated Hindu arhats with shaggy brows, princely Bodhisattvas glittering with strings of many-colored gems,[206] the ancient gods Indra and Brahma, shown as protectors both of the Law of the Buddha and of palatial Chinese gateways,[207] and other divine guardians—partly assimilated to Northern nomadic and to Chinese culture—such as Kuvera, Protector of the North, shown bearded and mustachioed, in Chinese armor.[208] Such pictorial amalgams were sometimes the result of the use of a Chinese model by a painter of exotic subjects, as when a geisha in the service of a great lord posed for the figure of a *devi*—a Hindu goddess—in a Buddhist scene,[209] as did the Italian courtesans who loaned their forms to Renaissance madonnas. With these pictures of hybrid beings too must be grouped the elaborate paintings of the ineffable paradises of Buddhism. like distant fairylands. One of the most eminent of painters of Buddhist icons in early T'ang was himself a foreigner, a Khotanese,[210] with the Saka name of Viśa Īrasangä,[211] called in Chinese Yü-ch'ih I-seng. He came to the Chinese court about the middle of the seventh century, recommended by his king, bringing with him a new painting style of Iranian origin, in which modeled and shaded polychrome figures seemed to stand out in relief, or even to float free from their background. A painting of a Devarāja by this master survives to our own day. His manner is said to have influenced the great master Wu Tao-hsüan, and to be traceable in the caves of Tun-huang.[212] He has also been credited with having helped bring the Western technique of using a line of unvarying thickness to outline figures—the "iron-wire" line—to the Buddhist temples of the great cities of China.[213] Not only did this Viśa paint in an exotic manner, but he painted exotic subjects, not disdaining to represent a "Dancing Girl of Kucha." [214]

EXOTIC LITERATURE

The peak of literary interest in the exotic lagged almost two centuries behind the great period of exoticism in the plastic arts. This new development began late in the eighth century, and was associated with the "old-style" movement in prose writing, a reaction against the "new" (that is, only a few centuries old) formal antithetical prose. But the taste for the strange appears in the poetry as well as in the prose of this era. Rich colors, strange fancies, and romantic images captured the attention of many of the best poets of the ninth century. Typical of the age was Li Ho, a poet of illusions and dream images and vivid coloration, prone to use hyperbole and synecdoche —"amber" for "wine," "cold reds" for "autumn flowers." It does not surprise us that this young man was devoted to reading the rich old classic *Ch'u tz'u* and the Zen sect's *Laṅkāvatāra-sūtra,* that he died young, and that the Sung critics spoke of his "demoniac talents." [215] Exotic flavors came naturally to him, as in his poem "The Ambassador from Kurung" or in his description of a barbarian boy with curly hair and green eyes.[216] Another like him was Tu Mu, an official also known for his military essay which advocated waging war on the Northern barbarians in the early summer when they were quiescent and unprepared.[217] Whatever his practical talents, Tu Mu was also a poet of the romantic group, and recollections of the splendid past are common in his verses:

> Looking back at Ch'ang-an, an embroidered pile appears;
> A thousand gates among mountain peaks open each in turn.
> A single horseman in the red dust—and the young Consort laughs,
> But no one knows if it is the lichees which come.[218]

This poem was suggested by the sight of the deserted palace at the hot springs near Ch'ang-an, where Hsüan Tsung and his Precious Consort passed the winter months long ago,[219] and refers to the special courier who brought lichees from Canton to satisfy the Consort's whim. A third poet characteristic of the times was Yüan Chen. This great writer longed passionately for the pure and classic standards of the imagined past. He deplored, for instance, the abandonment in the eighth century of the traditional stone from the banks of the Szu River, celebrated in the oldest literature as material for making chimes, in favor of some new stone; [220] alas, few moderns listen to the old music, he says, and though "Hsüan Tsung loved music, he loved *new* music." Even in his stanzas written to popular airs,[221] Yüan Chen laments the rage for new and exotic things. Despite their puritanism, however, these stanzas depend for their effectiveness upon the poet's treatment of such exotic subjects as imported rhinoceroses and elephants, Turkish horsemen, and Burmese orchestras. Yüan Chen was, in short, exotically anti-exotic.

But the history of exoticism in T'ang poetry has yet to be written. The prose tales on exotic themes, constituting an important variety of the T'ang wonder tale, are much better known. These flourished during the two decades on each side of the turn of the century. In particular, fantasy and marvels of every sort were à la mode during the early years of the ninth century. Fortunately many of them have survived into the twentieth. A common type is the tale of the wonderful gem, brought to China or sought for in China by a mysterious stranger. The stone has the power to clear muddy waters, to reveal buried treasures, or to bring fair winds to seafarers, or is endowed with some other equally gratifying property.[222] This taste for the fantastic,[223] which in late T'ang showed itself in astonishingly rugged and awe-inspiring landscape paintings,[224] necessarily also included the romantically foreign in the arts, and was exemplified in its purest form in stories of weird and lovely objects brought from abroad, most particularly the splendid oddities said to have been offered in former years as tribute gifts to the imperial court. We have to deal, then, not with the charm of genuine imports, but with the glamour of wares that existed nowhere on land or sea, with no truly golden gifts, but with their counterfeits—brummagem of the mind and tinsel of the imagination.

Imaginary gifts, which in turn feed the imagination, do not, of course, appear first in T'ang literature. From antiquity, we have the wonderful presents made to Mu, Son of Heaven; since his time, tales of marvelous gifts from abroad have appeared in every age. The two girls presented by the Red Raven people to archaic Mu, King of Chou by divine right, whom he took to be his concubines,[225] are prototypes of the two black maidens sent (or so we are told by a sophisticated thirteenth-century source), as tribute gifts from the Coromandel Coast,[226] whose fiery loins could rejuvenate the least potent of men. The antique charm of such wonders was enhanced by the old belief that foreign travel was full of physical hazards and spiritual perils, and that monstrous adventures were to be anticipated everywhere outside the confines of China. It was readily believed that spirits and monsters waited at every turn in the mountain trail and lurked beneath every tropical wave.[227] People and things from abroad naturally partook of this dangerous enchantment, and even as late as T'ang times it is probable that exotic gods were still invested with the aroma of uncertain magic and perilous witchery. But in every age, even our own, men are willing to credit every quaint superstition if it concerns distant lands. The notion of fantastic tribute, in short, was not novel in the ninth century. The books that told of it simply gave new life to old and natural traditions, but also found raw material in the events of the first half of the T'ang epoch, which had been unusual in the variety of exotic things that could be seen in China. Material and spiritual exoticism had flourished in the taste of the seventh and eighth centuries. Outlanders and their curious trappings were abundantly to be seen, and the vogue for them was everywhere prevalent. In this lively and expansive age, it even became necessary, from time to time, for the Son of Heaven to set an example for his unthrifty and credulous subjects by issuing bans on the submission of the weird, the wild, and the whimsical among articles of tribute. A notable instance of such exemplary simplicity is found in an edict of the founder of the dynasty, handed down in the first year of his reign.[228] This decree had the additional purpose, it should be noted, of pointing up the recklessness of the preceding regime, that of Sui. It concludes, ". . . such things as dwarfs, small horses with short joints, pygmy cattle, strange beasts, odd birds, and all things without actual utility: the presentation of these shall in every instance be discontinued and cut off. Let this be announced and published far and wide! Let everyone hear and understand!" This enactment did not remain effective for very long, but similar prohibitions issued from the throne again and again.[229] If not aimed at the odd, like the five-colored parakeets from Java, they were directed against the frivolous, like the snow-white hunting falcons from Manchuria.

But after the troubles of the second half of the eighth century, fewer rarities from overseas and overland could be found in the stricken country. There were even fewer after the depredations of Huang Ch'ao in the ninth century, such as the massacre of the foreign merchants during the sack of Canton. In that same century was the great persecution of foreign religions, which tended to remove from the sight of the average Chinese not only the foreign religions and the foreign priests and worshipers, but also foreign books and the images of foreign gods.

It is not surprising, then, that as the international age, the age of imports, the age of mingling, the golden age, began to pass away at the beginning of the ninth century, and the thirst for wonderful things from beyond the seas and across the mountains—whether for Buddhist manuscripts and medical books, or for costly brocades and rare wines, or perhaps just for the sight of an itinerant juggler from Turkestan—could no longer be readily satisfied, the ancient wonder tale gained new and vigorous life, and furnished to the nostalgic imagination what could not be granted to the senses.

The greatest number of T'ang tales about fictitious imports and fantastic tribute were written in the ninth century, when the authentic marvels had passed beyond reach.[230] So the vogue for the exotic in wares was replaced by the vogue for the exaggerated exotic in literature. To quote a modern critic:

We are no longer in the world of flesh and blood. We are in the Dreamland in which the soul glimmers like the flame of a candle. The landscape has been transformed into an "inscape." The world is drowned in the immeasurable ocean of Darkness, and there remains only "an odorous shade." [231]

Many of the stories pretend to tell of the reign of Hsüan Tsung, the fabulous king, most glorious monarch of a cosmopolitan age, himself a connoisseur of the exotic, and a symbol of everything romantic even before his own death.[232] In *his* day, one could *hear* the lutes of Kucha! In the next century one might only dream of them.

Here are a few examples of this kind of creative reminiscence:

Two white rings, the story tells, were given to an emperor of China by one of his vassals, among other "treasures which make firm the nation." [233] These were the rings of the "Mother who is King in the West," a dim and hoary figure associated with dreams of immortality in the mountains at the summit of the world. They resemble other magic rings well-known in folklore. Their possessor could expect with confidence the submission of all peripheral nations.[234]

Again, from Tongking came a piece of rhinoceros horn, as yellow as gold. This was set on a golden plate in the basilica, and the envoy who brought it explained that it had the virtue of dispelling cold—and indeed warm air radiated from it all around.[235] Similar were the hundred sticks of charcoal called the "charcoal of good omen," said to have been sent from the Western Liang, an ancient state in the Kansu area. These were as hard as iron, and would burn without flame for ten days, unapproachable because of the intensity of the heat.[236]

A royal gift from Kucha was a pillow coarsely wrought from a glossy stone much like agate. The fortunate head which slept on it was blessed with dreams of voyages through all lands and seas, even those unknown to mortal men. The tale tells that the head proved to be that of the upstart statesman Yang Kuo-chung, twice fortunate in being the favored cousin of the Precious Consort of Hsüan Tsung.[237]

The perennial demand for beautiful jade, the most magnificent of minerals, underlies the following story: Hsüan Tsung, midway in his reign, marveled that there was no artifact made from the almost legendary five-colored jade among the gifts recently received from the West, though he had in his treasury a belt decorated with plaques of this handsome stone, and a cup carved from it, both submitted long before. He commanded his generals in charge of the "Security of the West" to reprimand the negligent (but anonymous) barbarians who were responsible. The delinquent savages may have been natives of Khotan, the inexhaustible source of jade, and savages they seemed to the Chinese, despite the refinement of their music and the charm of their women. Whoever they were, they did not fail to start a shipment of the pretty polychrome stuff on its way to Ch'ang-an. Alas, the caravan was attacked and robbed of its cargo by the people of Lesser Balūr, turban-wearing lice-eating marauders from the frigid and narrow valleys on the fringes of the snowy Pamirs.[238] When the bad news reached the sacred palace, the Son of Heaven, in his wrath, sent an army of forty thousand Chinese and innumerable dependent barbarians to lay siege to the capital of the marauders and recover his jade. The king of Lesser Balūr quickly surrendered his booty and humbly sought the privilege of sending annual tribute to T'ang. This was refused, and his unhappy city of Gilgit was pillaged. The victorious Chinese general, leading three thousand survivors of the sack, set out for home. He was followed by a prediction of doom, pronounced by a barbarian soothsayer. And indeed the whole multitude was destroyed in a great storm, except for a lone Chinese and a single barbarian ally. The unfortunate Hsüan Tsung, thus finally deprived of his treasure, sent a party to search for the remains of his host. They found an army of transparent bodies, refrigerated prisoners and soldiers of ice, which melted immediately, and were never seen again.[239]

Those had been the magical years, when nothing was impossible. It was this dead glittering world of the eighth century that the writers of exotic fantasy tried to recreate in imagination.

The chief exemplar of this mode in fiction is a book written near the end of the ninth century. Unlike most T'ang wonder books, which exploit every sort of fantasy, this one is almost completely on the subject of *exotic* marvels. It is called *Assorted Compilations from Tu-yang*,[240] and was written by the scholar Su O in 876.[241] Here are some of the rarities he describes:

The "magic shining beans"[242] were sent from a country called "Forest of the Sun," possibly to be interpreted as "Source of the Sun," which is to say "Japan."[243] This land, far across the seas to the northeast, was most noted for a great shining rock, which reflected the internal organs of a man, like a modern X-ray machine, so that his physician might examine their condition and heal him the more quickly. The beans themselves were of a rich pink color, and radiated light over a distance of several feet.[244] Cooked with leaves of the sweet flag, they would grow to the size of goose eggs. The emperor himself tasted one of these excellent beans, and found them delicious beyond compare. Moreover, they freed him from hunger and thirst for several days.

Another marvelous food came from a country in the mysterious South Seas, which also sent a pillow of crystal, within which could be seen a landscape furnished with buildings and human figures; with the pillow was sent a brocaded coverlet, made of the silk of the "water silkworm,"[245] which expanded when dampened and contracted when heated. The food sent from this land was a fragrant kind of wheat which made the body light enough to ride with the wind, and some purple rice grains which restored youthful vigor and prolonged life.

Dragons, that is, water spirits, crystallized into miniature concretions, were another favorite gift. Examples are the "dragon horn hairpin"[246] and the "tread-water bead."[247] The wonderful hairpin was a gift that accompanied the "magic shining beans." It was made of a jadelike stone, of a deep plum color, and was carved in dragon shapes with inhuman skill. The Emperor Tai Tsung presented it to his favorite consort, the beautiful[248] Lady Tuku. One day, as he and she were boating on Dragon Boat Pond, a purple cloud formed over the pin. The sovereign took the pin in his palm and spat water on it, whereupon the vapor congealed into two dragons, which leaped into the sky and disappeared in the east. The "tread-water bead" was a black, perforated bead with an oddly scaly surface. Its bearer could pass unharmed through water. The emperor tested it by binding it with a five-colored cord (which poisonous dragons fear) to the arm of a good swimmer. This man walked on the surface of the waves, plunged under the water, and emerged dry. Later, when the women of the palace were playing with the bead in a pool, it turned into a black dragon.

Marvelous birds and bird spirits were desired tribute. One such was the "fire-rejecting sparrow," [249] a black passerine bird, sent as token tribute on the accession of Shun Tsung. The bird was immune to fire. It was, in short, a true phoenix, unlike the *feng-huang* of Chinese tradition usually miscalled "phoenix" in the West. That is, it was the *samandal* of India (said by the Arabs to be found also in Wāq-wāq) whose skin no flame could consume.[250] A crystal cage in the monarch's bedroom housed this prodigy. There the maidservants amused themselves in vain attempts to burn it with candles. Another country sent two dancing girls, one named "Light Phoenix" and the other "Flying Simurgh," [251] the most ethereal creatures imaginable. On their heads were golden crowns, adorned with the images of the fantastic birds for which they were named, or whose spirits they were. They dined on lichees, gold dust, and "dragon-brain" camphor.

Extraordinary heating devices form a special group. The "ever-burning cauldron" [252] cooked food without fire. This useful object, the tribute of a mythical kingdom, is described in a fantastic narrative that is full of references to countries named in the histories of Han, a millennium before. Related to it was the "fire jade," which was red and could be used like an ember of coal to heat a cauldron.

Contrariwise, sources of cold were equally wonderful and useful. The "ever-hard ice" [253] was found on a great mountain, whose glaciers were a thousand years old. It would not melt in the hottest sunlight. The "pine wind stone" was translucent, and within it could be seen the figure of a pine tree, from whose branches issued a cooling breeze. The sovereign kept it close to him during the summer.

Less desirable, but still to be wondered at, was the "daylight-altering herb." [254] It resembled a banana plant, and was always surrounded by an area of darkness. This uncanny virtue was displeasing to the emperor.

Among these literary marvels were some which could easily have been real, or at least adapted from reality. Such was the "pentachromatic carpet," [255] given to Tai Tsung of T'ang, as were many of these gifts, by the Korean kingdom of Silla. It was marvelously wrought to show the figures of dancers and musicians, and mountains and rivers. Among these things were shown every sort of bird and insect, which fluttered and flitted about when the least breeze blew through the room.

The "mountain of the myriad Buddhas" [256] was a jeweled construction carved from the aloeswood of Indochina, about ten feet high. This too had been sent by Silla. On the mountain were images of all the Buddhas, in a setting of buildings and natural verdure, all done in the minutest detail in pearls and precious stones. The emperor, a pious Buddhist, installed this cosmic symbol in a shrine, and spread the "pentachromatic carpet" on its floor. This wonderful object may not have been entirely imaginary.[257]

The "Chu-lai bird" [258] may also have existed in some form. Though the Emperor Te Tsung was often given trained animals and wonderful fowl, he ordinarily freed such creatures in accordance with Buddhist precept. But he did not release the handsome Chu-lai bird sent by a Southern country in 781. Its bill was red, and its purple-blue tail was longer than its body. It was very clever, and understood human commands. Its voice was high and piercing. This dandy of a bird, apparently a tropical magpie,[259] was much loved by the people of the court, who gave it the most costly delicacies to eat. It passed its nights in a golden cage, and spent its days flying about the courts of the palace, and "neither bold goshawk nor great falcon dared come near." Alas! one day it was caught and murdered by an eagle. The palace mourned it sincerely, and one courtier, a skilled calligrapher, made a copy of the *Prajñāpāramitā-hṛdaya-sūtra*[260] on paper speckled with gold for the good of its soul.[261]

An unknown country in the South Seas sent a girl of fourteen years, called the "Maiden of the Black Eyebrows," among whose remarkable skills was the talent of embroidering the seven scrolls of the *Lotus Sutra* in tiny, perfectly formed characters on a single foot-length of artist's taffeta. She too may have existed in the flesh.

The wonders just described are only a sampling from the splendid array displayed in Su O's book. As we have seen, some are attributed to such real countries as Japan and Silla, some to ancient nations long since unheard from, and some to lands altogether mythical. But if we survey the tribute records in reliable documents of the T'ang period, we find no mention of any of these gifts, even those from "real countries." The period covered by the narrations of Su O was the last half of the eighth century and the first of the ninth, ranging back over a century before his own lifetime, the late afternoon and the setting of the sun of T'ang's splendor. But the cold, unlovely days of Su O's own time were not yet come. During the years he claims to describe, there actually were horses from the Uighurs, dancing girls from P'o-hai, musicians from Burma, a rhinoceros from Champa, and pearls and amber from some remnant of the dismembered Persian empire. Su O has merely filled the gaps in the record of actual imports for these twilight years with things of magic and delight. His book, in short, deals with fairylands of commerce, and archaic wonder worlds of diplomacy. Its charm lies in its antiquarian exoticism, studded with doubtful gems and forgotten curios. Though conceivably some of these stories may have sprung, fertilized by the imagination, from accounts of actual embassies in the years of waning glory at the end of the eighth century, they are nonetheless delicacies for the use of a poet, not grist for the economist's mill.[262]

. . . cargo of gold, silver, jewels and pearls, fine linen, purple, silk and scarlet, all kinds of scented wood, all articles of ivory, all articles of costly wood, bronze, iron and marble, cinnamon, spice, incense, myrrh, frankincense, wine, oil, fine flour and wheat, cattle and sheep, horses and chariots, and slaves, that is, human souls.

Revelation 18:11

11= Men

WAR PRISONERS

CONSPICUOUS among the goods brought into China in the Middle Ages were human souls. Men, women, and children of foreign lands known and unknown were imported in large numbers to play parts for which they were not born, but which were allotted to them by evil chance or royal whim under the skies of T'ang.

During the seventh century, when the conquering Chinese hosts swept the hordes of the barbarians before them everywhere, a large number of the men sent into unwilling bondage in China were prisoners of war. Among these the Turks formed the largest group, having been taken by the thousand on the steppes of Mongolia and the deserts of Serindia. The peoples of Manchuria and Korea also fell into Chinese hands, and were sent off to toil for the Son of Heaven and his minions. Even civil populations might expect this fate. During the Chinese campaign against Koguryŏ in 645, fourteen thousand inhabitants of the city of Liao-tung were seized because they had dared to resist the imperial armies. They were condemned to slavery, but later pardoned by the exceptional clemency of T'ai Tsung.[1] But thousands of less lucky ones were sent to the capital to be displayed to the citizens in a triumphal progress, and presented by the victorious general to the Son of Heaven and his divine ancestors at the Grand Shrine (*T'ai Miao*).

On such an occasion, the victor, wearing the costume of a nomadic cavalier, drew up his armies in full panoply outside the East Gate of the capital, where the splendid palace guards were paraded to receive him. At a signal from the marshal, the procession began. In front went two mounted military bands, playing syringes, flutes, oboes, clarinets,[2] drums, and bells, and a chorus, which sang the four triumphal odes reserved for such grand occasions. The paean called "The Joy of Offering Congratulations at the Imperial Levee"[3] went as follows:

> The Four Seas are mantled by the Majestic Wind,
> For a thousand years made clean by that Virtue which endures.
> Barbarian clothes need not be worn again;[4]
> This day we report what our merits have achieved!

Choreography was designed for one of these compositions at least: the inaugural performance of the triumphal ode and dance "Breaking the Battle Line" was given in 632 by 128 boys in silver armor, in commemoration of the victories of T'ai Tsung.[5] Following the bands and the chorus came the happy troops, and after them, for the breathless admiration of the citizenry, the train of living trophies, the prisoners. They proceeded through the city to the palace, until they reached the gate of the Grand Shrine, where the musicians dismounted, and the throng waited outside the sanctuary for the monarch to conclude the holy rite of offering and thanksgiving to the shades of the deceased kings. Then the bands struck up again, and the conquering general and his officers advanced to the front of a tower where the Son of Heaven awaited them. Here they were formally received with renewed chanting of the triumphal odes. Finally the mob of unhappy captives was brought in to be displayed as examples of rebellion, obduracy, and barbarian manners, and to learn what fate was in store for them.[6] After these unfortunates had shuffled out of the august presence, the chief officers of the devoted army were rewarded according to their deserts, and could expect to be entertained at a great banquet.[7]

After the death of the great conqueror T'ai Tsung, his successor Kao Tsung, in celebration of the capture of Ashina Holu, Yabghu of the Western Turks, introduced a new ceremony into the triumph. He made a preliminary offering of the royal captive to the spirit of T'ai Tsung at the Radiant Tumulus,[8] the latter's sepulcher northwest of the city. This was followed by the customary rite at the Grand Shrine, in front of the assembled court and the chieftains of subject tribes.[9] This apparent novelty was probably a dimly understood revival of an archaic custom—the slaughter of a defeated king as a sacrifice to the royal manes. In this first case, which set a precedent for years to come,[10] however, Holu was graciously spared from death.

The pious motive for offering a noble captive at the tomb of an ancestor was reinforced by the political belief that a foreign chief was by the very nature of things a vassal of the Chinese monarch. In waging war against the emperor, he was in fact leading an insurrection against his rightful liege, and deserved death as punishment. Such was the crime and such the fate of the king of Tashkent,[11] captured by Kao Hsien-chih, the Korean general in Chinese employ, in 750.[12] But this dismal end seems not to have been the lot of most of the great personages taken by the Chinese captains. More typical was the case of Tuman, a chief of the Western Turks, who was captured by the great general Su Ting-fang in 660 and brought to the Eastern Capital, where the Chinese warlord himself pleaded successfully for the captive's life.[13] Indeed, special honors were sometimes the lot of noble prisoners, such as the king of Kucha, who was brought to the capital in 649. After he had been dedicated to the ghosts of dead emperors, he was released and awarded the title of Great Army Commander for the Militant Guards of the Left.[14]

Posthumous even though ambiguous honors were awarded to some royal prisoners—ambiguous in that they might be compared with the glory of a distinguished war horse whose fame depended on the personal history of the monarch who owned him. For instance: Wang Hsüan-ts'e, the ambitious and energetic emissary to India, revenged an offense against the honor of T'ang by mustering a motley host of Tibetans and Nepalese, sacking the splendid town of Magadha, and taking two thousand prisoners of both sexes, along with myriads of horses and cattle. Among the captives was the "usurping" king of Magadha, who was sent to China in 648. Two years later, on the death of T'ai Tsung, whose envoy Hsüan-ts'e was, the image of the contumacious Indian, carved in stone, was erected before the Radiant Tumulus of the late emperor.[15] So he found lasting fame—but as a trophy and emblem.

But the ordinary prisoner could usually expect only death or slavery.[16] Po Chü-i's poem "The Prisoner," written in 809, tells the whole story. The translation is Arthur Waley's.

> Tartars led in chains!
> Tartars led in chains,
> Their ears pierced, their faces bruised—they are driven into the land of Ch'in.
> The Son of Heaven took pity on them and would not have them slain.
> He sent them away to the south-east, to the lands of Wu and Yüeh.
> A petty officer in a yellow coat took down their names and surnames.[17]

Some prisoners of war were apportioned as personal slaves among the great officers of state, both civil and military, but most became "state slaves," subject to whatever employment was assigned by the rulers of the nation.[18] Under certain conditions, as when the prisoners were Chinese taken in a civil war, they might be freed by a special act of amnesty. This freedom might have its qualifications: not during T'ang times, but somewhat earlier, in 545, the fetters were struck from the wrists of a throng of war prisoners, who were then justly apportioned among the widows of the nation.[19] Such a fortunate outcome could not be anticipated by mere barbarians.

Whether his servitude was public or private, ethnic origin might determine the lifework of the unlucky prisoner. Nomads from Mongolia and Central Asia were frequently employed as horseherds, grooms, and outriders to noble carriages. Intel-

[handwritten: SLAVES GAINING FAVOR]

ligence and education could lead a state slave to an important industrial position, perhaps in textiles or ceramics or, better yet, to a position of trust in the imperial palace,[20] perhaps as a guard,[21] a translator, or a dancer. The worst that an enslaved prisoner could expect was to be sent off to the southern frontier, to labor among the feverish miasmas, the head-hunting aborigines, and the crocodiles, as were the Turks described by Po Chü-i, and the Tibetans and Uighurs sent to the Canton region in 851.[22] The ninth-century authorities, abnormally apprehensive about espionage activities, deemed these contaminated outposts the most suitable places of employment for captives native to alpine and boreal regions. It was easier to be liberal in the seventh century, when confidence in Chinese right and Chinese might was high. At best, however, a foreign slave, whether subject to a private gentleman or to the government, could hope to gain power and riches by talent or intrigue. Indeed, some household slaves with military abilities became important figures at the court. Such a man was Wang Mao-chung, son of a Korean rebel, who rose to giddy heights of authority, only to fall through excess of ambition.[23]

But unless they were lucky enough to be assigned to the households of highborn and meritorious subjects, war prisoners generally became slaves of the impersonal state. This was also the destiny of the families of persons convicted of treason, under the rule of collective responsibility. Prisoners and the relatives of traitors alike were obliged to pile rubble for the walls which protected the nation, or for the dikes which guarded its farmlands, until freed, perhaps, by a special indulgence or a general amnesty.[24]

[handwritten: GREAT WALL]

SLAVES

Chinese slaves to take charge of treasury and barn,
Foreign slaves to take care of my cattle and sheep.
Strong-legged slaves to run by saddle and stirrup when I ride,
Powerful slaves to till the fields with might and main,
Handsome slaves to play the harp and hand the wine;
Slim-waisted slaves to sing me songs, and dance;
Dwarfs to hold the candle by my dining-couch.

[handwritten: SELL YOURSELF]

These words occur in the dream of a young bridegroom, ambitious for the authority and luxury of a rich paterfamilias, translated from a Tun-huang manuscript by Arthur Waley.[25]

Probably most of the household slaves, used for domestic work ranging from that of lady's maid to gamekeeper, were supplied by merchants.[26] In late T'ang times a new source of slaves became important: hopelessly delinquent debtors and tenants sold themselves or their children to their landlords or other creditors for fixed periods—even for life.[27] But the typical T'ang slave was a foreigner whose sale put

money in the pocket of a dealer. The puritanical poet Yüan Chen, eternally curious
about exotic things, has described such a merchant of men in a long poem. He displays the huckster, his restless heart consumed with the desire for profit, driven
about the world by his greed, ready to sell anything at all, living or dead, if it be
to his advantage:

> In search of pearls, he harnesses the glaucous sea—
> He gathers his pearls, and ascends to Ching and Heng.
> In the north, he buys the Tangut horses,
> In the west, he catches Tibetan parrots.
> Fire-washed linen from the Continent of Flames,
> Perfectly woven tapestries from the Land of Shu;
> Slave girls of Yüeh, sleek of buttery flesh;
> Houseboys of Hsi, bright of brow and eye.[28]

The sensible slave trader steered clear of trading in the native-born. Ancient custom,
supported by law, made it hazardous to sell a Chinese. If the slave had been kidnaped, the criminal merchant was liable to execution for his pains. Nonetheless,
the head of a household might, when driven by necessity, sell one of his women or
children, his will being their will.[29] It was generally quite safe to deal in foreign
slaves, however, and not a burden on the conscience, since they were not quite
human, in the best sense of the word.[30] Therefore, any breed of alien was salable,
provided that no current law exempted him. The salesman's wares might be Persians,
seized with other loot by the pirate Feng Jo-fang and kept in the slave villages near
Wan-an on the island of Hainan.[31] They might be Turks, not prisoners of war but
human merchandise exported from Transoxania by the Sāmānids,[32] or peaceful
herdsmen or their children, kidnaped and carried over the Chinese frontier—a
practice not tolerated during the high years when T'ang was at peace with the
troublesome nomads.[33] It is even possible that some of the Slavonic slaves exported
by Khwārizm found their way to the Far East.[34] Or the slaves might be Koreans,
especially female Koreans, girls of the states of Koguryŏ and Silla, who were in great
demand as personal maids, concubines, and entertainers in rich houses.[35] This last
luxury commerce supported a horde of pirates on the waters of the Yellow Sea, and
occasioned the protests of the governments of the Korean peninsula. In 692, the
Chinese governor of the Shantung region, where the slaves were set ashore, asked
that such crimes against the friendly kingdom of Silla be suppressed, and it was so
ordered.[36] But there must have been sighs in some quarters. The beauty of these
girls was celebrated, even though sometimes inveighed against by the narrow-
minded. For instance, in 646 Koguryŏ sent a mission to T'ai Tsung to give thanks
for the sparing of the citizens of the besieged city of Liao-tung the previous year.
As a thank offering, the ambassadors brought two beautiful women. But the sovereign spoke to them as follows:

44

Go back and say to your master that although beauty and a fair appearance are made much of by men—and truly his gifts are voluptuously beautiful—I pity them, separated from father, mother, and brothers older and younger in their own country. To detain their persons while forgetting their families—to love their fairness while wounding their hearts—this I cannot do.   646 TAI TSUNG

And so he sent them home.[37]

But the greatest sources of non-Chinese slaves were the tribes of the south—enclaves of Thais and other aborigines among the newly dominant Chinese interlopers in Fukien, Kwangtung, Kwangsi, and Kweichow. Slave traders preyed upon these unfortunate "barbarians" without mercy, while edict after edict issued from the throne decrying this evil and forbidding it, apparently with little success.[38] Typical was the decree of Te Tsung, late in the eighth century, which indicates that young slaves were until then sent as ordinary annual tribute to the court from the remote town of Yung-fu, not far from the present Annamese border: ". . . to be the cause of their separation from the villages of their mothers and fathers, and to interrupt the love of bones and flesh, is truly inhumane. Let it cease!"[39] This may have finished the taking of aboriginal slaves under official auspices, but private dealings in them continued. In the middle of the ninth century, in a decree against all commerce in slaves in the far south, Hsüan[(1)] Tsung stated that he had heard that, since the simple natives there are no better than savages ". . . who till with fire and hoe with water, in want by day and starved by night," they are oppressed by taxes, and obliged to sell their sons and daughters. Therefore they are exploited by evildoers, and as a result, says the imperial order, ". . . males and females become wares and wealth, along with horn and ivory."[40] There is some indication that, SLAVE GIRLS equally among southern aborigines as among Koreans, young slave girls were most sought for. One of the first acts of the excellent governor, K'ung K'uei, when he took office in Canton in 817, was to ban the sale of women taken from the native villages.[41] The contemporary poet Chang Chi described one of them in these words:

> On the southern border, by the Bronze Pillars, where the spring brings poison herbs;
> How many days before the traveler will reach the Unicorn of Gold?
> Her ears pierced by jade rings, this girl—of what man's house?—
> Clasps the lute to herself, inviting the God of the Sea.[42]

Another great source of slaves for T'ang was trans-Gangetic India. Slaves imported from the Indies were styled "Kurung slaves," slaves from the lands of the *Kurung Bnam,*[43] "Kings of the Mountain," using the old Cambodian name, equivalent to Sanskrit *Śailarāja,* expressing the symbolic sway of the Khmer over the holy cosmic mountain, like that of the Śailendra kings of Java and Sumatra.[44] Southward from Champa, says the "Book of T'ang," ". . . all have curly hair and black bodies, and are collectively called *Kurung.*"[45] These slaves were "Malays" in the broadest sense. Judging from the "curly hair," they were often Veddoid types, but also Khmers and other wavy-haired peoples, possibly even with Dravidians and other men of the Indian Ocean. They were most noted for their talents as swimmers; they could plunge under the waves with open eyes, and retrieve lost objects from the bottom. Many must have been trained as pearl-divers.

Here is an account of the K'un-lun peoples by Hui-lin, the great Buddhist lexicographer of the eighth and early ninth century:

> They are also called Kurung. They are the barbarous men of the islands, great and small, of the Southern Seas. They are very black, and expose their naked figures. They can tame and cow ferocious beasts, rhinoceroses, elephants and the like. There are many races and varieties of them; thus there are the Zāngī, the Turmi [?], the Kurdang [?], and the Khmer. All are simple, humble people. Their nations have nothing of good form or social responsibility. They rob and steal for a living, and are fond of chewing up and devouring humans, as if they were some sort of *rakshas* or evil ghosts. The languages they speak are not correct and proper ones, being different from those of the several "bulwark"-nations. They excel when they go in the water, for they can remain there the whole day and not die.[46]

In this account we see some remarkable instances of Chinese ethnocentric prejudice, especially those against dark skins (they also called the Persians "black"!) and against relative nudity, which had been regarded as objectionable since Han times. Other sources classify *all* countries south of China as "Kurung," or make "Kurung" the equivalent of the *Dvīpāntara* of the Sanskrit books;[47] but Hui-lin's statement seems to limit the term to the Indonesians who had not received the "benefits" of Indian acculturation, that is, to the non-Hinduized aborigines of the Isles.

When the great Li Te-yü was exiled to Ch'ao-*chou* and lost his precious art collection in a shipwreck, he had a "Kurung slave" dive for it. It is not to the discredit of the barbarian swimmer that he failed because of the abundance of crocodiles.[48] Littoral Indians and aquatic Malays were favorite subjects for popular tales. In one of them,[49] the slave, a resourceful rogue, procures an assignation for the young hero with a beautiful courtesan by interpreting the ambiguous signs made by the lady with her fingers. Later the slave, having escaped his vengeful owner, is discovered selling drugs in the market of Lo-yang.[50] This sounds very much like an Indian or Arabian tale, with a Chinese veneer. It is characteristic of a special brand of exotic literature current in late T'ang times.[51]

It appears that Negro slaves were known to a small courtly group during a short period of the T'ang era. These rare beings were called *Zāngī* by the Chinese, using a term for Negroes that is universal in the Malay archipelago and has such alternate forms as *Zenj* and *Janggi*.[52] The name refers to the natives of "Zanzibar" in the oldest and widest sense, not just the island which now bears the name, but a large region in equatorial East Africa, an easy and natural terminus for ships coming from the Persian Gulf under the northeast monsoon. By extension, then, every Negro was a Zāngī. During the space of six years, from 813 to 818, three missions from the Javanese nation of Kalinga (whose king drank wine prepared from coconuts, and the country of the "poison women" [53] with whom it was fatal to sleep) came to the court of Hsien Tsung and presented, along with such rarities as a live rhinoceros and a five-colored parrot, a small number of Zāngī boys and girls.[54] The only other record is of a Zāngī girl sent by Śrivijaya, a world center of Sanskrit scholarship and Buddhist piety, to the Deva-putra of T'ang in 724.[55] These black youths and maidens left no mark on literature, and were given only the briefest notices in the histories. They were merely transitory curiosities for the cultivated courts of the eighth and ninth centuries, and never attained the lasting picturesque status of the small turbanned blackamoors of the European Rococo.[56] How they came into the hands of the king of Kalinga in the first place is not certain, though it has been generally assumed that they came from Africa. It is said that Indian pirates plundered a ship sent by the ruler of Ceylon to the Khalif in 712, and took "Abyssinian slaves" from it.[57] Black slaves, then, could be purchased along the shores of the Indian Ocean, and presumably brought as far as Java.[58] Possibly the T'ang coins found on Zanzibar and the Somaliland coast [59] were brought there by Chinese merchants in men. But all the Negroes sent from Java and Sumatra to China could equally have been enslaved in Southeast Asia, where there are Negritos even today. In T'ang times the Chinese knew a "Kat-kat Zāngī Country," which was an island off the northwestern corner of Sumatra, much feared by mariners because of the savagery of its inhabitants.[60] Such a place, close to Kalinga and Śrivijaya, could easily have been the home of the young blacks sent to Ch'ang-an.

DWARFS

Little men—dwarfs and pygmies—both native and exotic, were as fascinating to the Chinese of T'ang as to other medieval peoples. But the vogue for them seems not to have been more pronounced in T'ang than under earlier Chinese dynasties. Confucius himself fixed the classical size of a mannikin at three feet when he spoke of the height of the pygmy people called Chiao-yao,[61] whose name also means "wren." According to tradition, the little wren-people lived far to the southwest of China, though some said they were to be found on an island in the southeastern sea.[62] In ancient times they sent tribute of ivory, carabaos, and zebus to China. They were troglodytes and excellent swimmers.[63] It is not certain that the Chinese of Chou and Han times ever saw these tropical pygmies, who were either Negritoes or else wavy-haired men like the modern Senoi. But they did have their court dwarfs, who were entertainers, dancers, and musicians.

And so it was under the T'ang emperors too. The town of Tao-*chou,* in the southern part of what is now Hunan Province, was noted for the number of dwarfs born there, and was required to send specimens to the court each year as "tribute." Po Chü-i wrote of them in the ninth century. The translation is Arthur Waley's:

> In the land of Tao-*chou*
> Many of the people are dwarfs;
> The tallest of them never grow to more than three feet.
> They were sold in the market as dwarf slaves and yearly sent to Court;
> Described as "an offering of natural products from the land of Tao-*chou.*"
> A strange "offering of natural products . . ." [64]

A humane magistrate, Yang Ch'eng, terminated the submission of this unusual produce on his own initiative at the end of the eighth century. Naturally, a messenger from the capital soon appeared to ask why the expected tribute had not come. Yang Ch'eng wrote a formal reply in which he stated, probably with more cleverness than truth, that *all* of the natives of the place were abnormally short, and so he was at a loss to decide with equity which individuals to send off to the metropolis. At any rate, the requirement was officially abolished, and the name of Yang was blessed throughout the countryside. [65]

More astonishing and satisfying to the T'ang exquisites than such native dwarfs were pygmies imported from abroad, who reminded them of the "wren-men" of ancient times. In 724 the Sumatran thalassocracy of Śrivijaya, or Śrībhoja (as it was known to the Arabs and Chinese), sent a certain Kumāra (which means "Crown Prince," and perhaps he was that) [66] to Ch'ang-an with many rare gifts for the Son of Heaven, most of them human—such as musicians, a Negro girl (whom we have already noticed), and two pygmies. [67] In the same year a pygmy was sent from Samarkand, a fruitful land, rich in all wares and produce. [68] A race of pygmies called the "short men," who lived far to the northwest of that place, had been heard of in China since very early times. [69] Their land was said to be rich in pearls and phosphorescent gems. Another tradition said that they lived peaceful lives north of the Turks in Siberia, where their only enemies were great birds which ate them when they could, though the pygmies fought fiercely with bows and arrows. [70] These are, of course, the pygmies of the classical Greeks, but in this Far Eastern version of their story they are placed in eastern Europe or in Siberia, not in the depths of Africa. But the basic Western tradition which put them in Africa reached the Chinese too:

The Little People are to the south of Great Ch'in [Rome]. Their bodies are barely three feet long. At the season of plowing and planting their crops, they fear lest they be eaten by the cranes. But Great Ch'in provides guards to protect them, and the Little People exhaust their treasures to repay and reward them. [71]

But whence came the authentic nonmythical pygmy sent by the king of Samarkand?

HOSTAGES

Many kinds of alien men other than slaves found themselves subject to Chinese masters against their will. The Arab soldiers sent to help General Kuo Tzu-i put down the great rebellion of Rokhshan in the eighth century were one such bewildered group of puppets, as were the men of other nationalities whose lives were not entirely their own, and who provided a curious spectacle for the T'ang populace. Not so different from these foreign troops, except perhaps in social status, were the hostages kept in the capital to guarantee the friendly behavior of their noble and royal relatives abroad. Though Chinese tradition was opposed to the hostage system, the practicalities of international politics often required that this tradition be ignored. Indeed, the reasons commonly urged against the system were themselves practical rather than humanitarian. These reasons had their roots in conservative xenophobia: it was held that barbarians residing in China were likely to prove either trouble-makers or spies.[72] During the glorious imperialistic years of the seventh century, it was altogether an ordinary thing to require that a Turkish or Korean prince remain in the palace of Ch'ang-an as long as the T'ang government might think it prudent to retain him; even the Sāsānian prince Narsē [73] was held as a respected hostage, perhaps a willing one, after the death of his refugee father, Pērōz.[74] Such a period of obligatory residence might prove to be unendurably long, despite the worthless robes of honor and the accessible fleshpots. High-born male hostages whiled away their comfortable exiles, consoled perhaps by some nominal rank at court: the usual thing was a commission in the palace guards. No doubt these scions of foreign principalities looked wonderfully handsome in their colorful Chinese uniforms.[75] It was not until the peaceful reign of Hsüan Tsung that the authorities were instructed to send home the superannuated hostages who had been resident at the court for many decades.[76] The superficially honorable condition of these hostages in China, however, was regarded differently in their homelands. From that perspective, it was insult and slavery: "The sons of Turkish nobles became the slaves of the Chinese people, their pure daughters became bondswomen." [77]

HUMAN TRIBUTE

Even inferior to hostages in autonomy, since specific services were required of them, and hardly to be distinguished from slaves, were the men and women sent to the T'ang court as royal gifts or, as interpreted by the Chinese, as "tribute." Any extraordinary mortal might be thought suitable for this role, and indeed the Chinese towns had been accustomed since antiquity to send odd or monstrous objects of

HUMAN TRIBUTE (handwritten margin note)

every sort to the imperial court, and these might easily be human beings. Quite typical was the woman, submitted by a northwestern town early in the eighth century, whose whole body was covered with the shapes of temples and images of the several Buddhas, raised in relief on her skin.[78] Equally astonishing were the two "white-headed men" with skins like tallow, albino troglodytes sent by Cambodian Bnam.[79] But men from remote lands, given luster by distance and rarity, were sufficient curiosities in themselves. Such were the four Karluks from the region of Lake Balkash, sent to Ch'ang-an by the Uighurs in 822,[80] or the heavily bearded Ainus brought by a Japanese mission in 669,[81] or gifts of Turkish women,[82] or Tibetan girls sent as appropriate tokens of congratulation on a national holiday.[83]

IMMORTALITY POTIONS (handwritten margin note)

Best gifts of all were wise men from far countries, whose uncanny insights were the more believable because of their exotic source. Such was the "Great Musha," that is, one of the Manichaean Elect, a man profoundly versed in the "configurations of the heavens," sent with the recommendation of the king of Tukhāra in 719.[84] Such too was Nārāyaṇasvāmin, a compounder of drugs, brought from Magadha in 648 by Wang Hsüan-ts'e.[85] He claimed to be two hundred years old, and able to prepare elixirs of immortality. This sage had some fine tales for the T'ang courtiers: he told of a marvelous liquid found only in a stone mortar deep in the mountains of India. This potent water had the virtue of dissolving flesh, wood, and metal. It could only be removed in a camel's skull, and transferred to a calabash. Its source was guarded by a stone image, and death awaited any mountaineer who revealed it to a stranger.[86] This venerable taleteller was well received by the Chinese emperor, given honorable lodging under the supervision of a high official, and politely instructed to prepare his life-extending drugs. His powers had waned, it seems, for his efforts failed, and he was finally discharged from the imperial service. He spent the rest of his life in Ch'ang-an, no doubt supported by a considerable clientele.[87] Another such wonder-worker was the priest, sent by a Western nation in the seventh century, who had the power of bringing the dead to life by incantation. T'ai Tsung found guardsmen to "volunteer" for trials of these alleged powers. The foreigner put them to death by his spells, and then revived them by the same means. The story goes that a virtuous minister told the monarch that this was an evil art which could not hurt a truly good man (himself, of course), and indeed the foreign sage fell dead when he chanted his jargon at this exemplary courtier.[88] The unfortunate miraclemonger was evidently a skilled hypnotist, but the manner of his death has certainly been garbled (and improved) in transmission.

BRING PEOPLE BACK TO LIFE. (handwritten margin note)

MUSICIANS AND DANCERS

But of all the specialists of ambiguous social status who were sent to China by a foreign government, the most popular and influential were the musicians—instru-

mentalists, singers, and dancers—and the instruments and musical modes they
brought with them. When a historical text records that in 853 Japan sent "music"
to the T'ang court,[89] we must understand that the word includes musical forms and
compositions, which were regarded as being as transferable as real property, as well
as the performers and tools of their trade. For many centuries, the music of the West
had had its admirers in China, but under the Sui emperors there was a great vogue
for it, which continued into T'ang times. As Western nations were brought under
Chinese control, their music was "captured," as it were, and subsequently was demanded as "tribute" from them. Foreign orchestras were incorporated into the mass
of court employees and were required to perform for courtiers and vassals in "informal" palace entertainments. "Formal" ceremonies, in contrast, required traditional tunes, played on ancient Chinese instruments, especially bells, stone chimes,
and zithers.[90]

The habit of listening to exotic sounds, and of expressing fashionable enthusiasm
for them, spread from the court among the aristocrats, and so among all classes
of urban society:

> At the head of the wall, the mountain fowl sings kok! kok!
> In Lo-yang, in house after house, they study Western music.[91]

The unflattering comparison of the poet was not likely to reverse the modish trend.
The prime agencies which diffused "upper class" musical fashions among the people
were the two official "Instruction Quarters"[92] in Ch'ang-an, comparable to the Gion
and Pontochō quarters in modern Kyoto. One quarter specialized in song, the other
in dance.[93] Here gifted players, singers, and dancers, with a status like that of the
"official prostitutes,"[94] geisha of the most exalted kind, were trained in informal
music for the pleasure of those whom the Son of Heaven was pleased to favor. From
them, the new music was passed on to high-class independent courtesans, and so
down the scale of the demimonde and, by way of the gay blades of the town, into
the great stream of T'ang culture. These queens of popular music were careful to
study the latest tunes, and to set brighter words to old favorites. They could sing to
such popular melodies as "Music for Releasing a Goshawk," "Floating the Dragon
Boat," "Crushing the Southern Barbarians," "The Green-Headed Duck," and scores
of others, to the great admiration of high and low—unless prudence required that
the ladies be scorned, as during the unpredictable but brief periods when the sovereign expressed his determination to limit extravagance in court circles, and issued
an edict against such follies as gathering pearls and jade, wearing fancy sashes, and
giving performances by female musicians.[95] But if the regime was not too puritanical,
the girls were inspired to produce such tunes as "The Three Platforms of the Turks,"
"South India," "Music of Kucha," and "Watching the Moon in Brahman Land."[96]
These songs were suggested by melodies played by foreigners, especially by the
"tribute" musicians, but appropriately modified so as not to offend popular taste

too much. They were, we may imagine, pseudo-exotic compositions, like our own "Song of India," "Where the Ganges Flows," and "Pagan Love Song."

This not-quite familiar music with an exotic "content" and "style" was characteristic of the seventh century.[97] In the eighth century the pseudo-exotic gave way to the truly exotic, and Chinese popular music began to sound like the music of the city-states of Central Asia. Indeed, the famous song "Rainbow Chemise, Feathered Dress," which will always remind us of Hsüan Tsung (a royal music-lover who is said to have employed thirty thousand musicians) was actually only a revision of the Serindian song "Brahman." So the musical styles of Kucha and Qočo and Kashgar, of Bukhāra[98] and Samarkand, of India and Korea, were alloyed with the traditional music under official auspices. In the ninth century, when the sober classical music was again emphasized in court circles,[99] the stream of exotic influences was cut off, and although some Indochinese music, especially that of Burma and the kingdom of Nan-chao, was brought to China, it seems to have had virtually no effect on the music of T'ang.[100]

Of all the musical cultures of Serindia, it was the Kuchean which had by far the greatest influence on that of T'ang. Refined and vulgar citizens alike were avid for the "drum dance" tunes of the Kuchean bands.[101] The instruments used by the performers of Kucha were also preferred. Most important of these was the Kuchean four-stringed bent-neck lute, upon whose technique and tuning were based the twenty-eight modes of T'ang popular music, and the melodies developed from them.[102] The oboe and the flute were also important in Kucha, and therefore popular in China.[103] Best liked of all the Kuchean instruments was the little lacquered "wether drum,"[104] with its exciting music, and the exotic songs in mispronounced Sanskrit which were sung to it.[105] The great Hsüan Tsung himself, like many other noble persons, was a trained performer on the wether drum.[106]

Best known of all was the hybrid music of "Western Liang," the frontier town actually called Liang-*chou* in T'ang times. This music was a curious amalgam of the music of Kucha with traditional Chinese music, displaying such incongruities as the Kuchean lute conjoined with the classical lithophone. It was celebrated by the poets of the eighth century and later.[107]

The music of T'ang's Northern neighbors, felt to be both "sad" and "robust," had its influence too, but almost entirely on military bands. These concerts of "drum and blast"[108]—lively emotional music played on horns, drums and gongs—was most suitable for court celebrations, official triumphs, and other patriotic occasions.[109]

Music of Indian origin came to China otherwise than through Central Asia: the nations of Indochina, that is, of Champa, Cambodia, and Burmese Pyū, also sent their orchestras and dancers, who performed compositions on themes from the Buddhist scriptures, such as "The Mudras of the Buddha," "The Victory of the Fighting Ram," and "The Peacock King."[110]

Some of these dance pantomimes, which were the delight of the people of

52

T'ang, still survive in altered and fossilized choreography and are performed by musicians and dancers of the twentieth-century Japanese court, and also by some amateur lovers of the classics in Japan, though the ballets are now extinct on the mainland of Asia.[111] The orchestras which now accompany the Japanese survivals must resemble those of T'ang rather closely. They consist of three groups of instruments: first, woodwinds, including horizontal flutes, oboes, and "mouth organs," playing the melody in the high register, and illuminating it with chords; second, the percussive group, including the gong, the little "wether drum" on its stand, and the "grand drum" suspended from a vermilion frame crowned with a golden flame; third, the low-pitched strings, zither [112] and lute. This orchestra plays compositions with clearly distinguished parts, including usually a free prelude which establishes the mode of the piece from the pitch set by the "mouth organ," then a broad development, and a rapid coda.[113] One of the T'ang music dramas, preserved in nineteenth-century Japanese part books and still performed, is "Kalaviṅka," [114] named for a divine bird of the Buddhist paradise. It is said that the drama was revealed to mankind by an angelic being. Created in India, it was transmitted to China, probably by way of Champa,[115] and finally came to Japan, where it was very popular in the ninth century.[116] It was even performed in 861 at the dedication of the new head for the image of Vairocana at Tōdaiji temple in Nara, with choreography by an expatriate Chinese dance master, and new music, in the Cham manner, by the flute master Wanibe Ōtamaro.[117] The dance is now performed in Japan by four boys, fitted with wings and wearing flowery crowns; they play little cymbals in imitation of the thrilling celestial voice of the Kalaviṅka bird.[118] Another T'ang pantomime that is still performed in Japan is called *Po-t'ou*.[119] It shows a youth in plain clothing, with wildly loosened hair, searching for the wild beast which has eaten his father. This too came to Japan from China, but was ultimately Indian.[120] Among other pantomimes are "The Barbarian Drinks Wine," showing a drunken barbarian chief; "Bhairava Breaks the Battle Lines," a deed of the god Siva in his terrible aspect; and "Music for Striking the Ball," an enactment of a polo game.[121] Most entertaining of all in its original form must have been "Sprinkling the Barbarian with Water as He Begs in the Cold." [122] This was a winter solstice dance, done by naked youths, both Chinese and foreign, leaping about in fantastic masks to the clamor of drums, lutes, and harps, and sprinkling each other, and the passers-by as well, with cold water. This rowdy show was such a scandal to virtuous citizens that Hsüan Tsung was obliged to order its abolition early in 714.[123]

For that matter, the performances of acrobats and prestidigitators were not generally regarded as less noble than these musical plays. The illusions and spectacles of conjurers, tightrope dancers, contortionists, fire-eaters and performing dwarfs were collectively styled "Unclassified Music," [124] and many such performers were introduced from Turkestan and India to the cities of T'ang.[125] Shows of illusion, including apparent self-maiming, were regularly given at the temples of Ahura-Mazda in Liang-*chou* and Lo-yang.[126] Though often officially tolerated, or even encouraged by such an exceptional monarch as Hsüan Tsung, the shows of these alien tricksters were sometimes proscribed by the mighty. Kao Tsung, for instance, ordered the removal from the soil of China of a certain Indian, who was dazzling the populace with illusions of self-disembowelment and amputations, and commanded that no more of his stripe be sent to the T'ang court from beyond the frontier.[127]

Marionette plays are thought to have been first brought to Ch'ang-an in the seventh century from Turkestan, though shadow plays of parchment dolls had been seen in China since antiquity.[128]

Though the Chinese learned the new musical arts as best they could, the foreign masters, especially those of Transoxania and eastern Turkestan, were always welcome connoisseurs, though Chinese vanity was offended at the notion that native genius could not triumph over foreign cunning. So while an actor from Bukhāra, a flute player from Samarkand, an oboist from Khotan, a dancer from Tashkent, or a composer of songs from Kucha, were all assured employment in the Far East,[129] it was still possible for a well-known writer to produce an anecdote in which a palace maidservant of T'ai Tsung, after a single hearing of the performance of a lute song by a distinguished foreign musician, reproduced it with perfect fidelity. The discomfited artist left the country, and ". . . when this was heard among the nations of the West, several tens of them offered their submission!"[130] Such was the cultural majesty of T'ang.

Many of these entertainers were brought as gifts from distant kings; such men and their music were registered in the annals of T'ang. But there were also many free musicians who achieved fame in China. Although their music was not incorporated into the official court music like that of Kucha and Samarkand, it was highly popular among the people. Such was the case of the anonymous musicians of Kumādh below the Pamirs, whose art was ignored by the official archivists; or the musicians of Kabūdhān, called Ts'ao by the Chinese, mostly lutanists, who outnumbered all other nationalities among the foreign musicians in China.[131] We must ignore these independent and far-wandering artists, and consider our proper subjects here, the musicians who were chattels, whether of kings or of commoners.

The least of these talented slaves were the small boys who were favorites among the patricians as players of the cross flute,[132] such as the Western "chick" kept by Hsüan Tsung among his entertainers of the "Pear Garden."[133]

The Western boy with curly hair and green-irised eyes,
In the high tower, when the night is quiet, blows the transverse bamboo.[134]

The greatest of the musical bondsmen were the mature masters, who were in demand both as performers and as instructors. For some instruments at least, it was deemed essential for a cultivated person to have a foreign teacher in order to learn the true refinements of the art. We read of an accomplished Chinese lute player of the eighth century who was asked by an admiring listener, who had detected a foreign quality in his interpretation, "Is that not the mode of Kucha?" To this the gratified player replied, "My master was indeed a man of Kucha."[135] One such eminent master was the Kuchean Po Ming-ta (though it is not known if he was slave or free).[136] This man composed the popular ballet "Trill of the Spring Warbler," which was strongly colored by Kuchean music, was celebrated in the poetry of Yüan Chen, and is still performed in Japan.[137]

Beautiful girls trained as musicians, dancers, singers, and instrumentalists had been sent as presents from one lord to another since ancient times in China, though conventional morality of the "Confucian" sort regarded them as the most frivolous and corrupting of gifts. Nonetheless many T'ang rulers accepted them from lesser princes, and particularly from the Indianized nations of Turkestan. Such were the "female musicians" sent in 733 by the king of Khuttal, a country in the mountains of the upper Oxus, rich in horses, red leopards, and mines of black salt.[138]

Most admired of all the performers imported from Central Asia were the dancers, young boys and girls. Their shows were conventionally classified in two groups, the "pliant" dances and the "vigorous" dances.[139] Po Ming-ta's "Trill of the Spring Warbler" was typical of the former class, of poetic, graceful, and refined dances. But it was the group of "vigorous" dances which had the greatest popular following, and were therefore most frequently mentioned by the T'ang poets. Three of these are quite well known. One was the "Western Prancing Dance,"[140] usually performed by boys from Tashkent wearing tight-sleeved Iranian shirts and high peaked hats sewn with sparkling beads. They were girded with long belts whose ends floated high and free, as they crouched, whirled, and leaped to the rapid accompaniment of lutes and transverse flutes.[141] The "Dance of Chāch,"[142] named for its place of origin near modern Tashkent,[143] was done by two young girls, dressed in gauze caftans embroidered in many colors, with silver girdles. They wore the typical tight-sleeved blouses of the Far West, had peaked hats decorated with golden bells on their heads, and red brocaded shoes on their feet. They appeared first to the audience emerging from the opening petals of two artificial lotuses, and danced to the rapid beating of drums. It was an amorous dance: the maidens ogled the spectators and, at the end, pulled down their blouses to reveal their bare shoulders:[144]

> Matched pair spread flat—the brocaded mats unroll;
> Linked beats of triple sounds—the painted drums drive on.
> Red wax candles are taken away, peach petals rise;
> Purple net shirts are set in motion—the Chāch (dancers) come!
> Girdles droop from gilded thighs, flowered waists are heavy,
> Hats revolve with golden bells, snowy faces turn.
> I watch—too soon the tune is done, they will not be detained;
> Whirling in clouds, escorted by rain, they are off to the Terrace of the Sun.[145]

This poem on the "Geisha of Chāch,"[146] by Po Chü-i, a good example of the exotic in early ninth-century poetry, reveals its erotic theme in the last verse, where the old symbols of "clouds and rain" and "Terrace of the Sun" connect these fairy-like creatures with the myth of a fertility goddess, and hint at the conjunction of the sexes. The strangely rising peach petals appear to have been a display of fireworks.[147]

Most loved of all these young dancers from the Far West were the "Western Twirling Girls,"[148] many of whom were sent as gifts from the rulers of Kumādh, Kish, Māimargh, and especially Samarkand, during the reign of Hsüan Tsung, that is, during the first half of the eighth century.[149] These Sogdian girls, clad in crimson robes with brocaded sleeves, green damask pantaloons, and boots of red deerskin, skipped, tripped, and twirled on the tops of balls rolling about on the dance platform, to the delight of the surfeited hearts of the rich and noble. Hsüan Tsung was very fond of this dance, and both the Lady Yang and Rokhshan learned to perform it.[150] Indeed, the rage for watching such whirling dervishes was regarded in some quarters as an ominous aberration of manners.[151]

Fewer musicians and dancers came from other parts of Asia. Nonetheless, among the nations of Indochina and Indonesia, Nan-chao on the southwestern frontier sent a band to perform for the Chinese emperor in 800;[152] this exotic orchestra may already have had a hybrid character, since a Chinese emissary to Nan-chao a few years earlier had observed performers of Kuchean music, sent to Nan-chao long before by Hsüan Tsung, still playing in the orchestra.[153] After the way to T'ang was opened at the end of the eighth century by the Chinese conquest of Nan-chao,[154] Pyū of Burma presented an orchestra of thirty-five performers in 802, which played compositions based on the Buddhist scriptures, marking time by clenching their fists, and accompanied by conch shells and beautifully engraved bronze drums, like those owned by well-to-do "barbarians" of south China;[155] Sumatran Śrībhoja sent a company of musicians to Hsüan Tsung's court in 724;[156] and a company of Javanese female musicians came from Kalinga in the second half of the ninth century.[157] Eleven Japanese dancing girls were forwarded to the Chinese court in 777 by the representatives of the kingdom of P'o-hai;[158] on another occasion a Japanese embassy brought sacred conch horns as gifts.[159]

When Koguryŏ and Paekche were vanquished in the seventh century, the music of these Korean nations was made captive, and whole bands, with their instruments and texts, were taken to China in triumph.[160] The performers from Koguryŏ and their descendants continued to play faithfully for the Chinese court for over a century, but of the twenty-five compositions they knew at the end of the seventh century, only one was still remembered at the end of the eighth, and the native costumes of the musicians' captive ancestors had all been lost. The performers from Paekche, on the other hand, were all dead or dispersed by the beginning of the eighth century.[161] The greater durability of the northern Koreans (those of Koguryŏ) may be attributed to the fact that two groups of their fellow countrymen, now subject to Silla, were transmitted with their instruments to the Chinese court in 818, invigorating the feeble expatriates.[162] Silla, the rising state on the peninsula and the good friend of T'ang, sent a pair of desirable girls, distinguished as much for their beautiful hair as for their musical talent, to T'ai Tsung in 631. The monarch uttered some sentientious remarks, such as "We have heard that the pleasures of sound and color are not to be compared with the love of virtue," [163] and went on to tell the patient ambassadors how he had sent back to Champa the royal gift of a white Moluccan cockatoo, and concluded his speech by declaring that these lovely maidens were more to be pitied than an exotic parrot, and so back they must go to Silla.[164]

iii=Domestic Animals

HORSES

HORSES WERE of tremendous importance to the rulers of T'ang, whose high estate and far-flung majesty among the peoples of Asia depended in large measure on the availability of quantities of horses to carry soldiers and supplies against mobile enemies, especially the nomadic peoples, their voracious rivals. The doctrine of the final dependence of the state upon a huge number of war horses is plainly pronounced in the *Book of T'ang,* which states, in connection with the death of 180,000 government horses by disease, "Horses are the military preparedness of the state; if Heaven takes this preparedness away, the state will totter to a fall." [1] When the dynasty was founded early in the seventh century, the victors found themselves in possession of only five thousand horses pastured in the grasslands of Lung-yu, that is, in modern Kansu. Of these, three thousand were inherited from the fallen house of Sui, and the rest were booty taken from the Turks. [2] Through the care of the magistrates charged with carrying out government policy on horses, the nation could claim, in the middle of the same century, 706,000 horses, divided among the eight great pasturelands north of the Wei River, in the countryside above the Western Capital. [3] From then on every effort was made to keep the horse population at this high level. The only important change came after the reign of Hsüan Tsung, in the middle of the eighth century, when the disasters of war left the countryside waste. After these calamities, which accompanied the breakdown of central authority, the great nobles and high provincial officials acquired enormous holdings in livestock, which finally outnumbered those of the imperial government.[4]

The paramount need for horses did not, however, make it necessary for the sovereign to accept any gift of them. He might, out of conviction or expedience, reject an expensive present, whether dancing girl or dancing horse, as unworthy of his virtuous and incorruptible reign. The first three rulers of T'ang frequently did so.[5] Or again, the princes of foreign nations often sought the advantage of a family alliance with T'ang during the seventh century, and accordingly sent herds of the much-desired horses to accent a suggestion of marriage with a Chinese princess. Therefore, for the Chinese monarch to accept the gift was to announce a foreign policy. Consider, for example, the difference in the treatment of two Turkish governments: the Tölös sent three thousand horses in 642, asking a royal wedding, but after protracted argument T'ang rejected the humiliating concession.[6] But the very next year an alliance was contracted with the Sir-tardush Turks, who had sent a royal prince with fifty thousand of their grizzled black-maned horses,[7] along with great numbers of oxen, camels, and goats.[8]

Coupled with the notion of the horse as an instrument of diplomatic and military policy was the conception of horsemanship as an aristocratic privilege— a prejudice which the government tried to enforce by edict in 667, in prohibiting artisans and tradesmen from riding horseback.[9]

Still, this patrician animal owed his unique status to more than his usefulness to the lords of the land. He was invested with sanctity by ancient tradition, endowed with prodigious qualities, and visibly stamped with the marks of his divine origin. A revered myth proclaimed him a relative of the dragon, akin to the mysterious powers of water. Indeed, all wonderful horses, such as the steed of the pious Hsüan-tsang which, in later legend, carried the sacred scriptures from India, were avatars of dragons, and in antiquity the tallest horses owned by the Chinese were called simply "dragons."[10]

Most honored of all antique horses were the uncanny mounts of Mu, Son of Heaven, named the "Eight Bayards."[11] "Bayard" represents the Chinese designation of any pure-bred and magnificent horse, and has the frequent implication of supernatural origin or enigmatic parentage from the divine horses of the West and even, metaphorically, a human hero. Artistic representations of the abnormal but angelic animals which accompanied the great king through the wastes of hallowed K'un-lun were an important theme in the fantastic art of medieval China, and their grotesque images, painted in the fifth century, were treasured by T'ang connoisseurs, who explained their bizarre appearance by pointing out that the holy sages of antiquity, even Confucius himself, did not look like natural men. Divine creatures, whether human or equine, must not only be, but look, weird and otherworldly.[12]

In the Far West lived the great Horses of Heaven, "bayard-boned dragon-decoys," that is, with bones made to carry the wings of an ideal Western bayard, and precursors and inviters of dragons.[13] This is how Li Po described them:

> The Horses of Heaven come out of the dens of the Kushanas,
> Backs formed with tiger markings, bones made for dragon wings.[14]

The belief in the dragon-horses of the West goes back to the second century before the Christian era, when Wu Ti of Han, seeking to guarantee his own divinity and immortality, whether by magical foods prepared by alchemists or by elaborate rituals of incredible (and dubious) antiquity, longed for a set of unearthly steeds to draw him up into Heaven.[15]

The legend of water-born horses was known in various parts of Turkestan. In Kucha, for instance, when that city was visited by Hsüan-tsang in the seventh century, there was a lake of dragons in front of one of its temples. "The dragons, changing their form, couple with mares. The offspring is a wild species of horse (*dragon-horse*) difficult to tame and of a fierce nature. The breed of these dragon-horses became docile." [16] This story must have had its origin farther west in Iranian lands, where winged horses were familiar in art and myth.[17] Even the long-legged small-bellied horses of the "Tajik," that is, of the Arabs, were said to have been born of the conjunction of dragons with mares on the shores of the "Western Sea." [18] By Wu Ti's time the exemplars of the divine horses had been placed in Farghāna on the Jaxartes, cousins of the Nisaeans bred in Medea for the kings of Persia, "blood-sweating horses" renowned both East and West.[19] It is quite likely that the envoy who opened up the West to Chinese penetration in the second pre-Christian century, the famous Chang Ch'ien, was in fact a personal envoy of the emperor, charged with finding the wonderful horses which would usher in the Age of the Dragon for the people of Han.[20]

Though Chang Ch'ien may not have brought them, the Chinese had, by the second century of our era at least, obtained a fine, handsome kind of horse from the West,[21] which they identified with the dragon-horses of legend. Even if these steeds did not have wings, they had "bones made for dragon-wings." Though larger than the Mongolian pony and its domestic varieties familiar in China, these were perhaps not great battle chargers, but delicately nurtured animals kept for ritual purposes.[22] The zoölogical identity of these wonder-horses is uncertain. They have been described by one authority as "Aryan horses," a large, fast breed known around the Caspian Sea in antiquity.[23] Perhaps we can recognize their descendants in the modern Turki horse:

The Turkoman, or Turki, horse takes its name from Turkestan, its original home, although it has spread into Persia, Armenia, and Asia Minor. There are several strains, of which the finest inhabit the country to the south of Lake Aral and the Sir Daria, or Oxus. Standing from 15 to 16 hands in height, and capable of great endurance, these horses have large, Roman-nosed heads, ewe-necks, slender bodies, and long limbs. Although generally bay or grey in colour, some of them are black with white feet. The speed of these horses and such beauty as they possess are due to Arab parentage, grafted on an original stock, doubtless more or less nearly akin to the Mongolian tarpan . . .[24]

The Arab element is revealed in the "double spine," observed by the Chinese in Han times [25]—two ridges of muscle on both sides of the backbone, which made bare-back riding more comfortable, a much admired feature in classical antiquity in the West.[26] The "tiger markings" of Li Po's poem, on the other hand, reveal an atavistic element; "eel marking," that is, a dark stripe down the back, is characteristic of many primitive horses, like the Norwegian dun, and is very pronounced in the Asiatic onager.

The people of T'ang believed that the horses which they imported from well-watered Samarkand as breeders for their battle steeds were of the stock of the original bayards of Farghāna,[27] and they had heard of horses of the "dragon seed" in the snowy, windless valley of Kashmir.[28] In a story told at the beginning of the eleventh century we learn that six of the true blood-sweating horses were sent from Farghāna to the court of Hsüan Tsung in the middle of the eighth century. These were named "Red *Cherpādh*," "Purple *Cherpādh*," "Scarlet *Cherpādh*," "Yellow *Cherpādh*," "T-aromatic [clove] *Cherpādh*," and "Peach Flower *Cherpādh*," *cherpādh* meaning "quadruped" in the language of the Sogdians. The sovereign received them with delight, gave them new and less barbarous names, and had their pictures painted on the walls of one of his great halls.[29] It would be tempting to attribute this pretty tale solely to the nostalgic fancy of its author, Ch'in Tsai-szu, a literary man who lived three centuries after the alleged event. He has used, for instance, the romantically archaic name Ta-yüan for the homeland of the colored horses. But his story cannot be rejected outright. For one thing, the Chinese were prone to cherish obsolete names for foreign countries, and for another, there is an authentic account of a gift of horses (unfortunately not described or named) from Farghāna to Hsüan Tsung in an historical record.[30] Moreover, the epithet "red *cherpādh*" appears more than once in eighth-century literature—indeed, it was even applied to a unique variety of Chinese cat, bred at Ling-wu in Kansu.[31] I am inclined to believe in these T'ang blood-sweaters, and in the equestrian murals of Hsüan Tsung. But real or not, horses of that lineage inevitably had a dreamlike character.

The horse familiar to the Chinese since antiquity was the big-headed pony with erect mane, shaggy in winter, which once ranged most of Northern Asia and Europe, and was familiar to the Stone Age men of France and Spain. It is the wild horse of the steppes of Asia, whose bones have been discovered in Pleistocene deposits of the Ordos of north China,[32] but which is now restricted to Dzungaria,[33] and on the verge of extinction.[34] This tarpan (*Equus przewalskii*) also has domestic relatives scattered about the world, either relatively pure, like the Norwegian dun, or much altered by admixture of Arab blood.[35] The domestic Mongolian pony, on which the Chinese chiefly rely, is mainly tarpan but has a long flowing mane, a fore-lock, and a thick tail, again presumably the result of interbreeding with the Arab.[36]

From this basic stock, possibly with the help of other unknown races, many varieties of color and pattern were developed in ancient times, such as the white horse with a black mane traditionally associated with Hsia, the black-headed white of Shang, and the red-maned yellow horses of Chou. The richness and complexity of the vocabulary of horse types even in Chou and Han times testify to the high state of the art of breeding in Chinese antiquity.[37]

Despite the greed of the men of T'ang for the larger Western horses, they seem to have retained some admiration for the wild pony, for in 654 the Tibetans considered the gift of a hundred wild tarpans to be suitable for the reigning Son of Heaven.[38] From the same primitive stock, with greater or lesser admixture of Far Western strains, came also the few distinctive types of medieval China, such as a white horse with "vermilion" mane, bred in Shensi in T'ang times [39] and possibly a relic of the classic horse of Chou, and the wiry pony of Szechwan, a specialty of Sui-*chou* under the T'ang but known many centuries earlier to China's Western neighbors.[40] Many of the "national horses," that is, the government's breeding stock —post horses, war horses and the like—were hybrids of tarpan and Arab, some predominantly Arab. Sometimes there were too few of these carefully tended horses for the purposes of the nation, and then it became necessary to replenish them from abroad, as when Hsüan Tsung, early in the eighth century, issued an edict authorizing trade in horses with the "Six Western Barbarian Tribes." [41] But Arab blood was at a disadvantage in China, and hard to maintain against the flood of Mongolian ponies close at hand. The strains of Western steeds began to disappear after the end of T'ang, and vanished in early modern times with the great influx of ponies during Yüan and Ming.[42]

Foreign horses of these two sorts, then, Northern ponies and Western chargers, and many intermediate blends and varieties, poured into China during the rule of the T'ang empire. The Chinese loved and admired them. Part of their exotic taste in horses can be attributed to the tradition of the dragon-horses of the West, and part to the Turkish and distantly nomadic affinities of the ruling clan. Moreover, since there were never enough horses pastured in China for the needs of a great empire and of an equestrian, polo-playing aristocracy, the preference for foreign varieties followed naturally from the necessity for them.

Stories about the excellent horses of far countries were welcome to the men of T'ang, the believable along with the barely credible. They had heard, for instance, of a "Dappled Horse Country" (*Po ma ḳuo*) far to the north, where the snow was always heaped high upon the ground. The Chinese name of the nation seems to translate the name of a Turkish tribe, Ala-yondlu, "Those with piebald horses." [43] We do not know whether any of these spotted beasts, which in their homeland were subject to the indignity of being hitched to plows, ever reached the soil of T'ang.[44] Even more remote were the lands of the Arabs, whose admirable destriers could understand human speech.[45] Envoys of the Muslims brought some of these pure-blooded steeds to China in 703,[46] but we know nothing of their later adventures.

More dependable supplies of horses came from the northeast, from Tungusic and Mongolic peoples, such as the Mo-ho of P'o-hai,[47] who ranged south of the Amur;[48] the Shih-wei,[49] who dwelt to the west of the Mo-ho people;[50] the Hsi of southern Manchuria, who sent a gift of their agile horses in 816, and regular tribute missions after that year;[51] the Khitans, also in Manchuria and the destined conquerors of north China, who sent many embassies with their small horses, adept at forest-coursing, in the seventh and eighth centuries.[52]

To the north were the Turkish peoples, the chief source of T'ang's horses. They supplied a versatile and cunning breed, close to the ancient tarpan stock, hardy for long journeys and peerless as hunters, tamed long ago by the pristine masters of the steppe, the Hsiung-nu.[53] So important was the Turkish stock to the proud Chinese that they were obliged to humble themselves in many little ways to obtain badly needed animals. On one occasion, during the dynasty's early years, a Chinese prince demeaned himself by calling in person on the Turkish Khan in his distant camp, and was received with a display of haughty and imperious manners until the prince revealed his rich gifts (bolts of silk and jugs of wine were surely among them), at which the reception suddenly became ceremonious and warm, and a return mission was sent to the T'ang court with a herd of horses.[54] There were other little favors which could be done for the Turks. Material gifts were not always needed to elicit the desired return of well-bred horses. When, in the winter of 731–732, Bilgä Qaghan, the mighty lord, sent fifty fine horses to the T'ang capital, they were in the nature of a thank offering. The Qaghan's younger brother had recently died, and a band of six Chinese painters had gone to the tent-city on the steppes, there to render a likeness of the dead prince, which moved the lord to tears. His welcome herd accompanied the happy artists back to T'ang.[55] So, by one means or another, the Turkish tribes of the North, whether the Sir-tardush or the Toquz-Oghuz—the "Nine Tribes"—or some other group, were induced to send enormous numbers, sometimes as many as five thousand at once, to the imperial corrals.[56] But greatest and most arrogant of the suppliers of horseflesh to the Chinese were the Uighur Turks, who dominated the horse market after the middle of the eighth century, when incessant wars, both domestic and foreign, had created an insatiable demand in the shrinking T'ang empire. The Uighurs and the Tibetans had become the chief foreign enemies of T'ang and natural rivalry and Chinese diplomacy had turned the former against the latter. After the Tibetans had herded off all of the thousands of Chinese horses from the government ranges in Lung-yu[57] and even captured the capital city of Ch'ang-an, those insolent Turks, who had driven out the highlanders only to their own advantage, were deferred to in countless ways by the humiliated Chinese. Despite endless complaints about the Uighurs' haughty manners, extending even to attacks on the persons of Chinese on their own soil, the foreigners were rewarded for their services by a monopoly of the lucrative trade in horses.[58] No longer did an obsequious Turkish embassy bring a free gift of blood horses to Ch'ang-an, hoping for the good will of the masters of the East. Now it was hard-headed business, with the cultivated but effeminate Chinese (as they appeared to the outlanders) showing proper deference, and paying the seller's price. In the last decades of the eighth century, the ordinary price of a Uighur horse was forty bolts of Chinese silk, a stupefying expenditure.[59] In the early part of the ninth century, it was not unusual for the shattered nation to pay out a million bolts of taffeta in a year in exchange for a hundred thousand decrepit nags, the dregs of the northern marches.[60] Once in a while the Chinese emperor would attempt to limit this exhausting commerce. In 773 the Uighurs sent a special agent with ten thousand horses for sale. Their cost was more than the annual income of the government from taxes. Therefore Tai Tsung, a thoughtful monarch, ". . . not wishing to double the afflictions of the people, ordered that the authorities calculate an import budget, after which he allowed the purchase of six thousand of them." [61]

Hovering dangerously on the northern edges of the Turkish lands were the Kirghiz,[62] bane of the Uighurs in the ninth century, described as large men with pale faces, green eyes, and red hair.[63] They managed to get their horses across hostile territory to the Chinese frontier in the last half of the seventh and first half of the eighth century.[64] And all across Central Asia, from the Jade Gate of China to the Aral Sea, were the Western Turks and their Aryan subjects, and they too sent horses to the grand stables of T'ang.[65]

From the broad plains and rich cities of Transoxania and the nearby mountains came horses rich in Arab blood, especially in the eighth century during the vivid reign of Hsüan Tsung: from Samarkand,[66] Bukhāra,[67] Farghāna,[68] Tukhāra,[69] Chāch,[70] Kish,[71] Kabūdhān,[72] Māimargh,[73] and Khuttal.[74]

From the borders of Tibet the Mongolic T'u-yü-hun, much reduced from their former proud state, sent a gift of horses in 652,[75] and the Tibetans themselves sent a hundred two years later.[76] But the Tibetans did not become an important source of horses until the early decades of the ninth century, after they had been humbled by the Uighurs,[77] and even then they sent very few in comparison with those haughty Turks.

The city-states of Serindia also sent fine specimens to China, Kucha on several occasions,[78] and Khotan at least once.[79] The victorious Arabs sent their elegant steeds once later in the seventh century,[80] and once early in the eighth, as we have seen, and several times during Hsüan Tsung's golden reign.[81] Even distant Kapiśa (ancient Gandhāra), a hot rice-growing country on the northwestern frontier of India, rich in elephants and Buddhism but ruled by Turks, sent horses to China in 637, when T'ai Tsung, the Tängri Qaghan, dominated the world.[82] The rising state of Nan-chao in the Southwest too sent a gift of sixty horses of unknown breed to the Chinese in 795.[83]

64

The important trade in horses with the nomads of the North was systematized in 727 by the authorization of "exchange marketing" (*hu shih*) under government supervision on the frontier in the Ordos region. The purpose of this policy was to increase the number of horses in China and to improve the quality of the "national horses" by interbreeding with desirable foreign stock.[84] The immediate occasion of its establishment was the receipt of a friendly gift of thirty fine horses from Bilgä Qaghan, along with a letter which had come to him from the Tibetans, urging him to join in raids on Chinese territory, but which was now handed over to Hsüan Tsung by the Turkish envoy. The sovereign was delighted with these tokens of friendship, loaded the envoy with rich gifts, and also

. . . authorized that a place for "exchange marketing" be created at the Walled Town for Receiving Surrender in the West, under the Army of the Boreal Quarter. Here several tens of myriads of bolts of heavy taffeta and other silks were delivered each year . . .[85]

This became the regular point at which the horses of the Northern tribes were brought to China. Henceforth we can read in the Chinese histories such statements as the following, which is appended to the notice of the presentation of sixty-four horses by the Toquz-Oghuz, the Kirghiz, and the Shih-wei early in 748: "The Commissioner at the Walled Town for Receiving Surrender in the West was ordered to brand them and take them in."[86] A similar trading post was established on the Tibetan frontier, at the Red Mountain Pass, in 729.[87]

But there was brisk private trading, too. The Tangut settlements along the northwestern marches in particular enriched themselves at it. Early in the ninth century ". . . itinerant merchants from far and near delivered silks and other commodities to them, taking sheep and horses in exchange."[88] Prosperity was an uncertain thing, however, for in the third decade of the same century the settlements were impoverished by avaricious Chinese officials, who compelled the enterprising Tangut to sell their livestock at ruinously low prices. This led naturally to Tangut banditry along the roads on the southern fringe of the Ordos.[89]

At the great government trading post, camels, asses, and sheep as well as horses were received and examined and registered by the imperial superintendent, and sent on to the appropriate pasture or to the imperial stables. On the road from the frontier the horses went by groups of ten, each group under a single herdsman.[90] From then on the horses were tenderly watched by the state, and the greatest care was taken lest any be injured, lost, or stolen. The person in charge of a government horse at any moment was responsible for its safety and welfare. Horses were not to die, but if one did, the procedure for establishing proof of its death, and for the degree of responsibility of the agent using it, was prescribed in the smallest detail. For instance, if a horse was being used for a long journey, that is, not as a regular post horse, and it died on the road, the meat was sold and the skin sent back to a government warehouse. But if the death occurred in the desert, where no buyer or storehouse was at hand, the rider need only bring back (if he could get back himself) a piece of skin bearing the government brand as evidence.[91]

Once received in the imperial pasture, the foreign horse was assigned to a herd (*ch'ün*) of 120 animals in one of the great pastoral "inspectorates" (*chien*), each of which cared for as many as 5,000. There the animal was looked after until it was wanted for state service, either as a war horse, as a post horse, or as a mount for a member of the ruling family or a favored courtier. The horse was branded on many parts of his body, to show his ownership, age, type, quality, and condition. All state horses bore the character *kuan*, "official," on their right shoulders, and the name of the inspectorate to which they were assigned beside their tails. There were brands to show the nation of origin of a horse; brands to show his agility and stamina, such as "flying," "dragon," and "wind"; and brands to show his proper work, as the word "sent forth" branded on the right cheek of army and post horses on duty, or the word "bestowed" on the right cheek of official horses given to private persons.[92] The herdsmen and officers set over them were required to maintain their quotas of animals at the proper level, and were expected to increase them. Severe punishment was inflicted on the officer whose register showed fewer horses than required by his quota: thirty blows of a bamboo staff was the certain penalty for the shortage of a single horse.[93]

If an imported horse merited the attention of the magistrates who tended the palace horses, the beast was sent from the pasture to the capital city, and assigned to one of the corrals (*hsien*) or stables (*chiu*) attached to the palace itself. According to his type and quality, the horse was enclosed in the "Horse Corral of the Flying Yellows," the "Horse Corral of the Auspicious and Well-Bred," the "Horse Corral of the Dragon Decoys," the "Horse Corral of the *T'ao-t'u*," the "Horse Corral of the *Chüeh-t'i*," or the "Horse Corral of the Heavenly Park." [94] Five of the corrals were named for noble horses of the past, remembered through literature and tradition,[95] while the "Heavenly Park" was a poetical name for the park of the Son of Heaven, where he hunted with his dragon-horses. From these corrals exotic steeds could be taken for the use of great warlords, for imperial hunts, for aristocratic polo games, for ceremonial processions, or for other splendid and noble purposes.

Polo, introduced from Iran by way of Serindia at the beginning of T'ang [96] or a little earlier, and transmitted from China to Korea and Japan, was called simply "hit-ball" [97] and was played with curved sticks, their ends shaped like crescent moons, and net bags as goals. Emperors, courtiers, ladies, and even scholars played the game, and the palace had its own polo field.[98] We do not know what horses were accounted best for polo playing by the men of T'ang, but the records show that a pair of polo ponies was sent to China by the city of Khotan in 717.[99] We may guess that the superior ponies came from lands where polo was played with enthusiasm,

66

such as Turkestan and Iran; the Tibetans were also held to be exceptionally skillful players.[100]

But the Chinese could dazzle the Tibetans in return:

In the time of the Central Ancestor [Chung Tsung], a banquet was spread for the Tibetans in the basilica, and a performance by the curvetting horses presented. These were all fitted and caparisoned with silk thread, pigmented in the five colors, with garnishings of gold. Unicorn heads and phoenix wings had been applied to the tops of their saddles. When the music was played, each of the horses followed it, fluently responsive, and when they came to the middlemost stanza, the performers of the music gave them wine to drink, at which they took up the cups in their mouths; then they lay down, and got up again. The Tibetans were greatly astonished.[101]

Even more celebrated than Chung Tsung's horses, which disported themselves to musical measures at the beginning of the eighth century, were the dancing horses of Hsüan Tsung, which performed some decades later. These last numbered a hundred, and were recruited from among the most talented of the tribute horses sent from abroad. They were dressed in rich embroideries, fringed with gold and silver, and wore precious stones in their manes. Divided into two troops, they danced their intricate maneuvers, with tossing heads and beating tails, to the music of the "Song of the Overturned Cup" (*ch'ing pei ch'ü*), played by two bands of handsome young musicians, clad in yellow shirts and jade-studded belts. They could dance on three-tiered benches, and would stand stock still when their benches were heaved up by athletes. It became the custom for these beautiful animals to perform annually at the Tower of Zealous Administration (*Ch'in cheng lou*) on the fifth day of the eighth month in honor of the sovereign's birthday, a holiday styled the "Period of a Thousand Autumns" (*Ch'ien ch'iu chieh*). The horses shared the limelight on these auspicious occasions with a battalion of guards in golden armor, the ceremonial orchestra, barbarian mountebanks, performing elephants and rhinoceroses, and a great bevy of palace girls in richly embroidered costumes, who played the eight-faced "thunder drums.[102]

When Hsüan Tsung was driven from his throne, the famous dancing horses were dispersed. Some were sent to the northeastern frontier by Rokhshan, and a few were assigned to military duties there, but could easily be distinguished from the other war horses by their tendency to begin dancing when martial music was played in the camp.[103]

Lu Kuei-meng, the ascetic poet of the ninth century, wrote of them, linking them with the almost fabulous dragon-horses of Farghāna:

Grandchildren of Dragons from the Dens of the Moon, four hundred hooves,
Proud prancers, lightly pacing, responsive to the golden war drums:
When the tune is done, seeming to want the affection of their sovereign lord,
They look back at the Red Tower—but do not dare to neigh.[104]

Lu Kuei-meng's "Dens of the Moon" are Li Po's "Dens of the Kushanas" in Western Turkestan,[105] and these dancers belong to the exotic wonders of mid-T'ang.

A recurrent theme in the puritanical edicts which appeared from time to time during the T'ang regime, especially during virtuously warlike and ostentatiously solemn reigns, was the interdiction of gifts to the throne of small and delightful things, which were regarded as trivial, since they did not serve the state. Such was the ban on small horses which was handed down during the first year of the dynasty [106] and rejected pretty ponies in favor of stalwart steeds. Nonetheless, three years later the same monarch, Kao Tsu, accepted miniature "*kuâ-ha horses" from Paekche, in the southwestern part of the Korean peninsula.[107] Evidently the inaugural gesture of grave sincerity had been forgotten. When the stern and militant regimes of the seventh century gave way to the milder and more frivolously "cultured" reign of Hsüan Tsung in the eighth, little horses, along with other delicate rarities, were welcomed by the court. In this century the ponies came from the dominant Korean kingdom of Silla.[108] But they must have been of the same race as the ponies of Paekche, diminutive tarpan stock, evolved on an island—the island of Quelpart in Korea Strait—like our familiar Shetland ponies and the "fairy ponies" of Öland.[109] Small horses of this name had been known to the Chinese since the first century B.C., when they were hitched to the carriage of a dowager empress.[110] In the second century of the Christian era these ponies were sent by the central Korean kingdom of Wei,[111] but a later tradition identified them with the horses of the hero Chu Mong, the legendary archer who founded the kingdom of Koguryŏ.[112] Whether all these ponies came from the stunting environment of Quelpart is conjectural. In T'ang times their name, *kuâ-ha, was written with Chinese characters meaning "beneath a fruit-tree," and the explanation then current was that it signified that one could ride them without mishap under the lowest branches of a fruit tree.[113] But the name must originally have been a word from some northeastern language, whose meaning was forgotten and then rationalized by the Chinese.[114] In the twelfth century it was even possible to apply the name to small horses from the tropical south of the empire.[115] It was also customary in T'ang times to say that Korean ponies were three feet high,[116] but this must have been a symbolic number for the height of all diminutive creatures; it had been applied to dwarfish men since antiquity,[117] and so we cannot tell the size of the little animals with precision. It is easy to guess that they were used in T'ang in much the same way as in Han—to pull carts for royal ladies, to grace formal processions, and to embellish the public appearances of all effete young persons. It is likely that these were the gaily decorated dwarf ponies which carried the gilded youth of T'ang to drinking parties in the gardens of the capital during the height of the spring flower-viewing season.[118]

Celebrated above all other exotic horses in the age of T'ang were the "Six Bayards" which carried T'ai Tsung through dangerous campaigns against rival claimants to the throne of China. These paragons are known to us through both literature and art. The sovereign himself, in his deep affection for them, wrote a short prose description of each of the six, or rather of their effigies, and a poetic eulogy of each.[119] Here is one of them:

The *Cherpādh* Red: its color pure red, ridden at the time of the putting down of [Wang] Shih-ch'ung and [Tou] Chien-te;[120] hit by four arrows from the front and by one arrow from the back. The Eulogy goes:

> Where Ch'an and Chien [121] were still unquiet,
> There ax and poleax extended my majesty;
> Vermilion sweat—impetuous feet!
> Blue banners—triumphant return! [122]

Poetry and sculpture commemorated this charger, but a war horse ridden by T'ai Tsung in this same campaign, named "Yellow Grizzled Roan,"[123] had a different role in the arts: after it died in the Korean wars, T'ai Tsung had music composed in its honor, called "The Doubled Song of the Yellow Grizzle," apparently in imitation of an old tune of Han times.[124]

By means of the image "vermilion sweat," the beloved *"Cherpādh* Red" was linked, at least in fancy, with the blood-sweaters of Farghāna. Though the imperial six all had Western blood in their veins, it is certain, in view of some of their names, like "Tegin Roan," that they came to T'ai Tsung from the Turks.[125] The renowned images of these renowned steeds, done in stone relief at the emperor's command in the winter of 636–637,[126] were based on drawings by the great Yen Li-pen. After T'ai Tsung's death the sculptures were installed next to his "Radiant Tumulus" in Shensi, but they have since been transferred to museums.[127] The stone horses have their manes cut or tied in bunches, like crenellated battlements, an ancient fashion in Central Asia and Siberia, though probably of Iranian origin, but obsolete in China since the days of the Han emperors. Its reappearance testifies to the Turkish origin of T'ai Tsung's steeds, and certifies the nobility of both horses and rider.[128] But the ideal pedigree of the Six Bayards goes back beyond the famous horses of Han to the Eight Bayards of King Mu of Chou, whose wonderful lineaments were still preserved, a model for great barbarian-subduing kings, in an old painting, a kind of T'ang national treasure.[129]

Not so well known as the Six Bayards, but marvels of their age, were the "Ten Chargers"[130] of T'ai Tsung. These rare and beautiful steeds came to the monarch late in his life, and therefore lacked the intimate relationship with him which gave special dignity and glory to their six predecessors in the old days of bitter trials and uncertain success. The new horses were personally chosen by the monarch from among a hundred sent by the Turkish Qurïqan nation in 647.[131] The boreal herdsmen who raised them, dwellers in a land full of lilies north of Lake Baikal, bred them as sinewy and powerful horses, similar to those of the Khirghiz, and sent them unbranded, but with oddly docked ears and marked noses, to the great ruler of China.[132] T'ai Tsung himself chose names for the elect ten:[133] "Frost

Prancing White," "Shining Snow Grizzle," "Frozen Dew Grizzle," "Suspended Light Grizzle," "Wave Plunging Bay," "Sunset Flying Roan," "Lightning Darting Red," "Flowing Gold Yellow," "Soaring Unicorn Purple," "Running Rainbow Red." [134]

Although we may imagine that the horses of Qurïqan must have been painted by some seventh-century master to delight the eyes of their lord, there is no record of such a project. This was before the time of the most eminent of all Chinese painters of horses, Han Kan, who lived in the next century, during the reign of Hsüan Tsung, himself a fancier of exotic horses. Han Kan prided himself that his vigorous representations were based directly upon nature, rather than on traditional pictures of regal horses. [135] From what we may read of older horse paintings, the preferred pre-T'ang style was symbolic and even fantastic, with the divine parentage of royal horses shown plainly in eccentric line and color. Han Kan, it seems, was the first great painter to adopt the principle of uncompromising realism in horse painting. This was a great change. The supremacy of the horse among the foreign domestic animals was due not only to its role in the security of the nation but equally to its affinities with legendary and supernatural creatures of the venerated past. In a sense, then, Han Kan brought it down to earth forever, and the Chinese of the eighth century were the last to see the dragon-horses of Heaven as stupendously believable animals. Naturalistic exoticism had triumphed forever over reverent symbolism.

CAMELS

At the beginning of T'ang rule the domestic form of the two-humped Bactrian camel had been known to and used by the northern Chinese for at least a thousand years. In Han times they had been used by the thousands in the commercial and military caravans which penetrated the newly won lands of Serindia. [136] In those classic days the Chinese had to depend on such pastoral outlanders as the Hsiung-nu to replenish their supply of these valuable animals, treasured for their reliability in transporting men and merchandise through the high desert wastes of Gobi and Tarim. [137] So also in T'ang times, when the empire extended once more far across Central Asia, the need for camels was equally great, and they, like horses, had to be found abroad to meet the enormous demands at home. Camels came as presents to the throne, as tribute, as commodities, and as war booty. The Uighurs [138] and the Tibetans [139] sent camels to T'ang; camels came with a mission from Chumul on the Manas River, [140] and from the Turgäch, [141] and Khotan sent a "wind-footed wild camel." [142] Indeed, among the Turkish tribes generally, camels were enumerated among things of the greatest worth, like gold, silver, virgins, and slaves, [143] and they appeared in omen lore and poetry as beneficent and noble animals. [144] They could be obtained in the city-states of the Tarim, along the old caravan roads; Kao Hsien-chih seized many camels, along with other treasures, at Chāch.[145] Fighting camels were a noted feature of the great festivals of Kucha,[146] and the Kirghiz, too, used camels in various sporting events.[147]

The vast camel herds of the Chinese government, enriched from these foreign sources, were presided over by hordes of officials, as were the imperial horses. The chief herdsman of each herd was in charge of only seventy camels, however, while the standard herd of horses was made up of 120 animals.[148] Along with the other large domestic animals, they were kept in the grassy provinces of Kuan-nei and Lung-yu, that is, in modern Shensi and Kansu. The exact size of the imperial herds is not known, but in 754 there were 279,900 cattle, sheep, and camels in the official herds of Lung-yu.[149] Private gentlemen of means also kept camels as riding animals and as beasts of burden. It is probable that most of the herdsmen, trainers, and cameleers, both in public and private employ, were foreigners from Mongolia, Central Asia, and Tibet, in accordance with Tu Fu's dictum, "Western boys have power over camels." [150]

Very fast and dependable camels, especially white ones, were assigned to officials entitled "Emissaries of the Bright Camels," for emergency use on state business, and in particular to bring news of a crisis on the frontier.[151] But these excellent post camels might be diverted to less serious ends, as in a tale about Yang Kuei-fei, the consort of Hsüan Tsung. The monarch, so the tale goes, gave ten pieces of Borneo camphor, which he had received as tribute from Chiao-chih in Indochina, to the Lady Yang. She secretly dispatched them by "Bright Camel Emissary" to Rokhshan, her lover (as he appears to have been), on a remote and dangerous frontier.[152]

There were also "Flying Dragon Camels" in the imperial stables. Late in the eighth century it was not deemed too ignoble to employ these fine animals to bring rice to the capital, when the supply of grain in the metropolis proved insufficient for the brewing of wine for the Son of Heaven.[153] Camels seemed destined for anomalous and bizarre purposes on Chinese soil.

But their association with the ruffianly nomads across the northern frontier could also make camels seem terrible animals. Early in the eighth century they appear in a street song of the capital as the "golden camels from north of the mountains," and represent the marauders from Mongolia with their pack animals laden with the rich spoils of T'ang.[154] Later in the century they became specific symbols of the barbarous rebels who followed Rokhshan: "They brought the Two Capitals low, and made a practice of loading the rarities and treasures of the Tabooed Repository on camels for storage in heaps and hills in Fan-yang." [155] The classic expression of this attitude toward the northern captains and their camel transports is in Tu Fu's poem "Lament for a King's Grandson," whose picture is of a prince of Hsüan Tsung's scattered household, hoping to escape death at the hands of Rokhshan's men; the poet tells him of the accession of Su Tsung, whose "sapient virtue" has obtained the aid of the Uighur Turks against the insurgents. The poet affirms that the sacred emanations from the tombs of the imperial ancestors give perpetual hope of the preservation of dynasty and prince alike.

> At the head of Ch'ang-an's wall is a white-headed crow,
> Which flies by night to the Autumn-Inviting Gate, and on it cries;
> And on it goes to the people's homes, and pecks at the housetops of the great;
> From under these housetops successful officials run out to escape the outlanders.
> Their golden whips are sheared and broken, their ninefold horse teams dead;
> Bone waits not for family flesh, but goads alike and gallops away.
> With precious bangles hung from his waist, made of blue coral,
> How pitiable is this king's grandson, weeping at the flank of the road.
> When I ask him, he will not tell his clan or name,
> But will tell only of affliction and torment, and beg to be made my slave.
> Already he has undergone a hundred days of skulking through thorn and bramble;
> On his body there is no skin or flesh left whole.
> But the sons and grandsons of the High Theocrat have all, like him, been high-beaked—
> So the Dragon Seed in this one marks him off from ordinary men.
> Now dhole and wolf are in the city, while these Dragons are in the wild,
> And this king's grandson will do well to preserve his thousand-metal-piece body.
> I dare not talk long here, close by the crossroads,
> But for the king's grandson I stand for just this moment:
> "Yesterday night a wind from the East blew us the stink of blood,
> Camels coming from the East filled the Old Metropolis.
> Our lusty youths from the boreal quarter, fine bodies and hands,
> Once brave and keen, but now how foolish!
> For my part, I hear that the See has now passed to the Grand Heir;
> His Sapient Virtue in the North has humbled the Khan of the South,
> Whose men of the Flower Gate gash their faces, and ask that they may purge our
>   shame snow-white!
> But take care lest any of this come from your mouth, for hostile men go by.
> Alas! king's grandson! Take care that you do not let go,
> For the Excellent Inspiration from the Five Barrows will at no time cease to be!" [156]

Along with his value as a beast of burden, the camel made other contributions to civilized living. His hair made an excellent cloth, often very soft, which was later much admired by Marco Polo. In T'ang times, such camlets were manufactured at Hui-*chou* in Kansu and Feng-*chou* out in the Ordos—both of them on the northwestern frontier, the chief source of raw materials—and sent regularly to the imperial court.[157]

Moreover, camels could be eaten, and the hump in particular was regarded as a delicacy. Tu Fu has written of "the hump of a purple camel emerging from a blue cauldron," and Ts'en Ts'an, telling of a feast at the frontier station of Chiu-ch'üan, wrote,

[margin handwritten note: EATING HUMPS]

> The Tibetan lads and Western boys blend their chants and songs,
> They broil yaks whole, and cook wild camels . . .[158]

Stewed or broiled camel could not have been an ordinary dish in the cuisine of north China, except where both camels and foreign fashions were common.

CATTLE

We do not easily think of cattle as important on the list of exotic goods needed or desired by the men of T'ang. Since antiquity the Chinese had had many varieties of oxen, including fantastic races with motley hides, developed for the manifold sacrifices to the archaic gods, most of them hardly remembered in T'ang times. But under this multiplicity lay the comparative simplicity of three great varieties. These three primordial types were recognized in T'ang, as they are now: the great eighth-century pharmacologist Ch'en Ts'ang-ch'i called them the "yellow cow," the "raven-black cow," and the "water cow," [159] this last being the carabao or "water buffalo." The yellow cow is thought to be a hybrid of the European cow and the Indian zebu.[160] It is of southern origin and remains most characteristic of the south, though it has spread all over China. Where its range overlaps that of the magnificent carabao, the yellow cow turns water wheels and plows light ground, while the buffalo turns up the thick clayey soils of the rice fields.[161] In T'ang times the yellow cow was even more important on the island of Hainan, a savage land then, newly under Chinese administration; there were no asses or horses there, so the people rode about on yellow cows saddled, bridled, and decorated like horses elsewhere.[162] The black ox of north China is something of a mystery; it may share the blood of one of the wild races of oxen native to the Far East, such as the gaur or banting.[163] At any rate, cattle of one kind or another were to be found everywhere in the lands of T'ang. CHINA ALREADY HAD CATTLE

The Chinese had also had their dwarf breeds of cattle, comparable to the "fairy cattle" of Corvo in the Azores,[164] since very remote times. The "millet ox" [165] and *gieu*-ox [166] of the Chou kingdom were supposed to have been miniature sacrificial animals.[167] Another kind of tiny cattle, called *p'i*-cattle, or "cattle under a fruit tree," like the fairy horses of Korea and Kwangtung, had been produced since early times at Kao-liang, southwest of Canton.[168] T'ang Kao Tsu's edict, published late in 618,[169] against the offering of dwarf cattle and other tiny beings to the throne, may have been aimed against the presentation of such Chinese pygmies as these, and possibly against foreign ones too, such as the beautiful little gynees of Bengal.[170]

Stories about the oxen of foreign countries, some colorful, some fairly prosaic, circulated among the men of T'ang. They knew that the red-haired, white-faced Kirghiz people, disavowing descent from wolves (a peculiarity of the Turks), claimed to be the issue of the mating of a god with a cow in a mountain cave.[171] But what sort of beast that totemic ancestor was, or whether the race of domestic cattle herded by the Kirghiz [172] resembled it, is not on record. The Chinese knew too that the natives of Kucha held ceremonial contests between fighting oxen (and horses and camels as well) during their New Year's festival. The outcome of these ritual battles gave the prognosis of the increase, or decrease, of their herds during the coming year.[173] But no one has made note of these gallant cattle in China. Nor is there any report that the giant wild oxen of Central Asia, white-haired, with tails like deer and the space of ten feet between the tips of their horns, was ever seen by a Chinese traveler, though their existence was authoritatively reported.[174]

But indeed, nothing reliable can be said about the character of even such plainly visible cattle as the thousands sent to T'ang by a Turkish Qaghan in 628.[175] As for the herds of "cattle" submitted by the rulers of the T'u-yü-hun[176] and of the Tibetans,[177] it appears that these must have been yaks, the only cattle reported among the domestic animals of these people in this age.[178] To be more precise, they were zobos, hybrid offspring of male yaks and female zebus. The large, brownish-black wild yak and its half-tame brother, which resembles it but is somewhat smaller, thrive only in the frigid air of the alpine massif. Only the shaggy little half-breed zobos, of variable color, can endure the oppressive lowlands.[179]

From the homeland of the T'u-yü-hun, rich in parrots and useful metals, around the great blue lake Kokonor,[180] had come tribute of yaks, unambiguously named, from the beginning of the sixth century, and also gifts of their famous grizzled colts. The Tibetans, who required their guests to shoot their own yaks before a great banquet,[181] also sent specimen yaks to the Chinese court early in the eighth century.[182] I take it that these solitary beasts were not the docile little zobos, but the dark and proud ancestral types,[183] sent for the admiration of the sophisticates of the capital.

The image of the yak in Chinese literature did not reflect the dangerous character of the wild type. Tu Fu wrote:

> Blue-green grass was rank and rife—is withered dead and gone;
> Horses of Heaven, with shambling feet, follow after the yak-cattle.
> So, from ancient days, our noble and honest ones were thinly treated by fate,
> While wanton cockerels and vicious youths all were patent-sealed as lords.[184]

In these lines the noble horses of divine blood are shown stricken by drought and famine (symbolizing the poor spiritual sustenance given the good-hearted in those trying days), and can only shuffle along with the humble zobos, pictured as dull-witted, cloddish beasts (symbolizing men of like temperament).

Since antiquity, when barbarians brandishing wands adorned with yaktails entertained the guests of the king,[185] yaktails had been greatly desired in the Chinese lowlands as standards and banners, as decorations for hats, and as ornaments for the carriages of the nobility.[186] Under the rulers of T'ang, they were sent to the court as regular annual tribute by the westernmost towns of Szechwan, where the great mountains rise into Tibet.[187] These tails were the bushy ones of the zobo, which also provided the chowries of India.[188] In T'ang, having been delivered at the palace, the tails might eventually come under the delicate care of the "Supervisor of Carriages," who tended the vehicles of the ladies of the imperial seraglio and the costly animals which pulled them: "he has carriages and chaises in charge, and umbrellas and fans for them, and decorative objects, feathers, and yaktails, which he must put out in the sun at the proper season." [189]

SHEEP AND GOATS

Many wonderful kinds of exotic sheep (or, it may be, goats, since these animals were classified together by the Chinese, as is entirely reasonable) were known by repute in the lands of T'ang. Probably the most astonishing were the "earth-born sheep" of Rome:

The lambs of certain sheep are born from within the earth. The people of that country wait until they are about to sprout, and then construct a wall with which to enclose them and prevent them from being eaten by wild beasts. But their navels are attached to the ground, and if they cut them they would die. However, if men clothed in armor run their horses there, with the beating of drums, and so startle them, these lambs will cry out in fright, at which the navels are separated, and they go off after water and herbs. [190]

One scholar has hoped to see in this an echo of the legend of the Argonauts (armed men) and the Golden Fleece, but the story has been confused with that of the pinna mussel, so that the men in armor might represent the crustacea which war on the mollusks and sever their lifelines. But we shall hear more of the pinna later. The "earth-born sheep" is also, in part, the story of the "planted sheep," that is, of the cotton plant which produces vegetable wool. [191]

It was also reported in China that sheep with great heavy tails, weighing as much as ten catties, were raised in Samarkand. [192] They are no myths, but are the fat-tailed dumba of Bukhāra and the Kirghiz steppe, whose young are the source of the famous astrakhan fur. These animals spread from this center through Persia and Syria at a very early date. [193]

A wild sheep of bluish tint was also reported from Kapiśa, with a "kingfisher-colored" tail. This must have been a variety of the great bharal or "blue sheep," of the strangely twisted horns. [194] This fine animal, whose slate-blue coloration serves as camouflage against the bare rocks of the high mountains, ranges from Baltistan through the K'un-lun Mountains, at altitudes of over ten thousand feet, to the confines of China. [195]

It is not easy to identify the huge sheep reported by the famous traveler Hsüan-tsang as being raised by villagers high in the snowy Pamirs. [196]

A prince of the Turks offered ten thousand sheep, along with a great herd of horses, to the Chinese emperor in 626, but the gift was not accepted, and indeed, quite aside from political reasons, it appears that the Chinese of this age stood in no great need of foreign sheep and imported very few. Goats they had known from early times, but sheep were more appropriate to the stinking nomads. We must guess that the rejected sheep of the Turks were the steatopygous breed with drooping ears characteristic of Central Asia and Siberia, and well-known to the Chinese.[197]

ASSES, MULES, AND ONAGERS

The ass, like the camel, appeared on the Chinese horizon only in late classical times, that is to say, toward the end of the Chou dynasty, having been transmitted by slow degrees from its North African homeland. But for the men of T'ang, a millenium later, it was a native domestic animal, not to be wondered at, and not, it seems, an article of import, unless we count the ass fifty feet tall, reported in a credible source to have been sent by the Tibetans in 654, along with a hundred horses.[198] But this gigantic donkey seems to have been born from an overexcited rumor or a copyist's pen, unless a myth has somehow become entangled with a real event. The pharmacologist Ch'en Ts'ang-ch'i also told of "asses of the sea," as well as horses and cattle of the sea, whose hair would rise on end when they felt the sea wind, but what traveler's tale he had heard I do not know. It must have been of some distant sea creature, whose hair was not wetted by water, like the sea elephant and the sea otter.[199]

Mules, like their paternal ancestors, were post-archaic introductions into China and even somewhat odd in Han times, but by T'ang they were so common that it was possible to mount an army on mules in a province which was deficient in horses.[200]

Cousin to the ass and the mule was an equine animal known to the Chinese only from specimens sent as token tribute from the Far West in the eighth century. These strange beasts had the name *lou,* which registered a linguistic affinity with both the ass (*lu*) and the mule (*lo*). The Chinese lexicographers have been at a loss to classify these creatures, which were sent from Tukhāristān in 720,[201] and from Persia in 734,[202] the latter being a land in which they were said to abound.[203] Some say it was a kind of horse, and some say a kind of ass, but indeed it must have been a variety of the almost intractable onager, the miscalled "wild ass" of Turkestan, Persia, and the Near East, related to the chigetai of Central Asia and Mongolia, and to the kiang of Tibet.[204]

DOGS

It has been thought that all varieties of domestic dogs descend from five ancient types.[205] Several of these primeval ancestors had descendants in China. The "chow," for instance, derives from the spitz prototype, which also has many offspring among the Samoyeds and the Tungus peoples, and even in the tropical lands of Indonesia.[206]

76

The greyhound, a very old kind of dog, is shown in stone reliefs of the Han dynasty; its forefathers surely came from Egypt in long-forgotten times.[207] Most popular of all in ancient China was the snub-nosed mastiff, with its tail curled up over its back, in the lineage of the Tibetan wolf, *Canis niger,* which also bred the hound of the Assyrians, the Roman *molossus,* the Saint Bernard, the Newfoundland, the bulldog, and especially the miniature breeds of China, such as the pug.[208] Even the great Yen Li-pen painted a mastiff brought as tribute in the seventh century, perhaps a gift from Tibet, the motherland of the breed.[209]

The nations of Turkestan also sent dogs to China: Samarkand in 713,[210] and again in 724;[211] Kucha in 721.[212] Presumably these were hunting hounds, which were in great demand among the Chinese courtiers, though we know nothing specific about them. If so they found their way into the imperial kennels of the palace at Ch'ang-an.[213] There were useless curiosities too, like the two-headed dog, a monstrous birth, sent to the court of the Empress Wu in 697.[214]

A breed of spotted dog which came from Persia was called simply the "Persian dog" by the Chinese, but its ancestry is a mystery.[215] The dogs known by this epithet in the sixth century were large, ferocious animals, capable of killing and eating human beings.[216] Presumably the spotted Persians of T'ang times were the same.

Another dog imported from Western Asia in T'ang times was the "dog of Hrom,"[217] that is, a "Roman dog," which first appeared early in the seventh century, the gift of the king of Kao-ch'ang, or Qočo. Here is the story:

He presented male and female dogs, one of each, six inches high, and a foot or so long. They were most clever. They could lead horses by their reins and carry candles in their mouths. It is said that they were originally bred in the Country of Hrom.[218]

Nothing certain can be said of the appearance of these small animals, but it has been proposed that they were none other than the classic lap dogs par excellence, of the ancient Maltese race,[219] and it may well be so. Those intelligent toys, ultimately of the spitz family, with their shaggy hair and pointed faces, were the favorites of Greek hetaerae and Roman matrons alike.[220] The strain had been remarkably conservative, a white variety being still extant today. It may be such a white dog of Melita which we see in a painting of the Sung dynasty, though there is no certainty of the identification.[221] Indeed, it is not at all certain that the pair of small dogs sent by Qočo had any descendants in China at all, though perhaps others like them came to replenish the stock in the Far East. Consider this story of Hsüan Tsung and his beloved:

One summer day His Highness was playing at *go* with a Prince of the Blood, and he had ordered Ho Huai-chih to strum a solo on the lute. The Precious Consort stood before the gaming board and watched them. At a point when several of His Highness' men were about to be carried off, the Precious Consort released a toy dog from the country of Samarkand from beside the seats. The toy dog accordingly went up on the board, and the men on the board were disarranged. His Highness was greatly pleased.[222]

The hero of this tactful enterprise was probably a Roman dog. We may see him again (but with no hint of his ancestry) in the words to a song by an anonymous T'ang poet, written to the tune of "The Drunken Lordling." [223] The verses show a light-of-love, perhaps a courtesan, expecting her young gentleman's arrival:

> Outside the gate the toy doggy barks—
> I know that it's Master Hsiao who's here.
> With socks peeled off I go down the scented staircase,
> But—my dear oppressor is drunk tonight. [224]

The Chinese word which I have translated "toy dog" in these passages is related to the word for "dwarf," [225] and so gives us no clue to the geographic origin of the creatures. The Samarkandian origin of the Consort's dog points to Rome and thence to Malta; [226] we cannot be so positive about the lap dog which announced Master Hsiao, though some authorities have thought that all dogs called "dwarf dogs" (my "toy dogs") were of "Roman" origin. In any case, the modern snub-nosed toys of China do not seem to show Maltese blood, but perhaps unnoticed traces of it remain. [227] But these dwarfish pets, whether native or not, were favorite subjects for poems, or favorite images in them, from T'ang times down to the seventeenth century. [228]

IV=Wild Animals

ELEPHANTS

THE ELEPHANT was not always an exotic
animal to the Chinese. In the Age of Bronze, when the kings of Shang ruled in the
valley of the Yellow River, it was one of the commoner wild animals, and was evidently captured and tamed for useful purposes.[1] But as the forest cover of north
China was reduced and the human population increased, the great beasts retreated
toward the south, and during historical times were to be found only in pockets in
the remoter parts of the Yangtze watershed, and south of there. They were still
abundant in the mountainous parts of Kwangtung in the ninth century,[2] and on
the warm coasts of that province in the tenth:[3] an inscription of 962, in a pagoda at
Tung-kuan, east of Canton, commemorates the trampling of the peasants' crops by
a herd of elephants.[4] These Cantonese elephants were noted both for the pink color
of their tusks, well suited to the manufacture of ceremonial writing tablets, and for
the delicate flavor of their trunks, which were prized by native cooks.[5] More interesting, because more mysterious, was a black race of elephants, sometimes described
as "blue-black," denizens of the Yangtze valley, where they were given the humiliating name of "river pigs."[6]

During these centuries from the fall of Shang to the rise of Sung, the elephant, though only an occasional spectacle for the people of the north, was sometimes useful to the people of the south, but only in warfare, and that rarely. The warriors of Ch'u sent elephants against their enemies in 506 B.C.; the southern state of

Liang employed them, armed with cutlasses, in A.D. 554; and the rich state of Southern Han used an elephant corps in great battles of 948 and 971.[7]

But these exceptional instances could not blur the image of the elephant as a monster and a thing of wonder, whose real home was on the far side of China's southern frontier. In Han times it was said that the men of the Annamese coast rode elephants into the sea to find and bring back the treasures of the deep, in particular the beautiful pearls which were the tears of the shark people.[8] In T'ang times elephants were still regarded as peculiarly Southern animals, emblematic of the hot lands of Indochina, as the poet Chang Chi wrote of them:

> The Countries of the Sea, where they mount elephants in battle,
> The Island-provinces of the *Man,* where they use silver in the markets.[9]

Here elephants are paired with silver, since both were as abundant in Indochina as they were uncommon in China, which was still a land of war horses and copper coins. Chiao-*chou,* modern Tongking, then a protectorate of China, was the closest of these "Countries of the Sea." The ninth-century poet Tu Hsün-ch'üeh wrote verses full of exotic images from the South, verses like these: "Flower grottoes echo the songs of the *Man,*" [10] and "Where (even) the names of all the flowers and birds are different." [11] and "The wind plays in the red banana—with sound of leaf on leaf." [12] He did not fail to mention the elephant in one of his visions of Annam, seen as a land of exile, where

> Argosies are laden with slaves from the sea, ears weighted down with rings;
> Elephants are burdened with women of the *Man,* bodies wrapped in bunting.[13]

Beyond the Chinese colonies lay the great kingdom of Champa, and there elephants played an even greater part: the royal guards, five thousand strong, clad in rattan armor, and carrying bows and arrows of bamboo, went forth to battle on the backs of elephants, and elephants were used as instruments of execution, to trample criminals to death.[14] Above all, the king was surrounded by elephants when he appeared in public,[15] borrowing might and power from the massive beasts. We read of King Bhadravarman III, in a Sanskrit inscription of 909:

He, the king of Champā, like the sons of the Pāṇḍu, shines by his splendour in the battlefield . . . in the four regions of which the sounds of war-drums were drowned by the roars of gigantic beautiful elephants . . . Having mounted an elephant, surrounded by innumerable forces both in front and rear, he shone in his majesty, while his own splendour, like that of the Sun, was screened by the umbrella of peacock-feathers raised over him.[16]

In Cambodia too the elephant had regal status: the king of Bnam—that is, of the old south Cambodian nation—rode forth on an elephant.[17] The king of Chinrap, the northern nation, ancestral to the later dynasties of Angkor, had, like his cousin in Champa, a corps of five thousand war elephants. These had wooden howdahs lashed on their backs, each of which carried four archers. The best of these elephants of war enjoyed, instead of the normal vegetable diet, repasts of flesh.[18] The god-king Jayavarman III, ruling from his capital of Hariharâlaya in the middle of the ninth century, was himself a great hunter of elephants, as befitted a Cambodian king.[19]

The P'an-p'an nation, now long since vanished, but once powerful on the Malay Peninsula, was also known to the Chinese of T'ang for its army elephants, organized into centuries, with four men to the howdah, as in Cambodia, armed with bows and lances.[20] The Thai and Burmese peoples to the southwest were also notable elephant users: Liu Hsün, author of the *Ling piao lu i*, on an official mission to Yünnan, was astonished to find that aristocratic families there owned elephants, which they used as beasts of burden, as the men of T'ang used horses and cattle.[21]

There was a four-tusked white elephant said to live in a country called Kaga:[22] this fine animal made fertile the country it trod on, so it was suggested that the T'ang emperor, Kao Tsung, send troops to capture it. The sovereign rejected this costly adventure as unworthy of a ruler committed to a policy of thrift, and besides, as he said, "What use have We for an odd elephant?"[23]

Along with the general exoticism investing the elephant in China, there were also titbits of lore, presumably brought in by hunters and traders in ivory, though it is impossible to say how widely they were believed: elephants dislike the barking of dogs, so that Southern hunters frighten their prey into exhausting immobility by imitating that sound, and finally are able to kill them by stabbing them behind the ear;[24] elephants have long memories and will weep if they see the skin of one of their young;[25] the bile of the elephant is mobile, being lodged in a different foot in each season.[26]

Though wild elephants might be seen by unlucky southern peasants, and merchants could supply elephant tusks for the artisans of the cities of China, tame and living elephants came chiefly with embassies from the nations of Indochina, in particular from Champa. That country sent trained elephants to the court at Ch'ang-an on repeated occasions in the 650's, during the first reign of Kao Tsung,[27] in the 680's and 690's during the reign of the Empress Wu,[28] and in the first half of the eighth century, under Chung Tsung and Hsüan Tsung.[29] This last period was distinguished by two gifts from the Cham kings of the famous white elephants, in 709 and in 735.[30] After this we hear no more of elephants from Champa coming northward in the normal way. But early in the ninth century, the Chinese general Chang Chou, after retaking a pair of Annamese border towns from the Chams and removing thirty thousand heads, captured, along with such booty as suits of armor and royal princes, a number of Cham war elephants.[31]

Occasionally trained elephants came from other countries: from Cambodia in 651 and 771;[32] from an otherwise unknown country near Cambodia named *Ẓiäm-pâk in 657;[33] from Sumatran Jambi in 853;[34] and even from such an unlikely place as "Persia" in 746, most likely a secessionist town in Khurāsān or Transoxania.[35]

These tribute or gift elephants were kept in the imperial stables and were given a daily ration of rice and beans, and clothed in sheepskins and felt blankets in winter, there to await the imperial pleasure.[36]

We should expect that the behemoths of Champa would have a notable position in imperial progresses. During the fourth and fifth centuries state processions always featured elephants from Vietnam, guided by native mahouts and drawing carriages of musicians. This custom was revived by Sung, after the tenth century, but, despite the great number of docile elephants received by T'ang from its Southern neighbors, there is no evidence that they were employed in this way.[37] Indeed, they were sometimes not used at all. As we have noted earlier, the T'ang monarchs suffered from spasmodic attacks of puritanism, which impelled them to get rid of "costly fowl and strange beasts" brought by barbarian embassies. When Te Tsung took the throne in 780, he signalized the austerity of his new reign by ordering the release of thirty-two Cambodian elephants, along with his hawks and hounds, and over a hundred palace women. The elephants were all sent to "the sunward side of Mount Ching," that is, to the habitat of the black breed of Chinese elephant on the central Yangtze, there, presumably, to enrich the native stock with the rare Cambodian strain.[38]

The usual role of elephants imported into T'ang was a rather frivolous one: they performed in royal shows of fighting and dancing. Chung Tsung himself watched elephants fight at the Southern Gate of Lo-yang in 705.[39] The reign of Hsüan Tsung was, however, the most remarkable for its performing elephants. At the great palace entertainments given by that monarch elephants danced and made obeisance to strains of music, along with entertainments by dancing horses, picturesque floats, and the exhibitions of athletes and acrobats.[40] These regal animals came to a barbarous end. After he had captured Lo-yang, Rokhshan held a banquet for his allied chieftains, and boasted that he would show how all animals, even foreign elephants, would turn toward a true Son of Heaven, namely himself. He ordered the dancing elephants of Hsüan Tsung to be led in, but they refused to perform. The outraged rebel had them all put into a pit, and done to death by fire and halberd. It is reported that the falconers and musicians of this savage court were unable to refrain from open weeping.[41]

But for the men of T'ang the elephant was more than a symbol of the great nations of the tropics and their crushing battle lines, made humble by the civilizing force of the Chinese way of life; that was the secular image, represented, perhaps, in a painting by Yen Li-pen, which showed a barbarian priest scrubbing an elephant with a great brush, "exceedingly strange."[42] But equally vivid was the spiritual image with which the secular was intermingled—the Buddhist vision of the elephant, very much in evidence in the religious literature of T'ang. The Gajapati, "Lord of the Elephants," a cosmic guardian of the South, the Gajarāja, "King of Elephants," symbolizing the Buddha in all his majesty, and a Bodhisattva who

82

rejoiced in the epithet of "Aromatic Elephant," are typical examples; they must have been represented in painting as well as in pious prose.[43] Indeed, with the Gajarāja, the *Hsiang Wang* of the Chinese, we bridge the gap between the Enlightened One, the Buddha, and the imposing figures of the Indochinese kings, who also partook of the essence of elephants.

RHINOCEROSES

The rhinoceros, like the elephant, was a familiar animal in north China in prehistoric and perhaps early historic times, but was already a rarity by the time of the ages illuminated by books. It is likely that two of the three Asian species of rhinoceroses were familiar to the archaic Chinese: we have small sculptures of both a one- and a two-horned kind surviving from Shang, Chou, and Han times; these must represent the Javanese (or Sunda) rhinoceros and the Sumatran rhinoceros respectively, both once widespread on the mainland and in the islands, but now restricted to remote parts of Indonesia, and on the verge of extinction.[44]

In China during T'ang times, the rhinoceros was confined to a rather broad area south of the Yangtze, comprising most of western and southern Hunan, and adjacent corners of neighboring provinces.[45] Two-horned rhinoceroses also survived in remote parts of Lingnan, contiguous with their main range in Indochina.[46]

The Chinese probably never captured their indigenous pachyderms for training: performing rhinoceroses were, like performing elephants, exotic marvels. Indeed, Tuan Ch'eng-shih, a great collector of marvels, wrote with astonishment of the wooden traps used to catch rhinoceroses in the homeland of a certain sea captain, who had described them to a physician in Canton. The doctor in turn had brought the story to Ch'eng-shih.[47]

Tamed rhinoceroses, then, came as astonishing royal gifts from the great nations south of China to the T'ang emperor, like the one sent by "the *Man* of the South" in 854, which was promptly sent back.[48] It is no surprise to learn that Champa was the most important source of them: the Chams sent a tame rhinoceros to Ch'ang-an early in the seventh century,[49] then eleven of the kind called "Heaven-communicating" (probably the great one-horned Indian rhinoceros) in 640,[50] and still another in 793.[51] This last was displayed in the Grand Shrine, for the delight of the dead sovereigns as well as the living. And then there were trained rhinoceroses from *Zi̯äm-pâk (a country unknown to us) in the seventh century,[52] the Khmer kingdom of Chinrap in the eighth,[53] and Kalinga (along with the famous black girls) in the ninth.[54] Less expected were gifts of rhinoceroses from some Western state still calling itself "Persia" early in the eighth century, one in the company of a royal prince.[55] And one came from the Tibetans, with other wild animals, in 824.[56]

These tropical monsters did not always find the climate of north China congenial: one brought to the capital in 796 died of the cold in the imperial park the following winter.[57] Some of the beasts, however, managed to survive, and they performed, along with elephants, in the great palace entertainments of Hsüan Tsung. Perhaps one of these was the model for the two-horned Sumatran rhinoceros shown in mother-of-pearl inlay on the back of a mirror in the Shōsōin.[58]

But as an exotic image the rhinoceros was unimportant—the animal was rather an emblem of China's antiquity, a kind of classical behemoth surviving among the barbarians. It was its horns and their magic virtue which had a significant role in the history of exoticism, as we shall see later.

LIONS

The history of the Asiatic lion is a tale of lamentable decline. The great cat was a familiar animal in ancient India, Persia, Babylonia, Assyria, and Asia Minor, and was even to be found in Macedonia and Thessaly in classical times.[59] Since then its range and numbers have steadily decreased; in the nineteenth century it could still be found in parts of Mesopotamia, in Persia south of Shīrāz, and in Gujerat, but it has now disappeared from all of these places except the last; a few lions still survive precariously on the Kathiawar Peninsula.[60]

Many specimens of this lordly animal were brought to China both in antiquity and in medieval times. Two words for "lion" followed the animal into China. The first, a word sounding like *suangi,[61] obsolete except as an intentional archaism during T'ang, came from India to China before the Christian era. The second, a word like *śiśäk,[62] came some centuries later from Iran; it was the common medieval name for the beast. It is curious that the latter form occurs most commonly in medieval literature as the name of the country we now call Ceylon. The island (once manless, inhabited by ghosts) was also known to be ". . . abundant in rare jewels," [63] having "a mountain of jargoon and diamonds," [64] the fame of which gave it the ancient Indic name of Ratnadvīpa, "Island of Gems," and the ninth-century Arabic name Jazīrat al-Yaḳūt, "Isle of Rubies," [65] but despite the fame of its gems in China, no like name for Ceylon was adopted there. But there was an old native name, Sinhala, "Lions' Abode," from which came, it seems, the name given it by mariners from the Persian Gulf, Sarandīb (from Sinhala-dvīpa?).[66] The Chinese name for Ceylon was "Country of Lions," because there, it was said, ". . . they are able to tame and raise lions." [67] This name must derive directly from the Singhalese name itself, or from some legend on which it is based, as the one in which ". . . the daughter of the Vanga King cohabited in the forest with a lion," [68] for lions were not actually known on the island.

The lion made a profound impression on the Chinese imagination, as the most powerful and terrible of all animals. In the year 635, the emperor T'ai Tsung received a lion from Samarkand, and ordered Yü Shih-nan to compose a rhapsody in its honor.[69] The scholar-poet turned out a characteristic *fu* couched in ornate language, expressing the awestruck attitude of the medieval Chinese toward the King of Beasts:

> It glares its eyes—and lightning flashes,
> It vents its voice—and thunder echoes.
>> It drags away the tiger,
>> Swallows down the bear,
>> Splits the rhinoceros,
>> Cleaves the elephant;
> It crushes the mighty gaur between gums and palate,
> It bends the boa snake between finger and palm . . .[70]

We have another rhapsody on this very same lion, written, much later, by Niu Shang-shih. Unlike Yü Shih-nan, he knew the animal only from a written account of this embassy, a glorious event in the past.[71]

The Tocharians sent lions to T'ang on three occasions, once in the seventh and twice in the eighth century;[72] the embassy of 719 is especially interesting in that two lions were presented by a Tocharian magnifico on behalf of Rome;[73] a few months later a "Roman" priest "of Great Virtue" was received in Ch'ang-an. Leo the Iconoclast was reigning at Constantinople, but we cannot be sure that these were his agents, since "Rome" or "Rūm" connoted especially Syria, now subject to the Arabs.

Other tribute lions came from Māimargh,[74] from "Persia" (possibly part of troubled Khurāsān),[75] and from the Arabs, all during the prosperous first half of the eighth century. The last-mentioned of these, the Arabian lion, gave the monarch Chung Tsung an opportunity for some characteristic moralizing: he had already shown his pious concern for preserving life, in accordance with the precepts of the Buddha, by rejecting falconry and hunting. Now, consistent with this policy, he rejected the carnivorous gift, not forgetting either that one of his ministers had pointed out the great expense of feeding the beast.[76]

For the Chinese of T'ang then, the lion was a Western animal, and undoubtedly partook of the same spiritual essence as the tiger, emblem of the West. Indeed, as the poem of Yü Shih-nan shows, the lion was even more savage than the tiger, and its awful majesty must have been accentuated by distance and rarity, so that its spiritual potency was exaggerated in Chinese eyes beyond that of the traditional tiger. We may even see in this puissant image a clouded reflection of the pre-Islamic lion-god of the Arabs, Yaghuth,[77] though the association would be remote and indirect at best; it is doubtful that the Chinese knew the deity. The following anecdote illustrates the spiritual forces at the disposal of a lion:

> At the end of [the reign] "Opened Prime," a Western nation offered us a lion. When they came onto the West Road of Ch'ang-an, they tied it to a tree at the post-station.

Now this tree was close to a well. The lion roared horribly, as if it were disquieted. All of a sudden, there was a great onset of wind and thunder, and a dragon actually came from the well and made off.[78]

Clearly the lion, an alter ego of the Tiger of the West, had supernatural faculties attuned to the effluvia of the Dragon of the East, its opposite number.

The frightful power of the lion, whether physical or spiritual, showed itself in other ways; in particular, mere parts of the beast exuded a terrible aura. Flies and gnats did not dare to light on a duster made from a lion's tail, which would have disposed of them quickly in life.[79] If a musician strummed a zither strung with lion sinews, all other strings in the orchestra would break, this idea apparently being related to the lion's terrifying scream.[80] The excrement of a lion was a powerful drug, thought, in one tradition, to be identical with storax, but the T'ang pharmacologist Ch'en Ts'ang-ch'i corrected the belief.[81] The genuine article (which must have been very rare indeed) would, if taken internally, break up coagulated blood. It also had power over all crawling things, and was burned to drive away demoniac beings.[82]

Even the painted representation of a lion was awe-inspiring. The eighth-century court painter Wei Wu-t'ien was celebrated for his ability to paint strange animals, and

. . . when foreign countries presented lions to the court, he made paintings of them that were strikingly lifelike. Later the lions would be returned to their homes, and only their paintings were kept; even so, whenever the pictures were unrolled, any other animal that caught sight of them would be terrified.[83]

The works of this artist were much in demand by collectors of the ninth century,[84] and indeed tribute lions seem to have been a popular subject among T'ang artists. We know, for instance, of a "delineation in white" of a lion sent from Khotan, done by Li Po-shih.[85] Most famous of all were the tribute lions depicted by the master of this kind of art, Yen Li-pen. Apparently the great man painted more than one, for we may read of one "resembling a bear, with simian hair and a long tail," whose color was black,[86] and indeed Tuan Ch'eng-shih tells us that there was a black variety of lion in the West.[87] Yen Li-pen also did a group of lions, in a scene with a barbarian king enthroned among a group of courtesans holding musical instruments; these beasts were "tiger-headed with a bear's body, and yellow-brown in color, radiant with divine coloration . . ."[88] Chou Mi, who wrote these descriptions, pointed out that in both paintings the lions shown were not the kind familiar from other paintings of his time, the thirteenth century, though he adds, referring to the black lion, "I hear that those sent recently as tribute by outside countries are of this very kind!"[89] If Chou Mi was describing authentic paintings by Yen Li-pen, we must suppose that the common lion of Southern Sung and Yüan paintings was a fanciful or degenerate stereotype, in striking contrast to the pictures of Yen Li-pen, which were made from life.[90]

The lion also had a religious symbolism: like the elephant, the lion in China evoked images of India and Buddhism. Its roar was a recognized metaphor of the voice of the Buddha instructing the beings of all universes in his law. Moreover, since the Buddha was a lion among men, wherever he sat was styled the "seat of the lion," an image extended to eminent Buddhist ecclesiastics, and made real by the craftsmen who built their thrones. Therefore Li Po, writing in honor of a priestly friend, referred to "the lion of yellow gold which holds your exalted seat." [91] Finally, icons of Mañjuśrī himself, a popular figure in religious art, showed him mounted on a lion.

LEOPARDS AND CHEETAHS

The Asiatic leopard, in several forms,[92] has been familiar to the Chinese since the earliest times, and the leopard played an important role in the traditional system of symbols. In antiquity it was an emblem of valor and warlike nobility, and was accordingly painted on the targets shot at by great lords in the ritualized archery contests. An old adage compared the noble person with the leopard in his "permutations," although the standard interpretation of this saying saw in it only the meaning that good men are humble and ready to adapt to circumstances and make concessions. But an older meaning of "leopard-like" was probably "crafty" or "foxy," as we would say, perhaps especially "wily in battle." This artless image reminds us of the abstract animals of medieval European allegory, emblematic of the Christian virtues, like the stag as symbol of the soul thirsting for baptism. The connotation of "full of fighting spirit" remained at any rate, with the result that in T'ang times the soldiers who had once been called "Valorous Cavalry" were renamed "Leopard Cavalry," [93] and the "Awesome Guards" became the "Leopard Scabbard Guards" [94] ("Leopard Scabbard" was the name of a section of a standard book on strategy). And, like the lion's image, the very picture of a leopard had power over evil spirits, a virtue which inspired a T'ang princess to make herself a pillow in the form of a leopard's head.[95]

Many tribute gifts of leopards came from the Western regions, all of them during the first half of the eighth century. They were sent from southern India,[96] from Māimargh,[97] from Kish[98] and Kandahar,[99] these last being *red* leopards, and from Bukhārā,[100] Samarkand,[101] Persia,[102] and the Caliphate.[103] Leopards, in short, despite their respectable history in the Far East, were nonetheless exotic animals.

A clue to this popularity of foreign specimens of a familiar animal—not nearly as rare as a rhinoceros, much less a lion—may be found in the account of the tribute from Samarkand in 713, described as consisting of "dog- and leopard-kind," or "the like of dogs and leopards," in language which suggests that they are much the same sort of thing. The only similarity between the two is that both are trained as hunting animals. We meet precisely the same phrase in a different context: in the year 762 the Emperor Su Tsung issued an edict "discontinuing tribute of gos-hawks and sparrow hawks, of dogs and leopards." [104] Or again, the court had fixed regulations regarding the value of rewards to be given to foreigners in return for their presents of "goshawks and falcons, dogs and leopards." [105] Goshawks, sparrow hawks, falcons, and dogs, all were familiar to the Chinese as hunting animals, and we can only conclude that the leopards were, too.

The hunting leopards, or cheetahs, [106] have been tamed and trained by men for a very long time, especially for hunting antelope. The Sumerians used them, it seems, but the bold Hittites tamed even the true panthers for hunting. [107] Cheetahs appear in Egyptian art of the eighteenth and nineteenth dynasties, wearing costly neckbands. [108] They have been used in India, in Persia, in Armenia, in Abyssinia, and in North Africa, and in Germany in the seventeenth century and in France in the eighteenth. [109] A Mongol Khan would take a thousand of them on a great hunt. [110] Such was the popularity of the animal in Western and Southern Asia, that it was inevitable that it should become known to the Chinese of T'ang. But the scarcity of literary allusions to hunting cheetahs in the texts of that age indicates that their use must have been restricted to court circles, and for a very short period. But we must remove the true leopard from the history of Far Eastern exoticism, and put the dash-ing cheetah in its place.

SABLES OR ERMINES

The tribute records of T'ang show that early in the seventh century envoys came from Manchuria with gifts of an animal styled *"feng tiao."* Two missions had been sent by the Khitans, [111] and one by their northern neighbors on the Kerulen River, whom the Chinese knew as *Siet-ĵʷei* (modern Shih-wei). [112] The animal's name, unfortunately, is rare in T'ang literature, though fairly common in fifth and sixth-century texts, especially poetic ones, where it refers, by metonymy, to the handsome, glossy tails of a marten-like animal. The tails were used, along with cicadas, in ac-cordance with ancient custom, to decorate various formal or ceremonial hats, espe-cially those of military officers. The mode seems to have grown up under influence of the Northern nomads. [113]

The epithet *feng,* regularly attached to the animal which yielded these rich and desirable tails, connotes "sleek; plump; fat and glossy," and therefore "prime, choice." The name *tiao* is given to the marten, the weasel, the stoat, and the like, though in north China most commonly to the stone marten. Our tribute animals, then, were "prime martens" or "choice weasels," Manchurian and Siberian animals which yielded the most desirable appendages to the hats of noble chiefs in the North; most likely they were sables, or possibly ermines. Both "black *tiao*" and "white *tiao*" (both sable and ermine) appear commonly in medieval literature. The tribute specimens (presumably living ones) may have been intended only for display and admiration in the imperial park, or possibly as breeding stock, to provide a source of tails on Chinese soil. But we shall have more to say about the tails and skins of marten-kind later.

GAZELLES OR CHAMOIS

The mysterious embassy of "Rome" to T'ang, through the agency of the Tocharian intermediaries, has already been mentioned because of the fine gift of a pair of lions it brought. The same envoys brought a pair of animals which the Chinese called *"ling* goats." [114] The identification of the goats is not helped by the fact that in the Chinese context the meaning of the name is quite clear: *"ling* goats" (sometimes written with the character *ling* "holy; numinous") are gorals, sometimes called "mountain goats" in Chinese. In the Western world they and their relatives, which include the European chamois and the American "mountain goat," are collectively called "goat antelopes," since they resemble both. [115] But the goral is unknown in Western Asia and Europe. Gorals live in mountainous parts of China, both north and south, [116] and their flesh was eaten by both northerners and southerners in T'ang times, by the southerners especially as an antidote for snakebite. [117] The horns of the animal were important in the T'ang materia medica: they were sent to the court as "local tribute" from the mountain towns of southern Shensi and northern Szechwan—taken powdered in honey, they would relieve all kinds of severe fever. [118]

The horns of the *ling* goat have another virtue: there was an old story that they alone had the hardness to break the amethyst-colored diamonds of Cambodia. [119] We have a variant of the tale from the seventh century:

During [the reign] "Honorable Outlook" there was a Brahman mendicant who said that he had obtained a tooth of the Buddha, and that there was no thing hard enough to stand being struck by it. [120] Fu I heard of this and said to his son: "That is not a Buddha's tooth. But I have heard that the adamantine stone is the hardest thing of all, and that nothing can match it except the horn of the *ling*-goat, which will crush it. You might go and try this out!" The mendicant kept . . . sealed most strictly, [121] but [the youth] implored him obstinately, and after a good long time he revealed it. [The youth] produced the horn and rapped it, and it fell to bits responsive to his hand. [122]

Was this a goral's horn? And did the credulous monk have a Buddha's tooth or a diamond, or neither? The brash experimental spirit of Fu I's son solves none of these problems. What indeed were the *ling*-goats of Rome? It would be no great marvel if they were actually chamois from the Caucasus or Carpathians, those far relatives of the serow and goral. But then they may have been some other attractive and exotic animal, not too unlike the goral, such as the Persian gazelle, the Arabian gazelle, or the pretty little Dorcas gazelle of Syria, whose docile and affectionate nature make it a frequent pet in the Near East.[123]

Doubtful Ungulates

The "horse-hoofed goat," presented jointly by the Tibetans and Turks to the T'ang court in 647,[124] may have been some strange antelope.

A deerlike animal with oxlike horns, the gift of the Sir-tardush in the same year, had the name *barlan or *ballan.[125] The name may be related to Bulan, the unicorn known to the medieval Turks, whose horns were a gathering place for rain and snow [126]; it may even be the same flesh-eating unicorn which was killed (in later legend) by the Uighur hero Oghuz Qaghan.[127] Or perhaps it was the *guran* of the Tungus and Mongols—the ugly big-nosed saiga antelope.[128] Or the bharal?

A Doubtful Carnivore

A country named *Gaviyap(?) [129] (perhaps related to Sanskrit *gavya,* "suitable for cattle"), not now identifiable, sent to Kao Tsung upon his accession a fearful bear, called *t'ien-t'iet (maybe registering *tenter or something like that), which was accustomed to prey on white elephants and lions.[130] A fiercer beast than this could hardly be imagined. In the sixteenth century Li Shih-chen was sufficiently impressed to write of it: "So however ferocious and savage the lion may be, there is still something which can control him!" [131] This mighty creature was hardly a brown bear, which though large is primarily vegetarian. The mountain-dwelling Himalayan black bear is somewhat smaller, but is a fierce eater of flesh. Conceivably it was he who had acquired a reputation as a lion-eater.

Marmots

Perhaps we ought not to include the Himalayan marmot among exotic animals, since, though it lives at about fifteen thousand feet on the edges of Tibet, part of its range falls within the boundaries of the Chinese provinces of Szechwan and Yünnan. The men of T'ang called this little animal by its Mongolian name, *tarbagha,*[132] which is more properly applicable to its gregarious cousin in Mongolia. In English also we know the latter as "tarbagan." [133] The Tibetans of T'ang times liked to dig the little rodents from their rocky burrows and eat them, and indeed Ch'en Ts'ang-ch'i prescribes stewed tarbagan for sufferers from scrofula, so we suppose that they were imported from Tibet for this purpose.[134] In any case, marmots were sent to the court as "local tribute," along with musk and flakes of gold, from the town of Lan-*chou*.[135] This place, in Lung-yu Province (modern Kansu) lies between the ranges of the Mongolian and the Tibetan marmots, so that we cannot tell whether these "*tarbagha* rats," as the notice of tribute calls them, were of the former or the latter species.

MONGOOSES

In that year, the country Kapiśa sent a mission to present a **noudyi* rat. It was sharp of snout and its tail was red, and it could eat snakes. Should someone suffer a bite by a poisonous snake, the rat will smell it without fail, and urinate on it. The wound will heal forthwith.[136]

This was in 642. About ten years later the same nation sent another of the talented animals to T'ang.[137] These were certainly Indian or Javan mongooses,[138] whose Sanskrit name is *nakula*, and which are called *newal, neolā, nyaūl*, and the like, in various Indic dialects. South China has a mongoose of its own, the crab-eating mongoose,[139] but it seems not to have been associated with the fierce little foreigners. We do not know if the Indian mongooses lived up to their reputation, or bred any descendants for the T'ang imperial family.

There are persons who cherish the animal and have it sleep with them, although it is ill-tempered, for they prefer to be bitten by a mangus to being killed by a snake.[140]

That is a philosophic Indian opinion, probably not shared by the Chinese.

A WEASEL OR FERRET

The country of Persia presented a **gharnoudja* whose shape was like a rat, but bluish colored. Its body was seven or eight inches long, and it could go in holes to catch rats.[141]

This sounds like a ferret, which had been used in classical antiquity in the West to catch rats and rabbits, having been tamed both by the Greeks and by the Romans;[142] even the mighty Genghiz Khan did not disdain to hunt with ferrets.[143] On the other hand, the weasel, a grand mouse-catcher, was kept in homes, especially as a lady's pet, in the classical world.[144] Which would have been a more likely gift from the Persians I cannot say.

Golden-winged, silver-winged,
*   Winged with flashing flame,*
Such a flight of birds I saw,
*   Birds without a name:*
Singing songs in their own tongue—
*   Song of songs—they came.*

        Christina Rossetti, *Birds of Paradise*

v= Birds

THE CHINESE of the T'ang era trained birds for useful tasks (hawks as hunters and pigeons as carriers), and ate birds, and used them in medicine, and, above all, admired them. The larger and more handsomely colored fowl of course received most of the pleased attention, and the birds brought from remote places were most admired, since they were more stimulating to the imagination. Consequently they appear in literature, as we shall see presently, and were represented in art: we know, for instance, that Yen Li-pen painted "Exotic Birds in the Spring Park," [1] though unfortunately this picture has not survived.

T'ang gardens and parks were stocked with curious or charming birds, and imperial collectors, with their immense resources, could acquire great numbers of birds, and costly ones at that, for their pleasure and that of their courts. An example was the talented and impulsive Hsüan Tsung, who, in 716, sent eunuchs into the region south of the Yangtze

. . . to take Pond Herons and Tufted Ducks, desiring to place them in his Park. Wherever these agents went, there was vexation and trouble. Now as he made his way through Pien-*chou*, Ni Jo-shui said to His Highness, "Though farms and mulberries are in a critical state just now, they capture birds and wildfowl in their nets to supply frivolities for garden and pond. From far beyond the river and the mountain passes, these are transferred under escort by water and land, and fed with millet and meat, so that watchers by road and highway cannot but take it that Your Enthroned Eminence esteems birds while despising men! To Your Enthroned Eminence a Phoenix must surely be an ordinary bird, and a

Unicorn an ordinary beast—how much more so a Pond Heron or Tufted Duck! In what way are they so worthy of esteem?" His Highness issued an encyclical by his own hand, in which he gave thanks to Jo-shui, and he bestowed on him forty pieces of rich cloth, and had the birds set free to go where they would.[2]

Ni Jo-shui may have been a sententious moralizer—his argument is all too typical of conservative opinion in medieval China—but real hardships may well have been created by these great birding expeditions, and it was characteristic of Hsüan Tsung, a sensitive man, that, despite his fondness for luxury, he should be quick to respond to a humane appeal.

HAWKS AND FALCONS

Hawking was an art known to the Chinese from the third century B.C.; the great minister Li Szu, it is said, spoke of his favorite gray goshawk when he was about to be put to death.[3] After that time, the sport enjoyed increasing favor in north China, especially under the "Tatar" rulers of the fifth and sixth centuries of our era, when Chinese culture was richly infused with the customs and arts of the northern steppes and forests. This was particularly true of the state of Northern Ch'i in the sixth century.[4]

The sport continued to be popular under the T'ang monarchs, especially when a vigorous ruler, such as T'ai Tsung or Hsüan Tsung, set an enthusiastic example.[5] But things must have been different when an earnest sovereign fell under the spell of the traditional morality, in which hawking was regarded as frivolous. So, in the seventh century, Kao Tsung ordered an end to the regular tribute in hawks and falcons;[6] in the eighth century, Te Tsung emptied the imperial mews along with the imperial theater;[7] and in the ninth century Hsi Tsung signalized the virtue of his accession by following the example of Kao Tsung.[8]

In the great mews at the palace, adjoining the kennels of the hunting dogs, were kept four kinds of hunting hawk. Most rare, noble, and impressive were the eagles, chiefly the golden eagle.[9] Most elegant and aristocratic were the black-eyed, long-winged falcons: sakers to capture herons and other large game birds, and peregrines for ducks and other waterfowl. Especially prized was the white "Greenland" gyrfalcon;[10] T'ai Tsung himself had one of these, which he named "Army Commander."[11] A choice kind of gyrfalcon, imported from Manchuria, was the "frosted falcon":

> Slicing over the sea—the clouded goshawk,
> Crossing under the void—the frosted falcon.[12]

Next came the sparrow hawks, small short-winged accipiters, favored for hunting quail and other small game birds in wooded places.[13] Finally, most popular hunting birds of all, were the goshawks, yellow-eyed, large relatives of the sparrow hawks and, like them, primarily forest hunters, taking the traditional game, pheasants and rabbits.[14] A white variety of goshawk, brought from Manchuria, was valued most highly.[15] But a black goshawk was prized too; Tu Fu wrote a pair of poems on the white and black goshawks, of which this is the second:

> A black goshawk is not to be found staying among humankind;
> She passed over the seas, I suspect, coming from the Northern Pole;
> Her straightened quills beat the wind as she crossed over the purple borderland,
> At winter's onset she stayed some nights at the Solar Terrace.
> The foresters' nets were all out for her—but they applied their arts in vain;
> The geese of spring which go back with her surely see her with misgivings.
> A myriad miles in the cold void—it takes just a single day;
> But these golden eyeballs and these jade talons are of no usual stock.[16]

One of Hsüan Tsung's princes had a red goshawk, to match the yellow falcon of another royal youth; both were styled "cloud-bursters" by the imperial falconer.[17]

Undoubtedly a good supply of hunting hawks came into T'ang from beyond her borders, many of the best of them as "tribute" to the sovereign. In 866 Chang I-ch'ao, the independent governor of Tun-huang, sent four "green-shank" goshawks, along with two Tibetan women and a pair of horses;[18] in 715 a Manchurian chieftain sent a pair of white goshawks;[19] and during the eighth century P'o-hai, at the head of the Korean Peninsula,[20] sent many goshawks and falcons. The poet Tou Kung has described a rare hunting bird sent from Silla, also in Korea:

> The autocrat's horse is newly mounted—it is autumn in the Tabooed Park,
> His white goshawk comes from the eastern head of the sea.
> When the Illustrious One of Han, free of affairs, rightly finds leisure to hunt,
> Like a flurry of snow she strives to fly to the gauntlet on his brocaded arm.[21]

Korea and Manchuria were the prime sources of superior hawks and falcons; Mongolia and Turkestan were secondary sources. But the hawks of northern China itself were not to be despised, and those from north of Tai, in what is now Shansi, were especially regarded as noble birds. Of these the black falcons and sparrow hawks taken at Hua-*chou* near the confluence of the Wei River with the Yellow River in what is now eastern Shensi, must have been choicest of all, since they were demanded as tribute by the imperial court.[22]

We know a great deal about the T'ang way of classifying native hawks from a little treatise on falconry (the oldest surviving one) by the ninth-century writer to whom my book owes so much, Tuan Ch'eng-shih, himself an amateur austringer.[23] He has described the several kinds of Chinese goshawks and given their varietal names. These were color names in the main, but some also point to the native home of the bird. Among them were the "white rabbit goshawk," a first-rate hunter, the "skylark yellow," the "red spot engouted," the "redbud den white," from the sandy wastes of northern Shansi, the "Fang-shan white," from the poplars of northwestern

Hopei, the "earth yellow," from the deciduous oaks of the north, and the "white inky black," from the northern arborvitaes.[24]

The medieval Chinese themselves understood the art of catching and training hawks for the hunt, and did not have to rely on foreign experts.[25] So, when the young hawks were in passage, they took them with pigeon spies and decoys, and with cunning nets, dyed with yellow phellodendron and oak liquor to camouflage them against the earth and protect them from insects.[26] Or, for more tractable pupils, they took nestlings from their oaks and poplars.[27] In either case, they provided their goshawks with tail bells of jade, gold, and chased metals, and their sparrow hawks with embroidered collars. All their hunting birds were fitted with jesses of leather or green silk or "clouded brocade," leashes with jade swivels, gilded perches, and carved and painted cages.[28]

Hawks and falcons, whether native or foreign-born, were favorite subjects for T'ang painters. Li Yüan-ch'ang, the brother of T'ai Tsung, was said to be a better painter of birds even than Yen Li-pen and Yen Li-te.[29] And under Hsüan Tsung's golden reign there were many great hawk painters, the best being Chiang Chiao (himself a favorite of the sporting emperor), whose painting of a "horned goshawk" became the subject of a poem by Tu Fu.[30] (The "horned goshawk" seems actually to have been a "hawk eagle" or "crested eagle," the "royal goshawk" [*Shāh-bāz*] of the Persian falconers' handbooks.) [31]

Hawks and falcons and eagles also figure prominently in T'ang poetry, often symbolically. ". . . in metaphor and simile: the flashing eye, the lightning attack, the paralyzing blow, are as familiar in Chinese verse as in Western. So also is the image of the hawk as a ruthless predator, liable to sententious treatment in verse." [32] The poet Chang Hsiao-p'iao sees the trained hawk as an emblem of a bold and free spirit held in shackles:

> She imagines the level plain afar—where the hares are plump just now;
> She turns her honed bill a thousand times—and shakes her feather coat;
> Just let her peck loose this knot in her silken cord. . . !
> But unless she got the call of a man she would not dare to fly.[33]

Hunting hawks also had conventional associations with the cardinal directions, sometimes with the West, a rather artificial and traditional link: "West" was the direction of "autumn" and it was in this season that ". . . the hawks left their boreal eyries to migrate southward over the plains of China." [34] More realistic was the association with the North, the natural home of the hawks, and the home of the barbarians who brought them into China.

> The Bird of Viet comes from the South,
> But Hawk of Hu makes the Northern passage . . .[35]

These are the words of Li Po. Now here is a little quatrain about a soldierly youth, written by Hsüeh Feng. In it, the *hu* (barbarian of the North or West) goshawk has greenish eyes (a bit of freedom here—the goshawk's eyes are yellowish, to be contrasted with the black eyes of the falcon), suggesting the ruthless green or blue eyes of the barbarians themselves. This picture is matched in turn with the exotic images of the mottled horse and the ermine fur:

> A green-eyed *hu* goshawk treads his brocaded gauntlet;
> With five-flowered grizzled horse and white ermine furs,
> He goes and comes in the three markets, but there is no man he knows;
> And he throws down his gold-handled whip, and ascends the tower of wine.[36]

In the same way, the Uighurs were "whirling falcons," [37] and "the leopard is the younger brother of the tiger, as the goshawk is the older brother of the sparrow hawk," [38] and a certain harsh official could deserve the epithet of "ink-black eagle." [39]

These fierce birds were visible emblems of valor: the crimson shirts of the commanders of several companies of the guards of the Empress Wu had figured on them lions, tigers, and leopards, and goshawks and falcons.[40] A more primitive form of the same conception explains the use of goshawks in T'ang medicine: the flesh was eaten to quell the attacks of "wild foxes and perverted goblins"; the talons were reduced to ashes and taken in water for the same purpose (and also to cure the piles); [41] even the feces were burned and taken in a spoonful of wine as an antidote to demonaic influences (though the patient was on no account to be told what the medicine was).[42] So the savage, half-alien essence of the hawk, the terror of the animal world, was communicated to the sufferer to give him power over ghosts and demons.

PEACOCKS

In antiquity, that is, before the Han dynasty, the only peafowl known to the Chinese was the Indian peafowl.[43] One tradition tells that a specimen of this handsome bird was sent by an unidentified Western state to the second king of Chou. This would have been at about the beginning of the first millennium B.C.[44] Perhaps we can place little faith in this story, but there is no doubt that the Chinese of Han times regarded the peacock chiefly as a Western bird, which had its home in the Kashmir [45] and in some part of the dominions of the Parthian kings.[46] But the bird was known then only by report, probably from descriptions brought by travelers. This was at a time when, at the other end of the world, in Italy, Indian peafowl were being raised on little islands planted with trees, and were eaten by the luxurious.[47] But soon the new lands, which were to become the tropical south China of modern times, were opened up, and there the Chinese found the green peacock of Indochina. By the third century specimens of this beautiful creature, clothed in metallic green and gold, were brought from the confines of Champa, along with incenses, pearls, ivory, and parrots.[48] The demand for the wonderful birds increased rapidly. In 262, the southern kingdom of Wu sent an officer into Tongking to collect a tax of three thousand peafowl. This and similar depredations by the magistrates stationed among the Vietnamese (if they may be so called at this early period) led to an uprising and the murder of the tax legate in the following year.[49]

But as the tropical coast of Lingnan became familiar to Chinese settlers it was found that the desirable birds were as abundant on Chinese soil as on Indochinese, and in T'ang times they were sent to Ch'ang-an as annual tribute from Lo-*chou* and Lei-*chou*, on the Luichow Peninsula, along with fancy bamboos, parrots, and silver.[50] The peacock became for the Chinese the "bird of Viet," a standard symbol of the South—indeed, in the tenth century, the bird fancier Li Fang named it "Visitor from the South,"[51] and it flaunted its iridescent plumes   he gardens of the North:

> It moves—and sways its golden halcyon-blue tail,
> It flies—and dances in the shadow of the jade pool.[52]

"Bird of Viet" was more a symbolic and literary epithet than a common name. The peacock was ordinarily styled *"k'ung* sparrow," a name which is as mysterious as it is old. We may recall that the Greeks named the ostrich "Libyan sparrow" and "Arabian sparrow," and especially "sparrow-camel," and the Latins called it "overseas sparrow."[53] These names seem to embalm folk jest in serious language. The old Chinese tradition is that *k'ung* meant "great," but I cannot judge whether this accepted etymology was well-founded. If it was, "great sparrow" does seem comically inappropriate for such a splendid fowl.

An important study of the geography and natural history of south China, the *Nan fang i wu chih,* written by Fang Ch'ien-li in the ninth century, is unhappily now lost, though excerpts from it survive as quotations in other books. One of these is a brief compendium of T'ang peacock lore:

K'ung sparrows are very abundant in Chiao-chih, and in Lei- and Lo-*chou*. They live in the tallest trees in the high mountains. In largeness they are like geese, and when three or four feet tall are not inferior to cranes. They are thin of neck and arched of back. The head bears three feathers, an inch or so long. They fly in flocks of several tens. They roost and roam among ridges and mounds. At daybreak the sounds of their voices inter-blend. Their call is *"tughu."* The hen is short of tail, and lacks the gold and halcyon-blue. The cock's tail is still short after three years, but in five years it will be two or three feet long. In summer, it molts its plumage, but by spring it will have grown again. From its back to its tail there are round markings, pentachromatic, with gold and halcyon-blue encircling each other like coins. It is in love with its own tail, and when it roosts in the mountains, it first chooses a place to lay the tail. When it rains, the tail is heavy and it cannot fly high, and so the men of the south go out to catch it. Sometimes they wait in hiding for it to pass, and cut off the tail alive; and this is a local product of theirs. But if [the birds] look back, the gold and halcyon colors will suddenly diminish. The mountain men raise their chicks to act as decoys, or sometimes they find the eggs and have a hen brood and hatch them. These are fed with pigs' entrails, fresh greens, and the like. If they hear a man clap his hands and sing and dance, they will dance. They have jealous natures, and if they see someone in colorful costume, they will be sure to peck at him.[54]

The decoy peafowl were staked out with cords tied to their legs, and when the wild birds flew down beside them, the hunters threw nets over them.[55] These southerners had other uses for the birds, whether wild or tame, than supplying the feather trade: like the epicureans of Rome, they ate them, but not as a rare delicacy: "sometimes they give them to people for filling of mouth and stomach, or else they kill them to make preserved meat and charqui."[56] This flesh had the excellent virtue of being efficacious against both vegetable and animal poisons, and peacock blood was an antidote to the virulent, half-magical poison called *ku*.[57]

The sexual life of these scintillating birds obsessed the southerners. "They neither pair nor mate, but should voice or shadow come together, then pregnancy occurs,"[58] wrote a T'ang student of southern affairs. The movements of the ether seem to have been particularly influential, for, again, if the female calls down wind, and the male calls up wind, the female (it was said) will conceive;[59] but according to Tuan Ch'eng-shih, who cites Buddhist sources as authoritative, peahens become pregnant at the sound of thunder.[60] It was also alleged that a peacock would copulate with a serpent.[61]

We have noted Fang Ch'ien-li's report about the peacock's proclivity to dancing to music. This is a persistent theme in medieval literature. As early as the third century we hear of a peacock, sent from the Western Regions, which understood human speech and would dance at the snapping of fingers.[62] In one tradition, pheasants (or phoenixes, which were much the same) would dance when they saw their images reflected in a mirror, and this idea seems to explain the appearance of these birds in designs on the backs of T'ang mirrors.[63] Dancing peacocks, exhilarated by their own images, exemplified the cliché "vain as a peacock" in its medieval Chinese counterpart. Peacocks were presented by the king of Silla at the end of the eighth century. Their shimmering dance was depicted by the great nature painter Pien Luan.[64] This famous artist, who later deserted the court to become a Bohemian painter, made many other peacock pictures, a number of which survived into Sung times; the Emperor Hui Tsung's catalogue records his "Banana and Peacock," "Peonies and Peacock," and a number of others.[65]

The imagery of the peacock was much enriched by Buddhist literature, especially by the conception of the Peacock King: the pilgrim Hsüan-tsang had told the story of the Buddha incarnate in a peacock, bringing healing water miraculously from a rock[66]; and a Burmese dance, transferred to T'ang, commemorated the holy Peacock King.[67] Another peacock deity was the *Mahā-mayūrī vidyārājñī*, a goddess much favored by the spellbinding Tantrists. In China she had power to bring rain and overcome the demons of disease; sometimes transformed into a male, this potent spirit was shown seated on a lotus on the back of a peacock.[68] There were many Chinese translations of sutras devoted to her—in T'ang times, we have one by the famous I-ching, and another by Amoghavajra,[69] and there were paintings of this "Luminous Prince" by such eminent artists as Yen Li-pen[70] and Wu Tao-hsüan.[71]

PARROTS

The ancient Chinese had their own flocks of autochthonous parrots, which lived in the Lung Mountains near the old caravan route along what is now the Shensi-Kansu border. These classical birds, sometimes called "Holy Birds of the Western Regions," because of their ability to speak, were most likely a variety of the green parakeet with violet breast, called the Derbyan parakeet,[72] nowadays a native of Szechwan, Yünnan, and eastern Tibet, but not now known to be north of about 30° North Latitude.[73] But, unhappily, the aboriginal Lung Mountain colonies were raided for cage birds in medieval times, and the race has since then become extinct. In the ninth century P'i Jih-hsiu wrote pityingly of the men of Lung, who were obliged to hazard their lives to catch parrots as "local tribute" for the "Gilded Terrace" of the imperial court:

> The Mountains of Lung—a thousand myriad fathoms—
> The parrots nest on their peaks.
> Were all of their perils explored and their hazards followed to the end,
> These mountains would still not be comprehended.
> Doltish and dull-witted these people of Lung,
> With their hanging passageways—as if they would climb to Heaven.
> Should they spy such a nest up in the void,
> They will fight tumultuously to bring it down into their hands.
> Of a hundred birds they do not get one;
> Of ten men, nine die at it.
> By Lung Stream are the garrison recruits;
> The garrison recruits are not idle either:
> Under the Mandate, they must take up the carved cages,
> And go straight to the front of the Gilded Terrace.
> But this plumage has no value to itself,
> This tongue does not speak for itself.
> To what end this slighting of man's fate,
> To offer up such trifles for play and pleasure?
> I have heard that an ancient king, a paragon,
> Let each of his costly birds go free;
> Yet now the likes of these people of Lung,
> Must weep floods of tears each year.[74]

From about the second century of our era, new breeds of parrots, southern birds, symbolically allied to the peacocks, began to appear in the north, sent from the newly Chinese lands of Lingnan and Vietnam. In T'ang itself, the rose-ringed parakeet, the red-breasted parakeet, and the blue- or blossom-headed parakeet, as attractive as their names, were to be found on the Luichow Peninsula and nearby parts of western Kwangtung.[75] Like the peacocks, these showy little birds provided a casual article of diet for the natives of this zone, but only because of their abundance—a trivial motive for eating such flamboyant creatures, and to be contrasted with the destiny of the parrots of India, which were eaten by the brahmans as noble and holy food, or those brought to Rome and consumed, along with roast flamingo, by such gourmets as Elagabalus, as worthy of his elegance and luxury.[76] Some were sent away, however, to vie with the familiar parrots of Lung in the cages and gardens of northern bird fanciers. The classic birds must still have been abundant, however, since the parrots in the tenth-century garden of Li Fang were named "Visitors from Lung."[77]

But from the third century, parakeets of both the northwest and the south had dazzling rivals who quickly replaced them in the favor of connoisseurs wealthy or noble enough to obtain them. These were the parrots of Indochina and Indonesia,[78] splendid fowl sent as gifts from the mighty ones of the tropical nations to the Chinese emperor, or brought in (as parrots have been everywhere and in all times) from the ends of the earth by far-traveling sailors and merchants, visible proof that distant realms are more highly colored than the hills of home:

> Now the Eastern curtain draws;
>> Now the red'ning splendour gleams,
> Now the purple plum'd maccaws,
>> Skim along the silver streams.

Chatterton's "An African Song," from which these verses are taken, caught the eternal glory of exotic places—but the macaw is an American, not an African, bird and was unknown in the Old World until modern times. The parrots brought into T'ang by seafarers and diplomats were new kinds of parakeets, lories and cockatoos.

Most celebrated for their beauty were the parakeets and lories styled "five-colored parrots" in China. In medieval India the lories of the Moluccas were named *pañcavarṇagini,* "five-colored parrots," [79] for the same reason—they flashed with all the colors of the rainbow. Perhaps, even, the Chinese epithet was a translation of the Indian.

> With my becke bent, my littil wanton eye,
>> My fedders freshe as is the emraude grene,
> About my neck a circulet like the riche rubye,
> My littil leggis, my feet both fete and clene,
>> I am a minion to wait uppon a quene . . .

So the central figure of John Skelton's "Speak, Parrot." And so, it might be, an exotic parakeet in China. "Red parrots" arrived, too—these were certainly the scarlet lories and rosy cockatoos of Australasia, east of Wallace's line, which separates the two great faunas of Oceania. The "white parrots" of Chinese literature were plainly cockatoos from those remote lands.

No record of gifts of "red parrots" survives from T'ang times, though they had been imported earlier. The "South Indian Nation," however, sent a talking pentachromatic parrot with an embassy in 720: this embassy is well reported; it requested a Chinese army to punish the Arabs and Tibetans for numerous outrages, and the Indian ambasador was clever enough to point out that robes and girdles were the only sure marks of Chinese favor among the "barbarians"; he was accordingly invested by Hsüan Tsung with a brocaded caftan and a girdle of gilded leather.[80] In the previous century, a five-colored parrot presented by Champa had astonished T'ai Tsung, who ordered a "rhapsody" composed in praise of it.[81] This and a white parrot which accompanied it complained frequently of the cold, and by special decree these intelligent birds were manumitted and sent home again.[82] A mountainous country on the Malay Peninsula, rich in elephants,[83] sent a five-colored parrot in 655.[84] In the eighth century parrots came from Śrivijaya[85] and from Tukhāristān (brought by the great lord "Rama," on behalf of neighboring Kapiśa),[86] and twice from Kalinga early in the ninth century.[87] One of these multicolored creatures, which knew how to talk, remained the pet of the great Hsüan Tsung; it was suggested to him that this might even be the fabulous bird of good omen called "Joy of the Season," which had been shown in an old illustrated book with "cinnabar head, pink breast, vermilion cap, and green wings."[88]

As for white cockatoos, we have already mentioned the one from Champa (but it is not native there—it must have been caught in the furthest part of Indonesia). This was the bird, "refined in understanding, discriminating in intelligence, and excellent at answering questions," which T'ai Tsung, out of pity, returned to its native forest.[89] This bird, and the five-colored one which accompanied it, were painted by Yen Li-pen. Chou Mi, the Sung writer and critic, claimed that he owned this picture:

My household has long had in storage a "Picture of Prum Irap Presenting Parrots." These must have been the ones presented in the time of "Honorable Outlook" of T'ang. Since they longed for return, T'ai Tsung let them go back to their country, escorted by two women. This, then, is a true relic of Yen Li-pen.[90]

Another famous white cockatoo preserved in paint was "Snow-Garbed Maiden," the pet of Yang Kuei-fei. According to a widely repeated anecdote, the Consort flew it at the gaming board when Hsüan Tsung was in danger of losing at "double six," disarranging the men and preventing the inevitable blow to imperial pride.[91] This touching scene (another form of the story of the toy dog of Samarkand) was recorded by the master Chou Fang.[92]

More spectacular than these was the cockatoo with ten long pink feathers on its crown, surely the elegant rose-crested cockatoo of Ceram and Amboina,[93] the gift of an island nation far over the sea, five months from Canton, probably one of the Moluccas.[94] The envoys of this remote country brought camphor as well as the parrot, and asked for horses and bronze bells in return, and it was decreed that they be given them.[95]

As for parrot lore generally, there was an old tradition that stroking a parrot led to mortal disease. The disease was psittacosis, which is actually transmitted to the lungs by dust contaminated with the parrot's feces.[96] Then there were well-known tales, probably mostly of Indian origin,[97] of parrots as spies on household servants and errant wives. Finally, the parrot was the image of caged intelligence—best not to be wise! But ". . . loss of freedom may be voluntary and altruistic, as when the parrot becomes a symbol of the bride who surrenders her liberty to her husband, or the vassal who gives up his private interests for his lord's. Again, fine plumage, a source of vanity to its owner, may lead to capture, imprisonment, and sorrow."[98]

OSTRICHES

No foreign animal was a greater marvel in China than the ostrich, but no fewer than two came to T'ang in the seventh century. The monstrous birds were known by repute, since the Parthians had sent one as a gift as long ago as A.D. 101.[99] They were doubtless specimens of a Tocharian race of ostriches similar to the one which inhabited, until its extinction in 1941, the Syrian and Arabian deserts.[100] The head and neck of the adult male were red or pink, the body feathers glossy black, with white plumes in tail and wing. This was the bird called *ushtur murgh,* "camel-bird," by the Persians,[101] a name which, translated into Chinese, became the common medieval name for the ostrich in the Far East, replacing the ancient title "great sparrow of T'iao-chih," a name which reminds us of the Greek and Latin names of the ostrich.[102] The old name was not extinct, however, for the report of a mission from the Khan of the Western Turks in 620 states that the envoys presented "a giant bird of T'iao-chih."[103] More famous is the "camel-bird" presented by Tukhāra in 650: its ability to run 300 Chinese miles in a day, beating its wings the while, and to digest copper and iron, were widely reported.[104] The last-mentioned ability led to the adoption of camel dung into the T'ang materia medica: it was recommended that a man who had inadvertently swallowed a piece of iron or stone swallow some of the unlikely drug to dissolve it.[105]

This handsome Tocharian bird was offered by Kao Tsung to the manes of his glorious predecessor, T'ai Tsung, at the latter's tumulus,[106] and its image in stone stands today at the tumulus of Kao Tsung himself.[107] A camel-bird of unknown origin, but like the other shown plainly and realistically, clearly modeled from life, stands at the tomb of Jui Tsung.

A mystery altogether is Li Po's ostrich:

Birds

> Tapestried camel-bird at Autumn Estuary—
> As rare among men as up in Heaven:
> The Mountain Fowl is abashed before limpid water;
> Not daring to see its feather coat reflected.[108]

As was well known, the pheasant is enamoured of its own beautiful reflection. In this quatrain it is put to shame by the ostrich, "tapestried" in red, white, and black. Indeed "tapestried" is originally an epithet of pheasants: the golden pheasant is sometimes called "mountain fowl" as it is here, and sometimes "tapestried fowl" for its burnished polychrome plumage.[109] Was Li Po writing of an ostrich seen, not merely an ostrich reported? Or does the bird simply image a gifted literatus?

Kalaviṅkas

In Buddhist literature there are many references to the *kalaviṅka* bird and its melodious voice. This wonderful singer appears, not for its own sake, but as a stereotyped image of the Buddha and his voice, telling all beings the great truths about the nature of suffering and the impermanence of the physical world.[110] Of the bird itself, the great Buddhist lexicographer Hui-lin wrote: "This bird is aboriginal in the Snowy Mountains. It is able to sing while it is in the egg. Its voice is harmonious and courtly. One listens without satiety." [111]

The divine bird is found ambiguously in Far Eastern religious art, being confused with the *kinnara,* which is really a very different creature.[112] It was represented in a Chinese ballet of Indian origin called "Kalaviṅka" (we have referred to it already), which is still performed in Japan by winged boys.[113]

It might be supposed that a creature whose whole existence seems confined to religious metaphor and iconography would be sought in vain in the real world. The assumption would be mistaken, for early in the ninth century a mission came to the T'ang court from the kingdom of Kalinga and presented to the throne, along with a parrot, a number of "Zanj" youths, and many rare incenses, a *kalaviṅka* bird.[114] What then was this Indonesian bird? In seeking to identify it, we must find a bird that occurs naturally in both Indonesia and in India and that has a clear, melodious voice. These conditions are almost too easy to satisfy, since, allowing for specific and varietal differences, the two regions have many birds in common, and some are even fair singers. But the field has been narrowed down by a Chinese writer of the twelfth century. Chang Pang-chi, writing of a Buddhist temple in Chekiang, has this to say:

On the Basilica of the Buddha there were two *kalaviṅka* birds which built a nest between beams and ridgepole. They were as large as the black drongo,[115] and their body plumage and feathers were deep indigo, with kingfisher iridescence. Their voices were clear and shrill, like jade when it is struck. Each year they bore young, but they always led them away—where, we do not know.[116]

Our bird of mystery, then, is comparable to the common drongo of China, and like it has metallic plumage, but deep blue instead of black. Its voice is notably high and resonant. Does such a bird occur both in the Islands and in India? Yes, the paradise drongo,[117] or, as it is more commonly (and vulgarly) known, the great racket-tailed drongo. A Javanese race, *Dicrurus paradiseus formosus,* "beautiful paradise drongo," has glossy purplish black plumage, long sweeping outer tail feathers, and ". . . a series of melodious whistles and notes and great power of imitation."[118] Of the Indian race it has been said that it is ". . . perhaps the best singing-bird of the East."[119]

All the conditions are satisfied: in India the voice of this beautiful and fearless bird, with its shining plumage glossed in blue, ringing through the hill forests, became the symbol of the law-giving voice of the Enlightened One; a mated pair of an Indochinese or Yünnanese subspecies came wandering into Chekiang in the twelfth century, to the astonishment of Chang Pang-chi; and the king of Kalinga sent his beautiful "drongo of paradise" to Ch'ang-an as a natural wonder and equally as an emblem of the faith.[120]

She was a gordian shape of dazzling hue,
Vermilion-spotted, golden, green, and blue;
Striped like a zebra, freckled like a pard,
Eyed like a peacock, and all crimson-barr'd;
And full of silver moons, that, as she breathed,
Dissolved, or brighter shone, or interwreathed
Their lustres with the gloomier tapestries—
So rainbow-sided, touch'd with miseries,
She seem'd at once, some penanced lady elf,
Some demon's mistress, or the demon's self.

John Keats, *Lamia*

vi=Furs and Feathers

THE DISPOSITION to wear pelts and plumage stripped forcibly from their rightful owners may be as old as man, but the fashion shows no signs of obsolescence. In the beginning, at any rate, it was an admirably simple way of acquiring ready-made suits of clothes. Moreover, the wearer acquired both wild beauty and magic power along with warm comfort—in a sense he *became* a bear or a fox or a swan and shared their astonishing virtues.

In ancient China furs worn about the shoulders had a special dignity, and the "Great Furs" were the prerogative of the Son of Heaven, who wore them with his crown when he worshiped the high gods.[1] His holy pelisse is said to have been made of lambskin and to have been adorned with symbolic figures and images of the planets, mountains, and earthly creatures.

In the course of centuries furs became the mark of the northern nomad, or the Chinese fighting man, or even merely the winter costume of a northerner. In T'ang times a bewildering variety of fur garments was in use. There were white fox furs, marten furs, black sable furs, tiger furs, "furs worth a thousand metal-pieces," "purple forest furs," "halcyon-blue furs," and even "white linen furs," "tapestry furs," "cotton furs," and "woolen damask furs."[2] These last expressions, apparently self-contradictory, seem to refer to capes and warm cloaks partly of textile fabrics, lined or faced with animal skins, or perhaps even to thick cloth substitutes for furs.

Within the T'ang realm itself the greatest producer of furs was the province of Lung-yu, that is, roughly modern Kansu. The official tribute list states that, along with gold, whetstones, wax candles, musk, and cotton, this province supplied the court with "the horns, feathers, plumage, skins and hides of the birds and beasts."[3] Nothing comparable is reported of any other province. But furs for courtiers also came from as far away as Japan.[4] In the main, however, imported furs had a northern origin, though some came from the Far West; all were imbued with the flavor of the barbaric.

DEERSKINS

Distant Khwārizm was a famous exporter of furs: ". . . sables, miniver, ermine, and the fur of the steppe foxes, martens, foxes, beavers, spotted hares, and goats . . ."[5] Though there is no evidence that Transoxania had any considerable trade in furs with T'ang, ambassadors from Khwārizm did bring purple-dyed deerskins to Ch'ang-an in 753,[6] and the artisans attached to the imperial palace obtained crimson deer hides for their workshops "from Persia to Liang-*chou*,"[7] that is, from Iran through the great reach of Serindia to the T'ang frontier. These Iranian deer are given the name of *ching*. *Ching*-skins were also a native Chinese product, much favored for making boots.

Boots had had a long history in China. They had been adopted from the nomads in classical times, and used primarily for military costume. But their alien character had never been entirely forgotten. Even in T'ang we read of a Ch'ang-sha courtesan's daughter that, after performing the Chāch dance,

> She then took off her barbarian [*Man*] boots,
>   and removed her crimson veil.[8]

Indeed, until the boot with decorated felt uppers was invented in the first half of the seventh century, boots were tabooed within the sacred precincts, the basilica (*tien*) of the palace.[9]

The best boots were made of the skin of the *ching*-deer of Kuei-*chou,* in what is now northern Kwangsi. They were articles of local tribute to the court during T'ang,[10] though we know also that they were made in Fukien in 938.[11] It seemed to me once that the *ching,* whose soft skin was so popular among the bootmakers of T'ang, was the little tufted deer,[12] which is similar to the muntjac, and has long canines and almost invisible antlers. This pretty animal lives along the Chinese coast south of the Yangtze, and in the uplands of the southwest. I am no longer so confident of the identity of the *ching,* since the evidence is confusing: certainly the *ching* of Iranian Central Asia could not be the tufted deer.

In any case, red-dyed deerskin boots were à la mode during T'ang. Their distant relatives still survive in Japan, where the Shōsōin treasury preserves a pair of ceremonial shoes made of scarlet leather, decorated with gold ribbon, silver flowers, pearls, and colored beads.[13] These are said to have been worn by the Emperor Shōmu. In the reign of Tai Tsung, late in the eighth century, palace ladies wore high boots of scarlet brocade,[14] which must have been copied to make boots of Khorezmian or Kuei-*chou* deerskin dyed with Cambodian lac for palace dandies.

HORSEHIDES

From the Kansu corridor, the Ordos, and the Mongolian marches under T'ang control, horsehides came regularly to the capital as token tribute of the provincial towns.[15] Since early times this material had been important in the manufacture of small hide boats or coracles, for crossing northern rivers, and for making "saddle cloths."[16] We shall see later that horsehide armor was imported from the Turkish lands,[17] and it may be that the Chinese, who had an ancient tradition of making hide armor, were still using the skins of horses for this purpose in T'ang times.

SEALSKINS

The ribbon seal, called "sea leopard" by the Chinese because of its spots,[18] forages and frolics about the Sea of Okhotsk.[19] During the first of the two reigns of Hsüan Tsung the skins of this animal were sent from the kingdoms of the P'o-hai Mo-ho and Silla.[20]

SKINS OF MARTENS AND THEIR KIN

We have already noticed the continuance in T'ang times of the ancient custom of attaching the tails of martens and the like to the costumes, especially the hats, of warriors. Some high civil officials of T'ang also wore these badges of valorous distinction.[21] But it was the daring youths who went out to the Tatar frontier, or returned to their native soil for hawking and hunting, whose special mark these were:

> Interlinking gold mail armor
> Ear-covering marten-rat garb.[22]

Such phrases are common in T'ang poetry. The spiritual orientation of marten and ermine skins, handsome and warm but possibly also evocative of the bloodthirsty nature of their original owners, is always toward the North and the cold, and the milk-drinking barbarians, and the hazards of frontier warfare. Here they are in a "Song Below the Border" by Li Ch'i:

> Yellow clouds at Goose Gate Canton—
> Where sun sets behind wind and sand;
> A thousand horsemen in black sable furs—
> All styled "Boys of the Feather Forest."
> Gold clarinets blow through boreal snow,
> Iron horses neigh by clouded waters;
> Under the tents they are drinking the grape—
> And this is the very inch-big heart of their lives.[23]

Whether martens, sables, or ermines, small furs were imported in quantity for the T'ang military establishment. Even the Chinese frontier provinces sent them regularly to the imperial saddlery to be made into paraphernalia for the cavalry.[24] The soft warm skins were sent by the Ulaghun,[25] a people dwelling west of the Mo-ho, east of the Turks, and north of the Khitans, in the seventh century, and particularly from the Tungusic Mo-ho tribes, on the Sungari and the Amur, in the eighth century, sometimes in quantities of a thousand.[26]

LEOPARD SKINS

In 720 "South India" (Pallavas?) submitted a leopard skin to the T'ang court,[27] and four years later Silla sent another, this one doubtless taken from a long-haired Siberian leopard.[28] It was all very well for the lucky owner of a spotted furpiece to follow the poet's example: "The cold is right for being wrapped in leopard furs." [29] Warmth was desirable, but might be dangerous. The fierce leopard-nature could have an ill effect on the wearer, for the pharmacologist Ch'en Ts'ang-ch'i warns that "one should not lie on one to sleep, for it will frighten a man's soul"; moreover, if the hairs get into an ulcer or wound, they will poison it.[30] Some ignored this advice; such a one was the hermit Chang Chih-ho, who, in the best Taoist manner, ". . . when, matted on leopard and shod with coir, he dropped his fishhook, he put on no bait, for his ambition lay not in the fish." [31]

Leopard skin had an everyday academic use, too; just as a scholar's ink palette should be covered with a piece of patterned damask to keep the dust off, so should his ink stick be kept in a leopard-skin bag, against the dampness.[32]

LION SKINS

"In the fourth month, the Yabghu Qaghan of the Western Turks sent envoys who offered up a lion's skin." [33] The year was 622, and the pelt a trophy worthy of Nimrod or Hercules.

OTHER SKINS

It is said that Hsüan Tsung owned the fur of an animal whose barbaric name meant "indigo and fragrant," the gift of a distant nation in the times of T'ai Tsung.[34] This beast was said to be a hybrid between a leopard and a fabulous beast of ancient China, called *tsiəu-ngiu;* its pelt was more deeply blue than Persian indigo, and its aroma could be detected many miles away.[35] The problem of its identity is made all the more difficult by the fact that we do not know the identity of one of its parents, though the not quite fabulous panda has been suggested.[36] The Tibetan "blue bear" comes to mind.

Finally, in the eighth century, the Mo-ho of high Manchuria sent the skins of white rabbits, relics of their snowy forests, along with the pelts of their martens.[37]

SHARKSKINS

Shark's skins were a product of the whole coast of China south of the mouth of the Yangtze, and are included here as an exotic product only because they were also a product of Tongking, itself a Chinese protectorate.[38] Ancient tradition told of shark-people who lived under the sea off the coast of Champa; they were rich in pearls (which were their tears) and weavers of a strange pongee.[39] But sharkskins served prosaic ends, and seem not to have been invested with any special glamour, despite the fabulous mermen who may have worn them. A kind of plate armor had formerly been made of sharkskin, and the stuff made a useful abrasive, but in T'ang it was in demand mostly as a decorative and efficient wrapping on the hilts of swords, since its pearled surface would not readily slip in the hand.[40] Swords of the T'ang period, adorned with such other precious materials as gold, silver, and mottled rhinoceros horn, and with hilts wrapped in shagreen, may still be seen at Nara in Japan.[41]

ANIMAL TAILS

As a symbolic decoration, the tail of an animal could signify the whole animal and contain its essence, as a sword might hold the mana of a king, or a scalp the spiritual sap of an enemy. But of course some tails were simply badges of honor; among these must be numbered the yaktails imported from Tibet or those T'ang lands adjacent to Tibet in the West (modern Szechwan and Kansu),[42] and even from the Chinese protectorate in Mongolia in the north.[43] White horse tails from the northwest [44] and fox tails from the west [45] may have been richer in holy power, but there was no question about leopard tails—they were charged with mana and apotropaic energy.[46]

The *yin-yang* school of diviners recognized a "God of the Leopard Tail," and leopard tails were part of the ceremonial insignia surrounding the Son of Heaven.[47] The leopard tail had been an archaic military device, which by Han times had become a marker of the limits of a sacred procession which, like the palace precincts themselves, must not be profaned. Under the T'ang emperors it became an important element in the imperial regalia in its own right; suspended from a vermilion-lacquered pole, it was carried in its own carriage by an officer wearing a military crown, a vermilion costume and leather belt, and attended by a dozen soldiers.[48] This carriage had a place in all ceremonial processions: from a demon-dispelling auxiliary, the leopard tail had become a revered palladium. Much later, in Sung times, it disappeared, to be replaced by a merely symbolic banner of yellow cloth, adorned with painted spots.[49]

FEATHERS

To be like a bird is, in some ways, more desirable than to share the attributes of any other kind of animal. The freedom of the body, the flight of the soul, the soaring of the imagination, were equally ancient and important ideas, and still living ideals in T'ang. Though these images were most elaborately developed in the tradition we call "Taoist," whose ideal being was the "plumed man," airy and angelic, they also were a portion of the dreams of every Chinese. Accordingly, like the skins of animals, the plumage of birds could be used to adorn, and simultaneously to transform, the persons of the medieval Chinese, or at the very least to beautify the body and, at the same time, to stimulate the fancy.[50]

Fairy feathers, plumes to satisfy the heart, had to be beautifully colored. So, like the royal artisans of Hawaii, who plundered the nectar-eating drepanids, the royal artisans in Ch'ang-an desired such feathers as the glorious yellow ones of the oriole,[51] and the iridescent turquoise ones of the kingfisher. Kingfisher feathers were by far the most important, and had been used since the earliest times in jewelry and the richest kind of decoration, whether of the human body or of dwelling places. T'ang literature abounds in references to objects as large as tents or canopies[52] and as small as finger rings and other ladies' trinkets embellished with pieces of kingfisher plumes:

> Mud stuck to her pearl-sewn shoes;
> Rain wet her halcyon-plume hairpins.[53]

Some of the highly prized feathers of this enameled bird came from a remote part of Lingnan,[54] but most were a product of Annam, where an uneasy T'ang protectorate still ruled.[55]

Bird feathers (I do not know what birds contributed them) were also used in "painting": of Chinese inspiration if not Chinese manufacture is the screen panel showing a lady standing beneath a tree, from the Japanese emperor Shōmu's palace, and the panel bearing calligraphic maxims, both done in feathers and now in the Shōsōin.[56]

Then there were the plumes of the white egret of Annam,[57] long ago used to make the ceremonial wands of the dancers of Chou, and now required for military insignia.[58] Among the splendid standards displayed by the guards of honor at receptions for foreign princes, the ensigns marking the soldiers of the seventh file (who were clad in yellow jackets and hats ornamented with cloud symbols and flowers, and carried small lances) were particularly resplendent—they were made of the plumage of the wonderful five-colored parrots imported from the Indies.[59]

But most honored for military uses since antiquity were the feathers of the beautiful races of pheasants and other galliform birds, which had multiplied exceedingly in China, especially in the west and south, and in adjacent parts of East Asia.[60] Consider what marvels were available: the David's blood pheasant [61] in the Ch'in-ling Mountains, with its crimson tail; Temminck's tragopan [62] in west China, with its horns, white-spotted plumage, and blue face; the silver pheasant [63] of Lingnan, with its blue-black crest, its red cheeks and long white tail; the blue-eared pheasant [64] of Kansu and Kokonor, with its white horns, red cheeks, and bluish gray body plumage, glossed with iridescent green and purple; the golden pheasant [65] of the west and northwest, golden-crested, with a green and yellow back and scarlet belly; and perhaps most splendid of all, Lady Amherst's pheasant [66] of Tibet and southwest China, glowing in red, white, blue, yellow, and black, and especially in scintillant green. And there were a great many others. Which among these flamboyant birds lost their feathers to the official artificers of T'ang is not certain. Certain it is that the most notable in ancient tradition were the tail feathers of Reeves's pheasant,[67] a handsome golden-brown bird, spotted and striped with white and black, with a black-masked white head and an extremely long tail. The fowl is indigenous to north China and since the dim and glorious past has lent its flaunting plumes to ceremonial and military artists for wands, standards, and hats. For T'ang, we may observe them in demand by the department of stables and armories at the palace,[68] doubtless for the traditional insignia, for courtly fans,[69] and for the most elegant parasols.[70]

But here again we are still only on the fringes of the exotic world.

Peacock Tails

No tail feathers were more desired than those of the peacock. They were imported, along with rich silks and shellac, from the towns of Annam.[71] The natives gathered the feathers, "golden and halcyon-blue," for making fans and dusters. They were prone to cut the whole tail from the live peacock, since, as they said, this prevented the colors from fading.[72]

It was the responsibility of the officer in charge of the imperial carriages to arrange the disposition of the one hundred and fifty-six peacock-tail fans at the great state receptions. In T'ang these were somewhat novel (though not unprecedented), since they replaced the more classical fans made from the tail feathers of Reeves's pheasant. A mood for economy in the court early in the eighth century led to their replacement by embroidered replicas of peacock tails.[73] When the emperor made a progress, he was accompanied by one group of four and another group of eight peacock-tail fans, among such other bright banners as the "vermilion painted round fans."[74] The peacock fans seem to have been square, to judge from a description of a painting of a T'ang emperor, alleged to have been the work of Wu Tao-tzu. It refers to a ". . . square *k'ung*-sparrow fan, laid horizontally between the two elbows."[75] These fans were used on all manner of occasions marked by exceptional dignity or holiness. One such was the presentation of a patent conferring a posthumous title of honor on the Son of Heaven. We have a poem on this theme, written in the ninth century: two emperors were to be honored simultaneously, in front of one of the great royal halls, or basilicas, on the grounds of the palace:

> The *k'ung*-sparrow fans part—the incense table appears;
> Robe of state and dragon dress move—the patent envelope comes.[76]

The gorgeous fans appear quite commonly in poetry; I have observed them particularly in the verses of Wen T'ing-yün, as signs and symbols of imperial magnificence or idle elegance. Here is an example:

> On arching dikes the tender willows stare afar at each other;
> The "sparrow" fans, all round about, cover the fragrant jades.[77]

Or again:

> With embroidered hubs—courtesans from a thousand doors;
> With golden saddles—mark-lords from a myriad gates;
> Thin clouds tilt the "sparrow" fans,
> Light snow violates the sable furs.[78]

Needless to say, "sparrow" is short for "*k'ung*-sparrow," that is, "peacock."

FEATHER GARMENTS

Our modern stoles of maribou feathers and capes of ostrich feathers are vestigial and perhaps impotent. But the magical power of feathers was once abundantly obtained by dressing in them completely; a cloak or a suit of feathers brought one closer to the bird-spirits, or to birds in their spiritual form, or to birds conceived of as ideal forms, than any mere feather ornament could do. It is hard to say whether the bird-people of folk tales are human beings with bird coats, or birds with removable plumage. Probably the question is superfluous. At any rate, the theme of the swan maiden and her sisters is very widespread, but the story of the refined beings who can at will become either beautiful women or cloud-winging birds is only one expression of the universal image of the bird as spirit. In its more carnal and popular form we know of it in the tales of *The Thousand and One Nights,* where we may read about the bird-maidens in "The Story of Janshah" and in "The Tale of Hasan of Bassorah." Then there is the Persian story of Bahram-i-Gúr, who seized the dove-coat of the Peri, and there is another form of the legend in India.[79] And bird-women and their allies—feathered fairies, Taoist sylph-men, and other beings like them—are a commonplace of early Chinese culture.[80] Here is an example from T'ang times:

"The Roving Women Who Go by Night" are otherwise called "Daughters of the God-king in Heaven," and otherwise named "Star Anglers." They fly by night and remain hidden by day, like ghosts and spirits. They don plumage to become flying birds, and cast off the plumage to become women. They have no children, and take pleasure in seizing the children of men. There are teats on the front of their breasts. When ordinary humans give sweetmeats to little children, it should not be in an exposed place, nor should the clothes of little children be exposed to sunlight, for if their plumage falls into the clothes, it is likely to create a bird demon. Sometimes they spot these clothes with blood, which is a sign of them. Some say that they are the transformations of those who have died in childbirth.[81]

The old myths had their reflexes in other worlds than those of the imagination: the T'ang pilgrim Hsüan-tsang, observing the Sivaites of India, remarked that in addition to the naked ones and the ones who wore necklaces of skulls, there were ascetics who dressed in the plumage and tails of peacocks. He does not say what inspired this costume.[82] This eccentricity hardly surprises us, but we are less prepared for the reality of feather costumes in China. Though we know that *yü i,* "feather-clothed," is a metaphor for "full-fledged Taoist" (as it were), especially one already transformed to his new ethereal condition, we are surprised to learn that living professors of the Taoist faith actually wore garments of feathers, and even that respectably secular persons did so too, and at quite late periods of history.

In the almost archetypal days of the second century B.C., when Wu Ti of Han was dazzled by the pretentions of the Taoist wonder-workers, the term "feathered men" was no idle metaphor. The alchemist Luan Ta, for instance, was given a jade seal of authority by an imperial messenger who wore feathered clothes, and Luan Ta himself, "standing by night on white floss grass, was dressed in a dress of feathers."[83] On this point the T'ang scholiast Yen Shih-ku wrote: "In using the plumage of birds to make his dress, he was seizing on the conception of the flying and soaring of a divinity or sylph-being."[84]

But what are we to make of one Chao Kang, a great aristocrat of the Later

Han, who came to a banquet with a suite of a hundred retainers, and ". . . girded with a patterned saber, and mantled with a dress of feathers"? [85] Or of the imperial prince of the late fifth century of our era, in the state of Southern Ch'i, who was skilled at many delicate and subtle crafts: he tailored a "furpiece"—presumably a cape—of peacock feathers, which ". . . in its glowing colors, golden and kingfisher-blue, surpassed even the head of the pheasant." [86]

The story is told that late in the seventh century the municipality of Canton presented the Empress Wu, "Heaven Patterned," with a "furpiece" made of king-fisher feathers, ". . . rare and gorgeous, and different from the ordinary." The sovereign gave this rarity to a favorite, who bet it against the purple silk robe of another courtier. The Heaven Patterned took pains to point out that the feather cape was much more valuable than the robe, at which the owner of the robe went off in indignation, asserting stoutly that the pretty garment of a court minion was not to be compared with the robe of an honorable vassal.[87] We may detect in the attitude of this purple-clad one more than haughtiness toward a man preferred for reasons other than simple merit; there is also something of the antireligious scorn of the respectable clerk, stalwart in his bookish orthodoxy, who senses the "superstitious" glamour of a coat of feathers, the ancient garb of the Taoist heaven-seeker, like a Puritan struck aghast by miter and cope and other evidences of popery.

On rather better textual authority we learn that a skillful princess of T'ang tailored two skirts from the feathers of many birds. These showed ". . . one color looked at directly, and one color looked at obliquely; they made one color in the sun, and made one color in the shade; moreover the shapes of the hundred birds could all be seen there." The lady also made a saddlecloth of similar intricacy out of the fur of the "hundred beasts" (a purely formal number). Though conservative opinion stigmatized such creations as "monstrosities of costume," the feather skirts were much admired, ". . . and most of the noble vassals and rich households copied them, so that the furs and feathers of the singular birds and strange beasts from River and Mountain Pass [that is, in the Far South] were gathered almost to the point of their extinction." [88]

The story of the brocade of "Phoenix Feather Gold," made from feathers of a soft golden hue, which had been sent to Hsüan Tsung as tribute, is of much later date, and perhaps apocryphal: ". . . many garments were adorned with them in the palace; at night they emitted a brilliant light. Only Yang Kuei-fei was presented with a sufficient quantity to have them made into a dress and a screen, dazzling like sunlight." [89]

It was natural that tales of feathered garments should cluster around the Taoist court of Hsüan Tsung and his fairy-like consort. The well-known song of "Rainbow Chemise, Feathered Skirt," to which the Lady Yang danced for her lord's delight, was fairy music; for this a dress of feathers was congenial and in-evitable. Though tradition says that the emperor saw the original of this dance performed by moon-maidens in their palace in the night sky and that he gave the dance its name because of their costumes, it was actually the old Central Asiatic tune "Brahman," reworked and renamed by the monarch. The scientist Shen Kua, in the eleventh century, reported that in his day one could see a text written on the lintel of a high pavilion, ". . . in the horizontal script, resembling Indic characters, of a man of T'ang." Though no one could decipher these letters, tradition said that it was the text of the Rainbow Chemise dance.[90] If tradition did not err, this would rather have been the text of "Brahman," the original melody, in a Serindian script. But we cannot be sure. In any case the dance and song are now dead and gone. But the name of the dance, and its association with moon-fairies, bird-creatures, Hsüan Tsung, and Yang the Precious Consort, are still alive. They survive not only in China, but also in Japan, in the Nō called *Hagoromo*. The story of this dance-drama is in part like the ancient and universal tale of the mortal who stole the angel's feather cloak (a T'ang version of this "swan-maiden story" has a white crane as the heroine, and the feather cloak becomes a dress of white silk when the creature assumes human form).[91] The Japanese poetic drama also incorporates some version of the medieval Chinese "Rainbow Chemise, Feathered Skirt" dance, which the Japanese angel performs for the bumpkin in return for getting her feathers back. Arthur Waley has translated the Nō:

> Sky-cloak of feathers fluttering, fluttering,
> Over the pine-woods of Mio,
> Past the Floating Islands, through the feet of the clouds she flies,
> Over the mountains of Ashitaka, the high peak of Fuji,
> Very faint her form,
> Mingled with the mists of heaven;
> Now lost to sight.[92]

It would be agreeable to see the sylphine dance of Lady Yang still alive here, but again, we cannot be sure if the "Rainbow Chemise" in its Japanese form is a genuine relic or a pleasing but artificial archaism.

INSECT ORNAMENTS

Among the precious materials required by the court artisans to embellish the clothes and utensils of their haughty clients—along with such things as ivory and jade and tortoise shell—were the wing cases of a beetle, called the "blue-green insect," which was collected in Lingnan and Annam.[93] Sometimes called "jade insect," and sometimes "little gold tortoise," this gold and turquoise beetle was especially identified with the towns of Kwangsi, north of the great West River.[94] In this region the insect's iridescent chrysochlorous beauty, like that of the kingfisher and the peacock, lent itself to the decoration of ladies' costumes, and especially of their hair ornaments. More important even than their superficial charm was their virtue as love talismans.

The little creatures ". . . like to secrete themselves within the vermeil althaea flowers, where they copulate one with the other." [95] This insect heat was transferred, by sympathetic magic, to the persons of romantic ladies all over China. It appears in a poem by Li Ho in this typical guise:

> In grotto-like chamber her thoughts are no more tabooed
> They do as the bee-child does in the hearts of flowers,
> While ashes grow warm by the crumbling perfumed wick,
> And hair grows cool with its blue-green insect pins.
> When night is far gone, and the lamp flame is short,
> Then sleep matures where the small screen is deepest;
> How pleasant to make up a paired-duck dream—
> But by the South Wall—*do* stop pounding that block! [96]

These shining wing cases of *Chrysochroa* beetle played a similar role in Korea and Japan (where it is called *tamamushi* "jewel insect"). Its usefulness was extended beyond decoration of the person: everyone knows the fine "Tamamushi Shrine" in Nara, and the Shōsōin Treasury contains a dagger with a hilt of ivory and braided bark, whose wooden sheath is adorned with the gold-green wing cases of the *tamamushi*. [97]

Chrysochroa was not the only insect to lend itself to the jeweler's art, though it seems to have been the most popular. A "golden insect," also green-gold, but bee-like, was used by country women to decorate their bangles and hair ornaments. [98] Certain spotted grasshoppers or locusts, thought to be powerful erotic charms when collected on the fifth day of the fifth month (the time of their incredible mating with the earthworms) also became jewels on the clothing of girls. [99] But now we have drifted from the exotically enchanting to the familiar and captivating.

Groves whose rich trees wept odorous gums and
*   balm;*
Others whose fruit, burnished with golden rind,
Hung amiable—Hesperian fables true,
If true, here only—and of delicious taste.

John Milton, *Paradise Lost*, Book IV

vii=plants

I HAVE MADE the golden peaches sent to seventh-century T'ang from Samarkand the deputies and proxies of all exotic goods in medieval China.[1] They came from a distant and nominally tributary kingdom, and their golden color made them acceptable for planting in the imperial orchards. It is suitable that these fine fruits should serve as representatives of the whole group of foreign plants, from great to small, which were introduced into China in these times, to take hold in garden and orchard, some permanently, some only for a brief period. There is no record that the golden peaches were ever propagated beyond the walls of the sacred park in Ch'ang-an, or even that they survived in the park itself beyond the seventh century. Nevertheless, it is curious that "golden peaches" *were* bred in China, perhaps in imitation of the original Samarkandian peaches, or perhaps developed independently by an illiterate gardener. It was claimed that they could be bred by grafting a peach branch to a persimmon tree. More curious still, the art of producing the golden peaches by grafting was known to the most famous of all Chinese gardeners, "Camel Kuo," the hunchback of Ch'ang-an, whose negligent, Tao-inspired skill brought him the patronage of all the rich and noble citizens of the capital, as we are told in an elegant allegory composed by Liu Tsung-yüan.[2] The statement about the persimmon-colored peach appears in a book entitled *The Book of Planting Trees*, which carries as the name of its author "Camel T'o." [3] But however pleasing the attribution may be, a close study of the available texts of this book shows it to be a product of the Yüan dynasty. If a living prototype of Liu Tsung-yüan's fictional Camel Kuo actually existed, we can have no confidence that he developed a golden peach to match the beautiful Sogdian import. Real or not, it must have been the prestige given his name by Liu Tsung-yüan which led its true author to enhance the reputation of the *Book of Planting Trees* by adopting the nom de plume of the fabulous gardener.[4] But we shall soon see the hunchback again, and again in connection with an exotic plant.

Still, a royal peachtree seedling *might* have been transplanted beyond the confines of the palace grounds, and such a gardener *might* have propagated it, or copied it. Exotic plants were introduced as royal gifts from abroad, and did spread through the empire. On one famous occasion, in the year 647, foreign vegetable products were solicited directly from the nations "tributary" to T'ang, and, as a result, a considerable variety of new plants, edible and otherwise, were brought to the capital, where their names and qualities were carefully set down in the archives.[5] Many survived and became part of the common domestic flora of China. In addition to these royal imports, the resources of many private gentlemen must have enabled them to purchase exotic specimens, some of which were destined to establish races on Chinese soil. Two verses of Chang Chi, written at about the beginning of the ninth century for a friend leaving to take up a post in Canton, indicate that this was particularly true in the southern cities, where opportunities for the introduction of new species, especially the attractive tropical flowers and fruits, would have been most abundant:

> There they have flowers from overseas, and herbs from the *Man* throughout the
> winter—
> Wherever you may go, no household will not have a garden full of them.[6]

New garden plants were also established by foreigners living under the protection of T'ang, whether in the south or in Ch'ang-an. They must have found it as impossible to live without their favorites from home as European immigrants to America found it to leave their pinks and primroses and tulips behind. Moreover, though such introductions and influences are now difficult to detect, even foreign garden designs must have been translated to China during T'ang times.[7] Fortunately, tradition had created a climate of taste favorable to the acceptance of such novelties. Since Han times, if not earlier, as we know from the ornate rhapsodies of Szu-ma Hsiang-ju, the imperial gardens were in effect magical diagrams, vegetable cantrips binding the several natural realms of the whole world under the spiritual sway of the Son of Heaven. Although pleasure gardens became more secularized, as it were, during the post-Han centuries, the great imperial parks never entirely lost their magical character, and gardens of the citizenry generally imitated on a lesser scale those great examples of exoticism.[8]

Geoffrey Grigson has shown how native plants are used in English poetry to reflect and stimulate the deeper human emotions, while exotics, lacking the long and intimate interrelation with the English people, can do little more for a poet than make an exciting and colorful splash in his verses.[9] So it was also in China. The plum, promising spring and the renewal of vitality and hope, or the peach, embodying fecundity and immortality in lore and legend, exemplify a host of old familiars, rich in human associations. Not so the lichee, for instance; though known to the north since Han times, even in T'ang poetry it is still treated as an exotic, colorful and romantically charming, but only feebly expressive of ordinary dreams and passions— how much less so the novel fruits and flowers, beginning with the golden peaches, which are the subject matter of this chapter. Though they are secondarily enriched with exoticism for us, in coming from medieval China, their true role in T'ang imagination was like that of the hibiscus in our South Seas fantasies; they are not to be compared with our lilies and roses, whatever their native glory may have been in their homelands.

PRESERVATION AND PROPAGATION

As is well known, Lady Yang, the Precious Consort of Hsüan Tsung, craved fresh lichees, and was able to obtain them, though they had to be transported by post horse from Lingnan over the whole length of China. Nonetheless, these delicate fruits, which change color in one day and loose their aroma in two, reached the lady in Ch'ang-an with color and taste unimpaired.[10] How was this possible?

We shall tell presently of the delicious "mare-nipple grapes" which were transported fresh and intact from Qočo across the fringes of the Gobi Desert to Ch'ang-an. If we ask how this feat could have been achieved, we shall find no ready answer in T'ang literature. But we may find useful clues there and elsewhere. For instance, the watermelons at Khwārizm, exported in the ninth century, were packed in snow inside leaden containers.[11] It must be supposed, then, that the grapes of Serindia were brought in snow and ice from the Mountains of Heaven nearby. This does not explain the preservation of the lichees, coming from the tropical southern border of China; some other, and yet unexplained, cooling device must have been used. Nor can we say with certainty what means were used to keep alive the plants from distant nations (supposing they were not brought in as seeds) until they reached Chinese soil. Without hoping to find specific answers to these questions, let us look briefly at a few vestiges of T'ang customs having to do with cooling and plant preservation.

Hung Hsi-wen, a poet of the first half of the fourteenth century, saw a painting which showed Hsüan Tsung and Lady Yang taking their ease on a hot day,[12] and wrote a quatrain describing the scene, entitled "Picture of the Illuminated Illustrious and Grand Verity Escaping the Heat, with Ease and Pleasure":

A Gold Millet melon is already split in its basin of ice,
The snowy water is swirled and blended—they try the cooling tea.

The palace houris, not yet grasping that the Lord's loving favor has become ardent,
Still take the blue jars to draw flowers from the well.[13]

In short, the maidservants are too dull to see that the monarch is eager to be alone with his lady. Unfortunately, we know neither the name nor the dates of the artist; the picture may have been a Sung or even a Yüan work, and therefore worthless as evidence of iced melons and snow-cooled tea in the eighth century. Fortunately, whatever the case for snowy tea, there is abundant evidence of the use of ice for cooling foods in summer in T'ang times; indeed, the practice goes back to the Chou dynasty. Ice was sometimes even eaten in the summertime; Ch'en Ts'ang-ch'i advises against this practice as a source of illness—ice, he says, may only be used to cool food and drink, and is not itself to be ingested.[14] But melons were certainly kept in ice in T'ang times: they were kept primarily in icehouses or ice pits, which were of ancient origin, and secondarily in ice pots or ice urns.[15] The melons, popular in Ch'ang-an summers, and the ice-filled urns, sometimes made of jade, are both mentioned often by T'ang poets; indeed, the image "clear as the ice in a jade urn," [16] was even before T'ang times a stereotype of the transparent purity of a true gentleman. Some sort of icebox was in use too, for an eminent alchemist states that the limestone of stalactites is suitable for making "ice bins," [17] presumably to store perishable reagents for laboratory experimentation.

As for icehouses and ice pits, probably none could compare with those of the imperial palace. They were in charge of the "Office of His Highness' Forest," that is, the office in charge of the imperial parks, gardens, and orchards: here each winter the authorities stored a thousand blocks of ice, each three feet square and a foot and half thick, cut in cold mountain valleys and sent to the capital by the local magistrates.[18]

With such resources available to ensure the delectation of the court, we may be confident that equally adequate arrangements secured the safe transport of fruits, flowers, and desirable seedlings from remote places under T'ang jurisdiction. Sui Yang Ti had tangerines sent from Szechwan with their stems sealed in wax;[19] and in the eleventh century the prime peonies of Lo-yang were prepared for the trip to the Sung capital at K'ai-feng in the same way, as Ou-yang Hsiu tells us: "We pack them in little bamboo baskets, covered over with layers of green vegetable leaves, so that they will not be moved or shaken under the horse; and we seal the stems of the flowers with wax, so they will not fall in several days." [20] We may be sure that this was a T'ang practice also. Moreover, since tangerines were transported wrapped in paper at the beginning of the ninth century,[21] it is equally safe to say that other vegetable products were similarly protected in transit.

By methods such as these, then, exotic plants came to Ch'ang-an, where they were taken in charge by the Commander of His Highness' Forest, to await the needs of His Highness, whether for private banquet, public celebration, or holy sacrifice.[22]

So it was with the golden and silver peaches from Samarkand: "A Decree: It is ordered that they be planted in our parks and plantations."[23]

The Tabooed Park is situated to the north of the Great Interior Palace. On the north it approaches Wei Water, on the east it is curbed at Ch'en Stream, while on the west all ends at the wall of the ancient [Han] metropolis. Its circumference is one hundred and twenty *li*.[24] Birds and beasts, vegetables and fruits—not one is not grown therein.[25]

This great nursery and pleasaunce, nourished itself by the gardens of the world, was also the important source of plantings about the empire. When, in 740, during a special campaign to beautify the metropolitan cities of north China, Hsüan Tsung brought it about that "fruit trees were planted on the roads of both capitals and in the parks within the city walls,"[26] it is highly likely that these trees came from His Highness' Forest.

While not comparable to the great imperial park, some private parks and gardens must have been very extensive and very rich in species, even exotic ones. A glimpse of these private resources is afforded by a description of an innovation made by the young men of the household of Yang Kuo-chung, brother of Lady Yang. They constructed a movable garden of wood, mounted on wooden wheels, on which were planted "renowned flowers and strange trees." This flowering carriage, displayed to the public in spring, rotated as it moved, so that one and all could see the wonders it contained in detail.[27]

Finally, another source of plants introduced from abroad was the imperial herb garden, directed by the "Master of the Medicinal Garden," himself under the jurisdiction of the "Commander of the Office of the Grand Physician." This institution, located in the capital city, had as its special province the cultivation and harvesting of plants which provided useful drugs. Here young men from sixteen to twenty years of age, in a practical gardening environment and under the instruction of a "Catholic Gentleman of Medicine" (himself a lecturer in the various branches of medicine, not only in materia medica), studied *yin-yang* theory as applied to drugs, the geographic distribution of herbs, proper gathering seasons, the properties of the several parts of plants, poisonous and nonpoisonous herbs, the composition of medicines, and other subjects.[28] This specialized garden must have been an important supplementary distribution point for a great number of useful herbs demanded by the people of T'ang.

Date Palms

The golden and silver peaches were not the only fruit trees introduced from the West during T'ang. There was also the date palm. Dates had long been known as a Persian product,[29] and in T'ang were actually imported. The crisp, sugary character of

Persian dates imported into Canton were well described by a ninth-century writer,[30] and they had already been praised in a pharmacopoeia of the eighth century as beneficial to the complexion and to health generally.[31]

Dates were known under a variety of names, the most common of which, it seems, was "Persian jujube." [32] But two borrowed names had some currency, perhaps not much: one, something like *gurmang or *khurmang, was of Persian origin; the other, *miu-ləu, is more mysterious, but one scholar has hoped to see in it a cognate of Egyptian *bunnu* and even of Greek *phoinix*.[33] The "thousand-year jujubes" brought to T'ang in 746 by envoys of the king of warm and fertile Tabaristan on the Caspian Sea,[34] were dates, but it is not clear whether the trees or just the preserved fruits were brought. The trees would hardly have thrived in the climate of Ch'ang-an, but we have it on good authority that the trees were planted in the suburbs of Canton in the ninth century.[35]

PEEPULS

Less novel, though of more spiritual import, were the bodhi trees, the sacred fig trees of India. An Indian king sent one to the Chinese emperor in 641,[36] and one came from Magadha in 647.[37] It was entirely suitable that Magadha should be the giver of such a tree because it was the home of wonderful trees. Sacheverell Sitwell has described it:

It is not enough that the champak drenches the airs with the odour of its blue flowers. This is the paradise of flowering trees. The rose apple and the great tree of roses, a town of flowers, are like lights upon the brilliant air.[38]

Of the bodhi tree from Magadha, the Chinese sources remark that its leaves resembled those of the "white poplar," and that its name was said to be *pala*. This name is a contraction of Sanskrit *pippala*, or as we should say "peepul," which is the common name of the "Tree of Enlightenment," *bodhidruma*, an epithet which reminds us that it was under one of these that Gautama was illuminated. The original tree at Bodh-Gayā in Bihar was, according to a prevailing story, burned by the great Aśoka before his conversion, and then miraculously reborn from its own ashes. Other disasters befell the holy tree, but it has been continuously propagated by replanting slips, we are told, down to the present day. Its most famous descendant is the sacred tree at Anurādhapura in Ceylon, thought to be the oldest tree with a documented pedigree in the world. It has become almost a universal symbol of a tree of wisdom and even in Indian has other names, as *Puṇḍarîka* and *Aśvattha*. In Buddhism the tree of wisdom is not necessarily a peepul fig, but may appear as a luminous object of gold, crystal, and precious stones.[39] Tuan Ch'eng-shih, always inquisitive about Buddhist lore, has left us an account of the miraculous history of the greatest of all peepuls—how it shed its leaves when the Buddha entered Nirvana, how it was burned by Aśoka, of its resurrection, of the attempt of King Śaśānka to destroy it in the sixth century, its various names, and much else. He reports also:

The height of the tree is four hundred feet. Under it there is a silver stupa, and it has coiled about this, girdling it all round. The men of that country burn incense and scatter flowers here constantly through the four seasons, and do reverence by going all around the tree. During [the reign] "Honorable Outlook" of T'ang, we repeatedly despatched envoys thither, to set offering at the temple office and also to distribute *kaṣāya*. In the fifth year of "Manifest Felicity" [660] we erected a stele at the temple office, thereby to commemorate its holy virtue.[40]

The peepul had been introduced to China before T'ang times, and was often planted on temple grounds, where it was revered as the symbol of the Buddha and the enlightenment he offered to all men. Moreover, the Chinese name "bodhi tree" had been transferred to other species, especially the linden.[41] Whether any of the true sacred figs was an actual offshoot of the veritable Enlightenment Tree of Gayā, I do not know. If Magadha kingdom had sent such a wonderful cutting, we may be confident that its special quality would have been noted in the archives, but there is no such record. Therefore we must suppose the sacred Chinese figs to have been quite ordinary peepuls, only "bodhi trees" by courtesy—a courtesy which was generally extended to all individuals of the species, all the more readily, we may imagine, as piety was reinforced by distance from India. P'i Jih-hsiu left a quatrain "in the form of Ch'i and Liang" referring to such revered immigrant trees at the chief temple of the T'ien-t'ai sect in Chekiang; this temple was named *Kuo ch'ing,* "The Country Is Clarified" or "The Nation Is Pure and Clear":

> Ten miles to a piney gate—the road to "Country Clarified";
> Up on a platform one feeds the apes—by the tree of *Bodhi.*
> Marvelous they come, the mist and rain, falling from a cloudless sky—
> But, after all, it is the wind of the sea which blows this cloth of spray.[42]

SAUL TREES

Saul wood gets its name from Hindi *sāl.* It is the wood of *Shorea robusta,* a fine tree with yellow flowers, which produces a heavy, dense, dark wood much favored in India, especially where forests of it grow on the edges of the Bengal plains.[43] The tree has close relatives in Indochina and Indonesia, some of which (known nowadays by such misleading names as "mahogany," "Borneo cedar," "Singapore cedar," and the like),[44] are even superior in durability to the more widely known Indian species. Although the tree was introduced to China in medieval times and widely planted, there is no evidence that its timber was used there, in T'ang times at least. It was admired for its exotic source, its handsome flowers, and its important religious associations, since, like the bodhi tree, it was entangled in the career of Gautama himself.

The Lord passed into Nirvana at Śālavana, a grove of *sāl* trees near Kuśinagara, and he has gained the epithet of Śālendra-rāja, "King of the *Sāl* Trees," as has also the father of Avalokiteśvara (Kuan-yin), Śubhavyūha.[45] The great Hsüan Tsung, magically transported to the crystal palaces of the moon, saw a heaven-piercing *sāl* tree there: "The color of its leaves was like that of silver, and its flowers were the color of clouds." [46]

This holy tree seems to have been a pious introduction to China before T'ang times; [47] parts of the tree had early been accepted as valuable gifts: thus the king of Bnam, the "Malayan" nation [48] on the Gulf of Siam, sent envoys to Liang in 519 with gifts of various aromatics, and ". . . a lucky image of sandal, and leaves of the *śāla* tree." [49] But even as late as the eighth century, the tree was still uncommon enough to be regarded as an exotic. In 723 Li Yung wrote a commemorative inscription for a *sāl* tree of Huai-yin-*hsien* in Ch'u-*chou,* which had been made famous by the pilgrim I-ching, who had sojourned beside it when he returned from the West at the end of the seventh century. The poet remarks that ". . . the *sāl* tree is no thing of Central Hsia," [50] that is, of China.

A few decades later, early in the "Heavenly Treasure" reign of Hsüan Tsung, the imperial representative in the Far West sent two hundred cuttings from saul trees, obtained in Farghāna, to Ch'ang-an, stating in the accompanying memorial that the tree ". . . is not to be compared with common herbs; it gives no roost to birds of evil. Its upthrust trunk is not shamed by pine or thuja; the shade it makes is not humiliated by peach or plum." [51] Some years later, Tai Tsung reigning, more of the trees were sent from the West by Chinese authorities there, and a fine specimen was propagated in the great Buddhist temple of Compassion and Grace (*Tz'u en szu*) in the capital city, where it was observed by Tuan Ch'eng-shih in the following century.[52] Since references to the saul tree become very frequent in Sung literature, it seems probable that many of these cuttings took root, and that the efficient introduction of the tree must be put in the middle of the eighth century.

SAFFRON CROCUS

One of the rarest, most expensive and aristocratic flowers of antiquity was the saffron crocus. This fragrant purple, autumn-blooming flower apparently had its original home in the vicinity of Persia and northwest India, regions in which it has been intensively cultivated since antiquity. An aromatic dye produced from its deep-orange stigmas was an important article of ancient commerce. It was grown in Greece and Sicily in Pliny's time, and used by the Romans to flavor sweet wines and to diffuse as a fine spray to perfume theaters; [53] it was favored as a hair dye by Roman ladies, and naturally disapproved of by the Fathers of the Church.[54] The plant was introduced into China in the Middle Ages, and the fragrant powder was in demand there in T'ang times as a drug to cure internal poisons, and as a perfume, but it is not certain whether it was used as a dye.[55]

The Chinese called it *"yü* gold aromatic," meaning "a golden substance as sweet-smelling as the *yü*-plant used in making sacrificial wines in antiquity." Unfortunately the name *"yü* gold" had already been given to imported turmeric, though the "aromatic" was not suffixed in that case. Nonetheless, the two were often confused, as they were also in other parts of the world where they were known only in powdered commercial form.[56] For that matter, saffron was also confused with safflower, which was much used to adulterate saffron and had been introduced into China much earlier, and with zedoary, a fragrant rootstock of India and Indonesia, a close relative of turmeric, and important in the perfume trade.[57] (It should be remembered that drugs, perfumes, and incenses were not clearly distinguished in medieval times, and in putting a plant under one heading or another here, I am forcing a modern distinction on medieval culture. It has seemed best to treat the saffron crocus neither under the "drug" rubric nor under the "aromatic" rubric, but here among the introduced plants, in order to emphasize that the living flower was known to the people of T'ang.)

India sent saffron to T'ang in 641, and Bukhāra sent it in 734, but we do not know whether they sent the dried stigmas or the whole plants. We have a better record for 647:

The Country of Kapi [Kapiśa?] offered *"yü* gold aromatic." Its leaves resemble those of the *mo-men-tung* ["black leek," *Liriope graminifolia*]. The flowers open in the ninth month, and their aspect is lotus-like [cup-shaped]. Their color is deep purplish blue, and their fragrance can be smelled over several tens of paces. Though it flowers, it does not fruit, and if you wish to plant it, you must take the the root.[58]   MISTAKE ✱

On this occasion, then, whole plants were sent to China.

In any case, prepared saffron, whether an exotic import or from the newly domesticated herb, was used to perfume garments and hangings. Lu Chao-lin, a poet active during the second half of the seventh century, has left these lines:

> Pairs of swallows, flying paired, go round the painted beams,
> In netted curtains and halcyon-blue coverlets is *yü* gold aromatic.[59]

Or again, Ch'en T'ao, writing in the ninth century:

> In light awning a fragrant smoke—the aroma of *yü* gold.[60]

This example suggests some kind of incense, or perhaps a sprayed mist. A saffron oil perfume existed at the beginning of the tenth century at least. We read of a band of geisha at that period whose allure was enhanced with the most costly substances, among which were an essence of aloeswood impregnating their clothing, and saffron oil combed into their earlocks.[61]

Like some Roman wines, certain T'ang wines were flavored with saffron. Li Po described one such fragrant beverage:

> Best wine of Lan-ling, with *yü* gold aromatic—
> Comes in brimful cups of jade, amber shining.[62]

The poets of the ninth century were fond of color images and were prone to invent new ones, though sometimes they found them in embryo, as it were, in the verses of earlier men. The amber-colored wine of Li Po's poem, just quoted, gave birth to Li Ho's use of the metaphor "amber," meaning wine. Another verse by Li Po prefigured a common ninth-century "saffron" metaphor. He wrote:

> Languid willows on River dike, with *yü* gold branches.[63]

This is a vision of red-yellow foliage, or, as our own dictionaries say, defining the color "saffron yellow," "yellowish red-yellow in hue, of high saturation and high brilliance." In short, a fine and intense orange-yellow. A century later Wen T'ing-yün wrote of "Spring trees' *yü* gold red," [64] not even as daring as Li Po's image; but in the same century Li Shang-yin could fancy a garden of peonies in the forms of dancing girls, the petals forming their skirts, using this language: "With bent waists, dancing in competition, in *yü* gold skirts." [65] "*Yü* gold"—or "saffron"—no longer suggested exotic odors, but a lovely color. The technical question "was the dye which inspired the trope actually saffron, or was it turmeric?" is unhappily left unanswered.

Nāga-Flowers

Then there was the *"nāga*-flower," translating *Nāgapushpa* it seems. This Indian "snake flower," wrote Tuan Ch'eng-shih, resembles ". . . our 'Three Chine'; it has no leaves, and its flowers are white in color with yellow hearts and six petals. It comes to us by argosy." [66] But *Nāgapushpa* is the name of several Indian flowers, and we cannot tell which came to Tuan's attention. He was an omnivorous reader and something of a dilettante, and inasmuch as he was an amateur of Buddhist lore and well-read in Buddhist literature, it is likely that a great deal of his information on exotic plants came to him from reading rather than observation.[67] But perhaps an Indologist may yet recognize the flower from his description.

"Buddha's Land Leaf"

Another unidentifiable Indian plant is the "Buddha's land leaf," [68] specimens of which were sent to T'ang by Gandhāra in 647. They are described as follows: "five leaves on the stalk; the flower is red, but the central heart of it is perfectly yellow, while the stamens are purple colored."[69] The Chinese name translates Sanskrit *Buddhakṣetra,* an expression variously interpreted in the several Buddhist sects and Mahayanist eschatologies. It means a land where the authority of the Buddha is recognized and his precepts obeyed, but also a mystically conceived holy nation, where his law will ultimately prevail—a "City of God" in our terms—and sometimes even a Paradise to which the devout believer may aspire, especially the Western Paradise of Amitabha.[70] Did the five leaves of the holy plant then represent the five Buddha lands or paradises, or was the divine plan mysteriously mapped on each leaf?

Narcissus

The narcissus was a Roman plant to the medieval Chinese. But its Chinese name **nai-gi,* like the Greek name *narkissos,* seems to have come from Persian *nargis.*[71] The variety described by Tuan Ch'eng-shih had a pink flower with an orange center. That indefatigable researcher adds that ". . . they take these flowers and press them to make an oil, with which they anoint their bodies to expel 'winds' and 'airs.' The king of Rome Country as well as the noblemen within that country all make use of it."[72] Pliny too had noted that an oil derived from the narcissus had a warming effect on frostbite,[73] a complaint included within the Chinese notion of "wind" diseases. But, to tell the truth, there is no evidence that either flower or oil was ever seen by Tuan Ch'eng-shih, who remains our only informant, though we may guess that some traveler showed him a specimen.

Lotuses

The Sung philosopher Chou Tun-i, in his celebrated poetic essay in praise of the lotus,[74] assigned to the chrysanthemum the quality of a virtuous hermit among flowers, neglected in modern times, in contrast to the peony, the popular favorite of T'ang, the choice of the *haute monde* and the vulgar mob alike. He alone, he claimed, gave the lotus, that prince of flowers, the admiration which was its due. There is some justice in this adjudication, but the lotus was by no means lacking in T'ang admirers, although it was not as universally praised as the peony. The value placed on the lotus is illustrated by the survival of a considerable number of poems about it, especially lyrical effusions about gathering lotuses from boats. The great T'ai Tsung himself wrote verses on this theme, and even the strait-laced formal history of his reign records his visit to a lotus garden.[75] And here is Po Chü-i, watching lotus-gatherers:

> Up among the little peaches are the little lotus boats,
> Half picking pink lotuses, half white lotuses;

Unlikely are evil wind or waves from south of Kiang
Here at Nelumbo Pool, before the couch on which I lie.[76]

It was appropriate in stanzas on this subject to show the great blooms being picked
by beautiful girls of the southern lake country, whose pink and white complexions
provided inevitable comparisons with lotuses white and pink; these were the ir-
resistible "seductresses of Yüeh, belles of Ching," or "courtesans of Wu, seductresses
of Yüeh" of conventional poetic language.[77] Despite the fact that "Indian" lotuses,
both pink and white, had been known in China since long before T'ang, they still
retained an exotic flavor. Ch'en Ts'ang-ch'i wrote of them in his pharmacopoeia as
". . . living in the Western countries; the Westerners bring them here." [78] It is therefore not surprising that the poets of late T'ang, who favored exotic and romantic
themes, wrote many poems on the lotus; notable among them were Wen T'ing-yün
and Lu Kuei-meng. The painters of the end of T'ang also found something congenial in the lotus—such men as Tiao Kuang, who painted flowers and bamboos on
the walls of Buddhist temples in Szechwan; his picture of "Lotuses and Tufted
Ducks" survived into Sung. Another late T'ang artist, Chou Huang, left two paintings on the same subject, and another of lotuses and various other birds.[79]

The exoticism lingering in the lotus flower was maintained by the continuing
flow of Buddhist imagery from India. The lotus as symbol of a self-created entity was
original to pre-Buddhist religion in India. As an image of Brahma transferred to
the Buddha, it represented a pure being, rising uncontaminated from the slime and,
in the Amitabha cult, signified immaculate rebirth in the Western Paradise.[80] In
particular, the Bodhisattva *Padmapāṇi,* whose name, translated into Chinese, was
"Lotus-Flower Hand Bodhisattva," exemplified the permeation of Mahāyāna Buddhism by lotus imagery, as does the name of the "Lotus Sect" of T'ien-t'ai, whose
gospel is the *Saddharma-puṇḍarīka-sūtra,* in Chinese the "Miraculous Law Lotus
Flower Sutra." This church, immensely influential during T'ang, is supposed to have
been founded by the mendicant Hui-yüan late in the fourth century, at "White Lotus
Pool," but this "lotus" was most likely a water lily.[81]

But whether true lotus (*Nelumbo/Nelumbium*) or water lily (*Nymphaea*),
the Chinese "white lotus" was well-established in T'ang, and its less usual varieties,
like other plant oddities, were regarded as auspicious, and were likely to become
subjects of laudatory odes. Two blossoms on a single stalk, multi-petaled flowers, and
the like, were celebrated in this way, and were also favorite subjects for painters. The
pink lotus was the common kind, and next to it was the white. "Double" white lotuses, as we would style them, or "thousand-petaled" white lotuses as they were called
in T'ang, were an admired feature of a lake in the grounds of Hsüan Tsung's Great
Luminous Palace in Ch'ang-an.[82] But these magnificent flowers seem not to have
existed outside the palace, and, with this exception and indeed despite literary references (perhaps because of confusion with white water lilies), it appears that white
lotuses were not grown in north China. A scholar of the twelfth century tell us that

there were no white lotuses in Lo-yang before the ninth century, when the gardener-poet Po Chü-i first brought them from Chekiang and planted them there,[83] and indeed Po has many verses about white lotuses in his poems. His contemporary Li Te-yü boasted that he had written the first "rhapsody" (*fu*) on the subject of the white lotus: "Men of old," he said, "rhapsodized only the pink lotus—there has never been such a composition as this one . . ."[84] In short, the white lotus was still something strange even in the ninth century, and even then noticed mostly by such gardening enthusiasts as Po Chü-i and Li Te-yü. P'i Jih-hsiu used Indian exoticisms in his short poem, here prosaically translated, called "White Lotus":

> Even ghee, I fear, hardly matches its purity;
> I can only acknowledge that the *champaka* may equal its odor.
> Half-drooping, golden powdered—I know what it is like:
> A quiet and docile girl leaning over a torrent, which reflects the yellow of her
> forehead.[85]

The yellow dust on the brow of the girl in the simile was a popular cosmetic, colored by massicot, or perhaps by orpiment.

The pink lotus was familiar and the white lotus was not an everyday sort of flower, but the yellow lotus and the blue lotus were both great rarities. Yellow is not a normal color among Old World lotuses, although there is an American lotus which is yellow. It was known to the people of T'ang, if at all, chiefly in religious art: we have, for instance, a painting found at Tun-huang, which shows a female Bodhisattva —perhaps Tārā or a feminized Avalokiteśvara—in a pink skirt, with a yellowish-brown scarf over her breast, and wearing a gray girdle and stole. This divine creature is shown seated, ". . . with feet lightly crossed at ankles," on a yellow lotus.[86] This lotus was a product of Indianized reverence. Actual yellow lotuses, though well-known to the flower fanciers of Sung, were seldom seen in T'ang. Chao Ku tells, in a poem written in the middle of the ninth century entitled "On an Autumn Day I Look at Yellow Lotuses in Wu-chung," how he found them in a lake full of red ones: "The rest of the lotuses—flake on flake of pink."[87] Were they sports? Or were they the creations of the skilled gardeners of Chekiang, a region where gardening was a popular art? Most likely the latter. But there are references to "yellow lotuses" even before T'ang. For instance, an old book of wonders, written in about the fourth century, tells of "yellow lotuses" in mountain streams in Hunan.[88] But in all likelihood these were not lotuses at all, but their lesser, unassuming relatives, the yellow pond lilies, or spatterdocks.[89]

Yellow lotuses, then, were merely rarities and natural wonders. Blue lotuses, on the other hand, are infused with the supernatural, and in T'ang they seem to exist in the real world only as the productions of almost magical arts; though this should not incline us to reject them as unreal. Most of the lotuses which appear in the religious scroll paintings from Tun-huang as holy thrones and divine attributes, are white, or pink, or scarlet, but a few of them are blue. There is an Avalokiteśvara, "in purely Tibetan style," with gilded flesh, and sprays of blue lotuses in his hands.[90] Or again, we have a representation of Mañjuśrī, shown clad in tomato red and other vivid colors, and seated in a blue lotus, which is in turn ". . . raised on a pedestal on a lion's back—the lion's mane, beard and tail are green." [91] But blue lotuses had a humbler application too: they appear on the toes of the shoes of two painted clay "ladies in waiting," who also have flowers in their double-coil chignons, and wear long-sleeved jackets with "Medici collars." [92]

There are no blue lotuses in nature. Nonetheless, there are persistent claims in T'ang and Sung literature that it was possible for men to grow them. An early Sung encyclopedia repeats the story (no source given, but it is presumed to be of T'ang date) of a family of dyers in Hu-*chou* who could make blue lotuses. (We are all the more ready to credit this tale because Hu-*chou* is in northern Chekiang, the garden center of China.) The chief magistrate, we are told, sent a quantity of their seeds to the capital, where they were planted in palace ponds—but some of them sprouted pink blooms.

So they marveled at it, and sent a writing to inquire of the artisan of dyes, and the artisan of dyes said, "In my household there is a gentleman who is hereditary curator of the jar of indigo. It is his practice to take lotus seeds and soak them at the bottom of the jar, then he awaits the passage of a twelvemonth year, after which he plants them. Now if the seeds of the blue lotuses which he so plants are themselves planted, they will be your pink ones. It seems that they revert to their basic mode, and why is this a matter for amazement?" [93]

In this way, the paradisiacal flowers of the Bodhisattva were realized in secular gardens. Even our hunchbacked gardener, Camel Kuo, is credited with the art of producing deep blue lotus flowers by soaking the seeds in a vat of indigo dye.[94] Is it possible that the little man is no myth after all?

Even more remarkable is the tale of Han Yü's notorious nephew, a skilled adept of the Taoist arts, who in the popular lore of later generations became Han Hsiang-tzu, one of the "Eight Immortals" and the patron of fortune-tellers, and is shown in iconography carrying bamboo drum and clappers, or with a basket of flowers or the peach of immortality, or playing a flute.[95] This young wonder-worker (as reported by Tuan Ch'eng-shih in the ninth century) treated the roots of peonies with such chemical reagents as lac and calomel to produce, after a period of weeks, blue or purple or yellow or red flowers, as he desired. Some blossoms, it is alleged, also showed complete poems in clear purple characters.[96] Probably many readers of the present book will have made their hydrangeas blue by impregnating the soil about their roots with iron salts, produced by the simple device of burying old nails or cans, and so they will not be very astonished at young Han's method of making artificially colored flowers. Perhaps, however, they will not have noticed a Roman method described by Pliny:

There has been invented also a method of tinting the lily . . . the stalks are left to steep in the lees of black or Greek wine, in order that they may contract its colour, and are then planted in small trenches some semi-sextarii of wine-lees being poured around them. By this method purple lilies are obtained . . .[97]

The sober translators of this passage share the frequent opinion held of Pliny, that he was too prone to accept nonsense without question. They observe in a footnote: "Fée remarks that the extravagant proceeding here described by Pliny with a seriousness that is perfectly ridiculous, does not merit any discussion." We may hope that Pliny's detractors are becoming fewer as, with the growth of imaginative science in our times, the bounds of the possible are less confined.

Blue flowers, in any case, seem always to have aroused skepticism. Robert Fortune, the great collector of Chinese plants, in a letter to John Lindley, secretary of the Horticultural Society of London, wrote of "peonies with blue flowers, the existence of which is, however, doubtful." [98] Perhaps blue peonies survived in China only as a folk memory of the artifice of Han the Taoist. But we may now read of colchicine, a poisonous drug extracted from a plant related to the meadow saffron and autumn crocus,[99] which will induce mutations in other plants, such as many-petaled varieties. The secrets of the Taoists are in danger of becoming commonplaces.

WATER LILIES

Blue water lilies, on the other hand, are quite normal flowers, though exotic to the Chinese. A report for the year 647 reads:

The country of Kashmir offered up *nīla-utpala* flowers. Its petals were akin to the petals of the lotus, like interrupted circles. The color of these flowers was deep blue, while the stamens were yellow. Its aroma made fragrance for several tens of paces.[100]

This Indian water lily, sometimes called "blue lotus" (the confusion is universal—it is also the "Egyptian blue lotus") is shown in the hand of Mañjuśrī.[101] Its true international name is *Nymphaea caerulea*.

In the same year the neighboring kingdom of Kapiśa, home of fierce heroes dressed in wool,[102] ". . . sent emissaries to offer up *Kumuda* flowers. They were vermilion and white intermingled, and their aroma could be smelled from afar." [103] If we go by its name in Sanskrit, this exotic was *Nymphaea esculenta*, a white water lily (or perhaps it was *N. alba*), but from its variegated color we may judge it to have been a rare mutant from the typical species. The white water lily is a carriage for the goddess Lakshmi, and also for Avalokiteśvara. The latter is shown in a silk painting of the tenth century, found at Tun-huang, seated on a white water lily.[104] But this beautiful flower had more than a borrowed divinity. It was the visible image of a god, the *deva* of the moon, *Candra,* or, as he is sometimes called, *Kumuda-pati,* "Lord of the White Water Lily." [105] This flower, then, though we must always remind ourselves that it was not always clearly distinguished from the larger white lotus in literature and iconography, must be ranked with the sacred Egyptian lotus, its cousin *Nymphaea lotus,* in divine worth. Though it must have been familiar to the men of T'ang through Buddhist art, there is no evidence that the Indian water lily, whether blue or white, was ever solidly established in medieval China, and it seems to be an uncommon exotic even today.

But China has a native water lily, confined to the far south, and in T'ang times hardly more than a flower of vague rumor and report. It was called "sleeping lotus" in Chinese,[106] but it is in fact *N. teragona,* the "pygmy water lily." It shows a small white flower, and its name comes from the fact that

. . . it opens on summer days, but at night it contracts and goes below into the water, then comes forth again by day. The "herb of dreams" enters the earth by day and then comes forth again by night—so the two are just opposite; but the color of the herb of dreams is red; it is the one which Fang-shuo offered to Wu Ti.[107]

So even this native was akin to the creatures of the otherworld.

My lord contemptuous of his Country's Groves,
As foreign Fashions foreign Trees too loves:
"Odious! upon a Walnut-plank to dine!
No—the red-vein'd Mohoggony be mine!
Each Chest and Chair around my Room that
stands,
Was ship'd thro' dangerous Seas from distant
Lands.

Thomas Warton, *On Luxury*

viii·Woods

THE MEN of T'ang had a fine variety of native woods to provide them with the useful artifacts to which they were accustomed: a native rosewood[1] for axe-hafts; sour jujube, tough and fine-grained, for axles, spoons, and chopsticks; camphorwood from south of the Yangtze to make boats;[2] paulownia from Szechwan to make the zithers (furnished with jade pegs, and strings of silk from Chekiang) and beautiful harps of medieval China.[3] We are fortunate in having an "extinct" T'ang harp, restored with great finesse at the Shōsōin; it is made of paulownia, inlaid with birds and flowers of mother-of-pearl, and has twenty-three strings attached to pins of deer bone.[4] It will serve as an example of the excellence of T'ang woodworking.

The wood products of the southernmost part of the empire were much in demand, since more of the original forest remained there than in the north, and that subtropical land was rich in hardwoods. Many of these trees were to be found in Indochina as well as in China, and their woods may be counted as "semi-exotic." The feather palm, called "gomuti," of Lingnan and Indochina, is one of these;[5] besides providing coir for lashing the planks of ships, and sago for cakemakers, it yielded a handsomely veined purple-black wood, especially favored for the manufacture of gaming boards. From this same half-Chinese region came one of the most useful of all woods, the bamboo, source of a myriad utensils. Many kinds of bamboo grow in central and south China, but most highly valued in wealthy and aristocratic households were objects made of the "spotted bamboo," [6] which has purplish maculations on its stem and is adapted to all sorts of decorative purposes, but was used especially for the handles of the most elegant writing brushes. We have examples of these last in the Shōsōin: they are ornamented with ivory, gold, silver, or red sanders.[7] The handsome spotted bamboo was imported from Huan-*chou* in Tongking.[8] Its prestige was so great that it was sometimes faked. In the Shōsōin treasury are objects made of imitation spotted bamboo; this ambiguous substance (not otherwise identified) overlays, for instance, a box of black persimmon wood for keeping inksticks.[9]

Early in the eighth century unheard-of heights of luxury were achieved in building and furnishing the mansions and palaces of the members of the imperial family and of the great aristocrats, and the important Buddhist monastic establishments. The demand for fine woods was enormous, and stupendous sums were expended to denude whole mountains to obtain them.[10] These extravagant needs not only increased the consumption of native timbers but brought the importation of foreign woods, especially colored and aromatic ones, to new heights. It became fashionable among the aristocratic classes to have everyday utilitarian objects made from such exotics, so that the households of the great reeked of tropical fragrance. An example is provided by Li Ho's description of the excursion of a royal princess: he pictures her and her attendants panoplied as for war; her slave girls are shown on horseback, wearing linked-chain armor of shining bronze; they carry banners of net gauze suspended from poles of aromatic wood, decorated with gold.[11] To provide for such prodigal displays and also for the solemn ceremonies of states, the artisans of the palaces had to be supplied with great quantities of the rare woods of the Indies, which consequently poured into T'ang by way of the Annamese protectorate and the great seaport of Canton. Chief among these were sanderswood, called "purple rosewood" in T'ang; flowered rosewood, called "*lü*-wood"; and sandalwood, called "white sandal" or "rosewood aromatic."

SANDERSWOOD

"The purple *candana* comes from the valleys of Kurung and P'an-p'an, and although it does not grow in Central Hsia, men have it there everywhere."[12] The T'ang pharmacologist Su Kung, in telling of the universal occurrence of red sanderswood in T'ang, called it by a part-Indian name, "purple *candana*," that is, "purple sandal," since this excellent cabinetwood was regarded in medieval China as related to sandalwood on the one hand, and to rosewood on the other. The semantic connection was signalized by a linguistic linkage, since *candana* was transcribed by an old Chinese character for "rosewood." The Malayan sanders,[13] the common kind in China, has a yellowish or reddish wood with a roselike odor. Probably some of its more distant relatives sometimes came into medieval China too—such woods as Andaman padouk,[14] a fine timber, and Indian sanders,[15] whose odorless wood, besides serving in architecture, provides a colored powder for caste marks. Sanders, in fact, is almost as notable as a dye as it is a wood. The dyewood from the Indian sanders was used in medieval Europe to color sauces,[16] and that of the Malayan sanders was used in T'ang to color clothing.[17] "Purple rosewood" was the preferred substance for making stringed musical instruments, above all the lute. T'ang poetry is full of allusions to sanderswood lutes; Meng Hao-jan, for instance, wrote of one decorated with gold dust.[18] At Nara, in the Shōsōin, handsomely decorated sanderswood lutes of various kinds may still be seen, such as the T'ang five-stringed lute (the only one in existence) made of sanders and embellished with floral inlays of mother-of-pearl, tortoise shell, and amber.[19] There too may be seen a *juan-hsien* (Japanese *genkan*), or "lute of Ch'in," named for one of the ancient "Seven Sages of the Bamboo Grove" and also made of sanders, and inlaid with parrots and other figures in the same three precious substances.[20]

But the lovely sanderswood was employed for a multitude of other small objects, and fortunately many examples of these survive. In the Shōsōin are a rectangular box for making offerings to the Buddha, with gold inlay following the grain of the wood, and rock crystal plaques inset over colored paintings of flowers; an armrest used by the Emperor Shōmu, decorated with gold, camphorwood, and stained ivory; a *go* gaming board inlaid with animal figures and rosettes of ivory; a "double-six" gaming board with floral designs in gold and silver leaf under transparent tortoise shell; a long-handled censer with flowers, birds, and butterflies in gold, rock crystal, and green glass—all of these marvels are constructed of red sanders.[21] Literature provides us with descriptions of other rich objects: a worthy of the ninth century had a set of *go* counters, half of Borneo camphor, half of sanders;[22] a court beauty of the same period had a resonant plate of "white jade" suspended from a sanders frame, which she struck with a mallet of rhinoceros horn;[23] the poetic monk Kuan-hsiu, who lived for eighty years in the ninth and tenth centuries, wrote of a pagoda (presumably a miniature one) of "red *candana*";[24] the Emperor T'ai Tsung, an extravagant admirer of the calligrapher Wang Hsi-chih, kept examples of his writing mounted in the form of a scroll book, tied up in purple net gauze, on a sandalwood roller, with terminal knobs of red sanders.[25]

ROSEWOOD

By "rosewood," strictly speaking, we mean members of the genus *Dalbergia,* which are universally prized by makers of furniture for their fine dark color and attractive mottled patterns; the name is for the odor, not the color. Species of *Dalbergia* (some are called "blackwood" because of their dark brown color) occur in Asia, Africa, and in tropical America. Particularly notable kinds are *Dalbergia sissoides* of Java, and *D. latifolia* and *D. sissoo,* both of India.[26] The last named of these costly rosewoods was in demand in ancient Persia, under the Achaemenid dynasty; it was employed in Susa, for instance, along with cedar and cypress, for luxurious chairs and bedsteads.[27]

Some kinds of rosewood were used by the cabinetmakers of T'ang. Much of this wood could have been *D. hainanensis,* called "flowered *lü*-wood" and shipped, as the name suggests, from the island of Hainan to Canton; but probably other Indochinese *Dalbergias* were involved. "It comes," writes Ch'en Ts'ang-ch'i in the eighth century, "from Annam and Nan-hai, and is used to make couches and taborets. It resembles 'purple sandal,' but its color is red, and its nature is hard and admirable." [28] The beautiful patterned wood was also desired for medicinal reasons: pillows made of it could cure headaches.[29]

SANDALWOOD

Sandalwood is the white or yellowish heartwood of a small parasitic tree [30] of India, Java, and the Sunda archipelago.[31] "It is like our rosewood," writes Ch'en Ts'ang-ch'i,[32] meaning that it is comparable to the yellowish wood of the Chinese *Dalbergia.* And, indeed, despite the frequent epithet "white," yellow is the natural color of the fragrant wood, desirable because of the fragrance itself and because the close-grained wood, preserved by its own oil,[33] is perfectly adapted to making finely carved objects of virtu, such as small religious images, boxes for jewels, and other such small treasures. It was the religious applications which were most characteristic—the role of sandal in southern and eastern Asia was like that of cedar in the ancient Near East, where the wood of Solomon's temple and of Egyptian mummy cases stood for the immortality of the spirit.

The chief sources of sandalwood in T'ang times are not known with certainty. The raw wood and worked-up artifacts alike came from India and the Indies, but the exact sources and the proportional amounts they contributed are a mystery.[34] An Indonesian country, named *Dabatang,* perhaps Sumatran, sent sandalwood to the court in 647,[35] but otherwise imports of the stuff seem to be concealed under textual references to tribute and gifts of "rare aromatics" and other collective expressions.

Sandal had a significant place in Oriental medicine. Ch'en Ts'ang-ch'i states that it was used to quell "demoniac vapors" and to "kill crawling creatures." [36] The former virtue has been interpreted as carminative, and indeed the medieval Arabs also used sandal to relieve intestinal colic.[37] This usage was undoubtedly Indian in origin, as was the custom of using powdered sandal as a cosmetic,[38] which spread among the "Hinduized" countries of Indochina.[39] But medicines and cosmetics were not properly separate things in the medieval world: as Pāramiti put it in the Chinese translation he made of the Tantric *Śūraṅgama-sūtra* in 705: "plaster the body with white *candana,* and you will be able to get rid of feverish distresses one and all." [40]

The divinely sweet odor of sandal expressed to the senses the antidemoniac properties concealed within its godlike body. For the same reason, sandalwood was the most suitable substance out of which to carve the fragrant body of divinity, such as the sandalwood image of Avalokiteśvara seen by Hsüan-tsang. [41] Other sandalwood statues, great and small, were venerated through the East. And, extending the idea, sandal could become the epithet of a living god himself, as it was of the Buddha of the South, one of ten spirits of the directions, who was styled "Shining with Sandal and Pearl." [42]

The wood, and the emotions and imagery associated with it, were brought into China under the influence of Indian Buddhism, some centuries before T'ang. The word *candana,* "sandal," appears in China in 357, but only as the name of a country in the Indies; [43] as the name of a tree it appears in 454. [44] The exotic word was first spelled out in Chinese characters sounding approximately like *candana,* semanticized as "oriflamme rosewood" and "true rosewood." This was possible because the name of the Chinese rosewood was **d'an.* [45] The mature name, reserved for the fragrant heartwood, "rosewood aromatic," developed naturally and easily.

In T'ang, the acme of Buddhist culture produced a multitude of carved images, many of them of sandalwood. Consider the apocalyptic vision of the nine assemblies of divine beings described in the *Buddhāvataṃsaka-sūtra,* done in sandal by a foreign (and unhappily anonymous) master, with the help of sixty artisans, and adorned with jewels. This wonder of woodcarving was installed in the K'ai-yüan temple in Canton by Hsüan Tsung, where it was seen by the pilgrim Chien-chen. [46] Another pious traveler, the Japanese Ennin, tells of an image of Shakyamuni, three feet high, carved in sandalwood at the order of the powerful mandarin Li Te-yü and installed in the K'ai-yüan temple in Yang-*chou.* Ennin sipped tea with the great man (seated on chairs!) in the "Gallery of Auspicious Images," which had been restored with the aid of contributions from the Persian and Cham mercantile communities. [47]

Less expected than these was the story of the Buddhist priest Pu-k'ung, who, at the instance of Hsüan Tsung, ". . . burned an aromatic dragon of white sandal" while praying for rain. [48] The venerable Chinese custom of burning the rain spirit, whether in the form of a human surrogate of the deity, as in remote antiquity, or in an image, as in this case, [49] was thus adapted by a Buddhist to proper Indian usage.

Utilitarian objects of sandal ranged in size from small objects like an eight-lobed box in the Shōsōin [50] to large ones like the "Gallery of *Candana*" in Li Po's poem. [51] Sandal was a wood of luxury as well as a wood of religion. When Hsüan Tsung had a fine house built for Rokhshan in Ch'ang-an in 751, he had it furnished with the richest objects, such as gold and silver utensils, and among the furnishings were two couches, ten feet long and six feet wide, appliqued with sandalwood. [52] Even more splendid than these were the high seats presented to the monks of the An-kuo

("Country Stabilizing") temple by the Emperor I Tsung in 871, to be used by lecturers on the sutras. The seats were twenty feet high and framed in sandalwood and aloeswood.[53] Of the same magnificence was the meditation platform at the T'ien-t'ai monastery on Mount Wu-t'ai in the ninth century; it was covered with a sandal paste, so that the breezes blew its fragrance over a considerable distance.[54]

Sandal also supplied the poets with an easy, even rather ordinary, exotic image: such a pairing as "modeled in *candana* aromatic" and "copied on *pattra* leaves" [55] (the second of these, intended for "palmyra palm leaves," being literally redundant) gave an automatic picture of an Indian or a Hinduized milieu. A much greater rarity is the metaphor "sandal mouth" in the erotic verses of the talented harlot Chao Luan-luan,[56] clearly meaning "her mouth fragrant as sandal."

EBONY

Many trees of genus *Diospyros,* relatives of the persimmon and natives of India and the Indies, yield the handsome black hardwoods collectively named "ebony." [57] Some kinds of ebony, under the name of "raven wood," were imported into China by Persian argosies as early as the fourth century.[58] Again, in the twelfth century, we hear of imported ebony; one writer, for instance, describes the distinctively shiny black surface of antique zithers as ". . . like the raven wood which is brought for trade by overseas argosies." [59] But no direct evidence of the importation of ebony in T'ang appears, though the period is straddled by the eras just mentioned. We might reasonably expect to find objects of ebony in the Shōsōin, if it were important among exotic woods used in eighth-century China. The catalogues of that treasury allude frequently to elegant cabinetwork—a hexagonal stand and a cabinet with hinged doors are instances—[60] of "black persimmon," but this does not seem to be a proper ebony but rather a paler *Diospyros,* stained with sapan juice.[61] The question is open.

Manna and dates, in argosy transferr'd
From Fez; and spiced dainties, everyone,
From silken Samarcand to cedar'd Lebanon.

John Keats, *The Eve of St. Agnes*

ix= Foods

JUST AS NO hard and fast line can be drawn between cosmetics and drugs in the civilization of the medieval Far East, so any attempt to discriminate precisely between foods and drugs, or between condiments and perfumes, would lead to frustrated misrepresentation of the true role of edibles in T'ang culture. This role was not simple but complex.[1] Every food had medicinal properties, which were carefully studied by learned doctors, and especially by the Taoists for whom diet was closely related to the fight against time, and who aimed at prolonging ruddy and robust youth. Spices in particular—and exotic ones above all—because of their aromatic nature, infusing their wonder-working properties by means of unmistakable effluvia, were ranked high among the useful drugs, and were no mere taste-sharpeners for Lucullan banquets, though they were that too. But it is important to remember that even this statement oversimplifies the picture: spices and perfumes had their parts to play in religion as well as in medicine, and also in daily life, to preserve food, to repel unpleasant insects, to purify noxious airs, to clean the body and beautify the skin, to evoke love in an indifferent beloved, to improve one's social status, and in many other ways.[2] The variety and multiplicity of these purposes, rather than some easy and condescending characterization such as the "luxury trade," as if only the rich desired health and beauty, must be taken as the real basis of the great medieval commerce in exotic seasonings and relishes. They were at once charms and panaceas, and much else besides.[3] So saying, I will perversely proceed to divide up these edible aromatics or aromatic edibles quite arbitrarily, and treat them under separate rubrics, according to whether they seem to be most important in cookery, in perfumes and incenses, or in medicine. Sometimes the catalogu-

139

ing will seem strange, not only because it is arbitrary and one-sided, but because it defies modern usage and belief. Cloves and nutmegs can be given as examples: these will be discussed in the next chapter, on "Aromatics," rather than here under "Foods," where we should be most inclined to put them. There is no evidence that these spices were much used in T'ang cookery, but a great deal of evidence that they were important in the manufacture of perfumes and drugs.

The monkish traveler, I-ching, who had much experience with the cookery of Indonesia and India, reported, with evident relish, on the richly prepared fare available in those lands, as contrasted with his own: ". . . in China, people of the present time eat fish and vegetables mostly uncooked; no Indians do this. All vegetables are to be well cooked and to be eaten after mixing with the assafoetida, clarified butter, oil, or any spice." [4] Probably we should accept this account of the character of the Chinese cuisine in the seventh century, since it is given by an excellent observer. But it goes against contemporary opinions of Chinese cooking, especially that of the south. I-ching's description makes T'ang cookery sound like modern Japanese cookery —plain food, sometimes raw, with few savory mixtures or interesting sauces, we would guess. If so, the best of modern Chinese cooking has developed in relatively recent times, and we easily suppose, if that is so, that the rich character we find in it was only beginning to appear in T'ang times, undoubtedly under the influence of foreign taste and custom in foods, in particular those of India and the Indianized lands of the Desert and the Isles.

But, to tell the truth, very little is yet known about T'ang eating habits. In the sentences which follow it is not possible to do more than suggest, largely by giving examples, what sorts of things were usually or sometimes eaten. But nothing as to how they were prepared will be forthcoming—this important task remains for a future historian.

We know then that certain staples, such as millet, rice, pork, beans, chicken, plums, onions, and bamboo shoots were very widely used. We may also read of local specialties, and suppose that T'ang gourmets sampled these village dishes in the course of their travels for business and pleasure—such delicacies as frogs, a favorite food in Kuei-yang, far in the south (though it is reported that sophisticated northerners ridiculed the natives for this preference).[5] And there were the sago cakes of Kwangtung,[6] the dried oysters taken with wine in the same region,[7] and the "ground-chestnuts" of Chekiang.[8] When a local dainty attracted favorable attention at court and capital, it was added to the lists of local tribute and thereafter was received regularly by the imperial kitchens: the summer garlic of southern Shensi, the deer tongues of northern Kansu, the Venus clams of the Shantung coast, the "sugar crabs" of the Yangtze River, the sea horses of Ch'ao-*chou* in Kwangtung, the white carp marinated in wine lees from northern Anhwei, the dried flesh of "white flower snake" (a pit viper) from southern Hupeh, melon pickled in rice mash from southern Shensi and eastern Hupeh, dried ginger from Chekiang, loquats and cherries from southern

Shensi, persimmons from central Honan, and "thorny limes" from the Yangtze Valley.[9]

As the expansion of imperial T'ang brought new lands and diverse cultures under her control, it was natural that the lists of comestibles demanded in Ch'ang-an (and certainly elsewhere too, as the court set the fashion for the provinces) were lengthened to include new and strange delicacies, such as the aromatic jujubes of Hami,[10] the "thorn honey" which exuded from a leafless desert plant[11] and was sent by Qočo, the almonds of Kucha,[12] and the bananas and betel nuts (their Malay name of *pinang* was adopted in Chinese) of Annam.[13] These foods, and others like them, constituted a transitional group of "semi-exotics," being, so to speak, culturally foreign but politically Chinese. In due time they became culturally Chinese as well. And following them came the true exotics.

The importation of food (which was handled in the same way as drugs) was under strict government supervision. Each foreigner who entered the frontier had the wrapping or box of his "gift" of medicine or victuals sealed and stamped by the competent magistrate at the frontier post, the contents being described plainly for the information of court officials or market authorities, to aid in fixing their value.[14] The best of these exotic delicacies were turned into viands for the imperial tables under the supervision of a dignitary styled the "Provost of Foods" (*shang shih*). Assisted by eight dieticians and sixteen butlers, he provided the necessaries for the feasts and fasts of the Son of Heaven in strict accordance with seasonal taboos, and meals of appropriate character for state banquets, informal entertainments, and the like:

When he submits the food, he is obliged first to taste it. He must discriminate the names and quantities of all the sweets and nutriments, rarities and oddities, submitted by the several *chou* ("island-provinces") of the Subcelestial Realm, and prudently conserve and supply them.[15]

As the knowledge of these rarities spread outwards from the palace, the taste for them grew in town and city, and the commerce in them increased. Let us look at some of them.

GRAPES AND GRAPE WINE

The Chinese, like the other peoples of the earth, had, since they first brought cereals under cultivation, been familiar with the fermented drinks extractable from them— beer comes with bread. They had their beers (or "wines," as we like to call them) of millet and rice and barley, plain drinks for daily use; they had fruit drinks, and kumiss of fermented mare's milk;[16] they had delicacies like ginger wine and mead,[17] and several kinds of perfumed hippocras, dedicated to the gods. Some of these ancient brews were still made in T'ang; some were long obsolete. But in the main rice had become the staple source of alcohol.

By reputation, at least, a variety of exotic beverages were known: it was reported that the Chams made a wine of betel sap;[18] a toddy was made in Kalinga from juice extracted from the coconut flower;[19] the Tanguts brewed a beer of rice, which they had to import for the purpose.[20] But there is no evidence that any of the cheering foreign liquids were drunk in China, with the sole exception of the grape wines of the West.

Chang Ch'ien, the heroic traveler of early Han times, introduced grape seeds to China, where they were planted in the capital and the fruit grown on a small scale for eating purposes.[21] According to one T'ang tradition, these were of three kinds, yellow, white, and black.[22] They were reported to have been doing well in the vicinity of Tun-huang in the fifth century.[23] But grapes were not an important crop, and the wine made from them remained a rare and exotic drink.

So it was until the beginning of the rule of T'ang, when suddenly, as a result of rapid T'ang expansion into the Iranian and Turkish lands of the West, grapes and grape wine alike became well known in China. Even then, the fruit retained spiritual affinities with the West: clusters of grapes had been used as exotic decorative motifs in polychrome damasks for centuries, and "Hellenistic" grape patterns on the backs of T'ang mirrors are familiar to everyone.[24] Moreover, the Romans, the Arabs, and the Uighur Turks of Serindia were all known as great grape growers and drinkers of wine.[25] But after the T'ang conquest of Serindia, some of the exotic flavor of the grape and its juice was lost, like that of the "semi-exotic" almonds and betel nuts. Quite a variety of the products of the grape were demanded from Qočo by way of annual tribute to the great court at Ch'ang-an: "dried," "crinkled," and "parched" were three distinct varieties of raisins; a sirup was also imported, and, of course, wine.[26]

But most important of all, a new wine-making grape was introduced to China, and with it, knowledge of the art of making grape wine, and the foundation of a new industry. This was the famous "mare teat" grape. Our first dated reference to this variety tells of a gift from the Turkish Yabghu, who sent a bunch of these long purple grapes to the emperor in the spring of 647.[27] The name indicates their elongated shape, as distinguished, for instance, from a spherical variety called "dragon beads (or pearls)."[28] It has an imagistic parallel in one of the five poems describing vividly the more bewitching parts of a woman's body, written by the Ch'ang-an courtesan Chao Luan-luan; the five are "Cloudy Chignons," "Willow Brows," "Sandal Mouth," "Cambric Fingers," and "Creamy Breasts." In the last of these, the nipples appear under the metaphor "purple grapes," but respectful courtesy demands that we see in some other kind of grape the original underlying the tasty image, smaller and better proportioned than the "mare teat."[29]

Cuttings of the Western "mare teat" grapevine were brought to China after the conquest of Qočo in 640, though the exact date of the introduction is unknown.

THE ACCOUNT OF TA YÜAN

They were successfully planted in the imperial park,[30] and we may presumably discern their progeny in the two "Grape Gardens" in the Tabooed Park at Ch'ang-an, toward the end of the seventh century.[31] In due course they spread beyond the holy premises, so that we find them in a poem of Han Yü, who reproaches the owner of a dilapidated vineyard:

> The new twigs aren't yet everywhere—half are still withered;
> The tall trellis is dismembered—here overturned, there uplifted.
> If you want a full dish, heaped with "mare teats,"
> Don't decline to add some bamboos, and insert some "dragon beard." [32]

We do not know where this vineyard was, but vines were extensively grown in arid Kansu, and we shall tell presently of the wines of Western Liang in that province. The other paramount grape-producing region of T'ang China was the T'ai-yüan district of northern Shansi, "where charmers of Yen offer goblets of grape." [33] Local varieties were developed in these much-praised vineyards; in addition to wine grapes, we read of a large edible grape of Ho-tung (Shansi) in the tenth century, so delicate that it became worthless when transported to the capital.[34]

Grapes were sufficiently well known in the seventh century to deserve the published opinions of professional dieticians: Meng Shen avowed that eating too many produced symptoms of anxiety and darkened the eyes, though grape juice was useful in lowering a fetus which was pressing against the heart.[35]

But grapes were still not quite familiar fruits. Even in the eighth century, when they were well established in Chinese soil, Tu Fu could employ them in a series of images of a strange, non-Chinese country, pairing "grapes ripening" with "alfalfa abounding" (both rather classical figures, as both had been introduced by Chang Ch'ien in the second century B.C.); these were matched in turn with "Tibetan women" and "Western lads." [36] Probably Tu Fu was writing of some frontier town like Liang-*chou*. And indeed the wine of Liang-*chou* (an exotic enclave in T'ang, like Chinatown in San Francisco) was regarded as a fine, rare drink with glamourous associations. Even in Tun-huang, however, further out on the camel road, grape wine was an expensive addition to an important celebration, like champagne for our festivals.[37] The unofficial life of Yang the Precious Consort shows her drinking grape wine, the gift of the town of Liang-*chou*, from a glass cup decorated with "the Seven Gems." [38] A cup of this admirable wine was given to the emperor Mu Tsung early in the ninth century, and he remarked of it, "When I drink this, I am instantly conscious of harmony suffusing my four limbs—it is the true 'Princeling of Grand Tranquillity'!" [39] The title is suggestive of the honorific name of Lao Tzu, and also seems to echo the Greek notion that wine is a god.

The admiration for the wines of the West had a respectable history: some were imported during the Han-T'ang interval,[40] and the old encyclopedia, *Po wu chih*, which is full of third- or fourth-century wonders, says:

The Western Regions possess a grape wine which is not spoiled by the accumulation of years. A popular tradition among them states that it is drinkable up to ten years, but if you drink it then, you will be drunk for the fullness of a month, and only then be relieved of it.[41]

In T'ang times there was the strange wine made from the myrobalans of Persia, available in the taverns of Ch'ang-an;[42] the "dragon fat" wine, as black as lacquer, brought from Alexandria(!) at the beginning of the ninth century,[43] was, however, probably a product of the fertile mind of the romancer Su O. Grape wine, made in the Iranian fashion, undoubtedly came from Chāch in the eighth century,[44] when grape wine technology was already established in China.

When the king of Qočo, along with such other trophies as his best musicians, was brought captive before T'ai Tsung early in 641, a three-day drinking holiday —a kind of public bacchanal—was declared in the capital.[45] The character of the celebration was well adapted to the occasion, for it was from the new dependency of Qočo, renamed "Island-Province of the West" (Hsi-*chou*), that the art of making grape wine was introduced to T'ang and the eight "colors" (varieties) of this highly pungent and aromatic beverage became known to the people of north China.[46] The "mare teat" grapes seem to have been important to the new industry, and the manufacture of wine was an appendage of the vineyards of T'ai-yüan, which submitted quantities of the delicious drink annually to the imperial court.[47] The high repute of the wines of T'ai-yüan, made from "mare teat" grapes, appears in a poem of Liu Yü-hsi, charmingly rendered into English by Theos. Sampson in 1869 as "The Song of the Grape." The "men of Tsin" are the men of the T'ai-yüan region in Shansi.

> The grape vine from untrodden lands,
> Its branches gnarled in tangled bands,
> Was brought the garden to adorn
> With verdure bright; now, upward borne,
> The branches climb with rapid stride,
> In graceful curves, diverging wide;
> Here spread and twin, there languid fall,
> Now reach the summit of the wall;
> And then with verdure green and bright,
> Enchanting the beholder's sight,
> Beyond the mansion's roof they strive,
> As though with conscious will alive.
> And now the vine is planted out,
> It climbs the wooden frame about,
> The lattice shades with tender green,
> And forms a pleasant terrace screen.
> With dregs of rice well soak the roots,
> And moisten all its leafy shoots,
> The flowers like silken fringe will blow,
> And fruit like clustered pearls hang low.
> On "mare's milk" grapes the hoarfrost gleams,

Shine "dragon scales" like morning beams.
Once hither came a traveling guest;
Amazed his host he thus addressed,
As strolling round he chanced to see
The fruit upon th' o'er-hanging tree:
We men of Tsin, such grapes so fair,
Do cultivate as gems most rare;
Of these delicious wine we make,
For which men ne'er their thirst can slake.
Take but a measure of this wine,
And Liang-chow's rule is surely thine.[48]

The new art of making grape wine was even transferred to a small wild Chinese grape, which has purplish black fruit and still grows in Shantung. Its name is *ying-yü*. The herbals of T'ang tell of a wine made of this fruit, just like that from the exotic grapes of Kansu and Shansi.[49] It may be that these very grapes are the ones of which Tuan Ch'eng-shih tells in an anecdote about "Grape Valley" (but he uses the imported word for "grape"). The valley was apparently in Shantung; [50] there the fruit could be picked freely, but the eater was likely to lose his way. The fruits were known as "grapes of the Royal Mother," linking them with the fruits of immortality on the world mountain. In the middle of the eighth century, a certain Buddhist monk, who had converted a piece of this vine into a temporary staff, planted it at his temple, where it flourished mightily and produced an arbor studded with purple fruits, which was called "Canopy of the Vegetable Dragon Pearls." [51]

MYROBALANS

In 746 a joint mission from the Turgäch, Chāch, Kish, Māimargh, and Kapiśa brought to the T'ang court, among other valuables, an offering of emblic myrobalans.[52] More usually, however, these fruits were imported by the sea routes of the South, especially on Persian ships.[53]

The three classical myrobalans of India were collectively called *triphalā,* the "Three Fruits," in Sanskrit; [54] in Chinese they were named the "Three Fruits" and also the "Three **-raks,*" **-rak* being the final syllable of each of their names in the Tocharian tongue,[55] an important Indo-European language of Central Asia; it was from this direction, it seems, that the Chinese obtained their names. The three are "emblic myrobalans," Sanskrit *āmalakī;* [56] "belleric myrobalans," Sanskrit *vibhītakī;* and "chebulic myrobalans," Sanskrit *harītakī.*[57]

To these three astringent fruits the Indians and Tibetans, and other peoples under Indian influence, ascribed the most wonderful properties. A Tibetan text describes them collectively as an elixir of life, and says of the chebulic myrobalan, which grows on the Perfumed Mount of the God Indra, and is everywhere the one most extravagantly admired,[58] that ". . . when ripe, it has six tastes, eight efficacies, leaves three (tastes) upon digestion, accomplishes the seventeen qualities, and dispels all varieties of illness." [59] The belleric kind, however, is in India thought to be inhabited by demons; but all have genuine worth in tanning and in medicine, especially as purgatives when ripe, and as astringents when unripe.[60]

The pharmacologists of T'ang, especially the official reviser of the pharmacopoeia, Su Kung, state that all three of these important drug plants grew in Annam, then under Chinese control, and that the emblic and belleric, at least, also grew in Lingnan.[61] The Sung pharmacologist, Su Sung, states that in his time, the eleventh century, the chebulic myrobalan also grew in south China, especially around Canton.[62] It seems likely, however, that, though the classical "Three Fruits" were imported by Indian ships on the Persia run, other species, peculiar to Indochina and possessing the same essential properties, were imported from close at hand. But perhaps we must accept the identifications of the learned Su Kung, and concede that the three fruits were also cultivated in the environs of the great southern port. The sea-roving monk, Chien-chen, also tells that he saw a *harītakī* tree, with fruits like large jujubes, at the Buddhist office-temple of the Great Cloud at Canton,[63] and it may be that he was right in his identification. But it seems likely that related species from closer at hand were often confused with them, both preserved fruit and transplanted tree.

Whatever their source, the natural properties of the fruits, and the complex of beliefs about them, brought from India with Buddhist civilization, made them important in Chinese medicine. We are not surprised to find them, much shriveled, among the medicinal treasures preserved from the eighth century in the Shōsōin in Nara.[64] The emblic myrobalan will blacken the hair, wrote Chen Ch'üan, a doctor of the early seventh century; [65] this was clear evidence of its youth-restoring properties. Foreigners make a hot liquor of the peachlike fruit of the belleric myrobalan, wrote the eminent Su Kung; [66] this may refer to a drink, apparently alcoholic since it was classified as a "wine," which enjoyed some popularity in northern China; the art of making it was said to have been learned from the Persians.[67] "Astringent gaffer" was a playful name given to the chebulic myrobalan early in the tenth century [68]— "gaffer" must refer to the wrinkled skin of the commercial product. Perhaps the name was an allusion to ripe old age; the eighth-century poet Pao Chi, when he was taken ill, received merely the leaf of the tree which bears that fruit as a gift from a sympathetic friend, and wrote a set of extravagant verses praising its divine qualities, "age- and ill-dispelling." [69]

VEGETABLES

A number of vegetables, leafy and otherwise, were introduced into China in the T'ang period, some actually transplanted, some only as cut edibles. Spinach was one of a number of rare transplants sent in 647 by the king of Nepal—known to the men of T'ang as a cold country inhabited by perfidious men.[70] The plant seems ultimately to have been of Persian origin, and indeed was called by the Taoists "Persian herb," as a kind of cabalistic name, though this may not have been until after T'ang.[71] The Taoists do seem to have taken a special interest in this novelty, for Meng Shen, the specialist on dietary problems, says of it that ". . . it releases the poisons of wine, and men who dose themselves with cinnabar stone do very well to eat it."[72] That is to say, Taoist adepts who try to make themselves immortal by taking cinnabar elixirs may counteract the unpleasant effects of ingesting a mercury compound by eating spinach. In any case, say the histories, the taste of spinach is improved by cooking.[73] The name given the new vegetable by the Chinese seems to register a foreign name like *palinga,* and pseudo-Kuo T'o-t'o's *Book of Planting Trees* says that this is the name of a country.[74]

Then there was the kohlrabi, a kind of cabbage, which Ch'en Ts'ang-ch'i calls both "sweet indigo" and "indigo from Western lands," having observed something about the broad leaves which reminded him of the Chinese indigo plant. He recommends it as a general tonic.[75] Kohlrabi is ultimately a European plant, and clearly came to China by way of the Serindians, the Tibetans, and the Kansu corridor.[76]

Among the new plants sent from Nepal in the seventh century were a white plant "like the onion" (possibly a leek or shallot),[77] a "bitter leaf vegetable" resembling lettuce,[78] another broad-leafed vegetable called "vinegar leaf vegetable,"[79] and an aromatic "Western celery."[80] None of these are really Nepalese plants; all were evidently fancy exotics passed on by the king of Nepal to his distant cousin of T'ang.

The "rattan worth a thousand metal-pieces" brought by the composite mission from the Turgäch and others in 746 is a mystery now—Ch'en Ts'ang-ch'i tells of a number of Chinese plants known by the same complimentary name.[81]

A modern scholar thinks that the sugar beet, under a Persian name, may have been introduced to China during T'ang, ". . . perhaps by the Arabs."[82]

None of this practical greenery was noticed by the poets.

DELICACIES

The large, sweet, and aromatic seeds of the Korean pine,[83] called "sea pine seeds," or "Silla pine seeds," were imported, peeled, and eaten.[84]

The pistachio, a favorite nut in Sogdiana, Khurāsān, and Persia, where several species grow, was also imported and, from about the ninth century, was grown in Lingnan.[85] It was styled "hazelnut of the Westerners" by the men of T'ang,[86] though strange-sounding Iranian names for it were sometimes heard. It was not only tasty but was reputed to increase sexual vigor, and the glow of health generally.[87]

From Nan-chao in the Southwest came a "creeping" walnut, which tasted like a proper walnut; it was sometimes styled "seed of the rattan from among the *Man*."[88] The true walnut was called "peach of the Westerners."

The olive was known in China, at least by reputation, under the Persian name *zeitun,* as a fruit of Persia and Rome, where it yielded a useful cooking oil,[89] but there is no proof that either fruit or oil was ever brought to T'ang. The so-called "Chinese olive" is, of course, no olive at all, but the fruit of two native trees; [90] the sap of one of them (*Canarium pimela*) yields a black brea or elemi, which was used in varnishes and for calking ships.

From Sumatra came an aromatic and acrid kind of seed, apparently the dill.[91] It was known in T'ang by the name *jila,* which is either Sanskrit *jīra* or Middle Persian *žira.*[92] Indeed, Li Hsün the pharmacologist quotes an old book which says that it came from Persia, but this was often said of things formerly brought in Persian ships. Li Hsün reported that dill seeds were wonderfully stimulating to the taste, but that ". . . they should not be eaten at the same time as asafetida, for they will rob it of its flavor." [93]

The chieftain of the Tsang-ko tribe in what is now Kweichow, then a mountainous wilderness, sent a gift of pickled meat.[94] Lacking further information about it, I have optimistically included it here among the "delicacies."

SEAFOODS

The striped mullet,[95] which lived both in rivers and seas and is a favorite food of the otter, was well known to and liked by the medieval Chinese. In T'ang times it was netted off the coast,[96] but it must be counted also among the exotic foods of T'ang, since the P'o-hai Mo-ho sent envoys from Manchuria in 729 with a gift of this fish for the emperor.[97] The Chinese of the south made from the striped mullet a kind of sauce or relish which had the curious name of "leaping fish sauce" (*t'iao t'ing*). The salted fish were "touched with vinegar and dipped in wine," which gave the preparation a delicious taste. One explanation given for the name was that the mullets traveled in enormous shoals, ". . . like clouds in battle array," so that it was not necessary to put out the nets, for the fish leaped into the fishing boats in great numbers, even endangering them with their weight.[98]

Some years later, the same Manchurian fisherfolk sent a hundred dried "striped fish." [99] The name has a mythological ring to it: it appears in the *Li Sao,* the great epic of the soul in flight: "Riding the white turtle, ah! chasing the striped fish!" We find it again early in the third century of our era, in Ts'ao Chih's "Rhapsody on the Goddess of the Lo":

> There is prancing of striped fish to warn that she rides by,
> There is calling of jade simurghs as they go away together.

(The "jade simurghs" are harness bells.) But a connection between these classical swimmers and the anonymous preserved fish from the Northeastern barbarians can be shown only in fancy.

Finally, the medicine men, at any rate, knew of and could probably obtain a kind of Korean bivalve mollusk from Silla, where it was an article of diet. Ch'en Ts'ang-ch'i recommends a soup made of these and the edible laver called *kompo* [100] as a remedy for "knotted-up breath." [101] This is undoubtedly a Korean recipe, but we do not know whether it was eaten except on the advice of a physician. The name of the shell is **tâm-lâ,* which is evidently the old name of Quelpart Island, or Cheju, that is, *Tamna.* [102] The island is famous for its shellfish, and the Chinese have plainly transferred the name of the place of origin to the tasty mollusk itself.

CONDIMENTS

Before the Chinese had pepper they had their own pungent condiment, fagara. [103] Various kinds of fagara take the place of true pepper in India, China, and Japan, where the fruit wall, sometimes along with the seed, is used both in cookery and in medicine. [104] "Fagara of Ch'in," [105] the variety used in antiquity, had a number of applications in medieval medicine. It could, for instance, help delayed menstruation, cure certain dysenteries, and grow hair; [106] Tuan Ch'eng-shih says that it also had the rather peculiar virtue of attracting quicksilver, but how this was put to use is not stated [107]—perhaps it was a mineral prospector's indicator. Closely allied to it was "fagara of Shu," the Szechwanese fagara, which grew as far north as the Ch'in-ling, south of the capital, but one authority states that the best of this kind was brought in from the "Western Regions." [108]

This familiar seasoning, like other aromatic herbs, was added to sacrificial wines and meats, both to preserve them and to make them attractive to the gods. [109] In particular, a nectar spiced with fagara was an ancient and medieval libation appropriate to the rites of the New Year. [110] But drinks and dishes seasoned with fagara and other aromatics were gradually secularized, and went from the altars of the gods to aristocratic tables, [111] and even to quite ordinary tables. It is reported that the emperor Te Tsung (late in the eighth century) used curds and fagara in his tea, [112] and the mysterious Buddhist poet Han-shan (also of the eighth century), describing with scorn the viands on a selfish gourmand's table, writes of

> Steamed shoats dipped in garlic sauce,
> Roast duck tinctured with fagara and salt. [113]

This makes good sense to us, attuned as we are to pepper and salt together. The combination may have been especially characteristic of southern cooking then, anticipating the rich preparations we now recognize as "Cantonese." Han Yü, poetizing on his first introduction to the southern cuisine, wrote:

Coming here I fended off goblins,
So it's right that I taste southern cookery—
Blended with saline and sour,
Mixed with fagara and oranges.[114]

Pepper did not come as a complete novelty, then, but as an exotic and probably expensive substitute for fagara. Indeed, the name created for it emphasized its proxy status: "fagara of the Westerners."[115] At the same time, just as "fagara of Shu" (as opposed to the homely old fagara of Ch'in) was regarded as an excellent variety, so *"hu* fagara" was even better—but all were used for the same purposes. But the new variety probably brought new dishes with it; we read, for instance, of the pepper ". . . which comes from the country of Magadha, where they call it *maricha* [116] . . . the seeds are shaped like those of the fagara of Han, but it is acrid and pungent in the extreme. It is gathered in the sixth month. Men of our time always use it when they make 'Western plate' meat dishes."[117] Foreign recipes demanded foreign spices.

Black pepper is prepared from the berry spikes of *Piper nigrum* ". . . piled into heaps for fermentation, during which they turn black, and are then spread on mats to dry." White pepper is made from the same berries, the largest and best being soaked in water until the outer surface sloughs off.[118] The pepper plant is native to Burma and Assam, and has been introduced into India, Indochina, and Indonesia,[119] and from India into Persia, whence Persian ships carried it, along with sandal and drugs, to all parts of medieval Asia.[120] The T'ang pharmacopoeia says simply that it grows among the Western *Jung*,[121] that is, among the barbarians, but we have already noticed that it had an especial association with Magadha, and indeed "Magadha" is an epithet of "pepper" in Sanskrit,[122] and we must suppose that the region was a great center of production. The immense value of pepper in late medieval and early modern times, bringing wealth to the merchants who monopolized its trade, is now a familiar fact of history. But the spice appears to have been very costly in the eighth century too, for when the confiscated property of the disgraced minister Yüan Tsai was registered in 777, it was found that he possessed, among other rich goods (such as five hundred ounces of stalactite, a powerful medicine), one hundred piculs of true pepper—a tremendous quantity, and evident index of his riches.[123]

In the main, the medicinal value of pepper, once nearly as important as its worth as a condiment, depends on its irritant action, which stimulates secretion in the intestines, and so helps digestion.[124] Meng Shen recommends taking it in pure wine for "coldness and pains in heart and belly."[125] But it had its drawbacks too, for, writes another expert, ". . . if eaten in quantity it damages the lungs, and makes people spit blood."[126]

The Chinese of T'ang also knew another pepper, "long pepper."[127] They called it by its Sanskrit name *pippali* [128] or, more commonly, shortened this to *pippal* (mispronounced *pitpat* or *pippat*). Our word "pepper," of course, comes from the same source.[129] Long pepper spread through southern Asia even before ordinary black pepper,[130] and in Rome of Pliny's time it was more valuable than black pepper.[131] Tuan Ch'eng-shih tells us that it grew in Magadha, like black pepper,[132] but Su Kung calls it a product of Persia, because of its importance in the "Persia clipper" trade. He adds that ". . . the Westerners bring it to us; we use it, for its flavor, to put in food." [133] It seems not to have been planted in China during T'ang, and does not appear in T'ang poetry, but it was grown in Lingnan in the eleventh century,[134] and the great Sung poet Su Shih mentions it frequently because of its aroma. In fact, long pepper is even more fiery than betel pepper, which it resembles, and in consequence was regarded as a more potent drug than the other peppers. It was prescribed as a tonic for loins and legs, as a digestive aid, to abolish coldness in the stomach, and so forth.[135] After T'ai Tsung himself, suffering from an intestinal affliction, had tried the recipes of his doctors in vain, a concoction of long pepper simmered in milk, suggested by an officer of his guards, proved efficacious.[136]

The leaves of the betel pepper [137] are widely chewed in Southeast Asia, normally along with a slice of the nut of the betel palm,[138] as a mild stimulant and a sweetener of the breath. The commercial product was sometimes called "betel sauce" in T'ang, referring to the way it was prepared in Lingnan, where betel-chewing was an ancient custom; [139] but sometimes it was called "earth *pippala.*" [140] It was taken as a condiment in wine and in food, and was also prescribed for stomach disorders, like the other peppers.[141] Su Kung states that it also grew in Szechwan, and that foreigners from Western countries sometimes brought it in.[142]

Another pepper known to the men of T'ang was the cubeb,[143] a native of the Indies. In T'ang times it was brought from Śrivijaya,[144] and it was in Indonesia that the medieval Arab traders obtained it; in India it came to be called *ḳabab chini,* that is, "Chinese cubeb," possibly because the Chinese had a hand in the trade,[145] but more likely because it was important in the "China trade," vaguely so-called. Cubebs were also used as a spice in early medieval Europe.[146] In China this pepper was called both *vilenga* (apparently the name of an adulterant of black pepper in an Indic dialect, transferred to this Malayan plant) [147] and *viḍanga,* the cognate Sanskrit word. Li Hsün thought it grew on the same tree as black pepper.[148] In any event, the physicians of T'ang administered it to restore the appetite, to cure "demon vapors," to darken the hair, and to perfume the body.[149] There is no evidence of its use as a condiment, but I include it here to keep it with the other peppers.

The Chinese have a native mustard,[150] but in T'ang times a Western species of this plant, which is closely related to the cabbage and turnip, was brought in by foreign traders. This was "white mustard," [151] which they called by that name, and also "mustard of the Westerners." [152] It is a native of the Mediterranean world, but was being grown in Shansi by the eighth century.[153] The large, very pungent white grains were given in warm wine for respiratory disorders,[154] but, as with cubebs, their role in cookery is unknown.

SUGAR

Sweets were very popular in T'ang times, and honey was commonly used to make them. Southern Shensi produced honeyed bamboo shoots,[155] and honeyed ginger was made in both Yang-*chou* and Hang-*chou* near the mouth of the Yangtze.[156] A honey-water potion, taken over a long period of time, was thought to impart an admirable rosy glow to the face.[157] Yet, despite its antiquity and familiarity in China, a superior kind of honey was imported from the Tibetan peoples.[158]

Cereals were another familiar source of sugar in China. Such grains as glutinous millet and rice provided the ancients with tasty sirups and confections, and "barley sugar" was made at least as early as the second century B.C.[159] By T'ang times these must have seemed rather tasteless, inferior products, since they are not mentioned in the tribute lists. An important reason for this was that the juice and crystals extracted from the sugar cane had long since been introduced to the Chinese, and welcomed.

Cane sugar is the most widely popular of all plant sugars, although the extract of the sugar beet, sorghum, and palmyra have their many devotees. Innumerable races of the sugar cane grow in tropical Asia and Oceania. From this vast region the plant was transmitted westward, reaching Persia, it seems, by the fifth century, Egypt by the seventh, and Spain by the eighth.[160] Sugar could be extracted from the cane in several ways. The simplest way was to chew it, or to crush it to make a pleasant drink. On a more sophisticated level, the juice could be boiled down to make a solid substance, suitable for sweetening foods. Finally, impurities could be removed by a refining process, to prevent deterioration.[161] Each of these three stages is represented in Chinese cultural history.

Sugar cane was known to the people of late Chou and Han as a product of the warmer parts of the South, especially of Annam.[162] The "sugar liquor" mentioned by Szu-ma Hsiang-ju may even refer to a drink fermented from it by the southerners. At any rate, the Chinese liked the juice, and in time learned to grow the plant, so that by T'ang times it was growing well in central Szechwan, northern Hupeh, and coastal Chekiang.[163] Even so, it was not an everyday sort of plant, and stalks of sugar cane remained costly in the north. This was so even as late as the eighth century; we may read how Tai Tsung gave twenty sticks of sugar cane to a subject as a rare and wonderful gift.[164] Moreover, the sugar cane was one of the many natural things, like the peacock and lotus, which were involved in complicated imagery surrounding the Buddha: Shakyamuni was surnamed *Ikṣvāku*, "sugar cane," since one

of his ancestors was said to have been born from that plant,[165] and Wei Kao, conqueror of the Tibeto-Burman tribes on the Burmese frontier, sent to the court of
T'ang, along with other dances of Nan-chao, one called "King of the Sugar Cane,"
". . . which means that the instruction of the people by the Buddha is like the sugar
cane in its sweetness, and all rejoice in its flavor." [166]

One form in which sugar was prepared for everyday consumption was as little
cakes or loaves which passed under the name of "stone honey." These were made in
Tongking as early as the third century from sugar produced by drying the juice of
the cane in the sun.[167] Sometimes these were shaped into little men, tigers, elephants,
and the like. The "lion sugars" of Later Han are an example of these sweet figurines,[168]
but it is not certain that the sugar in them came from the Southern cane. In T'ang
times this "stone sugar" was manufactured in several towns; sugar cakes destined for
the imperial tables came from Lu-*chou* in southeastern Shansi, which sent them
northward, along with ginseng, linen, and ink; [169] they also came from Yüeh-*chou*
in northern Chekiang, along with cinnabar, porcelain, and damasks,[170] and from
Yung-*chou* in southern Hunan, along with kudzu, arrow shafts, and interesting
fossils.[171]

Though the source of sugar in these preparations differed from place to place,
milk was a constant ingredient. A good, lasting variety was made near the capital
from white honey and milk curds; [172] in some places it was prepared by boiling rice
powder in carabao milk, which produced a hard, heavy cake; [173] but the finest and
whitest was made from sugar cane and milk, a process employed exclusively in
Szechwan and among the "Persians." [174] These "Persians" must have been east
Iranians generally, since there were gifts of "stone honey" to the emperor from
Bukhāra and Khwārizm in the eighth century.[175] Samarkand had it too, for we read
of that place:

The people are addicted to wine, and like to sing and dance in the streets. Their king
has a hat of felt, decorated with gold and various jewels. The women have coiled chignons,
which they cover with a black kerchief sewed with gold foil. When one bears a child,
she feeds it with stone honey, and places glue in its palm, desiring that it speak sweetly
when grown up.[176]

The superior quality of the "stone honey" from the Far West induced T'ai
Tsung to send envoys to Magadha to learn its secret, which seemed to depend on a
superior ingredient. The art was accordingly imparted to the sugarmakers of Yang-
chou. They prepared a sugar by boiling the juice of the cane, which ". . . was in
color and taste far beyond that which was produced in the Western Regions." [177] It
was called *sha t'ang,* "sandy (or granular) sugar." [178] This seems to have been no
more than a rather good "brown sugar," granular, but not truly refined. Sugar cakes
made of unrefined sugar contain much else besides sucrose, and will decompose into
a sticky mess fairly soon.[179] A pure, white, crystalline sugar must be made by repeatedly and efficiently removing the scum from the boiling liquid. It does not

seem that this was done in T'ang times, even by the methods imported from Magadha.[180] Refined crystalline sugar was called in Chinese *t'ang shuang,* "sugar frost," and seems to have been a development of Sung times.[181] But tradition tells that one man knew the method in T'ang, and he may well have been the father of the Sung refining industry. In the sixties or seventies of the eighth century, a certain monk named Tsou came to live on Umbrella Mountain, just north of the town of Hsiao-ch'i ("Little Torrent") in central Szechwan. He knew the art of making "sugar frost" and passed it on to a farmer named Huang; in time there were many sugar refiners operating by the cane fields about the mountain.[182]

Who is this that cometh up out of the wilderness
  like pillars of smoke,
Perfumed with myrrh and frankincense,
With all powders of the merchant?

Song of Solomon 3:6

x= aromatics

INCENSE AND BRAZIERS

IT IS WORTH SAYING again that in the medieval world of the Far East there was little clear-cut distinction among drugs, spices, perfumes, and incenses—that is, among substances which nourish the body and those which nourish the spirit, those which attract a lover and those which attract a divinity. In this chapter we are concerned with those substances whose most important feature was their odor, whether this appealed primarily to man or to god. In T'ang, a man or woman of the upper classes lived in clouds of incense and mists of perfume. The body was perfumed, the bath was scented, the costume was hung with sachets. The home was sweet-smelling, the office was fragrant, the temple was redolent of a thousand sweet-smelling balms and essences.[1] The ideal and imaginative counterparts of this elegant world were the fairylands, paradises, and wonder-worlds of folk tale and poetry, especially those inspired by Taoism (but Buddhist legend is richly perfumed too). These dreamlands are always revealed suffused with marvelous odors, which were conceived as a kind of sustenance of the soul, and therefore uplifting and purifying in their effects, and making for the spiritualization of life and the expansion of the higher faculties.

The holy atmosphere which invested the rites of the Confucian cult was accordingly strengthened by the liberal use of odoriferous gums and resins and of compound perfumes. The center of the cult was the "emperor," that is (more rightly considered), the divine king, nexus of the spiritual forces emanating from Heaven, and responsible for the well-being of all creatures. An illustration: in 775, a certain warlord, a former follower of Rokhshan, seeing as inevitable the elevation to the throne of Rokhshan's rival, Li Cheng-chi (a Korean general in Chinese employ), released Li's envoys from prison, sent him rich gifts, "had a likeness of Cheng-chi drawn, and did service to it with burning incense, at which Cheng-chi rejoiced." [2] In short, the warlord offered the fortunate Korean divine honors. Incense marked the presence of the royal afflatus, breathing supernatural wisdom through the worlds of nature and human affairs. Or it represented the purifying breath of the gods on the affairs in which the emperor acted as their proxy: in 847, the new emperor Hsüan[(1)] Tsung, desiring to restore court etiquette to a more strict and seemly condition, issued a decree in which, among other reforms, he required of himself that he peruse memorials and petitions from his vassals only after he had washed his hands and burned incense.[3] The important symbolic role of incense at the holy court is revealed in its essence by the requirement that at the great levee, when the archaic robes and ceremonial mats had been laid out in the basilica, the "table of aromatics" was to be placed before the Son of Heaven. The great councilors of state then stood before this table and, perfused with the magical fragrance, proceeded to conduct the business of state.[4] Or again, on a lower level, when the candidates for the title of "Advanced Gentleman" were to be examined, chief examiner and candidates alike saluted each other at the aromatics' table by the examination hall.[5] Here too the table showed the presence of the divine and kingly grace.

The sovereign displayed his grace to his favored vassals and honored servants by giving them aromatic gifts. Examples of "manifestoes" addressed to the throne by great courtiers, thanking their lord for gifts of scented drugs, pomades, and rare perfumes, still survive. We have one, for example, written by Chang Chiu-ling, thanking Hsüan Tsung for bestowing certain aromatic drugs and facial unguents on him.[6] The text of a similar document of thanks from another official, for aromatics presented on the occasion of the sacrifice to the Hundred Deities shortly after the winter solstice, lists among the imperial gifts ". . . aromatic drugs in two gold-flowered silver caskets, one casket of facial unguent, two bags of aromatics for perfuming clothes, and one bag of 'washing legumes.'" [7]

Incenses also played a significant part in the worship of the immaterial gods not visible on an earthly throne. Here is a story recorded as told by Rokhshan to his sovereign when he was received at court early in 743:

"During the past year, insects ate the grain sprouts in Ying-*chou*. Your vassal burned aromatics and invoked Heaven in these words: 'If your vassal's management of his heart has not been right, nor his service to his liege-lord loyal, may the insects be made to eat your vassal's heart. But if he has not turned his back on the gods celestial and chthonian, may the insects be made to scatter.' At this there was a flock of birds which came from the North and ate the insects, finishing them off instantly. It is requested that this be deemed suitable for referring to the recording officers." This was complied with.[8]

Whether or not the general's humility (for so it seems in retrospect) shows the whole speech to be an invention, it still serves to illustrate incense-burning as a familiar and ordinary part of the worship of the Chinese gods, wafting a petitioner's words sweetly heavenward.

Buddhism and immigrant Indian culture had brought a number of new odors to the Chinese temples, and with them a rich store of customs and beliefs about incense and perfumes, reinforcing and elaborating the old tradition. It is true that these new manners and attitudes did not have the overwhelming effect in China that they had in Indochina, where a simpler native culture could absorb much more. For instance, the Indianized gentry of the "Red Land" in Malaya (perhaps the Raktamrttika, in modern Province Wellesley, known from a fifth-century inscription) [9] anointed their bodies with aromatic oils, and the kings of Tan-tan plastered their persons with aromatic powders.[10] Things did not go quite that far in T'ang, but this was the climactic age of Buddhism in China, and incenses played a great role, not only in liturgical observances but in literature and the worlds of the imagination. Buddhist books were permeated with aromatic images, and indeed the Sanskrit word *gandha,* "aromatic," often means simply "pertaining to the Buddha." A temple was called *gandhakuṭī,* "house of incense"; the pyre on which the Buddha was cremated became a "fragrant tower"; "Fragrant King" and "Fragrant Elephant" were epithets of Bodhisattvas; and on *Gandhamādana,* "Incense Mountain," dwelt the gandharvas, gods of fragrance and music.[11] All these expressions, and many others like them, were translated into Chinese, enriching T'ang thought along with the T'ang lexicon.

Pleasant odors also entered into secular life, especially the social life of the gentry. We read of a luxurious prince of the eighth century who would not speak to his guests unless he had aloeswood and musk in his mouth, ". . . and then, when he opened his mouth and entered into the conversation, the aromatic breath sprayed over the mat." [12] Such a man would in all likelihood have already bathed in scented hot water before joining the company.[13] Men were as competitive in their perfumery as ladies nowadays with their cakes and jellies: at an elegant party of Chung Tsung's reign the choicest aromatics of his courtiers were displayed, and a kind of fagara paste took the prize.[14] The height of elegance was achieved by Han Hsi-tsai, a tenth-century sybarite, who allowed incenses to blend with the fragrance of his garden flowers, each according to his notion of its suitability—as camphor with osmanthus, aloeswood with bramble, "four exceptions" with orchid, musk with magnolia, and sandal with michelia.[15]

It is not far from these elegances to the use of odors to attract love and to enhance the pleasures of love-making. The aphrodisiac use of perfumes was familiar to the courtesans of T'ang. A lovely and popular Cyprian of eighth-century Ch'ang-an, named "Lotus Fragrance," perfumed herself so delightfully that when she went out of doors ". . . bees and butterflies followed her, obviously in love with her fragrance." [16] Then the story is told about a courtesan under the protection of the great minister Yüan Tsai (he whose confiscated possessions contained so much valuable pepper, as we have seen); she was a very jade-fleshed fairy, who had no need of the artificial aids required by others of the sisterhood, since her farsighted mother had fed her perfumes when she was a child; as a result her body was naturally aromatic, as if she were a true immortal sylph-maiden. Alas! this erotic vision of perfumed flesh, with its Taoist overtones, is from Su O's "Tu-yang Miscellany," and can only be taken as an ideal which fashionable ladies might emulate, but never attain.[17]

It was natural that aromatics should have a more direct role in love medicine, in accordance with their important place among drugs generally. When Hsüan Tsung, who was no longer young, was first infatuated with Lady Yang, Rokhshan made him a gift of a hundred aphrodisiac pills. They were red, no larger than grains of rice, and made from "passion flower aromatic." The monarch would put one in his mouth when he retired to his bedchamber, ". . . to help his passions to develop into excitement, and the strength of his sinews not to flag."[18]

The Chinese produced a not inconsiderable number of perfumes and incenses from their native plants and animals. Cassia, camphor, and liquidambar (or "rose mallow")[19] were extracted from Chinese trees; from Chinese grasses were pressed the essences of sweet basil,[20] whose production was centered around Yung-*chou* in southern Hunan,[21] and citronella,[22] which was used with peach petals to scent hot baths (though the citronella brought from overseas was reputed superior).[23] Among Chinese aromatics of animal origin were civet, much used in medicine to calm the spirit and banish nightmares,[24] and especially musk, snatched from the little musk deer which is widespread in northern and western China. But even the use of musk was faintly tinged with exoticism, for gifts of this persistent perfume came in the eighth century from the barbarian chieftains of Yünnan,[25] and from the Manchurian Hsi, who had been settled at Jao-le;[26] and it was known that even such a distant people as the Persians anointed their beards and spotted their brows with musk during their worship of Ahura-Mazda.[27]

But despite the excellence of these and other native products, it cannot be denied that the array of wonderful aromatics imported from distant lands was spectacular, especially the resins and gum resins: sandalwood and aloeswood, Borneo camphor and patchouli, benzoin and storax, and frankincense and myrrh.[28] Though these treasures came to T'ang from all parts of the world, most of them arrived by ships coming over the South China Sea, such as the cargo of "exotic aromatics" sent by Kalinga in 815.[29] This freight made Canton one of the great incense markets of the world, and next to it Yang-*chou*. The quantities imported must have been tremendous, in view of the extravagant uses of the aristocracy, which extended even to aromatic architecture.[30] The acknowledged superiority of the Indochinese aromatics, besides which those of China were "beggar's incense,"[31] and the apparently inexhaustible sources of perfumes and incenses from "groves whose rich trees wept odorous gums and balms"[32] in the vaguely defined "South Seas," gave rise to the idea of a kind of incense tree, which bore all the important aromatics together. Its roots were sandal, its branches were aloeswood, its flowers were clove, its leaves were patchouli, and its gum was frankincense. One form of the tale puts this tree on Mount Ch'i-lien, the old Mountain in Central Asia, and calls it a "sylph tree," [33] connecting it with a Taoist paradise; but the eleventh-century pharmacologist Su Sung, commenting on this belief of the "men of old," stated that the idea came originally from the people of Bnam, the old pre-Cambodian kingdom on the Gulf of Siam.[34] But this simply puts the holy tree in a different Eden on another cosmic mountain—the kings of Bnam were the kings of the mountain par excellence.

The ancient Egyptians worshiped the sun god Rê at his setting in the West ". . . with an elaborate confection called *ḳuphi,* compounded of no fewer than 16 ingredients, among which were honey, wine, raisins, resin, myrrh and sweet calamus." [35] Blended aromatics were common in the ancient Near East, and in medieval China as well. Indeed, simple, unmixed scents appear to be a comparatively modern preference. The difference between the blends of West and East lay in what ingredients were most readily available: in the West, chiefly frankincense, with myrrh, galbanum, and onycha; in the East, chiefly aloeswood, with frankincense, sandal, cloves, musk, and onycha. So states one modern authority, though the official pharmacopoeia of T'ang makes aloeswood, frankincense, cloves, patchouli, elemi, and liquidambar the six essences most relied on by the blenders of aromatics.[36] An example of a T'ang blended incense, prepared for use in the *Hua tu szu,* a Buddhist establishment in the northwest of Ch'ang-an, near the Nestorian temple, survives: the recipe calls for 1½ ounces of aloeswood, 5 ounces of sandalwood, 1 ounce of storax, 1 ounce of onycha, ½ ounce of Borneo camphor, and ½ ounce of musk. These were ground fine, strained through gauze, and mixed with honey to make a paste.[37] Such aromatic amalgams appear frequently in poetry under the name "hundred-blend aromatics," a name which is much older than T'ang.[38] So Tu Fu has "The exhalations of the flowers mix like 'hundred-blend aromatics,' " [39] and Ch'üan Te-yü, a poet of the late eighth and early ninth centuries, describing a beautiful girl in her boudoir, writes:

> At the green window, pearl screened, embroidered with Mandarin ducks,
> An attendant slave-girl first burns a "hundred-blend aromatic." [40]

Kneaded incense blends from T'ang were also much esteemed in Japan; the exported product normally contained aloeswood, sugar, and plum meat.[41]

It appears that a similar concoction was *imported* into T'ang: Tukhāra sent envoys in 724 with a present of two hundred *"gandhaphala"* of exotic drugs.[42] *Gandhaphala,* "fragrant fruit," is a name given in India to a number of different trees with aromatic fruits, but in our texts, if my reading of the Chinese transcription of the Sanskrit name is right, we have to do with pastilles of mixed aromatic drugs, molded in the shapes of fruits.

Once arrived on the soil of T'ang, the sweet-smelling exotic substances were put to various uses, according to their natures and the needs of their owners. Luxurious fashion demanded that the woody materials be turned over to the carpenter and cabinetmaker. The most notable example of this kind of extravagance was a "gallery" built of aloeswood by Hsüan Tsung's minister Yang Kuo-chung; it had sandalwood railings, and walls plastered with musk and frankincense mixed with earth. It was the custom for the minister's fine guests to come to this odorous pavilion in the spring to view his peonies at the height of their bloom.[43]

But only the greatest wealth could command the materials for such prodigality; in the main, even gentlemen of considerable means turned these imports to the customary uses of incenses and perfumes.

It was pleasant to burn an aromatic candle in a bedroom or private chamber, and we often read about aromatic wicks and candles in the verses of the T'ang poets. A notable example was the fragrant candles of the emperor I Tsung, which, though only two inches long, would burn all night long, spreading a ravishing aroma all around.[44] A special form of the incense candle was the graduated candle, used to tell time during the night. This device may well have been first used by Buddhist monks at their vigils. It was well known before T'ang times, as a couplet by the sixth-century poet Yü Chien-wu testifies:

> By burning incense we know the o'clock of the night,
> With graduated candle we confirm the tally of the watches.[45]

Closely allied to these time-telling candles were the "incense clocks," as we would now call them, referred to in the first verse of Yü's couplet. These were elaborate traceries of powdered incense on a flat surface which had been incised with characters standing for the divisions of time. The time was read off as the fire burned its way through the narrow path of incense which led from sign to sign. These clocks were commonly called "aromatic seals," since the archaic figures made in incense were similar to those carved on a gentleman's personal seal. The courtly poet Wang Chien has made one the symbol of a lonely vigil:

> I sit at ease, burning a seal of incense;
> It fills the doorway with breath of pine and thuja.
> The fire is used up all round—and clear-cut now
> Are the letters on that blue-mossed stele.[46]

(The clock is burned out, dawn has come, and the poet can read the inscription on a stone tablet in his garden). The base on which the powder was poured and burned was normally of wood, as we find it in a tenth-century source, which describes a quaint modification: "If, when you are using a wooden mold, with incense fragments spread in a seal-character text, you quickly invert it, that makes 'winding river incense.'"[47] Some of the clock bases were of stone, however, and examples of these can still be seen in the Shōsōin: one is a circular stone slab, set in an elaborately carved wooden lotus, whose petals are gilded and painted with mythological figures.[48]

This museum piece was cut with Devanagari characters, not with Chinese seal characters, and this often appears to have been the case; it follows that the incense clock was much used in a Buddhist environment, or was even an Indian invention. Here is such a one in a couplet of Tuan Ch'eng-shih:

> Translated and clarified are the *gāthās* from under Western skies;
> Burned is the balance of incense in Sanskrit characters.[49]

But in homes and at ordinary rites, incense was burned in a brazier, sometimes made of precious substances, like the one of jade described in Li Ho's poem, "Strings of the Gods," which tells of a shamaness, strumming her lute with a plectrum of the wood called "thinking-of-you," and calling on a god to possess her:

> The girl-shaman pours a wine libation—clouds fill the void;
> From charcoal fire in the jade brazier, perfume—with her drum's "tong! tong!"
> Sea gods and mountain demons come into the seance,
> Paper coins, rustling, rattling, give voice in the whirling wind.
> With wood called "thinking-of-you," gold simurghs appliquéd,
> Each chatter, with drawing of brows, is doubled with one thrum;
> She calls the stars, she summons the demons, to savor of goblet and bowl—
> At feeding time of mountain goblins men shudder with the cold.
> At South End Mountains the sun's color pulls a curve into the horizon—
> The god, ah! how long is he here, between being and not-being!?
> At god's wrath, or god's joy, his mistress alters her face—
> Then, escorting the god, a myriad riders go back to the blue mountains.[50]

Braziers of the more traditional sort were in the shape of "Universe Mountains," whose slopes were sometimes populated with divine forms. A particularly grand example of this ancient style was kept in front of his bed by Wang Yüan-pao, a lover of luxury, who also had a hall with aloeswood railings: "two sculptured dwarf lads, holding up a Universe Mountain brazier, done in the Seven Jewels: he burned incense in it from fall of darkness right through until daybreak."[51] This was nothing, however, when compared with the "hundred-jewel incense brazier" in a Buddhist temple in Lo-yang; the gift of a royal princess, it was three feet high and had four mouths; it was adorned with pearls, carnelian, amber, coral, and every kind of precious gem, and chased with the figures of birds and beasts, gods and devils, angelic beings and divine musicians, and every sort of mythological being. This stunning production cost thirty thousand in cash, and exhausted the treasury of its precious substances.[52]

A popular kind of brazier was shaped like a bird or animal, real or imaginary—lions, unicorns, and the like—sometimes with the fragrant smoke issuing from their mouths. Especially common were ducks[53] and elephants.[54] And, to judge by a poem of Li Shang-yin, some braziers were provided with windows of mica.[55]

The Chinese had used long-handled censers since Han times. One variety had handles decorated with lions, was also known in medieval Central Asia and Gandhāra, and was ultimately, perhaps, derived from ancient Egypt.[56] Censers were exported from China to Japan, and handsome examples are preserved in the Shōsōin and in the Tōshōdaiji temple in Nara. They are usually made of copper alloyed with other metals—for instance, antimony and gold—but there is a sumptuous example of sanderswood, with floral decorations in gold, silver, and gemstones.[57]

"Censing baskets" were globes of hollow metal, pierced with intricate floral or animal designs; within the globe, an iron cup, suspended on gimbals, contained the burning incense. They were used to perfume garments and bedclothes, and even to kill insects. Examples made of silver and of bronze survive in the Shōsōin,[58] and we may read of them in Wang Chien's lyrics on court life, as in the verse "In the bottom of the silver censing basket the fire is flurried like snow." [59] But this kind of thurible was not the only device used to impregnate clothing with scent. The wife of the minister Yüan Tsai devised the following procedure:

She took forty blue and purple silk cords, each one ten-foot long, and set out on all of them her finery of net and taffeta and damask and embroidery. Beneath each strand of cord she placed an array of twenty gold and silver braziers, with exotic aromatics burning in each, and the aroma pervaded her garments.[60]

The custom of hanging sachets and scent bags of all kinds in the clothing, especially on the girdle, goes back to ancient times in China, as does the custom of perfuming aristocratic carriages. The tradition was well maintained in T'ang, when sweet basil formed a standard basis for costume scents.[61] Court ladies especially were profusely scented, and contemporary sources say that the odor of a court procession could be detected over a distance of several miles.[62] Here is a monkish picture of the perfumed ladies of T'ang, by "Cold Mountain" (Han-shan):

> Myself came briefly down the mountain,
> And went inside the city wall and fosse.
> I chanced to see a gaggle of girls,
> Erect and straight, fair of feature and form.
> Their heads bore flowers in the style of Shu,
> They were sleek with rouge and powder-daubed;
> Their golden bracelets—chased with silver blossoms,
> Their gauzy garments—pink and puce and purple;
> Their vermeil faces—akin to goddesses and sylphs;
> Their perfumed girdles—richly fuming vapors.
> Being men of the age, all looked back to stare,
> And doting affection dyed their hearts and minds.
> The words they said were "matchless in the world!"
> As with soul and shadow they followed them away.
> Like dogs which gnaw on lumps of rotten bone,
> They vainly licked their very lips and teeth,
> Not knowing how to turn to thought and reason—
> In what do they ever differ from livestock?
> Now those will become white-haired crones,

Old and ugly, just like ghosts and goblins.
These, prompted from first to last by currish hearts,
Will not leap out to the land of escape and freedom.[63]

It was not unmanly to be well perfumed: a poem of the ninth century tells of a young soldier embarking on an evening of pleasure with foreign courtesans in the capital; he rides a white horse, has a shirt with a phoenix pattern, and "the famous aromas of strange countries fill his sleeve with scent." [64] Even the emperor wore perfume bags, especially at the festival of the winter solstice, when it was a matter of convention.[65]

A famous scent bag was the one buried with Yang Kuei-fei. After his return from Szechwan, Hsüan Tsung sent an emissary to remove her body secretly from the wayside grave at Ma Wei. This agent found the bag still there and brought it to the sovereign, who wept from grief.[66]

Usually these sachets were made of some colored or flowered stuff, especially of fine gauze. There are several small ones in the Shōsōin, of gauze net and of linen.[67] Finally, there were the aromatic balls, mentioned in poetry, which were tossed skillfully about by dancing girls of T'ang.[68]

ALOESWOOD

Agaru, the Sanskrit name for the favorite aromatic substance of T'ang, has spawned a considerable progeny of English synonyms. From Malay *gahru,* Hebrew *ahaloth,* Portuguese *aguila,* and the like, we derive "garroo" (in trade jargon), "aloes," "eagle-wood," and even "agalloch." [69] These words and their relatives stand for a product of various trees of genus *Aquilaria,* native to Southeast Asia.[70] The aloeswood of the incense trade is heavy, dark, diseased wood, distinct from the lighter, softer wood around it. It is saturated with resin and richly scented. Sometimes these pathologically fragrant patches occur in the shapes of men and animals, which increases their market value greatly.[71]

The Chinese name for the best of this precious wood was "sinking aromatic," because it was heavier than water. One T'ang writer tells how the Chams obtained it: "They chop them down and stack them up for years upon twelvemonths. When they have rotted and disintegrated, so that only the heart and joints remain, they place these in water, at which they sink, and so we name this 'sinking aromatic.' " [72] But, adds another, "If it floats, and the patterning in its flesh has black veins, it is *tsïän* aromatic. Both 'chicken bone' and 'horse hoof' are kinds of *tsïän* aromatic, and neither has any special virtue [in medicine]; they are only fit for fumigating clothes and expelling odors." [73] These last are names for various cheaper commercial varieties of the incense.

In the West, China was the reputed source of aloeswood. We hear, for instance, of an Ibāḍite merchant of Oman who went to China in the eighth century and bought it there.[74] But despite the fact that the city of Canton sent garroo to Ch'ang-an regularly as local tribute, along with silver, orchids, lichees, and python bile,[75] it seems almost certain that the aloeswood was obtained on the Annamese marches.[76] The "China" of the Muslims was not a primary producer but a great emporium. Probably most of the aloeswood used in China was imported, especially from Champa, whose kings sent it to Ch'ang-an during the eighth century, including one gift of thirty catties of "black" lignaloes.[77] It seems likely that the civilized Chams relied heavily on the aboriginal tribes of the mountains to find the diseased trees, then as now. In the nineteenth century the *gahlao,* as the Chams call it, was gathered ceremoniously by a single village of Muslim Chams in Binh-Thuan province, in close collaboration with the *orang glai,* "forest men." Even as recently as that it was very important in both Cham and Annamese rituals.[78]

Aloeswood had a strong place in Chinese medicine, being employed to alleviate all sorts of internal pains, to drive out evil spirits, and to purify the soul. For these purposes, it was supposed to be decocted in wine; it was also added to ointments for application to external lesions.[79] The prevalence of aloes in T'ang incenses and fumigants indicates that the odorous smoke was thought, as in India,[80] to have a beneficial effect on ulcerations and wounds. Whether the report of Abū Zayd of Sīrāf, early in the tenth century, that the kings of China were buried in a preparation of aloes and camphor, has any actual foundation, I have not been able to learn.[81]

In any case, the importance of aloeswood in medieval Chinese incenses for every sort of ritual and private purpose was enormous. A quatrain by Li Ho will serve to illustrate this importance in miniature. It shows a young lordling awaiting the dawn in his lonely room:

> Curling, swirling—the smoke of "Sinks-in-water,"
> A crow cries out—the spectacle of a worn night,
> A winding pond—the ripples among the lotuses.
> The waist-girding white jades are cold.[82]

A scented water prepared from garroo is said to have been used to "dye" the garments of certain courtesans,[83] presumably to make the ladies more stimulating to the senses, but a more extravagant use of the precious wood was to perfume buildings. The aromatic was made into a powder and applied to the desired part—in the case of one Tsung Ch'u-k'o, to the walls of his mansion, to overwhelm the visitor when the door was opened.[84] None of this perfumed architecture has survived, but in the Shōsōin there is a long hexagonal sutra-box, which is coated with aloeswood powder and decorated with cloves and the red "love-seeds" of "wild licorice,"[85] a suitable container for the fragrant words of the Buddha.

It was natural that small and precious objects should be made of garroo—an example is the writing brush, partly of aloes and partly of spotted bamboo, bound by birchbark strips, which is kept in the Shōsōin.[86] It seems incredible that pieces large enough to provide the timbers of a building could exist, and yet this is precisely what is reported in reliable sources of the ninth century. A Persian merchant seaman[87] presented the new emperor Ching Tsung, a stripling with luxurious tastes, with enough aloeswood to make a kiosk—a bit of folly for which the young sovereign was severely reproved by one of his officers.[88] This costly pavilion had its prototype in one built for Hsüan Tsung a century earlier, in front of which the imperial collection of tree peonies—red, purple, pink, and white—was planted. But it was alleged that Yang Kuo-chung's aloeswood kiosk was the most richly beautiful of all.[89] The undiseased wood of *Aquilaria* is fragrant when freshly cut, and even pieces only partly impregnated with resin may be used as incense, though this is not the true "sinking aromatic."[90] Perhaps it was planks of this healthier and less odorous wood which went into the framework of the pleasure buildings.

LAKAWOOD

Another woody incense material used in T'ang was *kayu laka,* or lakawood, the scented heartwood of a rosewood liana, imported from Indonesia.[91] "Its aroma is like that of sapanwood," wrote the pharmacologist Li Hsün, "but it is not very aromatic when you first set fire to it. But if you take a variety of aromatics and blend them with it, it is outstandingly fine."[92] In T'ang it was named "purple liana aromatic" (but the wisteria was also called "purple liana"!), and above all it was the "aromatic which brings down the True Ones." The "True Ones" are the immortal sylphs of Taoism, nourished on dew and air, and the name shows the special importance of this incense in Taoist temples.[93] In a poem on a Taoist theme, Ts'ao T'ang matched a longevity potion with the god-bringing incense:

> Reddish dew gives me an image of upturning "the wine which extends life,"
> Whitish smoke puts me in mind of burning "the aromatic which brings down
> the True Ones."[94]

The magical or medicinal uses of lakawood are hard to distinguish from the religious: it was burned to get rid of all that was "weird and strange in house and home," and pieces were attached to small children to fend off evil vapors.[95]

ELEMI

The medieval Chinese were familiar with more than one of the oleoresins yielded by tropical trees of genus *Canarium*. These are called elemis, or breas. The brea of the "Chinese olive,"[96] a native of Kwangtung, was used as a calking varnish in T'ang. Because of its texture, it was called "kanari sugar."[97] But the Chinese had another elemi, which was among the products submitted by the metropolitan area of Canton.[98] This was called *"trâm*-sugar aromatic," *trâm* being Annamese for "kanari" (i.e., *Canarium* tree). It was the elemi of the copaliferous kanari [99] which in T'ang times grew in some parts of Lingnan, presumably near the Annamese border. But Tongking is the center of production. It is a whitish granular substance, redolent of lemon and turpentine; [100] but the incense is usually black because of an admixture of carbon.[101] "It resembles the bitter-peel tangerine," wrote Su Kung, "and the branches are decocted to make the aromatic, which resembles granular sugar, but is black. It comes from Kuang and Chiao and south of there." [102] It must have been used in Ch'ang-an, as it was in Tongking, to burn on the altars of the gods.

CAMPHOR

Chinese (or "Japanese") camphor [103] is "dextro-camphor," a crystalline substance taken from the wood of a large tree of China, Japan, and Tongking. Borneo (or "Sumatra") camphor [104] is "laevo-borneol," a similar product extracted from a tall Indonesian and Malayan tree.[105] It is the latter which is in most demand in China, and it was the camphor of the trade with Europe from medieval until modern times.[106]

Two names for Borneo camphor were current in medieval China. One of them transcribed *kapur Baros,* "camphor of Baros," from Malayan trade jargon; sometimes it was called simply "ointment of Baros." [107] Baros was a settlement on the west coast of Sumatra, once a chief place of camphor export.[108] The other name was "dragon brain aromatic." Strange and precious substances brought from overseas were easily related in imagination to the dragons who ruled the seas, and so ambergris was called "dragon spittle." Attempts were made in T'ang to distinguish "Baros ointment" from "dragon brain," none too successfully. Some said that one came from fat trees, and the other from lean trees, though it was not certain which was which.[109] Others said that "Baros" was the clear sap of the tree, while "dragon brain" was the dried product.[110] Indeed, the word "ointment," usually applied to "Baros," suggests that it was marketed as a more or less unctuous product, as distinct from the crystalline "dragon brain." In addition to these, the empire of Śrivijaya produced a "dragon brain oil." [111]

The home of Borneo camphor was obscure to the men of T'ang. Was it Baros, or was it Bali? The names were almost identical in Chinese transcription.[112] Then it was said that the Persians produced it [113]—but this, as so frequently happened, was to assume that the products brought by Persian merchantmen were themselves Persian. The good monk Hsüan-tsang reported that camphor was produced in a place called Malakūta on the Malabar coast: [114] ". . . in form like 'cloud-mother' [mica], its color was like ice or snow." [115] Presumably the camphor tree had been successfully introduced there. It was reported that in eastern Kalinga the dead had their mouths stuffed with gold and were cremated on a fire loaded with camphor.[116]

As for known imports, the king of Dagon, a dependency of Dvāravatī, sent gifts of Baros ointment in the seventh century;[117] the great nation of Udyāna, rich in gold, iron, and saffron, sent "dragon brain" in the same century, and received in return an imperial letter of thanks;[118] even the Arabs, though far from the source of supply, sent it, but that was a century later.[119] All in all, camphor brought the warm odor of the South.

In late medieval times camphor was packed for export in joints of bamboo, so that the traveler Ibn Baṭṭūṭa thought it grew that way.[120] It is likely that the commercial camphor which came to T'ang was treated in the same way. Once in China, camphor was stored in a mixture of glutinous rice, charcoal, and red "love-seeds."[121]

The odor of camphor was extravagantly admired in T'ang, and it was an ingredient of many scents and incenses. The most famous of its kind was the "auspicious dragon brain" (as it was called in the palace) sent as tribute from Tongking to Hsüan Tsung. This highly aromatic camphor was molded into the forms of cicadas and silkworms, as amulets to be worn in the clothing, and the monarch gave ten of these to his favorite, the Lady Yang. Here we may continue the story of the *go* game, accompanied by the lute music of Ho Huai-chih, which was interrupted by a pet dog—we began it in an earlier chapter:

At this time, the wind blew the neckerchief of the Precious Consort on top of the kerchief of Ho Huai-chih. Then, after a good while, it fell off as he turned his body. When Ho Huai-chih returned home, he became aware that his body was full of an unusually fragrant aroma. Accordingly he removed his headdress and stored it in a brocaded bag. Now when His Illustrious Highness returned to the "palace pylons" [from exile] he thought back unceasingly to the Precious Consort. Therefore Huai-chih submitted to him the headdress which he had in storage, and set forth the affair of that other day circumstantially. His Illustrious Highness opened the bag, and said, weeping, "This is the aroma of the 'auspicious dragon brain!' "[122]

Another anecdote shows how the odor of camphor was particularly relished in one's clothes. The boy emperor Ching Tsung made a bizarre game of shooting his concubines with paper arrows containing powdered borneol and musk, which gave a powerful fragrance to the lucky ladies who were hit.[123]

According to the official pharmacopoeia, camphor cured evil vapors in heart and belly, and was especially recommended for eye troubles, including cataract.[124] According to the eighth-century alchemist, Chang Kao, it should be mixed with musk (apparently a frequent combination) to cure "winds" which had settled in the bone marrow.[125] Indian prescriptions for the medicinal use of camphor followed the article itself into T'ang. The Chinese version of a Buddhist sutra honoring the Bodhisattva Avalokiteśvara advises a person who has been bitten by a poisonous insect to mix equal quantities of Borneo camphor and guggul in pure water, and ". . . chant the dhāraṇī 10 times in front of the image of Avalokiteśvara. As soon as chanted, one is cured."[126] This useful medicine had a more practical use too. Wang Yen-pin, nephew of the warlord who later founded the Min "empire" in Fukien, was chief magistrate of Zayton early in the tenth century. He added to the prosperity of his city and of the province by encouraging trade with the argosies coming up from the South Seas, and must be regarded as one of the founders of Zayton's fame and later ascendancy. He was, however, an esthete and good-liver, and had a standard remedy for overindulgence in liquor: he poured several vessels of liquid camphor over himself at the end of a party, and then slept until noon.[127]

Camphor was even used in food. A delicacy prepared for the imperial table in 825 (the youthful Ching Tsung again) was "clear wind rice." This was a smooth mixture of "crystalline rice," "dragon eyeball powder," "dragon brain fragments," and cow milk. The mixture was placed in metal tubs, which were lowered into an "ice pool." When thoroughly chilled it was removed from the refrigerator for the monarch's delight on the hottest days.[128] There must have been a magical meaning in the selection of the aromatic ingredient, as well as the others: camphor flakes look like "ice and snow," and therefore have a cooling effect.

The camphor insects sent from Annam have already been mentioned. The custom of making such figurines was known also in China, under T'ang or soon after. In the tenth century, T'ao Ku, author of *Ch'ing i lu,* wrote that, although he was familiar with Buddhist images made of camphor, he had never seen a colored one; nevertheless, he added, this rarity existed in a temple in K'ai-feng: it was the figure of a boy, carved with great skill, and painted in natural colors.[129]

STORAX

The classical storax[130] imported to China long ago from Rome and Parthia had been dark purple in color, and some said it was lion's dung—a fearful drug.[131] This scented resin was, it seems, popular and well-known in pre-T'ang times, and it is this substance which the archaizing poet Ch'en Piao had in mind when he wrote of an ancient king surveying his city:

> The palace pylons of the king of Ch'in, clouded with smokes of spring,
> The gemmy branches of a tree of pearls, approaching the indigo sky.
> The wafted aroma of the autocrat's air, revealing the storax there,
> The floating motion of the light from his screen, hung with watery crystal.
> Thin flurrying gauze and crepe follow his scented sleeve,
> Smooth flexing mermaid's silk pursues his jeweled mat.
> From this spot to Kumdan—a single turn of his head—
> The autumn colors of sunset clouds from a thousand years ago.[132]

The place of this Western resin in China can be compared with that of another, myrrh, but unlike it, myrrh was the least noted of the exotic resins. But when we come down to T'ang times, the substance which passed as "storax" was in fact a Malayan balsam, useful in making perfumes.[133] Its fanciful name, invented in the tenth century, is "God's tallow."[134] Like other perfumes, bits of it were carried about on the person, often suspended from the belt. Hence Li Tuan's couplet:

> Vagrant youths with pellets of storax;
> Glee-maidens with palm-leaf fans.[135]

GUM GUGGUL AND BENZOIN

Under the name of "Arsacid aromatic"[136]—that is, Parthian aromatic—the Chinese knew more than one substance. In pre-T'ang times it was given to bdellium, or gum guggul,[137] a widely used adulterant of frankincense. From the ninth century the same name was transferred to benzoin, or gum benjoin, an aromatic resin of Indochina and Indonesia.[138] This change and the change in the meaning of "storax" signalize the increasing importance of the products of the Indies in the economy of medieval China at the expense of the Syrian and Iranian ones. As a result the Chinese sources of T'ang times are full of ambiguities, since the name was applied to both the Western and the Southern aromatics, and both seem to have been used for the same purposes.

In the fourth century the wonder-working priest Fo-t'u Teng used "Arsacid aromatic," that is, gum guggul, in his rain-making ceremonies;[139] this is the first reference to it in China. In the fifth and sixth centuries it came from the Buddhist countries of Turkestan, and was especially associated with Gandhāra.[140] Gandhāra had been a great source of both Buddhist doctrine and exotic perfumery for the Chinese, though it provided the aromatics only as an intermediary in a profitable trade; it could not claim them as home-grown products. Moreover, the very name "Gandhāra" was interpreted as meaning "Aromatic Country." Therefore a fragrant gum coming from that land, itself once part of the Parthian domains, easily acquired the name of the dynasty which had ruled it.[141]

In mid-T'ang times, then, Sumatran benzoin, known to the Arabs as *lubān Jāwi,* "frankincense of Java," came to T'ang as a substitute for bdellium, and passed under the same Chinese name. So it was possible for Li Hsün to write that "Arsacid aromatic" was produced both in the South Seas and in Persia.[142] The confusion was easy: both substances could be and were palmed off as frankincense, and both were brought by commercial vessels, some of Persian origin, up through the South China Sea.

The attributes of gum guggul were passed on to benzoin. When Tuan Ch'eng-shih reported that the Persian tree which produces "Arsacid aromatic" was also called "tree which drives away perverse beings," [143] he meant gum guggul, the original incense of Parthia. The T'ang writers on drugs affirmed that "Arsacid aromatic" quells evil demons within the body,[144] and that if the genitals of a woman haunted by an incubus are fumigated with it, it will quit her forever.[145] Though they referred to the traditional apotropaic properties of guggul, the drug they prescribed, in some cases at any rate, was actually Indonesian benzoin.

FRANKINCENSE

Frankincense, or olibanum, is a gum resin produced by a south Arabian tree[146] and by a related tree in Somaliland.[147] The gum was known to the Chinese under two names, one going back to the third century B.C. and transcribing Sanskrit *kunduruka*, "frankincense,"[148] and the other a descriptive phrase, *ju hsiang,* "teat aromatic," given to mammillary pieces, of the kind described by Pliny: "The incense, however, that is most esteemed of all is that which is mammose, or breast-shaped, and is produced when one drop has stopped short, and another, following close upon it, has adhered, and united with it."[149] The cabalistic name "Floating Lard from the Holy Flower"[150] was probably used only by alchemists.

Frankincense seems not to have been particularly associated by the men of T'ang with either of its homes, the Hadramaut, where it was guarded by winged serpents,[151] or Somaliland, the Punt to which Queen Hatshepsut and other Egyptian rulers sent their expeditions. Su Kung reports a white kind from India, and a weakly aromatic kind with a green interior from Mongolia.[152] Li Hsün has it derived from Persia, as he does so many articles of commerce.[153] In some cases we have to do with pieces of the true frankincense which had circulated widely among the markets of Asia, and in others, no doubt, with fragrant forgeries.

Frankincense had been, with stacte, onycha, and galbanum, one of the ingredients of the sacred incense of the old Hebrew ceremonies, and it also found its proper place in Christian ritual.[154] In T'ang as well it was chiefly used as an incense, though to a much smaller extent. Moreover, it was very expensive. Feng Jo-fang, the Hainanese pirate, who lived lavishly among his Persian slaves, burned frankincense only to give light for his parties—a case of sumptuously conspicuous waste.[155] Similarly, as a grand gesture of contempt for worldly wealth, one Ts'ao Mu-kuang burned ten catties of the precious incense in a basin, saying, "Wealth is easily obtained, but the Buddha is hard to find."[156]

"Teat aromatic" had some place in medicine, and was prescribed for external ulcers and intestinal complaints;[157] Taoist doctors recommended it as a life-extending substitute for cereals.[158] A rather unexpected application was the invention of Chang Yen-yüan, the author of a history of painting: he mixed powdered frankincense with paste to glue paintings to their scrolls, claiming that it kept the mountings firm and bookworms out.[159]

Myrrh   A DRUG.

Myrrh,[160] like frankincense, is a gum resin of Africa and Arabia, of holy reputation in the ancient Near East. It is remembered particularly as one of the substances required by the ancient Egyptian embalmers,[161] a tradition continued by Nicodemus to preserve the body of Jesus. The dark red aromatic was little known in T'ang, and then primarily to druggists, who gave it in wine for wounds from metal blades and falls from horses, apparently as an analgesic,[162] and for miscarriages and pains following on childbirth.[163] It was known in T'ang only under an approximation of its Semitic name *murr*,[164] though in the tenth-century catalogue of drugs with odd names, it appears as "blood from the tongue of the *Man* dragon."[165] I have seen no record of its use in incense or perfume and, except for its fame, would have treated it under "Drugs" in the next chapter.   ?? SO WHY NOT TREAT AS DRUG?

Cloves

Cloves might have been discussed under "Foods" or under "Drugs," since the spice had as varied uses in China as in the West. But its aromatic character seems to have outweighed its other qualities, and, as it was often mixed into incense and the like by the men of T'ang, it has been included here.[166]

The older name for cloves was "chicken tongue aromatic," referring to the shape of the dried immature flower buds; a newer name was "nail aromatic," which also described their shape, just as does our word "clove," from Latin *clavis* through Old French *clou*, "nail."[167] "Nail aromatic" was the name originally given to the flowers of several native Chinese lilacs because of the form of their little blossoms, and in T'ang poetry it seems always to denote "lilac fragrance," not the imported spice. Contrariwise, "chicken aromatic," which means "clove" in our sense, was an abbreviated form that appeared in the verses of such late T'ang poets as Li Shang-yin and Huang T'ao, who were interested in the senses generally and odors particularly.

Cloves were imported from Indonesia. Li Hsün mentions the "Eastern Sea," apparently referring to their original home in the Moluccas.[168] Su Kung, on the other hand, asserts that cloves are also produced in Annam, from which we must conclude that the useful tree had been introduced there.[169]

An old and respected use for cloves, going back to Han times, was to sweeten the breath,[170] and great officers of state were required to have a few cloves in their mouths when they addressed reports to the Son of Heaven.[171] Cloves were also used

171

in complex incenses and perfumes, and one authority reports an aromatic essence made by "brewing" the flowers of the male tree.[172]

Though cloves were apparently not used in T'ang cookery to the same extent as nowadays in the West, there is a record of finely sliced meat "soaked in 'nail aromatic,'" that is, marinated in a liquor flavored with cloves.[173] Drinkers had a use for the spice too: chewing a clove was thought to increase one's capacity for wine, and to hold off drunkenness indefinitely.[174]

Cloves were used for a variety of medicinal purposes, including "killing insects, driving off evils, getting rid of wicked things," not to mention the cure of piles.[175] They were also applied with a ginger extract to patchy white beards to turn them richly black.[176] But above all they provided a sovereign remedy for toothache, famous through the ancient and modern worlds. Eugenol, the active ingredient in oil of cloves, occurs in "clove bark," which Li Hsün prescribed for toothache.[177]

PUTCHUK

Putchuk, or costus root, yields a volatile oil giving the unique odor of violets, and is of importance in perfumery.[178] It is called "wood aromatic" in Chinese.[179] It had been noted in China for its powerful fragrance and used there as early as the beginning of the Christian era. It was chiefly regarded as a product of the Kashmir, but in T'ang times was known as a product of Kabūdhān and Ceylon.[180] It does not appear on the lists of "tribute" from Kashmir, but perhaps it was concealed under the collective "Western drugs" received from that country early in the eighth century.[181] The official book of materia medica, however, states that the kind which came sea-borne by way of the Indies was the best quality, whereas that coming overland from the West was poor.[182] Costus root apparently played a minor role in making blended incenses and perfumes,[183] and was also used in medicine, especially for pains around the heart: "If a woman is stabbed to the heart by blood or breath, and the pain cannot be borne, give her a dose of it, triturated in wine."[184]

PATCHOULI

A Malayan mint[185] yields the fragrant black oil which was called *malábathron* or *phýllon Indikón*, "Indian leaf," in the classical West.[186] Its Sanskrit name is *tamālapattra*, but we know it by a name derived from Tamil, *paccilai*, "green leaf." In Chinese, patchouli was called "bean-leaf aromatic,"[187] from its appearance.

Patchouli was a product of Tenasserim in T'ang times,[188] but by the eleventh century it was growing in the Canton region,[189] where it can be found today.[190] It had been known in China from the same Malayan source since about the third century of the Christian era, and was used to perfume clothing.[191] It had been enthusiastically adopted in India, where it was also a perfume for ladies' hair.[192] Indeed, patchouli was so closely associated with Indian shawls during the Second Empire and the mid-Victorian period that Europeans insisted that they have this charming odor, and even used it as a test of the genuineness of the shawls.[193] The perfume is frequently referred to under its Sanskrit name in Chinese translations of the Buddhist scriptures (for instance, the Tantric *Śūraṅgama-sūtra,* translated in 705) as an ingredient in purifying baths and especially in sacred water for bathing the image of the Buddha.[194] The monks of T'ang presumably followed these rubrics.

JASMINE OIL

Two kinds of exotic jasmine were known to the men of T'ang, one under its Persian name *yāsaman,*[195] and another under its Indic name *mallikā.*[196] Both were established in the Canton region.[197] The aromatic flowers were associated with Persia, Arabia, and Rome, and symbolized love and beauty, especially lovely fairylike women.[198]

It was known in China in the middle of the eighth century that Islam pressed a smooth and fragrant oil from jasmine flowers.[199] It is in fact a famous Persian product, once manufactured at Dārābejird, Sābūr, and Shīrāz.[200] But although this oil was brought into the port of Canton in Sung times,[201] we do not know for certain that any of the almost fabulous perfume was brought to T'ang.

ROSE WATER

Nero is said to have had fountains of rose water, and Elegabalus is reported to have bathed in rose wine, but no rose water has been observed in China before 958, when King Śri Indravarman of Champa sent a certain Abū Hasan to the court of Later Chou, bearing "tribute" gifts which included, along with such marvels as eighty-four glass bottles of liquid "Greek fire," fifteen bottles of rose water. He affirmed that this perfume came from the "Western Regions," and that it was meant to be sprinkled on the clothes.[202] This mission has enjoyed some fame in our own times. But it seems not to have been noticed that there are earlier reports of rose water in China. Twenty or thirty years before the Cham embassy, the sovereigns of Later T'ang had a fantastically expensive artificial garden laid out in one of the great royal halls. Mountains and hills were made of aloeswood, rivers and lakes of rose water and storax, trees of clove and an unidentified aromatic,[203] walls and battlements of frankincense, buildings of rosewood and sanders, and carved human figures of sandalwood. The whole made a miniature city, over whose main gate was a signboard reading, "Nation of

Magical Scents." It was rumored that this fragrant landscape was booty from the state of Shu in Szechwan.[204]

But we can find rose water in ninth-century China. When Liu Tsung-yüan received a poem from Han Yü, his respect was so great that he would not read it until he had washed his hands in "rose dew."[205] In our own day "rose dew" is still made in China for a cooling drink.[206] It appears, then, that there was a native Chinese art of making rose water, well established before the first appearance in the Far East of the famous *gulāb* of Fars, unless perhaps the art had been introduced long before the Cham mission came. In any case, none of this was the famous "attar of roses," an essential oil which is thought to have been first made in India many centuries later.[207]

AMBERGRIS

Ambergris is a pathological secretion in the intestines of the cachalot, or sperm whale.[208] It is a gray, light substance, whose special value to perfumers is that it makes flower odors permanent.[209] Our name for it means "amber gray," but formerly it was simply "amber," from Arabic *'anbar*. This word reached China by the ninth century, and may be found in Tuan Ch'eng-shih's excellent book.[210]

The Arabs were the chief merchants of ambergris in medieval times. Ibn Khordadhbeh says that Arab traders gave iron to the natives of the Nicobar Islands in exchange for the precious concretions.[211] Tuan Ch'eng-shih, on the other hand, makes Somaliland its chief source:

The country of Berbera is in the sea to the southwest of us. They are unfamiliar with the Five Cereals there, but they are accustomed to puncture the veins of their domestic cattle and take their blood, which they blend with milk and drink raw. They have neither dress nor costume, using only some sheepskin below the waist to cover themselves. Their women are immaculately white, straight and upright . . .

He goes on to say that the chief commercial products of this strange people are "amber aromatic" and ivory, which they sell to bands of Persian merchants.[212]

The true source of ambergris was not understood in the medieval world. Some Persian and Arabic scholars ". . . saw in it the outflow of a submarine spring, others a dew which, emerging from the rocks, flowed into the sea and there coagulated; others yet maintained that it was the excrement of an animal."[213] The question seems not to have arisen in China until the end of the T'ang dynasty. In about the tenth or eleventh century [214] ambergris began to be called "dragon spittle,"[215] a phrase already in use in T'ang poetry, but only with reference to spume on dragon-infested waters.[216] The new usage probably coincided with the beginning of the importation of the substance itself into China, instead of mere tales about it, at about the beginning of Sung.[217] Whales were akin to dragons, since both were great sea spirits, related alike to the Indian *makara,* which had a jewel in its head.[218] Possibly ambergris was thought of as the saliva of a dragon because it was confused with spermaceti, which comes from the cachalot's head.[219] Ambergris, at any rate, joined the family of rare and wonderful goods like "dragon brain" camphor, "dragon scale" aromatic (a kind of agalloch), "dragon eyes" (a fruit like the lichee), "dragon beard" grass, and other units of draconian anatomy which enriched the Chinese world.[220] But, like jasmine oil, ambergris was still only an exotic rumor for the men of T'ang.

ONYCHA

Onycha is an aromatic derived from the operculum of a gastropod mollusk found along the shores of China south of the Yangtze. It was sent as "tribute" to Ch'ang-an by the coastal towns, among them Lu-*chou* in Annam.[221] We may therefore treat it as a "semi-exotic." The shell also contains succulent flesh, which was eaten by the southerners.[222] In Chinese, onycha was called "plate aromatic,"[223] from the shape of the operculum, and, mixed with aloeswood, musk, and the like, it formed an ingredient in a popular incense (as it did in the Mosaic incense).[224] This was called "plate decoction"[225] and was the incense which, according to tradition, was consumed like ordinary firewood in the palace courtyard of Sui Yang Ti, who was noted for his unthrifty ways.[226] A cosmetic ointment for the lips of ladies was also prepared from onycha, mixed with wax and the ashes of fragrant fruits and flowers.[227]

And show me simples of a thousand names,
Telling their strange and vigorous faculties.

John Milton, *Comus*

xi=Drugs

PHARMACOLOGY

ABŪ ZAYD REPORTED in the ninth century
that in China it was the custom to raise a great stone tablet in a public place, upon
which were inscribed the several maladies to which men were subject and a brief
account of their proper treatment. Thus all men might have reliable medical advice;
if a patient were poor, he could also receive the price of his medicine from the treasury
of the state. No contemporary Chinese counterpart to this admirable tale has yet
been found, but notices for the edification of the public were engraved in stone, and
there was intense interest in public charities, particularly in hospitals, under the
T'ang emperors.[1] The great inspiration for these humane interests and activities was
Buddhism. This foreign religion had become truly Chinese in about the sixth century,
and it was from that period that public charities became a regular, rather than merely
ephemeral, part of Buddhist practice in China. Food and other alms were distributed
to the needy by temple priests, and dispensaries were established to provide necessary
drugs for the poor. These charities formed a great part of the "field of compassion,"
which was now regarded as one of the two great areas of religious life, the other being the "field of worship," having to do with prayer, ritual, and the like.[2] In the
seventh and eighth centuries, the heyday of medieval Buddhism in the Far East,
hospitals and other pious establishments for the relief of the poor were regularly
founded in the larger cities, often at the command of the sovereign. The Empress
Wu, who was a fervent Buddhist, appointed special agents to oversee the charities
for the poor, the sick, the aged, and the orphaned.[3] The pilgrim Chien-chen created
charitable foundations in the commercial city of Yang-*chou* in the middle of the
eighth century.[4] Even Hsüan Tsung, a follower of Taoism, followed Buddhist ideals

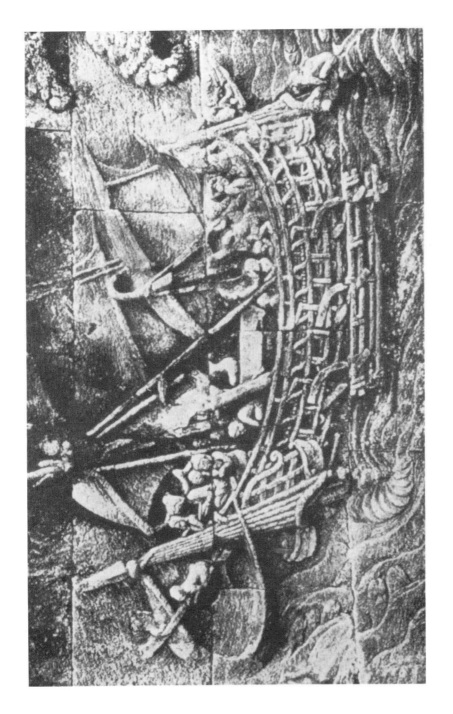

I. "... they cruised the Strait of Malacca toward the lands of gold, Suvarnabhūmi, the fabulous Indies." (p. 12) [relief, Borobudur, Java]

II. ". . . one cannot guess what token tribute was brought, or what symbols of submission were offered to the Chinese emperor . . ." (p. 25) [Yen Li-pen, "Foreign
Envoy Arriving with Tribute," possibly a late copy]

III. [Yen Li-pen, "Foreign Envoy Arriving with Tribute"]

IV. *". . . the ineffable paradises of Buddhism, like distant fairylands."* (p. 32) [Tun-
huang mural, paradise scene]

V. *"Their land was said to be rich in pearls and phosphorescent gems."* (p. 48) [ceramic, dwarf]

VI. *"In Lo-yang, in house after house, they study Western music."* (p. 51) [Tunhuang mural, Serindian orchestra]

VII. *". . . visibly stamped with the marks of his divine origin."* (p. 59) [Tun-huang manuscript, man leading caparisoned horse]

VIII. *". . . North, the natural home of the hawks, and the home of the barbarians who brought them into China."* (p. 95) [Hu Kuei, "Going Out to Hunt"]

IX. *"Camels coming from the East filled the Old Metropolis."* (p. 72) [ceramic, loaded camel]

X. *"Doubtful Ungulate."* (p. 90) [Chou Fang, "Exotic Gift from a Tributary State"]

XI. *"This divine creature is shown seated . . . on a yellow lotus."* (p. 129) [Tārā or
Avalokiteśvara seated on yellow lotus]

XII. *"Moreover, the Romans, the Arabs, and the Uighur Turks of Serindia were all known as great grape growers and drinkers of wine."* (p. 142) [ceramic, merchant holding wineskin]

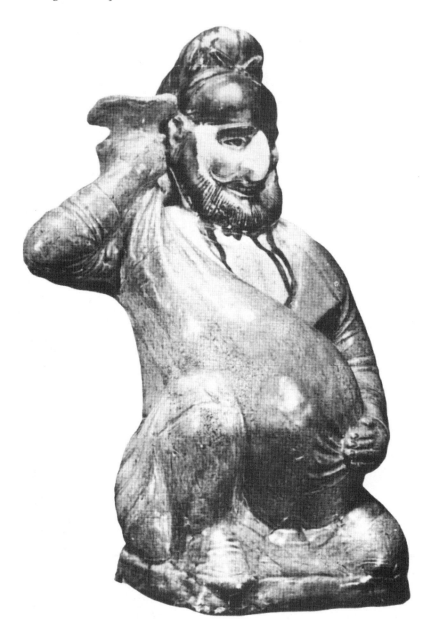

XIII. *"The Chinese had used long-handled censers since Han times."* (p. 161)
["Kuan-yin as the Guide of Souls"]

XIV. *"A popular kind of brazier was shaped like a bird or animal . . ."* (p. 161)
[elephant brazier]

XV. "... they seemed true shrubs of fairyland ..." (p. 246) [Lu Leng-chia, "Foreigners Presenting Coral Trees to Arhat"]

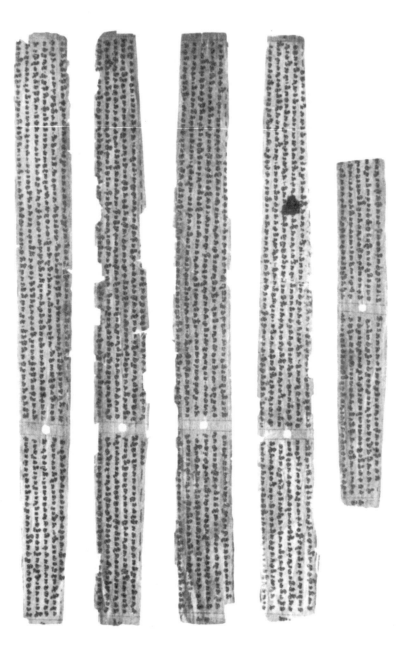

XVI. *"Some ancient scriptures, on pattra paper."* (p. 271) [*Prajñāpāramitā* in Nepalese script on palm leaves from Tun-huang]

in issuing a decree early in 735 for the founding of public hospitals in the capital city, with the additional purpose of ridding the metropolis of beggars.[5] After the great persecution of 845, the hospitals which had been managed by Buddhist temples were, at the suggestion of the minister Li Te-yü, provided with secular administrators, though later they were restored to the religious foundations.[6]

The T'ang penal code required that a doctor follow the ancient recipe books and official herbals strictly, and prescribed two and a half years of state servitude if a patient died because a medicine was improperly mixed;[7] the penalty was death by hanging if the patient was the emperor.[8] This official rigor made for conservatism, and explains why ancient formulas were slavishly copied into the newest pharmacopoeias—happily for the historical scholar, to whom many remedies would otherwise be lost, but not making for experiment and independence in medical circles. In view of the official emphasis on orthodoxy of treatment, it is surprising that a new and liberal mode of medical practice, which made the relief of suffering the doctor's primary incentive, was becoming influential, even in official and conventional circles. This was the result of the influence of Buddhist ethics on the attitudes of physicians.

An example of the best medieval physician, heroically devoted to the Buddhist principle of compassion,[9] was Sun Szu-miao, a learned and respected Taoist, who had rejected an invitation to the Sui court, and came to that of T'ang T'ai Tsung only in his old age, without accepting an official post.[10] This dedicated and unusual man wrote commentaries on *Lao tzu* and *Chuang tzu;* a collection of remedies in three hundred scrolls called *Ch'ien chin fang,* "Recipes Worth a Thousand Metal Coins";[11] the first Chinese treatise on ophthalmology;[12] and many other books. He advocated the employment of mineral drugs, anticipating the iatrochemists of Europe. He left a will asking for a cheap funeral without sacrificial animals or buried figurines, and was ultimately deified in the temples of medicine.[13]

A disciple of Sun Szu-miao also achieved a great reputation. This was Meng Shen, who, unlike his master, held various official posts, especially under the Empress Wu; at the end of her reign, he retired to the mountains to study alchemy and pharmacology, and died, greatly honored, at the age of ninety-three, during the reign of Hsüan Tsung. He left a number of important books of medical prescriptions.[14]

When touching on the condition of medicine, and more especially of pharmacology, in T'ang (leaving out, I fear, many worthy but more conventional practitioners), it is impossible not to mention Ch'en Ts'ang-ch'i, whose careful notes on many aspects of T'ang material culture not directly related to drugs have been of so much value to me. His great book, the *Pen ts'ao shih i,* was written, as the title indicates, to supplement the conservative official digests of drug lore. His successors of the Sung period criticized it severely for containing so much unorthodox material, but it is of immense value to us for the information it contains on new drugs which were just coming into use in early medieval times. His biography does not appear in the national collection—the penalty of his unconventionality. The T'ang history remarks unkindly that because he claimed that human flesh would help those who suffered from the "wasting disease" (tuberculosis?), sons and daughters of consumptive parents would sometimes go so far as to offer slices of their own flesh to them.[15]

Finally, we can hardly overlook, in a book devoted to the exotic, a physician of Persian origin, called in China "Li the Secret Healer," who went to Japan in 734 with the mission of Tajihino Mabito Hironari, and was one of the men of various national origins who were responsible for the upsurge of culture in the Nara period there.[16]

A wealth of pharmacological literature, new and old, was available to T'ang druggists. The basic library of T'ang materia medica consisted of at least the following: (1) *Shen nung pen ts'ao,* "Basic Herbs of Shen Nung," named for the god of domestic plants and animals, and dignified with the title of *ching,* "canon." This primordial work, possibly put together in Han, but containing much older materials, had come down to T'ang times in the edition of T'ao Hung-ching of the late fifth century, with the observations of that sage added to the primitive data. In its original form the canonical book was divided into three parts, which reveal Taoist emphasis: *superior drugs,* which lighten the body and lengthen life, such as cinnabar, azurite, mica, the divine *Fomes* fungus, tuckahoe, ginseng, musk, oysters, and so on; *middle drugs,* which are tonic and disease-resistant, such as orpiment, realgar, sulphur, ginger, rhinoceros horn, and deer velvet; and *inferior drugs,* some poisonous, used only to cure sickness, such as ocher, minium, ceruse, wolfbane, frogs, and peach seeds. (2) Among the pharmaceutical books of the Six Dynasties, by far the most important was the *Ming i pieh lu,* "Separate Account of Famed Physicians," of T'ao Hung-ching, which brought materials from the Shen Nung canon together with the post-Han authorities.[17] (3) The official T'ang book was the *Hsin hsiu pen ts'ao,* "Basic Herbs Compiled Anew," completed in 659 by a board headed by Li Chi but better known in the new edition, "Annotations on the T'ang Basic Herbs," of Su Kung. This great work included much new information acquired since T'ao Hung-ching's day, especially on southern plants, and was apparently the first *illustrated* herbal.[18] Truly exotic drugs must have been pictured, along with the southern ones, in the hand-illustrated manuscripts of T'ang; even the name of one of the medical illustrators is preserved: Wang Ting, of the seventh century, who painted "Pictures of Instruction and Admonition for the Basic Herbs" (*Pen ts'ao hsün chieh t'u*).[19] (4) We have mentioned the books of Sun Szu-miao, and must here add another of his, the *Ch'ien chin shih chih [fang],* containing dietary recipes "worth a thousand metal coins." (5) The *Pu yang fang,* "Supplementary Nurturing Recipes," of Meng Shen (early eighth century). (6) The *Shih liao pen ts'ao,* "Basic Herbs for Cures by Eating," by Chang Ting; an expansion of the preceding, and very influential in post-T'ang times.[20] (7) The *Hai yao pen ts'ao,* "Basic Herbs in Overseas Drugs," by Li Hsün (mid-eighth century), on exotic medicines.[21] (8) Wang T'ao's *Wai t'ai pi yao,* "Secret Essentials from the Outer Tribunal" (eighth century).[22]

The best of these human and literary resources were, of course, always available to the Son of Heaven, and it is about the imperial pharmacy that we have the most information. A considerable area in the capital city was set aside for the imperial herb gardens, which were placed in charge of a "Master," who, along with the authorities who supervised general medicine, acupuncture, massage, and magic, was one of the five" "Masters" under the "Grand Commander of Physicians."[23] He was given a number of apprentices between the ages of sixteen and twenty to assist him and to learn the properties of drugs, the parts of the empire in which useful herbs grew, the right way to plant and tend them, the best seasons to gather them, correct methods of storage, and the like.[24] From these gardens the herbs went to the palace, where, when needed, they came to the two heads of the court pharmacy, who were entitled "Purveyors to the Autocrat, Presidium of Medicines." These great pharmacists were responsible for diagnosis, prescription, and compounding. Their medicines had to be compounded in accordance with certain fixed rules: each medicine should contain one "superior" drug, monarchical and heavenly, to lengthen life, three "middle" drugs, vassal and human, to strengthen the organism, and nine "inferior" drugs, ministerial and earthly, to cure the disease. Moreover, the imperial pharmacists had to take account of the tastes of these reagents, as related to the Five Organs of the body, and other complex matters, such as the rule which determined that in maladies of the stomach and diaphragm, the royal patient should eat first and then take the medicine, while in diseases of the heart and belly, he should take the medicine first and eat afterwards.[25] The compounding took place in the watchful presence of the highest councilors of state and the commander of the guard, and the finished product was tasted by the chief pharmacists, by the great chamberlain (the pharmacists' superior), and by the crown prince (presumably lest he be too anxious to succeed), before going on to the sovereign's bedside.[26]

On the other hand, we know little about the way medicines came into the hands of ordinary men and women (other than that the Buddhist dispensaries had an important role), and virtually nothing about the retailing of drugs in T'ang times. An exception to this generalized ignorance (other than what we may surmise about the great markets of Canton, Yang-*chou,* and Ch'ang-an), is the case of the town of Tzu-*chou* in the plain of Szechwan. Beginning in the middle of the ninth century, dealers in drugs from all over the nation assembled in this town early in the ninth month of each year (it would be October in the West), and held a great medicine fair, which lasted for eight days and nights.[27]

But we are much better informed about the kinds of drugs which could be procured. All the resources of the vegetable, animal, and mineral kingdoms were exploited by the pharmacists. Hardly anything, even what was inert, or poisonous, or merely disgusting, did not have a role in healing the sick. From an enormous list, a few examples will serve to illustrate the diversity of the basic drugs of T'ang: aconite from Chekiang and Szechwan, cassia bark and buds from northern Kwangsi and southern Kiangsi, rhubarb from the northwest, ginseng from the north and Manchuria, lotus root from the mouth of the Yangtze, fritillary from Hupeh and Szechwan, sweet flag from southern Szechwan, licorice from the north and Mongolia, tuckahoe from Shensi, Spanish fly and oil beetles from Shensi, dragon bones from the mountains of Shansi, goral horns from the mountains of Szechwan and Kansu, musk from a wide belt stretching from northern Yünnan through Szechwan and the Tibetan foothills into north China, Mongolia, and Manchuria, ox bezoars from Szechwan and Shantung, rhinoceros horn from southern Hunan, python bile from Lingnan, wild boar bezoars from the Ordos, arsenic from T'ai-yüan in Shansi, stalactite from Shantung, Hupeh, and Kwangtung, gypsum from Shensi, Kansu and elsewhere, Glauber's salt from northern Szechwan, niter from central Shansi, mica from Shantung and northern Anhwei, rock salt from Kansu, Epsom salts from the gorges of the Yangtze, and kudzu powder from central China, especially Chekiang.[28]

We are fortunate in having some actual examples of eighth-century drugs preserved in the Shōsōin in Nara. These are kept with the weapons, games, household furniture, musical instruments, and other objects, most of which had been presented to the Emperor Shōmu by visiting foreigners. After his death in 756, his Empress Kōmyō presented all these things, including about sixty drugs, to the great Buddhist temple Tōdaiji, whose storehouse the Shōsōin is. A very large number of these drugs are of Chinese origin; some are from more distant parts of Asia: among the latter are cinnamon, cloves, gallnuts, and litharge from Iran; pepper and rhinoceros horn from India; and cantharides, fossil "dragon" bones, and much else, including some materials which do not seem to us to be drugs at all, such as aloeswood, sapan, cinnabar, and silver powder. Systematic scientific study of these rare drugs has been possible only since 1948. Among the important discoveries made since then have been the definite establishment of the identity of some medieval drugs for the first time. For instance, it had not been known before that "spiky niter" was an old name for Epsom salts, or that Epsom salts were used at all in medieval Chinese medicine.[29]

Even if only the best published authorities were followed, the medicines compounded numbered in the thousands, and they purported to deal with all known diseases. The true value of many of the old remedies has recently been the subject of much serious attention by scholars and scientists, and most of us nowadays have read how some "modern" specific was anticipated in the medieval Chinese herbals. Examples are the use in T'ang of *Pulsatilla sinensis* in the treatment of amoebic dysentery,[30] of calomel for venereal diseases,[31] and of infusions of gourd in wine for beriberi.[32] But we are not likely to be persuaded of the efficacy of the best dragon fossils, opalized in many colors, for incubi and succubi,[33] or to accept dried penis of white horse, with honey in wine, as a remedy for male impotence.[34] To stew a talisman written on holy peachwood and take it for demon possession seems to us more magic than medicine.[35] But a fair survey of the realities of T'ang medicine can be made only if we bury our "scientific" and "aesthetic" prejudices and try to see it all tolerantly, true and false, pretty and ugly, as a part of medieval life. Here is a sampling: if husband and wife both drink rain water before retiring to their chamber on the first day of spring, the lady will surely conceive; dew gathered from flowers is excellent for the complexion; an ointment made from an amalgam of tin and silver with mercury is a sedative in cases of extreme anxiety; calomel is excellent for "rum blossoms" on the nose; realgar is sovereign against all poisons; magnetite (a lodestone elixir, whose attractive powers simulate the sexual) will fortify the testicles and strengthen the loins; niter is prescribed for difficult urination and menstruation; licorice is the best of all herbs, and can be profitably mixed with any drug, especially in abdominal complaints; leaves of thoroughwort, an ancient apotropaion used in ritual aspergings, are mixed with oil for a woman's hair tonic; mallow makes an intestinal demulcent; rhubarb root is a bowel tonic; cooked leeks improve the appetite, and the juice of pounded leeks is applied to the bites of mad dogs and poisonous reptiles and insects; shallots facilitate childbirth; dried ginger opens up all internal passages; ferns make a soporific; yams make a sedative; dried apricots are useful in heart disease; dried peaches are useful in lung disease; an arrow, hidden secretly under the sleeping mat of a new mother, will relieve intestinal ulcers; if cramped muscles are struck three times with a spoon, they will relax; juice of crushed spiders is efficacious on snake bite; sea horses, held in the hand or tied to the body, facilitate labor; oysters help sexual disorders, such as nocturnal emissions; donkey meat stewed with condiments helps melancholy and madness; tiger flesh gets rid of all sorts of evil spirits, and gives travelers immunity from tigers; fat of wild boar, taken with wine, gives a woman abundant milk, so that she can suckle three or four children.[36]

An important subdivision of drug lore is made up of Taoist tradition and experiment, emphasizing the internal use of minerals (above all, of life-extending cinnabar); T'ang medicine is thoroughly infected with the views of the alchemical fantasts, both progressive and conservative. This accounts for the fact that handbooks of materia medica are frequently colored by rosy dreams of rejuvenation, desirable women, and unearthly powers. But "Taoist" prescriptions were not universally accepted: both Chen Ch'üan and Chang Kao, for instance, warn against the poisonous character of cinnabar.[37] Nonetheless, the times were favorable to the claims of the Taoists, and the more naïve of their supporters hoped to find panaceas, if not in the laboratories of T'ang scientists, at least in remote countries, mystically identified with traditional and paradisical homes of the immortal sylphs. In T'ang, therefore, the demand for foreign drugs was enormous, in contrast to the Six Dynasties period just preceding, when religious paraphernalia, such as Buddhist relics, images, and incenses, were paramount in overseas commerce.[38] Along with exotic drugs, the men of T'ang required exotic druggists, so that a sort of aristocratic craze for miracle men from India, learned devotees of yoga and tantric spellbinders, swept the land.[39] So, by a syncretic alchemy of the imagination congenial to the taste of the age, though it had its antecedents as early as Han, both Buddhists and Sivaites, equipped with wonderfully efficacious drugs, were seen as foreign equivalents of the native-born alchemists and cinnabar-eaters.

Accordingly, the influence of Indian medicine on China, which was already considerable, increased, and many Indian medical books, especially Buddhist ones, were translated into Chinese. An example from the seventh century is the *Avalo-kiteśvarakrta-Cikitsā-Bhaiṣajya-sūtra,* which contains both medical prescriptions and magical formulas (*dhāraṇī*).[40] It appears that ophthalmology was a field in which this influence made itself felt with especial force: the traveling monk Chien-chen consulted a foreign specialist in this field in Shao-*chou,* near Canton, when he came to Kwangtung in 748, and we have already mentioned the pioneering treatise on this subject written by Sun Szu-miao, apparently inspired by Buddhist work.[41]

The Indian pseudo-Taoists with their newfangled ways and scarcely believable pretensions were not always well received by the conservative gentlemen of the court, who were only too willing to accuse them of malpractice. As is well known, many of the T'ang emperors ate Taoist immortality elixirs, and some opinions held that their deaths from undiagnosed illnesses were actually due to poisoning by such potions. This suspicious attitude was directed against both Chinese and Hindu healers. Both T'ai Tsung and Kao Tsung had invited famous Indian doctors to prepare life-prolonging drugs for them. One of Kao Tsung's courtiers admonished him for swallowing such a barbaric preparation, and cited the story of his predecessor, for whom the drug had proved ineffectual—and indeed, there were dark rumors that T'ai Tsung's death was not unconnected with it.[42] Similarly, in 810, when Hsien Tsung asked his ministers for their views on the value of immortality elixirs, one of them replied with the formal statement that the history of alchemical tradition proved their danger. He cited the case of the late Te Tsung: that monarch had invited an Indian priest to prepare an elixir for him, and became violently ill after taking it. Later, when he was on his deathbed, his courtiers wished to kill the foreigner, whom they held responsible for the fatal illness, but refrained, ". . . lest they be laughed at by the outland barbarians."[43] Hsien Tsung seems not to have taken this interpretation of his grandfather's death seriously, for he himself suffered from poisoning by "gold and cinnabar,"[44] and more than one of his successors was thought to have perished as a result of faith in metallic elixirs.[45]

Belief in these powerful Taoist-Indian medicines continued unabated, and Chinese emissaries combed the world in search of new ones. In 716 a certain Westerner spoke to Hsüan Tsung of the wealth of the countries beyond the seas, and ". . . of the profit in merchant argosies." "He desired, moreover," he said, "to go to the Country of Lions [Ceylon] to find potent drugs, and also a crone skilled in

handwritten margin note: PAOIST DRUGS AND DEATH

medicine, and to install her in the palace wings." In this instance, however, the official who was told to accompany the ambiguous alien addressed a memorial to the throne urging the unkingliness of commerce, the doubtful efficacy of foreign drugs, and the unseemliness of a foreign lady in the harem; since none of these things tended to promote true virtue, he asked His Highness to reconsider. Hsüan Tsung abandoned the plan.[46] Pious aversion to these foreign nastinesses was as characteristic of the conservative lords of those times as the failure of the plan was untypical of the age. Exotic medicines continued to come into China in abundance. In particular, they tended to accumulate in Buddhist temples. It is perhaps a little surprising that this was true even in the ninth century, when overseas trade was much less regular than it had been in the preceding century. Yet Hsü T'ang, a poet of that century, wrote of exotic drugs in abundance in a Buddhist monastery,[47] and P'i Jih-hsiu told of a monk named Yüan-ta, over eighty years old, who had a garden in which he loved to plant rare medicinal herbs.[48] Plainly the herb gardens of the monasteries played an important role in the propagation of introduced drugs in China. And, of course, religious pilgrims played an important part in bringing the herbs in the first place. Many of these pious herb-collectors were foreigners in the service of the Chinese ruler. Such a one was Nandī, a Central Asian, who traveled widely in the south of Asia before coming to China by sea. He reached the capital in 655 with a large collection of Sanskrit manuscripts, but in the following year was dispatched to the Indies to bring back exotic drugs; on this trip he got no further than Canton; in 663 he went to Cambodia for the same purpose, but his career is a blank after that.[49] In biographies such as these, we frequently detect heroic qualities—men dared much to achieve their missions, and frequently lost their lives in the search for medicines for the Chinese.

Drugs came from abroad by ordinary commercial routes as well and, of course, by the quasi-commercial diplomatic missions carrying token "tribute" from distant princes to Ch'ang-an. These imported goods were strictly inspected at the frontier, and their sale price fixed according to their value and the requirements of Chinese policy.[50] Though we cannot guess their contents, we can imagine the size of the shipments of the best medicinal products of Asia which passed through these customs barriers, especially in the first half of the eighth century, when all the world seemed to turn toward T'ang: Tukhāra sent "strange drugs" several times,[51] a "Persian" prince brought "aromatic drugs" in person,[52] Kashmir sent "Western drugs," [53] Kapiśa sent "secret recipes and marvelous drugs," [54] and, in the ninth century, when the channels of commerce had different alignments, the Tibetans sent assorted drugs.[55]

As the pharmacologists of T'ang became acquainted with these novelties, the results of their studies were gradually incorporated in the published pharmacopoeias, and so, as practicing physicians learned of them, the demand for the drugs increased, and many of the plants which yielded them were transplanted in Chinese soil. Indeed, books devoted solely to these new and excellent ingredients were obtainable. The great work of Li Hsün, *Hai yao pen ts'ao,* has already been referred to;

fortunately, though the complete text is lost, it has been liberally excerpted in the medical books of Sung and later periods. Unhappily, the same is not true of Cheng Ch'ien's *Hu pen ts'ao,* "Basic Herbs of the *Hu*-Westerners," which was probably devoted in the main to Iranian medicines; it too disappeared after T'ang, but quotations from it are not easy to find.[56]

Citragandha

One of these Indic wonder-drugs was called *citragandha,* "of various fragrances," [57] sent to Ch'ang-an in the eighth century by a Buddhist king of north India; [58] more came from Tukhāra,[59] and with a joint mission from Turgäch, Chāch, Kish, Māimargh, and Kapiśa.[60] This preparation contained tamarisk manna, pine resin, licorice, root of Rehmannia, and "hot blood," and was (writes Ch'en Ts'ang-ch'i) to be taken in wine for wounds and for hemorrhages such as those attendant on childbirth. The foreigners had their own way of testing the efficacy of the drug: "they take a small child," he says, "and cut off one foot. They put the drug in its mouth, then have it step on the foot; if it is able to walk at that very time, it is of good quality." [61]

[handwritten margin note: TESTING DRUGS ON CHILDREN]

Thēriaca

In 667, ambassadors from Rūm presented the T'ang emperor with the true universal antidote, the *thēriaca,* a pill which, according to Pliny, had as many as six hundred different ingredients.[62] The Chinese observed that it contained the gall of swine, and was dark red in color; the foreigners seemed to respect it greatly, and Su Kung noted down that it had proved its usefulness against "the hundred ailments." [63] Whether this panacea contained such ingredients as myrrh, opium, and hemp, which were regularly present in the theriacas of medieval Islam, we do not know.[64]

CARDAMOMS

There are native Chinese cardamoms,[65] but those of tropical lands were more highly regarded and were consequently imported in quantity. The "black cardamoms," or "bitter cardamoms," called "wisdom-augmenting seeds" in Chinese,[66] were gathered both in Lingnan and Indochina,[67] and may therefore be considered a "semi-exotic." Eaten in dumplings of glutinous millet or rice with honey, they were supposed to strengthen the mind, hence their name.[68] But they also had more general tonic effects: they "increased the breath, stabilized the soul, and supplemented inadequacies"; in particular, taken parched with salt, they were marvelously efficacious in curing incontinence of urine.[69]

From Tongking came the "true cardamon": [70] the dried fruits had been traded into Greece from India, at least as early as the fourth century B.C., and were well known in Rome.[71] Li Hsün reports that the dried leaves, which have a bitter-sweet taste, were used in medicine as well as the husks and fruits.[72]

"Bastard cardamom," [73] a camphor-flavored cardamom of Indochina,[74] which was especially useful in the treatment of respiratory disorders, was also imported.[75]

The "round cardamom" or "cluster cardamom" of Java [76] came to China from a place named Qaqola,[77] apparently on the west coast of the Malay peninsula, and the name of this country is preserved in the Arabic word for "cardamom," *qāqulah*.[78] It appears that the plant must have been brought from Java and grown commercially on the peninsula; [79] it was established in Kwangtung by the eleventh century.[80] The Chinese called this "white cardamom" because, as Tuan Ch'eng-shih says, "the seeds make a cluster, like grapes, and are slightly bluish when they first appear, but when ripe they turn white; they are gathered in the seventh month." [81] They had a variety of important medicinal applications, including the relief of bronchial and lung congestions.[82]

The word "cardamom" is not uncommon in the poetry of the ninth and tenth centuries, in the verses of such men as Wu Jung, Li Ho, Tu Mu, and Han Wo: this was an age when poets were preoccupied with rich and exotic flavors, as well as strange colors and odors.

Nutmeg

Ch'en Ts'ang-ch'i was the first Chinese to describe the nutmeg,[83] which he called "fleshy cardamom." [84] He tells that the spice (though it seems not to have been used as a spice then) was brought up to T'ang in the great argosies and that, like cardamom, it was native to Qaqola.[85] According to Li Hsün, however, it was a product of "Kurung and Rome," [86] a statement which tells us little about where nutmeg was grown, but a great deal about the extent of the trade in it; East Indian nutmeg was known in Europe in the sixth century.[87] In T'ang, a kind of broth made from ground nutmeg was prescribed for various digestive disorders and for diarrhea.[88] The plant and its recipes were apparently well received, since it was being grown in Lingnan by early Sung times.[89]

Turmeric and Zedoary

Turmeric is the product of one of a number of pigmented and more or less aromatic rhizomes of genus *Curcuma*. In the narrowest sense it is a species [90] which is only slightly pungent and is most used as a dye; this common turmeric is believed to have been indigenous to southwest China. Closely related to it is a highly aromatic species of India and Indonesia known as zedoary,[91] which is used chiefly as a source of perfume. There are many other species in Indonesia and Indochina which are used as coloring agents, in medicine, in curries, and in aromatic preparations.[92] The collective Chinese name for these was *"yü gold,"* a name which was also given to saffron, as we have seen (p. 125), though saffron is described more specifically as *"yü gold aromatic."* In any case, they were commonly confused in trade and practice alike. In contexts where aroma is emphasized it can be assumed that we have to do either with saffron or with zedoary, and otherwise with turmeric.[93]

India, says the T'ang history, produced diamonds, sandalwood, and turmeric (or zedoary?), which she traded with Rome and Cambodia and Annam.[94] Or was it saffron? Most likely all three. Similarly, in T'ang times, *"yü* gold" was a product of Greater Balūr,[95] of Jāguda,[96] of Udyāna,[97] and of Kashmir.[98] In the case of these nations to the northwest of India, saffron is a distinct possibility, and in the case of Kashmir, the classic home of saffron, virtually a certainty.

The Persians, on the other hand, ascribed zedoary to China.[99] Possibly this is explained by the presence in China of a *Curcuma* named "ginger yellow," which was also imported from the West. Su Kung says that the Western barbarians called it **dź'i̯wĕt,* that is, something like *jud* or *jet;* elsewhere he says that they called common turmeric "horse **dź'i̯wĕt"* because they used it to treat horses.[100] Maybe this transcription registers the first syllable of "zedoary" in some Oriental language; in Arabic it is *jadwār.*

In T'ang medicine, turmeric was used primarily to break up congestions of the blood and to control hemorrhages.[101] Whether the *"yü* gold" which was used to dye women's clothes, and at the same time to give them a slight fragrance, was turmeric or saffron (also used as a dye in antiquity) is uncertain.[102] The powder which was spread, along with camphor, on the paths where the Son of Heaven was about to tread was either saffron or zedoary. (Compare a 1960 news dispatch from Brussels: "The Rue Neuve, busiest of central Brussels' shopping streets, will be sprayed with perfume for the wedding of King Baudouin and Doña Fabiola de Mora y Aragon on December 15.")[103] In T'ang, the custom was abolished by Hsüan[(1)] Tsung for reasons of economy in the middle of the ninth century.[104]

TACAMAHAC

A number of important but unrelated trees were called *t'ung* in Chinese. Basically the name denotes the paulownia, whose handsome purple blossoms account for the expanded name, "flowering *t'ung.*" Classed with this tree linguistically are the "phoenix tree," called *wu t'ung,* or "blue *t'ung"* (*ch'ing t'ung*),[105] the "wood-oil tree," called "oil *t'ung"* (*yu t'ung*),[106] the "coral tree," called "spiny *t'ung* (*tz'u t'ung*),[107] and the "balsam poplar," called "Western *t'ung"* (*hu t'ung*).[108] The resin of this last is called "tacamahac," a name also given to the resin of the balsam poplar of North America [109] and to an aromatic elemi yielded by an Indochinese tree which is not a poplar at all.[110] The resin of the so-called "Western *t'ung*," which was imported by T'ang, came from a poplar that also supplied a wood useful for making utensils,[111] and is found in northwest China and the Gobi Desert, and as far west as Europe. The tree got its Chinese name from its resemblance to the phoenix tree (*wu t'ung*), not to the paulownia.[112] The resin itself appeared on the Chinese market under the name "spittle of the Western *t'ung*" [113] or "tears of the Western *t'ung*." Some authorities thought that the bites of insects feeding on the tree produced the flow of sap.[114] It came, mixed with fragments of wood and alkaline earth, from Kansu,[115] from Hami,[116] and from various parts of Turkestan and Iran.[117]

This tacamahac was used by physicians to treat "great poisonous fevers" and abdominal swellings, and to provoke vomiting.[118] More important, perhaps, was its use by jewelers, especially those attached to the imperial palace, as a flux for gold and silver solders.[119]

MANNA

Ch'en Ts'ang-ch'i was the only T'ang pharmacologist to describe the "thorn honey" of Yarkhoto in Serindia. He says that it is secreted by a hairy desert plant, and gives a transcription of its native name, which has been interpreted as *khār-burra*, "lamb thorn," [120] reminding us of the "camel thorn" of Arabia. Ch'en, who apparently had studied the sweet exudate, prescribed it for a number of maladies, including violent and bloody diarrheas.

Similar to this, and possibly from the same source, was a sugary substance "from a remote region west of Pa [Szechwan]," which Ch'en Ts'ang-ch'i calls "sweet dew honey," connecting it with the miraculous and heavenly sweet dew of old Chinese tradition. He advocates it to cure fevers about the diaphragm, to clear the eyes, and to inhibit thirst.[121]

BALM OF GILEAD

Balm of Gilead is the sap of an Arabian plant, also called "balm of Mecca," which the Queen of Sheba is said to have introduced to Palestine. This fragrant greenish gum came to the attention of Tuan Ch'eng-shih in the ninth century; he reports that it is a sovereign cure for acariasis and adds, ". . . this oil is exceedingly precious, and its cost is double that of gold." He calls it a product of Rome, and indeed the Romans knew it, for the balsam tree which produces it was exhibited in the triumphs of

Pompey and Vespasian. Tuan records a Syriac form of its name, *apursāmā,* the source of Greek *bálsamon.*[122] There is no evidence that it ever came to China.

GALBANUM

Galbanum is a sweet gum resin, the sap of a tree related to that which produces asafetida.[123] Tuan Ch'eng-shih knew this substance, too. He records a Persian name for it, *bīrzai,* and a Semitic name cognate to Aramaic *khelbānita,* which is the name of one of the four ingredients of the sacred perfume of the Jews. It was also known to Pliny and other Roman writers. Tuan calls it a product of Persia and Rome (meaning, as usual, Roman Asia), and declares that it is used in various useful medicines.[124] But again, we cannot be sure that the balsam itself was ever seen in T'ang.

ASAFETIDA

Unlike galbanum, asafetida was well known in T'ang as a drug and flavoring.[125] It was commonly called by a Serindian name much like Tocharian *aṅkwa,*[126] but its Sanskrit name *hiṅgu* was also known. It was imported both as sun-dried cakes of gum and as sliced roots, the latter being regarded as inferior.[127] Many Asian countries supplied the valuable drug to China. Among them Jāguda figured prominently, and also Persia, along with various unnamed countries of South and Central Asia;[128] it was submitted regularly as tribute by the Chinese garrison at Beshbalik on the edge of Dzungaria,[129] and came up through the South China Sea by merchant vessel.[130]

Asafetida is a nerve stimulant and promotes digestion, but the property most exploited in T'ang was its strange ability to neutralize foul odors, though it is very odorous itself.[131] It was also a powerful antihelminthic,[132] and it was boiled with jujubes in cow's milk or meat extract and swallowed as an antidemoniac.[133]

Judging from the poem "An Idle Stay by the T'ung River," written by the monk Kuan-hsiu, talented painter and poet who lived eighty years in the ninth and tenth centuries, asafetida was taken with tea:

> In the quiet room I burn a sandal seal;
> In the deep brazier I heat an iron flask.
> The tea, blended with *aṅkwa,* is warming,
> The fire, sown with thuja roots, is fragrant.
> Some few single cranes have come flying,
> A good heap of sutras is read through;
> What hinders me from stealing away like Chih-tun—
> From riding a horse up into the blue darkness?[134]

The "sandal seal," of course, is an incense clock. Chih-tun was a hermit monk of the fourth century, and a great admirer of horses.

I have suggested from time to time that Tuan Ch'eng-shih's notes were based more on extensive reading in many languages than on personal observation, and that accordingly we cannot take a reference to a plant or animal in his book to mean that it had been seen in China. But it does appear that the knowledge of this most interesting man was based on more than books. In his rather detailed account of the tree which yields asafetida he refers to conflicting information given him by two priests, one a "Roman" named Wan, the other a certain "Deva" from Magadha.[135] The presence of the informant Wan, possibly an Anatolian or Syrian, suggests that Tuan relied on other unnamed foreigners for oral information on exotic affairs.

CASTOR BEANS

"Tick hemp,"[136] says Su Kung, is so called because its seeds, which are imported from the West and also grown in T'ang, look like cattle ticks.[137] This was the castor bean, which was important for its oil in many parts of the ancient world; it is thought that it may have been first domesticated in Egypt, where the oil was used in lamps.[138] In China both the seeds and the oil pressed from them were used in medicine.[139]

PURGING CASSIA

"Indian laburnum," or "golden shower," or more prosaically "purging cassia,"[140] was for the Indians "gold-colored" and "king's tree," and for the Arabs "Indian carob" or "cucumber of necklaces."[141] The tree, which has beautiful flowers and bright red seeds in long pods, is a native of India, but was transplanted to all tropical lands quite early because of the popularity of the black pulp surrounding the seeds as a remedy for constipation.[142] In T'ang it was called "Brahman black pod,"[143] or "Persian black pod,"[144] because it resembled the Chinese honey locust[145] or "soapbean tree," which was named "ink-black pod" in China. The Indian name *āragvadha*[146] was also well known to the T'ang doctors, who prescribed the seeds for a number of internal complaints.

SEAWEEDS

Edible marine algae were no new thing in China; red laver,[147] for instance, which makes an excellent soup, was a familiar product of the coastal waters of central and south China, and was sometimes brought from Japan.[148] Green laver, a "sea lettuce" from the shallow waters of the southern seas, was known in T'ang as "rock water mallow."[149] It was used as a diuretic, and its place in the materia medica of the "Westerners" was noted and copied down.[150]

Sweet tangle[151] is a brown alga, or kelp, rich in iodine, potassium, and sugar. It was regularly imported, under the name *kompo,* from Silla on the Korean Peninsula, and came as tribute from the Tungusic tribe called Mo-ho of P'o-hai.[152] It was reported to be a favorite and health-giving food of the "men of the sea islands," but made "men of the north" ill; it was recommended to the Chinese as a cure for various swellings, and it must be assumed that goiter was one of these.[153]

GINSENG

The true vegetable elixir of traditional Chinese medicine was the anthropoid root of the ginseng.[154] The "divine herb,"[155] or "returned cinnabar with the wrinkled face" (a pseudo-alchemical name suggestive of its wonderful powers),[156] grew on the Mountain of the Purple Cluster,[157] in the T'ai-hang Range in Shansi, but the most and the best was brought in from the Korean kingdoms of Koryŏ, Paekche, and Silla, and from the nations of Manchuria.[158]

That which is given as tribute by the country of Silla has hands and feet, and is shaped like the human figure; it is over a foot long. It is fixed between pieces of Cunninghamia wood, and decorated with bindings of red silk thread.[159]

It was customary to give gifts of this panacea to friends, as one might give a poem or a painting or a precious stone, and many poems of the T'ang period which express thanks for just such a present still survive. P'i Jih-hsiu, for instance, claimed, in extravagantly worded verses, life-extending virtues for the root far beyond the powers of the Taoist alchemists.[160] "It masters the Five Labors and the Seven Lesions . . . it augments the Five Organs and the Six Viscera . . . ," wrote the pharmacologists, and much else besides.[161] The fantastic claims made for this Sino-Korean rival of the Graeco-Arabian mandragora seem not to be so fantastic in the light of recent studies by Chinese scientists, which indicate that it actually contains a stimulant of both sympathetic and central nervous systems, and of the genitourinary system.

ASSORTED HERBS

The yellow root of a plant of the fumewort family[162] was imported from Manchuria, and prescribed for kidney complaints.[163]

The slightly poisonous brown tuber of a Far Eastern species of the "physic nut"[164] came from Korea and the sands of outer Kansu; it was used for "pains in the heart."[165]

The root of one of the "star grasses,"[166] presented to Hsüan Tsung by an Indian monk, was called "Brahman ginseng," meaning that its tonic and restorative powers rivaled those of ginseng. It was planted in China in late T'ang or early Sung, and well established in Kwangsi by the twelfth century.[167]

The bark of the *kân-d'â* tree, whose name was said to mean "brown," was used to dye the robes of Buddhist monks, and came from "the West"; "Annam also has it," writes Li Hsün.[168] The name could be either Sanskrit *gandha*, "aromatic," or *kanthā*, "monk's patch-robe."[169] In T'ang it was taken in wine to warm the bowels and stomach.[170]

"Yellow detritus,"[171] imported from Annam, was used as a yellow dye and also to allay pectoral and abdominal pains. It was apparently a powdered rosewood or something very similar.[172]

A "Western *Coptis*"[173] from the seacoast of Persia provided roots useful for intestinal disorders and for piles. Its identity is uncertain.[174] It was established in Shensi and Kansu in Sung,[175] but seems now to have disappeared.

The somewhat poisonous seeds called "crane lice"[176] were brought from the Far West, including Persia. Foreigners called them "swan lice." They were used as an antihelminthic and for various ulcers and swellings.[177]

A bitter crystalline extract of aloes,[178] an African succulent, was called "elephant gall" because of its taste, and was given to small children for anemia with fevers. It was said to grow in Persia.[179]

A white mushroom[180] from the reedy salt marshes of Manchuria was imported and taken with wine for tapeworm.[181]

And there were other mysterious and unknown herbs, such as the unidentifiable weeds brought by monkish envoys from north India and Tukhāra for the delectation of the court,[182] and others listed by those specialists in exotic materia medica, Ch'en Ts'ang-ch'i and Li Hsün—among them an "herb which sways alone without wind," which should be worn to induce a husband's love.[183]

BEZOAR

Among the drugs of animal origin none had more repute in China than the bezoar. Rightly so-called, the bezoar is a concretion found in the fourth stomach of many ruminants, notably the bezoar goat; it enjoyed a great reputation in the Near East as an antidote for poisons. The "bezoars" of medieval China, called "ox yellow" there, did not always match this classic definition. Some, if not most, were biliary calculi, taken from the gall bladders of oxen.[184] The role of these calculi in medicine was almost more spiritual than physical; indeed, it is no surprise to read of a "yellow" disgorged by an ox, inside of which ". . . . there was a thing like a butterfly which flew away."[185] Indeed, "ox yellow calms the heaven-soul and settles the earth-soul; it rids one of perverse goblins and puts an end to internal evils." [186] These valuable objects were produced in China, largely in Shantung, many of whose towns sent parcels of them annually to Ch'ang-an as tribute along with stone utensils and edible mollusks. Some were produced in Szechwan, too. [187] These Chinese "bezoars" were in great demand as far away as Persia, where they were much prized as talismans and remedies. [188] On the other hand, T'ang received a considerable quantity of Korean bezoars from Silla during the eighth century, [189] and some also from Manchuria and from Nan-chao. [190] A draconic concretion, styled "serpent yellow," sent by Farghāna in 761, must have created great excitement. [191]

Olnul

Li Hsün preserves a quotation from an old gazetteer which describes an animal, called *olnul* in Korean: [192]

It comes from the waters of the Eastern Sea. Its appearance is like the figure of a deer, but its head resembles a dog's, and it is long of tail. Each day they emerge to float on the face of the water, and the Kurung householders shoot them with bow and arrow. They take their "external kidneys" and dry them in the shade; in a hundred days their taste is sweet and their aroma is admirable. [193]

The "external kidneys," are, of course, the animal's testicles. The "K'un-lun-ers" (for a variant translation)—that is, Indonesians—are puzzling in the seas between China and Japan, unless the term was generalized to mean only "expert hunters on the seas." The animal is plainly some kind of seal, [194] or possibly, if we take the long tail seriously, a sea otter. It was taken mostly in the seas off Silla. [195] The drug was taken with herbs in wine for demon possession, fox spirits, copulation with ghosts in dreams, and for various forms of male sexual weakness. [196]

It is probable that castoreum and civet were marketed under the same name, and not distinguished in China. [197]

PYTHON BILE

No fearful hunters of human bile roamed the T'ang towns as they did in Champa, [198] but the black-tailed pythons [199] of Chinese-occupied Annam yielded their gall bladders for the physicians of the T'ang capital, [200] and the reptiles were robbed in the same way by the professional bile gatherers of P'u-an, in what is now Kweichow Province. [201] Liu Hsün, a close observer of southern life, saw himself how, on the fifth day of the fifth month of each year, the "rearers of serpents" obtained the drug:

All of them were within a great basket, in which was a matting of pliant herbs, and they were coiled and bent round on top of these. A pair of men lifted one of them out on to the ground; then they took ten stakes or so and turned its body over, starting at the head, and then held it down with the stakes, so that it was unable to turn over on its side. Then they sliced some inches or a foot along its belly, using a sharp blade, and the liver and gall bladder burst out. At that they cut away the gall bladder, which in all of them is the size of a duck's egg. This they put out in the sun to dry, looking forward to sending it up as tribute. But they folded the liver back inside, and threaded the mouth of the wound together. Then they gathered it up and put it in the basket. Some say that they carry it back and release it among the streams and meres.[202]

Python lore came to the ears of Tuan Ch'eng-shih, who notes an easier way of catching the beast:

When it has swallowed a deer, and the deer has been completely digested, it will wind round a tree, and then the bones in its belly will be pushed out through the scales. Its tallow and lard are very good indeed while it is nursing these wounds.
Some toss a woman's dress to it; it will coil round this, and not get up.
The gall bladder is close to the head in the upper decad of the month, close to the heart in the middle decad, and close to the tail in the lower decad.[203]

Other kinds of gall were substituted for the genuine material on the drug market, but the expert pharmacists had a test to detect them: one should put a bit of the stuff in pure water. The true python's bile will float on the surface, moving about in circles, while pig's bile or tiger's bile, the common counterfeits, will sink.[204]

The use of the gall in medicine in China links that country with Indochina; in Cambodia and elsewhere it has an important role too. The T'ang physicians prescribed it for bloody diarrhea, hemorrhages caused by worms, and a variety of other maladies.[205]

White Wax

The white wax of Annam was ordinary yellow beeswax bleached in sunlight.[206] Even this has its medicinal uses: taken in wine with an egg it would stop hemorrhages in a pregnant woman (a kind of magical sealing?) and grow black hair where white has appeared.[207]

Human Hair

Considerable quantities of human hair were sent to Ch'ang-an from Manchuria and Korea [208] during the eighth century. One wonders what might have been the peculiar virtue of these foreign tresses which made them superior to the native product, and whether it is possible that they were put to uses other than the magico-medical ones, which are comparatively easy to trace. Hairs are powerful, and even dangerous: Chen Li-yen, a younger brother of Chen Ch'üan and like him a physician, had to administer a saving dose of realgar to a Taoist who had swallowed a hair which had naturally turned into a snake.[209]

If the hair of a living man is suspended on a fru. tree, such birds as crows will not dare to come and eat its fruit. Or again, if a person runs away, take his hair and put it on a carriage placed transversely, and turn it backwards; he will then be bewildered and confused, and not know where he is going. All such things as these are divine transformations.[210]

But most of the recipes are of the same kind as that which prescribed the cord with which a man has hanged himself in a cure for epilepsy.[211] Those which call for the hair of the head depend on the notion of binding, tying up, and holding fast. If a child is given to crying out in alarm, he should be given the ashes of hair with oil in milk or wine; if a man bleeds without apparent reason, he should take a spoonful of ashes of hair and fingernail parings in wine.[212]

BLUE VITRIOL

A "green salt," produced in the Qarašahr region of Central Asia and in Iran, and also brought to T'ang by ship, was similar to the natural blue copper carbonate, azurite, and like it was used in the treatment of eye diseases. This must have been crystallized copper sulphate, sometimes called "blue vitriol," a supposed cure for trachoma. A substitute for this, green verdigris (a copper acetate) was prepared by the Chinese from metallic copper and vinegar, but physicians were warned that it was not to be used in medicine.[213]

My hangings all of Tyrian tapestry;
In ivory coffers I have stuffed my crown;
In cypress chests my arras counterpoints,
Costly apparel, tents and canopies,
Fine linen, Turkey cushions boss'd with pearls,
Valance of Venice gold in needlework . . .

William Shakespeare, *The Taming of the*
Shrew, Act II, scene 1

xii=Textiles

WHEN, in the middle of the ninth century, the representatives of the "Country of the Female *Man*-barbarians," as splendid as princely Bodhisattvas, brought offerings to the palace in Ch'ang-an (so goes the romantic tale of Su O), they had "luminous sunset-clouds brocade" among their gifts.

They asserted that this was made from "refined water fragrant hemp." It was shining and radiant, infecting men with its sweet-smelling aroma. With this, and the intermingling of the Five Colors in it, it was more ravishingly beautiful than the brocades of our Central States.[1]

The wonderful textiles offered by these beaded Amazons seem to be imaginative transformations of the fabrics styled "morning sunrise-cloud" brought from Indonesia and Indochina—fine cotton goods, of which we shall have much to say later. The notion that there could be textiles more lovely than any manufactured in T'ang testifies to the extravagance of Su O's fancy, since China was at this time the very home and headquarters of rich stuffs and elegant weaves.

The fiber most used for textile making in T'ang was silk, both the long filaments reeled from the cocoon of the domestic silkworm, and the short broken fibers from the cocoon of the wild silkworm which needed to be spun into thread. There were also a number of vegetable fibers from which both plain and fancy linens could be made, including ramie, kudzu, hemp, banana, and bamboo. Wool was used mostly for felt in the Far East, woolen textiles being more characteristic of the Iranian sphere of culture.

The number of weaves in which these threads were employed was very large: an idea of them is given by the official list of goods purveyed by the imperial Office of Weaving and Dyeing: there were ten textiles, including pongees, damasks, nets, and gauzes, along with linens and woolens; five kinds of cords and ribbons; and four kinds of spun threads, including tussah.[2] The most characteristic T'ang weave was a weft twill. Some scholars think that this was a new introduction from the West, where twills are ancient; the weft twill was especially important in Sāsānian weaving. In ancient China, twills had not been much used, though the warp twill was known; satin, a T'ang invention, is a warp twill in which many fine warp threads completely cover the weft.[3] The beautiful patterned fabrics which we often call "brocades" were actually polychrome damasks, mostly weft rep twills, though some were still done in the old warp style.[4] However T'ang also produced some true brocades, with gold leaf twisted on silk threads. Tapestry weave seems to have been introduced in the eighth century, by way of the Uighur Turks.[5] T'ang also had printed textiles. These were done by the "negative" method: the design was cut in wooden blocks, the fabric was pressed between them, and the dye poured into the hollows; this technique was known from the eighth century. It contrasts with the typical wax resist printing of India and the West.

As an example of the luxuriance of T'ang textiles, consider *"k'ung*-sparrow net," or, as we would say, "peacock net." This was a fine, rich, apparently iridescent fabric manufactured at Heng-*chou* in Hopei.[6] It had been a favorite material among ladies of luxurious taste since the sixth century.[7] Here it is in one of the "Ten Demands" which the Sui courtesan "Sixth Maiden Ting" addressed to her lover:

> A skirt tailored of *k'ung*-sparrow net,
> Red and green intermingled, contraposed,
> Refulgent as with fish-scaled dragon's brocading,
> Clear-cut and luminous, admirably strange:
> How coarse or fine, you know, my lord, yourself—
> I demand of you, young man, a dress and sash![8]

The great centers of the T'ang textile industry were around the mouth of the Yangtze River, and in Szechwan. In these regions large numbers of workers plied their looms to produce immense quantities of fancy fabrics demanded by well-to-do persons of the empire. It is said that seven hundred weavers were devoted entirely to providing the fabrics required by Yang the Precious Consort. From time to time this huge industry was attacked, and in part reduced, as tending to corrupt public morals. In 771, for instance, Tai Tsung decreed that the manufacture of certain cloths with complicated figures, including both monochrome and polychrome damasks and patterned gauzes, was to be stopped, for the reason just given, and also because this detailed work ". . . was harmful to the female artisans." The woven images of dragons, phoenixes, unicorns, lions, peacocks, heavenly horses, and divine herbs were prohibited, though ". . . the regularly current white 'brocade of Koryŏ' and the brocades of mixed colors, as well as the regularly current damasks and brocades with small figures and graphs and the like, may still be allowed in conformity with old precedent." [9] A similar edict of Wen Tsung, promulgated in 829, went so far as to order the burning, on the first day of the new year, of all the looms and reeds which produced gaudy and frivolous textiles.[10]

It is curious to find a Korean weave (if indeed this was more than a mere descriptive name) among those allowed to circulate by Tai Tsung. Exoticism, it seems, did not necessarily taint the Chinese spirit. Despite the excellence of the T'ang textile industry, or perhaps because of it (since it stimulated interest in rare goods), many cloths of foreign make were imported. Inevitably, T'ang, the purveyor of fine goods to all of Asia, came under the influence of these imports, and shipped abroad articles of her own manufacture which show the impress of exotic ideas. Therefore the handsome T'ang fabrics preserved in the Shōsōin and Hōryūji at Nara in Japan, and the almost identical ones found near Turfan in Central Asia, display the popular images, designs, and symbols of Sāsānian Persia, usually thoroughly adapted to T'ang culture.[11] One of the fabrics of Hōryūji, for instance, is patterned with roundels, in each of which are four bearded Sāsānian kings, mounted on horseback and carrying bows, but with Chinese characters branded on the flanks of their steeds.[12] Again, a prose poem of the end of the eighth century, entitled "Rhapsody on the Figured Brocades Offered by Men from Overseas," describes a pattern of dancing "phoenixes," ". . . with double corollas and layered leaves intermingled conformably with them, so as to make a pattern." [13] The animal shown in a floral scroll or roundel is a typically Iranian device, and these royal gifts must have been the prototypes of well-known T'ang brocades showing "phoenixes" in floral roundels.[14]

A SUIT OF GOLD

It might almost have been predicted that Kao Tsung would reject such an extravagant article as the golden costume presented to him by ambassadors from Tukhāra early in 682.[15]

WOOLENS

The wools of Turkestan, both eastern and western, were famous in medieval times.[16] Woolens were familiar enough in T'ang (they are frequently mentioned in poetry, for example), but, except for rugs and carpets, they seem not to have been imported. Indeed, there was a sort of native industry in wool which may have sufficed for the limited purposes for which the Chinese required them. An exception was the woolen cloth—or perhaps we should say "hair cloth"—made from otter fur, sent by the Tibetans in the ninth century, along with other precious things, such as yaktails and gold vessels.[17] This unusual cloth (the alpaca of T'ang?) was exotic, though otters were not; there was even a Chinese of the same period, a professional fisherman, who had trained ten of the clever animals to do his fishing for him.[18]

The native T'ang woolens were almost as curious as the Tibetan: a "woolen" fabric was made of rabbit hair at Hsüan-*chou* near the mouth of the Yangtze,[19] and woolen goods of camel hair were manufactured in Kansu (Hui-*chou*) and the Ordos (Feng-*chou*).[20] The art of making these camlets had presumably been learned from the Iranian peoples of the West.

RUGS

In 726, the king of Bukhāra sent envoys to T'ang, asking help against Arab raiders. These emissaries brought with them a number of valuable gifts, such as saffron and "stone honey," and also a "Roman embroidered carpet." [21] The king's wife, the "Qatun," sent the Chinese empress two large rugs and one "embroidered carpet." [22] In return for these, Hsüan Tsung was asked to give a saddle and bridle, a robe and girdle, and various other regalia to the lord of Bukhāra, and a costume and cosmetics to his wife.[23] Other woolen rugs, including "dance mats," came to Ch'ang-an in the eighth century, the gifts of the potentates of Kapiśa, of Māimargh, of Turgäch, Chāch, and Kish.[24] Among the "embroidered dance mats" of Persia which arrived at the T'ang capital in 750, some were characterized as "great hair" and "long hair," terms which must refer to rugs with unusually deep and thick piles.[25] Possibly the dance mats decorated with gilded serpents, described in a poem by Li Ho, were of Iranian origin,[26] but another of the same poet's verses tells of an undoubted Iranian wool rug under the Sino-Persian name of *t'ập-tɘng:* we must believe that these were not uncommon in the houses of the well-to-do in the eighth and ninth centuries. The poem, "Song of a Palace Houri," is worth translating. In reading it, the reader must understand that a "palace warder" is a gecko: according to an old tradition these little lizards could be fed on cinnabar until they became red; then they were pounded up in a mortar, and the liquor obtained used to spot the body of the emperor's concubines; these marks were permanent, it was thought, unless the woman had sexual intercourse, after which they disappeared. Therefore the Son of Heaven could see plainly whether his women had remained faithful to him, and the geckos were accordingly called "palace warders." The "Seven Stars" are in the Great Dipper. A-chen was the favorite of a ruler of the third century, and the "houri" of our present poem means to say that she is as sad and lonely as that lady of a former age. "Long Island" is the name of a garden. The poem mixes contemporary and archaic images.

> The light of the candles, high suspended, shining through the gauze, is empty;
> In the flowered chamber, at night, they pound the "palace warders."
> The elephant's mouth blows incense, the *taptan* is warm;
> The Seven Stars hang over the city wall, I hear the gong of the water clock.
> The cold penetrates the silken screen, the shadow of the basilica is dark;
> The curtain's architrave, with its colored simurghs, shows marks of frost.
> Crying mole-crickets mourn the moon under the crooked balustrade;
> Bent-knee hinges and copper doorplate lock me, like A-chen, in.
> In dreams I enter the door of my home, and go up the sandy islet;
> At the place where the River of Heaven falls is the road to the Long Island.
> I wish that my Lord, bright and shining like the Great Luminary,
> Would release his concubine to ride a fish away, skimming the waves.[27]

ASBESTOS

The wonderful quality of asbestos was familiar to both Romans and Chinese from about the beginning of the Christian era. The men of Han regarded it as a Roman product, quite properly since this mineral fiber was very well known to the Romans, who also understood that it came from a rock. Here is Apollonius Dyscolus on asbestos napkins:

When these napkins are soiled, their cleansing is performed not by means of washing in water, but brush-wood is burnt, the napkin in question is placed over this fire, and the squalor flows off; while the cloth itself comes forth from the fire brilliant and pure.[28]

This natural but somewhat ostentatious display is said to have had its counterpart in China in the second century, when a man purposely soiled his asbestos robe, and hurled it into a fire with simulated anger, only to bring it out fresh and clean.[29] These anecdotes make the Chinese name for the mineral fabric understandable—it was "fire-washed linen." But asbestos was also called "fire hair," which illustrates another (and false) theory of the origin of the stuff. In the Hellenistic Orient it was sometimes thought to be of vegetable origin, like cotton, but among the Chinese, until the sixth century, and after that among the Arabs, the most popular theory was that it was the fur of the salamander-rat (but sometimes the phoenix) which was cleaned and renewed by fire.[30]

A Persian gift to the T'ang emperor in 750 was a "fire hair embroidered dance mat," that is (as it might be conceived), a rug made of salamander wool.[31] To judge from a couplet in a poem of the same period, asbestos was sometimes used in clothing; the verses describe the costume of a rich aristocrat:

A fire-washed single garment, with embroidered square collar;
A "dogwood brocade" girdle, with jeweled plates and wallet.[32]

Asbestos seems to have been particularly associated with Lingnan, presumably because of imported stuff in the hands of dealers there. In a poem on that region, Yüan Chen (of the early ninth century), describing such typical articles of that region as sago and elemi, also has these lines:

Fire linen when dirty or dusty needs washing in fire,
Tree floss is warm and soft, right for padding clothes.[33]

"Tree floss" is kapok, another typically southern product.[34]

FELT

The arts of making and using felt had been known to the Chinese since the end of the Chou dynasty, but in Han times it was still conceived to be a rather barbaric stuff. Its true home was among the Iranians, where the ancient Magi and the Achaemenian Shahs wore high felt hats, as did their latter-day imitators in Sogdiana.[35] Even in T'ang times the material was not completely naturalized, though it was widely used for curtains, draperies, tents, mats, saddle covers, boots, and all sorts of coverings. Somehow it was regarded as more characteristic of the nomadic peoples, like butter, and T'ang descriptions of nomadic life invariably emphasize its presence. High-ranking Tibetan soldiers lived in huge felt tents, which could accommodate several hundred men;[36] but the great King Srong-btsan-sgam-po, to please his Chinese consort, ". . . discarded his felt and fur robes which had to give way to Chinese silk and brocade"[37]—this was the beginning of a seventh-century trend; not many years after, during Kao Tsung's reign, the Tibetans asked for and received Chinese craftsmen in sericulture, wine making, mills, paper, and ink.[38] The red-haired, blue-eyed Kirghiz (they regarded black hair as unlucky) carried whetstones at their belts and wore hats of white felt.[39] The Turks cut the image of their god from a piece of felt, and kept it in a skin bag, plastered with fragrant ointments, as they moved about the country, and worshiped it suspended from a pole.[40]

But felt boots were made in Ch'ang-an itself;[41] scarlet felt for Chinese use was brought in from the garrison at Kucha,[42] and white felt was a regular product of inner Kansu and the Chinese Ordos.[43] Early in the seventh century, Chang-sun Wu-chi (codifier of the T'ang statutory laws) was responsible for a widespread mania for men's hats of felt made from the wool of a black sheep,[44] and among the many rich gifts given to Rokhshan by Hsüan Tsung was "felt embroidered with goose feathers."[45] In short, though it savored somewhat of the wild horsemen of the steppe, felt was as commonplace in north China as Scottish woolens are in England.

LINEN

If "linen" is used in its broadest sense, meaning a fabric woven from threads spun of vegetable fibers, the Chinese had many excellent linens of their own, especially those of hemp, ramie, and kudzu. But they imported some too: they used the "Western (*hu*) woman linen," of the Ordos and Mongolia and of their own provinces of Shensi and Shansi, but though the name indicates that it was made by non-Chinese weavers, we do not know what sort of thread they used.[46] From Silla and nearby Manchuria came another unidentified linen (hemp seems the likely fiber).[47] For that matter, cotton cloth fits our definition of "linen," and the Chinese regarded it as of the same class of textiles. But that is another story.

Varṇakā

Varṇakā, whose Indian trade-name indicates that it was a "colored" stuff,[48] was the product of "Lesser Brahman," a land of vegetarians just beyond Pyū in Burma,[49] and also was brought to Ch'ang-an from Samarkand in the eighth century.[50] Although Sung texts tell of "white *varṇakā*" (a seeming contradiction) of Baghdad, and "*varṇakā* with gold characters" of Rūm,[51] we have no hint of the nature of this "colored" linen (a cotton?) of T'ang times.

PONGEE

T'ang, the land of silk, accepted some foreign silks. Early in 839, a shipment of a plain weave of raw silk (which can conveniently be called "pongee") [52] crossed the Yellow Sea, the gift of the ruler of Japan to his cousin of T'ang.[53] This kind of material would have been most suitable as a ground for court painters.

BOMBYCINE

T'ang, and other Far Eastern countries as well, made bombycines, or tussahs, of thread spun from the silk remnants left when the wild tussah moth cuts its way out of the cocoon.[54] Toward the end of the eighth century, Nan-chao offered tribute of Tibetan tussah to T'ang.[55] From both Annam and Japan came tribute of a coarse bombycine, or what we might call by our naturalized word "shantung." [56] Japanese shantung was of two kinds, and there were two hundred lengths of each kind. One was named for the *kuni* or "province" of Mino, and the other was styled "water woven." This last mysterious epithet, otherwise unintelligible, takes us into the world of the "water silkworms," which we shall encounter again presently.

But before that let us look at some fancy tussahs from Silla. Several times during the eighth century that Korean nation offered textiles called "sunrise clouds of morning bombycine" and "fish tusk bombycine."[57] The latter was also sent by the "Black Water Mo-ho" and the Shih-wei.[58] The name "sunrise clouds of morning," connoting the radiantly pink color of white clouds illuminated from below, was a familiar epithet, applied to popular cotton cloth much imported from the Indies. It is to be supposed that this Korean tussah was attractively colored to deserve the same name. As for the "fish tusk," this designated a yellowish veined or grained appearance, with larger yellow flammulations, suggestive of the appearance of a cross section of walrus ivory, and so the name.[59]

POLYCHROME SILKS

Tapestries, brocades, and other sumptuous stuffs ornamented with colored figures, especially fancy silks, were classed together in T'ang, under a term which I have translated "brocade." They will be briefly treated together here, but it must be remembered the while that China was a world-renowned source of these splendid goods, and gave much more than she received. Persia was a great rival of China in fine fabrics, and embassies from Khuttal and Kapiśa were undoubtedly proud to offer "Persian brocades" to the Son of Heaven.[60] Here too we must mention the "caftan woven with gold threads," a true and noble brocade, the gift of the " 'Amīr al-Muhminīn Sulaymān" (that is, of the Ummayad Commander of the Faithful) to Hsüan Tsung in 716.[61] Even the manner of the Byzantine Greek was represented in the Far East—an example is a fabric decorated with eight-pointed stars, found in a grave at Astāna, near Turfan.[62] And among the oddities belong a "hair brocade," the gift of Samarkand,[63] presumably a fine woolen or perhaps a muster (silk and wool mixture), and a brocade from Silla commemorating the victory of that country's hosts over the men of Paekche. On this latter piece was woven a paean in five-word form, eulogizing Kao Tsung of T'ang in the most fulsome manner, and it was presented to Kao Tsung by the younger brother of the king of Silla.

WATER SHEEP AND ICE SILKWORMS

In our discussion of exotic and fantastic sheep we have noted down the story of the "earth-born sheep," the *Agnus scythicus* of Roman legend. That story, possibly presenting a pale reflection of the episode of the Argonauts and the Golden Fleece to the Far East, has become entangled with the story of the "water sheep," whose "wool" was the raw material of a real industry, the production of *pinikón* around the shores of the Indian Ocean during the early centuries of the Christian era. The fabric known by this name was woven from the tough, thin anchoring filaments, called byssi, of the pearl-bearing mussel *Pinna squamosa,* and was probably an outgrowth of the pearling industry about the Persian Gulf and Ceylon.[64] These pinna textiles had ". . . a uniform gold-brown or dull cinnamon hue." [65] In China, where the paramount animal producer of textile fibers was the silkworm, not the sheep, we have stories of a marvelous thread from across the seas, produced by a "water silkworm," most probably the pinna mussel. The beautiful Yang Kuei-fei had a lute, whose wood was mirror-glossy, with figures of two phoenixes inlaid in red and gold, and this precious instrument was strung with ". . . the silk threads of the strained-water silkworm," the tribute of a remote nation some 250 years earlier.[66] Or again, there was the coverlet of "divine brocade," woven from the silk threads of the water silkworm, also called the "ice silkworm." This useful animal (so went the tale) was fed its favorite leaves in pools lined with multicolored tiles, in its home in the South Seas; the blanket made from its cocoon had the virtue of expanding in contact with water and contracting when it touched fire.[67] This tale was the production of our old friend Su O. That the "water silkworm" is sometimes an "ice silkworm" is probably due to the fact that the graphs for the words "water" and "ice" differ by only a single dot, and are regularly confused in Chinese texts. In this case, the confusion was accepted the more readily in that there was an ancient tradition of "ice silkworms" in China itself. A fourth-century tale told of ice silkworms, horned and scaled, seven inches long, which lived on a round cosmic mountain. When covered with frost and snow, they spun multicolored cocoons that could be turned into patterned textiles which were not wettable by water and were unconsumed by fire; the archaic culture hero Yao received some of this material from "men of the sea" (a term which sometimes means only "men from overseas"), and wove himself ceremonial robes of it.[68] This imaginary cloth (or is the pinna mussel behind this too?) was easily confused, at least in the minds of innocent men of letters, with a perfectly real "ice taffeta," or "glacé taffeta," [69] a fine white fabric made during the first Christian century in Shantung. In the name of this product, " 'ice' means that its color is as fresh and clean as ice." [70] Accordingly, when a *literatus* of the ninth century wrote "Rhapsody on the Offering of Ice Silkworms by Men from the Sea" on a rhyme scheme which can be translated "Now That the Four Barbarians Are Put in Order, the Seas Do Not Hide Their Treasures," praising, of course, the world-wide effects of the imperial charisma,[71] a one-time governor of Zayton could also write, on the identical rhyme scheme, "A Rhapsody on the Offering of Ice Taffeta by Men from the Sea." [72] So colored cloth from the monstrous worms of the frozen world-mountain was effectively merged with the old Han glacé taffeta, while keeping the fantastic qualities of the ice-worm's filaments: ". . . neither scorched nor dampened, only to be compared with the fire-rat in significance; sometimes vermilion, sometimes green . . ." Even the asbestine salamander is pulled into the story.

The panegyrical language of these two "rhapsodies" prevents us from being certain whether the tribute "ice taffeta" was to be taken merely as symbolic of the revival of the good old days of Yao, or whether something actually describable as a cloth made from the cocoons of the ice (or water?) silkworm had in fact been received from overseas during T'ang. If the latter, it may well have been *pinikón*.

COTTON

From about the beginning of the ninth century, words for cotton appear commonly in Chinese poems. To give a few examples: P'i Jih-hsiu wrote of Buddhist priests "kerchiefed with *karpāsa*-linen, catered to with morsels of *candana*," [73] where "*karpāsa*-linen" means cotton cloth; Chang Chi described Kurung slaves brought to China by "*Man*-barbarian visitors," black-skinned, wearing their hair in long curls, heavily earringed, and caped in "tree floss"; [74] Po Chü-i tells how he drinks, unrepentant, in the early morning hours in his sky-blue Turkish tent:

> A short wind-screen covers the head of the couch I lie on,
> With raven-black hat, and this blue felt, and white cotton cape;
> I drink one goblet at the *mao*-hour, and sleep one nap;
> What affair is there—out in the world—which isn't dim and remote? [75]

Cotton was well enough known from mid-T'ang times, it seems, but more as a popular novelty than as an old familiar thing. Let us look at its history in the Far East.

True cotton is the product both of the annual "cotton plant" (*Gossypium herbaceum*) and of the perennial "cotton tree" (*G. arboreum*), which occur as wild and cultivated plants in tropical Asia. The useful fibers of these plants are often confused in literature, both Western and Chinese, with the floss known as simal, the product of the "silk-cotton tree" (*Bombax malabaricum*), and with kapok, which comes from another "silk-cotton tree," the ceiba (*Ceiba pentandra*).[76] Both simal and kapok, which also grow widely in southern Asia, serve to stuff cushions and the like but are useless for spinning into thread.

True cotton, then, is not native to China, but is endemic to many tropical lands close by. However, it cannot be cultivated in lands which have rain throughout the year, since it is subject to mildew; for this reason it is not found growing in southern Malaya, Borneo, Sumatra, or western Java. It is grown, like sandalwood, in places which have a dry season (approximately April to September), such as eastern Java, Bali, the Sunda Islands, and northern Malaya.[77] Most likely it was first domesticated in India.[78]

Cotton was introduced to China as an article of commerce in about the third century A.D., by two different routes: through Serindia and through Indochina.[79] Cotton planting followed by the same routes. It was cultivated by non-Chinese peoples of what was later called Yünnan in later Han times, and in Chinese Turkestan by the beginning of the sixth century.[80]

The cotton of Qočo in Serindia was especially well known in T'ang: it was grown, spun, and woven into cloth by the natives of that city, and imported thence.[81] Administratively, this was Chinese territory, and its conquest must have stimulated the creation of a Chinese cotton industry. But the cottons of Indochina and the Isles enjoyed much greater repute in T'ang. It was reported of Champa, for instance, that "its king wears *bagtak* [and] *karpāsa* [that is, cotton], draped slanting from his upper arm, and wrapped above his waist. To this he adds true pearls and golden chains made into beaded pendants. He crowns his curled hair with flowers." [82] Bali was known to grow its own cotton and to make cloth of it: there ". . . all the men have curled hair, and they cover themselves with '*karpāsa*-linen,' using a horizontal length to wrap around their thighs." [83] Hsüan-tsang, the great traveler for the Faith, reported cloth made of *karpāsa* in India, but mistakenly described it as made from "the thread of a wild silkworm"; [84] of the timid and ugly Tocharians he wrote, "they wear much cotton, but are little costumed in wool." [85] And cotton was imported from many places in the South: cotton thread from Nan-chao; [86] "flowered" and other cotton fabrics from Champa; [87] and fine cottons from Ceylon.[88] Island kingdoms in the Southern ocean, whose names are now difficult to identify, sent cottons: [89] mysterious *Dabatang* was such a land—there, on the seas west of Kalinga, they wrote their books on palm leaves, and the mouths of dead men were filled with gold, after which their bodies were burned on pyres of Borneo camphor. This nation sent cotton cloth to T'ang in 647.[90]

We have seen the foreign words *bagtak* and *karpāsa* in passages just quoted. In T'ang the tree, the floss, and the cloth were known by a variety of names. One of the earliest was *t'ung,* in use from later Han to T'ang.[91] The origin of this name is unknown; it was obsolete in late T'ang. Better established by that time were Chinese phonetic renderings, by way of some Malayan language, of Sanskrit *karpāsa,* "cotton," [92] and of an old Iranian word cognate to Modern Persian *bagtak,* related somehow to Pali *patāka*.[93] If a distinction was made between the two, *karpāsa* (or rather its Chinese transcription) meant a coarser cotton cloth, and *patāka* a finer, but the difference was not always observed. These words, as we have seen, appear in late T'ang poetry and, looking at these poets again, it seems an inescapable conclusion that a cotton industry was established in Lingnan by the beginning of the ninth century. The poet Wang Chien, who was writing at that period, in a poem composed on the occasion of the departure of a friend for Canton, has these verses:

> At the head of the frontier garrison, shops for Dragon Brain;
> At the mouth of the customs barrier, heaps of elephant tusks.

And then,

Bagtak woven by family on family,
Red bananas cultivated in place after place.[94]

Another poet, a tenth-century one, wrote of "Southern Yüeh," the same region as the one described by Wang Chien, in these terms:

In kitchens at daybreak they boil insipid greens,
With loom reeds in spring they weave the cotton flowers.[95]

"Sunrise Clouds of Morning"

The expression "sunrise clouds of morning" has already been noted as the name of a pink tussah silk imported from Korea. "Sunrise clouds" might equally be rendered "clouds flushed with dawn," to suggest the lovely peach color of an Indochinese and Indonesian cotton dye, and was used also of some silks, as when Li Ho writes, "One length of light chiffon, dyed with the pink clouds of morning." [96] It is only coincidence that Théophile Gautier, writing "A une robe rose," asked

Est-ce à la rougeur de l'aurore,
A la coquille de Vénus,
Au bouton de sein près d'éclore,
Que sont pris ces tons inconnus?

The phrase occurs also in direct reference to the rosy dawn in a quatrain by Wang Po, but even there its application to a textile cannot be forgotten, since this dawn is divinely woven:

As on a fragrant screen spring herbs are painted;
As by a sylph-man's reed the morning flush was woven.
What is quite like a road by hill and water—
Where against my face the flowers go flying? [97]

The rosy cotton was imported directly from the Annamese protectorate,[98] and gifts of it were received even from such an unlikely place as Tibet.[99] But, like other cotton goods, it was above all a product of the Indianized nations of the South. Consider for instance the cotton culture of the Burmese country of Pyū, also called Śrîkshetra. In the seventh century its people practiced a kind of Buddhism based on Sanskrit scriptures, a rival to an older sect whose holy books were written in Pali; the ashes of their dead were buried in inscribed terra-cotta urns,[100] and ". . . for clothing and costume they use only *bagtak* made into 'morning sunrise-clouds,' and simply wrap it around their waists. They do not dress in silks or satins, saying that these come from the silkworm, and this would be to injure living things." [101] Similarly, the wives of the king of Champa ". . . are costumed in morning sunrise clouds *karpāsa*, which they make into a short skirt; they carry golden flowers on their heads, and their bodies are adorned with beaded pendants of golden chains and true pearls." [102] In short, they dressed much like the king.[103] Not only the dyed cloth of these dark peoples but also their barbaric costumes could be seen in the northern capitals: when the orchestras of Bnam and India, with their phoenix-headed harps, lutes, cymbals, flutes, conchs, and many drums, played at court receptions in Ch'ang-an, the dancers were costumed in the dawn-flushed cotton, which for the Indians was cut as the cassocks of Buddhist monks.[104]

For Newton's notion of colours is αλογος *unphilo-*
sophical.
For the colours are spiritual.

Christopher Smart, "Rejoice in the Lamb"

xııı=Pigments

THE COURT DYERS at Ch'ang-an recognized
five official colors other than white: blue, red, yellow, black, and purple.[1] There were
ancient and honorable vegetable dyes to supply them: Chinese indigo,[2] madder,
gardenia, acorns, and groomwell. There were even alternates for some colors, as the
yellow of the "Amur cork tree," [3] of the "smoke tree" (fustet),[4] and of the barberry,[5]
to supplement the gardenia. Mineral pigments, on the other hand, were used primarily by painters to color their pictures, and by women to tint their faces. In this
group the traditional substances were azurite for blue, malachite for green, cinnabar
(and sometimes minium, or "red lead") for red, ocher for yellow, carbon for black,
and ceruse for white. New pigments introduced from foreign countries were mostly
vegetable colors. Other cultures exploited exotic plants, but there were few new
mineral colors to be found abroad. Rocks and their components do not vary much
from clime to clime, or rather, they vary in abundance much more than in kind.
Accordingly, the pigments imported by T'ang were mainly plant products.

GIBBON'S BLOOD

Some medieval Chinese pigments were fanciful, either in origin, in name, or in
reputation. We may have our doubts about the frost from a southern mountain
which could be used as a purple dye, and the dew from a mountain lake which produced a red dye: "These are the crown of the Subcelestial Realm, and it is regrettable

208

that men have no knowledge of them." [6] But the dye color called "gibbon's blood" existed on a different level of reality than these, or rather, it was paradoxically mythical and real at the same time. This was the blood (it was said) of an animal called *hsing-hsing:*

The *hu* of the Western countries take its blood for dyeing their woolen rugs; its color is clean and will not turn black. Some say that when you prick it for its blood, if you ask, "How much will you give me?" the *hsing-hsing* will say, "Would two pints be truly enough?" In order to add to this amount, you thrash it with a whip before asking, and it will go along with an increase, so that you can obtain up to a gallon. [7]

This agreeable anthropoid was described in ancient books as able to understand human speech, and even able to speak itself; some said it was the naked white-skinned "wild woman" (known to haunt the jungles of Annam); [8] its lips were a delicacy for the gourmet; it was addicted to wine, and this failing helped the natives of the southern forests to catch it. Apparently it also had a sense of humor: a T'ang story tells how a number of the beasts were captured and put in a pen, to be cooked for the magistrate of a Tonkinese town. They picked the fattest of their number and thrust it weeping forth, to await the magistrate's pleasure in a covered cage: "The Commandant asked what thing this was, and the *hsing-hsing* spoke from within the cage, and said, 'Only your servant and a jug of wine!' The Commandant laughed, and cherished it." Of course the clever, winebibbing animal became a treasured pet. [9]

Though its story may have been merged with an alien story and an exotic tradition, there can be little doubt that the *hsing-hsing* was a Chinese gibbon, [10] and in all probability its name was collective and composite, referring equally to the three gibbons of south China and Indochina, the "black, crested, or Indo-Chinese gibbon," the "white-handed gibbon," and the "hoolock gibbon." [11] The hoolock is still to be seen in southwest China, and the crested gibbon may occur there; the white-handed gibbon tends to range further to the south. In poetry of the eighth and ninth century, the *hsing-hsing* occurs in the Yangtze Valley, and in Szechwan: "There one may sometimes see the *hsing-hsing* crying in the trees." [12] Evidently the hoolock or one of his cousins, like other mammals now pressed over the southern frontier of China, once ranged much further to the north than it now does.

It might be hoped that the origin of the gibbon's blood story could be found in the West, and the hope is supported by the Egyptian tradition that some cynocephali understand letters and are therefore dedicated to Thoth, the patron of writing; [13] this reminds us of the loquacious Chinese apes. Also, in the Classical world, monkeys were reputed to be overfond of wine, as Aristotle, Aelian, and Pliny observed, and their drunkenness made them easy to capture, [14] just as the people of the southwestern marches of China believed. On the other hand, apes were noted in the Western tradition for their lustfulness. The lechery attributed to baboons may be simply the result of attempts to explain Egyptian pictures showing them as ithyphallic, but in any case the red apes of India were also said to be lustful, and indeed the gibbons of that country were probably the originals of the Asiatic *satyri* described by Pliny and Aelian.[15] So while the Classical Pan was a lustful goat, the Classical satyr was a lustful ape. The image of the ape as "luxury," that is, sexual desire, became a late medieval stereotype in Europe.[16] Unfortunately our Chinese gibbon is not particularly "luxurious," nor is the blood of the Western ape useful as a textile dye.

Indeed, the source of the tradition of the bloody dye, if it existed at all outside the Far East, has yet to be traced. But we can find Western analogues, none of them anthropoid. Our vocabulary retains, in such words as "crimson" and "cramoisy" (a crimson cloth), the name of the kermes insect, the source of an ancient dye, like the cochineal insect. A variety of kermes, called "St. John's blood," used in Germany and Poland since the twelfth century, even bridges the gap between a dye and a primate's blood. And then there is "dragon's blood," a name given in the West to a variety of vegetable pigments. But we have no apes in all this. Nonetheless, Chinese usage makes it clear that "gibbon's blood" was the name of a fine bright scarlet observed in imported Western textiles, and not the name of a dye used by the Chinese themselves. Perhaps it meant "kermes dye," but we cannot explain how the insect was transformed into a mammal.

Although "gibbon's blood" was used long before T'ang as the name of an exotic textile dye, it was only in late T'ang times that it was generalized as the name of a color. Then a camellia blossom could be the color of "gibbon's blood,"[17] a "gibbon's color" screen might be painted with broken boughs,[18] and a fashionable lady's rouge was styled "gibbon nimbus."[19] We shall observe the new expression in the poetry of the ninth and tenth centuries, when we come to discuss "ultramarine" (lapis lazuli pigment), a color with which it was often contrasted.

LAC

The Chinese of T'ang used a dye which actually had an animal origin. This was lac, a substance secreted by the "lac insect"[20] on a number of Indochinese trees. The insect also deposits a resinous substance on the branches; this is the source of commercial shellac, and was used by the jewelers of T'ang as an adhesive,[21] just as more recently the Malays have used it to fix kris blades to their hafts.[22] In T'ang, the pigment was called either "purple mineral" (showing that the source of the dye had once been wrongly understood), or *lakka,* using a loan word.[23] Lac was imported from Annam,[24] and from Cambodia.[25] It was used as a silk dye and in cosmetic rouge.[26]

DRAGON'S BLOOD

The effusion of the lac insect was in turn confused with the blood of a mythical or semi-mythical animal, the Chinese "unicorn." One of the red kinos which was traded about the Old World under the name "dragon's blood" was in China styled "unicorn gutta" and was thought of as desiccated blood.[27] It was the product of the fruit of an Indonesian rattan palm,[28] but in the trade it was confused with Socotran dragon's blood, the resin of an entirely different plant,[29] and with a different Indonesian kino,[30] and also with lac. In T'ang it was used as an astringent drug and prescribed for hemorrhages, partly at least on the principle of imitative magic, because of its bloodlike color.[31] It cannot be said with certainty that it was also used as a dye, but it was commonly employed in this way in its Malayan homeland,[32] and the Chinese pharmacologists emphasize that it was used in just the same way as lac.[33]

SAPAN

"Brazilwood"[34] was known to the Chinese as "sapanwood," a term now generally current in the Orient. It comes from an Indonesian word cognate to Old Javanese *sapan,* "red," because of the red heartwood which yields the dye.[35] Sapanwood had been imported from Champa and Cambodia for many centuries,[36] and these were still the important sources for it in T'ang, where it was in great demand.[37] The Sāsānian Persians also used it as a dye, and the Hainanese pirate Feng Jo-fang had heaps of it among the treasures he had looted from Persian merchant vessels.[38] The Chinese of T'ang dyed cloth with it,[39] and used it to stain wooden objects; this was the color used on the handsome boxes of "black persimmon wood" in the Shōsōin.[40]

MUREX PURPLE?

The palace women of the last sovereign of Sui were issued a daily allotment of a cosmetic named "snail kohl" (or mascara), which was imported from Persia. They used it to lengthen their eyebrows, as was the fashion.[41] Nothing is said of the color of this pigment, but the Chinese name strongly suggests the Classical Tyrian purple obtained from the *Murex* shell. I have no record of this for T'ang (though a few pots of the Sui cosmetic must have survived the conquest!), but the possibility that this famous dye reached the Far East may justify this note.

INDIGO

In addition to the old source of vegetable blue—the native "indigo" taken from one of the knotweeds [42]—the cosmetic makers of T'ang had also an imported Persian dye, called "blue kohl," derived from the true indigo.[43] This deep blue is thought to be of Indian origin, but it was in use very early in Egypt, and later also among the Iranian nations.[44] In T'ang it was known as a product of Kabūdhān, along with putchuk and gum guggul,[45] and of Farghāna, where the ladies painted their eyelids with it.[46] The rulers of Samarkand sent indigo with other valuable gifts to T'ang in 717.[47]

The exotic cosmetic was used by the women of T'ang as by their Western sisters, as we may see in a poem of Li Po:

Grape wine—in golden beaker—
A houri of Wu, just fifteen, borne on a slender horse,
Eyebrows painted with blue kohl, and red brocade boots;
The words she speaks are not correct, but the songs she sings are pretty;
She is drunk in my bosom on the tortoise-shell banquet mat—
What now, my lord, below the lotus hangings?[48]

Indigo was required for the "moth eyebrows" of the palace women of Te Tsung, late in the eighth century.[49]

By the beginning of the ninth century, the expression "blue kohl" had been generalized by the poets into a color appropriate to distant mountains. Po Chü-i has "The mountain named 'India,' a heap of blue kohl,"[50] and Yüan Chen has, even more strikingly, "Flowery mountain, brushed with blue kohl."[51] The exotic color image, like "gibbon's blood," is characteristic of the age.

Bhallātaka

"Marking nuts," under the Sanskrit name of *bhallātaka*,[52] were imported from "the Western seas and the country of Persia," and used to strengthen the loins and to dye the hair black.[53] The marking nut tree, a native of north India, was widely used there to make black marks on cloth and also to provide a dark gray dye.[54] It is not certain that the men of T'ang used it for this last purpose.

OAK GALLS

The round excrescences stimulated by Cynips insects around the buds of the "dyer's oak"[55] and other oaks are rich in tannin, which readily forms a bluish-black ink in conjunction with iron salts, and so they are widely demanded for both inks and dyes. The Chinese had obtained their tannin from the bark and acorns of native oaks since archaic times, but the galls imported from Persia, under an Iranian name like *muzak* or *mazak*, were properly regarded as superior.[56] Su Kung reports that galls also grow on tamarisks in the sandy deserts of the West.[57] Though the pharmaceutical books state only that oak galls were recommended for various tonic medicines and to darken the hair, we may readily assume that, like *bhallātaka*, they were also used in dyeing.

GAMBODGE

Gambodge is named for Cambodia, its true home. This pigment is the solidified sap of an Indochinese tree related to the mangosteen.[58] This sap yields a fine yellow pigment, highly esteemed in the Far East: "It makes the golden yellow ink of Siam, which is used for writing on locally made books of black paper." [59] It was the only vegetable pigment much used by the medieval painters of China, where it was named "rattan yellow." [60] Li Hsün reports that it was needed by alchemists as well as by artists; [61] it must therefore have been imported, most likely from Cambodia.

FLAKE BLUE

The basic carbonates of copper, malachite and azurite, were the traditional green and blue pigments of the Chinese painters. A variety of names, both popular and technical, for several grades of these two bices was current in medieval China: a traditional distinction is that between coarse grinds, which tend to be dark, and fine grinds, which are lighter. Azurite was ordinarily called "stone blue," but alchemists called it by the whimsical name of "blue-waisted girl," [62] and dark, coarsely ground preparations were "great blue." The "flake blue" [63] brought, according to Su Kung, from the Southern lands of Champa and Bnam by commercial argosy, was thought by the pharmacologist himself to be a malachite [64] but was most likely a coarse, flaky, deep blue azurite.[65] Indeed, in the cant of the alchemists, azurite was simply "K'un-lun," [66] as we would say "Indochina."

ORPIMENT

The beautiful yellow arsenic sulphide named orpiment (from *auripigmentum*), also called "king's yellow" by Western painters, was in China "hen yellow" [67] because it was found associated with realgar, which was "cock yellow." [68] The alchemists called it, in their cabalistic jargon, "blood of the divine woman" or "blood of the yellow dragon," [69] and they claimed that the kind like "spat blood" brought up by ship was superior to the native mineral mined in Hunan.[70] It was also named "sperm of gold," because of supposed mineralogical relation with gold, as azurite was "sperm of copper." [71] This fine color had been imported from Champa and Cambodia at least as early as the fifth century, and was therefore also called "Kurung yellow." [72] Accordingly, we are not surprised to find it as the golden yellow of the paintings on silk brought back from Tun-huang.[73] The vicinity of Mastūj was reputed in T'ang to be rich in orpiment and grapes,[74] but we do not know if either of these products was exported thence to China.

Among the fashions most popular with T'ang ladies was the application of "forehead yellow," as we know from the literature of manners.[75] It seems likely that a yellow lead, like massicot, was most commonly used for the purpose, but it is not unlikely that golden arsenic was sometimes applied, though, like lead paint, it is injurious to the skin if left on too long.[76] Yellow, like blue and even black, was perfectly proper on the faces of highborn ladies. Such fanciful vogues as these, some of foreign origin, provoked both the merriment and the indignation of the poets. Here, in "Foreign Fashions," is the view of Po Chü-i on the mode in cosmetics and coiffures at the beginning of the ninth century, in Arthur Waley's translation:

> The fashions of our day
> Spread from the City to the four corners of the world.
> At present a custom prevails far and near
> Of cheeks unrouged and faces without powder.
> With muddy grease the ladies smear their lips;
> Their eyebrows tilt to the shape of a painted roof.
> Beautiful and ugly, dark and fair, lose their natural form;
> All present, when they leave their rooms, the same countenance of woe.
> Their round coils, brushed back from the temples, are piled up behind;
> They do not mitigate the yellow of their skin by any touch of red.
> Wild tresses once were seen by the rivers of our Eastern Town,
> And sorrow seized those who saw, for they knew there were Tartars in the land.
>
> Prince, take note! The head-fashions of this period Yüan-ho—
> These heaped tresses and unpowdered cheeks—are no Chinese way! [77]

Your stone, your med'cine, and your chrysosperme,
Your sal, your sulphur, and your mercury,
Your oil of height, your tree of life, your blood,
Your marchesite, your tutie, your magnesia,

. . . . .

And worlds of other strange ingredients,
Would burst a man to name?

Ben Jonson, *The Alchemist,* Act II

xiv=Industrial Minerals

IN MEDIEVAL INDIA a great variety of trade goods had names prefixed with *cini* or *cina,* as signs that they came from China and had the excellent qualities of imports from that rich and talented land; so the T'ang pilgrim Hsüan-tsang observed that in India peaches were called *cinani,* "from China," and pears were styled *cina rajaputra,* "Chinese king's son." [1] But in fact many of these expressions designated not true Chinese products but articles which were of some importance in the China trade, just as "Persian" wares in T'ang were often Malayan or Indian in origin. Among the nominally Chinese goods were *cina pishta,* "Chinese flour," a name given to minium or red lead, and *cina vanga,* "Chinese lead," a name for lead. These names may have been deserved, in that the Chinese of T'ang did in fact exploit lead mines, and they did have the secret of making red lead, which they regarded as a kind of cinnabar, mysteriously produced from lead instead of from quicksilver. In any case the names show the prestige which Chinese industrial minerals enjoyed in medieval Asia. [2]

China is rich in minerals of many kinds, and most of them were converted to practical purposes by the artisans of T'ang. Indeed, the ancient Chinese had investigated the mineral kingdom with admirable thoroughness. The study of mineral drugs and their properties was a field in which they led the world. But they were also richly supplied with the materials needed by painters, tanners, lapidaries, and other craftsmen, who required minerals of superior quality and understood their properties. Of course, the excellent knowledge which alchemists and artists and physicians had of mineral substances did not prevent confusion in the public marketplace, where some merchants were ready to sell substitutes to the unwary. Thus the modern scholar is as confused as the medieval buyer, since the scholar has had transmitted to him quite conflicting accounts of what are nominally specimens of the same mineral. Fortunately, Su Kung and other compilers of the T'ang pharmacopoeia have carefully noted down many of these falsifications; for example, they tell us that merchants of the seventh century regularly sold calcite (calcium carbonate) under the name of gypsum (hydrous calcium sulphate).[3] But less careful pharmacologists sometimes recorded, with painstaking honesty, the properties of both substances under the name of one, to the despair of the twentieth-century student.

Some foreign varieties of minerals which were also mined in T'ang were regarded as more pure or more active than their Far Eastern counterparts; realgar is a case in point. Others which were much needed did not occur at all in China—borax for instance. Still others were manufactured reagents, not yet provided by Chinese industry—litharge was one such. All these products had to be imported; they and some others are the subject of this chapter.

SALT

China produced enormous quantities of salt. Ch'en Ts'ang-ch'i wrote, "Within the Four Seas, what place lacks it? It is rather scarce only among the several barbarians of the Southwest."[4] The chief source of the useful mineral was sea water, and the great center of the evaporation industry in antiquity had been the coastal state of Ch'i (modern Shantung), which remained important in T'ang times.[5] But since the Han dynasty both brine and natural gas had also been obtained through deep boreholes in Szechwan,[6] and the Chinese also had deposits of rock salt for mining, and dry salt lakes on their frontier. For instance, the non-Chinese settlements along the Mongolian frontier just inside the great bend of the Yellow River, around Feng-*chou,* gathered over 14,000 piculs (or "hundredweights") of salt annually for the Chinese government.[7] Among the recognized varieties of salt used in medicine, cookery, and industry were "*Jung*-barbarian salt," "shining and luminous salt," and "seal salt." The first of these was actually a mixture of salts, including hydrous sulphates of magnesium, calcium, and sodium, along with potassium and sodium chlorides, variously colored by impurities and gathered from "alkali soils" in arid regions of the northwest in Kansu and Kokonor;[8] it was, in short, a crystalline deposit left in the dry beds of ancient lakes. "Shining and luminous salt" was rock salt.[9] "Seal salt," named for its appearance, was an artificially refined salt, in large rectangular crystals, shaped like ordinary Chinese documentary seals;[10] the "seal salt" of Ling-*chou* in western Shensi was of sufficiently high quality to be acceptable as "local tribute" in Ch'ang-an.[11]

With rich native salt resources available through the government monopoly, it is surprising to read of the importation of salt. But this commerce was not, in fact, very important, and was apparently limited to colored salts considered especially desirable for medicinal purposes. "Green salt" was one of these, but it had nothing to do with table salt (sodium chloride), and has been discussed in chapter xi under the heading "Blue Vitriol."

"Black salt" came as tribute in the joint mission of Turgäch, Chāch, Kish, Māimargh, and Kapiśa in 746 (along with "red salt"),[12] and in 751 and 753 also came from Khwārizm, south of the Oxus, a nation famous for the oxcarts used by its merchants to traverse the countries of Asia.[13] The identity of this substance is unknown.

ALUM

Alum was used in the ancient world, both East and West, by physicians (its astringent properties are most familiar), by dyers as a mordant to transform soluble dye substances into insoluble lakes, and by leatherworkers to make animal skins supple. The T'ang papermakers also glazed their fancy papers with alum.[14]

In T'ang, alums were graded according to their color. "White alum" was pure alum; the colored varieties contained various impurities, but sometimes they must have been other hydrous sulphates, superficially similar to ordinary alum. Some white alum was produced in northern and northwestern China, but the best quality was imported from Qočo in Central Asia [15] for the imperial paper finishers. Byzantium and Persia were also noted for their excellent white alums, crystal clear with acicular patterning; this kind was much desired by the Chinese alchemists, and Persian alum was much favored by druggists.[16]

"Yellow alum," possibly the hydrous sulphate of iron and aluminum called "halotrichite," perhaps mixed with alunogen,[17] was sent as tribute from the northwestern towns of Sha-*chou* and Kua-*chou*,[18] and was in demand for alchemy and for "dyeing skins."[19] "Green alum" was also produced at Kua-*chou*.[20] It was apparently melanterite,[21] colored like beryl-green glass; it could be oxidized by roasting into "crimson alum."[22]

From Persia came an elegant variety of alum, permeated with golden threads; this too was favored by the alchemists,[23] but what mineral this was and whether it had practical everyday uses in the Far East are equally unknown.

Sal Ammoniac

Ammonium chloride, or "sal ammoniac," occurs naturally about fumaroles in volcanic regions, but may also be prepared from the dung of domestic animals. The men of T'ang imported it, "shaped like odontoid niter, and bright and clean," from the Western Regions,[24] and above all as tribute from the Chinese protectorate at Kucha.[25] They called it *njau-ṣa,* an Iranian form, probably Sogdian, related to Persian *naušādir.*[26] The T'ang goldsmiths used it as a flux for soldering gold and silver.[27] It had a notable role in medicine, and indeed it first appears in the materia medica of T'ang.[28] Although the pharmacologists warned that it was poisonous and ought to be taken sparingly, they emphasized its importance for relieving bronchial congestion and other catarrhs.[29]

Borax

Borax crystallizes on the shores of lakes in arid regions west of China, in particular in Tibet.[30] It was brought to T'ang from these regions for the use of metalworkers, who exploited its property of dissolving metallic oxides for their gold and silver solders.[31] It does not, however, appear in the T'ang books of materia medica.[32]

Niter, Glauber's Salt, and Epsom Salts

The T'ang pharmacologists followed old tradition in lumping Epsom salts (a hydrous magnesium sulphate) with Glauber's salt, or mirabilite (a hydrous sodium sulphate), and both of them with niter (potassium nitrate), all being distinguished by name, but thought to be closely related in substance. They were imported from the arid lands of Central Asia, where they were formed by the evaporation of alkaline lakes.[33]

Of these, niter was the best known and the most important in technology, being vital, because of its fluxing properties,[34] to the Taoist alchemists, and used in pyrotechnical compositions. The men of T'ang had "flame flowers," "silver flowers," and "peach blossoms," all apparently pretty fireworks, and there was also some kind of Catherine wheel.[35] All of these probably required niter. The Arabs of the thirteenth century held niter and fireworks to be so much Chinese in character that they called niter *thelj as-Sin,* "Chinese snow," and a rocket *sahm khatāī,* "Cathayan arrow."[36]

Mirabilite was named "crude niter,"[37] but its place in medicine was much overshadowed by Epsom salts (epsomite), named "spiky niter"[38] from the shape of its pointed crystals and extracted from impure mirabilite by distillation.[39] A very pure reagent was obtained in this way, as we know from a sample preserved in the Shōsōin.[40] Its purgative properties were understood, and it was frequently prescribed by the T'ang physicians.[41]

SULPHUR

The physicians of T'ang needed sulphur for their preparations; the alchemists needed it even more for their cinnabar elixirs, and it went into fine vermilion required by the painters of pictures and purveyors of cosmetics. Sulphur was also used in the manufacture of pyrotechnical devices.

Sulphur was useful in the treatment of skin diseases, and it was for this reason that hot springs containing sulphur compounds had been popular since Han times.[42] The element was also believed to have calorific properties, which heated the water of the thermae; for the same reason it was used in medicines to heat the body—for instance, to cure coldness around the waist and kidneys.[43] Since ancient times cups made of sulphur were supposed to have rare virtues, including that of prolonging life. Yüan Tsai, the great minister of Tai Tsung who took his *hot* viands from porcelain utensils floating in cool water, ate and drank *cold* preparations from sulphur bowls, aiming at the perfect balance between hot and cold influences thought to be necessary for bodily health.[44] A certain Taoist alchemist, Wei Shan-fu, even claimed to be able to relieve men of their lusts through the agency of sulphur, ". . . and therefore his art was much practiced."[45]

Sulphur for these purposes had been imported by ship from Indonesia for many centuries;[46] it was presumably gathered in volcanic regions there. The yellow mineral was named "fluid yellow."[47] It comes as no surprise to find this expression applied to a colored textile by a poet of the ninth century, an age in which new color images were much in vogue. Wen T'ing-yün has

> A small woman, cloaked in fluid yellow,
> Ascends the tower, and strums her jeweled zither.[48]

But, in fact, though this kind of literary figure was congenial to the age, it was not new at all, only revived. The term had been used in an ancient poem, written long before T'ang, to denote a yellow pongee.[49]

REALGAR

Like orpiment, realgar is a compound of sulphur and arsenic, and (also like orpiment) it was thought to be a "seed of gold," all the more so because it was found

near gold deposits.[50] In alchemical lore it was believed to have the power of trans-
forming copper into gold, and even to become gold itself.[51] Therefore realgar played
a fundamental role in the Taoist laboratories, and in the preparation of the elixirs
of long life it represented the color yellow in its mystical meaning.[52] The ordinary
name of realgar was "cock yellow," but its Taoist name was "soul of the cinnabar
mountain." [53]

Realgar also had an important place in the materia medica, being recommended
as a cure for skin diseases, as an antiseptic for poisoned wounds, as a rejuvenator, and
as an apotropaion; a prepared realgar egg in the Shōsōin collection of old medicines
may be supposed to have had the last-named role. In particular, the drug was
effective against the incubi which haunted mad women; the sufferer was relieved by
fumigating her genitals with a burning ball of realgar and pitch.[54]

Realgar had been mined, with orpiment, in several parts of China in early
times, but in T'ang the best was imported from unnamed countries in the West.[55]
There were important deposits of the arsenic sulphides south of Ta-li in the country
of Nan-chao; [56] possibly some came into T'ang as well.

LITHARGE

The oxide of lead which we call "litharge" and which was known in T'ang under
its Persian name *mirdāsang* (more rarely as "yellow flower of lead," "yellow tusks,"
and "yellow dragon") [57] had two primary uses. First of all, it was a drug, prescribed
for piles, wounds made by metal weapons, and other lesions; it was also good for
facial blemishes, and therefore it formed an ingredient in facial ointments.[58] Secondly,
it was required by the decorators of wooden furniture as a drier for oil paints. T'ang
oil paints normally contained perilla oil, and were often used in conjunction with
transparent lacquers; [59] among the medieval objects painted in oil which we know
through literature was a food storage box given to Rokhshan by Hsüan Tsung.[60]

Heavy crystals of litharge, "shaped like the teeth of yellow dragons," were
imported from Persia. It was not until Sung times that the Chinese learned to prepare litharge as a by-product of the smelting of galena for its lead and silver,[61] though
possibly it had already been done in the secret crucibles of the alchemists.

SODA ASH

A yellowish earthy substance, used in laundering clothes and as an ingredient in
colored glasses, was imported from the "shores of the Southern Seas." [62] This was
a crude sodium carbonate, perhaps made by the incineration of a saltwort, like the
barilla of the medieval European glassmakers. The Chinese called it "natural ash"

and employed it to these ends as early as the third century.[63] But even in T'ang times, nonspecialists like Ch'en Ts'ang-ch'i misunderstood how it was used, conceiving that agate and jade (mistaking the artificial products for the natural) were "softened" to a claylike consistency by being buried in this stuff, so that they could be modeled with ease.[64]

DIAMONDS

A belt hook set with diamonds was the guerdon of the Chinese general who defeated the Hsiung-nu (nominally "Huns") early in the second century A.D.; the hook may have been the booty of battle rather than of Chinese manufacture, since the diamond is not a Chinese stone.[65] Again, the ruler of Kĕlantan in fifth-century Java sent a diamond finger ring to the Chinese sovereign of the southern state of Sung, along with a red parrot.[66]

If such decorative diamonds were ever brought to T'ang, they have left no trace in the historical records. T'ang diamonds are industrial diamonds. Some of them must have found their way to China from India, which was the chief supplier of diamonds (as of sandalwood and saffron) to the Roman Orient, to Bnam, and to Annam.[67] But pre-Cambodian Bnam itself, on the shores of the Gulf of Siam, produced some diamonds: ". . . in appearance they are akin to 'purple stone nobility'; they grow on the rocks at the bottom of the water, and men plunge into the water to get them; jade can be cut with them." [68] The handsomely named "purple stone nobility" is usually amethyst, but one authority has suggested that in this instance smoky quartz might be intended by the name.[69] However appropriate the comparison to colored quartz crystals, the passage quoted rightly illustrates the true significance of the diamond in T'ang—as a lapidary's tool. Diamonds were used to cut hard stones and to perforate pearls.[70] Diamond points for jade drills were also imported from Central Asia for the imperial workshops in Ch'ang-an.[71] Even closer at hand, the Uighurs of Kan-*chou* in the northwest produced diamond drills.[72]

Next to this workaday purpose, the diamond was best known in China in Buddhist imagery. Its name in Chinese is "hardness of [or from] gold," as it was said to form inside gold.[73] The name was a partial adaptation of Sanskrit *vajra,* the all-cleaving thunderbolt of Indra, also called his "diamond club." The indestructible body of the Buddha was a "diamond body," and after that lord had attained enlightenment, he sat on a diamond throne. In T'ang, the "Diamond Sutra," a condensation of the *Prajñāpāramitā-sūtra,* first translated by Kumārajīva, enjoyed the highest popularity.[74]

But though the diamond was a wonderfully hard exotic substance, it was not the symbol of wealth and romance it is with us.

. . . the wealth of Ormus and of Ind,
Or where the gorgeous East with richest hand
Showers on her kings barbaric pearl and gold . . .

John Milton, *Paradise Lost*, Book II

xv = Jewels

A REIGNING MONARCH could hardly do better than to send a rich jewel, or many of them, if he wished to win the good will of another sovereign, and the history of T'ang is studded with references to the transfer of such diplomatic gems to Ch'ang-an. Unfortunately, the gems are seldom identified by name in the historical records, or at best their quality is concealed under some ambiguous compliment such as "rare jewel" or "famous treasure." Examples of royal gifts of jewels are the following: in 619, a jeweled belt from Kapiśa;[1] in 627, a golden belt with inset jewels and "a myriad nails," from the Khan of the Western Turks;[2] about 650, Kao Tsung being newly enthroned, objects of precious metals and gemstones, from King Srong-btsan-sgam-po of Tibet;[3] about 712, a belt set with gems, presented by an ambassador of Islam, the same notorious one who refused to bow to Hsüan Tsung, reserving that honor for Allāh;[4] in 744, gems and horses from many Western nations—Islam, Samarkand, Kish, Kabūdhān, Māimargh, Jāguda, Tukhāra, and Turgäch;[5] in 746, many jewels, from King Śīlamegha of Culā-vaṃsa in Ceylon via the monk Amoghavajra;[6] in 815, from Kalinga, famous jewels.[7]

The receipt of these precious objects seems always to have been invested with an ambiguous air of guilt, however welcome they were as signs of T'ang prestige in the remote parts of the world. Instances of the rejection of expensive and marvelous gifts by the Son of Heaven, to the tune of puritanical avowals of "virtue before wealth," have been noted already. Even the finest jewels did not escape this ascetic treatment. An example: when the Khan of the Western Turks was invested with

222

a princely title by the Chinese emperor in the first year of the T'ang empire, he sent the theocrat Kao Tsu, the "High Forefather," a great pearl; the jewel was returned with these words: "The pearl is truly a treasure, but what we give weight to is a true-red heart; we have no use for the pearl." [8]

Somehow the craving for gems, however desirable, was demeaning, and difficult to justify under the traditional moral code. On the other hand, foreigners, especially Westerners, and most particularly Persians, were imagined to be true gem lovers and gem owners, and it was this that distinguished them from the men of T'ang. "A poor Persian" was a laughable contradiction in terms, [9] and the Iranian Magus stalks the pages of T'ang popular stories, invested with the glamor of the sorcery he was reputed to practice, and above all enriched by the magical gems he was believed to carry. The Persian gem dealer was considered the last word in connoisseurship, and at the same time a worshiper of valuable jewels. [10] He was at once an object of envy and of contempt. This attitude is illustrated here in a short tale which has also the flavor of a Taoist fairy story.

Once a man of Lin-ch'uan, of the Ts'en clan, traveling over hill and dale, saw two white stones in the water, as large as lotus seeds, each rapidly pursuing the other. He caught them, took them home, and put them in a kerchief case. That evening he dreamed that two beautiful women in white garments, calling each other elder and younger sister, came and attended him on left and right. When he woke he understood that they must have abnormal forms of the two stones. So he kept them tied up in the girdle of his dress. Afterward he came to Yü-chang, where there was a Westerner of Persia who accosted him and asked, "Has the lord a treasure?" And he said, "Yes," and, producing the two stones, showed them to him. The Western man sought to purchase them for three myriads. Although Ts'en treasured them, they were useless to him, and he was pleased to get the cash, so he gave them up. Using the cash as life capital, he became prosperous and well-provisioned, but only regretted that he could not have asked about the stones and their use. [11]

The jewel-seeking foreigners could even become images of wordly avarice, as they appear in a poem by the eccentric monk Han-shan, in which blue-eyed merchants seek to buy his crystal bead, a Far Eastern "pearl of great price," symbolizing the purity of simple Buddhist faith. [12]

JADE

Strictly speaking, our word "jade" means both nephrite, a tough amphibole, [13] and jadeite, a tough pyroxene. The classical Chinese jade was nephrite—the use of jadeite in China is a modern development. The jade of the Aztecs was jadeite; the jade of the Maoris was nephrite. There was a kind of convergence of the two great barbaric civilizations with Chinese culture in their ritualistic use of kingly jade and godlike feathers. Sacheverell Sitwell has remarked this:

For, here, the Maori warriors have a static calmness against their setting which is like the ghosts of great men; the shades of the *Iliad*. The unruffled plumes exaggerate their stature and in their right hands they hold scepters of jade, the symbols of their kingly power.[14]

However, unhappily for any hopes we may have of simple mineralogical identification in medieval texts, the Chinese word which we usually translate "jade" means little more than "fine ornamental stone" in some contexts, and has also been given to a variety of stones—such as the precious silicified serpentine—merely because they resemble nephrite. We have also "white jade" for marble, and "black jade" for jet, while other such soft materials as steatite and pyrophyllite have been given the respectable name of *ngi^wok,* the T'ang word which underlies modern Mandarin *yü,* "jade." Most famous of these false jades was the so-called "beautiful jade of Indigo Field," actually a green and white marble quarried at "Indigo Field" in the Chung-nan Mountains south of Ch'ang-an.[15] The accomplished Lady Yang, who loved to play the classical lithophone, was given a set of chimes made from this handsome stone by the devoted monarch Hsüan Tsung.[16]

However ancient and honorable the art of jade cutting was in China, the material itself was not Chinese. Even in old lore and in imagination, jade was the stone of the holy mountains at the center of the world-continent. The *Canon of the Mountains and Seas* described, among the mountains of the West,

A Jade Mountain, which is the dwelling-place of the Royal Mother of the West. The Royal Mother of the West has the appearance of a human being, but is leopard-tailed and tiger-toothed; she is a skilled whistler, and wears a riband on her tangled hair.[17]

The profane counterpart of this immortal mountain of dreams was the old city of Khotan (called Gaustana or Gostana in early T'ang, and Yüttina in the ninth century) on the southern silk road through Serindia, whose king lived in a "painted house," ruling over a people full of artifice and extravagant speech.[18] This was the ancient source of all nephrite used in China,[19] and the white jade and deep green jade required by the lapidaries of T'ang continued to come from that city.[20] Pebbles of the precious nephrite were picked from the beds of two rivers, which join near Khotan before they empty into the Tarim River. These are the Kara-kāsh ("Black Jade") and the Yurung-kāsh ("White Jade") rivers. In these waters, ". . . the men of that country are certain to obtain the beautiful jade in places which they see to be full of moonlight," [21] so it has been said that the jade of Khotan is crystallized moonlight.[22]

Nephrite had already achieved a notable place in the Neolithic culture of China, but only as part of a general polished stone industry. By Chou times the mineral was already rich in royal and divine associations, and was reserved mainly for ceremonial and magical objects. Among these were the old pointed royal scepters, descended, it may be, from archaic axes; there were the "astronomical jades" with which the royal stargazers took their sightings; there were the tablets, full of mana, which announced the accession of the Son of Heaven; there were "funerary jades" which closed the apertures of the dead man's body; there were cap and girdle ornaments for men, and buckles, sword fittings, scabbard mounts, and finger rings.[23] Perhaps these last mentioned objects, secular and personal in purpose, had once been talismanic and apotropaic in function too. A great deal of their meaning was lost by Han times, but much of the archaic sense of these things was saved, though greatly altered. The king-shaman, who compelled the attendance of the rain-dragons with his wand of green nephrite,[24] still remained, but encrusted with the newer paraphernalia of the monarchy. Moreover, a set of poetic and metaphorical images had grown up around the beautiful stone: its glossy luster typified the beneficent, morally enriching character of the Confucian virtue of "humanity," and its toughness and fine texture symbolized the virtues of the upright man.[25] In less elevating literature, jade, especially suet-white jade, stood for the physical beauty of women, representing the ideal appearance of their flesh, as if they were marble goddesses of the Mediterranean world.

These made up the received heritage of the meanings and uses of Khotanese nephrite for the people of T'ang, some more or less elegantly embalmed, some very much alive. Among the latter was the custom of making ritual implements, repositories of divine power, of jade.

The most sacred and secret of such objects were the tablets deposited on Mount T'ai in Shantung by the Son of Heaven when he celebrated the ancient sacrifice of Feng and Shan, in which he gave thanks to the great gods, including his own divine ancestors, for the blessings bestowed on himself and his dynasty.[26] When, in 666, Kao Tsung, as was his prerogative, opened up the channels leading to Heaven by performing this holy rite, he used ". . . three letters patent of jade, all bound with gold. Each tablet was one foot two inches long, one inch and two parts broad, and three parts [of an inch] thick. The characters cut on them were filled with gold; moreover, they made a casket of jade to store them."[27] Similar sanctified tablets, some with gold-armored warriors represented on them in polychrome, were among the treasures found in the tomb of Wang Chien, ruler of Szechwan at the beginning of the tenth century.[28]

An edict of the second reign of Hsüan Tsung deplored the use of inferior substitutes in lieu of jade for ceremonial utensils, since the practice tended to disturb the divinely established harmony. Accordingly, it was ordered that

From now and hereafter, for the Six Utensils for honoring the deities, and for Oblation Jades of the ancestral shrines, you shall uniformly employ the true jade; but in the ordinary sacrifices you may use jade substitutes. If jade should be hard to get, it is preferable to reduce the cut and measure of the larger things in order to retain the true.[29]

This must have been a reluctant economy measure, for jade was clearly prescribed by the rubrics for all vessels used in the worship of the gods.

In T'ang, jade was also used for every sort of small object of utility and pleasure by those persons who could afford to buy them. These included little vases and boxes, sometimes cut in the archaic rectangular manner of late Chou, often in the yellow or brownish jade favored in antiquity,[30] but like as not in the more "natural" modern style, and in the more conventional green or white material. Palace ladies, for instance, kept aromatics in jade boxes of the shape of tortoises.[31] Not all these objects were the work of T'ang artisans: a small "Kurung jade wine cup" may have been named for a style of decoration rather than its place of origin,[32] but a jade goblet, ". . . quite precious and singular," obtained in Tibet, was certainly the product of the Central Asian highlands.[33]

Body ornaments of jade were in the old tradition, even if they might have a new form. We have, surviving from T'ang, ladies' hair ornaments such as jade bird forms embellished with gold and silver, and comb backs of jade decorated with human and animal figures in relief.[34] Jade girdle ornaments in the form of fish were newly popular as symbols of rank and prestige.[35] Some of these gauds came from abroad, such as a white jade finger ring, the gift of Samarkand to Hsüan Tsung.[36]

A new vogue among the nobility was to wear girdles made of jade plaques, in place of the older leather belts or those composed of metal rings, worn formerly under Sui. Even these were sometimes the gifts of foreigners, as was the jade belt sent to T'ai Tsung by the king of Khotan in 632, designed, under Persian influence, to show the forms of the full and crescent moon in its twenty-four green plaques.[37] And during the first half of the ninth century, the Tibetans several times sent jade girdles to the rulers of T'ang.[38] A royal belt with seven plaques of dragon-carved jade was found in the tomb of Wang Chien, who ruled Szechwan before and after the collapse of T'ang in 907.[39]

Much small sculpture was done in jade during T'ang: camels, lions, tortoises, rabbits, and various birds, as well as mythological and symbolic creatures like the Chinese "phoenix."[40] The favorite horses of Hsüan Tsung were represented in jade—images known from later illustrated books as well as in literature.[41] Yang the Precious Consort, because she was plump (we are told) suffered from "parching of the lungs" during the summer heat, and kept a little jade fish in her mouth to relieve this condition.[42] Another little jade animal was equally famous, but had an emblematic and prophetic role rather than a healing one: the story goes that when several princelings were at play in the palace, the imperial grandmother laid out before them a number of jade objects, ". . . which were the tribute of Western countries," to watch them struggle for possession of them. Only one boy remained aloof and impassive—this was the future Hsüan Tsung, whom the lady then characterized as destined to be "Son of Heaven of the Grand Tranquillity," that is, bound to reign with universal peace. She gave him a little jade dragon to mark the event, and in later years the sovereign prayed to this precious talisman in times of drought.[43]

Images of divine beings were sometimes made of jade: in the Buddhist temple named "Exalting the Good"[44] there was a jade statue of the Buddha, one foot seven inches tall, with bodhisattvas and "flying sylphs" of the same material.[45]

226

A special use, of ancient Taoist origin, for the jade of Khotan was as a drug to lighten the corporeal frame and extend its life. This was soberly listed among the medicines of the imperial pharmacopoeia. The best form of edible jade for such rare purposes was the kind reduced to a liquid, in accordance with an old alchemical recipe; but the mineral could also be ingested as a powder or in small grains, to cleanse the inner organs of impurities.[46]

JADE IN ALCHEMY

CRYSTAL

By "crystal" or "rock crystal" we mean a pure, transparent, crystalline quartz, that is, uncolored natural silica. Its Chinese name is "germ [or sperm, or essence] of water," a linguistic conception not alien to the traditional Chinese belief that the mineral was petrified ice, a notion also familiar to Pliny.[47] Rock crystal is a mineral of wide occurrence, and is highly valued only when perfectly clear. This quality, along with unusually fine workmanship, will have characterized the objects of crystal imported into T'ang, such as the rosaries brought as gifts by the Japanese monk Ennin,[48] or the objects of rock crystal (including drinking cups) which came to T'ang as royal gifts from Samarkand several times in the eighth century,[49] and a crystal cup sent by Kapiśa.[50]

But indeed rock crystal served the same purposes as any other hard ornamental stone. It was also, because of its hyaline beauty, a suitable material for the artisans of fairyland. The "fire-rejecting sparrow," an item in Su O's bizarre tribute list, was brought in a basket of crystal,[51] and the Moon Maiden of a ninth-century poem ". . . let fall a water-germ aigrette from the indigo void," [52] a souvenir for her earth-bound lover.

Crystal lends itself well to description by simile and metaphor, and objects of crystal appear often in poetic images as ice or water or drops of dew, or even moonlight. The following excerpt from a poem on a crystal rosary is characteristic:

> Good craftsmen rubbed and scrubbed, and formed a string of beads,
> Limpid through and through, pellucid, void and clear—look, and they seem not there,
> Star flashing, moon beaming, nothing surpasses them . . .[53]

Or this one, also on a monk's string of beads:

> Uniformly executed of spring ice, polished and buffed.[54]

Or again:

> Pour it into the petals of a lotus—
> Sometimes, as you look, it is dew.[55]

Or Wei Ying-wu's quatrain in praise of crystal:

Reflecting things, it takes on their complexion's hue,
Enclosing void, it lacks outside and in.
I hold it up, turned to the luminous moon;
Translumined—I'm anxious lest it turn to water.[56]

Different from these is the description of a white-flowering walnut tree, transformed in the imagination into the figure of a monk telling his beads; this is by Li Po:

Against a red gauze sleeve—distinct and clearly seen;
Within a white jade dish—quite gone when you look;
I can fancy it an old monk at rest, reciting from memory—
Before his wrist he pushes down beads of water germ.[57]

Color images derived from minerals are probably more common than anyone has supposed (if anyone has thought of such a thing). The old stereotyped metaphors are from dyes (like our indigo, purple, and stammel), but by T'ang times most of them had lost their freshness. While no medieval Chinese poet may ever have gone as far as Marlowe, for whom "things green are emerald; those blue, sapphire; yellow is golden, or topaz; white, ivory; while the clear transparence of stream or fountain is invariably silver or crystal," [58] but only a little exploration shows that the Chinese were at least as prone to find unexpected gem stones in the trees and birds and flowers as were the bards of Tibet, where ". . . on the plain where diamond rocks glitter is a lake with a mirror like turquoise and gold." [59]

CARNELIAN

By "carnelian" we mean a reddish variety of chalcedony, that is, of translucent cryptocrystalline silica. Here the word is used to translate Chinese *ma-nao* (etymologized as "horse brain"), a word which has more often been Englished as "agate." "Agate" is a name given to banded chalcedony, the bands being in contrasting colors—say, bluish gray and white. But *ma-nao* is (in T'ang at least) usually some shade of red, and if we say that *ma-nao* is "agate" it is necessary to explain that we mean an agate in which that color is prominent. But it is simpler to say "carnelian." Here are examples of the redness of *ma-nao*: in 846, "P'o-hai sent as tribute a *ma-nao* casket, three feet square, and deep madder in color; the skill of the workmanship was incomparable." [60] Again, a man who had smashed a *ma-nao* plate sent the little pieces to a friend, saying that they were pomegranate seeds, and the friend tried to eat them.[61] Finally, *"ma-nao* is the metamorphosis of ghost's blood." [62] Madder, pomegranate, and blood—certainly "carnelian."

Carnelian was imported in some quantity from the West, and all of it was used to make small utensils.[63] We have specific instances of carnelian (including a vase of that material) sent to the court from Samarkand [64] and from Tukhāra.[65] The latter nation offered the raw mineral as a worthy gift, and it must be assumed that this was turned over to the T'ang court lapidaries. A Persian embassy of the eighth century (some government in exile?) presented a couch of carnelian.[66] But the precious mineral also came from the East: the P'o-hai Mo-ho sent a carnelian cup in 730,[67] and earlier, in 655, a huge lump of the red stone was brought from Japan.[68] But evidently Japanese export "carnelian" was sometimes not genuine.[69]

T'ang literature abounds in references to cups, dishes, bowls, jars, and other kinds of vessels ground out of carnelian; we may even see a T'ang "agate" dish, in the form of a broad leaf with prominent venation, in the Shōsōin.[70] It appears that the T'ang lapidaries excelled at turning out small utensils of this kind, as the jewel engravers of Khotan, for their part, specialized in cutting intaglios with small animal figures in carnelian and chalcedony.[71]

MALACHITE

Malachite, the green basic carbonate of copper, may be treated in technology as an ore of the metal, or ground up to make a painter's pigment, or, especially when it is emerald green and handsomely banded like agate, it may be cut into a variety of ornamental and useful objects; the most famous in modern times was the fine malachite of the Urals, used in Russia for making table tops and elegant inlays. It was used for all these purposes in China, depending on the quality of the mineral. Malachite, and its blue congener azurite, were mined for paints at Tai-*chou* in northern Shansi during T'ang.[72] The copper mines at Hsin-*chou* [73] in what is now eastern Kiangsi undoubtedly produced malachite (a very common manifestation of copper), but gem-quality malachite seems not to have been found there until the eleventh century, when a local industry in costume jewelry flourished in the town.[74] Hsüan-*chou* (southern Anhwei) also produced malachite, which was submitted as local tribute, but whether for lapidary work or for pigments is not known.[75] There is a tale of a mirror stand of malachite in the eighth century,[76] but in fact the mineral seems not to have been carved much, and it appears in literature only rarely. Its claim to mention in a discussion of exotic goods is based on a gift of "stone green" (as malachite was ordinarily styled in China) from Rome in 643.[77] Here too, our sources fail to tell the shape of the gift.

Malachite appeared in a new role in the tenth century. Though this takes us just beyond the limits of the T'ang period, the subject is sufficiently interesting to deserve a few words here. It became the fashion to display miniature mountains, especially rugged and craggy ones, on trays and dishes. The custom had ancient antecedents. Incense braziers in the form of "universe mountains" were familiar to the men of Han. From about the beginning of the seventh century, however, the idea of making these of ordinary stone, instead of an artificial product like metal or earthenware, to lend a naturalistic effect to the little mountain appeared somewhere in the

Far East. A prototype was the brazier-mountain, of real stone, set in a bowl, given by the Korean state of Paekche to the Empress Suiko of Japan. This was one of the ancestors of the little rock gardens called "bowl mountains" [78] in Sung times; the term was not yet in use in T'ang, though we read of "bowl lakes," apparently miniature gardens built around a pool in a pot.[79] Three centuries later (early in the tenth century) we begin to read of tiny mountains constructed out of expensive blue and green minerals:

The wealth of General Supervisor Sun Ch'eng-yu of Wu-yüeh overmatched that of the levee of the usurper itself. He expended a thousand metal-pieces to acquire in the market a lump of "stone green" whose heaven-given mode was jagged like a mountain. He commanded his artisans to work it into a "universe mountain" incense brazier. On the point of its peak they made a hidden hole, from which the smoke emerged, to gather on one side, from which a tuft went directly up through empty space. It was, in fact, a beautiful sight to see, and his friends and intimates copied it, calling it "Unduplicated Mountain." [80]

This malachite mountain was not Sun's only rare creation in that form: he also had a miniature of Mount Li, the site of the famous thermae near the Western Capital, made of Borneo camphor cooked in milk.[81]

In the same age, the early decades of the tenth century, a prince of the Khitans, rulers of southern Manchuria, purchased a stone worked into several peaks, a landscape named "hollow bice repository." [82] ("Hollow bice" was an ancient name for azurite, the blue form of basic copper carbonate, malachite's brother.)

Over a hundred years later, the nation of Ta-li, successor state to Nan-chao in Yünnan, sent envoys to the Sung court to offer, along with swords, rhinoceros hide armor, carpets, and saddles and bridles, a "mountain" of a deep blue (or deep green) stone called *pi k̲an*.[83] Whether this was malachite or colored glass (as a T'ang source suggests) or a blue-green coral (there is strong evidence for this), or maybe precious green serpentine, is not yet known.[84] The admired and enigmatic *pi k̲an* was, in T'ang times, brought in from the remote Southwest, through the aboriginal nations of Yünnan and Burma, but was also a product of Khotan.[85]

LAPIS LAZULI

The role of lapis lazuli in Far Eastern civilization has been a mystery, largely because no Chinese word for the mineral could be identified in texts earlier than the Mongol period. It now appears that the word *se-se* (Ancient Chinese *$\ast$ṣvt-ṣvt*), given to deep blue [86] gemstones by the men of T'ang, usually meant "lapis lazuli" (lazurite), but sometimes the blue feldspathoid "sodalite," [87] which is hardly to be distinguished from it, and occasionally even "sapphire." The argument for the identification will be suppressed here to a longish note, but in what follows, all reference to lapis lazuli based on *Chinese* sources assumes the correctness of the identification.[88]

It appears that the men of T'ang bought their lapis lazuli in Khotan, the city of the quintuple forts, dear to the earth goddess, whose rivers were rich in jade.[89] Late in the eighth century the emperor of China sent his agent Chu Ju-yü (whose name means "Pearl Like Jade"!) to procure objects of jade for him in Khotan. The envoy came back with a scepter, girdle ornaments, a pillow, hairpins, cosmetic boxes, bangles, and other things of the finest nephrite, and also brought back with him ". . . a hundred catties of lapis lazuli, along with other treasures."[90] The merchants of Khotan, it seems, enriched themselves as entrepreneurs of gems, as well as by the sale of their native jade. Lapis lazuli was known in China centuries later as "stone of Khotan,"[91] a name which indicates that the gem bazaars of Khotan monopolized the Far Eastern trade in that gem, as well as in "other treasures."

The real home of lapis lazuli was salubrious and well-pastured Badakhshan, its ancient and classical source.[92] Here in the valley of the Kokcha, a branch of the Oxus River, the mineral azure, sometimes fine indigo-blue, sometimes pale blue, sometimes green or gray, was chopped out of its limestone matrix. Here too were mined the red spinels, called "balas rubies," which enjoyed equal fame in the medieval Orient.[93] The existence of these mines was known to the Chinese, who placed them correctly southeast of Chāch (modern Tashkent), the home of the celebrated dancers.[94] Kao Hsien-chih, the Korean general in charge of the Chinese forces in the West, took quantities of fine lapis lazuli, along with gold, camels, and blood horses, when he plundered Chāch in 750.[95]

Though the principal supplier for Central and East Asia was Chāch, and its eastern market was Khotan, the Chinese thought of lapis lazuli as the *Persian* gem par excellence.[96] They were not mistaken in the attribution. Not only was lapis one of the common minerals from which Sāsānian gems were cut, along with sard, agate, garnet, and jasper, as we know from archaeology,[97] but it had a special significance in Persian sky symbolism. We see it in the Takhtītākdēs, the "throne in the shape of a cupola," of Khusrō II, over which was a baldaquin of lapis lazuli and gold, showing the stars and planets against the blue of the sky, the forms of the zodiac and the climates of the world, along with the shapes of ancient kings.[98]

As for the Romans, it was reported in China that the palace of the Basileus had door leaves of ivory, floors of gold, beams of aromatic wood, king posts of crystal and colored glass, and pillars of lapis lazuli.[99] The tale may reflect the distant news of a kingly hall or great church in Constantinople, of the sixth or seventh century, with golden tesserae in its floor mosaics, and its pillars adorned with ultramarine. Pliny had described lapis lazuli, under the name *sapphiros,* especially the pyrite-studded variety: "In sapphiris enim aurum punctis collucet caeruleis," he wrote, reminding us of the name "gold star stone," a Chinese synonym for "stone of Khotan" in Sung times. He wrote that the best comes from Media.[100]

In China itself, pieces of lapis lazuli were lordly gifts. The sister of Yang Kuei-fei, a princess noted for her extravagance, gave a great quantity of the mineral, heaped in a golden bowl, to the carpenters who had raised a new mansion for her.[101] The finest jewelry was made of it. It is reliably reported that when Hsüan Tsung's court moved to his winter palace at the hot springs of Mount Li in the tenth moon of every year, the brilliant cortege filled the valley with brocaded colors and exotic odors, and left a trail of gilded slippers and strings of lapis lazuli beads along the highway.[102] A belt, studded with plaques of violet-blue lapis lazuli, preserved in the Shōsōin, probably represents a typical courtier's girdle of the eighth century. The same treasure house contains a "wish-fulfilling wand" of mottled ivory horn, decorated with horn and blue lapis lazuli.[103]

The Chinese were not alone among the Far Eastern peoples in their admiration for the blue mineral. The Tibetans valued it above all others, even ahead of gold,[104] and those highlanders saw in it the image of the azure sky, and said that the hair of their goddesses had its color.[105] Both men and women there wore it on their heads.[106] A later Chinese report (of the tenth century) states that Tibetan men of that age wore Chinese hats, while their women wore beads of *se-se* in their plaited hair.[107] Some of these last were the fabulous "beads worth horses," first mentioned in that century, and perhaps not lapis lazuli but dark sapphires, cut in spheres or cabochons.[108]

Lapis was also a favorite hair ornament among the ladies of Nan-chao, along with shell and amber, and their king sent lapis lazuli and amber to the Chinese Son of Heaven.[109] Similarly, the ladies of T'ang preferred lazurite in their hair: the ninth-century poet Wen T'ing-yün devoted a whole poem to the theme of "Lapis Lazuli Hairpins," describing the gems set, ". . . like halcyon-dyed ice," in the "falling clouds" of a woman's black hair.[110] The blue mineral was equally suitable to the decoration of holy objects; for example, it studded the gorgeous banners which accompanied the gilded and perfumed cart in which reposed a venerable bone, a relic of the Buddha, to an imperial welcome in the year 873.[111] Lapis lazuli could even be fashioned into artifacts of considerable size—or else they were encrusted with it—as a pillow, which, along with a golden bed, belonged to an official of the salt and iron monopoly in Fukien.[112]

We do not read, however, of the use of lapis lazuli in Chinese architecture, though this may be an accident of the transmission of medieval documents. Nothing comparable to the azure pillars reported for Oriental Rome are reported for the basilicas of T'ang. Indeed, this is somewhat surprising, since lapis lazuli lends itself to the decoration of buildings, and especially to structures adorned with cosmic symbols. We have seen it in Byzantium, and in the artificial sky over the Persian king, and we can see it again, centuries later, in the cathedral of St. Isaac in St. Petersburg, with ". . . its pillars of lapis lazuli at the entrance; and the columns of malachite at the altar," or again, in the same atavistic culture, at Tsarskoe Selo, which had

". . . a room of which the panelling is formed of amber, in homage to the Baltic and its sandy shores; and a hall of lapis lazuli with a parquet of ebony inlaid with wreaths of mother-of-pearl." [113] From the perspective of medieval China, this description would have fitted a Persian rather than a Russian picture, for the Chinese associated both lapis lazuli and amber with Persia, though they were mined elsewhere. But the image is not duplicated in China itself, as far as we can tell, though the T'ang attempt to duplicate the archaic "Luminous Hall," the ceremonial temple of the Son of Heaven, with its blue heavenly dome, should have inspired the application of the azure stone, and in fancy we may believe that it did.

But lapis lazuli could be used to decorate a royal garden. Hsüan Tsung, who was accustomed to spend his winters with his favorite and his whole court at the thermae of the Floriate Clear Palace in the wooded hills east of the capital city, built a microcosmic island-mountain of lapis lazuli in one of the mineral pools there, around which the girls of his seraglio sculled boats of sandalwood and lacquer. [114] This rich and splendid piece of landscaping represented the height of aristocratic fashion in gardens, at a time when the first use of rough natural rockeries to represent the World Mountain was still a century in the future, the creation of such eccentrics as Po Chü-i and Niu Seng-ju. [115]

In the twelfth century an artificial *se-se*, presumably a blue paste, was in circulation. [116] This pseudo-lapis was probably being made even in T'ang times, [117] and much of the translucent *se-se* of T'ang may be false lapis. In the same way, the ancient Egyptians had made imitation lapis lazuli for use in inlays, as on the burial masks and other furniture in the tomb of Tut'ankhamūn, [118] and there are many Assyrian texts of the seventh century B.C. which give recipes for paste jewelry, including one for making *ṣipru* (= *sapphiros*), that is, lapis lazuli. [119]

The popularity of this beautiful gem stone brought from the Far West led to the creation of a new color image, corresponding to the deep saturated blue of ultramarine. [120] A name for this specific color was needed in poetry: the old word *pi* (**piǎk*), originally a mineral name too, now stood for all the dark hues of the blue-green range of the spectrum. The more precise image was the creation of the poet Po Chü-i. He made the name of a color from the name of a mineral by exactly the same process which made our "azure" a color word, when it had once been a mineral name. Po Chü-i, then, precedes Chaucer, the first English poet to use "azure" (from the Persian *lāžward*) in the sense of "blue," instead of in its traditional value "lapis lazuli." [121] Such mineral metaphors were not new to Chinese poetry. For instance, the Emperor Chien Wen Ti of Liang, in the sixth century, wrote this couplet:

> The wind opens the carnelian leaves,
> The water moves the berylline waves. [122]

Here "carnelian" is *ma-nao*, standing for an orange-red color, and "berylline" is *liu-li*, artificial beryl or lapis lazuli perhaps, a blue or green-blue paste.

The double *se-se* (*ʂɐt-ʂɐt*) itself had been used in poetry before the ninth century, but without reference to color: it was an onomatopoetic form, representing such sounds as the rustle and whisper of the wind in foliage. The sixteenth-century critic Yang Shen was the first to reveal that this term, which occurs abundantly in the poems of Po Chü-i, did not, as his contemporaries universally believed, have the usual meaning in that author's writing, but was rather a vivid color image.[123] Like the Liang emperor's blue glass, Po applied "lapis lazuli" or "deep azure" or "ultramarine" (all are possible translations) to the color of ripples moved by the wind, and also to a stone in his garden and to "autumn" (surely the dark autumn sky). In this last image, the ultramarine of autumn is presented in striking contrast to the red of autumn leaves, analogous to the carnelian leaves of Chien Wen Ti. This opposition of colors in the early ninth century was a truly exotic figure, but it gradually became a stereotype among the exquisite poets of the tenth century, who adopted Po Chü-i's invention, and paired it with the rich scarlet which was styled "gibbon's blood." We find the new parallel in a poem by Fang Kan (fl. 860), in which a deep ultramarine forest is set off by a gibbon's blood garden of flowers; in a poem by Wei Chuang (fl. 900), which contrasts the deep azure ("lapis lazuli") waves of a river with the blood red ("gibbon's color") of a water-colorist's palette; and in a poem by Yin Wen-kuei (fl. 904) we read:

> The dew in the flower's heart is washed with gibbon's blood
> The wind on the water's face spreads lapis lazuli gauze.[124]

And here is a complete quatrain, one of a set of four fairyland poems by the talented monk Kuan-hsiu (he was equally famous as poet and painter), in which the lapis color is contrasted, rather, with "golden."

> Three or four sylph maidens,
> Bodies clothed in lapis-blue garb,
> Hands holding luminous moon pearls
> For knocking down gold-colored pears.[125]

The new color is as perfectly appropriate to this dream of the late ninth century, as the Taoist imagery is to a Buddhist prelate of this age. All these couplings of colors were rejuvenations of the ancient cliché, now dull and dusty, of *ch'ing tan,* "azurite and cinnabar," already faded to "blue and vermilion," an ordinary metaphor for "polychrome painting."

"Germ of Metal"

In 643, T'ai Tsung received envoys from the "king of Rome,"[126] who carried gifts of red and green glass, malachite, and something called "germ of metal."[127] The Romans told of the incursions of the Arabs into their country, and were well received by the emperor, who gave them a letter bearing his seal, and fine damasks. Again, in

741, Tukhāra sent a mission to Ch'ang-an, bearing colored glass, raw (uncut) carnelian, and raw "germ of metal." [128] The same mysterious stone (for it appears to have been a precious stone) was sent to China by the king of Shighnān, [129] and it was reported in Ch'ang-an that it had been taken by "polishers of stone" from a river of Kurān, adjacent to Tukhāra. [130]

Since the expression "germ of metal" as the name of an imported gemstone did not, it seems, survive the T'ang dynasty, we must look to early literature for an explanation of it, and clues to the identity of the stone. A typical occurrence, from the early part of the fifth century, tells of the apparitions of white animals, including wolves, rabbits, sparrows, pheasants, and doves: ". . . these were taken to be good omens of 'white,' given birth by 'germ of metal.' " [131] This means that the startling albino creatures were manifestations of the "white" principle, signifying the West and the "element" metal—an application of the popular "Five Element" doctrine. Here is another example, this one from T'ang:

The germ of the Metal Star fell west of Scepter Peak in the Chung-nan [Mountains], and therefore it is called "Grand White Mountain." This "germ" was transformed into a white stone, in appearance like beautiful jade . . .[132]

"Metal Star" and "Grand White" are both names of the white planet Venus, here made the cosmic source of a stone resembling white jade in color and translucency. Or again, the poet P'i Jih-hsiu wrote of water in these terms:

> Limpid with the cleanness of "jade marrow,"
> Buoyant with the freshness of "metal germ." [133]

"Jade marrow" was an old term for Taoist and fairy liquors of melted jade; it also came to mean "chalcedony." These verses reinforce the conception of "metal germ" as a watery or pearly white stone, comparable to white chalcedony or jade.[134]

It is not easy to say what this strange stone, briefly imported during T'ang, might have been. It was pictured, as we have seen, as a concretion of the metaphysical "germ of metal," that is, of the principle of the West and autumn, and as the essence of lunar whiteness, as azurite was the germ of copper and realgar the germ of gold. In short, it was a rather uncommon, semiprecious stone, of a beautiful lustrous white color. A real possibility is moonstone, also called adularia, a kind of orthoclase feldspar, which is characterized by its pearly, chatoyant, milky whiteness. Perhaps this is the *ceraunia* which Pliny lists among the white gems, and ". . . which received light and luster from not only the sun and the moon but also from the stars," and came from Kirmān in Persia.[135]

GLASS

Glass had been familiar to the Chinese for centuries, and had been manufactured by them since late Chou times.[136] Their language distinguished two kinds of glass, *liu-li* and *po-li*. *Liu-li* was colored glass, either opaque or only dully translucent, or even a colored ceramic glaze; it was akin to the lead glass which we call "paste," and like paste was thought of as a substitute for natural gemstones, especially for green and blue ones.[137] Indeed, it was sometimes confused with real minerals, such as lapis lazuli, beryl, and, no doubt, turquoise. *Po-li,* on the other hand, was transparent, either colorless, like rock crystal, and compared with water and ice, or else palely tinted. *Liu-li* was already old in China, but blown vessels of *po-li* were a novelty in T'ang.[138]

Little need be said of the false gem *liu-li*. It was familiar in both life and literature, and was doubly exotic in that it came occasionally with embassies from the West,[139] and was also reported of distant cultures, such as Pyū in Burma, a country enriched both by excellent astronomers and the law of the Buddha, where the holy temples were decorated with tiles glazed with *liu-li,* and inlaid with gold and silver.[140] There was also a vogue for hair ornaments and bracelets of *liu-li* in late T'ang.[141] A late medieval report on the relative merits of Chinese *liu-li* and foreign *liu-li,* which may apply also to T'ang, stated that the native paste was freshly colored but brittle, while that brought from overseas was coarser and darker but very durable.[142] Its gemmy quality endeared it to poets, especially for picturesque descriptions of fairy landscapes, as "Palaces with basilicas of 'water germ,' tiled with *liu-li,*" [143] that is, made of rock crystal and colored paste.

Utensils of fine clear glass, however, were still considered exotic treasures. Therefore Ch'en Ts'ang-ch'i wrote: "It is a jewel of Western countries, and is akin to jade and other stones. It is born within the earth, and some say that it is water transformed after a thousand years; still this is not necessarily so." [144] Some thought it was petrified ice, like rock crystal.[145] Specimens of the wonderful stuff were sent to T'ang from Kapiśa; [146] indigo-colored *po-li* came from Farghāna,[147] pink and indigo *po-li* from Tukhāra,[148] and red and green varieties from Rome.[149] Some of these "tribute" articles may actually be the ones preserved in the Shōsōin. For instance, there is a deep blue glass beaker there, decorated with rings in relief, mounted on a silver pedestal and not at all Chinese in style, and there is a pale green ewer in the Persian style.[150] But perhaps these were of T'ang manufacture, in the Western manner, and indeed they appear at the same time as the development of soda glass in China, replacing the old lead and barium glasses.[151]

Though *liu-li* was primarily an ornamental glass, often molded or sculptured, and applied (as the T'ang poets tell) to every sort of rich object, *po-li* was most commonly the material of blown vessels—cups, pots, dishes, and the like. Many of the latter, possibly Chinese, possibly Western, are displayed in the Shōsōin, and kept in private and public collections in all parts of the world. To list only a few, there are dark green fish-pendants, with eyes, mouth, and gills in gold, possibly imitations of the tallies of T'ang officials; [152] a shallow green cup, with wavy edge; [153] a shallow brownish dish with a foot; [154] pieces for the "double six" game, yellow, indigo, green, and pale green; [155] a four-lobed red-brown pedestal cup, with "raised floral design and scrolls . . . derived from Sāsānian silver work"; [156] a greenish white bracelet in the form of "two confronting dragon heads holding a pearl," and another, amber-colored with red-brown stripes, also shaped as two facing dragons.[157] Possibly the pendants, double six pieces, and bracelets would have been described in T'ang as made of *liu-li;* that is, perhaps *liu-li* meant simply glass worked like stone.

FIRE ORBS

In 630 the empire of the Chams presented T'ai Tsung of T'ang with a crystalline "fire orb" (or "fire bead" or "fire pearl"), the size of a hen's egg, with the explanation that if held between the sun and a bit of punk, it would set the latter on fire.[158] The envoys said that it had been obtained in Rākshasa, a country of black men with vermilion hair, the fangs of wild beasts, and the talons of hawks.[159] A very similar description of the fire orbs of Bali is given in the T'ang History.[160] Another country of Southeast Asia, Dvāravatī, sent a fire orb with elephant tusks to the T'ang court, asking for horses in return.[161] The crystal globes were also reported to be a product of Kashmir,[162] a country known to the Arab mineralogists as rich in rock crystal.[163] When the pilgrim Ennin landed at Teng-*chou* in Shantung in 839 he offered a crystal orb to the great god of Sumiyoshi, praying for a safe and speedy return to Japan.[164]

The Chinese name of these crystal spheres reflects Sanskrit *agnimaṇi,* "fire jewel," the name given to burning lenses in India, which seems to have been the Oriental home of the spheres. India in turn probably got them from the Hellenistic Near East; Pliny had prescribed crystal balls for cauterization, and, long before, in the ninth century B.C., a rock crystal lens was kept in the palace of the Assyrian King Ashur-nasir-pal.[165] As for China, convex glass and crystal lenses were known by the first century A.D.[166] The classical equivalents to them, very familiar in Han times, were concave bronze mirrors, called *yang sui,* "solar kindlers" or "igniters using *yang.*"[167] Indeed, any instrument which could focus the energy of the sun, which itself concentrated the invigorating and holy light of Heaven, was revered as a divine object, a condenser of mana. The new fire globes, therefore, partook of this power. They were at the same time lunar symbols, or even miniature moons, and related to the "fire pearl" which was deemed to be the conventional plaything of the dragon. This dragon-pearl, familiar in art, was originally the full moon itself, which, ages ago, had risen at the first of the year by the horn of the Dragon of Spring, marked by the star Arcturus.[168] It was also the *cintāmaṇi,* the wish-fulfilling jewel of the Indian *nāgas,* serpent-princes identified in popular lore with the Chinese rain-dragons.[169]

As a globular source of light and radiant heat, standing both for sun and moon, the "fire pearl" was allied with other luminescent jewels. The Chinese lore of "luminous pearls" (or "beads") and "night-shining pearls" and luminous moon pearls" (see Kuan-hsiu's fairy poem a few pages earlier) goes back to Chou times, and may ultimately be of Indian origin. It has its parallels and analogues in many cultures, from the Manichaeans of Serindia, for whom the "treasure-bead of the luminous moon" was first among all the jewels, to the gem on the head of the image of the Dea Syrica in Hierapolis, which "flashes a great light in the nighttime." [170]

Actually, the luminescent "gems" seen in China were often the eyes of whales, which, like the body parts of many marine creatures, were naturally phosphorescent. These shining globes were also, no doubt, the wishing jewels of the Indian dragon-kings who lurked under the waters of Ocean. [171] They had been known in China since the fourth century, and were several times sent to the court of Hsüan Tsung in the eighth century by the Mo-ho peoples of Manchuria. [172]

But there were also luminescent gems of mineral origin; some stones have this quality continually, others only when rubbed or heated. During Hsüan Tsung's first reign, an embassy from Māimargh presented the monarch with a gem called simply *pi̯ṷk*. This was the name of an archaic flat stone ring, a symbol of the heavenly kingship in Chou times; but it was also a word used interchangeably with *pi̯äk*, "dark blue-green stone" and sometimes "luminescent blue-green stone." [173] If not a ceremonial jade ring, then, this gift was probably made of chlorophane, the thermoluminescent variety of fluorite, which was undoubtedly the material of the phosphorescent "emeralds" of classical antiquity, such as the green eyes of the marble lion on the tomb of King Hermias of Cyprus, [174] though the Hellenistic alchemists had methods, seemingly magical, of making night-shining gems by the application of phosphorescent paints to stones, the most famous being their "emeralds" and "carbuncles." [175]

The greatest of the fire orbs of T'ang shone on the summit of the Hall of Light. [176] This was a reconstruction of the cosmic ceremonial hall of the Chou Son of Heaven in his role as adjuster of the calendar and regulator of the seasons. Since ancient times the problem of the structure and decoration of this *regia* had been debated by antiquarians, architects, and theorists of monarchy. The argument raged through the early years of T'ang, but the actual building was not attempted until the Empress Wu, an anomalous female "Son of Heaven" (reminding us of Hatshepsut of Egypt) who desired to reinforce her charisma, razed a basilica in Lo-yang, the Eastern Capital, and in 687 began the construction of a Hall of Light on the site. The magical temple was completed on February 11, 688. [177] It was destroyed by fire in 695, but work on a successor was begun immediately, and it was completed in the spring of 696. The new building was 294 feet high and 300 feet square. Within it were nine newly cast bronze tripods which represented the dominion of the great lady over the Nine Island-Provinces. The gilded iron phoenix which first adorned its summit was destroyed in a windstorm, and replaced by a fire orb. [178] No less glorious was the massive cast-iron pillar built in 695, the "celestial axis" celebrating the empress' restored Chou dynasty, which was 105 feet high and carried a fire orb at its apex, supported by four "dragon men"; on the ball were inscribed the names of the great officers of her realm and the chiefs of the several subject barbarian tribes. This remarkable edifice was designed by a certain Mao P'o-lo, from his name clearly a foreigner.[179]

In 738, about forty-two years after the erection of the Hall of Light, a certain Ts'ui Shu, on the occasion of his examination for the degree of "Advanced Gentleman," composed a poem on "The Fire Pearl of the Luminous Hall":

> The right-placed See reveals a storied house,
> Which, up in the void, shows forth a fiery orb;
> When night comes, a pair of moons are full,
> But after daybreak, a single star stands alone;
> When sky is clear, its light is hardly extinguished,
> When clouds are born, it seems they wish not to be;
> Afar off, we recognize the succession of Grand Tranquillity,
> Where the nation's jewel lies on the famous city.[180]

This famous globe was reported to be of bronze;[181] if the report is true, it retained the name of the true heat-concentrating crystal sphere, while adopting the material of the archaic *yang*-converging bowls. This was a step in the direction of the finial balls on Buddhist pagodas, which came to symbolize the light of the Buddha's truth shining like a beacon to all quarters of the world.

A popular T'ang tale in the literary language refers to a fire orb under a hybrid name, showing that the orb was regarded as the legitimate successor of the ancient bronze bowl. The tale also illustrates the common belief in the wealth and magical powers of Persians. Only a short excerpt can be given here: the young hero has acquired a pearl in the course of a series of wonderful adventures with the ghosts of ancient notables in a kind of Taoist underworld or tomb-grotto near Canton; he comes to the city to sell his pearl in the "Persian Bazaar," and the buyer tells its story in these words:

"This is the Solar-Kindling Pearl, the treasure of my country Tadjik. Long ago, at the beginning of Han, Chao T'o sent a stranger to scale mountains and navigate seas, and he robbed us of it and returned to P'an-yü. That was just a thousand years ago. In my country there are persons skilled in arcane figures, and they said that in the coming year the national treasure would be returned. Therefore my king summoned me to equip a great argosy and to take weighty resources and go to P'an-yü in search of it. And indeed today it has come into my possession!" Then he produced jade liquor and washed it, and its brilliance illumined the entire room. Whereupon the foreigner embarked in his argosy and went back to Tadjik.[182]

IVORY

The pharmacologist Chen Ch'üan wrote:

In the Western Regions they stress the use of elephant tusks in decorating couches and chairs. In the Central Country we value them, and use them to make ceremonial tablets.

Whenever an elephant sheds its tusks, it buries and hides them itself. The men of the several countries of Kurung obtain them by surreptitiously substituting wooden tusks for them.[183]

The Chinese of T'ang obtained ivory from their own province of Lingnan,[184] from the T'ang protectorate of Annam,[185] and from the Nan-chao nation in Yünnan.[186] More remote sources were Champa,[187] *Pǝk-ịǝp* and *Dabatang* in the Indies,[188] and the Lion Country of Ceylon.[189]

Ivory was much used for making small and slender objects—such things as chopsticks, hairpins, and combs; it was also desired for the appliquéd ornamentation of larger objects. Sometimes it was stained in attractive colors, such as crimson, indigo, or green. A floral design might appear white where it had been incised through the pigmented surface of the ivory, or the design might be painted on an uncolored background.[190] There is in the Shōsōin a rectangular sanderswood box, decorated with geometric designs in marquetry of sanders, boxwood, black persimmon, white ivory, and green-stained ivory.[191] In the same repository, among many other objects of ivory, is a lute plectrum carved with a representation of mountains, animals, birds, and flowers, and dyed crimson, with touches of green and blue.[192] Among the various ceremonial objects required by the Son of Heaven on the different festival days, such as painted hen eggs on "Cold Food" days, and a "thunder carriage" at the summer solstice, a palace officer was required, on the second day of the second month, to present him with handsomely designed foot rules, some of painted sanderswood and some of incised ivory.[193] A rule of scarlet ivory, elaborately carved with flowers, birds, and animals, which is kept in the Shōsōin, is undoubtedly one of these imperial Chinese objects, or a replica used by the Japanese sun king.[194]

Characteristic of T'ang were the ceremonial note tablets [195] with rounded tops, which were carried by court officials to imperial audiences. From the middle of the ninth century at least, privy councilors attending the levee picked up these ritual tablets from a rack at the doorway of the basilica, whereas lesser officials generally kept theirs in bags carried by flunkeys.[196] The tablets of lowly officers were of bamboo or wood, but those of high-ranking personages were made of ivory.[197] Some must have been richly ornamented: the heir to the T'ang throne, for instance, when he went to be "capped" at the age of twenty, wearing a kingly robe and crown and girded with a jade-furnished sword, a fire orb on its scabbard chape, carried an ivory tablet decorated with gold.[198]

Another special use for ivory was in the decoration of one of the five ritual carriages of the Son of Heaven. These were the carriages of jade, of gold, of ivory, of leather, and of wood. All had a symbolic blue dragon on the left side of the chassis, and a white tiger on the right, and were equipped with an embroidered blue umbrella in three tiers, surmounted by a "universal mountain." The ivory carriage was required when the monarch wished to make an ordinary progress along his roads; it was yellow, and ornamented with ivory.[199]

Ivory was sometimes used for small sculpture: we have a statue in that material of the goddess Hariti, suckling a nude, curly-headed child, apparently made in the eighth or ninth century. It shows the T'ang taste for a rather thick figure and swaying posture, but also the influence of the Gandhāran style.[200] We also have an ivory statuette of a dancing girl, painted in polychrome, apparently the work of a T'ang craftsman.[201]

RHINOCEROS HORN

The horn of the rhinoceros played a role in the minor arts of T'ang very similar to that of ivory, and indeed the two substances were regularly linked in language, particularly in parallel verse. The demand for rhinoceros horn was very great, so that, although many rhinoceroses still lived in Hunan, as we have seen, and their horns were submitted to the court as tribute, it was also necessary to import them. From close at hand, they were obtained in Nan-chao[202] and Annam;[203] more remotely, they came to the port of Canton from the Indies, and in such quantities that the near extinction of the Indochinese rhinoceroses in modern times can in large part be attributed to the China trade of T'ang.[204] It was reported that the rhinoceros was accustomed to bury a shed horn, which a hunter might obtain safely by substituting an artificial one,[205] but this story seems to be an adaptation of the same tradition applied to elephant tusks. The most desirable and costly horn was handsomely patterned and grained, sometimes showing, after being polished, the outlines of a living creature or some other interesting picture.[206]

Rhinoceros horn was important in medieval Chinese medicine, especially as an antidote for all kinds of poisons. Belief in its efficacy goes back to the fourth century, and may have originated in China, to spread to Western Asia and the Roman empire.[207] In T'ang, the horn was taken as a powder (it was believed that the raw material could be softened to make it easy to grind, by carrying it, wrapped in paper, in the bosom),[208] or even burned to ashes and swallowed in water.[209] It may be that in former times, when the horns were hollowed out to make medicinal cups, they copied the shape of archaic buffalo horn cups, which were naturally hollow,[210] but most known horn cups of T'ang age are small, round, and conventionally shaped,[211] and it cannot be said with certainty that these were expected to nullify the effects of poison. But there is a horn cup shaped like a short curved horn in the Shōsōin.[212]

The horn was in itself treated as a precious substance, suitable for the jeweler's art, and could be transformed into little boxes, bracelets, paperweights, knife hilts, and chopsticks, all objects which were also made from ivory.[213] Horn was also used to make decorative weights for curtains,[214] and we read of ". . . an ivory bed with gauze-like curtains and rhinoceros horn weights."[215]

Courtiers and high officials wore girdles decorated with plaques of rhinoceros horn, like black-veined amber, which they valued equally with jade and gold, to imperial audiences and banquets.[216] The enormous value of these belts was even noised about the harbors and bazaars of Islam,[217] and one belt, with mottled plates on black-lacquered leather, may be seen in the Shōsōin.[218] The Tu-yang Miscellany reports that the ninth-century emperor Ching Tsung had such a girdle, which shone by night.[219]

Another special use of rhinoceros horn was to make long, flat, "wish-fulfilling" wands, with curved tips, which were held by Buddhist priests in a dignified manner while expounding the holy scriptures.[220] There are many examples of these religious scepters in the Shōsōin; one is set with colored glass balls and lines of gold, and adorned with ivory pierced to show flowers and birds.[221] Another is painted with birds, butterflies, and clouds in silver, and has a handle of sanders inlaid with ivory.[222]

FISH TUSKS

Several times during the eighth century the T'ang palace received gifts of "fish tusks" from Silla.[223] And from the Tungus peoples of Manchuria came a substance called *kuttut* [224] by the Chinese. These names correspond respectively to Persian *dandān māhī*, "fish tooth," and Arabic *khutu*, both of which designate walrus ivory, and sometimes also fossil mammoth ivory from Siberia.[225] But the *kuttut* sent as tribute from Ying-*chou*, the chief Chinese garrison town in south Manchuria, and the "fish teeth" of Silla, though mostly walrus ivory, may also have included fossil narwhal ivory from the Siberian shores of the Pacific.[226]

PEARLS

The power and wonder of pearls was very great. But it seemed to the men of T'ang that their magical beauty was only fully understood and appreciated in distant lands. In those mysterious realms men knew how to exploit their special virtue, which was to control the watery element whose essence they contained. Therefore pearls led to wells in the desert, or to the treasures of dragon kings under the seas. Such a pearl was the "superior clarifying pearl" sent (or so it was reported) to Hsüan Tsung by the king of Kapiśa:

Its light radiated through the whole chamber, and quivering and moving within it were sylph men, and jade women, and cloud cranes. Should there be calamities of water, or drought, or men-at-arms, or dispossession, if devoutly prayed to, it would not fail to respond with the hoped-for results.[227]

This story is vouched for by usually reliable writers of the ninth and tenth centuries, so that we may have confidence that the "pearl" really existed. Perhaps it was a cunningly designed sphere cut from a luminescent mineral, with the shapes of birds and divine beings etched into it. But to the Chinese, it was a magic pearl from some dragon hoard.

Wonderful pearls figure in many popular tales of T'ang, frequently as owned by or desired by a Persian merchant. Here is one of them; it sounds like a sailor's yarn, tailored to the Chinese taste:

In this last generation a Westerner from Persia came to Fu-feng and looked up a hotel. He saw a square stone outside the host's door. He loitered about for several days until the host asked his reason. The Westerner said, "I desire this stone for pounding silks," and he sought to buy it for two thousand cash.

The landlord took the cash, rejoicing greatly, and gave him the stone. The Westerner carried the stone outside the town limits, and cutting it open got a pearl an inch in diameter. Then he took a knife and slashed his arm by the armpit, and hid it there. Then he returned to his country of origin, cruising the seas by ship.

They had proceeded for more than ten days when suddenly they began to founder. The boatmen knew that this was because of a sea god in search of a treasure, so they searched all around for one, but there was no treasure to give the god. At that they wished to drown the Westerner. In alarm, he cut open his armpit, and took out the pearl. The boatmen recited a spell, and said, "If you wish this pearl, it should be taken in charge!" At that the sea god stretched out its hand, which was very large and very hairy, took the pearl, and departed.[228]

Pearls, then, stood for wealth and beauty and supernatural power. In metaphor, accordingly, a pearl was also a person of great worth, as when the painter Yen Li-pen called Ti Jen-chieh "a pearl left by the glaucous sea," honoring a talented youth and future minister.[229] A pearl was also, especially under its Sanskrit name *maṇi*, a symbol of the Buddha and his law. In Sino-Indian lore it was also a wishing jewel, granting the desires of its possessors.[230] Moreover, Chinese and Indians alike saw a special affinity between the pearl and the moon. In China, the pearl was the congealed *yin* (female/negative/lunar matter) embodied in the oyster, and it was alleged that the "fetus of the pearl" within the oyster waxed and waned in accordance with the phases of the moon.[231]

In ancient times the Chinese had obtained some pearls from the waters off their central coast, but with the establishment of the Han dynasty the old province of Ho-p'u, in what is now southwestern Kwangtung, then a savage outpost, became the chief source of pearls. These, along with ivory, rhinoceros horn, silver, copper, and fruits, came to typify the luxury-providing south to the well-to-do northerners.[232] The pearl fisheries of Ho-p'u were worked so intensively that the supply was exhausted. The Grand Protector of the region in Later Han, Meng Ch'ang, was able to restore the people's livelihood by wise methods of control and conservation. He was deified and became the spiritual patron of the fisheries, and the theme of the "return of the pearls" to Ho-p'u was celebrated even in T'ang times in many "rhapsodies" (*fu*) illustrating the bad economic effects of avarice and unrestrained exploitation.[233]

The fisheries had varying fortunes under T'ang. At first they were required to send pearls as tribute to the court, but this order was halted on December 25, 655.[234] Apparently the requirement was revived again, since it was again terminated on August 27, 714. So Ho-p'u became chiefly a silver-producing region, until August 18, 863, when pearl gathering at its "Pearl Pool," the most productive offshore island, was once more permitted in order to restore the natives' livelihood. (It should be mentioned that the people there also relished the flesh of oysters, which they dried in the sun on bamboo splinters.)[235] Some pearls were also obtained from a freshwater bivalve in western Szechwan.[236]

But the pearls brought in merchant vessels from the South Seas were esteemed above all Chinese pearls for their color and luster.[237]

> In the southern land many birds sing;
> Of towns and cities half are unwalled.
> The country markets are thronged by wild tribes;
> The mountain-villages bear river-names.
> Poisonous mists rise from the damp sands;
> Strange fires gleam through the night-rain.
> And none passes but the lonely seeker of pearls
> Year by year on his way to the South Sea.

This is Arthur Waley's translation of Wang Chien's poem on "The South."[238] These exotic concretions from the lands of fire and fever were received with gladness and even with greed, and at the same time with assumed disdain, as the baubles of inferior cultures, accepted only as tokens of their free gratitude, in return for the benefits of whatever atoms of Chinese civilization might reach their humble shores. We find this ambivalent sentiment well exemplified by the sententious verses of a certain Lü Ying, in his "Rhapsody on the Inch-Through Pearl Offered by the Western Regions," written in the time of Ching Tsung, early in the ninth century.[239] It contains such characteristic lines as this: "And therefore they are converted to the ways of our Central Nation, which come to the outer barbarians like wind which humbles the grass."

Such was the meaning of the "great pearls" received from India in 642,[240] of the hundred pearls brought by the ambassadors of King Rudravarman II of Champa in 749,[241] of the unperforated pearls sent by the ghost-nation of Persia in 750 (and there were more in 771),[242] and the pearls of Ceylon (received in 750)[243] and of Japan (received in 839).[244]

Pearls, native or foreign, were primarily treated, in their material aspect, as rich embellishments of costume and household furniture, and their beadlike shape made them especially suitable for screens and curtains. To judge from tales written in the ninth and tenth centuries, a fine pearl, whether rounded or a baroque jewel in the form of a divine being, was regarded as a proper gift to a Buddhist temple.[245]

Pearls, like other substances fair and foul, did not escape the mortars of the T'ang pharmacist. In medicine, or rather in imitative magic, as we would say, they were taken for cataracts and other eye disorders, since they were shaped like the eye, and were as clear and luminous as the full moon. They were regarded with special favor by the Taoists, who counted them among the life-extending drugs. Before compounding an unpierced pearl in a medicine, it was necessary to grind it to powder.[246]

TORTOISE SHELL

The men of T'ang got tortoise shell,[247] for making ladies' hairpins and headdress ornaments and inlays in expensive household objects, from Lu-*chou* in Annam.[248] In addition, in 818 a shipment was brought, along with two Zenj girls and a live rhinoceros, with a mission from Kalinga.[249] A beautiful tortoise-shell plectrum for a five-stringed lute, in the Shōsōin, has the figure of a lute-playing Westerner, mounted on a camel, inlaid in mother-of-pearl.[250] This and other tortoise shell probably came to China from the warm seas of the South.

The shell also supplied a maculated image for the poets, as in these verses:

The pond water—berylline pure,
The garden flowers—tortoise-shell spotted.[251]

NEPTUNE'S CRADLE

The giant clam called Neptune's cradle[252] lends the stuff of its glossy white, deeply furrowed shell to the uses of the lapidary. In ancient China this "mother-of-pearl" (and perhaps others) was regarded as a stone, its source being unknown, and it was polished like jade. It was especially popular in early medieval times for making wine cups and other drinking vessels. Under the T'ang emperors nacre was reputed to be a product of Rome,[253] and it was known to be one of the Seven Precious Substances, the *Saptaratna,* of Indian tradition.[254] The chances are that the shell of this great scallop was still being imported in T'ang times, but the available texts are not conclusive.

CORAL

The T'ang history reports the "Roman" method of obtaining precious coral:

There is a coral isle in the midst of the sea. The men of the sea board great ships, from which they let down iron nets to the bottom of the water. When the coral grows first on the tops of flagstones, it is white like fungus, but after a year it is yellow, and in three years it is an interlocking structure of red branches, three or four feet high. Now its roots tie themselves to the net where iron is protruding, and they on the ship wind it up. Should they miss the season, and not get them, they will rot.[255]

This was, of course, the precious red coral of the Mediterranean, esteemed all over the civilized world. Coral, as the men of T'ang knew, also grew in the South Seas, and they imported it from Persia and Ceylon. Its Chinese name seems to derive from the Old Persian word for "stone," *sanga.[256]

The dendriform specimens had the strongest influence on the Chinese imagination, for they seemed true shrubs of fairyland and jewel trees from the paradises of the immortal gods. Wei Ying-wu, the fastidious poet who always burned incense where he proposed to sit,[257] has this to say in praise of coral (it is one of a series of quatrains on gem materials):

A crimson tree, lacking flowers and leaves,
Neither stone nor yet a gem-mineral,
In what place may the men of our age find it?—
For it grows on the summit of P'eng-lai.[258]

P'eng-lai is the island of the sylphine immortals in the Eastern seas, sought in vain oy the ancients of Ch'in and Han; in T'ang it was only a barely credible dream. But a coral tree in a garden pool could convey a vivid image of the vegetation of that dream world.[259]

Related to the trees of red coral in P'eng-lai were the trees of the mysterious mineral *lang-kan* in P'eng-lai's continental counterpart, K'un-lun, where the peaches of immortality grew. These trees of fairy gems, colored blue or green or blue-green, were well known in ancient days, and were reported in the classical books of Chou and early Han.[260] Though the *lang-kan* tree of the West was, for the medieval Chinese, another fable, like the coral tree of the East, and as Aladdin's jeweled tree is to us, nonetheless a substance called *lang-kan* was imported in T'ang times from the barbarians of the Southwest[261] and from Khotan.[262] Some said it was a kind of glass, that is, related to the colored paste called *liu-li*,[263] but others told of a stony *lang-kan,* which was a species of coral fished from the sea, red when fresh but gradually turning blue.[264] Perhaps some *lang-kan* was blue or green coral, and some a glassy blue-green mineral; in any case, it was related to "dark-blue *kan*," from which were made miniature mountains brought to China in the tenth century from Yünnan (as we observed when discussing malachite on p. 230).

Red coral from the West had been used since antiquity for rings, bracelets, and other jewelry, and for decorating the surfaces of other valuable objects. A repertory of such precious trinkets could be gleaned from the T'ang poets, ranging from the coral aigrette in the hair of a beautiful woman [265] to the coral pen rack in the study of a discriminating scholar.[266]

AMBER

The Chinese word for "amber," *xuo-p'vk*, has been pleasantly explained as "tiger's soul," a phrase which has the same pronunciation, and the etymology has been rationalized by the tale that the congealing glance of a dying tiger forms the waxy mineral. This reminds us of the Greek notion that amber was the solidified urine of a lynx. But Tuan Ch'eng-shih, our T'ang bibliophile and collector of curiosa, has this to say:

Some say that when the blood of a dragon goes into the ground it becomes amber. But the *Record of the Southern Man* has it that in the sand at Ning-*chou* there are snap-waist wasps, and when the bank collapses the wasps come out; the men of that land work on them by burning, and so make amber of them.[267]

This strange and ambiguous tale seems to contain an allusion to the wasps and other insects often found encased in amber, but the rest of it is incomprehensible. In any event, "tiger's soul" probably has nothing to do with the word *xuo-p'vk*, which seems to represent a loan from some language of western or southern Asia, in its original form something like *xarupah*, related to *harpax*, the "Syrian" form mentioned by Pliny.[268]

Although the legend of the relation between amber and the vital essence of tigers and dragons persisted into medieval times, the true nature of amber had been known since the third century, if not earlier. This scientific knowledge was familiar to the T'ang pharmacologists, and preserved in their compendia. The *Basic Herbs of Shu,* for instance, states: "Amber, then, as a substance, is the sap of a tree which has gone into the ground, and has been transformed after a thousand years." [269] Even poets knew this truth. Wei Ying-wu's brief ode to amber embodies it:

> Once it was the old "deity of chinaroot,"
> But at bottom it is the sap of a cold pine tree.
> A mosquito or gnat falls into the middle of it,
> And after a thousand years may still be seen there.[270]

The "deity of chinaroot" is a precious fungoid drug found among pine roots; it was believed that this was an intermediate stage in the development of amber from pine resin.[271]

The precious resin was known to be a product of Rome,[272] and it was imported from Iran.[273] This must have been the famous amber gathered on the shores of the Baltic Sea. But closer at hand was the amber deposit of upper Burma, near Myitkyina (and near the jadeite mines which would be exploited many centuries later); this material was acquired by the people of Nan-chao, where the nobles wore amber in their ears, like the modern Kachins.[274] There were even gifts of amber from Champa[275] and Japan.[276] A commercial variety brought up by merchants through the South China Sea was thought to be especially fine.[277]

Amber had a part in T'ang jewelry similar to that of coral, that is, it was readily converted into ornaments for ladies, and small but expensive objects of virtu for well-to-do households. Among the objects of amber in the Shōsōin are double six pieces, a fish pendant, rosary beads, beads for a ceremonial crown, and inlays in the backs of mirrors.[278] Medicine also had a place for amber, as it had for all precious substances which might conceivably lend their beauty and permanence to the human organism. Venerable pine trees were revered in themselves, and fresh pine resin was itself a life-prolonging drug. How much more so must amber be, which was pine resin subtly embalmed by a spiritual preservative.[279] More specifically, it was prescribed for "bad blood" and effusions of blood caused by weapons.[280] In short, recipes based on the ancient idea that amber was coagulated blood continued in use even in T'ang, despite the existence of better knowledge.

The T'ang poets found "amber" a useful color word, signifying a translucent red-yellow, and used it particularly as an epithet of "wine." We have already seen it used by Li Po, in our discussion of saffron (p. 126). A line by Chang Yüeh is another case:

In the Northern Hall they stress the value of amber wine.[281]

Li Ho, the precocious ninth-century poet, went a step further, and made "amber" stand for "wine" by metonymy. This usage was part and parcel of his well-known interest in color imagery for the intensification of emotion; he was unique in his abundant use of "golden," "silvery," "deep green," and in the way in which he used "white" to express intense illumination and emotional contrast in landscape descriptions (as in black and white photography, say): "the sky is white," and even "the autumn wind is white."[282] Here is his "Have the Wine Brought In!"

> In glass-paste stoup
> The amber is thick—
> From a small vat wine drips—true pearls reddened;
> Boiling dragon, roasting phoenix—jade fat dripping.
> Net screen, embroidered awning, encircle fragrant wind.
> Blow dragon flute!
> Strike alligator drum!
> Candent teeth sing—
> Slender waists dance—
> Especially now when blue spring day is going to set,

And peach flowers fall confused like pink rain.
I exhort milord to drink to besottedness by end of day,
Nor let the wine upset on the earth over Liu Ling's grave! [283]

Liu Ling, one of the ancient "Seven Sages of the Bamboo Grove," was a notorious winebibber, and bottles were buried with him; to spill wine on the ground now, as a libation, intended or accidental, would be like carrying coals to Newcastle.

JET

Another fossil of organic origin used in medieval jewelry was jet, sometimes, despite its softness, called "black jade." [284] According to an ancient tradition it represented a stage of development reached by amber after the passage of a thousand years. That it was ultimately woody could be told by its odor when burned. Pieces of jet were worn by small children to ward off evil spirits.[285] It was imported from a deposit south of Qočo in Serindia.[286]

xvi=Metals

METALS PLAYED an important part in T'ang culture, and metal technology was well advanced. Foreigners in China sought valuable metalwork to take home with them,[1] and, conversely, edicts were handed down prohibiting the export of gold, silver, copper, and iron, as well as the removal of coins by alien traders.[2] Some metals were always in short supply, despite the natural mineral wealth of China. One such was gold.

GOLD

In T'ang times, there were native sources of gold in Szechwan. It was found there as flakes in alluvial deposits, and called "bran gold."[3] The poet Hsü T'ang wrote of Lung-*chou,* in what is now the northeastern part of that province, where the waters are flying white and the birds are red, that

> What the soil generates is only fit for drugs,
> For the royal taxes there is only tribute gold.[4]

But more important than these were the gold deposits of Lingnan and Annam, often deep in rugged territory, inhabited only by the aborigines.[5]

> The men of the South say that it is where the teeth of poisonous snakes drop among the rocks; and they also say that where the dung of a serpent adheres on the rocks, or where the dung of the *Yüan*-bird adheres on the rocks, these are all broken, and the places which have received the poison become raw gold.

So wrote the learned pharmacologist Ch'en Ts'ang-ch'i, but he also stated that this "raw gold," which was reputedly a deadly poison, was to be distinguished from "yellow gold," which was harmless, for he himself had observed the following:

> I have regularly seen men taking gold: they dig into the ground to a depth of more than a ten-foot, to reach rock which is greatly disturbed. Here each lump of rock is all blackened and scorched, but beneath such rock is the gold. The larger is like a finger; the smaller resembles hemp seeds and beans; the color is like "mulberry yellow," and when you bite it it is extremely soft—this then is the true gold. But when a workman stealthily swallows some, I have not seen that it is poisonous. The "bran gold" comes from the midst of river sands, and is taken by washing it out on felt.[6]

Another source stated that the people who lived along the rivers of Fu-*chou*, Pin-*chou*, and Ch'eng-*chou* (all in southern Kwangsi) devoted their days to working placer deposits.[7] And there was a "gold pond" near Canton, where the natives suddenly began to raise ducks and geese, because "they had regularly seen flakes of bran gold in their feces, and in consequence raised them in abundance. They collect the feces and wash it out, and daily obtain about an ounce or a half ounce, and so are made wealthy."[8]

Gold prospectors continued to use the indicator plants designated in old collections of miners' lore; ginger, they said, indicated the presence of copper or tin; wild onions were a sign of silver deposits, and shallots grew where gold lay.[9] That metallic trace elements in the soil favor the growth of certain plants, whose presence accordingly indicates the possibility of workable deposits nearby, is a recently established fact in the West.[10]

That gold may be "hooked" by quicksilver was known,[11] but it is not known whether miners knew the art of extracting gold from sand or a crushed matrix by amalgamation. It may only have been a Taoist secret.

Before the advent of T'ang, both gold and silver were hardly ever worked as the basic materials of dishes, vases, or even of jewelry. Gold was made into some personal ornaments, in costly imitations of styles of ancient bronze prototypes, and for splendid inlays in large bronze vessels. But the Persian technique of beating gold and silver into elegant thin-walled forms captured the devotion of the T'ang metalworkers (and probably there were Persian goldsmiths in China, refugees from the Arabs, to teach them), replacing the classical methods of casting metal objects in molds. With the new and popular art came the designs and shapes of Sāsānid Persia: animals hunted in floriate landscapes, and symmetrical vine patterns and rosettes.[12] But despite the prevalence of the exotic vogue, the old methods of ornamenting metal were not forgotten: there were, for instance, silver-hilted swords with golden clouds inlaid in their blades, and daggers whose hilts were covered with aloeswood and whose blades were inlaid with flowers of gold.[13]

Gold leaf, gold foil, and "cut gold," [14] the last-named being a style of gold-leaf appliqué, were all employed by the artists of T'ang. Leaf gold was used in paintings, as we know from examples found at Tun-huang,[15] while the Shōsōin contains many objects beautifully decorated with it—for example, a "Silla zither" adorned with birds and plants in cut gold.[16] At least one of the towns where goldbeaters produced the materials for these gorgeous objects is known; it was Huan-*chou* in Annam.[17]

Precious metals were also inset in a lacquer base. This technique is now generally known by its Japanese name of *heidatsu*.[18] Extant examples from T'ang include boxes whose lacquered lids show flowers, birds, and clouds in gold and silver.[19] Literature reveals that this method was applied to all sorts of useful objects: when Rokhshan was in favor at Ch'ang-an, Hsüan Tsung gave him, along with other valuable utensils, spoons and chopsticks ornamented with rhinoceros horn and gold *heidatsu,* and a dumpling dish with both gold and silver *heidatsu;* his beloved consort gave the great barbarian a lidded box ornamented with precious stones and gold *heidatsu,* and an "iron-faced" cup with gold *heidatsu*.[20]

The art of gold granulation, known in several parts of the ancient world, was once thought to have been lost, but the secret was discovered in the twentieth century. It consisted of heating gold grains red hot in charcoal dust, producing a film of gold carbide which served to solder the granules to the gold surface on heating in air, when the carbide was reduced to pure gold again.[21] This technique was well known in ancient China, but its original home was probably southern Russia. A golden Chinese belt buckle (not the familiar belt hook!) was found at Lo-lang, the Chinese colony on Korea, which was decorated with turquoise gems, Chinese dragons, and patterns of little gold balls; its date is unknown, but it was found with lacquer objects dating from the third to the eighth century.[22] Typical T'ang granular work was, however, done with beaded gold wire, as in the details of a standing phoenix of sheet gold, once part of a golden headdress, or in an elaborate hairpin surmounted by a peacock in sheet gold and beaded wire.[23]

But in China, as elsewhere, medieval taste came to prefer filigree work to the ancient granulation. From T'ang we have beautiful hairpins of gold, mounted with pearls, turquoise, and other precious stones, mostly in filigree.[24]

Powdered gold had a significant role in T'ang painted decoration. It has been found in scroll paintings from Tun-huang; [25] on lotus petals cut from green paper, probably for use in Buddhist flower-scattering ceremonies; [26] and on a dagger sheath with a silver-gilt chape set with pearls, the sheath itself being covered with aloeswood and painted with birds, flowers, and clouds in gold.[27]

Gold-plating may have been a T'ang invention; it is referred to in several poems of the ninth century.[28] Gilded silver (as well as solid gold) was used for a great variety of utensils: ladies' cosmetic boxes,[29] wine jars in the shape of camels,[30] and the furniture of scabbards[31] are examples. And, of course, jewelry and all sorts of accessories for the toilet of ladies were made of gold: hairpins, combs, diadems, bracelets.[32] Golden birds, especially the holy birds we call "phoenixes" by rough analogy, were popular with ladies, above all on their headdresses.[33] We can still look at such beautiful objects as a T'ang golden crown, constructed of parallel bands showing butterflies, floral patterns, and foliate scrolls; a golden apsaras, shown flying, probably meant to be attached to a woman's clothing; and a wooden comb whose golden top shows foliate scrolls and a rampant lion in the Persian manner, executed in *repoussé*.[34]

In addition, gold was needed by the Taoists, who regarded it, in both liquid and powdered forms, as a powerful drug to stabilize the soul and lengthen life.[35] Meng Shen, the pharmacologist, reports that burning medicinal gold produces a five-colored aura, a fact which he himself verified.[36]

Gold was equally important in the realms of the imagination. Things of wonder and divine splendor were pictured as golden. These ideal images were much enriched during the climax of Chinese Buddhism in T'ang by ideas transmitted from India. The immortal sylphs of Taoism were golden, but so was the glorious Buddha, who was styled "Golden Man" or "Golden Ṛṣi," and his images too were covered with gold. Moreover, the language of the Buddha was said to be golden, and his lodgings and attributes were as "golden" as they were "perfumed." The heaven of Mañjuśrī was "golden-hued," and the bird Garuḍa, companion of Vishnu, had golden wings.[37]

On a more prosaic level, "gold" stood for all things of great worth, but human worth in particular. So T'ai Tsung praised his great minister Wei Cheng as a craftsman who could detect the gold in the raw mineral of the imperial person, extract it, refine it, and make it worthy of the good opinion of men.[38] Many rhapsodic *fu* were composed during T'ang on the theme "Opening Up the Sand to Cull Its Gold"; one such was written by Liu Tsung-yüan, on a rhyme scheme meaning "The Way of Seeking Treasure Is the Same as Picking Out Talents";[39] the basis of the simile is the gravity and splendor of gold, like the substantial and brilliant character of a virtuous man.

Such was gold in T'ang. But internal production did not meet the needs of the people, and the gold of Asia poured in over the frontiers. Though Iran may have been the ultimate source of the art of beating golden vessels and the ultimate inspiration of many of the designs worked on them by the artisans of T'ang, it appears that Tibet must also be given an important place among the nations whose craftsmen contributed to the culture of T'ang. To judge by records of tribute and gifts from Tibet to T'ang, which over and over again list large objects of gold, remarkable for their beauty and rarity and excellent workmanship, the Tibetan goldsmiths were the wonder of the medieval world. But it would be a daring scholar who would point to the evidence of their influence in China. Let us look at the descriptions of some of these extravagant imports, while hoping that future archaeologists will discover actual examples of Tibetan or Tibetan-inspired T'ang goldwork in the soil of China.

One of the largest gifts of Tibetan gold was one of the earliest. Late in 640, Mgar Stong-rtsan, the minister of the great King Srong-btsan-sgam-po, came to Ch'ang-an to arrange a marriage between his lord and a Chinese princess. To bind the engagement he presented golden vessels weighing a thousand catties, and many other precious things.[40] In the following year, an imperial daughter, later deified by the grateful Tibetans, went to join the ruler of the highlands—an event commemorated in paint by Yen Li-te, but unhappily not now recoverable.[41]

We do not know what the golden vessels of 640 were, but we are better informed about a gift sent by the same Tibetan king in 641 to his father-in-law, T'ai Tsung, in honor of his swift victory in Korea. This was a golden wine jug in the form of a goose seven feet high.[42] Early in 658 the Tibetans sent another marvel of metalwork: a golden city, populated by golden horsemen, and the figures of horses, lions, elephants, and other animals.[43]

There were many other such metallic wonders. Tibet was a golden land. In the ninth century its king lived in a sumptuous tent, decorated with tigers, leopards, and fierce reptiles executed in gold.[44] But other nations were rich in gold too: the Uighur Khan had a golden tent at Kharabalgasun which would hold a hundred men,[45] and the distant king of Rūm sat on a couch covered with gold foil.[46] Great quantities of gold and silver were sent by Silla,[47] and there were occasional gifts of these metals from the tribes of Manchuria,[48] the Nan-chao kingdom,[49] and many nations of Turkestan, including Chāch, Kish, and Māimargh.[50] From snowy Balūr came flowers of gold.[51] What is surprising in all this welter of gold is that we hear nothing of gold brought to China from the Indies. Somewhere in Malaya was Suvarṇadvīpa, the island or continent of gold, an almost fabulous El Dorado for the peoples of India.[52] But the tradition, which was a powerful factor leading to the Indian settlement of Southeast Asia, was absent from China.

PURPLE GOLD

Hsüan Tsung, in gratitude for the *Book of the Dragon Pool,* written by his son when a serious drought oppressed the region of the capital city, presented the prince with a "girdle of purple gold," taken in Korea by his ancestor, Kao Tsung, at the time of his victory over the kingdom of Koryŏ.[53] Other objects of purple gold appear from time to time in the literature of T'ang—objects of great elegance, such as the "purple gold hammer" in the sleeve of a young warrior who also boasted stirrups of "white jade,"[54] or the "wine vessel of purple gold," sent, with imperial robes and a jade girdle, to Chu Ch'üan-chung, virtually master of China in 903, by the hapless Chao Tsung.[55] Distant snowbound Balūr also "abounded in purple gold."[56]

This beautifully named metal had been known in pre-T'ang times, and also in Sung and later, though it appears that in Ming times only imitations of the fine original were possible.[57]

A clue to the identity of "purple gold" may be found in ancient Egypt. Among the rich objects discovered in the tomb of Tut'ankhamūn were ornaments of gold covered with a rose-purple film; for instance, rosettes of this material alternated with bars of pure yellow gold on one of the young king's slippers. The same unusual metal has been found in the diadem of Queen Tewosret, also of the nineteenth dynasty, and in the earrings of Rameses XI of the twentieth.[58] This proves to have been gold containing a trace of iron, which becomes violet on heating.[59] In later times, the ancient art of tinting metals to this and other colors was a treasured secret of the Hellenistic alchemists, about which we have learned from Alexandrian and Byzantine papyri.[60] Whether the purple gold of Balūr, China, and Korea represents a curious but accidental parallelism of technique in Eastern and Western alchemy, discovered independently in Egypt and China, and possibly elsewhere, or a case of the diffusion of the art across Asia, cannot yet be told. But borrowed or original, the Chinese purple gold will have been the product of the inquisitiveness of the Taoist alchemists.

SILVER

T'ang silver production was concentrated in Lingnan and Annam.[61] Apparently most of the white metal was produced by cupellation from galena, yielding only one or two parts of silver in 384 parts of lead.[62] At the beginning of the ninth century there were forty silver refineries in operation, producing 12,000 ounces annually; this number was increased to forty-two, with a production of 15,000 ounces, in the middle of the ninth century.[63]

The work of the T'ang silversmith was superb, at least up to the middle of the ninth century, when, because of the falling off of Iranian influences after the great religious persecution of 845, a period of decline set in.[64] The T'ang artisans made many designs, often "chased on a firmly punched background of tiny circles."[65] Sometimes the designs were made in repoussé relief; occasionally they were engraved. Often the whole object was made by soldering several pieces together, a technique used especially to make stem cups. Parcel-gilt and gold inlay were much used for the decoration of all kinds of silver vessels. The pictures shown on these bowls, dishes, boxes, and cups were usually mythological scenes or floral and animal scenes, and especially the "royal hunt," a theme closely related to the representations on Sāsānian silverwork and textiles.[66] Some silver objects, however, reveal an archaic native style, recalling the stone reliefs of Han.[67] A special technique was to apply silver foil, or silver-gilt foil, over a bronze mirror.[68] Silver *heidatsu,* that is, thin silver designs laid in lacquer, was also made. A notable example is a typically plump court lady, done in this material; she is shown standing beneath a tree, like some of her sisters on objects in the Shōsōin collections.[69] Other utensils made of silver were scissors, pincers, ladles, chopsticks, and grave figurines.[70]

The standard materia medica included a silver paste, called "silver tallow," apparently an achievement of the alchemists; it was an amalgam of silver and tin with mercury, prescribed as a tonic for heart and spirit.[71] The composition of "yellow silver," from which apotropaic talismans were made, is unknown, but it too must have been a Taoist creation.[72] Black silver was made by fumigating the metal with sulphur; seekers after immortality brewed their drugs in vessels made of this charmed material.[73]

Generally speaking, silver, like gold, was not used as currency, at any rate not as government issue. In Lingnan, however, where the metal was more common than elsewhere, it passed freely as a medium of exchange, as salt and silks did on the Tibetan marches, and cinnabar and quicksilver in mountainous central China.[74] Indeed, beyond "the Five Mountain-passes [which divide Lingnan from the rest of the country] buying and selling is wholly done with silver," [75] and so important was silver to the commercial life of the Canton region that when the mining of silver was outlawed in 808 (the emperor urging that, while copper is useful, silver is not), Lingnan was specifically excepted.[76]

Except for occasional gifts from other places such as Turkestan [77] and Manchuria,[78] most imported silver came from Silla [79] and from Tibet.[80] Presents from these lands were often in the form of handsome silver utensils.

Among the most valuable gifts sent to T'ang early in 658 by the Tibetan king was something called a "gold *pala."* [81] Again, in 761, the Kuchean king offered a silver *pala* at Ch'ang-an, and was given fine silks as a token of thanks.[82] Moreover, in the temple of a great god of Kabūdhān there were a number of objects of precious metals, reputed to be the gifts of the Chinese Son of Heaven in Han times. Among these was a golden image, and a "golden *pala"* fifteen feet broad.[83] But what a *pala* might be, whether gold or silver, is a mystery.

BRASS

The Chinese knew brass, the alloy of copper and zinc, as a product of Persia, and called it *"t'ou* stone" (or, as we might say, "tutty stone") signifying "zinc stone," from Persian *tūtiya.*[84] It was imported for the use of court artisans,[85] and was required for ornamenting the girdles of officials of the eighth and ninth grades.[86] Moreover, the alchemists used fragments of "Persian brass" in their mysterious amalgams.[87] Māimargh also sent brass as tribute to T'ang in 718.[88]

Rather large amounts must sometimes have been available, since there was a standing image of Vairocana, six feet high, done in brass, in a Ch'ang-an temple.[89]

But possibly the men of T'ang had learned the secret of the mixture: they certainly produced other fine alloys, such as "white copper," a silvery mixture of copper and nickel made since Han times;[90] there is a long-handled censer of this material in the Shōsōin.[91] Another censer in the same treasury is made of "red copper," reported to be an alloy of antimony, gold, and copper.[92] The Chinese "white copper" is Anglo-Indian "tootnague" (another word related to *tūtiya*), which the later Persians called *khār-čīnī*, "stone of China," saying that the Chinese valued it for mirrors and arrowheads, while the Muslims preferred it for lance heads, rings, and bells.[93]

GOLD AND SILVER COINS

The medieval Chinese minted no gold coins, saving the precious metals for objects of luxury and ostentation; the silver (and apparently gold) which was a standard medium of exchange in Lingnan was an exception. But the Chinese welcomed gold from abroad. Japanese ambassadors brought most of their assets to T'ang in the form of gold dust.[94] Gold and silver coins of the nations of Serindia, especially of Kucha, had circulated in China during the sixth century. They were certainly used throughout the Chinese protectorates in the West during the seventh and eighth centuries: evidence is a silver coin, found in the mouth of a dead man at Qočo, which shows a priest of Ahura-Mazda on one face and has the name of the Khalif Mu'āwiya on the other. This hybrid coin was accompanied by an ordinary coin of T'ang.[95]

Even the gold coins of Rome and the silver coins of Persia found their way into the hands of Serindian traders during this period, and some came into China itself to delight the curious with their images of foreign gods and kings. For instance, a gold solidus of Justin II was found in a Sui grave near Ch'ang-an,[96] and two silver coins of Khusrō II were found in a grave of the same period in Honan.[97] It seems, however, that these exotic pieces of money were not so common in T'ang as they had been in Sui, but this may be only an illusion dependent on the accidents of archaeological discovery. A tomb of T'ang date in the vicinity of Ch'ang-an has yielded a Byzantine gold coin,[98] and another grave nearby has produced a silver coin of Khusrō II.[99]

At the other end of the empire, in Canton, the gold dinars of Islam seem to have been used in trade, to judge from a T'ang book describing the city, which states that the Arabs uniformly use golden coins in commodity exchanges.[100]

xvii=Secular Objects

VARIOUS UTENSILS

DESPITE THE EXCELLENCE of Chinese craftsmanship in wood, ceramic, metal, and other materials, it was natural that the unique products of other lands should find favor in T'ang especially with the moneyed classes. Monks from Japan, for instance, found a welcome for their gifts of "knives decorated with silver, girdles, assorted writing brushes . . . ,"[1] and we may imagine that the "precious utensils" brought to Ch'ang-an by a "king's son" of that same nation in 853 were received with even more pleasure.[2] Not all imported wares, however, depended for their popularity on the rarity and value of the raw materials from which they were made: the rattan work of Annam, for instance, was in demand at the imperial court.[3]

Not only were there vessels in the Iranian style made in T'ang (some even colored ceramic imitations of metal ewers), but there were basins and ewers imported from the Far West, and we may suppose that some of the silver jugs and other fine examples of the metalworker's art now to be seen in collections were actually made in Iran for the China export trade.[4] Both Bukhāra and Samarkand sent ostrich-egg cups;[5] their use was as ancient as Babylon, and their beauty was praised by the Arab poets, who compared the ". . . delicate complexion of a lovely woman with the smooth and brilliant surface of an ostrich egg."[6] From the Arabs came a "ground-sprinkling jug" set with gems.[7] A golden pen from Kapiśa had the

258

text of Lu Szu-tao's "Song of the Swallow" engraved on it.[8] There was a little box of agate, cut to bring out its purple patterns, with the name of the king of Rome on it.[9] Samarkand gave a jeweled incense brazier and little jugs for eye medicines.[10] The king of Silla sent finely chased bells for the tails of hunting hawks.[11] Ceremonial banners came from the same country.[12] Bukhāra sent the emperor a jeweled couch.[13] The same Japanese prince (it appears) who brought gifts to the Son of Heaven in 853 was a skillful *go* player, and produced a board made from a gray stone which he called "catalpa jade," and counters which seemed cool in summer and warm in winter.[14]

LAMP-TREES

Of special interest are two "agate lamp-trees" brought to the court in the middle of the seventh century by the son of the king of Tukhāra.[15] These artificial "trees," which were also called "fire-trees," were used during the most brilliant of all T'ang festivals, the New Year's illumination, a celebration of three days or more held in the middle of the first month of the year. At this time, all families vied in hanging out beautiful lamps, and everyone sang and danced through the night. This appears to have been an outgrowth of the old New Year's festivals in Serindia, and indeed we have a mural of T'ang date from Qočo which shows a tree with branches in seven whorls, each carrying a row of lamps, and attended by a lady and her maid-servant.[16] By the sixth century, at least, the celebration had been introduced to China, and its date moved to the fifteenth of the first month, always a night of the full moon. An avowed objective of the celebrants was to outshine that orb with the brilliance of their artificial lights.[17] For the festival the usual curfew enforced in large cities was relaxed, and the nights given over to jollity.

A description of a large lamp-tree displayed in Ch'ang-an states that it was decorated with embroideries and precious metals, and held fifty thousand bowl-lamps; it was attended by over a thousand women of the district wearing flowered hairpins, and any number of maidservants as well. It is reported that the streets of Lo-yang were lined with wax candles and with "lamp towers" made of fine silks by the best craftsmen, each 150 feet high, hung with gold, silver, and gems and holding lamps in the shapes of dragons, phoenixes, tigers, and leopards. Another T'ang lamp-tree, cast in bronze, cost forty thousand strings of cash in wages for the artisans, and was dragged through the provinces for the admiration of all the people, at the cost of ten thousand strings for drayage.[18] A popular tale of T'ang tells that when Hsüan Tsung asked a Taoist adept which city had the most beautiful lamp festival, he was told that it was Yang-*chou,* and he was magically transported thither.[19] The monk Ennin, who visited Yang-*chou* in 839, described the splendor of the New Year's holiday, in which the Buddhist temples were actively engaged. Pious citizens left donations under the lamp-trees erected by religious foundations. Ennin tells of a "spoon and bamboo lamp" at one of the Yang-*chou* temples which was a tree made of bamboos, seven or eight feet high, with spoons, counted in the thousands, serving as lamps on the ends of the branches.[20] Just before he lost his empire to the founders of T'ang, Yang Ti of Sui set down his thoughts on a Yang-*chou* New Year's illumination in these words:[21]

> Wheel of the Law turns up in the sky,
> Indic sounds come up to the sky,
> Lamp-trees shine with a thousand lights,
> Flower flames open on the seven branches.[22]
> Moon image freezes in flowing water,
> Spring wind holds the nighttime plums;
> Banderoles move on yellow gold ground,
> Bells come out from beryl estrade.

ARMOR

The implements of war were very important to imperial T'ang, and as the government desired them for itself, so it tried to keep them from its neighbors. There was a considerable clandestine trade in weapons, especially with the nomads over the northwestern frontier,[23] though the transport and even the unauthorized possession of arms and armor were punishable by one to three years of penal servitude. A private individual found to have a suit of armor and three crossbows was liable to banishment to a distance of two thousand Chinese miles. Artisans who manufactured weapons without authorization were subject to even greater penalties.[24] On the other hand, all objects of military utility which came into the capital city, from what place soever, were registered by name and quantity, before going into the arsenal.[25] An important source of armor in China itself, perhaps the chief source, was the Yangtze Valley and the neighboring Huai area.[26]

The oldest kind of native armor was made from the tough hides of wild animals, rhinoceros hide and the skin of wild buffaloes being the most favored.[27] These kinds were still manufactured in T'ang times,[28] as was sharkskin armor (also an archaic type);[29] the torsos of the troops were even protected by armor of wood, of pongee, and of linen,[30] not to mention felt and paper.[31] An exotic variety was made from the thigh hides of wild horses, sent by the Turks of the Toquz-Oghuz.[32] "Sheet armor" of a new style, with round breast pieces, and a coat in a characteristic cut, is frequently seen worn by pottery knights and *dharmapāla* ("Protectors of the Religion") of T'ang times.[33] This same style is also to be found in figures from Serindia, and it is even possible that it was brought to China as an artistic form, not as an actual armorer's fashion.[34]

Plate armor of metal was the direct descendant of the ancient hide armor, and iron plate was the typical armor of T'ang.[35] One variety of iron armor, evidently polished to a brilliant luster, was styled "brightly shining armor."[36] This was a special product of Korea, perhaps of southwestern Korea, since the state of Paekche several times sent gifts of it, along with chased battle-axes, to Ch'ang-an in the first half of the seventh century,[37] and thousands of suits of it were seized during T'ai Tsung's wars in the peninsula.[38] But golden armor was more suitable to the glory of a tutelary god or a reigning Son of Heaven, or even to his household guards, and Paekche also sent such a splendid suit to T'ai Tsung.[39] Again, during that sovereign's campaigns in southern Manchuria, Paekche gave him a gold-lacquered suit of armor, and a suit of armor of "dark gold"[40] showing a quintuple pattern of mountains. The gentlemen in the suite of the Son of Heaven wore these expensive gifts when he joined forces with the general Li Chi, and ". . . the light of the armor was dazzling in the sun."[41] Such rich armor could not have been too uncommon in the more prosperous days of T'ang—and we may read of silver armor then, too. When Hsüan Tsung ordered military exercises at the foot of Mount Li, not far from the capital, in 713, two hundred thousand men-at-arms assembled there, and ". . . their battle-picks, javelins, and golden armor were so radiant that they illumined heaven and earth."[42] Or again, Tu Fu, a close observer of military life—it seems as if the drums always rattled in his ears and the spears flashed constantly in his eyes—describes the heroic young men of a patriotic family in these terms:

> The snow is still frozen to their golden armor,
> The dust is not spilled from their vermilion flags.[43]

Scale armor, made by sewing small iron plates to a coat in overlapping rows, was also worn in T'ang.[44] Scale armor is still worn by the Na-khi people of Yünnan, unlike their predecessors of Nan-chao, who wore leather sheet armor.[45] The medieval Tibetans wore armor of leather scales, usually lacquered in red and black, and indeed scale armor still survives in Tibet.[46] This may be related to the T'ang scale armor, but whether it represents a survival of a common embryonic ancestor, or is a vestigial descendant, cannot be told now.[47]

Early in the eighth century chain mail appeared in China. The first dated reference to it is for 718, when a gift of "link armor"[48] came from Samarkand.[49] But later in the same century, the Tibetans, dominant in the western marches, clothed their knights and horses alike in fine mail, leaving only their eyes free,[50] and the Koreans of the ninth century had a tradition that a suit of chain mail had fallen from Heaven long ago, "east of the walled city of Liao."[51] In any event, the armor was of Iranian origin.[52] A unique representation of Far Eastern mail may be seen in a painting from Tun-huang.[53] Though the chain was usually of iron,[54] other metals were also used:

> Discarded in the rain—gold chain armor;
> Beyond the moss—a lance sunken in the green.[55]

Or again:

> Grooms on horseback in yellow copper of linked chain armor;
> Net banners on aromatic staffs with gold painted leaf.[56]

SWORDS AND SPEARS

> I have a god's sword, by a strange man given—
> In the darkness, now and again, its subtle soul speaks.
> Philosophers know that it came from the Eastern Seas . . .[57]

These words from a song about a sword of Silla express the archaic belief in swords endowed with magic power—swords ensouled, like the Madjapahit blades of the Indies. Swords rich in mana were often the weapons of distant lands, where magicians, ghosts, and talismans were more abundant than in T'ang. Even the poisoned lances of the "Southern *Man*," which killed men without shedding their blood, were no mere chemical agents, but divinely activated, "rained down from heaven."[58]

The potent essences of Male and Female coöperated to produce a perfect sword, or indeed any important metal object, such as a temple bell. Ideally a virgin boy and girl should work the bellows which heated its metal. In the old times swords were made in pairs, male and female, *yin* and *yang,* soul mates of bronze, which could speak, sing, and move about by themselves; they could flash light, and were indeed dragon-spirits of a sort, and masters of the lightning.[59] In T'ang times the powerful bronze swords of K'un-wu, also called "treasure sabers," which could cut jade, were well remembered as the ancient prototypes of all magical and kingly blades, and were the frequent theme of poems rich in historical allusion.[60] Even if not named, these wonder-swords were thought of in poems like this one by Tu Fu, poet of battles, writing of an exotic sword fit for a hero-king who was to come to settle the storms which ravaged the realm:

> Brought here from an outlandish distant place,
> Yet not mounted with pearl or jade—
> In what are you strange and weird?
> Each night you spit a spike of light!
> Now tiger spirit should prance to heights,
> But dragon body will stay long stored;
> Should wind and dust not come to rest,
> I will keep *you* to offer to an enlightened king![61]

Among the bladed weapons recognized by the official armory of T'ang there were long ceremonial and processional swords, ornamented with gold and silver,[62] short swords girded on by soldiers,[63] and long infantryman's swords.[64] All of these (and some others) were single-edged knives and sabers,[65] the instruments of T'ang supremacy over the peoples of Asia. As for spears, there were the short lacquered lances of the cavalry [66] and the long wooden spears of the foot soldiers,[67] as well as more splendid varieties carried by the palace guards and ritual police.[68]

We may gain some idea of the beauty of medieval Chinese swords from specimens in the Shōsōin, with their hilts and scabbards thickly sewn with precious stones and metals, some lacquered and painted in oil with floral and animal designs: a good example has sharkskin wrapping on the hilt, while hilt and scabbard have gold and silver scrollwork set with round gems.[69] Some of these excellent weapons, at least, will have been of T'ang manufacture: "patterned sword and knife blades" were produced for the court in eastern Szechwan, near the gorges.[70]

Others were imports. The kingdom of Nan-chao sent a sword "forged by a vagabond"; poison had been added to the molten metal which went into its making, and the blade had been quenched in horse's blood; hilt and *quillons* were decorated with gold and rhinoceros horn, to make a weapon suitable to a dynasty of kings.[71] Iron blades came from the Black Water Mo-ho of Manchuria several times in the eighth century, but their magic is not reported.[72]

"Damascus steel" was known in medieval China, but whether it was imported in T'ang times or not is uncertain. It was described as "Persian" in the sixth century, and as "Kashmirian" in the tenth, and thought to be so ". . . hard and sharp that it can cut metal and hard stones." [73] Welding strips of steel together is not the only way to produce the moiré appearance of "damascened" blades; the same wavy patterns occur in high-carbon "wootz" steel of medieval India.[74] In China this metal was called "*pin* iron," probably a name from an Iranian tongue by way of an Indian Prakrit form such as *piṇa*.[75] It is probable that if the men of T'ang got "Damascus blades" it was from India, or from an Indianized intermediary.

Bows and Arrows

The Chinese word for "bow" is cognate to "dragon," to "rainbow," and to "vault of the sky," [76] and we may be sure that the linguistic relationship exemplifies a mythical relationship: bows have the power of the rain clouds, darting lightning. Among the many kinds of T'ang bows were the longbows of the infantry, made of mulberry wood; the small crossbow, also an infantry weapon; the great long-range crossbows; the painted ceremonial bows; and especially the "horn bows," strengthened with horn and sinew, the chief weapon of the horseman.[77] In ancient times these last had been the characteristic bows of the warriors of the steppe, enemies of the Chinese, but were long since thoroughly adapted to Chinese culture, and in T'ang were manufactured in Hopei and northern Shensi, admittedly close to the frontier and nomadic influences.[78] The handsome bows in the Shōsōin, of zelkova and catalpa wood, are presumably of Chinese manufacture.[79] But it is uncertain whether foreign bows, such as those of Khwārizm, "which only the strongest could bend,"[80] or the fine horn bows of the Shih-wei in Manchuria,[81] can be counted among important T'ang *exotica*.

The shaft of the T'ang arrows was made of bamboo, brought from the thickets of Kiangsi and Hunan, south of the Long River.[82] Wooden arrows were restricted to target-shooting and hunting; long steel-headed arrows were used to pierce armor in battle; crossbow bolts were short, and "feathered" with skin.[83] The terrifying whistling-head arrows of the nomads were made in a town near the Mongolian frontier, and sent to the capital as "tribute."[84] But again, though the fine stone arrowheads of the Black Water Mo-ho (an admired product of the Tungus lands since antiquity) were still well thought of,[85] and though there were wonderful tales of the baneful poisoned arrows of the forest savages close to Burma,[86] Chinese arrows seem to have had no important foreign rivals in T'ang times.

Quivers woven of the white kudzu vine, but usually lacquered in black or red, can be seen in the Shōsōin,[87] but it cannot be stated positively that these were the royal quivers manufactured at Kuei-*chou* in northern Hopei.[88]

All over the world, I wonder, in lands that I never
    have trod,
Are the people eternally seeking, for the signs and
    steps of a God? . . .
Here in this mystical India, the deities hover and
    swarm,
Like wild bees heard in the tree tops, or the gusts
    of a gathering storm.

> Sir Alfred Comyn Lyall,
> "Meditations of a Hindu Prince"

xviii=Sacred Objects

ALONG THE familiar trade routes through the
deserts of Central Asia, or through the Southern Seas, a great traffic in holy and
venerable objects passed from India and its cultural dependencies into T'ang.[1] Artisans
of many races, including the Chinese, were engaged in making religious objects in
the great Buddhist temples of Asia, and these temples had their own shops (as well
as hostels, pawnshops, and credit agencies) for the benefit of the faithful who traveled
these hazardous routes.[2] The goods they sold to the pious augmented the flow of
images, relics, and texts which went into the Far East from India, the true home
of the Law. As a result, a very diversified set of exotic objects enlivened the religious
landscape of T'ang, among them such things as a Buddhist shrine five feet high
sent as a gift from Tibet;[3] a model of the Nālandā temple brought from India itself
by a monk;[4] ". . . the five-fingered bell and vajra which were inherited from his
deceased Master, a silver plate, and rosaries made of seeds of the bodhi tree and
crystal beads," all these being the legacy of the great Tantrist Amoghavajra to Tai
Tsung;[5] a silver harp in the grotto of the T'ien-t'ai monastery at Wu-t'ai Mountain,
". . . which had 84,000 notes, and each of the 84,000 notes cured one of the worldly
passions."[6] An example of the collecting zeal of Chinese visitors to the holy places

of India is that of the famous I-ching, who, between his departure from Canton in 671 and his return to Lo-yang in 695, after traversing thirty countries, accumulated 400 collections of scriptures in the Sanskrit language, the texts of 500,000 anthems, and 300 holy relics.[7]

RELICS

The reverence shown to relics of the saints and masters of Buddhism, and even of the Buddhas themselves, was phenomenal, and what is more, these excellent objects fetched a great price in the public markets, as the following tale tells. This was one of a rich repertory of anecdotes told by the abbot of the Bodhi temple in the P'ing-k'ang Quarter of Ch'ang-an, adjacent to the home of the minister Li Lin-fu (here the minister "seated on the right"):

Li, the Right-Seated, whenever his birthday arrived, invited some monk of this office-temple to come in his turn to his home, where he laid out a maigre feast for him. There was Monk I, who once extolled the Buddha there, and was given a saddle, completely equipped, as alms. He sold it, and its materials were valued at seventy thousand! Then there was Monk Kuang, who had a name for his voice. After reciting the sutras for several years, it came his turn to extol the Buddha there. Accordingly, he went the limit in invoking the patriotic merit and personal virtue of the Right-Seated, expecting to get a heavy donation. When the maigre feast was finished, a painted hamper, in a scented net kerchief, was brought from under the curtain. In it rested an object like a rotten nail, several inches long. His expectations lost, the monk went back, and was several days in a state of mortification. But after a while he reflected that such a great vassal would be incapable of deceiving him, and so he took the thing to the Western Market, where he showed it to a Westerner of the merchant class. When this Western merchant saw it, he was astonished, and said, "Where did you obtain this object, High One? If you must make a commodity of it, I won't stint the price." The monk made a trial of asking a hundred thousand. The Westerner gave a great laugh, and said, "You haven't reached it! Go just as far as you will, and then speak again!" He kept adding, up to five hundred thousand, and even then the Westerner said, "This is worth a thousand myriads!" And so he gave it to him for that. The monk inquired after its name, and he said, "This is the Precious Bone!"[8]

Excess of enthusiasm for the fragments of precious bodies could even lead to acts of piracy: the Chinese "Master of the Law" Ming-yüan tried to steal the world-renowned tooth of the Buddha from its reliquary in Ceylon. Tradition said that if this powerful relic should leave the country, the whole island would be devoured by demons.[9] Fortunately, the pious zealot was frustrated by the intervention of supernatural powers.[10]

Such fanatical piety naturally provoked its opposite. There were many in T'ang who condemned the faith of the worshipers of relics, and despised the relics themselves as filthy objects of no worth. Han Yü, who wrote the malevolent memorial against the honors shown to the finger bone of the Buddha, was only the most eminent of these. This uncompromising anticleric represented the more cultured side of the xenophobia of the ninth century, which culminated in the great persecution of foreign religions, the destruction of religious art, and the beginning of the end of Buddhism as an important fertilizer of Chinese civilization.[11]

But meanwhile the enthusiastic search for saintly relics continued. The pilgrim Wu-k'ung returned to Ch'ang-an in 790 with a tooth of Shakyamuni obtained from a monastery in Udyāna.[12] In the ninth century there were teeth of the Buddha in four temples of the capital city, each with its special festival which attracted hordes of believers, who offered medicines, foods, fruits, and flowers, and, in fragrant clouds of incense, ". . . tossed cash like rain toward the storied hall of the Buddha's tooth." [13] The monastery at Wu-t'ai Mountain boasted the skull of a Pratyeka-Buddha, which (reported Ennin) ". . . is white and black in color and in appearance resembles Japanese pumice stone," with some few white hairs still attached to the crown.[14] There were even relics of historical personages, ranging in dignity from a bit of King Aśoka in a Ch'ang-an temple [15] to a piece of the Japanese monk Reisan, kept in a cloister on Mount Wu-t'ai. This last was a most curious object, consisting of a ". . . strip of skin from Reisan's arm, four inches long and three wide, on which the devout Japanese pilgrim had drawn a pictures of the Buddha." [16]

Although it must be admitted that such edifying objects seem to have had little effect on the effusions of the poets, they stimulated the imaginations of the learned tellers of stories. So we have a tale which revolves around a magic pearl sent to the Empress Wu by a Western country, along with the lower jawbone of the Heavenly King Virūpākṣa, as large as a folding chair, and the tongue of a Pratyeka-Buddha, which was blue, and as large as the tongue of an ox.[17]

IMAGES

Religious images, Buddhist ones above all, were much in vogue during T'ang, especially small ones of metal, wood, or clay, which any believer might own—a vogue which encouraged the artisans of T'ang greatly.[18] But for rich individuals and handsomely endowed institutions there were images brought from foreign places, and artistic treatment of foreign subjects, all of which both satisfied and modified the taste of the men of T'ang. The homemade exotic images were plentiful enough; they ranged from the symbolic (such as the figures of the Seven Planets [Manichaean?] painted by Yen Li-te) [19] to the naturalistic (such as the pictures of the musicians of Pyū sent to court by Wei Kao, conquerer of Nan-chao and the Tibetans).[20] "Realistic" representations of foreign subjects were regularly painted in T'ang, since official painters were assigned the duty of delineating the persons and costumes of all visitors to the court.[21] Such paintings, rolled on sandalwood cylinders tipped with white jade, amber, or crystal,[22] must have had an important effect on the taste of the times, at least in court circles. But the effect of objects of art actually imported from the studios of distant nations must have been even more widespread and penetrating.

Indeed, next to sutras and relics, a prime objective of Chinese pilgrims in the holy lands of the Indies was the acquisition of holy statues and images to edify the faithful at home and adorn the rich temples of T'ang.[23] Not all the exotic icons were from India, however. Many were from the workshops of other Buddhist nations, examples being the brass statue from Khotan kept in the temple of the Holy Flower [24] in Ch'ang-an, in a hall whose murals had been painted by divine beings,[25] and the figures of the Buddha, executed in gold and silver, brought by the son of the king of Silla as a gift to Hsien Tsung in 810.[26] Some were not even Buddhist; among the paintings found at Tun-huang there is what seems to be a Christian saint, with red mustaches, and a Maltese cross on his tiara, but perhaps he was conceived to be a Bodhisattva in the Far East.[27]

Among these introduced objects, however, the group which is most significant for its long-range effect on Chinese taste consisted of patterns and models of beings and symbols of religious worth, intended to guide the minds and hands of artisans not lucky enough to have been born in the lands which the Buddha and his saints had trod. When the painter Vajra Tripitaka, a native of Ceylon and skilled portrayer of holy figures, came to T'ang to exercise his craft,[28] we may be sure that he brought with him his books showing the standard proportions of religious figures. Whether he guarded them jealously or showed them proudly to his Chinese colleagues is not known. But certainly the Chinese were anxious to have such classical models, and certainly they used them: whole compositions are repeated in the different caves of Tun-huang, a phenomenon explainable only by the assumption that patterns were followed to guarantee a devout conformity to just ideals.[29] Special emissaries were sent abroad to obtain iconographic stereotypes; such a one was the man dispatched to Khotan by Hsüan Tsung to obtain the proper form of Vaiśravana, the Heavenly King of the North, a favorite divinity of the Turkish overlords of the city-states of Central Asia.[30] Divine patterns might also form an important part of the booty of war or diplomacy: the aggressive T'ang agent, Wang Hsüan-ts'e, who obtained many drawings of Buddhist images in India, took from Bodh-Gayā a copy of the image of the Buddha made by the Bodhisattva Maitreya himself; from this a gold-encrusted figure of that deity was modeled in Ch'ang-an in 665.[31] (Of course, the artistic influences operated in both directions: Chinese workers at the loom, goldsmiths, and painters worked for the Arabs in Mesopotamia in the eighth century—men such as the painters Fan Shu and Liu Tz'u, and the weavers Yüeh Huan and Lü Li.) [32]

The period of exotic influences on religious art passed, when, as part of the great persecution of 845, images both public and private were melted down for agricultural implements or for the uses of the treasury.[33] Ennin's words on this disaster were: "What limit was there to the bronze, iron, and gold Buddhas of the land? And yet, in accordance with the imperial edict, all have been destroyed and have been turned into trash." [34]

xix=Books

''Exotica''

THE PHYSICAL APPEARANCE of texts
brought from foreign countries impressed the men of T'ang with their oddness, but
often enough became naturalized and accepted. Alien scripts were strange things, all
the more so in suggesting to the impressionable mind all sorts of quaint ideas, bizarre
wisdom, and even fearful spells, concealed in their incomprehensible shapes. Not that
there were not peculiar native scripts: along with the old and familiar "seal script" and
the square "model script," there were "tiger claw script," "fallen shallot script," "supine
ripple script," "sun script," "moon script," "wind script," "worm-eaten leaf script,"
and a great many others, including such accepted introductions as "Westerner (*hu*)
script" and "Indian script." [1] But among the forms of writing used in the "Western
Regions" and sometimes to be seen by the curious in T'ang, were such scripts as "ass
lips," "lotus petal," "Great Ch'in" (that is, Roman), "riding horseback," "risen
corpse," "Heaven," "dragon," and "bird tone," to name only a few of a total of sixty-
four known to Tuan Ch'eng-shih. [2]

It was the same with the paper on which these several kinds of characters were
written. T'ang had its own papers, made from hemp, and kudzu, and paper mulberry, and even from pulp of bamboo and rosewood; these were tinted in various
shades (a thin, crisp, golden yellow was one of the most beautiful T'ang papers), and
sometimes scented; the sheets were glued together end to end to make long scrolls; the
best of them, perhaps, were mounted on sandalwood rollers with crystal knobs
(though there were also folded books by the ninth century, and stitched books by the

tenth). But the most elegant books were written on silk, venerable for its use in ancient times.³

Despite these excellent native resources, however, a use was found for many foreign papers. The T'ang poets often refers to *"Man*-barbarian note paper"; Koryŏ sent paper scrolls as tribute; Japan made a paper of pine bark; and from the lands south of China came white paper with "fish egg" pattern, and a paper made from seaweed called "slanted streak paper." ⁴ The art of making these papers had been originally learned from the Chinese; their exotic quality was therefore somewhat superficial. Whether any parchment found its way to T'ang from the distant West is uncertain, though the Chinese had known of its existence, or of something like it, since the second century B.C., when the great traveler Chang Ch'ien reported that the Parthians wrote in horizontal lines on the skins of animals.⁵ Leather was used for stationery in medieval Khotan,⁶ but was little noticed in China. But there was an alien writing material which was much in evidence in T'ang, and had some effect on the poetic imagination. This was the leaf of the palmyra, a fan palm of southern Asia.⁷ In T'ang it was known simply by the Sanskrit word for "leaf," *pattra*.⁸ The official history of T'ang reports that the Indians, skilled in the arts of astronomy and mathematics (as all men knew), ". . . write on leaves of the *pattra* tree to chronicle events." ⁹ Tuan Ch'eng-shih, who gives a correct etymology of the loan word, describes it as an evergreen tree of Magadha (perhaps because the manufacture of palm-leaf books was an important industry there), and adds that, if well cared for, scriptures written on palmyra will last five or six hundred years.¹⁰

A resident of the capital could see the tree which produced these useful leaves. This rarity, brought from a "Western nation," was planted on the grounds of the Buddhist temple called "Exalting the Good." ¹¹ This was famous for the grandeur of its buildings, reputed to be the largest in Ch'ang-an, and for its many other treasures, such as an image of the Buddha in Khotanese jade, a painting by the master Wu Tao-hsüan, and especially for its ancient pine trees. A branch of one of these last, carved in the shape of a dragon, had brought rain during a serious drought.¹² Late in the ninth century the poet Chang Ch'iao wrote some verses in praise of the revered paper palm.¹³ We wonder how it managed to survive so long in the climate of Ch'ang-an.

The books made up from properly shaped leaf material, called "ollahs," were bound between two boards, called "Indic presses" ¹⁴ in T'ang.¹⁵ They could not have been uncommon, in view of the vigorous collecting efforts of Chinese pilgrims to India. They were to be found most readily in the great monasteries of T'ang; Ennin observed a copy of the *Lotus Sutra* in this format at Wu-t'ai Mountain.¹⁶ Books could also be read in more secular surroundings: I Tsung, for instance, a pious believer, kept palm-leaf books in the palace, and chanted the sutras from them himself.¹⁷ King Śīlamegha of Ceylon sent a copy of the *Mahāprajñāpāramitā-sūtra*, inscribed on palmyra, to Ch'ang-an by the hands of the monk Amoghavajra in 746.¹⁸

Leaf books were especially to be venerated since they commonly were written in a language which, like the letters sent to T'ang by the king of Kurān in 646, ". . . was of a kind with the speech of the Buddha." [19] The Chinese workers in words found a nice exotic image in these sacred leaves, and they appear often in verses intended to evoke the atmosphere of Buddhist devotion. So Li Shang-yin, in "Superscription on a Monk's Wall," wrote, "If you believe in the true and substantial words on *pattra* . . ." (that is, in the words of the holy sutras).[20] Or, even better, we have already seen *pattra* paired with *candana,* "sandal." Here it is again, in P'i Jih-hsiu's picture of a garden-temple:

> A small basilica, with *kunduruka* incense;
> Some ancient scriptures, on *pattra* paper.[21]

Frankincense and palmyra—smell and feel of the religion of the warm West.

BOOKSHOPS AND LIBRARIES

In the eighth and ninth centuries, the citizens of T'ang could presumably get books about foreign places, dictionaries of foreign languages, and even foreign books in the shops of the large cities.[22] Unfortunately we still know very little about the bookshops of T'ang, having only such scraps as a reference in a popular story to a shop for classical books in the capital, patronized by candidates for the government examinations, and a poetical allusion to a bookshop in the Southern Market of Lo-yang.[23] It is also known that the new printed books (mostly on oneiromancy, astrology, and kindred arts) were sold at Ch'eng-tu in the ninth century.[24]

Since T'ang was an age of notable book collectors, rather more information is available about libraries. Of these, the most important was the library of the Son of Heaven. This was begun by T'ai Tsung in 628 at the urging of such eminent men as Wei Cheng, Yü Shih-nan, and Yen Shih-ku, who oversaw the accessions and engaged calligraphers as copyists. The new imperial T'ang library [25] contained two hundred thousand scrolls, many of them copies of very rare books. Another great effort was made under Hsüan Tsung, especially toward the copying of scarce books in private libraries, on the best hemp paper from Szechwan. Academies for the preservation of literature [26] were established in the two capitals. A new home for the imperial collection was found,[27] where the lately devised system of classifying all books according to four subjects was followed, with colored ivory labels (inscribed with title and volume number) to indicate the subject. "Classics" had a red tab, white ivory inlaid roller, and yellow tie; "Histories," a green tab, blue ivory inlaid roller, and light green tie; "Philosophers," an indigo tab, carved sanders roller, and purple tie; and "Collections," a white tab, green ivory roller, and vermilion tie.[28]

The first reign of Hsüan Tsung, that is, the peaceful first half of the eighth century, was the heyday of official T'ang book collecting. But when the historian Ou-yang Hsiu was preparing to write his history of T'ang in the eleventh century, he found that more than half of this great library had vanished as a result of civil disasters, especially the rebellion of Huang Ch'ao.[29]

No census of the libraries of T'ang religious establishments is available, but these collections too must have been considerable. A catalogue of extant Buddhist translations from the Sanskrit, made in 664, listed 2,487 different works, some of them very long.[30] If we consider that a single temple in Ch'ang-an had a thousand copies of just one of these, the *Lotus Sutra,* stored in a pagoda,[31] we may imagine the astronomical number of holy scrolls kept in the metropolis.

Private collectors were busy everywhere, and some of the oldest and rarest books were in their hands. These were men like Ni Jo-shui, the orthodox classicist, who had rebuked Hsüan Tsung for the frivolity of his bird collecting—his shelves would not hold his books, so he piled them in the window frames, totally excluding the light of the sun from the library.[32] There were men like Chang Ts'an, who devoted his old age to copying the Confucian classics, since, as he said, ". . . reading texts is not to be compared with copying texts."[33] There were men like Tuan Ch'eng-shih, a devotee of the curious, with a powerful memory: learning first all the secrets he could as a collator of the imperial archives, he later spent all his time with his household library, and became especially well-informed in Buddhist literature.[34]

With this kind of energy and enthusiasm, it is not suprising that private libraries were both large and good; for example, Li Pi's library contained thirty thousand scrolls, and the books collections of Liu Po-ch'u, Wei Shu, and Su Pien each contained twenty thousand scrolls.[35] These rich private libraries must have rivaled the imperial collections in the splendor of their furniture as well as in the rarity of their holdings. Consider the sumptuous volumes belonging to the collector Ts'ui Jen-liang, described by the poet Lü Wen, their wrappers studded with rock crystal ("water germ"), their paper glossed with mica ("cloud mother"):

> . . . Jade tower with precious racks, placed in the middle heavens,
> Sealed rarities and secret oddities—a myriad rolls and more;
> Wrappers stitched with "water germ," rollers inlaid in green,
> Paper pounded with "cloud mother," writing in yellow gold.[36]

Books of Travel and Geography

Some of the conceptions formed by the men of T'ang about foreign peoples and their lands were derived from books written by travelers abroad and by government geographers. The titles of many of these are still known, even though most of the books themselves are lost to us. Among them were *Treatise on Strange Things in Bnam* by Chu Ying; *Record of the Road Miles to the Western Regions* by Ch'eng Shih-chang; *Transmittal of My Travel in the Outer Nations* by the monk Chih-meng; *Record of the Nation of Forest City (Prum Irap)*,[37] author unknown; *Record of a Commission Undertaken in Koryŏ*, author unknown; *Register of Tibet and the Yellow River*, author unknown; *Treatise on Strange Things in the Southern Quarter*, by Fang Ch'ien-li; *Illustrated Record of the Western Regions* by P'ei Chü; *Record of the Silla Nation* by Ku Yin; *Record of Yünnan* by Yüan Tzu; *Illustrated Transmittal on the Tribute Offered at the Levee by the Kirghiz* by Lü Shu. A very important one was *Illustrated Treatise on the Western Regions*, in sixty scrolls, the work of many emissaries of Kao Tsung in Samarkand, Tukhāra, and such places, sent to study their customs and products and to draw maps; the materials thus collected were written up by the court historiographical office, under the supervision of Hsü Ching-tsung, and the final work presented to the throne in 658.[38] And there were a great many other books. Of the lost ones, whose names are therefore all the more exciting, we sometimes have a few passages, preserved as quotations in later books: such is fortunately the case with the important treatise of Fang Ch'ien-li, just mentioned; so it is also with the *Record of My Travel in Central India*, full of the marvels of India, by the rather piratical imperial agent Wang Hsüan-ts'e.[39]

The journals of pilgrims to India, who were often learned clerics, form an important part of the literature which informed (and only occasionally misinformed) the men of T'ang about distant places. Fortunately some of these have survived until the twentieth century, so that everyone who knows anything about medieval China is familiar with the names of Hsüan-tsang and I-ching. Indeed, the influence of Hsüan-tsang's travel book, *Record of the Western Regions*, has extended far beyond his own times, and beyond the realm of merely informative writing. In T'ang times this monk was widely celebrated, and his famous example inspired many others to take a deep interest in India and the cultures under Indian influence.[40] Centuries later a fictional version of his journey, titled *Record of an Excursion in the West*, but now widely known in Arthur Waley's translation as *Monkey*, became one of the great picaresque novels of the world, with an international reputation. It may also be considered one of the great works of exoticism in fiction.

RELIGIOUS BOOKS

The master Hsüan-tsang, who brought more than six hundred sets of the sutras and *abhidharmas* to T'ang,[41] described the perils of the passage between India and China, which so many devoted monks traveled to bring back the true words of the Buddha. In a letter to the Indian Iñānaprabha, written in 654, he said,

I should humbly like to let you know that while crossing the Indus I had lost a load of sacred texts. I now send you a list of those texts annexed to this letter. I request you to send them to me if you get the chance. I am sending some small articles as presents. Please accept them. The road is long and it is not possible to send much. Do not disdain it.[42]

The usual thing was for the pious travelers, after braving the material and ghostly hazards of the wilderness, to study at the great monastery of Nālandā in Magadha, which housed five thousand priests and novices in its halls and galleries of brick. Most of them also paid their respects to the bodhi tree at Gayā, where the Buddha was enlightened. An example is Tao-sheng (named Candradeva in Sanskrit), who went by way of Tibet to study Hīnayāna texts at the great intellectual center of Nālandā. He started back to T'ang with a great burden of books and images, but fell ill and died in Nepal.[43] Another such was Hsüan-chao, who went to central India, filled with holy zeal, but died there, being over sixty years of age, without achieving his objectives.[44] These men and others like them left no records of the strange things they saw, nor did they add new Indian books to the libraries of T'ang. But they were martyrs and victims for the glory of their religious community, whose contribution to knowledge, taken as a whole, was stupendous.

The search was often for an authentic and reliable text of whichever sutra was enjoying popularity or prestige in T'ang. The *Parinirvāṇa-sūtra,* for instance, an old favorite, found its place taken in general esteem during the second half of the seventh century by the *Lotus Sutra*.[45] Early in the eighth century I-ching's translation of the *Suvarṇa-prabhāsa-uttamarāja-sūtra* enjoyed considerable popularity, but it was superseded later in the century by the *Diamond Sutra*,[46] which was allotted the honor of providing for our own times the text of the oldest surviving printed book. Changes of fashion such as these inspired new efforts on the part of book-collecting pilgrims, sometimes with official blessings. Her own version being incomplete, the Empress Wu desired the original Sanskrit text of the *Avataṁsaka-sūtra*,[47] congenial to her exaltation of Mahāyāna. Accordingly she sent envoys to Khotan, where the book was said to exist. The emissaries found the book and brought it back, along with a competent Khotanese translator named Śikṣānanda, who was given the Chinese religious name of Hsüeh-hsi. The holy pages, pressed between boards, and the learned scholar were both installed in the palace in the Eastern Capital, and the latter set to work making a Chinese translation, with the lady sovereign sitting nearby—a presence which could not have made his philological work easier.[48] He will serve, however, as a specimen of the hundreds of foreign scholar-priests who were summoned to the splendid court of T'ang, clutching their precious books to their bosoms.

There were some who, unlike Śikṣānanda, achieved some fame in the world— the Tantric priests of the eighth century may stand for them. There was Śubhā-karasiṁha, who came to Ch'ang-an when he was eighty years old, claiming descent from Śākyamuni. He brought a considerable number of Sanskrit documents, enjoyed the favor of Hsüan Tsung for his mystic powers and skill in magic, and was employed as a rainmaker more than once.[49] There was Dharmacandra, who brought a new collection of spells along with sutras and *abhidharmas,* books on astrology, and Sanskrit medical texts.[50] Vajrabodhi, a king's son who taught among the Pallavas of southern India and then went to Ceylon, accompanied the Ceylonese mission which brought the *Mahāprajñāpāramitā-sūtra* to China.[51] Most famous of all the Tantric spellbinders was Amoghavajra, the disciple of Vajrabodhi; a brahman from Ceylon, he had a spectacular career at the T'ang court in the second half of the eighth century, enjoyed all sorts of special privileges, and died full of honor in his adopted land.[52] All brought their powerful cantrips, their incredible talismans, and their astonishing philters, along with the textual authorities which validated their use.

Not everything came from India: Silla was able to send a set of Buddhist sutras to T'ang early in the ninth century as a gift suitable to the sovereign.[53] Nor were all imported books derived from the teachings of Gautama. In 638 the Persian Nestorian *·Â-lâ-puən* brought his scriptures and teachings to lay before T'ai Tsung; the emperor praised them for their subtlety and profundity, and had a temple established in the capital for the heretic.[54] Again, in 807, the Uighurs obtained permission to erect Manichaean temples in Lo-yang and T'ai-yüan;[55] but after the power of the Uighurs was destroyed by the Kirghiz in the reign of the Taoist emperor Wu Tsung, ". . . the writings and images of Mani were burned in the streets."[56] The ancient gods were once more exalted, and the appeal of the exotic was at its nadir.

SCIENTIFIC BOOKS

The T'ang monks who visited the West brought back with them foreign writings on philosophy, mathematics, astronomy, and medicine, along with purely theological tomes.[57] Scientific studies were much in demand in T'ang, where the astronomical arts of India were held in high repute. Treatises on these subjects were as welcome at the palace as gold and gems. The ambassadors of Kapiśa, for instance, presented Hsüan Tsung with a volume of astronomical studies in 720, along with "secret formulas and singular drugs."[58]

In the eighth century, official calendrical calculations were virtually a monopoly of experts belonging to three Indian families, the Kāśyapa, Gautama, and Kumāra.[59] The most eminent of these Indian astronomers was Gautama Siddhārtha,[60] director of the royal observatory for Hsüan Tsung. This great man, who rejoiced in the name of the Buddha, rendered the *Navagrāha* ("Nine Planets") *Almanac* of India into Chinese,[61] and introduced more exact methods of predicting solar and lunar eclipses, the use of the zero symbol, and a table of sine functions. Unfortunately the last two innovations were resisted by conservative Chinese astronomers, and failed to be adopted.[62]

An *Almanac of the Seven Luminaries,*[63] also of Indian inspiration, was in use in the seventh century; it had antecedents under the same title, but in various permutations, as far back as Han times.[64] A statute of the middle seventh century forbade the private possession or study of this astrological calendar, along with charts of the heavens, books of divination, and treatises on the art of war;[65] this official secrecy limited the dazzling effects of astronomical exoticism to approved scientists and the politicians who managed them. Amoghavajra was influential in propagating the Indic methods of calendar computation; he translated into Chinese a *Sutra Spoken by Bodhisattva Mañjuśrī and the Sages on the Auspicious and Evil Days and the Good and Evil Planets and Lunar Mansions,* by which the positions of the planets could be accurately predicted.[66] The sage's Chinese disciple, Yang Ching-feng, published notes to this book in 764, in which he listed the planetary names of the days of the week in the Indian, Persian, and Sogdian languages. The Sogdian (Manichaean?) list of the "Seven Luminaries," written in Chinese characters, is a fascinating catalogue of vanished Babylonian gods: Mihr (Sun), Mâh (Moon), Bahram (Mars), Tîr (Mercury), Ormuzd (Jupiter), Nâhid (Venus), Kevan (Saturn).[67] Nâhid will be more recognizable as Anahata, the Old Persian form of the name, that is, as Anaitis, a Semitic Aphrodite; but it is doubtful that this wanton lady was ever envisaged in T'ang at the mention of the name of her planet. The Sogdian name for "Sunday" has been especially persistent: the Day of Mihr appears on a Chinese almanac published in Taiwan in 1960.[68]

Many other books of calendar science and astrology current during T'ang were based on the Western system. The great astronomer-monk I-hsing, co-builder of the water-powered armillary sphere, with its escapement mechanism to allow it to keep pace with the movements of the heavens,[69] also used the Near Eastern names of the planets in his books on astronomy.[70]

Books of medicine and pharmacology came from Indianized lands too. By Sui times many of these had been admitted to the palace library—books bearing such titles as *Drug Prescriptions Advocated by the Various Ṛṣi of the Western Regions; Drug Prescriptions of the Brahman [Countries]; Important Prescriptions Collected by Famous Physicians of the Western Regions.*[71] These titles do not appear in the official T'ang catalogue, and it must be assumed that they were destroyed during the civil wars which plagued T'ang from time to time, or perhaps in the xenophobic persecution of Wu Tsung. But new books on medicine continued to come from the outer world, especially books of "secret prescriptions," as we have seen. We even know of an illustrated herbal of foreign origin: in return for a pair of white parrots, an embroidered purple robe, fine inlaid vessels of gold and silver, and over three hundred pieces of fancy gauze and damask sent to him by Hsüan Tsung, the king of Silla sent a letter of thanks, along with the painted representations of the herbs and fungi of his country.[72]

TABLATURES AND MAPS

The popularity of Serindian music in T'ang, and the employment of Serindian music teachers, meant that Serindian musical scores using foreign notation were imported as well. The elder brother of Hsüan Tsung, styled prince of Ning, was an earnest musician; he played on the drums, and ". . . the books he read were the musical scores of Kucha." He was "intoxicated with music," as his imperial brother observed.[73] Though we do not have examples of these Kuchean musical texts, music for the lute written in the medieval tablature (quite different from the modern) was found at Tun-huang, and a score for the T'ang five-stringed lute is preserved in Japan.[74] These were written under strong Kuchean influence, and the prince's texts must have resembled them closely.

Map making in T'ang was closely related to strategy, and of the greatest interest to the military branches of the government. To facilitate T'ang success in subjugating new countries and retaining control of dependent ones, missions abroad were expected to consider cartography as one of their jobs—a conventional form of espionage. Moreover, all foreign visitors to the capital were closely interrogated by officers whose aim was to draw from them all possible information on the contours of their native lands, and these details were copied down on charts.[75] Occasionally a nation might voluntarily submit a map to the Son of Heaven, thus abjectly signifying its tributary status. So it was after the successful invasion of Magadha by Wang Hsüan-t'e; the victor visited Kāmarūpa, in what is now western Assam, and subsequently the king of that land sent envoys to Ch'ang-an with many rare and wonderful objects, including a map of his own country, requesting in return an image of Lao Tzu and the text of his *Tao te ching*.[76]

Notes

INTRODUCTION (Pages 1–6)

[1] Laufer (1919), 379; TFYK, 970, 11b; THY, 99, 1774; THY, 100, 1796.

[2] Reischauer (1955a), 82, referring to perishable goods taken by Japanese travelers.

[3] Soper (1950), 10, tells of a native of Silla in Korea who bought up large numbers of the paintings of the master Chou Fang and took them home with him.

[4] Takakusu (1928), 22.

[5] Balazs (1931), 52–54, has a general account of the foreign trade of China in this period.

[6] Coedès (1948), 68.

[7] Bagchi (1929), 77, 346–347.

[8] P. Pelliot, *Memoires sur les coutumes du Cambodge* (1951), p. 81.

[9] v. Gabain (1961), 17.

CHAPTER I (Pages 7–39)

[1] For an excellent summary of the history of this era, see Goodrich (1959), 120 ff.

[2] Prices were high for about the first ten years of the reign of the dynasty, but low during most of the seventh century, though slightly higher again in its final decades. Ch'üan (1947), 102–109. As to the taxes, see Balazs (1931), 43–55, and Pulleyblank (1955), 125. The *corvée* could be commuted by an extra portion of silk cloth. In remote parts of the empire, the tax was simplified; thus the peasants of Lingnan paid only rice, and the subjugated Turks sent sheep and coins. It was modified also in great commercial and industrial cities; the business center of Yang-chou paid its primary taxes in money instead of in grain and silk; the manufacturing town of Ch'eng-tu paid them both in silk. The three levies were named *tsu* (in grain), *tiao* (in cloth), and *yung* (in labor). There were also lesser taxes on land and household, proportional to the size of the holding.

[3] Pulleyblank (1955), 27.

[4] Pulleyblank (1955), 48–49.

[5] Ogawa Shōichi (1957), 97; Schafer (1951), 411. Characteristic were the "Old Style" prose (*ku wen*) and the imaginative short story. Pulleyblank (1960), 113, has tried to link the cultural renaissance with a movement toward a spiritual revival of the dynasty itself.

[6] Ch'üan (1947), 109–126, esp. 111–112. In the capital, rice cost 500 times as much in 764, during a period of inflation, as it did in 725, during the good times.

[7] Ch'üan (1948), 144–145.

[8] Ch'üan (1948), 145.

[9] Pulleyblank (1955), 35–36.

[10] STCH, 1, 26b–27a; Nakamura (1917), 352.

[11] Locally other goods would do as well, as cereals in Tun-huang in the northwest, or gold, cinnabar, and ivory in Canton in the remote south. Ch'üan (1948), 107–114.

[12] The result also of the opening of new copper mines and the improvement of methods of minting coins. Ch'üan (1948), 144–148. There were various edicts against the export of coins in the second half of the eighth century, but coins got out nonetheless, merchants being what they are. Reinaud (1845), 72–73; Kuwabara (1930), 34–35.

CHAPTER I (*Continued*)

[13] Ch'üan (1948), 133; Balazs (1931), 82–92. The eighth century was also notable for the first appearance of letters of credit to facilitate commerce; this useful instrument became a government monopoly early in the ninth century. Balazs (1960), 204.

[14] Balazs (1931), 82–92; Pulleyblank (1955), 30.

[15] Pulleyblank (1955), 55–56.

[16] In Chinese, "An Lu-shan" (see the Introduction), as it is now pronounced in the standard dialect. The name was Sogdian, and the rebel was of mixed blood.

[17] Pulleyblank (1955), 26–27, 75–81, 103.

[18] In the middle of the century the population of all China was about 52 million, according to the census of 754, the year before the Great Rebellion. The Western Capital, Ch'ang-an, contained about two million souls; the Eastern Capital, Lo-yang, over a million. Other great cities were Wei, also with over a million, and Ch'eng-tu with nearly a million. There were twenty-two other cities with over 500,000 inhabitants. But a rich port like Canton had only a little more than 200,000 inhabitants. The census records for the period after the Great Rebellion (for 764) show that only about one-third (16 millions) of China's population remained. The greatest reduction was in the north, to which the wars were confined and where about three-quarters of the population then lived. But this proportion is greatly exaggerated, the result of faulty census records after the wasting of the civil wars, and of the elimination from the census rolls of large numbers of untaxed persons: monks, merchants, foreigners, tenants, and so on. Balazs (1931), 14 ff., 23; Fitzgerald (1947), 6–11.

[19] For most of this, see Goodrich (1959) and Fitzgerald (1938). The Arabs and Persians who pillaged Canton in 758, coming by sea, were probably buccaneers from the island of Hainan. Schafer (1951), 407. For the whole subject of Muslims in China and Central Asia during T'ang, see Drake (1943), 1–40.

[20] Ch'üan (1947), 112–147; Ch'üan (1948), 129–133.

[21] Nakamura (1917), 558; Levy (1955), *passim*, esp. p. 117.

[22] See especially Pelliot (1904), 134, 141.

[23] See, among a host of references, especially Goodrich (1959), 129–131. Wright (1951), 33–47, discusses premature anti-Buddhist proposals as early as the seventh century.

[24] Wright (1957), 37.

[25] Schafer (1951), 409. In romanizing Middle Persian names, I follow Christensen (1936).

[26] Schafer (1951), 408–409.

[27] Pulleyblank (1955), 134.

[28] Quennell (1928), 92–95. Perhaps the fish was one of the fish-shaped tallies carried by ambassadors in T'ang times. There were Jews in China then, but the case of the ninth-century Persian Jew, Eldad ha-Dani, in Rabinowitz (1946), 236, is a rather shaky instance. Still, most of the Jews in medieval China must have been Persian. A. Stein (1907), 570–574, found a Persian business letter in the Hebrew script at Dandān-uiliq in Chinese Turkestan, which has been dated 708. Also of the eighth century is a sheet of passages from the Psalms and the Prophets found at Tun-huang by Pelliot; see White (1942), 139–140. See also Needham (1959), 681, for more on Jewish merchants in the medieval Far East.

[29] TS, 216b, 4135b. Copies of the Confucian classics and of the *Shih chi* were finally sent to Tibet, after much argument, in 731. TCTC, 213, 13a–13b.

[30] Reischauer (1955a), 277–281.

[31] Chao (1926), 961; Reischauer (1940), 146.

[32] Chao (1926), 961; Balazs (1932), 53; Reischauer (1940), 150–153.

[33] Balazs (1932), 53; Reischauer (1940), 156, 160–161. Until overwhelmed by Silla, the state of Paekche in the southwestern part of the peninsula sent its ships straight across the Yellow Sea to Yüeh-*chou*, on Hang-*chou* Bay in Chekiang. CTS, 199a, 3616a.

[34] Reischauer (1955a), 277–281.

[35] Reischauer (1955a), 143.

[36] Reischauer (1940), 162; Reischauer (1955a), 281, 284–285. In the ninth century, when the Japanese Tendai priest Ennin visited China, many of these expatriate Koreans had already merged with the Chinese population, and there were Korean boatmen in China who no longer spoke their native tongue. Ennin also found that he could stay at the "Cloisters of Silla," Buddhist monasteries intended primarily as hostels for Korean en-

voys, on the way to the Chinese capital. Rei-schauer (1955), 150.

[37] Kuwabara (1930), 48, 97.

[38] Kuwabara (1930), 48, 97; Hourani (1951), 74–75; Villiers (1952), 7, 56–57, 113–114; Wheatley (1961a), xviii–xx and 42–43. Kuwabara states his belief that the Chinese must have known the southwest monsoon as early as the second century A.D.; certainly it was used by the pilgrim Fa-hsien in the fifth century, en route from Indonesia to Shantung. In the seventh century I-ching sailed from Canton under the northeast monsoon.

[39] Hourani (1951), 61–64. There were pi-rates, however, in the waters around the mouth of the Indus River.

[40] Sauvaget (1948), 41; Hourani (1951), 69.

[41] Lewicki (1935), 176–181; Sauvaget (1948), 41. The former source tells of mer-chants of the Ibāḍite sect who went from Siraf to China in the eighth century. One of them, Abū 'Ubaida of Oman, looked to buy aloeswood there.

[42] Hourani (1951), 78.

[43] Pelliot (1912b), 105; Schafer (1950), 405. Persian replaced Sogdian on the land routes only in the thirteenth century.

[44] Braddell (1956), 13, says that the Mala-bar (western) Coast of India was a much more practical place of departure for sailing to the Indies, and therefore more busy in early times than the Coromandel (eastern) Coast.

[45] The monk Vajrabodhi found thirty-five Persian vessels in a port of Ceylon early in the eighth century, there for the purpose of trading in gems. Hasan (1928), 98.

[46] Hourani (1951), 70–72; Schafer (1951), 406; Wheatley (1961a), 45. See especially Schafer (1951) for the description of the Per-sia–Far East trade in the narrative of the monk Hui-ch'ao, and for other references to the great sea routes. Above all, see Pelliot (1904), 215–363, 372–373.

[47] Kuwabara (1930), 46–47. Sabaean Arabs probably opened up the Indian Ocean in an-tiquity; Sāsānian Persians extended the trade beyond Ceylon to the Far East. Hasan (1928), 85.

[48] By the twelfth century at least, Chi-nese ships were an important factor in this trade.

[49] Yamada (1959), 135–140. Yamada be-lieves that Chinese ships first went as far as India in the ninth or tenth century.

[50] Hourani (1951), 46–50; Paris, (1952), 275–277, 655; Wolters (1960), 346. Laufer's attempt to find a second "Persia" in Indone-sia was due primarily to his failure to under-stand this and to see that Persian seafarers might speak a trade jargon containing Malay words, wear costumes of assorted "South Seas" vintage, and convey the products of the In-dies, as well as their own, to China. See Lau-fer (1919), 468–487, and the just criticisms by Chang Hsing-lang (1930), vol. 4, 185–193. I agree with Pelliot that ". . . all the texts mentioning Po-ssu before the Sung dy-nasty refer in all likelihood to Persia . . . But, in the 11th and 12th cents., the name was sometimes misapplied to a Malay state . . . It may be the name Pase (Pasei or *Pasi) . . . which was then mistaken for Persia." Pelliot (1959), 87. ". . . Po-ssu ships, until about A.D. 1000, can only mean 'Persian ships' . . ." Pelliot (1959) 102.

[51] Hirth and Rockhill (1911), 28; Naka-mura (1917), 348–351; Chang Hsing-lang (1930), vol. 2/3, 181; Kuwabara (1930), 86–89; Hornell (1946), 143–146; Hourani (1951), 109. Some of the classical references to "shore-sighting" birds in India and the West in these sources have to do with birds which look for land, like Noah's birds, but do not carry messages. Nakamura has evidence to show that the minister Chang Chiu-ling, who had pigeons to carry letters for him, named "flying slaves," may have learned of them from Persian or Singhalese merchants in Canton. See KYTPIS (TTTS, 3), 43a. This would put the introduction of this idea into China late in the seventh century. But by the beginning of that century T'ai Tsung was sending messages between Ch'ang-an and Lo-yang by his favorite white falcon "Army Leader." See CYCT (TTTS, 1), 53b. There-fore the only novelty in the later develop-ment was the use of pigeons rather than some other bird. See Takakusu (1928), 466–467, for a description of the merchant vessels sixty or seventy feet high, which, according to the priest Chien-chen, came to Canton in the middle of the eighth century.

[52] As opposed to clinker-built, with over-lapping planks.

[53] Kuwabara (1930), 86–89; Hourani (1951), 88 ff.; Schafer (1951), 405–406. See

CHAPTER I (*Continued*)
Christie (1957a), *passim,* for a theory relating the *p'o* "argosies" of the medieval China Seas to Dayak warboats.

[54] TS, 39, 3724d; TPHYC, 70, 10b. A complete study of the strategic uses of this place will be found in Matsui (1959), 1397–1432. See Chao (1926), 960–961, for the great trade routes of T'ang. Chao counts seven in all. This one is the An-tung route via Ying-*chou.* See also Chia Tan's famous itineraries in TS, 43b, 3735d–3736d, and Pelliot's commentary on this text in Pelliot (1904).

[55] Miller (1959), 8.

[56] Chavannes (1905), 529–531; A. Stein (1925), 481, and photographs 34–36; A. Stein (1933), 160–162; Bergman (1939), 42; Miller (1959), 23.

[57] Part of this road is described in detail in an anonymous geographical text of the ninth century, found at Tun-huang. See Lionel Giles (1932), 825 ff.

[58] PS, 97, 3041b; Schafer (1950), 181.

[59] Pelliot (1904), 134, 141, 150–153, 175–178; Laufer (1905), 234, 237. Christie (1957), *passim,* discusses some details of the Burma route during T'ang.

[60] Bagchi (1950), 19.

[61] Pelliot (1904), 133.

[62] Ishibashi (1901), 1051–1063; Kuwabara (1930), 19–20; Balazs (1932), 53–54. The Lukin of the Arab geographers (for example, Ibn Khordadhbeh) is possibly the same place, the name corrupted from Lupin.

[63] Nakamura (1917), 361; Kuwabara (1930), 16–17.

[64] Nakamura (1917), 247, quotes many Buddhist texts to show that foreigners, especially Indians, applied the name "Cīna" to Canton and "Mahācīna," i.e., "Great China," to Ch'ang-an. Khanfu is from Chinese Kuang-*fu;* the official name was Kuang-*chou.*

[65] Balazs (1932), 23, 56. Though rich, Canton was not a large city. There were 25 cities of China with populations of over 500,000 in the eighth century. According to Abū Zayd (ninth century), there were over 120,000 foreign merchants resident in Canton.

[66] Balazs (1932), 55; Sauvaget (1948), 6.

[67] So says the Buddhist priest Chien-chen, who visited the port in 748. Takakusu (1928), 466–467.

[68] Chien-chen again. Takakusu (1928), 467. The Chinese text (here translated by me)

may be found in Nakamura (1917), 487–488. See also Ishibashi (1901), 1063–1074, for medieval Canton.

[69] Balazs (1932), 56; Sauvaget (1948), 7; Schafer (1951), 407.

[70] Nakamura (1917), 487–488.

[71] Takakusu (1928), 466. For a list of Indian Buddhist pilgrims to China in T'ang times, see Bagchi (1950), 48–55.

[72] Hourani (1951), 63. A tradition preserved by the geographer Marwazī, early in the twelfth century, says that these sectaries fled in 749 and settled on an island in a large Chinese river, opposite a port. This is surely Canton. But I give the tradition as fact with some hesitation.

[73] A wholesaler's godown or warehouse for the deposit of goods was called *ti;* a retail shop with goods on open sale was called *tien.* See Chu (1957), 13. Chou (1945), 23, makes it clear that the curfew was maintained in Canton as well as in other important cities. But the poet Chang Chi, in his verses addressed to a friend about to leave for an official post in Canton, wrote of ". . . the babble of barbarian voices in the night market." ChTs, han 6, ts'e 6. Since the purpose of the sunset drum was to send the people back to their own quarter of the city, whose gates were closed through the night, it may be assumed that Chang Chi's night markets were local, as contrasted with the city's great central market. But the markets of the larger cities were also allowed to remain open by night on important holidays, and were then scenes of gaiety. See, for instance, YHTC, 7, 50, which tells of a rich man visiting a night market incognito, with a great wallet full of ready cash, for a night of girls and wine. The great metropolitan markets opened at noon to the sound of 300 drumbeats, and closed before sunset with 300 strokes on a gong. TLT, 20, 13b.

[74] TS, 4, 3640d; TS, 116, 3942d; CTS, 89, 3357c.

[75] The exact year is unknown. See Kuwabara (1930), 8; Balazs (1931), 54.

[76] Nakamura (1917), 353.

[77] Nakamura (1917), 354, suggests that these may have been disgruntled Arab troops sent by the Khalif in 757 to help General Kuo Tzu-i put down an insurrection. But the presence of Persians in the gang, and the fact that the raiders left in ships, leads me to

think that they came under the guidance of the great pirate captain Feng Jo-fang, who captured great numbers of Persians and other foreigners, and installed them in slave villages on Hainan. Many Persian sailors must have joined his crews. See Schafer (1951), 407.

[78] Wang Gungwu (1958), 82–84.

[79] Nakamura (1917), 362.

[80] "Chu chiang," CCCCTS, 483.

[81] "Tzu p'ing," CCCCTS, 150. For discussion of the rebellion, see Nakamura (1917), 351–352, 355–356.

[82] CTS, 131, 3436d; Nakamura (1917), 356–357.

[83] It is reported that as he was leaving Canton to return to the capital, at the end of his term of office, he searched the baggage of his retainers, and threw into the river all the costly rarities from overseas which he found.

[84] CTS, 151, 3482b; TS, 170, 4042b; Nakamura (1917), 360; Balazs (1932), 57–58.

[85] Nakamura (1917), 363.

[86] Hsü Shen (in office 802 to 806), Cheng Yin (in office 811 and 812), and K'ung K'uei (in office 817 to 819), who abolished illegal taxes, reduced unnecessary imposts, were sparing in confiscation, and encouraged the worship of the "God of the South Seas," are all examples of good governors. K'ung K'uei especially is noted for his reforms, for which he received the praise of Han Yü, then in exile at Ch'ao-*chou.* Nakamura (1917), 364–365, 489–491.

[87] TS, 9, 3655d; Nakamura (1917), 559–560; Levy (1955), 114–115, 117, 121; Wang Gungwu (1958), 82–84. Ch'üan-*chou,* the Djanfu of the Arabs (and much later Marco Polo's Zayton), in Chekiang Province was just beginning its spectacular career as a port for international shipping. There is some tenuous evidence of the presence of Muslim missionaries in Ch'üan-*chou* in the seventh century. Certainly there were foreign merchants there in the ninth, and there was considerable development of the ports of Fukien under the independent warlords of the tenth century, who encouraged foreign shipping to call at Ch'üan-*chou* and Fu-*chou.* Schafer (1954), 78.

[88] Mei ling, so called because of the many plums there. It was also called Ta yü ling.

[89] Hsiang (1933), 33; Schafer (1951), 408, 413.

[90] Nakamura (1917), 254; Schafer (1951), 407 (n. 36). See especially Chang's essay in CTW, 291, 1a–1b. For a brief account of the roads and market towns of T'ang, see Yen (1954).

[91] Nakamura (1920), 252–261. The connecting link was the Holy Canal (*Ling ch'ü*), built in Ch'in times, in the third century B.C., to facilitate the conquest of the south and the transport of goods to the north. This important waterway was enlarged in Han times to transport provisions for the troops of General Ma Yüan. It was still being used in T'ang and Sung times, though it needed repairs at intervals.

[92] "Chiu tzu p'o wen che-ku." ChTS, han 9, ts'e 3, ch. 2, 13a.

[93] Paddle-wheel vessels, operated by treadmill and capable of moving against wind and current, were developed on these lakes by Li Kao, a member of the imperial family, about 785. They seem to have been used mostly as warships. Kuwabara (1930), 95–96.

[94] JCSP, 9, 88, quoting T'ang poetry. For medieval Yang-*chou,* see especially Ishibashi (1901), 1309–1314.

[95] Ch'üan (1947a), 153, 165–166.

[96] Ch'üan (1947a), 154–157.

[97] Ch'üan (1947a), 153.

[98] Ch'üan (1947a), 161–163.

[99] Ch'üan (1947a), 149–153; Chu (1957), 41–42.

[100] The epigram appears in JCSP, 9, 88.

[101] Contemporary literature tells of Persian shops. See Nakamura (1920), 244.

[102] CTS, 110, 3402d; CTS, 124, 3426b; TS, 141, 3988d. The total population was over 450,000 at this time.

[103] JCSP, 9, 88.

[104] Ch'üan (1947a), 166–175. Metalwork developed at Ch'ang-sha and Kuei-lin, and silk textiles at Hang-*chou.*

[105] JCSP, 9, 88.

[106] Pulleyblank (1955), 35–36, 183–187.

[107] Reischauer (1955), 20.

[108] Schafer (1951), 408.

[109] TS, 38, 3721b; Balazs (1931), 23. The official but less familiar name for Lo-yang was Honan-*fu.*

[110] *Shen tu.*

[111] TS, 38, 3721b.

[112] Katô (1936), 48. From such a street (*hang,* "row of shops"), where the merchants shared common interests, grew the later "merchants' associations," also called *hang.*

[113] Hsü (1902), 5, 33b; Drake (1940), 352.

Chapter I (*Continued*)

[114] Nakamura (1920), 246–247; Chao (1926), 953–954; Pulleyblank (1955), 37; TS, 134, 3978b; CTS, 105, 3393a. The creator of the pool was Wei Chien. The pool itself was named "Pool of Transport from Far and Wide" (*Kuang yün t'an*).

[115] It is reported that after the conquest of the Turks in 631, about 10,000 families came into T'ang and settled in Ch'ang-an. Hsiang (1933), 4. For T'ang Ch'ang-an, see also Sirén (1927).

[116] *Sārthavāk* is Sogdian, the apparent equivalent of Chinese **Sât-pâu* (Albert Dien, private communication of February 12, 1961, based on the work of H. W. Bailey and others).

[117] Katô (1936), 49–51, 60. The merchants of a bazaar and their headman became, in Sung times, the merchants' association with its president.

[118] TS, 196, 4087b. This is from the biography of Lu Yü, author of the *Ch'a ching*. His writing did much to bring about this new fashion.

[119] TCTC, 225, 4a. This was in 775.

[120] TFYK, 999, 26b; edict of Wen Tsung in CTW, 72, 2b–3a; Hsiang (1933), 34. Private usurers were limited to 6 per cent interest in T'ang, though the government rate was 7 per cent; Balazs (1960), 205.

[121] Ishida Mikinosuke (1932), 67; Gernet (1956), 228–232.

[122] Kishibe (1955), *passim*. The price was, of course, subject to general economic fluctuation and to the reputation of the lady. One elegant prostitute received a purse containing 300,000 copper cash from her admirer. YHTC, 1, 6.

[123] Chu (1957), 114–115. For a fuller account of the prostitutes' quarter in Ch'ang-an, and biographies of famous hetaerae, see PLC in TTTS, 8, 1a–22a, and Kishibe (1955). For "private" and "official" prostitutes, see Wang T'ung-ling (1930).

[124] Li Po, "Sung P'ei Shih-pa-t'u nan kuei Sung shan," in LTPWC, 15, 1a; Hsiang (1933), 36–37; Ishida Mikinosuke (1942), 54–63.

[125] Li Po, "Ch'ien yu tsun chiu hsing," in LPTWC, 3, 8a. The cliché "vermilion will seem . . ." refers to visual hallucinations: "we won't be able to see straight." The first line seems to refer to a classical song (see *Chou*

li. Ch'un kuan, Szu yüeh) about the ancient source of the best paulownia wood, the classic material for making the body of a zither. "Studs" is *chu*. This word properly applies to the bridges of a *se* or a *cheng*, which are other sorts of zithers. The zither of this poem is the *ch'in*, which has no bridges. "Western houri" is *hu chi*, which in Chinese connotes a beautiful lass, with gracious manners, of Western or Northern, probably Iranian, origin. *Chi*, formerly "noble lady of Chou," was in this age "courtesan."

[126] Nakamura (1920), 244–245.

[127] Ishida Mikinosuke (1932), 65–66; Drake (1940), 352; Schafer (1951), 408.

[128] TPHYC, 152, 4a.

[129] TPHYC, 152, 4a.

[130] Boodberg (1935), 11.

[131] TS, 40, 3726d. The last-named of these products came from the fragrant underground stems of the "hemlock-parsley" *Conioselinum univittatum* (*ch'iung-ch'iung*).

[132] THY, 100, 1798; TCTC, 225, 20b.

[133] TS, 182, 4062c; CTS, 177, 3538c.

[134] Schafer (1951), 410.

[135] Ishida Mikinosuke (1948), 75, 88. These puppets were called *chiu hu-tzu* or *pu tsui hsien*.

[136] Schafer (1951), 413–422.

[137] Reischauer (1955a), 220. See Chang Ch'ang-kung (1951), 6–7, for evidence of the political and social power of foreigners (including the Arab just mentioned) in late T'ang.

[138] Balazs (1932), 54 ff.

[139] See, for instance, Balazs (1932), 54; Reischauer (1955a), 40.

[140] Farquhar (1957), 61, writing of Ming times, makes this very clear.

[141] See Reischauer (1955a), 81, for the difficulties experienced by a Japanese embassy attempting to trade along the way to the capital.

[142] In some cases at least, express permission was needed; for example, "The Hsi [a Manchurian people] sent to beg that they might exchange wares in the Western Market. It was authorized." TFYK, 999, 25a. This was in 716. The same source gives other examples of formal requests to engage in trade in the capital.

[143] THY, 86, 1581. The same edict made it illegal to transport *any* metal across the northern or western frontier. This was doubtless

aimed at keeping the raw materials for weapons from possible enemies.

[144] Kuwabara (1930), 190.

[145] Schafer (1951), 409. See CTS, 8, 3081c. The priest was hand in glove with an imperial agent.

[146] So Abū Zayd. See Reinaud (1845), 34. Kuwabara (1930), 188, believes that this exorbitant impost was the so-called *hsia ting shui* of the *T'ang shu,* or *p'o ch'üeh* of the *T'ang kuo shih pu.*

[147] CTW, 75, 3a. It is interesting that the province of Fukien is mentioned as important in foreign trade at this early date.

[148] Nakamura (1917), 245. This, as Nakamura points out, seems to explain why popular tales of T'ang tell of a rich foreigner who, on the point of death, hands over some portable treasure, such as a gem, to a Chinese who has taken his fancy.

[149] THY, 100, 1796; TLSI, 2, 70–71.

[150] THY, 97, 1748. The year was 821; the princess was the T'ai-ho kung-chu.

[151] TCTC, 232, 18a.

[152] TLSI, 2, 40. However, if the litigants were of different nationality, say one from Silla and one from Paekche (though both "Koreans"), the case was adjudicated according to Chinese law.

[153] CTS, 198, 3614b.

[154] CTS, 197, 3609d.

[155] TFYK, 999, 13b–22a, has examples of requests for all of these things. The wallet was *yü tai,* "fish pouch."

[156] THY, 100, 1795. For a full discussion of these talismans, see Rotours (1952), *passim,* esp. pp. 75–87.

[157] THY, 100, 1798. An edict of 695 fixed these proportions.

[158] CTS, 10, 3089b.

[159] TLT, 18, 11a–18a. These hostels were managed by the *Chung-shu* ("Documents of the Penetralia") Department.

[160] The meaning of the archaic designation *hung-lu* was already obscure. It is said to mean "Transmission of Announcements," but, although *lu* sometimes has the sense of "set forth or transmit," still "announcement" (or something close to that) for *hung* (normally "wild goose") is hard to explain.

[161] During the period 684–705, this office was called plainly "Office for Overseeing Guests" (*Szu-pin szu*). For an account of the manner in which newly arrived envoys were received, see the description of the arrival of the Japanese mission in Ch'ang-an in 840 in Reischauer (1955), 283 ff.

[162] TS, 46, 3741b.

[163] Yü Kung-ku (1934), 8–9. Yü believes that Chia was a Manichaean, having learned the mysteries of that faith from visiting Uighurs.

[164] TS, 23a, 3677d.

[165] The Shih-chung, "Attendant on the Penetralia."

[166] *Fan,* "bulwark, fence, buffer," was an epithet intended to convey the proper role of a tributary state. In common usage, since in theory *all* foreign countries were bulwarks of China, *fan* came to mean simply "foreign."

[167] TS, 16, 3667c. This chapter of *T'ang shu* describes the ceremony in considerable detail.

[168] Reischauer (1955a), 79–80.

[169] In Sumatra. For the identification, see Pelliott (1904), 321 ff.

[170] Hsüan Tsung, "Pao tz'u Shih-li-fo-shih Kuo chih," CTW, 22, 17b.

[171] CTW, 17, 1a–1b. Reign of Chung Tsung.

[172] Hsiang (1933), 42; Ishida Mikinosuke (1942), 65–66.

[173] "Fa ch'ü," in YSCCC, 24, 5b.

[174] Fitzgerald (1938), 173–174.

[175] Liu Mau-tsai (1957), 199. This book, called *T'u-chüeh yü,* "Turkish Speech," survived in Japan until the end of the ninth century, perhaps longer. It is listed in Fujiwara Sukeyo, *Nihon-koku genzai-sho mokuroku* (891–897).

[176] Ogawa Tamaki (1959), 34–44.

[177] Hsiang (1933), 41; Soper (1951), 13–14; Acker (1954), 171, n. 2; Cheng Chen-to (1948), esp. pl. 113; Mahler (1959), 108–109 and pl. XXXI.

[178] *Wei-mao.* Mahler (1959), 109–110, pl. XV.

[179] Hsiang (1933), 42–43; Ishida Mikinosuke (1942), 65–66; Soper (1951), 13–14; Acker (1954), 171, n. 2. Another foreign style was a kind of tall conical hat with a rolled brim, but it is not certain that this was worn by Chinese. Hsiang (1933), 43; Mahler (1959), pl. XIX.

[180] Yüan Chen so stigmatized "piled-up" coiffures and "ocher" faces as un-Chinese. Hsiang (1933), 42; Ishida Mikinosuke (1942), 67; Mahler (1959), 18, 32, pl. VIII. Many

CHAPTER I (*Continued*)

other foreign fashions, mostly of Iranian origin, are described by Mahler. For the "Uighur chignons," see CHP (SF, 77), 2a.

[181] Waley (1960), 240.

[182] Ishida Mikinosuke (1948), 144–155; Liu Mau-tsai (1957), 203–204. On the whole, however, Chinese building, like the Egyptian, was resistant to foreign influence. Exotic ceilings in cave shrines, patterned according to Buddhist cosmology, could only be made, it seems, at places like Tun-huang, where no Chinese precedent was available. See Soper (1947), 238.

[183] Hsiang (1933), 41; Fitzgerald (1938), 173–174; Maenchen-Helfen (1957), 120.

[184] Hsiang (1933), 45–46; Reischauer, (1955), 297. For the importance of the vegetable oil industry, both for cakes and lamps, see Gernet (1956), 146–149.

[185] This is from the famous story *Jen shih,* a novelette about a fox-fairy by the eighth-century writer Shen Chi-chi. See TPKC, 452, 1b. The tale has also been translated in *Dragon King's Daughter* (1954), 7. See also the story about "The Foreigner Who Sold Cakes," whose central figure had been a wealthy man in his own country, but solitary and humble in China for many years. TPKC, 402, 9a–9b.

[186] SP, 72a. This book gives the bill of fare for a Lucullan banquet, called a "tail-burning" (*shao wei*), given on the occasion of the accession of a great minister to office. This particular banquet was for Wei Chü-yüan, the author of the book, himself. See also Edwards (1937), 1, 192–193.

[187] SP, 69a.

[188] Soper (1951), 9–11.

[189] HHHP, 8, 222–224.

[190] HHHP, 8, 225–228.

[191] Soper (1950), 11.

[192] Soper (1951), 74. The translations are Soper's.

[193] LTMHC, 9, 273; HHHP, 1, 60.

[194] Chou Fang did the most glamorous of all scenes, "Yang Kuei-fei Leaving the Bath." HHHP, 6, 166–172.

[195] HHHP, 5, 155–159; 6, 166–172. Both painters also did pictures of Yang Kuei-fei teaching her favorite parrot.

[196] HHHP, 10, 262.

[197] Mahler (1959), 81–84 and *passim.*

[198] HHHP, 1, 60.

[199] LTMHC, 10, 324; Soper (1950), 19.

Two other famous painters of foreign scenes were Li Heng and Ch'i Min. Ch'i Min sometimes appears as Ch'i Chiao. See LTMHC, 10, 313.

[200] Soper (1951), 25.

[201] HHHP, 6, 166–172.

[202] HHHP, 5, 155–159.

[203] Especially the mourners for the Buddha in cave 158, painted in the ninth century. Gray (1959), pl. 57.

[204] Grousset (1948), xxxiv–xxxv, describing mural paintings of Qyzyl, near Kucha.

[205] LTMHC, 10, 313, 324; Soper (1950), 19. Special examples of exotic influence on sculptured animals are marble representations of the zodiacal animals, in a "Siberian" or "Iranian" manner. "These reliefs in this respect present a *fashion* rather than a *style* . . . like all their counterparts in the T'ang cult of the exotic, are really apart from the normal chronological stylistic development of Chinese sculpture." Rowland (1947), 265–282. Whether this dictum would apply to *paintings* of exotic subjects, we cannot know.

[206] This type of costume had a curious effect in the history of music. The old song *P'u-sa* [*B'uo-sat] *man,* to whose tune many lyrics were written from time to time, was invented by an unknown popular entertainer of the ninth century. The name means "Bodhisattva Barbarians," or more exactly *"Man-barbarians* [dressed like] Bodhisattvas." According to Su O (TYTP, 2, 58b), the name derives from the appearance of the envoys sent from a certain Country of the Female *Man-*barbarians, who came bearing tribute, and wearing golden caps with strings of beads hanging down over their bodies, as in the traditional pictures of a Bodhisattva. The country cannot now be identified; no doubt it was a "matriarchy" of some kind in the Indies. Medieval Chinese sources frequently describe the costumes of men and women of Indochina and Indonesia in similar terms. Thus TFYK, 959, 17b, states that the king of Champa wore strings of beads, ". . . like the decoration on a Buddhist image." The Sung book *P'ing-chou k'o-t'an* states that the name *P'u-sa man* refers to "foreign" (Indonesian or Indochinese?) women living in Kwangtung; this is part of the truth. Hirth's suggestion that the name was a transcription of "Mussulman" must be rejected. All of the above can be found in Kuwabara (1930), 67–

69. See also Baxter (1953), 144. A recent study of this song form (Chang Wan [1960], 24) attempts to make the name a transcription of a Burmese ethnic name like *Pyusa-[wati]-Man;* this argument fails because it is based on modern Mandarin phonology, which is irrelevant here. As we shall argue later, most if not all of the tribute missions described in TYTP are mythical, or at best have been richly embroidered in the prose of Su O. It may be that the song had its origin, not in any real event, but in the fanciful narrative of Su O itself.

207 Soper (1951), 11, n. 122.

208 Jayne (1941), 7.

209 YYTT, hsü chi, 5, 218. Of paintings in the temple Pao ying szu in Ch'ang-an.

210 According to HHHP, 1, 63, and *T'ang ch'ao ming hua lu* (translated in Soper [1950], 11), he was a Tocharian. But LTMHC, 9, 278–279, makes him a native of Khotan; Nagahiro (1955), 71–72, supports this view.

211 From Sanskrit *Vijaya.* Hsiang (1933), 6.

212 Hsiang (1933), 6–7, 52–56; Ishida Mikinosuke (1942), 179–180; Soper (1950), 11; Bailey (1961), 16. For the difficult chronology of this painter, see Nagahiro (1955), 72–74. Some early T'ang figures in the Tun-huang murals (for example, those of 642, revealed in cave 220) have faces molded by means of highlights, and ". . . have weight and occupy definite positions in space . . ." Gray (1959), 54. This may be the kind of Indian or Serindian manner brought to the astonished court by Viśa.

213 Trubner (1959), 148.

214 In a Sung collection. YYKYL, a, 7.

215 Arai (1959), 5–6, 11–12. "Demoniac" translates *kuei,* which also connotes "uncanny" and "spiritual."

216 LCCKS, *wai chi,* 14b–15a.

217 CTS, 147, 3474c.

218 Tu Mu, "Kuo Hua-ch'ing kung," FCWC, 2, 6b.

219 A whole literature developed on this romantic theme. See Schafer (1956), 81–82.

220 "Lithophones from the Banks of the Szu" are mentioned in the *Shu ching,* and throughout the ages the Chinese tried to find the original rock in this region for the manufacture of the traditional chimes. See Schafer (1961), 50–51. The usurping material was called "Stone of Hua-yüan." See the poem "Hua yüan ch'ing" in YSCCC, 24, 4b. It ap-

pears that Hsüan Tsung liked to experiment with new materials for the classic chimes. He is reported to have had a set made from the "green jade of Indigo Field" (*lan-t'ien,* in the mountains south of Ch'ang-an). This last material was not jade, but a green-tinged marble. The chimes were cut for the Lady Yang, who was a skilled performer on the lithophone. KYTPIS (TTTS, 3, 76b).

221 *Yüeh fu.*

222 Schafer (1951), 417–421.

223 It has been suggested that this vogue extended even to the creation of hallucinatory images in painting by some artists of the period from the eighth to the tenth century: visions of beasts and men in rocky landscapes, presaging certain manifestations of surrealism in the West. See Baltrušaitis (1955), 212–213.

224 Loehr (1959), 171. This taste had given way to a more serene and quiet style by the end of the eleventh century.

225 MTTC, 10.

226 KHTS, b, 14a. The country was Ma-pa-erh (cf. YS, 210, 6596b, where the *erh* is written with "child" instead of "two"). It was a great nation, about 100,000 *li* from Zayton. The Chinese form seems to transcribe the name of a place whose Arabic name was Ma'abar. Professor Paul Wheatley tells me that it comprised part or all of Coromandel.

229 Kiang (1937), *passim.* This fascinating book deals with journeying conceived as a perilous spiritual enterprise, and shows how much ancient Chinese literature (representing probably only a fraction of oral tradition) was designed to show the careful traveler what to expect and what to avoid. The *Shan hai ching* is an example of such a Baedeker to the monsters likely to confront the traveler in remote places.

228 CTW, 1, 13b. See also TS, 1, 3634d, for November 29, 618.

229 For example, one by Chung Tsung; CTW, 16, 13a–13b. Another by Hsien Tsung; CTW, 59, 6b.

230 Ogawa Shōichi (1957), 112–114, has classified the typical poetic motifs of the twilight of T'ang as border clashes, civil war, and historical reminiscence. Our present theme of "fantastic tribute" is a subspecies of this last category.

231 John C. H. Wu (1939), 165. The passage quoted refers to the poetry of the last

Chapter I (*Continued*)

decades of T'ang—that of Li Shang-yin, Tu Mu, Wen T'ing-yün, and others.

232 Only slightly less favored in reminiscent literature of the ninth century is the reign of Tai Tsung, late in the eighth, regarded as something of a revival.

233 *Ting kuo pao.*

234 YYTT, 1, 3–4, for the reign of Tai Tsung. This story, despite the fantastic details and supernatural embroidery, was based on an historical event. The tale *Su Tsung ch'ao pa pao* (quoted in TPKC, 404, 1a–3a) gives a wonderful account of the jewels given to a Buddhist nun by a divine being, which brought peace and prosperity to the nation in the 760's. This moved the emperor to adopt the era name "Responsive to the Jewels" (*Pao ying*). The same story appears in shorter form in YYTT, the source of my present story of the rings. Now these jewels or treasures were actually presented to the throne in the manner described. See CTS, 10, 3090c; Yeh Te-lu (1947), 101–103.

235 KYTPIS (TTTS, 3, 42b–43a). See also Laufer (1913), 315–370, for the wonderful properties of rhinoceros horn.

236 KYTPIS, 45a.

237 KYTPIS, 41b–42a.

238 In Chinese the country is called "Little Po-lü." The king of the country resided at Gilgit. See Chang Hsing-lang (1930), 5, 160.

239 YYTT, 14, 109–110.

240 *Tu-yang tsa pien.*

241 See Su O's own preface in CTW, 813, 27a–27b. The author describes himself as a youthful admirer of such old wonder books as *Shih i chi* and *Tung ming chi,* who came to believe, even after the study of more serious works, that "within heaven and earth there is nothing which does not exist." The book is preserved in TTTS, 2, and has been briefly discussed in Edwards (1937), 83–85. Dr. Edwards has in turn quoted Alexander Wylie (1867), 194, to the effect that the book was "written after the style of the *Shu i chi,* and many of the statements have the appearance of being apocryphal." A remarkable understatement! Nonetheless, Po Shou-i (Po, 1937), in his study of the importance of aromatics during T'ang and Sung, quotes anecdotes from this book of wonder as if they were historical. Happily, Su O's tales remained in circulation and were still drawn

upon by writers of fantasy many centuries later, as by Yang Yü, for his *Shan chü hsin hua* in the fourteenth century. See Franke (1955), 306.

242 *Ling kuang tou.* There is an English version of this whole passage in Edwards (1937), 1, 84–85.

243 *Jih-lin,* maybe to be emended to *Jih-pen.* The name of the country and the story of the wonderful rock were taken by Su O from the fifth-century book of Jen Fang, SIC, b, 12b.

244 The X-ray rock was said to have been known in the third century b.c. but in China, not abroad, and named by the First Emperor "Bone-Reflecting Treasure." YYTT, 10, 73. The native name for the beans was "**k'iĕt-tâ* beads."

245 This creature and its product will be discussed in chap. xii on "Textiles."

246 *Lung chüeh ch'ai.*

247 See CTS, 52, 3281d.

248 *Lü shui chu.*

249 *Ch'üeh huo ch'üeh.*

250 Laufer (1915), 320–321. Quennell (1928), 148, describes the *samandal* of Wāqwāq, "like a green woodpecker, its plumage being speckled with red, white, green and blue." But our Chinese firebirds were black.

251 *Ch'ing feng* and *Fei luan.* The Persian *simurgh* should cause no more astonishment as an equivalent for the fanciful Chinese *luan,* which is thought by some to be an enriched version of the Argus pheasant, than the more conventional equation of the Occidental phoenix with the Chinese *feng.*

252 *Ch'ang jan ting.*

253 *Ch'ang chien ping.*

254 *Pien chou ts'ao.*

255 *Wu ts'ai ch'ü-shu.* The epithet "in the five colors" denotes "in all colors," or "rainbow-hued."

256 *Wan jo shan.*

257 Artifacts of this intricate sort were actually very popular in T'ang and Sung times.

258 *Chu-lai niao.*

259 The green magpie (*Kitta chinensis*) of Indochina has red bill, green plumage, and a green and blue tail with a white fringe. There are other species of magpie which would fit as well. The clever manner and raucous voice, along with the colors, all suggest this bird.

260 *To hsin ching.*

[261] This bird was held to be an omen of the rise to power of Chu Tzʻu, a warlord who drove the Emperor Shun Tsung from the capital and into Manchuria. Chu Tzʻu then declared himself emperor. The omen depends on the interpretation of the bird's name in Chinese: "Chu comes." Otherwise this sounds like a real gift.

[262] As by Yang Yü in the fourteenth century. Franke (1955), 306.

CHAPTER II (Pages 40–57)

[1] CTS, 199a, 3615d. See Wang Yi-tʻung (1953), 303, for civil populations enslaved en masse in pre-Tʻang times.

[2] Syringes (Panpipes) are *hsiao;* flutes are *ti;* oboes are *pi-li;* clarinets are *chia.*

[3] *Ho chʻao huan.*

[4] That is, battle dress, with boots and trousers in the fashion of the "barbarians." Cf. Waley (1923), 117–118. "Tatar" costume was normal battle garb.

[5] Fitzgerald (1933), 153–154.

[6] This ceremony is described in greater detail in THY, 33, 607–610.

[7] THY, 14, 321, tells of the feast for Li Chi and his subordinates after the presentation of the prisoners from Koryŏ in 669.

[8] *Chao ling.*

[9] THY, 14, 320–321.

[10] As in the case of Korean prisoners presented at the tumulus in 666. THY, 14, 321.

[11] *Shih kuo.*

[12] TS, 135, 3980b.

[13] THY, 14, 321.

[14] THY, 14, 320. For the cases of two other distinguished captives, both of them Turks, see THY, 14, 320 (for the year 650), and THY, 321 (for 681).

[15] CTS, 198, 3613d; YYTT, 7, 57.

[16] Wang Yi-tʻung (1953), 301.

[17] Waley (1941), 174. There is much more of this fine poem.

[18] Wang Yi-tʻung (1953), 302.

[19] WS, 12, 1932d.

[20] Medley (1955), 267–268. Medley observes that "when, in the eighth and ninth centuries, it was desired to cut down the number of slaves in the imperial service, many were disposed of in the market, where they commanded high prices. The palace-slaves were especially esteemed, not only for the quality of their work and for their general bearing, but also for their prestige-value and the scandal and gossip that they could relate."

[21] Enslaved war prisoners were enrolled in the private guards of Tʻai Tsung and Hsüan Tsung. Pulleyblank (1955), 142.

[22] THY, 86, 1573. Balazs (1932), 10.

[23] Pulleyblank (1955), 42, 46.

[24] Balazs (1932), 2–3.

[25] Waley (1960), 162.

[26] Balazs (1932), 11, has pointed out that slaves played little part in agricultural production in medieval China; the contrast with Roman slavery is striking. However, Wang Yi-tʻung (1953), 334–335, shows that, when land grants were made to prominent men in Northern Wei and Sui, a body of slaves was given to each for labor in the fields.

[27] Balazs (1932), 13.

[28] YSCCC, 23, 10a–10b. "Fire-washed linen" is asbestos. The "Continent (or Island) of Flames" is a poetical and mythical name for the lands south of China. Shu is Szechwan; the Hsi were a Manchurian tribe.

[29] Wilbur (1943), 90.

[30] Cf. Pulleyblank (1958), 206–207. A slave was not the equal of a free man under the law. He was subject to the death penalty for accusing his master of crime, truly or falsely; he suffered death for using violence on a free man; he was imprisoned for a term of years for making love to a free woman, even with her consent. Wilbur (1943), 151 n., 156. Foreign slaves were forbidden to marry Chinese or to be adopted by a free Chinese. Balazs (1932), 11; Wilbur (1943), 158. Fear of contamination by inferior blood was at the root of these laws. For Tʻang laws covering slaves, see Pulleyblank (1958), 212–217.

[31] Nakamura (1917), 488; Takakusu (1928), 462.

[32] Barthold (1958), 236, 240. The Sāmānid state issued licenses to traders in Turkish slaves, and Turkish slaves were important exports of Farghāna.

[33] A decree of 701 forbade this traffic. THY, 86, 1569.

[34] Barthold (1958), 235, from Maqdisī (tenth century).

[35] Wilbur (1943), 92–93.

[36] THY, 86, 1571. Two years later the ambassador from Silla petitioned the Chinese emperor to arrange the return of homeless

CHAPTER II (*Continued*)
Koreans left wandering on the Shantung coast.

[37] CTS, 199a, 3615d.

[38] Balazs (1932), 6–7; Pulleyblank (1958), 207, 217. In pre-T'ang centuries the aborigines of the provinces further north were enslaved. For instance, the Liao tribes of Szechwan were captured and made slaves as a matter of government policy. Wang Yi-t'ung (1953), 307–308.

[39] CTW, 50, 6b–7a.

[40] CTW, 81, 9b–11a.

[41] CTS, 154, 3486a; Nakamura (1917), 364.

[42] CSYSC, 6, 18a. The Bronze Pillars, like the Gates of Hercules in the West, here marked the traditional limit of Chinese civilization in the South. "Unicorn of Gold" appears to be a substitution for "Neighborhood of Gold." Both are *chin lin*. "Neighborhood of Gold" was the name of a T'ang garrison in Annam, and in former times a vaguely defined country far to the South, that is to say, Suvarṇadvīpa or Suvarṇabhūmi (Chin-*chou*), the Golden Chersonese. See Pelliot (1903), 226; Luce (1924), 151–154; Wheatley (1961a), 116–117.

[43] Christie (1957a), 352. Modern Khmer *krong phnom*. Hence the country of the Khmers was called *Bnam*, "The Mountain," by the Chinese; in the modern national language this has become an unrecognizable *Fu-nan* (see my Introduction).

[44] See Braddell (1956), 16, for survivals of this conception.

[45] CTS, 197, 3609d. The Chinese transcription used here is *k'un-lun*, the most common Chinese rendering of *Kurung*, though some others were more faithful to the supposed Khmer original. Such were *ku(t)-lun* (Kurrung?) and especially *ku-lung*, "ancient dragon," described by the Chinese as the family name of the kings of Bnam. Pelliot (1904), 230. Another has related *k'un-lun* rather to indigenous forms like Prum and Krom, reflected in Arabic Komr and Kâmrūn. R. Stein (1947), 238.

[46] ICCYI, 81, 835c. "Khmer" is Chinese *Kâp-miet*, following Pelliot (1959), 599. My "Turmi" is *T'uət-mjiɐ;* "Kurdang" is *Kuət-d'âng*.

[47] Pelliot (1959), 600; Wheatley (1961a), 183.

[48] Nakamura (1917), 263, citing LPLI. See also Chang (1929), 96, citing *P'ing-chou k'o t'an*. Chang Hsing-lang has been the chief protagonist of the doctrine that the *K'un-lun* slaves of medieval China were Negroes brought from Africa by Arabs. See Chang (1929), *passim;* Chang (1930), vol. 3, 48–81; Chang, (1930a), *passim.* He relies chiefly on Chinese texts which describe these people as "black," a term which the Chinese applied to all peoples darker than themselves, such as the Chams, and even the Persians, as many modern colonials do to all native peoples of the equatorial regions. Chang also relies on references to curly or wavy hair, but this is a common feature of diverse peoples of India, Indochina, and Indonesia. Negroes were clearly distinguished from these peoples of the Indies, as we shall see presently. A real puzzle are the "devil slaves" of the early twelfth-century (Sung) text, *P'ing-chou k'o t'an*, whose curly hair is "yellow." Chang, in the English version of his thesis, translates Chinese *huang* ambiguously as "tawny" instead of plain "yellow," and this helps not at all. These inky "devil slaves," of enormous strength, who are plainly separated from the "Kurung slaves," those daring swimmers, may have been some Negroid race from Papua or Melanesia, with bleached hair, as some tribes have nowadays. Conceivably some were African Negroes. Cheng Chen-to (1958), 5, identifies some T'ang ceramic grave statuettes of grooms as "*K'un-lun* slaves," chiefly on the basis of their curly hair. They wear a kind of dhoti or sarong; see Mahler (1959), 84, 88. As early as 1911 Hirth and Rockhill (p. 32) stated fairly enough that K'un-lun slaves ". . . were in all likelihood Malays or Negritos of the Malay Peninsula and the islands to the South." Pelliot was probably right in thinking that the curly-haired K'un-lun were gradually confused with the true Negro Zāng. "In other words, Indonesian negritos may have been called Zāngi without being African negroes, while African Zāngi came also to be known in China as K'un-lun." Pelliot (1959), 600.

[49] "The K'un-lun Slave," by P'ei Hsing, reproduced from his *Ch'uan ch'i* in TPKC, 194.

[50] *Dragon King's Daughter* (1954), 89. Chang Hsing-lang (1930a), 44–59, gives the text of this and other stories about the Kurung slaves.

[51] For the language of signs, see Burton (1934), vol. 1, 774, and note on vol. 1, 931, with special reference to "The Tale of Aziz and Azizah."

[52] The Chinese transcription is **səng-g'ji* or **səng-g'jie*. Schlegel (1898) went far astray in trying to show that this name meant "Siamese," as shown in Pelliot (1904), 289–291. Cf. Pelliot (1959), 597–603.

[53] For the natural history of "poison-damsels" see Penzer (1952), 3–71.

[54] Four boys in 813: THY, 100, 1782; TS, 222b, 4159c. Five boys in 815: CTS, 15, 3111b; CTS, 197, 3610a; TFYK, 972, 7a. Two girls in 818: CTS, 197, 3610a; THY, 100, 1782; TFYK, 972, 7b.

[55] TFYK, 971, 6a. The Indonesians translated the Chinese "Son of Heaven" as *devaputra*. Takakusu (1896), 136.

[56] Balazs (1932), 13, observes that Negro slaves (and in this group he includes the "Kurung slaves," accepting Chang's theory) played no important part in the Chinese economy. The truth is that the curly-headed Malay slaves (if such they were) seem to have been reasonably common as personal servants, but most of the "Zángī slaves" were the curiosities of a single decade.

[57] Mookerji (1957), 133.

[58] For the island of Zanzibar in Sung times, when it was called "Kurung Zángī Country" (Modern Chinese *K'un-lun Tseng-ch'i kuo*), that is, the Zāng (Negro) country of Kurung (the South Seas), see Chang Hsing-lang (1929), 97. See also Goodrich (1931), 138–139, for examples of Negro slaves in Yüan China, and Indonesian slaves (from Sunda) in Ming China.

[59] Mathew (1956), 52. At Mogadisciu in Italian Somalia, and at Kazerwa, in the Zanzibar Protectorate.

[60] TS, 34b, 3736c; Pelliot (1904), 349. Apparently off the west coast of the Malay Peninsula. Professor Paul Wheatley suggests the possibility of a relation to Ptolemy's Konko- or Kokko-nagara, somewhere in this region (private communication, October 19, 1959).

[61] There are various ways of writing the word; another form is *Chiao-liao*. The ancient readings are **dz'jäu-ngieu* and **dz'jäu-lieu*, respectively. Compare *chiao-nao* (**tsjäu-njau*) or *chiao-liao* (**tsjäu-lieu*) "small bird; wren." The root word evidently means "miniscule being." See TT, 7, 104–105, which also cites

the saying of Confucius from *Kuo yu* (Lu yü).

[62] TT, 7, 105a. For a general view of pygmies in Chinese history, see Wada (1947). YYTT, 10, 80, tells of a T'ang connoisseur who had a mummified mannikin, only three inches tall, thought to be a wren-man.

[63] TuT, 187, 1002b.

[64] Waley (1941), 168.

[65] TS, 194, 4083c.

[66] Pelliot (1904), 321, 335. Sriboza = Śrībhoja = Śrivijaya. From late in the ninth century the Arab travelers in the East spoke of Serboza and Zabedj, and the Chinese of **Sâm-b'iuət-dz'iei*. This was the "Isle of Gold" of the Indians; Wheatley (1961a), 177–183.

[67] TFYK, 971, 6a. A country of pygmies (Chu-ju kuo) far to the south of Japan is mentioned in the third century. See *Wei chih* as cited in TPYL, 378, 4a.

[68] THY, 99, 1775; TFYK, 971, 5b. The pilgrim Hsüan-tsang described Samarkand as a veritable paradise. See TTHYC, 1.

[69] See résumé in TuT, 193, 1042a, based largely on *Wei lüeh*. Cf. TPYL, 368, 4a.

[70] The story, apparently of Greek origin, appears in China first in the third century. Needham (1959), 505. For the present version see TuT, 193, 1042a, quoting *T'u-chüeh pen-mo chi*.

[71] TuT, 193, 1041c. See Hirth (1885), 202–204, for an account of these stories and their classical analogues. The pygmy-crane story is embedded in a version of the swan-maiden story from Tun-huang. See Waley (1960), 154.

[72] Yang (1952), 519–520.

[73] Chinese **Niei-niet-şi* has been so interpreted.

[74] Drake (1943), 7; TS, 221b, 4155b.

[75] Foreigners who became military officials in T'ang service were not required to reside within the palace, though some were officers in the imperial bodyguard and were stationed at the Black Warrior Gate. TLT, 5, 12a.

[76] Yang (1952), 510.

[77] Grousset (1932), 16, from the northern Turkish inscription at Kosho Tsaidam.

[78] CYCT, in TTTS, 1, 52b.

[79] Early in the seventh century. TS, 222b, 4159c. For traditions of albinos in Indochina, also known to Greek geographers, see Wheatley (1961a), 158–159.

[80] CTS, 16, 3116d.

CHAPTER II (*Continued*)

[81] Reischauer (1955a), 45.

[82] CTS, 16, 3116d.

[83] CTS, 19a, 3135a. Chang I-ch'ao, imperial legate at Sha-*chou* (Tun-huang) sent them along with four goshawks and two horses for the Yen-ch'ing Festival (possibly an imperial birthday). This was in 866. The following year an edict put an end to the submission of women as gifts on the occasion of this festival and the Tuan-wu Festival. TS, 9, 3655a.

[84] TFYK, 971, 3b; Ch'en Yüan (1928), 63–64.

[85] Pelliot (1923), 278–279. For Wang Hsüan-ts'e and other T'ang travelers, see Wu Lien-teh (1933), *passim*.

[86] See Pelliot (1912), 376–377, for the problem of this solvent's name, given in Chinese as **p'uân-d'a*, "ritual water" (Pelliot), and **b'uân-d'â-k'ia* "water." Needham (1954), 212, rightly considers this an early reference to a mineral acid, most likely sulphuric.

[87] YYTT, 7, 57; THY, 82, 1522. YYTT gives his tale of another marvelous Indian drug. Cf. Waley (1952), 95–96.

[88] CHL, in TTTS, 3, 15a.

[89] TFYK, 972, 10b.

[90] THY, 33, 609–610. See Kishibe (1948) for details of the incorporation of foreign bands into Chinese court music.

[91] Wang Chien, "Liang-*chou* hsing," in ChTS, han 5, ts'e 5, 21a. The name "mountain fowl" is usually applied to Reeves's pheasant (*Syrmaticus reevesii*).

[92] *Chiao fang.*

[93] The former, the "right" one, was in the Kuang-tse fang; the latter, the "left" one, was in the Yen-cheng fang. There were also two in Lo-yang, both in the Ming-i fang. CFC, in TTTS, 8, 80a.

[94] Wang Yi-t'ung (1953), 328, says of "singing girls" of all classes that they were "comparable to slaves."

[95] As in 714. TS, 5, 3644b.

[96] CFC, in TTTS, 8, 80a–90a. See Baxter (1953), 119–120.

[97] The foreign repertory of the early T'ang court musicians was virtually the same as that of Sui. Only the music of Kao-ch'ang (Qočo-Turfan oasis) was added.

[98] In China during this period Bukhāra was called by the old Parthian dynastic name of Arsak, abbreviated to "An" Country.

[99] The "Instruction Quarter" of the seventh century was reduced; the "Pear Garden" of the eighth century was abolished, though its functions were continued on a smaller scale in an institution called "Close for the Hallowed Music of the Sylphs" (*hsien shao yüan*), an elegant name with archaic, religious, and Taoist overtones.

[100] All of the above paragraph summarizes Kishibe (1952), 76–86. Kishibe reduces Western influences on Chinese music to three kinds: (1) Old Iranian, centered at Khotan; (2) Tocharian (newer Iranian), centered at Kucha; and (3) Sogdian, centered at Samarkand.

[101] THY, 33, 611.

[102] Hsiang (1933), 56; K'ung (1934), 44–46; and see especially a newer study, P'an (1958), *passim*.

[103] Hsiang (1933), 58–59.

[104] *Chieh ku.* But *chieh*, "wether," is also the name of a northern tribe, which conceivably had something to do with the origin of this drum. It was known widely in Turkestan and in India, but reached China from Kucha.

[105] K'ung (1934), 62–66. See Harich-Schneider (1954), 4, for a description of its modern descendant.

[106] Hsiang (1933), 58.

[107] Hsiang (1933), 58; K'ung (1934), 51–52.

[108] *Ku ch'ui.* The "three-stringed Hunnic fiddle" (*hu ch'in*), in use among the Sha-t'o Turks, may have been introduced into China as early as this. Eberhard (1948), 55.

[109] K'ung (1934), 30–31.

[110] K'ung (1934), 75–79.

[111] As part of the Japanese ceremonial music, which is collectively called *gagaku*, "courtly music" or, if it is danced, *bugaku*, "dance music." It includes ancient Japanese songs and dances (*utamai*), T'ang music (*tōgaku*), old Korean music (*komagaku*), Japanese folksongs set to Chinese orchestration (*saibara*), and Chinese and Sino-Japanese poetry chanted to instrumental accompaniment (*rōei*). I am here concerned only with *tōgaku*. Harich-Schneider (1954), 1.

[112] The unfretted variety, with moveable bridges, called *cheng* (*koto* in Japanese).

[113] Harich-Schneider (1954), 3–5.

[114] Generally called *Karyōbin* in Japanese.

[115] Takakusu (1928), 27–28; Demiéville (1925), 223–224.

[116] Harich-Schneider (1954), 4.

[117] According to Demiéville, the original music must have been Cambodian, brought with the ballet to China after the Chinese invasion of Champa in 605. But the Chinese did not care for Cambodian music (nor Cham music either, it appears), and so they reset the dance to music in the "purer" Indian style, as it was then known in China. Demiéville (1925), 223–224.

[118] Demiéville (1925), 226; Demiéville (1929), 150–157. Plate 16, fig. 1, in the latter source, displays the costume of the Kalaviṅka dancer.

[119] Ancient *puât-d'əu or *b'wat-d'əu. Takakusu (1928), 27–28, thought that this was a transcription of the name of the Vedic King Pedu, and that the dancer represented his serpent-killing horse. Hsiang (1933), 65, is skeptical of this explanation, and believes that Wang Kuo-wei was probably right in deriving the name from Pa-tou, a country in Central Asia.

[120] Harich-Schneider (1954), 5; Takakusu thought that this too reached China by way of Champa, as indeed much "Indian" music and dance did.

[121] Takakusu (1928), 27–28; Harich-Schneider (1954), 4–5.

[122] P'o hu ch'i han.

[123] Hsiang (1933), 65–69. In the Japanese version the dancers wear straw raincoats.

[124] San yüeh. I judge that the man with "loosened limbs" (chieh chih) sent to Ch'ang-an by the Yabghu of Tukhāra in 719 was a contortionist. See THY, 99, 1773.

[125] K'ung (1934), 59–62. See Lévi (1900), 327, for the example of five Hindus, skilled in music, magic, tightrope walking, and feigned mutilations, who came to Ch'ang-an in 646. Cf. Waley (1952), 90; Waley (1956), 125.

[126] CYCT, 3, 34.

[127] "Edict Prohibiting Shows of Illusion," in CTW, 12, 1a.

[128] Laufer (1923), 38–39.

[129] Kishibe (1952), 68–72, collected the names of thirty-one Western musicians in T'ang; the examples I give are all from his list.

[130] CYCT (TTTS, 1), 51b–52a.

[131] Kishibe (1952), 74. The national origin of other Western musicians can be determined by their Chinese names, which were derived from the names of their countries. Among those countries which supplied music and musicians to T'ang but are not listed among the officially recognized groups at court were Māimargh (Mi), Kish (Shih), Kabūdhān, Chāch (Shih), Merv (?Mu), Kushaniyah (Ho), Khotan, and Kumādh. Kishibe (1952), 86.

[132] Heng ch'ui; but by T'ang times it was already being called a ti, a name formerly restricted to the vertical flute.

[133] KSP, in TTTS, 4, 63b.

[134] Li Ho, "Lung yeh yin," LCCKS, wai chi, 14a.

[135] LMCTC, in TTTS, 10, 11a.

[136] Kuchean immigrants to China were normally given the surname Po, "White," which was also the name of the kings of Kucha. It has been suggested that the national name Kucha/Kutsi itself comes from an Indo-European word meaning "white." Bailey (1937), 900–901.

[137] Ch'un ying chuan. Hsiang (1933), 57. The poem is Yüan Chen's "Fa ch'ü" (in YSCCC, 24, 5b), part of which has been translated in chap. i.

[138] TFYK, 971, 95; TS, 221b, 4155a.

[139] Hsiang (1933), 59.

[140] Hu t'eng wu.

[141] Hsiang (1933), 60–61. The dance has been described in a poem by Liu Yen-shih (ChTS, han 7, ts'e 9, 4b), translated into Japanese by Ishida Mikinosuke, and thence into French by M. Haguenauer, in Ishida (1932), 74. Another poem on the same subject by Li Tuan also appears in French in Ishida (1932), 73.

[142] Identifications of Hsiang (1933), 95. His spelling is "Chaj." Chāch is a Persian form; the Arabic is Shāsh. Barthold (1958), 169. But Chavannes (1903), 313, thought that the Chinese version transcribed Chākar, a name for the elite troops of such states as Bukhāra and Samarkand.

[143] Barthold (1958), 171–172.

[144] Hsiang (1933), 61–62. There was also a solo version of the dance, and one done in Sung times by a chorus of boys, apparently quite different.

[145] Po Chü-i, in ChTS, han 7, ts'e 5, ch. 23, 8a. Po Chü-i has another poem on the same dance in ChTS, han 7, ts'e 6, ch. 25, 16a.

CHAPTER II (*Continued*)

[146] *Che-chih chi.*

[147] Related to "peach blossoms." See Wang Ling (1947), 164.

[148] *Hu hsüan nü* [*tzu*]. An attempt has been made to etymologize *hu-hsüan* as "Khwārizm." The evidence is slight.

[149] From Kumādh in 719 (TFYK, 971, 3b). From Kish twice in 727 (TFYK, 971, 7b; THY, 99, 1777). From Māimargh in 729 (TFYK, 971, 8a). From Samarkand in 713 (THY, 99, 1775) and in 727 (TFYK, 971, 7b).

[150] Ishida Mikinosuke (1932), 71; Hsiang (1933), 63–64; K'ung (1934), 54–55: YFTL, in TTTS, 11, 10a. For full details of the costumes of "official" foreign musicians in the T'ang court, see TT, 146, 762c. There are poems by Po Chü-i and Yüan Chen on the "Western Twirling Girls." There are French versions by Haguenauer in Ishida (1932), 68–69; and English versions based on Haguenauer in Mahler (1959), 147–149.

[151] TS, 35, 3716c.

[152] THY, 33, 620. Wei Kao, the governor who brought about the treaty between T'ang and Nan-chao in 794 and was responsible for sending the orchestra in 800, may have been the author of the "... earliest known description of an orchestra which specifies the tuning of the instruments. No similar document exists for western music until considerably later, and there is nothing comparable for any other Asian orchestra—ironically enough not even for a Chinese one." Twitchett and Christie (1959), 178.

[153] Twitchett and Christie (1959), 176.

[154] Coedès (1948), 179.

[155] CTS, 13, 3105a; THY, 33, 620; THY, 100, 1795; LPLI, a, 4; Twitchett and Christie (1959), 176–179. CTS, 197, gives the date as *chen yüan* 8 in error for *chen yüan* 18. A special Burmese instrument was the Indian *vīṇā*, a zither with a gourd resonator, called in Chinese a "gourd zither." A simple variety of bamboo *vīṇā* had been brought to China by Sui Yang Ti from conquered Champa, but it was found too uncouth for Chinese tastes. Larger instruments were richly decorated in polychrome. It is likely that the Burmese musicians were equipped with these. See Hayashi (1925), 444–452; THY, 33, 620. Po Chü-i criticized the imperial complacency about Chinese prestige abroad occasioned by

the appearance of this orchestra: "Music of P'iao, in vain you raise your din. Better were it that my Lord should listen to that peasant's humble words." These words are from Arthur Waley's translation of "The Imperial Secretary on the Occasion of a Burmese Pwe at the Chinese Court A.D. 802," in G. E. Harvey (1925), 14–15.

[156] TFYK, 971, 6a.

[157] TS, 222c, 4159d.

[158] CTS, 199b, 3619d; TFYK, 972, 3b.

[159] Reischauer (1955a), 82.

[160] THY, 33, 619.

[161] THY, 33, 619.

[162] TFYK, 972, 7b; THY, 95, 1709.

[163] "Sound and color" connote specifically music and female beauty.

[164] TS, 220, 4149c; CTS, 199a, 3616d.

CHAPTER III (Pages 58–78)

[1] TS, 36, 3718d.

[2] TS, 50, 3752d; Rotours (1948), 884.

[3] Distributed among Ch'i-*chou*, Pin-*chou*, Ching-*chou*, and Ning-*chou*. TS, 50, 3753a; Rotours (1948), 887. On the administration of the pastures, see Maspero (1953), 88–92.

[4] Schafer (1950), 182.

[5] For example, in 651 Kao Tsung ordered that gifts of dogs, horses, goshawks, and falcons no longer be offered to him. Here it was hunting which was condemned as frivolous. TS, 4, 3638c.

[6] CTS, 199b, 3617d–3618a.

[7] THY, 72, 1306. "Black-maned" translates *lo*. "Grizzled" translates *ts'ung*. See Tuan's commentary on *Shuo wen*.

[8] CTS, 3, 3070a.

[9] TS, 4, 3639c.

[10] Erkes (1940), 43.

[11] *Pa chün.*

[12] Liu Tsung-yüan, "Kuan pa chün t u shuo," LSSC, 16, 8a–8b.

[13] *Chün ku* and *lung mei* are two epithets conventionally applied to the Horses of Heaven.

[14] Li Po, "T'ien ma ko," LTPWC, 3, 5a. "Dens of the Kushanas" is *Yüeh-chih k'u*, a phrase developed by the poet from the more conventional term *yüeh k'u*, "dens of the moon," a metaphor for the Far West. The latter expression occurs in a poem of Lu Kuei-meng, which is quoted later.

[15] Waley (1955), 100.

[16] Beal (1885), 1, 20.

[17] They are represented on an Iranian silver vase preserved in Japan. Ishida Mikinosuke (1942), 186. Winged horses in stone sculpture near great tombs in China must be these Iranian types.

[18] CHC, 5a.

[19] B. Schwartz proposed that the bloody sweat was caused by a parasite, *Parafiliaria multipapillosa.* Dubs (1944), 132–135; Waley (1955), 102. The blood-sweaters of Medea are mentioned by Herodotus. See Dubs (1944), 135. Nisaean horses were noted for their great size; other and smaller "Medes" were noted for their strangely shaped heads. See Anderson (1961), 127.

[20] Waley (1955), 96.

[21] Yetts (1934), 242. Fernald (1959) states that the first Western horses obtained by the Chinese were Wu-sun horses, apparently hybrids between Bactrian horses and steppe ponies, and shown with "wings on Han tiles. These were the first "heavenly horses"; those of Farghāna came later.

[22] Waley (1955), 96, 101–102. Waley compares them to the masked yellow horses found preserved in ice at Pazaryk.

[23] Egami (1951), 94 ff. Egami believes that the blood-sweating horses of Farghāna are the same as the *chüeh-t'i* kept by the Hsiung-nu in Han times; he suggests that this latter name is cognate to Mongolian *külütei,* "sweating."

[24] Lydekker (1912), 148.

[25] Dubs (1944), 133.

[26] Vergil, *Georgica,* iii, 87: *At duplex agitur per lumbos spina.* See Anderson (1961), 26.

[27] THY, 72, 1306.

[28] TS, 221b, 4155a.

[29] CIL, 3, 6b. Compare the form *źiəp-b'įwɐt,* with the dental of the first syllable assimilated to the initial labial of the second. This appears in the name of one of T'ai Tsung's "Six Bayards" (see below, p. 68). Harada (1944), 389, took this to represent an Iranian *aspa,* which is impossible. R. N. Frye informs me that the word is a Sogdian form for "quadruped," used specifically for "horse," probably vocalized as *čərθpāδ* and heard in China as *čirpāδ,* hence the Chinese transcription and my spelling.

[30] In 741. TFYK, 971, 13a. Here Farghāna is transcribed *b'uât-γân-nâ.*

[31] As was another cat named for a horse, "blue-gray grizzled" (*ch'ing ts'ung*). YYTT, 8, 242.

[32] Andersson (1943), 29. Yetts (1934), 237, points out with reason that these horses, with their characteristic upright manes, are those shown on the Shang oracle bones.

[33] Lydekker (1912), 71–72; Egami (1951), 104–105. Egami gives this identity to the Chinese term *t'ao-t'u* of the ancient Hsiung-nu.

[34] *Derniers Refuges* (1956), 212.

[35] Lydekker (1912), 107. Perhaps "Arab" is too imprecise. Some say that modern breeds derive from Przewalski's and a *Libyan* strain. Yetts (1934), 251.

[36] Lydekker (1912), 107–108.

[37] Erkes (1940), 34, 41–44.

[38] TFYK, 970, 14b. Laufer thought that such "wild horses" were only semiferal, accustomed to being ridden but living on grassy plains, not fed in stables. See Laufer (1916), 371.

[39] TFYK, 971, 5a. This type came from Tan-*chou;* it was also reported elsewhere.

[40] TS, 42, 3730a; Sowerby (1937), 284. The horse of Shu, here referred to, was attributed to the T'u-yü-hun people of the fourth century; CS, 97, 1336c. The pony of modern south China, described in Lydekker (1912), 109–110, is presumably the same, or near it. See Phillips, Johnson, and Mayer (1945), 22, for a photograph of a modern Szechwan pony. This and other south China ponies ". . . are better muscled than Mongolian horses, and the neck is more fully developed and the head is carried somewhat higher . . . The animals are sure-footed and become very adept at running up and down stone steps that are so common in the Chungking area." Phillips, Johnson, and Mayer (1945), 21.

[41] *Liu hu.* TS, 91, 3899a.

[42] Sowerby (1937), 283.

[43] Pelliot (1959), 135. Pelliot has "piebald" for my "dappled," translating the Chinese name.

[44] TS, 217b, 4143b.

[45] YYTT, 10, 78.

[46] TFYK, 970, 18a. They are aptly called *liang ma. Liang* has an important connotation of "well-born."

[47] *Mo-ho* is Ancient Chinese *muât-γât,* possibly to be read *marghat.* They were a "Tatar" tribe (some at least were Tungus),

CHAPTER III (*Continued*)
sometimes identified (by metathesis) with the Moukri(t) of Theophilactus Simocatta.

48 Two herds of thirty each were brought in 730. TFYK, 971, 8b.

49 Thought now to be Mongolic, like the Hsi.

50 An unidentified number in the winter of 747–748, and a flock of fifty in the winter of 836–837. TFYK, 971, 16b; THY, 96, 1722.

51 TFYK, 972, 7a; CTS, 199b, 3619b. THY, 72, 1308, says that these horses were superior to those of the Khitans.

52 In 619 (THY, 96, 1717); 623 (CTS, 199b, 3618d); 719 (TFYK, 971, 3b); 724–725 (TFYK, 971, 6a); 730 (TFYK, 971, 8b). THY, 72, 1308, says that they were smaller than Turkish horses, and adapted to running in dense forests.

53 THY, 72, 1306; Egami (1951), 108.

54 TS, 78, 3872b.

55 TFYK, 999, 18b.

56 The great herd of the Sir-tardush has been mentioned above. From the Toquz-Oghuz (*chiu hsing*) came horses in 747 and 748. See TFYK, 971, 16a, 16b. From the "Turks," missions with horses, often numbering in the thousands, are reported for 626 (but rejected; TFYK, 970, 5b); 628 (TFYK, 970, 6a); 704 (reported as garbled; TFYK, 970, 18b); 717 (TFYK, 971, 2b); 727 (TFYK, 971, 7b); 731–732 (TFYK, 999, 18b).

57 TS, 50, 3753a; Rotours (1948), 898.

58 TS, 51, 3754a; Balazs (1932), 53; Levy (1951), 89.

59 TFYK, 999, 25a; TCTC, 224, 19a.

60 TS, 50, 3753a; TS, 51, 3754a; TFYK, 972, 7b; TFYK, 999, 25a–26a; Balazs (1932), 53.

61 TFYK, 999, 25a.

62 Represented in Chinese as *kien-kuən or *kiet-kuət, for some Altaic name like *kirkon/kirkot.

63 THY, 100, 1785. Referring to an embassy of 843.

64 In 676 (CTS, 5, 3074b; TFYK, 970, 16b); 724–725 (TFYK, 971, 6a); 747 (TFYK, 971, 16a); 747–748 (TFYK, 971, 16b).

65 From the "Western Turks" in 622 (TFYK, 970, 4b); 627 (CTS, 194b, 3599c); 635 (CTS, 194b, 3599d). The Tölös in 642 (CTS, 199b, 3617d). The Turgäch in 717 (TFYK, 971, 2b); 726 (TFYK, 971, 6b); 744 (TFYK, 971, 14b). The Chumul in 721

(TFYK, 971, 4b). The mission of the Western Turks in 627 brought 5,000 horses.

66 In 624 (THY, 99, 1774); 724 (TFYK, 971, 5b); 744 (TFYK, 971, 14b); 750 (TFYK, 971, 17b).

67 In 726 (TFYK, 971, 7a); 727 (TFYK, 971, 7b); 750 (TFYK, 971, 17b).

68 In 741 (TFYK, 971, 13a).

69 In 681 (TFYK, 970, 17a); 720 (TFYK, 971, 4a; THY, 99, 1773); 744 (TFYK, 971, 14b); 748 (TFYK, 971, 17a).

70 In 746 (TFYK, 971, 15b); 747 (TFYK, 971, 16a).

71 In 744 (TFYK, 971, 14b).

72 In 744 (TFYK, 971, 14b).

73 In 744 (TFYK, 971, 14b).

74 In 729 (TFYK, 971, 8a); 733 (TFYK, 971, 9b); 746 (TFYK, 971, 15b); 750 (TFYK, 971, 17b). Maqdisī remarks on the export of horses from Khuttal; Barthold (1958), 236.

75 TFYK, 970, 14a.

76 CTS, 4, 3075c.

77 In 817 (TFYK, 972, 7b; THY, 97, 1737); 827 (TFYK, 972, 8b); 836 (THY, 97, 1739); 837 (THY, 97, 1739).

78 In 631 (TFYK, 970, 7a); 676 (TFYK, 970, 16b; CTS, 5, 3074a); 721 (TFYK, 971, 4b).

79 In 742 and probably thereafter. TS, 110, 3933c.

80 TFYK, 970, 17a.

81 In 724 (TFYK, 971, 5b); 744 (TFYK, 971, 14b); 753–754 (TFYK, 971, 19b).

82 TFYK, 970, 8a; CTS, 198, 3614a. The Turks called the Chinese Son of Heaven, especially T'ai Tsung, "Heavenly Qaghan." Ishida Mikinosuke (1942), 5 and 20. Other Western countries from whom the Chinese received horses were Jāguda in 744 (TFYK, 971, 14b); Shighnān in 724 and 725 (TFYK, 971, 5b and 6b); "K'o-han-na" (a mistake of one character would give Farghāna or Ṣaghāniyān) in 733 (TFYK, 971, 9b); "Su-hsieh-li-fa-wu-lan" in 748 (TFYK, 971, 17a); and Tabaristan in 746 (TFYK, 971, 15b).

83 CTS, 197, 3611b; THY, 99, 1764. For other exotic breeds see THY, 72, 1305–1308.

84 TS, 50, 3753a; Rotours (1948), 895; Pulleyblank (1955), 106.

85 CTS, 194a, 3599b; TCTC, 213, 5b–6a. There were three frontier towns called "Walled Towns for Receiving Surrender" (*shou-hsiang-ch'eng*). The one in the west was in Ling-*chou* at the edge of the Ordos.

It was also under the jurisdiction of the Army of the Boreal Quarter (*Shuo-fang-chün*).

[86] TFYK, 971, 16b.

[87] TCTC, 213, 14b.

[88] CTS, 198, 3612a.

[89] CTS, 198, 3612a.

[90] One man was also assigned to ten cows, but a single herder could control only six camels, asses, or mules. On the other hand, he could manage a flock of seventy sheep. TLT, 22, 30a.

[91] Maspero (1953), 92, 113–149; Yang (1955), 150.

[92] THY, 72, 1305; TLT, 17, 24b–25a, 28a–28b; Maspero (1953), 88–89.

[93] Maspero (1953), 89.

[94] TS, 50, 3753a; Rotours (1948), 886.

[95] The "Flying Yellow" was a divine horse (*Huai-nan-tzu*); the "Auspicious and Well-Bred" (*chi liang*) was an ancient maculated horse (Commentary on *Shan hai ching*). We have already noted the "Dragon Decoys," the *t'ao-t'u* (ancient tarpans?) and the *chüeh-t'i* (ancient blood-sweaters?).

[96] Hsiang (1933), 74. This is the common opinion. T'ang Hao, however, states that the game was invented in China about the beginning of the second century A.D. and transmitted westward to Persia, to be developed under the Sāsānians, and then rediffused throughout eastern Asia. His evidence—mainly references to a field sport played on horseback in a poem of Ts'ao Chih—seems rather flimsy; T'ang (1957), 2–7.

[97] *Ta ch'iu* or *chi ch'ü*. Hsiang derives Chinese *ch'iu* (**g'i̯ə̆u*) from Persian *gui*. T'ang does exactly the reverse.

[98] Hsiang (1933), 74–79.

[99] TFYK, 971, 2b.

[100] Hsiang (1933), 76.

[101] CLWKC.

[102] TS, 22, 3677b–c; MHTL, in TTTS, 4, 8a–9a. See Waley (1952), 181–183, for a full translation of the story of the dancing horses and their unhappy end. See also Baxter (1953), 121–122.

[103] MHTL (TTTS, 4), 9a.

[104] FLHSWC, 12, 15a–15b.

[105] See n. 14 above.

[106] TS, 1, 3634d. Prohibitions such as these typify the beginnings of reigns which follow expansive and liberal ones, as those of T'ai Tsu (following Sui Yang Ti), Kao Tsung

(following T'ai Tsung), Chung Tsung (following Wu Hou), Su Tsung (following Hsüan Tsung), and Te Tsung (following Tai Tsung)—a remarkable pendulum.

[107] CTS, 199a, 3616a; TFYK, 970, 4b.

[108] A **kuâ-ha* horse in 723, and two in 724 (TFYK, 971, 5a; THY, 95, 1912). Two "small horses" in 734 (TFYK, 971, 10b). The T'u-yü-hun also bred "small horses"; (TS, 221a, 4156d). There is no record of their importation.

[109] Lydekker (1912), 110; Laufer (1913), 339–340; Sitwell (1953), 77–78.

[110] HS, 68, 0529a. As to the name, I follow Chang Yen, the third-century historian, quoted in Yen Shih-ku's commentary. The text has only "little horses." But **kuâ-ha* horses occur in the next century.

[111] HHS, 115, 0897a; SKC (Wei), 30, 1005b.

[112] PS, 94, 3033b.

[113] So say Li Hsien, the T'ang scholiast, and many others. HHS, 115, 0897a.

[114] Laufer (1913), 359; LS, 116, 5851b. Laufer (1916) 375, says that he tried in vain to find a Korean original for the name.

[115] KHYHC, 16a. Fan Ch'eng-ta says that the name **kuâ-ha* was given to small carriage-horses bred for the emperor, and that the tallest of them, brought from the Lung River at Te-ch'ing (in Kwangtung) were less than three feet. The best of these ponies had the double-ridged spine of the ancient Horses of Heaven, which would indicate a partially Arab ancestry. They were still sent as tribute from this region in Ming times. Laufer (1916), 375.

[116] PS, 94, 3033b; commentary on HHS, 115, 0897a.

[117] See above, p. 47.

[118] KYTPIS, in TTTS, 3, 49b; Ishida Mikinosuke (1942), 9. A Japanese scholar, Matsumoto Eiichi, is said to have noted this scene, transformed into a Buddhist setting, at Tunhuang. See Ishida (1942), 9. Unfortunately I do not have access to the original work (*Ton-kō-e no kenkyū*, pls. 78a–b).

[119] "Liu ma t'u tsan," in CTW, 10, 20a–21a.

[120] Rivals of T'ai Tsung for the throne.

[121] Rivers near Lo-yang.

[122] Compare the translation of Fitzgerald (1933), pl. 3.

[123] *Huang ts'ung p'iao.*

CHAPTER III (*Continued*)

[124] *Huang tsʻung tieh chʻü.* TS, 21, 3676d. In antiquity there was a piece for the flute called "Song of the Yellow Grizzle."

[125] *Tʻe-le* for *tʻe-chin;* see Harada (1944), 389.

[126] TFYK, 42, 12a–12b.

[127] "Radiant Tumulus" is *chao ling.* Two figures are in the museum of the University of Pennsylvania, four in the Provincial Museum at Sianfu. Fernald (1935), *passim;* Fernald (1942), 19–20, 26; Harada (1944), 385–397. The imperial eulogies were once engraved beside the images in the calligraphy of Ou-yang Hsün, but are now worn away. Waley (1923), 117–118, rightly observes that the sculptured figure shown pulling an arrow from a charger's chest is not, as has been supposed, a barbarian groom, but General Chʻiu Hsing-kung, wearing the "Tatar" military costume then customary in the Chinese army.

[128] Maenchen (1957), 119–138.

[129] Soper (1951), 73–74.

[130] *Shih chi.*

[131] CTS, 3, 3070b; TFYK, 970, 12b.

[132] TS, 217b, 4143a; CTS, 3, 3070b; CTS, 199b, 3618b; YYTT, 1, 1; THY, 72, 1305.

[133] The names are listed in TS, 217b; CTS, 3; and CTS, 199b. These sources do not agree on four of them. In general, TS, 217b, and CTS, 199b, agree, and I follow them, but the form of CTS, 3, seems preferable for the "Soaring Unicorn Purple" (*hsiang lin tzu*). Here TS, 217b, has *hsiang* "auspicious" for *hsiang* "soaring," and CTS, 199b, has *ao* "soaring," a form normally bound to *hsiang.*

[134] Here "bay" is *yü* and "yellow" is *kua.*

[135] LTMHC, 9, 303–305; Soper (1950), 12.

[136] Schafer (1950), 174, 176.

[137] Schafer (1950), 177.

[138] In 816. TFYK, 972, 7b.

[139] In 837. THY, 97, 1739. Presumably Bactrians, but the Tibetans also had swift one-humped Arabian camels; TS, 216a, 4135a.

[140] In 721; TFYK, 971, 4b.

[141] In 717; TFYK, 971, 2b.

[142] TFYK, 971, 2b.

[143] Roux (1959), 46.

[144] Roux (1959), 59.

[145] CTS, 104, 3391a.

[146] YYTT, 4, 37.

[147] TS, 217b, 4143c.

[148] TLT, 17, 24b–25a. Herds of horses and cattle had 120 animals; herds of camels, mules, and asses had 70. There were 620 sheep to a herd, however.

[149] Schafer (1950), 182. Compare this figure with the 325,700 horses in the same region at that time.

[150] Schafer (1950), 185.

[151] Schafer (1950), 182.

[152] Schafer (1950), 272. The story is in *Yang Tʻai-chen wai chuan,* written in Sung times.

[153] Schafer (1950), 182. The whole story, which concerns Te Tsung, may be found in TS, 53, 3756a.

[154] TS, 35, 3716b.

[155] TS, 225a, 4173b.

[156] CCCCTS, 44. Compare the translations of this poem in Ayscough (1929), 220–222; von Zach (1952), 85–86; and Hung (1952), 101–102.

[157] Schafer (1950), 283.

[158] Schafer (1950), 184–185, 273.

[159] Quoted in PTKM, 50a, 19a. Chʻen recognized that this classification was very old even in his time.

[160] Sowerby (1937), 286; Phillips (1958), 54. This cross has even been named *Bos sinensis* by Swinhoe.

[161] Sowerby (1937), 286.

[162] LPLI, b, 15.

[163] Sowerby (1937), 286.

[164] Sitwell (1953), 77–78.

[165] *Chi niu.*

[166] Actually **gʻiəu,* modern *chiu,* of uncertain meaning. Often written as *huan,* "white silk."

[167] PTKM, 50a, 19a.

[168] SIC, b, 17b; KC, quoted in TPLY, 898, 1b.

[169] TS, 1, 3634d.

[170] See Yule and Burnell (1903), 407.

[171] YYTT, 4, 36.

[172] TS, 217b, 4143b.

[173] YYTT, 4, 37.

[174] YYTT, hsü chi, 8, 241.

[175] TFYK, 970, 6a.

[176] In 637. TFYK, 970, 8a.

[177] In 837. THY, 97, 1739.

[178] TS, 221a, 4151d; TS, 216a, 4135a.

[179] Lydekker (1898), 54–55; Lydekker (1912a), 191. The zobo is black and white, or gray and white, or all white. There is also a "small black-polled breed."

[180] PS, 96, 3039d.

[181] TS, 216a, 4135d.

[182] In 817; TFYK, 972, 7b. In 824; TFYK, 972, 8a.

[183] The wild yak is now menaced with extinction; *Derniers Refuges* (1956), 213.

[184] "Chin shu hsing," CCCCTS, 193–194.

[185] *Chou li,* "Ch'un kuan," *mao jen.*

[186] PTKM, 51a, 27a.

[187] From the provincial headquarters of Chien-nan-tao, and from Chi-*chou,* Wei-*chou,* and Pao-*chou.* TS, 42, 3729d, 3730b–c.

[188] Lydekker (1898), 54–55; Lydekker (1912a), 191.

[189] TS, 47, 3743d.

[190] CTS, 198, 3614c. A shorter version of the tale appears in TS, 221b, 4155c.

[191] Laufer (1915d), 115–125, gives a study of this legend, best preserved in China. He has been corrected and improved by Pelliot (1959), 507–531, who shows how the stories have been confused. Pelliot is to be thanked for the Argonaut idea. The tales were known in China from the third century.

[192] YYTT, 16, 135.

[193] Lydekker (1912b), 171–177.

[194] *Pseudois nahura,* a species midway between sheep and goat.

[195] Lydekker (1912b), 305–306.

[196] YYTT, 16, 135.

[197] Lydekker (1912b), 194–195.

[198] CTS, 4, 3071c.

[199] As suggested by Li Shih-chen in the sixteenth century. PTKM, 50b, 22a.

[200] This was in Ts'ai-*chou* and vicinity. TS, 214, 4127b.

[201] THY, 99, 1773; TFYK, 971, 4a.

[202] Two of them. TS, 221b, 4153d.

[203] TS, 221b, 4155b.

[204] Lydekker (1912), 180, 183; Sowerby (1937), 285. Chigetai and kiang are varieties of *Equus hemionus.* Bones of this species have been excavated from Bronze Age deposits in China itself. Andersson (1943), 29. Egami (1951), 122, alleges plausibly that the *t'o-hsi* and the *chü-hsü,* familiar among the Hsiung-nu of Han times, belonged to this species.

[205] Otto Keller (1909), 91. These are the spitz (derived from the jackal), the sheep dog (perhaps from *Canis alpinus*), the greyhound (perhaps from the Abyssinian wolf), the pariah (also from the jackal), and the mastiff (from the Tibetan wolf).

[206] Conrad Keller (1902), 49–50.

[207] Laufer (1909), 267–277.

[208] C. Keller (1902), 76; Laufer (1909), 248, 262–263; Laufer (1923a), 445.

[209] Yen Ch'ang-yen, "Yen Li-pen chih kung t'u," in *T'u shu chi ch'eng,* "ch'üan," i-wen, 2, 2b. This Yen lived under the Chin ("Gold") Dynasty.

[210] THY, 99, 1775.

[211] TFYK, 971, 5b.

[212] TFYK, 971, 4b.

[213] See TS, 47, 3743a; Rotours (1947), 222.

[214] TFYK, 970, 17b.

[215] CTS, 198, 3614b.

[216] PCS, 12, 2216c.

[217] Modern *Fu-lin kou.*

[218] TuT, 191, 1030c. Similar accounts appear in CTS, 198, 3612a; TFYK, 970, 5a. These sources are explicit in stating that it was the first appearance of this kind of dog in China.

[219] Collier (1921), 143.

[220] Otto Keller (1909), 94.

[221] Sirén (1928), pl. 21.

[222] YYTT, 1, 2. There is more to this story, but it will be told under the subject of camphor, where it is more appropriate (p. 167).

[223] *Tsui kung-tzu.*

[224] ChTS, han 12, ts'e 10, ch. 11, 2a.

[225] *Wo,* cognate to *wo,* "dwarf," as suggested by Laufer (1909), 277.

[226] Shiratori (1956), 254, is confident that the Consort's lap dog was a Roman dog, not a native of Samarkand.

[227] Collier (1921), 128–131, thinks that they do; Laufer (1909), 278–281, was uncertain as to how well the strain had persisted.

[228] The words *wo-tzu* and *wo-erh,* these diminutive forms being the rule, are now obsolete. Another term for a toy dog is *pai kou-tzu,* but I am not convinced that this represented a specific variety, much less the Roman toy alone, as Shiratori (1956), 247–249, suggests. Whether it can be equated with a Szechwanese toy of the tenth and eleventh centuries, called the "dog of Lo-chiang"—a little reddish dog with a short tail—is another open question; see THPL, 12, 89. The identity has been suggested, however. For these matters, see Laufer (1909), 277–280; and Collier (1921), 130–131. It has also been supposed that the "dog of Lo-chiang" is ancestral to the little Japanese toy spaniels called *chin* (said to be from *chiisai-inu*).

Chapter IV (Pages 79–91)

[1] Schafer (1957a), 289.

[2] LPLI, 1, 8a.

[3] SS, 287, 5264b.

[4] NHCSC, 2, 21.

[5] LPLI (TTTS, 7), 40a; PHL, 7, 63a.

[6] LPLI (TTTS, 7), 40a; YYTT, 16, 131. H. T. Chang (1926), 105, asserts that the elephant was absent from the Yangtze valley in T'ang times; he seems to have overlooked these texts.

[7] Schafer (1957a), 290–291.

[8] TMC, in HWTS, 1b. Of the country named (in Archaic Chinese) *B'iwăd-lǝk.

[9] "Sung nan ch'ien k'o," ChTS, han 6, ts'e 6, ch. 3, 2a.

[10] ChTS, han 10, ts'e 8, ch. 1, 7b.

[11] ChTS, han 10, ts'e 8, ch. 1, 14b.

[12] ChTS, han 10, ts'e 8, ch. 3, 2b.

[13] "Tseng yu jen pa chü fu Chiao-chih p'i ming," ChTS, han 10, ts'e 8, ch. 2, 8b.

[14] TS, 222c, 4159b; CTS, 197, 3609d.

[15] CTS, 197, 3609d.

[16] Majumdar (1927), 118–119. The inscription is from Hoá-Quê, near Tourane.

[17] TS, 222c, 4159c.

[18] TS, 222c, 4159c; CTS, 197, 3610a.

[19] Coedès (1948), 178.

[20] TS, 222c, 4159b.

[21] LPLI (TTTS, 7), 40a.

[22] The place is unidentified.

[23] [C]TS, quoted in TPYL, 890, 6a; YYTT, 16, 131. The report of the elephant is attributed to the envoy from a "Chou-ch'eng Country" in 671.

[24] YYTT, 16, 132.

[25] YYTT, 16, 131.

[26] Left front in spring, right front in summer, left rear in autumn, right rear in winter. YYTT, 16, 131–132.

[27] CTS, 4, 3071c; TFYK, 970, 14a; THY, 98, 1751.

[28] TFYK, 970, 17a–17b.

[29] TFYK, 970, 19a–19b; 971, 1b, 9a, 11a; THY, 98, 1751.

[30] TFYK, 970, 19b; 971, 11a.

[31] TS, 222c, 4159b.

[32] TFYK, 970, 13b; THY, 98, 1752; CTS, 11, 3094b. The earlier group from Chinrap, the later from *Miuǝn-tân, that is, "Chinrap of the Land" or Upper Chinrap.

[33] TFYK, 970, 15a. The name is garbled in the text, but is given clearly in TS, 222b,

4159d, with an alternative form lacking the final -k; it is described as country abounding in herds of wild elephants. Professor Paul Wheatley, in a private communication of November 12, 1959, suggests the identity of this place with the *Sâm-b'âk of Chou Ch'ü-fei.

[34] THY, 100, 1795.

[35] TFYK, 971, 15b. The text says that Persia sent the animal with an envoy who was the lord of a great city in *Xuo-dz'i, which sounds suspiciously like a variant of Kucha/Kuci.

[36] TLT, 17, 20a–20b.

[37] TuT, 64, 364c; SS, 148, 4833b–4833c.

[38] TS, 222c, 4159c; CTS, 12, 3096c.

[39] TS, 4, 3643a.

[40] TCTC, 218, 17b, especially the commentary of Hu San-hsing. See also the poem of Lu Kuei-meng, "Tsa chi" ("Various Skills"), in FLHSWC, 12, 15b.

[41] MHTL, quoted in PSMC, p. 1. I have not seen this passage in surviving editions of MHTL. PSMC is a twelfth-century work.

[42] YYKYL, b, 50.

[43] Soothill and Hodous (1937), 390–391.

[44] *Derniers Refuges* (1956), 212; Jenyns (1957), 35, 43. See Jenyns (1957), 33–35 for the controversial philological history of the rhinoceros in China; it has been, it seems, confused with various kinds of ancient wild ox, especially the gaur and the water buffalo, and perhaps even the yak.

[45] Based on records of local tribute of rhinoceros horn from the T'ang province of Chiang-nan. TS, 40, 3725b; 41, 3729b–3729d. They were found in much of western and southern Hunan, with some adjacent parts of Szechwan, Hupei, and Kweichow.

[46] LPLI (TTTS, 7), 39a–39b. This source gives a T'ang classification of several varieties of rhinoceros in Lingnan, but considers them to be subdivisions of the two-horned (Sumatran) type.

[47] YYTT, 16, 133–134.

[48] CTS, 18b, 3131d.

[49] CTS, 197, 3609d. This was at the beginning of T'ai Tsung's reign.

[50] THY, 98, 1751. According to tradition, the "Heaven-Communicating" (*t'ung t'ien*) rhinoceros had a single horn over a foot long.

[51] CTS, 13, 3103a; TFYK, 972, 5b; THY, 98, 1751.

[52] TFYK, 970, 15a. For the place, see n. 33 above.

[53] TFYK, 971, 18a; THY, 98, 1752.

[54] CTS, 197, 3610a; TFYK, 972, 7b; THY, 100, 1782.

[55] In 730 (TFYK, 971, 8a) and 746 (TFYK, 971, 15b).

[56] TFYK, 972, 8a.

[57] Yüan Chen's poem "Hsün hsi" ("Tame Rhinoceros"), YSCCC, 24, 6a.

[58] TCTC, 218, 17b; Shōsōin (1960), no. 5 in the south storehouse.

[59] Otto Keller (1909), 35, 37–38.

[60] Derniers Refuges (1956), 212.

[61] Ancient Chinese *suân-ngiei, Archaic Chinese *swân-ngieg.

[62] This is Tocharian A, after Pulleyblank (1962), 109.

[63] TS, 221b, 4155b.

[64] Quennell (1928), 154–155.

[65] Yule and Burnell (1903), 181.

[66] Yule and Burnell (1903), 181.

[67] TS, 221b, 4155b.

[68] Yule and Burnell (1903), 181.

[69] CTS, 198, 3614a; CTS, 2, 3068a; TFYK, 970, 8a; THY, 99, 1774.

[70] CTW, 138, 1b–2b. "Bear" for the mysterious p'i is misleadingly simplified; szu may once have meant "gaur," but its identity was lost by T'ang times; "boa snake" is arbitrary and whimsical for "pa snake."

[71] CTW, 398, 3a. I do not have the poet's dates; he was middle or late T'ang.

[72] In 657 (TFYK, 970, 15a); twice in 719 (the first time: TS, 221b, 4155c; CTS, 198, 3614c; TFYK, 971, 3a; THY, 99, 1779; the second time: TFYK, 971, 3b).

[73] TS, 221b, 4155c; CTS, 198, 3614c; THY, 99, 1779.

[74] TS, 221b, 4154a; TFYK, 971, 7b.

[75] CTS, 8, 3082c; TFYK, 971, 5a.

[76] TS, 102, 3918b; CTS, 89, 3353b.

[77] Hastings (1927), I, 521.

[78] KSP, a, 2a.

[79] YYTT, 16, 131.

[80] YYTT, 16, 131; EYI, 18, 192.

[81] YYTT, 16, 131; PTKM, 51a, 25a.

[82] Ch'en Ts'ang-ch'i, quoted in PTKM, 51a, 25a.

[83] Translation from Soper (1958), 13.

[84] Soper (1958), 14.

[85] YYKYL, a, 23.

[86] YYKYL, a, 30.

[87] YYTT, 16, 131.

[88] YYKYL, b. 50.

[89] YYKYL, a, 30.

[90] One of Yen Li-pen's pictures of tribute lions was preserved in the Hsüan ho collection of Sung Hui Tsung. HHHP, 1, 60. It is not unlikely that it was one of those later described by Chou Mi.

[91] LTPWC, 7, 9a. "O-mei shan yüeh ko sung Shu seng yen ju chung ching."

[92] Panthera pardus fusca of India, Indochina, and south China; P. p. fontancirii of north China; and P. p. orientalis of Siberia and Manchuria.

[93] TLT, 24, 21a–21b.

[94] TS, 49a, 3747d.

[95] TS, 34, 3713b.

[96] TFYK, 971, 4a.

[97] TFYK, 971, 8a.

[98] TFYK, 971, 7b; THY, 99, 1777.

[99] TS, 221b, 4154d.

[100] TS, 221b, 4153d; TFYK, 971, 6b–7a. They were brought by two missions.

[101] TFYK, 971, 7a–7b; THY, 99, 1775. There were three missions with leopards.

[102] TFYK, 971, 16a.

[103] TFYK, 971, 16a.

[104] TS, 6, 3647d.

[105] TS, 48, 3746a.

[106] There are two kinds, the African cheetah, Felis guttata (or Cynailurus guttatus), and the Asiatic cheetah, F. jubata (or C. jubatus).

[107] Friederichs (1933), 31.

[108] Otto Keller (1909), 86.

[109] Werth (1954), 92. According to the Sacramento (California) Bee for October 2, 1959, an attempt is being made to introduce the African cheetah into India, where the native species has become extinct.

[110] O. Keller (1909), 87.

[111] One in 619 (THY, 96, 1717), and one in 623 (CTS, 199b, 3618c).

[112] In 629. CTS, 199b, 3619b; TFYK, 970, 6b. The version of TFYK also refers to tribute of "feng leopard," a term whose interpretation depends partly on the solutions of the problem here under discussion.

[113] See, for instance, SuS, 12, 2373a, on the proper decorations for military caps, and especially the "Rhapsody on the Floriate Sable" ("Hua tiao fu") by the sixth-century poet Chiang Tsung, in CLCC, 1, 6a, which sums up all these associations.

[114] TS, 221b, 4155c; CTS, 198, 3614c;

CHAPTER IV (*Continued*)
TFYK, 971, 3a; THY, 99, 1779. THY gives the date as 722, an error for 719.

[115] The goral is *Naemorhedus goral*. The name *"ling* goat" is apparently sometimes also applied to the two Chinese relatives of the goral, the serow (*Capricornis sumatraensis*) and the takin (*Budorcas taxicolor*).

[116] Sowerby (1940), 67, observes that ". . . it is strange that such animals as the serow and goral do not appear in Chinese art, as both are fairly common in mountainous areas . . ." It is certainly strange, but perhaps they have not been looked for by art students who could recognize them.

[117] Meng Shen, the seventh-century pharmacologist, quoted in CLPT, 17, 19b.

[118] Su Kung and Meng Shen, quoted in PTKM, 51a, 28a–28b. Su Kung also observes that the horns of the "mountain goat" make good "saddle bridges." The horns of the goral are short, and, since the name "mountain goat" is also used of other kinds of wild sheep and goats, we must assume that this passage does not refer to the goral. Similarly, in modern times, the horns sold in Chinese pharmacies under the names *"ling* goat" and "mountain goat" come from various kinds of antelope; for instance, in 1948 the horns of the saiga of Siberia fetched as much as $250 on the Chinese drug market. Bridges (1948), 221.

[119] Laufer (1915c), 21–22. The tale is quoted from Pao P'u-tzu in PTKM, 10, 5a. See also PTKM, 51a, 28a, on the goral and its horn. Laufer thought that "ram's horn" (as he translates the term) was a corruption of "ram's blood," which, according to Pliny, could soften a diamond so that it could be broken; in medieval poetry ram's blood becomes a symbol of the power of the blood of Christ. Laufer (1915c), 24–26.

[120] The sentence is not very plain in Chinese, though it may be so in my translation.

[121] This sentence appears to be garbled in my text.

[122] KSTI, in TuSCC, "Yang" (goats), chi shih, 11b. Fragments of this lost book can be found in the *Han fen lou*, SF, ch. 67, but not the one here translated. The title sometimes appears as *Kuo shih i tsuan*. The author is unknown, but the book appears to have been written in the late T'ang or early Sung.

[123] Sclater and Thomas (1897–1898), 107.

[124] TFYK, 970, 12a; THY, 100, 1796.

[125] TFYK, 970, 12a; THY, 100, 1796. Ancient Chinese *b'wât-lân.

[126] Brockelmann (1928), 42. I owe the linguistic suggestion to P. A. Boodberg.

[127] Bang and Rachmati (1932), 687–688. I owe this reference to P. A. Boodberg.

[128] Ramstedt (1949), 125. There is also Turkish *qûlân,* "wild ass." Stephenson (1928), 22.

[129] Or *Gabiyap, or *Gavyapa. Ancient Chinese *g'ia-b'ji-i̯äp.

[130] YYTT, 16, 134; TFYK, 970, 13b.

[131] PTKM, 51a, 25a.

[132] Ancient Chinese *t'uo-puât and *d'â-b'uât.

[133] The "Tarbagan marmot" is *Marmota bobak;* the "Himalayan marmot" is *M. himalayana.*

[134] Quoted in PTKM, 51b, 35a. Li Shih-chen points out that marmot skins make warm fur coats, but we do not know if they were used for this purpose in T'ang times.

[135] TS, 40, 3726c.

[136] TFYK, 970, 9b. A virtually identical passage occurs in TS, 221a, 4153c, and CTS, 198, 3614a. The name of the "rat" is here given as *ńźi^wok-źi, though TS has -d'ək, apparently in error for -źi, in the second syllable. But I believe we should substitute nəu- (as given in THY) uniformly for ńźi^wok- in these transcriptions.

[137] TFYK, 970, 13b; THY, 99, 1776. For January/February of 652. In TFYK the name is given as *ńźi^wok-d'i̯ə.

[138] *Herpestes edwardsii* and *H. javanicus,* both common in South Asia.

[139] *H. urva.*

[140] Yule and Burnell (1903), 596, quoting *A History of Ceylon* (Paris, 1701).

[141] THY, 100, 1796. Similar passages in TS, 221b, 4155b, and TFYK, 970, 12a. The name is *γuât-nəu [or ńźi^wok]-dźi̯a, presumably registering an Iranian form.

[142] Otto Keller (1909), 163–164; A. P. D. Thompson (1951), 471.

[143] A. P. D. Thompson (1951), 476.

[144] O. Keller (1909), 164–165.

CHAPTER V (Pages 92–104)

[1] Li (1956), 44.
[2] TCTC, 211, 12b.
[3] Schafer (1959), 295.

[4] Schafer (1959), 297.

[5] Schafer (1959), 298.

[6] TS, 3, 3638c; Schafer (1959), 303–304.

[7] Schafer (1959), 304.

[8] TS, 9, 3655b.

[9] Schafer (1959), 306.

[10] *Falco gyrfalco grebnitzkii* of northeast Asia.

[11] Schafer (1959), 308–309.

[12] Lu Kuei-meng, "Feng ch'ou Hsi-mei . . . ," FLHSWC, 1, 11b.

[13] Schafer (1959), 309.

[14] Schafer (1959), 310.

[15] *Accipiter gentilis albidus*. Schafer (1959), 311. A prime source of these birds was the Mo-ho nation; see, for instance, TS, 219, 4146d.

[16] "Chien wang chien . . . ," CCCCTS, p. 495.

[17] KYTPIS, 3, 68a.

[18] CTS, 19a, 3135a.

[19] Su T'ing, preface to "Shuang po ying tsan," CTW, 256, 12b.

[20] In 722 (TFYK, 971, 5a), 737 (TFYK, 971, 12a), 739 (TFYK, 971, 12b), 741 (TFYK, 921, 13b), 749 (TFYK, 971, 15a), 750 (TFYK, 971, 15b), 777 (TFYK, 972, 3b).

[21] Tou Kung, "Hsin-lo chin po ying," ChTS, han 4, ts'e 10, p. 23a. Tou Kung lived ca. 762–821.

[22] TS, 37, 3719d. Ling-*chou*, to the northwest, annually submitted "eagles, falcons, white feathers," but I am not certain whether this should be construed as "white feathers of eagles and falcons," or as "eagles and falcons; white feathers."

[23] Schafer (1959), 318–319. The booklet appears as the last chapter of modern editions of YYTT, with the title *Jou chüeh pu*, "Section on Predators of Flesh." A Han treatise on falconry, the *Ying ching*, "Goshawk Canon," disappeared during T'ang.

[24] Schafer (1959), 325–334.

[25] Schafer (1959), 298–299.

[26] Schafer (1959), 320.

[27] Schafer (1959), 298.

[28] Schafer (1959), 312–314.

[29] Schafer (1959), 300–301.

[30] Schafer (1959), 300–301.

[31] Schafer (1959), 307.

[32] Schafer (1959), 300.

[33] Schafer (1959), 299.

[34] Schafer (1959), 300.

[35] Li Po, "Tu lu p'ien," LTPWC, 4, 1a.

[36] Hsüeh Fang, "Hsia shao nien," ChTS, han 8, ts'e 10, p. 16b. The poet lived in the ninth century.

[37] Schafer (1959), 308.

[38] "Ku yüeh fu," in TPYL, 926, 5a.

[39] TS, 128, 3968a. Said of Wang Chih-an at the beginning of the eighth century.

[40] CTS, 45, 3258c.

[41] Ch'en Ts'ang-ch'i, in PTKM, 49, 12a.

[42] Su Kung, in PTKM, 49, 12a.

[43] *Pavo cristatus*.

[44] Chou Ch'eng Wang. ChS, quoted in TPYL, 924, 4b. Erkes (1942), 34, thought there were tame peacocks in Ch'u in the fourth century B.C., on the slender evidence of the phrase "peacock baldachin" in the *Chiu ko*. At best this means only that the people of Ch'u got peacock feathers from *some* source. He also concludes that the birds must have been brought from India, ". . . denn wilde Pfauen scheint es in China nicht zu geben." Nothing could be more wrong.

[45] HS, 96a, 0606d.

[46] HsHS and HC, quoted in TPYL, 924, 5a. Both these sources place the peafowl in T'iao-chih, whose identity is still uncertain. Chavannes thought (*T'oung Pao*, 8, 176) that it was the Arab kingdom of Characène at the mouth of the Tigris, which submitted to the Parthians at the beginning of the second century A.D.

[47] Otto Keller (1913), 150–151. They are known to have been raised by the Romans in the second century B.C.

[48] SKC (Wu), 8, 1048b. *Pavo muticus* occurs also in Java. It is more stately and richly colored than the Indian peacock. David and Oustalet (1877), 402–403; Delacour (1951), 311. This bird has been found in Yünnan, but some authorities say that the Indian peacock occurs there too. Read (1932), 78–79. For peacocks in medieval Yünnan see TC, 197, 3164c. White peacocks, reckoned good omens, have occasionally been reported in China, for example in 461. I know of no T'ang examples. See PHL (HHLP), 1a–1b. Recently a third species of peafowl, the Congo peacock (*Afropavo congensis*) has been found in Africa. Delacour (1951), 311.

[49] SKC, 3, 1038c; CS, 57, 1234d. The latter source places these events some years later, apparently in error.

[50] TS, 43a, 3731c–3731d; PHL (HHLP, ts'e 91), 1a–1b. Su Kung, in PTKM, 49, 11b, says that there were many peacocks in Lingnan and Tongking.

CHAPTER V (*Continued*)

51 PTKM, 49, 11b.

52 Untitled poem by Wu Yüan-heng (eighth and early ninth centuries), in ChTS, han 5, ts'e 7, ch. 1, 7a.

53 O. Keller (1913), 174.

54 NFIWC, quoted in PTKM, 49, 11b.

55 PHL (HHLP, ts'e 91), 1a–1b; LPLI (in TPKC, 461), 1b.

56 LPLI (in TPKC, 461), 1b.

57 TMJHPT (tenth century), in PTKM, 49, 11b.

58 PHL (HHLP, ts'e 91), 1a–1b.

59 PHL, in PTKM, 49, 11b.

60 YYTT, 16, 127.

61 CW (ninth century), in TPKC, 461, 2b.

62 CS, quoted in TPYL, 924, 5a.

63 Hansford (1957), 82.

64 Soper (1958), 224.

65 HHHP, 15, 398–402.

66 Hackmann (1951–1954), 307–308.

67 TS, 222b, 4160d.

68 Hackmann (1951–1954), 307–308. See de Visser (1920), for the whole story of this peacock queen.

69 Nanjio (1883), 79.

70 HHHP, 1, 59.

71 HHHP, 2, 70.

72 *Psittacula* (or *Palaeornis*) *derbyana*.

73 Schafer (1959a), 271–273. The parrots of medieval Yünnan and Tibet are mentioned in TC, 195, 3130b, and 197, 3164c.

74 Schafer (1959a), 273–274.

75 They are *Psittacula krameri, P. alexandri*, and *P. cyanocephala*, respectively. Schafer (1959a), 275.

76 Schafer (1959a), 278; Otto Keller (1913), 49.

77 Schafer (1959a), 274.

78 Schafer (1959a), 275–277.

79 Yule (1903), 521–522.

80 TS, 221a, 4153c; CTS, 8, 3082b; CTS, 198, 3613d; TFYK, 971, 4a; THY, 100, 1787.

81 TS, 222b, 4159b; CTS, 197, 3609d.

82 TS, 222b, 4159b.

83 Its name is given as *Kiu-ləu-miĕt.

84 TS, 222b, 4159c; THY, 100, 1794.

85 TFYK, 971, 6a and 7b.

86 TS, 221b, 4155c; TFYK, 971, 3b. My "Kapiśa" attempts to explain the *Xâ-b'ji-śie of the text.

87 TS, 222b, 4159c; TFYK, 972, 7b.

88 Schafer (1959a), 278.

89 CTS, 197, 3609d; THY, 98, 1751.

90 YYKYL, hsü chi, 5.

91 Schafer (1959a), 281.

92 Soper (1951), 10.

93 *Kakatoë moluccensis*.

94 Its name is given as *Nəu-d'â-γuân.

95 TS, 222b, 4159d; CTS, 197, 3610a; THY, 99, 1779. THY confuses this mission (of 647) with an earlier one of 644.

96 Schafer (1959a), 279. See Wheatley (1961), 123, on Chao Ju-kua's account of the powder on parrot's wings, which was wrongly thought to be the source of the disease.

97 Schafer (1959a), 279–280.

98 Schafer (1959a), 280.

99 HHS, 4, 0659c; HHS, 118, 0904d.

100 Called *Struthio camelus syriacus*. See Waley (1952), 74.

101 Hirth and Rockhill (1911), 129.

102 TFYK, 970, 13b states specifically that it is called "camel bird" by the "barbarians." The Han history and other sources call it "great sparrow of T'iao-chih." Compare my remarks on names for the ostrich in the West above, under the discussion of the peacock. The T'ang commentary adds: "namely the 'camel bird' of today." In Pan Ku's *Hsi tu fu*, LCCWH (SPTK), 1, 10b, it is called simply "bird of T'iao-chih." On this, the T'ang scholiast Li Shan says, "a great bird, whose egg is like a water jar." This gloss derives from KC (see quote in PTKM, 49, 11b). For T'iao-chih, see n. 46 above.

103 CTS, 1, 3065c.

104 TS, 221b, 4154d; CTS, 4, 3071a; TFYK, 970, 13b; Ch'en Ts'ang-ch'i in PTKM, 49, 11b.

105 Ch'en Ts'ang-ch'i, in PTKM, 49, 11b.

106 CTS, 4, 3071a.

107 Laufer (1926), 29–33; Schafer (1950), 288.

108 "Ch'iu p'u ko," LTPWC, 7, 5a. There are seventeen poems in this set. The poet lived at "Autumn Estuary."

109 It is *Chrysolophus pictus*. Read (1932), no. 271.

110 Demiéville (1929), 153; Soothill and Hodous (1937), 317; Hackmann (1951–1954), 70.

111 ICCYI, 23, 456c. Cf. also ICCYI, 25, 463a.

112 Ecke and Demiéville (1935), 61–62. The authors state that the humanoid figure with wings, claws, and the tail of a bird at the granite pagoda in Zayton, which looks like an Indian *kinnara*, is in fact a *kalaviṅka*,

and that the *kinnara* is never birdlike in China and Japan.

[113] See the picture of their costume in Demiéville (1929), pl. xvi.

[114] Two sources (TS, 222b, 4159c, and THY, 100, 1782) place this event in 813; two others (CTS, 197, 3610a, and TFYK, 972, 7a) place it in 815. I am instinctively inclined to accept the later date.

[115] There are many variant forms of the name of the common black drongo of China (*Dicrurus cathoecus*): *pjię-kap, *p'iei-kap, *p'iei-kiep, *b'ji-g'jəp, etc. The bird has metallic black plumage and a long black tail; it sings through the night until dawn, and is noted for its bravery—it will attack even hawks and crows. It is a widespread resident of China, but the name may also sometimes be applied to the hair-crested drongo (*D. hottentotus*), a migrant. The specific identity of the Chinese name was first suggested by Mollendorf (see Read [1932], no. 295A); cf. PTKM, 49, 10a; Wilder and Hubbard (1924), 171.

[116] MCML (TSCC), 5, 57.

[117] *Dicrurus* (or *Dissemurus*) *paradiseus*. Several subspecies occur in India, Burma, Laos, Vietnam, and Yünnan, as well as in Indonesia. See Delacour and Jabouille (1931), 84–86.

[118] Delacour (1947), 340–342.

[119] Fletcher and Inglis (1924), 31.

[120] Laufer (1915b), 284, discusses the possibilities for the identity of the *kalaviṅka* from Kalinga; he comes to no definite conclusion.

CHAPTER VI (Pages 105–116)

[1] CL, T'en kuan, *Szu fu.*

[2] See TuSCC, Li i tien, 340, *passim,* for examples.

[3] TLT, 3, 17a.

[4] Li Po, "Sung Wang-wu shan jen Wei Wan huang Wang-wu," LTPWC, 14, 2b.

[5] Barthold (1958), 235–236, quoting Maqdisī (tenth century).

[6] TFYK, 971, 19a. The identity of the deer is a puzzle. The text gives *t'ung, an otherwise unattested form; presumably this is an error for *liang, a recognized alternate of *ching. The problem of the identity of *ching

is treated in the immediately following paragraphs.

[7] TLT, 22, 14b–15a.

[8] ChTS, han 11, ts'e 10, chi nü, 2b.

[9] The old military boot was made of skin, with a short upper, which gradually became longer. In the first half of the seventh century Ma Chou created a boot with felt uppers, and in the first half of the eighth century P'ei Shu-t'ung made them of goatskin, lined with *ching,* and with ties added. See the short history of boots in China in Hu San-hsing's commentary on TCTC, 221, 12a.

[10] TS, 43a, 3732b. See also Li Ch'ün-yü's poem on boots of *ching-*hide from Kuei. ChTS, han 9, ts'e 2, 12b–13a.

[11] Schafer (1954), 69.

[12] *Elaphodus cephalophus.*

[13] Mosaku Ishida and Wada (1954), pl. 119.

[14] Soper (1951), 14.

[15] TS, 37, 3720c–3721a, and 40, 3727a.

[16] Or so we should call them; they were placed under the saddle. Nakano (1924), 59–60.

[17] TFYK, 971, 3b.

[18] *Phoca equestris.*

[19] Laufer (1913), 340.

[20] Five skins from P'o-hai Mo-ho in 730 (TFYK, 971, 8b); unspecified number from Silla in 723 (TFYK, 971, 5a); sixteen from Silla in 734 (TFYK, 971, 10b).

[21] The *Shih-chung* and *Chung-shu-ling.* It is not always easy to tell whether the animal meant is a marten, a kolinsky, a sable, or an ermine. All are known by the same collective name. PTKM, 51b, 35b; Han Chüeh (1953), 391.

[22] Ts'ui Hao (eighth century), "Ku yu hsia ch'eng chun chung chu chiang," ChTS, han 2, ts'e 9, 1a.

[23] Eighth century. ChTS, han 2, ts'e 9, 1, 1a.

[24] TLT, 22, 18a.

[25] **Uo-lâ-ɣuən. Perhaps cognate to Mongol *ulaɣan,* "red."

[26] Several missions from P'o-hai Mo-ho (TFYK, 971, 8b; 971, 12b; 971, 13a). In the first two of these texts "marten-rat" has been garbled to "leopard-rat." Eight missions from the Black Water Mo-ho (TS, 219, 4146d); one from the "Great (or *d'ai-?) p'iuət-niet Mo-ho (TFYK, 971, 4a). The Black Water Mo-ho seem to have been the modern Goldi, whom the Khitan people called *weji,* "forest men." See Wada (1955), 16.

CHAPTER VI (*Continued*)

27 THY, 100, 1787. No doubt the southern race, *Panthera pardus fusca.*

28 *P. p. orientalis.* THY, 95, 1712.

29 Li Hsien-yung (ninth century), "Ho Yin Ya t'ui ch'un lin chi shih," ChTS, han 10, ts'e 2, 2, 12a.

30 Ch'en Ts'ang-ch'i, quoted in PTKM, 51a, 26a.

31 TS, 196, 4087a.

32 YHTC, 1, 6.

33 TFYK, 970, 4b.

34 Called *Lịəm-źie* Country. The beast's name is given as *sịän-g'ị^wo* "indigo," *źịang-tsị^wo* "fragrant."

35 MHTL (TTTS, 4), 16b.

36 Duyvendak (1939), 402 n. 1; suggested with much hesitancy.

37 TS, 219, 4146d; TFYK, 971, 4a.

38 TS, 43a, 3733a.

39 Schafer (1952), 156, 159–160.

40 So NYC (quoted in PTKM, 44, 31a), long before T'ang, says ". . . the skin has pearls, and may embellish sabers and swords." And Su Sung (quoted in the same source), after T'ang, wrote ". . . it may embellish the grip of a saber."

41 For example, *Shōsōin* (1928–), IV, 37; Mosaku Ishida and Wada (1954), pl. 25.

42 TLT, 22, 18a; TS, 42, 3729d, 3730b–3730c.

43 TS, 37, 3721a.

44 TLT, 22, 18a.

45 TS, 42, 3730b–3730c.

46 Ch'eng Ts'ang-ch'i, in CLPT, 17, 30a.

47 TPT, in PTKM, 51a, 26a.

48 TLT, 17, 17a; SS, 149, 4837a.

49 SS, 149, 4837a. Even in T'ang some, like the pharmacologist Su Kung, regarded the imperial leopard tail as merely emblematic, not worthy of respect in its own right. TPT, in PTKM, 51a, 26a.

50 On a different level were the white eagle feathers of what is now northern Shansi, used by the court fletchers to give wings to their arrows. Li Shih-chen, PTKM, 49, 12a; Schafer (1959), 307.

51 *Oriolus cochinchinensis* [= *chinensis*]. TLT, 22, 14b–15a.

52 For instance, the satirical rhapsody composed on such things in the eighth century by Wang Yin. See TS, 76, 3868d.

53 Li Hua, "Yung shih," ChTS, han 3,

ts'e 2, p. 4a. The poem describes a lady caught in a storm.

54 Ch'in-*chou* in westernmost Kwangtung. TS, 43a, 3732a.

55 Chiao-*chou* and Lu-*chou*. TS, 43a, 3733a. Hirth and Rockhill (1911), 235–236, tell of a governmental prohibition of 1107 on gathering the feathers for applying to textiles.

56 Mosaku Ishida and Wada (1954), pls. 33, 34.

57 Several species were available. Cheng Tso-hsin (1955), 15–17.

58 TLT, 22, 18a.

59 TS, 23a, 3678a.

60 The following examples are taken from Delacour (1951), *passim;* but cf. Read (1932), nos. 269–273, and Cheng Tso-hsin (1955), 90–109. But the reader would do best to read Sitwell (1947), 186–196, on the tragopans and pheasants.

61 *Ithaginis cruentus sinensis.*

62 *Tragopan temmincki.*

63 *Lophura nycthemera nycthemera.*

64 *Crossoptilon auritum.*

65 *Chrysolophus pictus.*

66 *C. amherstiae.*

67 *Syrmaticus reevesii.*

68 TLT, 22, 18a.

69 TS, 48, 3747a.

70 SWCY, 8, 290, quoting TuT.

71 TLT, 22, 18a; TS, 43a, 3733b. Poem of Li Tung (ninth century), in ChTS, han 11, ts'e 2, ch. 3, 11a, states that they come from "Nan-hai," that is, Lingnan via Canton.

72 LPLI, in TPKC, 461, 1b.

73 TLT, 11, 30b.

74 WHTK, 117, 1054a.

75 YYKYL, a, 24.

76 Hsüeh Feng (fl. 853), "Hsüan cheng tien . . . tsun hao," ChTS, han 8, ts'e 10, pp. 12a–12b, describing the ceremony of awards to Shun Tsung and Hsien Tsung.

77 Wen T'ing-yün, "Wan kuei ch'ü," ChTS, han 9, ts'e 5, ch. 2, 1a.

78 Wen T'ing-yün, "Kuo Hua ch'ing kung," ChTS, han 9, ts'e 5, ch. 6, 5b.

79 Burton (1934), 2924.

80 Eberhard (1942), Vol. II, 156, 287–289. For modern Chinese versions of the swan maiden story, see Eberhard (1937), 55-59.

81 YYTT, 16, 130.

82 TTHYC, 2, [4b].

83 SC, 12, 0043d.

84 Yen Shih-ku's commentary on the identi-

85 HHS, 107, 0872a.

86 NCS, 21, 1705b. Of the Wei hui T'ai tzu.

87 CIC (TTTS, 17), 18a–18b. Feather garments were still being made in Kwangtung by non-Chinese aborigines at the end of the eighteenth century: ". . . among them is the celestial goose velvet, the foundation of the fabric being silk; into which the feathers were ingeniously and skillfully interwoven, on a common loom, those of crimson hue being the most expensive. Of these wild goose feathers, two kinds of cloth were made; one for winter, the other for summer wear. Rain could not moisten them; they were called 'rain satin,' and 'rain gauze' respectively. Canton men initiated the manufacture, employing feathers of the common goose, blending them with cloth." See Macgowan (1854), 58–59, for this very interesting account of the art of plumagery. Macgowan also mentions ladies' capes of peacock feathers in the Canton area, but the art of making these was lost by the middle of the nineteenth century. LPLI, a, 5, describes goosedown quilts made in Lingnan in T'ang times, but says nothing of feather capes. Still it is reasonable to assume, in view of the other evidence of the importance of feathers here in ancient and modern times, that plumagery was a medieval as well as a modern specialty of Lingnan. Colored feathers were introduced into the textiles of fourteenth-century Islam, according to Qazwini; Stephenson (1928), 62, 83. Possibly the art was of Chinese origin.

88 TS, 34, 3713a. Cf. Laufer (1915d), 114. In 1107 the Sung government was obliged to prohibit gathering kingfisher feathers because of the excessive slaughter to provide embellishments for an elaborate silk brocade. Hirth and Rockhill (1911), 235–236.

89 Laufer (1915d), 114, translated from *Lang hsüan chi* as quoted in TuSCC.

90 MCPT, 5, 32.

91 Waley (1960), 149–155, and 258–260. The story was known in China from at least A.D. 300.

92 Waley (1922), 177–185.

93 TLT, 22, 14b–15a.

94 Ch'en Ts'ang-ch'i, quoted in PTKM, 41, 16b. They were especially gathered at Pin-*chou* and Ch'eng-*chou*.

95 Wang Ch'i, commentary on Li Ho's poem translated just below.

96 Li Ho, "Hsien Hsiu-ts'ai . . . szu shou," ChTS, han 6, ts'e 7, ch. 3, 2a (the third of four), and LCCKS, 3, 7a–7b.

97 *Shōsōin* (1928–), VI, 26.

98 Wang Ch'i, commentary on Li Ho, "Nao kung," LCCKS, 2, 30b. The place was Li-*chou*.

99 Ch'en Ts'ang-ch'i, in PTKM, 41, 16b.

CHAPTER VII (Pages 117–132)

1 See Introduction to the present book and also, especially, THY, 100, 1796.

2 Liu Tsung-yüan, "Chung shu Kuo T'o-t'o chuan," LHSC, 17, 2b. Cf. translation by H. A. Giles as "Pas trop gouverner," in H. A. Giles (1923), 142–144.

3 CSS, in SF, ts'e 212, 7a (han 106).

4 Mr. Gari Ledyard did the textual study which leads to these conclusions.

5 TFYK, 970, 11b–12b; THY, 100, 1796; Laufer (1919), 303–304.

6 Quoted in Nakamura (1917), 567, from ChTS, han 6, ts'e 6.

7 Murakami (1955), 77.

8 Schafer (1961), 4–5.

9 Grigson (1947), 79–85.

10 TCTC, 215, 13b, for the seventh month of 746. The commentator Hu San-hsing states that since the days of Su Shih (eleventh century) men have said that the lichees come only from Fu-*chou* in southern Szechwan. Hu quotes Po Chü-i to the effect that the lichee's color is altered in one day, its aroma in two, and that color, aroma, and taste are all lost in four or five.

11 Mahler (1959), 73–74, based on Barthold. It seems that the Chinese were not familiar with the watermelon, which they called "Western melon," until the middle of the tenth century. See Laufer (1919), 439.

12 Hung Hsi-wen, "Ming huang T'ai chen p'i shu an le t'u," YSH, ch'u chi, ts'e 14, 10b.

13 "Gold Millet" is the name of a place near Ch'ang-an, and I have so taken it here. But it could mean "granulated with gold."

14 Ch'en Ts'ang-ch'i, PTKM, 5, 22b, also quotes a *Shih p'u* on this point.

15 Ishida Mikinosuke (1942), 215–216.

16 The words are those of Pao Chao (fifth century).

17 TFCY, quoted in CLPT, 3, 13a. This book, by Tu-ku T'ao, was apparently written

CHAPTER VII (*Continued*)
in the seventh century—some sources say Sui,
some T'ang.

[18] TLT, 19, 19b.

[19] Yeh Ching-yüan (1958), 159.

[20] LYMTC, p. 6a.

[21] Yeh Ching-yüan (1958), 159.

[22] TLT, 19, 15b; TLT, 7, 13a–13b.

[23] TFYK, 970, 8b.

[24] This edition of TLT inserts a gloss:
"TFYK states that it was twenty-seven *li*
(Chinese miles) east and west, thirty-three *li*
north and south."

[25] TLT, 7, 13a–13b.

[26] CTS, 9, 3085a.

[27] KYTPIS (TTTS, 3), 53b.

[28] TLT, 14, 51a–51b, 52a–52b.

[29] Laufer (1919), 385. They are mentioned
in WS and SuS.

[30] Liu Hsün in his LPLI; see Kuwabara
(1930), 53.

[31] Ch'en Ts'ang-ch'i, in PTKM, 31, 15a.

[32] Laufer (1919), 385. The name occurs in
YYTT and Ch'en Ts'ang-ch'i.

[33] Laufer (1919), 385–386.

[34] TFYK, 971, 15b.

[35] Liu Hsün again; Laufer (1919), 386–387.
Yü Ching-jang (1954), 193–195, discusses the
sources already studied by Laufer, without
adding anything new.

[36] TFYK, 970, 9a–9b.

[37] TS, 221a, 4153c; TFYK, 970, 11b; THY,
100, 1796.

[38] Sitwell (1936), 181.

[39] Demiéville (1929), 90–91.

[40] YYTT, 18, 149–150. A *kaṣāya* is a Buddhist priest's cassock.

[41] *Tilia miqueliana*. Demiéville (1929), 90–
91.

[42] P'i Jih-hsiu, "Chi t'i T'ien t'ai Kuo ch'ing
szu Ch'i Liang t'i," ChTS, han 9, ts'e 9, ch.
8, 7b.

[43] Yule and Burnell (1903), 798; Burkill
(1935), 2005.

[44] *Shorea kunstleri et al.*; Burkill (1935),
2001–2005.

[45] Soothill and Hodous (1937), 323.

[46] Waley (1952), 140. An episode in a
Taoist tale of late T'ang.

[47] For instance, a foreign monk is reported
to have identified a saul tree at a temple in
Hunan early in the fifth century. YYTT, 18,
147.

[48] A. Christie tells me that he is convinced

of its close relation to Champa, where a
Malayan tongue was spoken.

[49] NS, 78, 2730c.

[50] Li Yung, "Ch'u chou Huai yin hsien
Sha-la she pei," CTW, 263, 1a.

[51] Chang Wei, "An hsi tao chin sha-la shu
chih chuang," CTW, 375, 2a–2b. A shortened
version of this memorial appears in YYTT,
18, 147–148.

[52] YYTT, hsü chi, 6, 227.

[53] *Historiae Naturalis*, Bk. XXI, chap. 18.
Ch'en Ts'ang-ch'i states that saffron grows in
"Great Ch'in," that is, in Roman Asia; quota-
tion in PTKM, 14, 40a.

[54] Laufer (1919), 309–329, contains a full
discussion of the saffron problem, especially
its confusion with turmeric. Cf. PTKM, 14,
38a.

[55] Ch'en Ts'ang-ch'i, in PTKM, 14, 40a.
Laufer (1919), 312, makes the curious assertion that saffron seems not to have been imported or used in China before Yüan times,
but there is abundant evidence to the
contrary.

[56] Yü Ching-jang (1955), 33–37, discusses
the confusion, but adds no new ideas.

[57] Laufer (1919), 322–323; Burkill (1935),
714–715. Safflower is *Carthamus tinctorius*;
turmeric is *Curcuma longa*; zedoary is *C.
zedoaria*. There is also a *C. aromatic* which
has properties similar to those of zedoary.

[58] THY, 100, 1796. Also in TFYK, 970,
11b, where the sentence "the flowers open
in the ninth month" has been corrupted into
unintelligibility.

[59] Lu Chao-lin, "Ch'ang-an ku i," ChTS,
han, 1, ts'e 9, ch. 1, 10a.

[60] Ch'en T'ao, "Fei lung yin," ChTS, han
11, ts'e 4, ch. 2, 16a.

[61] YHTC, 1, 7.

[62] Li Po, "K'e chung tso," LTPWC, 20, 2a.

[63] Li Po, "Ch'un jih tu tso chi Cheng
Ming-fu," LTPWC, 11, 11a.

[64] Wen T'ing-yün, "Ch'ing ming jih,"
ChTS, han 9, ts'e 5, ch. 9, 10a.

[65] Li Shang-yin, "Mu-tan," ChTS, han 8,
ts'e 9, ch. 1, 26b.

[66] YYTT, hsü chi, 9, 246.

[67] His biographies are in TS, 89, 3896a;
CTS, 167, 3515a.

[68] Laufer (1919), 402, has "vegetable
greens" (*ts'ai*) instead of "leaf," apparently
from a misprint in some edition of the chief
sources which I have not seen.

[69] TFYK, 970, 12a; THY, 100, 1796. The texts are identical, except for a metathesis in TFYK.

[70] Soothill and Hodous (1937), 226; Hackmann (1951–1954), 204; and especially Demiéville (1929), 198–203.

[71] Laufer (1919), 427–428.

[72] YYTT, 18, 153.

[73] *Historiae Naturalis,* Bk. XXI, chaps. 12 and 75.

[74] Chou Tun-i, "Ai lien shuo," CLHC, 8, 139.

[75] TS, 2, 3637b. It was the winter of 633–634.

[76] PSCCC, 28, 7b.

[77] The Chinese clichés are *Yüeh yen Ching shu* and *Wu chi Yüeh yen.*

[78] Quoted in PTKM, 33, 23a.

[79] HHHP, 15, 403 and 405.

[80] Lessing (1935), 44–47. Here may be found a complete account of the lotus symbolism in Buddhism.

[81] Therefore the *Saddharma-puṇḍarīka-sūtra* is called "White Lotus Sutra" (that is, "White Water Lily Sutra") in a poem of the monk Kuan-hsiu found at Tun-huang. Wu Chi-yu (1959), 356.

[82] KYTPIS (TTTS, 3), 64b. This was the *T'ai i ch'ih,* "Pool of the Grand Liquid."

[83] YFL, 9, 2a–2b.

[84] Li Te-yü, "Po Fu-jung fu," CTW, 696, 5b.

[85] P'i Jih-hsiu, "Po lien," ChTS, han 9, ts'e 9, ch. 8, 3b. The *champaka* is a fragrant flower, *Michelia champaka,* compared by the Chinese to the gardenia. Soothill and Hodous (1937), 465.

[86] Waley (1931), 160 (no. CLX in Stein collection).

[87] Chao Ku, "Ch'iu jih Wu-chung kuan huang ou," ChTS, han 9, ts'e 1, ch. 2, 1a–1b.

[88] SCC (SF, han 60 = ts'e 122), 1a–1b.

[89] *P'ing p'eng ts'ao; Nuphar japonica.*

[90] Waley (1931), 150–152 (no. CXL). Waley adds: "This is the earliest known painting in the style that we later associate with Tibetan art."

[91] Waley (1931), 265 (no. CDXLIV [in Delhi]).

[92] Figure in Field Museum, Chicago.

[93] TPKC, 409, 8a–8b.

[94] CSS, in SF, han 106 (= ts'e 212), 14a.

[95] Van Gulik (1954), 121–123. This nephew, who was actually a Taoist, met the great poet more than once. Van Gulik (1954), 136–137.

[96] YYTT, 19, 157. Cf. Van Gulik (1954), 135. Van Gulik says that "His method of treating the roots of trees with dyes was followed in China until recent years." He believes that the part about the purple characters was ". . . an embellishment added by the narrator."

[97] Bostok and Riley (1856), 317.

[98] Cox (1945), 80. Cox includes these among such other Chinese plants, worthy of special investigation, as the "Peaches of Pekin, cultivated in the Emperor's garden and weighing 2 lbs."

[99] *Colchicum* sp., of the family Melanthaceae.

[100] TFYK, 970, 11b–12a; THY, 100, 1796. Both texts contain errors, which are fortunately easily corrected by mutual comparison. "Kashmir" is **g'ia-siĕt-piĕt,* placed between Kapiśa and Gandhāra in THY, and must register a form like **Kashpir.*

[101] Soothill and Hodous (1937), 265.

[102] Beal (1885), I, 54.

[103] THY, 99, 1776; the year is here given erroneously as 648. Cf. THY, 100, 1796; TFYK, 970, 11b.

[104] Davidson (1954), pl. 26.

[105] Soothill and Hodous (1937), 156.

[106] *Shui lien.*

[107] PHL (TTTS, 7), 71b. YYTT, 19, 159, also has a note on this flower. Li Shih-chen thought it akin to the spatterdock; see PTKM, 19, 3b.

CHAPTER VIII (Pages 133–138)

[1] *Dalbergia hupeana.*

[2] Ch'en Ts'ang-ch'i, quoted in PTKM, 35a, 37a; 36, 46a; and 34, 29a.

[3] Li Ho, "Li P'ing k'ung-hou yin," LCCKS, 1, 1b, and commentary by Wang Ch'i; also "Chui ho Liu Yün," LCCKS, 1, 11a.

[4] Mosaku Ishida and Wada (1954), no. 131.

[5] *Kuang-lang (Arenga sacchariſera).*

[6] *Pan chu,* probably *Phyllostachys puberula* var. *boryana.* This variety grows in central China, and I am not certain that the Annamese kind, here referred to, is the same.

[7] *Shōsōin* (1928–), 38–42.

[8] TS, 43a, 3733a.

CHAPTER VIII (*Continued*)

[9] *Shōsōin* (1928-), 38-42.

[10] Gernet (1956), 19.

[11] Li Ho, "Kuei chu cheng hsing yüeh," LCCKS, 2, 18b.

[12] Su Kung, quoted in PTKM, 34, 28b.

[13] *Pterocarpus indicus*. Burkill (1935), 1830.

[14] *Pterocarpus dalbergoides*. Burkill (1935), 1829.

[15] *Pterocarpus santalinus*. Burkill (1935), 1832-1833. *Pterocarpus marsupium* is another useful Indian sanders.

[16] Yule and Burnell (1903), 789-790.

[17] Schafer (1957), 131.

[18] Schafer (1957), 131. Cf. Li Ho, "Kan ch'un," LCCKS, 3, 23a, and especially Wang Ch'i's eighteenth-century commentary.

[19] Mosaku Ishida and Wada (1954), pl. 1 (in color). In Japanese publications sanders is called *shitan*, i.e., "purple rosewood."

[20] Mosaku Ishida and Wada (1954), pl. 31.

[21] Ishida and Wada (1954), pls. 2, 20, 37, 39, 94.

[22] YHTC, 4, 30.

[23] LCC (SF, han 78 = ts'e 157, 2a). This source is of about A.D. 1000.

[24] Kuan-hsiu, "Shu shih pi ch'an chü wu pi," ChTS, han 12, ts'e 3, ch. 12, 15b.

[25] FSYL, 10, 146.

[26] Burkill (1935), 753-756.

[27] Gershevitch (1957), 317-320; Burkill (1935), 753.

[28] Ch'en Ts'ang-ch'i, quoted in PTKM, 35b, 41b. Cf. Schafer (1957), 132.

[29] Schafer (1957), 132. Readers of some Japanese publications should beware of interpeting the characters for *hua-lü*, "flowered lü," as referring to the Hainanese rosewood, as they do in medieval China. Mosaku Ishida and Wada (1954), for instance on p. 68, use these same graphs to represent the Japanese word *karin*, "Japanese quince" (*Chaenomeles* sp.). Therefore articles in the Shōsōin described as made of *karin* ("*hua-lü*") may not be made of rosewood.

[30] *Santalum album*. The Malay name *chĕndana* (Sanskrit *candana*) is also applied to *Pterocarpus santalinus*, a relative of red sanders, and Malay *chĕndana puteh*, "white sandal," is sometimes used for the wood of *Eurycoma*; "yellow sandal," however, is always the true *Santalum*. Burkill (1935), 1953-1955.

[31] Other species of *Santalum* grow in Australasia and Oceania.

[32] Quoted in PTKM, 34, 28b.

[33] Burkill (1935), 1956.

[34] Yamada (1957), 405, states that, up to T'ang, India was the chief source, but, beginning in Sung, the Flores Archipelago, especially Timor, supplied China with most of her imports. Nonetheless, the T'ang evidence is ambiguous; perhaps it should be regarded as a period of transition, or of universal trade.

[35] CTS, 197, 3610a. Paul Wheatley (private communication) thinks it may be in Borneo.

[36] In PTKM, 34, 28b.

[37] From the eleventh century. Huard and Wong (1958), 59.

[38] Burkill (1935), 1955.

[39] Li Shih-chen (PTKM, 34, 28b) states that all the chiefs of the various Southwestern barbarians in his time plastered their bodies with it.

[40] LYC, quoted in PTKM, 34, 28b.

[41] Hackmann (1951-54), 30.

[42] Hackmann (1951-54), 30.

[43] CS, 8, 1095c.

[44] Schafer (1957), 130.

[45] Schafer (1957), 130.

[46] Takakusu (1928), 466.

[47] Reischauer (1955a), 213.

[48] YYTT, 3, 32.

[49] Schafer (1951a), *passim*, reconstructs the history of this custom.

[50] Mosaku Ishida and Wada (1954), pl. 74. It is curious that objects of sandalwood are very rare in the Shōsōin collection, in contrast to those of sanders, which are abundantly represented.

[51] Li Po, "Tseng Seng Hsing-jung," LTPWC, 11, 7a.

[52] YYTT, 1, 3; TCTC, 216, 8b.

[53] TCTC, 252, 6a; Po (1937), 49.

[54] Reischauer (1955), 255.

[55] Wei Ch'an, "Yüeh lu Tao-lin szu," ChTS, han 9, ts'e 3, 4b-5a.

[56] ChTS, han 11, ts'e 10, chi nü, 8b. I take *t'an k'ou*, literally "rosewood mouth," to stand for "*candana* mouth."

[57] Burkill (1935), 826-832. These trees also contain hydrocyanic acid, widely used as a fish poison. Burkill lists twenty-six species, of which the best is usually considered to be the unstreaked black of *Diospyros ebenum* of south India and Ceylon.

[58] KCC, in PTKM, 35b, 41b. Burkill (1935), 826, states wrongly that ebony is not mentioned in early Chinese literature, before Sung and Yüan. See also Pelliot (1959), 101–102.

[59] TTCLC, p. 3. The author's *floruit* is 1180–1240.

[60] Mosaku Ishida and Wada (1954), pls. 65 and 81.

[61] Ishida and Wada (1954), pl. 65, note.

CHAPTER IX (Pages 139–154)

[1] Yamada (1957), 2, discusses this problem. He uses the term *kōyaku*, "aromatics/drugs," for perfumes, spices, and medicines collectively.

[2] Yamada (1957), 4 ff., discusses all these things.

[3] Yamada (1957), 4.

[4] Takakusu (1896), 137.

[5] YHTC, 6, 44; 7, 49.

[6] LPLI, b, 11.

[7] Schafer (1952), 161.

[8] *Scirpus tuberosus.* SLPT, in CLPT, 23, 24a.

[9] These are only a few examples from many which appear in the tribute lists of TS "ti li chih."

[10] Variety of *Zizyphus vulgaris.*

[11] *Alhagi maurorum.*

[12] Called "flat peach pits" in Chinese, but the Persian name *bādām* was also known in China. See Laufer (1919), 405–409.

[13] TS, 40, 3727a–3727b, for the Central Asiatic contributions, TS, 43a, 3733a, for the Annamese. See also Su Kung in PTKM, 31, 14a, for the betel (*Areca catechu*) of Annam.

[14] TLT, 18, 17a.

[15] TLT, 11, 9b.

[16] Ling (1958), *passim.*

[17] Meng Shen, in PTKM, 25, 24a.

[18] CTS, 197, 3609d.

[19] CTS, 197, 3610a.

[20] CTS, 198, 3611d.

[21] PTKM, 33, 20b; YYTT, 18, 148.

[22] YYTT, 18, 148.

[23] T'ao Hung-ching, quoted in PTKM, 33, 20b.

[24] It has also been suggested that Chin. *b'uo-dâu,* "grape," may be cognate to Gk. *bótrys,* "bunch of grapes." Ishida Mikinosuke (1948), 246. However, Chmielewski (1958),

35–38, reasonably derives the loan-word from a hypothetical Farghanian *bādaga,* related to Khotanese Saka *bātaa,* "wine." A better Greek relationship appears in Athenaios (*ca.* A.D. 200): *batiákē,* "Persian word for 'cup.'"

[25] Laufer (1919), 223.

[26] TS, 40, 3727a.

[27] TFYK, 970, 11b; THY, 100, 1796; Laufer (1919), 232.

[28] YYTT, 18, 149; PTKM, 33, 20b.

[29] The texts of the poems appear in ChTS, han 11, ts'e 10, chi nü, 8a–9a.

[30] THY, 100, 1796–1797; Laufer (1919), 247.

[31] TLCCFK, 1, 25a.

[32] HCLC, 9, 29.

[33] Ishida Mikinosuke (1948), 248. The line is by Po Chü-i. HHPT, 17, 243, makes Kansu, especially the Tun-huang region, the most important grape-producing area.

[34] ChIL, a, 42b.

[35] SLPT, in PTKM, 33, 21a.

[36] Tu Fu, "Yü mu," CCCCTS, p. 323.

[37] As in the Tun-huang wedding song, in Waley (1960), 196.

[38] YTCWC, quoted in Harada (1939), 62. *Ch'i pao,* "seven gems," is an old term with Buddhist associations; it is read *shippō* in modern Japanese, and means "cloisonné." The term occurs frequently in medieval Chinese literature for some kind of many-colored jewel-like ornamentation. In view of the astonishing cloisonné-backed mirror in the Shōsōin, which is hard to explain away, the name seems to stand for a primitive kind of enamel work in the Chinese tradition, before the well-known introduction of Western enamel technology in about the fourteenth century. Molten colored glass was, in this pre-T'ang and T'ang technique, dripped into the cloisons and fixed by an adhesive; Blair (1960), 83–93. For an ingenious idea of how champlevé technique might have originated in a T'ang pottery technique, see Davis (1960), 650.

[39] ChIL, b, 37a.

[40] THY, 100, 1796–1797.

[41] Quoted in TPYL, 845, 6a.

[42] Hsiang (1933), 47.

[43] Hsiang (1933), 48. Hsiang accepts the genuineness of this wine.

[44] TFYK, 971, 7b.

[45] TS, 2, 3637c.

[46] TFYK, 970, 12b; THY, 100, 1796–1797.

CHAPTER IX (*Continued*)

There is also a report of a gift of frozen wine from Qočo. The implications of this, which might have some reference to the manufacture of brandy, are not clear. See Laufer (1919), 233, discussing a quotation from *Liang szu kung chi* in TPYL, 845, 5b–6a.

[47] TFYK, 168, 11b, notes the cessation of the tribute, no doubt temporarily, early in 837.

[48] Sampson (1869), 50–54. The original text will be found in LMTWC, 9, 5a–5b. It may be worth noting that CSS, by the pseudo-"Camel Kuo" (in SF, 212, 7a–7b), which we have noted in connection with blue lotuses (p. 130) has an interesting discussion of viticulture in which it also recommends the application of a rice liquor to the roots of the grapevine to improve the quality of the fruit. If not actually a T'ang book, then, CSS preserves some T'ang techniques.

[49] TPT and SPT quoted in CLPT, 23, 10b–11a. The vine is *Vitis thunbergii*.

[50] "South of Pei-ch'iu [Shell Mound]," an ancient place in that province.

[51] YYTT, 18, 148–149.

[52] TFYK, 971, 15b.

[53] The pharmacologist Hsiao Ping tells of black six-cornered myrobalans brought by "Persian argosies," but his assertion is listed in PTKM, 35b, 39a, under the Sino-Sanskrit name for chebulic myrobalans, which are five-cornered. A mistake has been made somewhere, possibly by Li Shih-chen.

[54] Yule and Burnell (1903), 607–610; Wayman (1954), 64.

[55] Laufer (1915a), 275–276. For Sanskrit *haritakī*, "chebulic myrobalan," Laufer gives Tocharian **arirāk*, and for Sanskrit *vibhītakī*, "belleric myrobalan," he gives Tocharian **virirāk*. Both these reconstructions are based on the Chinese **χâ-liei-lək* or **χâ-lji-lək*, and **bji-lji-lək*. Unfortunately he does not give a Tocharian form for Chinese **·â-ma-lək* or **·âm-muâ-lək* (Sanskrit *āmalakī*); presumably it would be **amalāk*. Ch'en Ts'ang-ch'i (in PTKM, 31, 13b) registers the Chinese transcription of still another name of this last of the three, apparently Indic. There was also what appears to be a native Chinese name *yü kan*, "sweetness of the excess," explained by Ch'en Ts'ang-ch'i as meaning that, though the emblic myrobalans taste bitter at first, they seem sweet later. It is this name which

is given in the notice of tribute from Turgäch *et al.*, above.

[56] Wayman (1954), 64. The Chinese name, presumably of Tocharian origin if Laufer's argument can be extended, is easily confused with **am-la*, from Sanskrit *āmra*, "mango," and indeed Asahina (1955), 491, makes the mistake of taking the former for the latter; this same source also confuses the chebulic with the belleric myrobalan.

[57] The three are *Phyllanthus emblica*, *Terminalia bellerica*, and *T. chebula*. Actually there are a considerable number of tropical trees which belong to this group, all characteristically having tannin in their tissues, which accounts for the stringent taste of the fruits. Burkill (1935), 2134–2135.

[58] Burkill (1935), 2135.

[59] Wayman (1954), 67.

[60] Burkill (1935), 2135.

[61] Quoted in PTKM, 31, 13b.

[62] Quoted in PTKM, 35b, 39a. See also Huard and Wong (1958), 56.

[63] Takakusu (1928), 466.

[64] Asahina (1955), 491 and 494.

[65] Quoted in PTKM, 31, 13b.

[66] Quoted in PTKM, 31, 13b.

[67] KSP (TTTS, 4), 56b. Cf. Hsiang (1933), 47.

[68] YP, 62a–67b.

[69] Pao Chi, "Pao ping hsien Li Li pu tseng ho-li-le yeh," ChTS, han 3, ts'e 9, 4a.

[70] TFYK, 970, 12a; THY, 100, 1796 and 1789. See Laufer (1919), 392–398, for discussion. The characterization of Nepal is Hsüan-tsang's; see Beal (1885), II, 80–81.

[71] Li Shih-chen, in PTKM, 27, 34a.

[72] Quoted in PTKM, 27, 34a.

[73] TFYK, 970, 12; THY, 100, 1796.

[74] CSS (SF, ts'e 212, 12a). Laufer (1919), 392, accepts this source as authentically T'ang.

[75] Quoted in PTKM, 16, 22a.

[76] See remarks of Li Shih-chen in PTKM, 16, 22a.

[77] TFYK, 970, 12a; THY, 100, 1796. TFYK has "sweet" for THY's "white." A foreign name is given, which Laufer (1919), 303–304, equates with Middle Persian *gandena*, possibly "shallot," but Laufer's translation is inaccurate in several respects.

[78] TFYK, 970, 12a; THY, 100, 1796; Laufer (1919), 401. Laufer's speculations about the antiquity of chicory in China seem aside from the point. There is a "bitter leaf vegetable"

(that is, lettuce) which is old in China; see PTKM, 27, 35b. A Chinese-Sanskrit vocabulary gives *kākamāci* as the Indian equivalent, which Pelliot identifies as *Solanum indicum.* Bagchi (1929), 88 and 301.

[79] TFYK, 970, 12a; THY, 100, 1796. Laufer (1919), 400–402, has various suggestions for its identity, none of which seem to be provable.

[80] TFYK, 970, 12a; THY, 100, 1796; Laufer (1919), 402. The latter suggests garden celery or parsley.

[81] TFYK, 971, 15b; Ch'en Ts'ang-ch'i, quoted in PTKM, 18b, 46b.

[82] Laufer (1919), 399–400.

[83] *Pinus koraiensis.*

[84] Li Hsün, quoted in PTKM, 31, 14a; Hsiao Ping, quoted in the same place.

[85] Laufer (1919), 247–250 and 410–414.

[86] Ch'en Ts'ang-ch'i, in PTKM, 30, 11b.

[87] Li Hsün, in PTKM, 30, 11b. See Laufer for possible etymologies of the transcribed Persian names.

[88] YYTT, 19, 160. Laufer (1919), 270, mentions this plant but does not attempt to identify it.

[89] Laufer (1919), 414–419, based on YYTT, 18, 152.

[90] *Canarium album* and *C. pimela.*

[91] Ch'en Ts'ang-ch'i, in PTKM, 26, 33b. Laufer (1919), 383, thinks it was cummin, but I rely on Yamada (1957), 468, and other recent authorities.

[92] Laufer (1919), 383–384.

[93] Quoted in PTKM, 26, 33b.

[94] TFYK, 971, 12a. The word here translated "pickled meat" is *la,* which has that meaning in Sung times; here I assume that it already had it in T'ang.

[95] *Mugil cephalus,* a kind of "gray mullet," which is entirely distinct from the "red mullet." The Chinese word is *tzu.*

[96] Perhaps also in the Yangtze. "Mullet skins," use unknown, were sent to the court as local tribute from Soochow. TS, 41, 3728a.

[97] TFYK, 971, 8a.

[98] LPLI, b, 17.

[99] TFYK, 971, 12b.

[100] Chinese *k'un-pu,* but apparently not a Chinese word. It is not clear if Ainu *kompo,* the form I have used, is a loan word or a native. See Ramstedt (1949), 123. This seaweed will be discussed in the section on "Seaweeds" in chap. xi.

[101] Quoted in PTKM, 46, 38a.

[102] I owe this identification to Mr. Gari Ledyard.

[103] *Zanthoxylum* sp.

[104] Burkill (1935), 2284–2285.

[105] *Zanthoxylum piperitum.*

[106] Chen Ch'üan, quoted in PTKM, 32, 16b.

[107] YYTT, 18, 148.

[108] Su Kung, in PTKM, 32, 16b.

[109] Yamada (1957), 22–23.

[110] See articles *chiao chü,* "fagara wine," and *chiao hsü,* "fagara holy rice/holy wine," in any standard encyclopedic dictionary. I observe the use of fagara wine at New Year's both in Han and Sung, straddling our period.

[111] Yamada (1957), 22–23.

[112] So says YHCC, as quoted in PWYF, p. 771b, and in TuSCC, article on peppers, ts'ao mu, 250. But I am unable to check the original of the quotation. There is a (T'ang) *Yeh hou wai chuan* in SF, 113 (ts'e 225), and in KCSH, but without the present passage.

[113] Untitled poem in ChTS, han 12, ts'e 1, p. 21b.

[114] Han Yü, "Ch'u nan shih i Yüan Shih-pa hsieh lü," HCLC, 2 (ch. 6), 69.

[115] In addition to the identifiable peppers imported during T'ang, note should be taken of an "acrid-smelling drug" among the strange plants sent from Nepal in 647. It is described thus: in appearance it is like the orchid; it is green in frozen winter; it is gathered and dried and made into a powder; it tastes like Kuei fagara; its root can cure diseases of the "breath." TFYK, 970, 12a; THY, 100, 1796. This may have been a pepper.

[116] Sanskrit "pepper." Our text has *muâi-lji-tsię,* possibly from a feminine form in *-ī.*

[117] YYTT, 18, 152.

[118] Burkill (1935), 1746–1751.

[119] Burkill (1935), 1746–1751.

[120] Laufer (1919), 374.

[121] Su Kung, in PTKM, 32, 17b.

[122] Laufer (1919), 374.

[123] TS, 145, 3994d.

[124] Burkill (1935), 2285.

[125] SLPT, quoted in PTKM, 32, 17b.

[126] Li Hsün, quoted in PTKM, 32, 17b.

[127] *Piper longum = Chavica roxburghii.*

[128] Transcribed *piĕt-puât-lji.* YYTT, 18, 152, gives this name, and also one purporting to be Roman.

CHAPTER IX (*Continued*)

[129] See Burkill (1935), 1744–1745, for other Indic names.

[130] Burkill (1935), 1746–1751. There is also a Javanese long pepper (*Piper retrofractum*), which is more pungent than either Indian long pepper or black pepper and is important in pickling, making curries, and in medicine. Much is exported to China; Burkill (1935), 1751–1752. We may readily suppose that this species came to medieval China as well, under the same name as the Indian species.

[131] Burkill (1935), 1744–1745.

[132] YYTT, 18, 152.

[133] Su Kung, quoted in PTKM, 14, 37a.

[134] Su Sung, quoted in PTKM, 14, 37a.

[135] Ch'en Ts'ang-ch'i, quoted in PTKM, 14, 37a.

[136] TTSL, quoted in PTKM, 14, 37a.

[137] *Piper betle* or *Chavica betel*.

[138] Burkill (1935), 1737–1742. See Penzer (1952), 187–300, for much betel lore. The best chewing leaves are those on upper branches; the lower ones are inferior and are used primarily for medicine. The flavor is improved by bleaching the leaves in the sun.

[139] Penzer (1952), 274.

[140] Su Kung and SLPT in PTKM, 14, 37a.

[141] Li Hsün, quoted in PTKM, 14, 37a.

[142] Quoted in PTKM, 14, 37a.

[143] *Piper cubeba*. The unripe berries are dried for use.

[144] Ch'en Ts'ang-ch'i, quoted in PTKM, 32, 17b. Su Sung (quoted in PTKM, 32, 17b) says it was grown in the Canton region in the eleventh century.

[145] Yamada (1959), 139.

[146] Burkill (1935), 1743–1744.

[147] The Sanskrit word is applied to *Emelia ribes*. Laufer (1915b), 282 ff.

[148] Quoted in PTKM, 32, 17b.

[149] Ch'en Ts'ang-ch'i, in PTKM, 32, 18a. Cubeb stimulates the mucous membrane of the genitourinary tract, and can be used as a diuretic; it was used as an aphrodisiac in sixteenth-century Goa. Burkill (1935), 1743–1744.

[150] *Brassica juncea*. Burkill (1935), 358–363, tells of this and other oriental mustards. *B. nigra* is our table mustard.

[151] *Brassica* (= *Sinapis*) *alba*. Burkill (1935), 358–363, states that this "extends as a weed to China."

[152] SPT, quoted in PTKM, 26, 29b.

[153] Ch'en Ts'ang-ch'i, in PTKM, 26, 29b. Cf. Laufer (1919), 380.

[154] Sun Szu-miao, quoted in PTKM, 26, 29b.

[155] TS, 40, 3726a.

[156] TS, 41, 3727b, and 41, 3728a.

[157] Chen Ch'üan, quoted in PTKM, 39, 5a.

[158] Su Kung, quoted in PTKM, 39, 4b. The pharmacopoeia calls this "earth honey" and sometimes also "stone honey," i.e., "honey taken from among the stones." Unfortunately "stone honey" also meant "stonelike honey," i.e., hard sugar cakes—a source of abundant confusion. See below.

[159] Shih Sheng-han (1958), 77–79.

[160] Burkill (1935), 1932–1933.

[161] Burkill (1935), 1925.

[162] JCSP, 6, 48–49.

[163] Local tribute from these regions; see TS, 40, 3725c; 41, 3728c; 42, 3729d–3730d. The tribute from Szechwan is actually called "cane sugar," as if the sugar had been extracted before submission.

[164] JCSP, 2, 19. Hung Mai, from the vantage point of Sung, discusses historical examples of the high value of cane sugar in the north, and cites this as an instance.

[165] Soothill and Hodous (1937), 195.

[166] TS, 222b, 4160d.

[167] See NFTMC.

[168] PTKM, 33, 21b. They were called [*suan*]-*ni t'ang*.

[169] TS, 39, 3723c.

[170] TS, 41, 3728b.

[171] TS, 41, 3729b.

[172] Su Kung, in CLPT, 20, 3a.

[173] Su Kung, in PTKM, 33, 21b.

[174] Meng Shen, in PTKM, 33, 21b; SPT, in CLPT, 23, 28a. Su Kung regards the cakes of the south as superior to those of Szechwan, and imperial preference supports him. But Meng Shen regards those made in Szechwan and Persia with cane sugar as the best.

[175] TS, 221b, 4153d; TFYK, 971, 19a.

[176] TS, 221b, 4153d.

[177] TFYK, 970, 12a–12b; THY, 100, 1796.

[178] An Indic form *gunu* (Sanskrit *guḍa*) appears as its equivalent in a T'ang vocabulary. Bagchi (1929), 90.

[179] Burkill (1935), 1934.

[180] Burkill (1935), 1935, states that the Arabs produced a refined sugar in the seventh century.

[181] It was also called *t'ang ping*, "sugar ice," in Sung.

[182] This story is given by Hung Mai in JCSP, 6, 49. I owe much of the immediately preceding account of the history of sugar refining in China to the ideas of Hung Mai. Cf. Shida (1957), 126.

CHAPTER X (Pages 155–175)

[1] Yamada (1957), 22, thinks that, whatever the use of incenses in the Far East, little use is made of perfumes for the body as compared with the West. He ascribes this to the fact that the Mongoloid races gave comparatively little body odor, and in medieval times remarked repeatedly the strong odor of the Caucasians of Turkestan. But, in fact, the ancient and medieval Chinese used scents on their persons abundantly.

[2] TCTC, 225, 5a.

[3] CTS, 18b, 3130b.

[4] TCTC, 220, 3a. Commentary of Hu San-hsing on a "table of aromatics" used at a levee in 757. Cf. TS, 23a, 3678c–3678d. The table carried *hsün lu*, "censing braziers."

[5] MCPT, 1, 5.

[6] CTW, 288, 7b.

[7] "Washing legumes" is a soaplike preparation, using peas as a base. Shao Shuo, "Wei Kuo ling kung hsieh la jih szu hsiang yao piao," CTW, 452, 12b.

[8] TCTC, 215, 5b.

[9] Pelliot (1904), 231, n. 2; Coedès (1948), 89; Wang Gungwu (1958), 68; Wheatley (1961a), 32 ff.

[10] TuT, 188, 1009c and 1010c.

[11] Soothill and Hodous (1937), 319.

[12] KYTPIS (TTTS, 3), 70a.

[13] See the poem of Han Wo (tenth century) in praise of baths ("Yung yü"), in ChTS, han 10, ts'e 7, 4, 5b.

[14] ChIL, b, 59a.

[15] ChIL, a, 37a. "Bramble" (*Rubus rosifolius*, or *R. commersonii*) is *t'u-mi*, and "magnolia" (*Magnolia fuscata*) is *han hsiao*. I cannot identify the substance named *szu chüeh*, tentatively translated "four exceptions." It is referred to elsewhere in ChIL (b, 61b) as a Chinese incense, along with *san yün*, "three equal portions."

[16] KYTPIS (TTTS, 3), 40b.

[17] TYTP (TTTS, 2), 33b.

[18] KYTPIS (TTTS, 3), 47a.

[19] From Sanskrit *rasa-mālā*, "perfumed garland." Yule and Burnell (1903), 770.

[20] The famous "aromatic of Ling-ling" (*Ling-ling hsiang*), apparently an especially fragrant variety of *Ocimum basilicum* (*lo-le*), perhaps developed locally. But there is a possibility that it was *Ocimum sanctum,* the "sacred basil," devoted to Vishnu, which is widespread in tropical Asia.

[21] TLT, 20, 18a–18b.

[22] *Cymbopogon* (= *Andropogon*) *nardus,* or a closely related species. "Lemon grass" is one of the "floss grasses" called *mao* in Chinese. "White floss grass" was imported from Annam, and was apparently a distinct variety. See article in PTKM, 14, 40a.

[23] Ch'en Ts'ang-ch'i and Li Hsün, quoted in PTKM, 14, 40a.

[24] Ch'en Ts'ang-ch'i, in PTKM, 51a, 31a.

[25] TFYK, 971, 10a–10b.

[26] TFYK, 971, 5b.

[27] CTS, 198, 3614b.

[28] In China, as contrasted with usage elsewhere, some aromatic imports, such as myrrh, were regarded more as medicines than as incenses and perfumes. See Yamada (1957), 25. Huard and Wong (1958), 58, observe a correspondence between the five principal perfumes of Muslim Spain (musk, camphor, aloeswood, ambergris, and saffron) and the five aromatic drugs of Asia, including China. But the correspondence cannot be maintained; ambergris played only a slight role in Chinese medicine, and the part of saffron was minor.

[29] TFYK, 972, 7a; CTS, 15, 3111b. Readers interested in the medieval names of incenses, spices, and the like are referred to the *Suvarṇa-prabhāsa-sūtra*, translated by I-ching as *Chin kuang ming ching*. It gives the names, synoptically in Chinese and Sanskrit, of thirty-two substances used in a ritual apotropaic bath. See TSDZK, XVI, no. 665, p. 435.

[30] Po (1937), 48–49.

[31] ChIL, b, 61b.

[32] *Paradise Lost*, IV, line 248.

[33] *Hsien shu.* YYTT, 18, 148.

[34] PTKM, 14, 40b.

[35] *Derniers Refuges* (1956), XII, 131. The Egyptians also used a long-handled censer. We shall see this in use in medieval China. Is it possible that a whole complex of incense-culture was transmitted eastward from the ancient Near East?

[36] Yamada (1957), 26; HHPT, 12, 108–109.

[37] HP, b, 28.

CHAPTER X (*Continued*)

38 *Po ho hsiang.* The term appears in a couplet in an "Old Poem" (*ku shih*), where it is described as a blend of saffron, storax, and thoroughwort.

39 "Chi shih," CCCCTS, p. 430.

40 Ch'üan Te-yü, "Ku yüeh fu," ChTS, han 5, ts'e 8, ch. 9, 3b.

41 Yamada (1957), 336 and 361.

42 TFYK, 971, 6a; THY, 99, 1773; TS, 221b, 4154d. TFYK says "three hundred"; THY and TFYK say "Western (*hu*) drugs." The Chinese transcription is *kân-d'â-b'uâ-lâ.* *Gandhabhala* leads nowhere, but *gandhaphala* is a well-established word. Chavannes (1903), 158, mistook **b'uâ* for **sâ,* which led him to some vain speculations about an "essence de parfum" which "peut être Gandhasâra."

43 KYTPIS, 3, 71a.

44 Po (1937), 49.

45 Yü Chien-wu, "Feng ho ch'un yeh ying ling," YTCC, 29b.

46 Wang Chien, "Hsiang yin," ChTS, han 5, ts'e 5, ch. 5, 2a. Cf. HP, b, 22, which describes "hundred graduations incense" and "incense seal-characters" of the Sung dynasty.

47 ChIL, b, 59a.

48 Yamada (1957), 330, and see *Shôsôin* (1928), XI, pls. 22–26, 27–31.

49 Tuan Ch'eng-shih, "Tseng chu shang jen lien chü," TSPMCCC, ts'e 25, 4b.

50 Li Ho, "Shen hsien," LCCKS, 4, 21a–22a.

51 KYTPIS (TTTS, 3), 54b. See n. 38 in chap. ix above for the "Seven Jewels." These braziers were called *po shan lu.* They were once thought to be a Han invention, but it now appears that they go back to Chou times; we have a bronze example, richly decorated with gems, from about the fifth to third century B.C.; Wenley (1948), 8. A more general name for incense braziers was *hsiang lu,* or *hsün lu,* "censing braziers."

52 CYCT, 3, 37.

53 For example, Hsü Yin, "Hsiang ya," ChTS, ts'e 1, 1, 3a, which has "hundred blend" smoking in its mouth.

54 See, for instance, Li Ho's poems "Kung wa ko," LCCKS, 2, 22b, and "Ch'a tseng," LCCKS, 3, 21a. Also the commentary of Wang Ch'i. Or Wen T'ing-yün, "Ch'ang-an szu," ChTS, han 9, ts'e 5, 3, 2a. There are flat-bottomed circular bowls used as incense braziers, kept in the Shōsōin. They are made

of white marble and of bronze. See *Shôsôin* (1928), VII, pls. 26–30. I do not know the Chinese name for these.

55 Li Shang-yin, "Shao hsiang ch'ü," ChTS, han 8, ts'e 9, ch. 3, 34a.

56 Yamada (1957), 328–329. See Le Coq (1925), fig. 14, for a long-handled bronze censer from Central Asia of the second century; Le Coq compares it with Egyptian types. Long-handled censers are shown in a Tun-huang painting found by Aurel Stein, and in the hands of Lohans at the Lung-men and T'ien-lung-shan caves.

57 Yamada (1957), 328–329; *Shôsôin* (1928), XI, pls. 32–37.

58 Yamada (1957), 329–330; *Shôsôin* (1928), III, pls. 43–47, and VII, pls. 23–25. Yamada traces these back to the *Hsi ching tsa chi,* which says that they were made by a Han artisan. "Censing baskets" are *hsün lung* in Chinese.

59 Wang Chien, "Kung tz'u," ChTS, han 5, ts'e 5, ch. 6, 4a; another appears on p. 9a of this same series.

60 *Yün hsi yu i,* quoted in Po (1937), 48.

61 TPT, in CLPT, 9, 36a.

62 Po (1937), 48.

63 Untitled poem in ChTS, han 12, ts'e 1, 17b.

64 Chang Hsiao-p'iao, "Shao nien hsing," ChTS, han 8, ts'e 4, 8a.

65 TLT, 22, 14b.

66 TS, 76, 3869b. There is also a poem on this theme by Chang Hu, "T'ai-chen hsiang nang-tzu," ChTS, han 8, ts'e 5, ch. 2, 18b. This ninth-century poet wrote many poems about the reign of Hsüan Tsung, on such subjects as musical instruments, songs, festivals, and dances (including several on the Chāch dance). Hung Mai, in JCSP, 9, 89, remarks on the importance of this writer for preserving information on these customs.

67 See Mosaku Ishida and Wada (1954), and Yamada (1957), 490–491.

68 For example, in Chang Hu, "P'ei Fan hsüan ch'eng pei lou yeh yen," ChTS, han 8, ts'e 5, ch. 1, 10b. It is also thought that little lidded caskets in the Shōsōin were boxes for aromatics. See Yamada (1957), 330.

69 Yule and Burnell (1903), 335.

70 Chiefly *Aquilaria agallocha* of Indochina; among others are *A. malaccensis* (Malaya), *A. moszkowskii* (Sumatra), and *A. grandiflora* (Hainan). Species of genus *Gonystylus*

(Borneo and Sumatra) afford substitutes for the real thing. Burkill (1935), 198–201.

[71] Burkill (1935), 197–199.

[72] TuT, quoted in CLPT, 12, 48b.

[73] Ch'en Ts'ang-ch'i, quoted in PTKM, 34, 27b. Cf. Su Kung, quoted in same place. Another variety was named "*dẓ'an* aromatic"; see TuT, quoted in CLPT, 12, 48b.

[74] Hourani (1951), 63.

[75] TS, 43a, 3731a.

[76] It was also submitted by Huan-*chou* in Annam. TS, 43a, 3733a.

[77] TFYK, 971, 17a; this was in 749. See also TFYK, 971, 10b (for 734) and THY, 98, 1751.

[78] Aymonier (1891), 276–280.

[79] Li Hsün, quoted in PTKM, 34, 27b. Cf. Huard and Wong (1958), 59.

[80] Burkill (1935), 198, refers to the medicinal use of aloes incense in early medieval India.

[81] Sauvaget (1948), 16.

[82] Li Ho, "Kuei kung tzu yeh lan ch'ü," LCCKS, 1, 12b.

[83] YHTC, 1, 7. The same women of whom we have already reported that they put saffron oil in their hair.

[84] Po (1937), 49, quoting CYCT, 3, 37.

[85] *Abrus precatorius.* Mosaku Ishida and Wada (1954), no. 51.

[86] Ishida and Wada (1954), no. 52.

[87] His name is given as Li Shu-sa, partly or wholly, it seems, a transcription from a foreign tongue.

[88] TS, 78, 3871d; TCTC, 243, 8b; Po (1937), 52. The reproof came from Li Han, a member of the imperial family.

[89] HP, b, 21; KYTPIS, 3, 71a.

[90] Burkill (1935), 202.

[91] Burkill (1935), 754–755; Schafer (1957), 134. The plant is *Dalbergia parviflora.*

[92] Li Hsün, quoted in PTKM, 34, 28b.

[93] Schafer (1947), 134.

[94] Ts'ao T'ang (ninth century), "Sung Liu tsun shih chih chao ch'üeh t'ing," ChTS, han 10, ts'e 2, ch. 1, 5b, the third of three.

[95] Li Hsün, quoted in PTKM, 34, 28b.

[96] *Canarium album* or *C. pimela.*

[97] Chinese "*kan-lang* sugar."

[98] TS, 43a, 3731b. The Ancient Chinese version of *trâm* is *tsïäm.*

[99] *Canarium copaliferum.*

[100] The local name is *trâm trăng,* "white kanari."

[101] Crevost (1925), 28; see pp. 28–29 for a complete account of this product.

[102] TPT, quoted in PTKM, 34, 31a.

[103] *Cinnamomun camphora.*

[104] *Dryobalanops aromatica.*

[105] Burkill (1935), 338.

[106] Burkill (1935), 546 and 862–864. See also Han Wai-toon (1941), 3–17, and Penzer (1952), 196. Camphorwood has recently become more valuable in commerce than camphor itself; Burkill (1935), 548 and 864. The tabulation of camphors in Huard and Wong (1958), 59, is so confused as to be worthless.

[107] *P'o-lü kao.*

[108] See Yule and Burnell (1903), 69 and 151–153; Pelliot (1904), 341–342; Hirth and Rockhill (1911), 194; Laufer (1919), 478–479; and especially Pelliot (1912a), 474–475.

[109] YYTT, 18, 150.

[110] Su Kung, in PTKM, 34, 31a.

[111] Li Hsün, in PTKM, 34, 31a. Camphor oil is distilled in modern China. Bryant (1925), 230.

[112] Assuming that P'o-lü is indeed "Baros," and P'o-li is Bali. Su Kung (in PTKM, 34, 31a) gives the former, Tuan Ch'eng-shih (YYTT, 18, 150) gives the latter, apparently in error.

[113] YYTT, 18, 150.

[114] Soothill and Hodous (1937), 335, identifying Hsüan-tsang's transcription, in accordance with Eitel.

[115] TTHYC, ch. 10 (no pagination).

[116] TS, 222c, 4159d. Cf. Burkill (1935), 866: "The Malays use it in the ceremonial purification of a corpse . . . and so do the peoples of Sumatra. The body of a Batak Raja may be preserved in camphor until it is auspicious to bury it."

[117] Dagon is *[Nəu-]d'â-γuân.* CTS, 197, 3610a; TFYK, 970, 11b; THY, 99, 1779.

[118] TS, 221a, 4153c; TFYK, 970, 9b.

[119] TFYK, 971, 5b.

[120] Yule and Burnell (1903), 151–152.

[121] Su Kung, quoted in PTKM, 34, 31a.

[122] YYTT, 1, 2. Another version of the tale, given in TCWC (TTTS, 13), 77a, strikes a less pleasant note: the Consort sent three of her ten pieces to her reputed lover, Rokhshan, by secret camel messenger.

[123] Po (1937), 49, quoting ChIL, b, 35b.

[124] TPT, quoted in PTKM, 34, 31a.

[125] Chang Kao, quoted in PTKM, 34, 31a.

CHAPTER X (*Continued*)

[126] Sen (1945), 85–86.

[127] Schafer (1954), 16 and 78.

[128] ChIL, b, 52b.

[129] ChIL, b, 58a.

[130] *Styrax officinalis.* In Chinese "storax" is *su-ho.*

[131] Ch'en Ts'ang-ch'i, in PTKM, 34, 30b; YYTT, 16, 131.

[132] Ch'en Piao (fl. 831), "Ch'in Wang chüan i," ChTS, han 8, ts'e 4, 2a.

[133] The product of *Altingia excelsa* (= *Liquidambar altingiana*) of Indonesia, and *Altingia gracilipes* of Tongking. Laufer (1919), 456–460; Burkill (1935), 117–118. Ch'en Ts'ang-ch'i distinguished the two substances, but Su Kung, though recognizing that storax came both from the West and from Indonesia, sticks to the description of the hard purple *Styrax.*

[134] *Ti k̲ao.* YP, 62a–67b.

[135] Li Tuan, "Ch'un yu yüeh," ChTS, han 5, ts'e 3, ch. 1, 1a. Here the "palm leaf" is *p'u-k̲'uei* (*Livistona chinensis,* a fan palm).

[136] *An-hsi* (**·ân-si̯ǝk*) *hsiang.*

[137] *Balsamodendron hook̲,* and *B. roxburghii.* Yamada (1954), 14–15; Yamada (1956), 231–232.

[138] *Styrax benzoin.* Laufer (1919), 464–467; Yamada (1954), 2.

[139] Yamada (1954), 7.

[140] Yamada (1954), 7–8.

[141] Yamada (1954), 11–12.

[142] Li Hsün, quoted in PTKM, 34, 30b.

[143] YYTT, 18, 150.

[144] Su Kung, in PTKM, 34, 30b.

[145] Li Hsün, in PTKM, 34, 30b.

[146] *Boswellia carteri* of the Hadramaut. Yamada (1958), 208.

[147] *Boswellia frereana.* Yamada (1956), 208. Related plants of India, *B. serrata* and *B. glabra* produce a false frankincense, used to adulterate the true. Yamada (1956), 231–232.

[148] **K̲i̯uǝn-li̯uk̲.* Boodberg (1937), 359, n. 60.

[149] Bostock and Riley (1855), 127, translating *Historiae Naturalis,* Bk. 12, chap. 32. A modern scholar believes that "teat aromatic" was a name first given to the desirable resin of *Pinus merk̲usii* of Indochina and Indonesia, and later transferred to frankincense; see Wolters (1960), 331 and 333. He also notes that the same name has in modern times been

applied to *Pistacia,* a mastic; Wolters (1960), 324 and 330–331. I do not find the first of these contentions entirely convincing.

[150] *Ling hua fan yü.* YYTT, 2, 12.

[151] Hastings (1927), VII, 200–201.

[152] Su Kung, quoted in PTKM, 34, 29b. My "Mongolia" is, in the text, "the Shan-yü."

[153] Li Hsün, quoted in PTKM, 34, 29b.

[154] Hastings (1927), VII, 200–201.

[155] Takakusu (1928), 462.

[156] YHTC, 8, 62.

[157] Ch'en Ts'ang-ch'i, quoted in PTKM, 34, 29b.

[158] Li Hsün, quoted in PTKM, 34, 29b.

[159] Acker (1954), 244–245.

[160] *Balsamodendron myrrha* and *Commiphora abyssinica.* Yamada (1956), 211.

[161] Hastings (1927), VII, 201; Lucas (1934), 94–95.

[162] Chen Ch'üan, quoted in PTKM, 34, 30a.

[163] Li Hsün, quoted in PTKM, 34, 30a.

[164] So in Arabic; Hebrew has *mōr.* Chinese **mu̯ǝt,* for **mu̯ǝr.* See Laufer (1919), 460–462.

[165] YP, 62a–67b.

[166] See the recipes in HP, ch. b. Cloves are the dried flower buds of *Carophyllus aromaticus* (= *Eugenia aromatica*).

[167] Chinese writers on pharmaceutical matters were not always certain that the two names referred to the same product, though Ch'en Ts'ang-ch'i (PTKM, 34, 28a) considered them simply varietal names. Pharmacologists after him, however, continued to debate this vexed problem. Their identity was definitely proved by Shen K'ua. See MCPT, 26, 175–176.

[168] Li Hsün, quoted in PTKM, 34, 28a.

[169] Su Kung, quoted in PTKM, 34, 28a.

[170] HKI, quoted in TPYL, 981, 6b.

[171] MCPT, 26, 175–176.

[172] So TPT, in PTKM, 34, 28a; cf. Chen Ch'üan in *ibid.*

[173] SP (TTTS, 10), 70a.

[174] YHTC, 3, 19.

[175] Li Hsün, in PTKM, 34, 28a.

[176] Ch'en Ts'ang-ch'i, in PTKM, 34, 28a.

[177] Li Hsün, in PTKM, 34, 28a. Cf. Stuart (1911), 95. But Yamada (1959), 142, thinks "clove bark" is a name for an Indonesian cinnamon, whose oil was also used as a dental anaesthetic. The Chinese pharmacologists, however, treat it as the bark of the tree which produces cloves.

[178] From *Saussurea lappa* (= *Aplotaxis lappa*).

[179] *Mu hsiang*. A T'ang synonym was "blue wood aromatic" (*ch'ing mu hsiang*), but this expression is now used for the rhizome of *Aristolochia contorta*. Laufer (1919), 462–464; Asahina (1955), 498. *Mi hsiang*, "honey aromatic," is sometimes considered a synonym (Li Shih-chen, PTKM, 34, 28a; cf. Hirth and Rockhill [1911], 211), but this was, according to the T'ang pharmacologists, a product of Indochina. Because of the similarity of the name, it has also been confused with myrrh. Laufer (1919), 462–464, says, "The Chinese term, indeed, has no botanical value, being merely a commercial label covering different roots from most diverse regions." I suspect that this was not entirely true, and that we must look for "honey aromatic" among the plants of Southeast Asia. Many modern sources make *mu hsiang* refer to *Rosa banksia* (e.g., Stuart [1911], 43, 49, and 380; Read [1936]), a confused usage already noted by Li Shih-chen in PTKM, 14, 35a.

[180] TS, quoted in TPYL, 982, 1b and 2b; that is, CTS. See also Wheatley (1961), 62.

[181] TS, 221b, 4155a.

[182] Su Kung, quoted in PTKM, 14, 35a.

[183] HP, b, 32, lists a (Sung) recipe conjoining costus root with camphor, musk, cloves, cassia, pepper, and several lesser ingredients. Similar concoctions were probably made in T'ang.

[184] Chen Ch'üan, quoted in PTKM, 14, 35a.

[185] *Pogostemon cablin* is the common patchouli of the Malay peninsula, once cultivated there. *P. heyneanun* of southern India is called "Indian patchouli" but is common in Malaya and may have been introduced thence into south India. Burkill (1935), 1782–1783.

[186] Laufer (1918), 5.

[187] *Huo hsiang*. Other plants now have this name, unhappily for students of history. In Indochina it is applied to betony (*Betonica officinalis*); see Laufer (1918), 35–36. Stuart (1911), 247 (and other modern botanical references) all give giant hyssops (*Agastache rugosa* = *Lophanthus* sp.), but this is an American plant. TuT (quoted in CLPT, 12, 84b) describes a "bean-leaf aromatic" which comes from the rotting wood of a large tree —and sounds very much like aloeswood.

[188] Li Shih-chen quotes a "History of T'ang" (*T'ang shih*), in PTKM, 14, 40b. Cf. Laufer (1918), 29.

[189] Su Sung, quoted in PTKM, 14, 40b.

[190] Hou (1957), 167, notes the presence of "Cantonese patchouli" (*Pogostemon cablin*); this is the common Malayan species.

[191] KC, quoted in PTKM, 14, 40b; NFIWC, quoted in TPYL, 982, 3b.

[192] Laufer (1918), 38.

[193] Burkill (1935), 1780.

[194] Quotations in PTKM, 14, 40b.

[195] *Jasminum officinale*. Yāsaman (actually *ia-sâi-muân*) occurs in CHC. The Arabicized form *yāsmīn* was also current in T'ang, for example, *ia-siĕt-mi^weng*.

[196] *Jasminum sambac*. The transcription is *muât-lji*.

[197] Schafer (1948), 61 ff.

[198] Yamada (1958), 600–601. Yamada has traced a number of stories about the transformation of beautiful princesses into jasmine flowers to Champa and to the Philippines.

[199] CHC, 5a. Cf. Yamada (1958), 593. YYTT, 18, 153, attributes the oil to the Persians in the ninth century. Cf. Schafer (1948), 61.

[200] Laufer (1919), 332–333.

[201] Laufer (1919), 332–333; Schafer (1948), 62.

[202] TFYK, 972, 22a–22b; TPHYC, 179, 17b; CLC (TTTS, 10), 22a; Kuwabara (1930), 130–131.

[203] The text has *ch'in huo*.

[204] ChIL, b, 58b.

[205] YHTC, 6, 46. "Rose" here is *Rosa multiflora* (*ch'iang-wei*), a fragrant white or pink climber; other famous Chinese roses are *R. rugosa* (*mei-kuei*), with pink or magenta flowers, and dense prickly foliage which turns orange in autumn; *R. chinensis* (*yüeh chi*), red, white, or yellow, and very fragrant; and *R. banksia* (*mu hsiang*), a white or yellow climber. See H. L. Li (1959), 92–101.

[206] Li (1959), 96.

[207] Hirth and Rockhill (1911), 204. An endnote seems an appropriate place to bury some unidentified vegetable aromatics. These are all new listings by Ch'en Ts'ang-ch'i, who seems to have had access to specimens and information not available to, or possibly rejected by, the official pharmacologists. These include "*b'ieng* aromatic" (PTKM, 14, 40a),

CHAPTER X (*Continued*)

an herb from the South Seas with anti-demoniac properties, used with ginger and mustard in baths; "*kɐng* aromatic" from the Wakhsh (Oxus) country (PTKM, 14, 40a), with the same properties as the preceding; Li Shih-chen, without real reason, lists both of these as varieties of *p'ai ts'ao hsiang* (app. *Lysimachia* sp.) of Indochina (*L. foenum-graecum* is an aromatic Chinese herb used by women to scent their hair; see Burkill [1935], 1375); *ngiʷɐn-dz'i-ək* (PTKM, 34, 31b) is a Persian resin similar to camphor, used in heart disease, hemorrhages, and so on; *kiet-ṣat* (PTKM, 34, 31a) is a fragrant flower from the West, put in medicinal pomades with walnut; Li Shih-chen, quite unreasonably, includes it under *trâm*-elemi.

208 *Physeter macrocephalus.* Yamada (1955), 3; Pelliot (1959), 33.

209 Yamada (1955), 3.

210 Yamada (1955), 9–11; Yamada (1957), 246; Pelliot (1959), 33. The Chinese transcription was *·â-muât* (for *·amar*).

211 Yamada (1957), 15. Cf. Gode (1949), p. 56.

212 YYTT, 4, 37. Cf. TS, 221b, 4155d. See Duyvendak (1949), 13, for a translation of the whole passage.

213 Pelliot (1959), 34.

214 Yamada (1957), 200, on the basis of rather ambiguous evidence, believes that the new name was given to it in the ninth or tenth century; Pelliot (1959), 35, finds it first definitely in an eleventh-century poem of Su Shih.

215 *Lung hsien.*

216 Yamada (1957), 199.

217 See Yamada (1957), 246 and 249; Yamada (1956a), 2–5. The latter especially has details of Sung customs and technology related to ambergris.

218 Yamada (1957), 197–198.

219 Pelliot (1959), 38.

220 Yamada (1957), 198.

221 TS, 43a, 3733a. The shell is *Eburna japonica.* A picture of it may be seen in CLPT, 22, 39a.

222 Su Sung, in PTKM, 46, 39a.

223 *Chia hsiang.*

224 PTKM, 46, 39a.

225 *Chia chien.*

226 See the poem of Li Shang-yin, "Sui kung shou sui," ChTS, han 8, ts'e 9, ch. 2, 9b.

227 Ch'en Ts'ang-ch'i, in PTKM, 46, 39a.

CHAPTER XI (Pages 176–194)

1 Sauvaget (1948), 20. The Arabic manuscript attributed to Sulaymān tells of a medical stele of 851. The oldest known in China aws erected at Lung-men in 575, under Buddhist auspices. See Rudolph (1959), 681, 684.

2 Gernet (1956), 214–216. The two "fields" were *pei t'ien* and *ching t'ien.*

3 THY, 49, 863; Gernet (1956), 217. For a superior account of hospitals in T'ang, see Demiéville (1929), 247–248.

4 Gernet (1956), 217.

5 TCTC, 214, 3a; Gernet (1956), 217.

6 THY, 49, 863; Demiéville (1929), 247–248. Hospitals were termed *ping fang* or *yang ping fang.*

7 TLSI, 4, 32 (ch. 26).

8 TLSI, 2, 78 (ch. 9).

9 Huard and Wong (1957), 327–328.

10 He died in 682; his official biography says that he was over a hundred years old.

11 Honored in the Taoist canon as Sun Chen-jen, *Pei chiu ch'ien chin yao fang.*

12 *Yin hai ching wei. Yin hai,* "silver sea," is a Buddhist term for the eye.

13 Biographies in TS, 196, 4085d–4096c; CTS, 191, 3590c–3590d.

14 TS, 196, 4086a–4086b; CTS, 191, 3591b.

15 TS, 195, 4084a.

16 Schafer (1951), 409.

17 T'ao Hung-ching also had a *Shen Nung pen ts'ao chu* (annotations on the canon) in seven scrolls, but this was lost by T'ang; a partial manuscript has been found at Tunhuang.

18 See TS, 59, 3971a: Li Chi, *Pen ts'ao yao t'u.*

19 LTMHC, 9, 279–280; TS, 59, 3770b.

20 This book survives today only in quotations, but a fragment was found at Tunhuang.

21 Huard and Wong (1958), 16. It survives only in quotations. Some say it was written by Li Hsün's younger brother Li Hsüan.

22 Kimura (1942), *passim;* Huard and Wong (1958), *passim.*

23 TLT, 14, 50a ff.

24 TLT, 14, 51a–51b.

[25] TLT, 11, 12a.

[26] TS, 47, 3743a.

[27] SWCY, 8, 309.

[28] See Schafer and Wallacker (1961), for many others.

[29] See Kimura (1954), *passim,* and Asahina (1955), *passim.*

[30] In CCF (see the 1955 edition of this text, published in Peking, p. 280).

[31] Huard and Wong (1957), 308.

[32] Lu and Needham (1951), 15.

[33] TPT, in CLPT, 16, 2b.

[34] Meng Shen, in CLPT, 17, 1b.

[35] Meng Shen, in PTKM, 29, 4a.

[36] All examples from T'ang pharmacologists, quoted in PTKM.

[37] Quoted in PTKM, 9, 37b and 38a.

[38] Wang Gungwu (1958), 113.

[39] Bagchi (1950), 172–173.

[40] Sen (1945), 71. The translation occurs in the Taisho Tripitaka, 1059.

[41] Ch'en Pang-hsien (1957), 150.

[42] CTS, 84, 3347a; Ch'en (1957), 150.

[43] THY, 52, 899; CTS, 14, 3108d.

[44] CTS, 15, 3113b. Ho and Needham (1959a), 223.

[45] Ho and Needham (1959a), 224.

[46] TCTC, 211, 13a–13b.

[47] Hsü T'ang (fl. 862), "T'i Kan lu szu," ChTS, han 9, ts'e 8, ch. 2, 9b.

[48] P'i Jih-hsiu, "Chung hsüan szu Yüan-ta nien yü pa shih hao chung ming yao . . . ," ChTS, han 9, ts'e 9, ch. 6, 13b.

[49] Biography in HKSC, no. 4; Bagchi (1950), 216. Cf. Bagchi (1950), 76, for another seventh-century monk, "Hiuan-chao," who gathered rare medicines in southern India for the emperor of China.

[50] TLT, 18, 17a; TS, 48, 3746a.

[51] TS, 221b, 4154d; TFYK, 971, 8b; THY, 99, 1773.

[52] TFYK, 971, 8a. His name is given as *Kiei-χuət-b'â,* which would register something like *Kihorba.*

[53] TS, 221b, 4155a.

[54] TS, 221a, 4153c; TFYK, 971, 4a; THY, 99, 1776.

[55] THY, 97, 1739.

[56] TS, 59, 3771a; Laufer (1919), 204; Huard and Wong (1958), 16.

[57] This is my interpretation of Chinese *tsi̯ět-γân.*

[58] CTS, 198, 3614a; TFYK, 971, 8a; THY, 100, 1787.

[59] TFYK, 971, 13b; THY, 99, 1773.

[60] TFYK, 971, 15b.

[61] Ch'en Ts'ang-ch'i, quoted in PTKM, 34, 30b.

[62] CTS, 198, 3614c; THY, 99, 1779. Transcribed in Chinese as *tiei-ia-ka.*

[63] Quoted in PTKM, 50b, 24b.

[64] Hirth (1885), 276–279; Ch'en Pang-hsien (1957), 158; Huard and Wong (1958), 15; Needham (1954), 205.

[65] *Tou-k'ou* is a collective term and includes native as well as foreign species. Read (1936), 207–208, includes "Chinese cardamon" (*Amomum costatum*) and "wild cardamom" (*A. globosum,* Chinese *ts'ao tou-k'ou,* "herbaceous cardamom") among the native kinds. But the taxonomy of the cardamoms is a very confused problem. See also Wheatley (1961), 87–88.

[66] *I chih tzu.* The same name has also been applied to the longan. Read (1936), 207–208; Stuart (1911), 35–36, both have *Amomum amarum.*

[67] Ch'en Ts'ang-ch'i, in PTKM, 14, 37a.

[68] Ch'en Ts'ang-ch'i, in PTKM, 14, 37a, and see Li Shih-chen's comment.

[69] Ch'en Ts'ang-ch'i, in PTKM, 14, 37a.

[70] *Elettaria cardamomum,* indigenous to southwest India and Tongking and found wild in both places, though widely cultivated in the tropics. Burkill (1935), 910–915. These must be the cardamoms which were sent as local tribute from Feng-*chou* in Annam. TS, 43a, 3733a.

[71] Burkill (1935), 910–915.

[72] Li Hsün, in PTKM, 14, 36a.

[73] *Amomum xanthioides,* which is also confused with "hairy cardamom" (*A. villosum*), was called *ṣiuk-ṣa-mi̯ět* in China.

[74] Laufer (1919), 481–482; Read (1943), 481; Burkill (1935), 136.

[75] Ch'en Ts'ang-ch'i, in PTKM, 14, 36b. Li Hsün, oddly enough, has it imported from the "Persian" lands in the West and from the head of the Gulf of P'o-hai. This is out of the question, since the plant grows only in Indochina and Oceania, unless we regard these imports as in the hands of Persian traders, and so "Persian."

[76] *Amomum kepulaga.*

[77] This name, found in Ibn Baṭṭūṭa, has

CHAPTER XI (*Continued*)

been transcribed into Chinese and appears in YYTT, 18, 152, and Ch'en Ts'ang-ch'i, quoted in PTKM, 14, 36b. See Pelliot (1912a), 454–455.

[78] Pelliot (1912a), 454–455.

[79] Burkill (1935), 133–134, and 912, notes that it is cultivated in Sumatra, but is not nowadays grown in the Malay Peninsula.

[80] CLPT, 9, 53b.

[81] YYTT, 18, 152.

[82] Su Kung, in PTKM, 14, 36b; cf. Burkill (1935), 134.

[83] Hirth and Rockhill (1911), 210.

[84] *Jou tou-k'ou. Myristica fragrans,* or *M. moschata.*

[85] Ch'en Ts'ang-ch'i, in PTKM, 14, 37b. Cf. Hirth and Rockhill (1911), 210; Stuart (1911), 276.

[86] Li Hsün, in PTKM, 14, 37b.

[87] Burkill (1935), 1524–1525.

[88] Chen Ch'üan and Li Hsün, in PTKM, 14, 37b. Cf. Burkill (1935), 1529, for nutmeg in Muslim and Indian medicine.

[89] Su Sung, in PTKM, 14, 37b.

[90] *Curcuma longa = C. domestica.*

[91] *Curcuma zedoaria.* The English name may include *C. aromatica* of India.

[92] Burkill (1935), 705–710; cf. Laufer (1919), 309–314.

[93] YP, 62b–67a, gives "exuviae of the Golden Mother" as a synonym of *"yü gold,"* but it cannot be told whether this refers to saffron or to turmeric or to both.

[94] TS, 221a, 4153b.

[95] TS, 221b, 4154c.

[96] TS, 221b, 4154d.

[97] TS, 221a, 4153c.

[98] TS, 221b, 4155a.

[99] Laufer (1919), 544.

[100] Su Kung, in PTKM, 14, 38a.

[101] TPT, in PTKM, 14, 38a.

[102] CLC (TTTS, 10), 29a.

[103] The *Observer* (London), November 27, 1960.

[104] CTS, 18b, 3133b; cf. Po (1937), 49.

[105] *Firmiana simplex = Sterculia platanifolia.*

[106] *Aleurites fordii.*

[107] *Erythrina indica.* This tree later gave its name to Zayton.

[108] *Populus euphratica.*

[109] *Populus tacamahac.*

[110] *Calophyllum inophyllum.* A sample of

"Western *t'ung* tears" in the Shōsōin has not been definitely identified. Asahina (1955), 496.

[111] TPT, in CLPT, 13, 33b.

[112] Su Kung, in PTKM, 34, 32a. Su Kung also observes that the wood was used for making utensils.

[113] *Hu t'ung chin. Chin,* "spittle," is frequently corrupted into *lü,* "statute," the two graphs being much alike.

[114] TuT, quoted in CLPT, 13, 33b; Yen Shih-ku, commentary on HS, 96a, 0606a.

[115] Su Kung, in PTKM, 34, 32a.

[116] TS, 40, 3727a.

[117] TLT, 22, 14b–15a; Laufer (1919), 339, quoting LPLI, b, 13.

[118] Su Kung, in PTKM, 34, 32a.

[119] TLT, 22, 14b–15a; Yen Shih-ku, commentary on HS, 96a, 0606a; Su Kung, in PTKM, 34, 32a; Laufer (1919), 339.

[120] Ch'en Ts'ang-ch'i, in PTKM, 33, 21b; Laufer (1919), 343, identified the name, and makes the plant *Hedysarum alhagi.*

[121] Ch'en Ts'ang-ch'i, in PTKM, 5, 22a. See Laufer (1919), 345.

[122] YYTT, 18, 153; historical and linguistic notes from Laufer (1919), 429 ff. The plant is *Commiphora opobalsamum.*

[123] *Ferula galbaniflua,* and other species.

[124] YYTT, 18, 152; historical and linguistic notes from Laufer (1919), 362.

[125] It is *Ferula fetida* and other species.

[126] Laufer (1915a), 274–275. This is Tocharian B, so-called. The Chinese reconstruction is **â-ngj{ʷ}ɐi.*

[127] Su Kung, in PTKM, 34, 31b.

[128] YYTT, 18, 151; Su Kung, in PTKM, 34, 31b; Laufer (1919), 353–362.

[129] TS, 40, 3727a.

[130] Li Hsün, in PTKM, 34, 31b.

[131] Burkill (1935), 999; Su Kung, in PTKM, 34, 31b.

[132] Su Kung and Li Hsün, in PTKM, 34, 31b.

[133] TYF, quoted in PTKM, 34, 31b. Burkill (1935), 999, observes that in Malaya its fumes are used to drive away devils.

[134] Kuan-hsiu, "T'ung Chiang hsien chü tso" (the third of twelve), ChTS, han 12, ts'e 3, ch. 5, 5b.

[135] YYTT, 18, 151.

[136] *Pi ma (Ricinus communis)*; *ricinus* means "tick."

[137] Su Kung, in PTKM, 17a, 28a.

[138] Laufer (1919), 403–404.

[139] Stuart (1911), 378–379, is wrong in writing that "The oil is expressed by the Chinese, but was not especially used in medicine apart from the pulp . . . ," as the articles in PTKM show.

[140] *Cassia fistula.*

[141] Laufer (1919), 420–424.

[142] Burkill (1935), 475.

[143] Ch'en Ts'ang-ch'i, in PTKM, 31, 15b.

[144] YYTT, 18, 152.

[145] *Gleditsia sinensis.*

[146] *·â-lǝk-b'uǝt* is the transcription of Ch'en Ts'ang-ch'i (allowing for metathesis of the second and third syllables), explained by Laufer (1919), 420–424. YYTT has a similar one, called "Roman," and a "Persian" one which registers a different and unidentified form.

[147] *Tzu ts'ai,* "purple leaf-vegetable" (*Porphyra tenera*).

[148] Ennin brought some, along with powdered tea, from Japan as gifts for the Chinese. Reischauer (1955a), 82.

[149] *Shih ch'un* (*Ulva lactuca* [or *U. pertusa*]).

[150] Ch'en Ts'ang-ch'i, and Li Hsün, in PTKM, 28, 41b.

[151] *Laminaria saccharina.* See n. 101 for chap. ix.

[152] Li Hsün, in PTKM, 19, 4a; TFYK, 971, 13a. Li Hsün also says that the "Westerners" (*hu jen*) "twist it to make cordage." Does he mean foreigners generally?

[153] Meng Shen, in PTKM, 19, 4b.

[154] *Jen-shen* (*Panax ginseng*). *P. repens* of Japan has been substituted for it. *P. quinquefolius* of America was exported to China early in the nineteenth century.

[155] So-called in a poem by P'i Jih-hsiu, "Yu jen i jen-shen chien hui yin i shih hsieh chih," ChTS, han 9, ts'e 9, ch. 7, 4b.

[156] YP, 62b–67a. "Returned cinnabar" was ultrarefined cinnabar elixir, with the constituent mercury and sulphur recombined.

[157] *Tzu t'uan shan.* Li Hsün (PTKM, 12, 15a) also mentions a variety from Sha-*chou* (Tun-huang), ". . . short and small and not worth using."

[158] Su Kung, in PTKM, 12, 15a; TFYK, 971, 5a and 10b; THY, 95, 1712–1713. The "Black Water Mo-ho" and the "Yellow-Headed Shih-wei" sent it in 748. TFYK, 971, 16b. Su Sung (in PTKM, 12, 15a) tells us

that the herb grew widely in Shansi and in the mountainous parts of Shantung by the eleventh century, evidently the result of intensive cultivation in China during late T'ang and early Sung.

[159] Li Hsün, in PTKM, 12, 15a.

[160] P'i Jih-hsiu, "Yu jen i jen-shen chien hui yin i shih hsieh chih," ChTS, han 9, ts'e 9, ch. 7, 4b.

[161] Chen Ch'üan, quoted in PTKM, 12, 15a.

[162] *ịän-ɤuo-sâk* (*Corydalis ambigua*).

[163] Ch'en Ts'ang-ch'i, and Li Hsün, in PTKM, 13, 28b.

[164] *Po ju tzu* (*Iatropha janipha*). "Physic nut" is properly a name for the American *I. curcas.*

[165] Su Kung and Li Hsün, in PTKM, 17, 33a.

[166] *Hsien mao* (*Curculigo ensifolia* [= *Hypoxis* sp.]).

[167] KHYHC, 17a.

[168] Li Hsün, in PTKM, 37, 55b.

[169] Soothill and Hodous (1937), 342.

[170] Li Hsün, in PTKM, 37, 55b.

[171] *Huang hsieh.*

[172] Ch'en Ts'ang-ch'i, in CLPT, 12, 58b; TS, 43a, 3733a.

[173] *Hu huang lien. Huang lien* is *Coptis teeta.*

[174] Stuart (1911), 65, has *Barkhausia repens. Read* (1936), has *Picrorhiza kurroa.* Laufer (1919), 199–200, notes that *Barkhausia* does not grow in Persia.

[175] CLPT, 9, 45a.

[176] *Ho shih.* From *Carpesium abrotanoides,* according to Read (1936), no. 20a, but other authorities give a different identity.

[177] Su Kung, in PTKM, 15, 9b.

[178] *luo-uâi* or *nuo-uâi.* Laufer (1919), 480–481, says that this is from "Arabic Greek *alua alwā.*"

[179] Ch'en Ts'ang-ch'i, and Li Hsün, in PTKM, 34, 32a.

[180] *Kuan chün.* Unidentified.

[181] Su Kung and Chen Ch'üan, in PTKM, 28, 43a.

[182] TFYK, 971, 8a and 12a.

[183] Several from Li Hsün and Ch'en Ts'ang-ch'i, in PTKM, 21, 9a.

[184] So in YYTT, 10, 80; see Su Kung, in PTKM, 50b, 24a. Shiratori (1939), 47–48, states that the *buâ-sât* of PHL is from Persian *pāzahar,* "anti-poison"; Laufer

Chapter XI (*Continued*)
(1919), 525 ff., does not think this is the bezoar.

[185] YYTT, 10, 80.

[186] Chen Ch'üan, in PTKM, 50b, 24a. Sun Szu-mo credits it with similar powers, but adds, more specifically, that it has a tonic effect on liver and gall bladder.

[187] Su Kung gives a list of these places in PTKM, 50b, 24a; tribute from Teng-*chou*, Lai-*chou*, and Mi-*chou* in Shantung, and from Li-*chou* in Szechwan; see TS, 38, 3722b–3722c; 42, 3730b.

[188] Laufer (1919), 528.

[189] TFYK, 971, 5a and 10b; 972, 2b; THY, 95, 1712–1713.

[190] The former were sent by the Black Water Mo-ho and the Yellow-Headed Shih-wei; TFYK, 971, 16b; for the latter, see TFYK, 971, 10a–10b; TS, 222a, 4157a.

[191] TFYK, 970, 16b.

[192] Chinese *·uət-ni̯uk or *·uət-nᵂat.

[193] Li Hsün, quoting LHC, in PTKM, 51b, 34a.

[194] The illustration in CLPT, 18, 16a, shows a seal; Kimura (1946), 195–196, calls it *Otoes* (= *Callorhinus*) *ursinus,* and this is possible, though there are a number of other candidates, e.g., *Pusa hispida* (or *P. foetida*), the "ringed seal" of the Manchurian coast and northern Japan, and also found in Lake Baikal and the Caspian Sea. Old males have an odor "between asafetida and onion," but the testicles of any species would presumably provide musklike steroids. For the various seals of the coast of East Asia, see Scheffer (1958), 57, 61, 82–84, 93–94, 95–102, 103, 109.

[195] Chen Ch'üan, quoted in PTKM, 51b, 34a. He calls the animal a "dog of the sea," which ordinarily denotes a seal.

[196] Ch'en Ts'ang-ch'i, *et al.,* in PTKM, 51b, 34a.

[197] Ch'en Ts'ang-ch'i, and Li Shih-chen quoting TS, tell of an animal called *ḵuət-nᵂat of Manchuria, the Turkish lands and the West. Ch'en Ts'ang-ch'i says that it resembles a fox, and produces a musklike aromatic, orange-colored, looking like rotten bone. Probably the *nᵂat sent from Khotan in 717 is the same (TFYK, 971, 2b). Hirth and Rockhill (1911), 234, think that it was civet that was imported from the West, and castoreum from the North. A name given by

Ch'en Ts'ang-ch'i, *·â-dz'i-b'uət-t'â-ni, they take to be Arabic *al-zabād,* "civet," but another cognate is indicated. See also Laufer (1916), 373–374, and Wheatley (1961), 105–106. The civet cat *Viverra zibetha* lives in south China and Indochina, as well as in southern Asia. Its Chinese name is *hsiang li,* "aromatic *Nyctereutes*" or "fragrant raccoon-dog." "They take the sacs adjoining the water-passage [urethra], pour wine on them, and dry them. The effluvium is like true musk." So wrote Tuan Ch'eng-shih, YYTT, 16, 134. Khwārizm exported castoreum in the tenth century, according to Maqdisī (Barthold [1958], 235), and it may be that some found its way to China.

[198] See Aymonier (1891), 213; human bile was sprinkled on the royal war elephants.

[199] Or Indian pythons, *Python molurus;* Chinese *jan she.*

[200] TS, 43a, 3733a; tribute from Chiao-*chou* and Feng-*chou.*

[201] This was T'ang Chien-*chou;* see TS, 42, 3730d. The source lists no python bile as local tribute from this remote place (which sent gold dust, kudzu powder, and other valuables to the capital), but the passage translated just below indicates that it was on the tribute list for some part of T'ang.

[202] LPLI, b, 22–23.

[203] YYTT, as quoted in PTKM, 43, 23b–24a. Cf. YYTT, 17, 143, where a few words are omitted.

[204] So says Su Kung in PTKM, 43, 24a; but Meng Shen states that they too will move on the water, but more slowly.

[205] Ch'en Ts'ang-ch'i and Meng Shen, in PTKM, 43, 24a. Cf. Burkill (1935), 1847–1848.

[206] Tribute from Feng-*chou* and Fu-lu-*chou.* TS, 43a, 3733a. Cf. Hirth and Rockhill (1911), 48, for the importation of Annamese beeswax. A white wax was also made from the production of the wax insect of China.

[207] Chen Ch'üan, in PTKM, 39, 5b.

[208] Specifically, from Silla, the Black Water Mo-ho and the Yellow-Headed Shih-wei. TFYK, 971, 5a, 10b, and 16b; THY, 95, 1712–1713. One shipment of hair from Silla weighed a hundred catties.

[209] TS, 204, 4106a.

[210] Ch'en Ts'ang-ch'i, in PTKM, 52, 37a; partly also in YYTT, 11, 84. The "carriage

placed transversely" is a bit dubious as a translation.

211 YYTT, 11, 86.

212 CCF, in PTKM, 52, 37a. The association with nail clippings is common in other parts of the world. See Hastings (1927), VI, 475. Su Kung, in PTKM, 52, 37a, gives a variety of other cures; in each the hair is taken in the form of ashes.

213 Su Kung and Li Hsün, in PTKM, 11, 8a. Laufer (1919), 510, and Read and Pak (1928), 76, identify "green salt" as Persian *zingār,* that is, green verdigris; and indeed this acetate may have been sometimes shipped as a substitute for the sulphate, accounting for the confusion in colors.

CHAPTER XII (Pages 195–207)

1 TYTP (TTTS, 2), 58b.

2 TLT, 22, 20b–21a.

3 For a survey of this whole question, see Simmons (1956), *passim.* She points out that weft twill appears in Chinese textiles of the sixth or fifth century B.C. from Pazyryk in Siberia, so that this weave seems also to be ancient in China.

4 The polychrome damasks of Han had been warp reps. "Brocade" customarily translates Chinese *chin.*

5 Yang (1955a), 275.

6 TLT, 3, 13a. There was also a "*k'ung*-sparrow linen," the tribute of Ch'u-*chou* in Huai-nan. This must have imitated the brilliant luster of the peacock's tail, or perhaps even had feathers worked into the fabric.

7 See PS, 47, 2904a, for the biography of Tsu T'ing, a gay blade and frequenter of courtesans late in the sixth century; he was, however, a well-educated man, and understood several foreign languages; he owned many bolts of "*k'ung*-sparrow net."

8 Ting Liu-niang, "Shih so," *Ch'üan Sui shih,* 4, 10a, in CHSKCNPCS.

9 Tai Tsung, "Chin tuan chih tsao yin ch'iao chao," CTW, 47, 6b–7a; cf. TS, 6, 3648d.

10 TFYK, 56, 16a.

11 A. Stein (1921), 907–913; A. Stein (1928), 674–680.

12 Simmons (1948), 12–14.

13 Li Chün-fang, "Hai jen hsien wen chin fu," CTW, 536, 21b–22b.

14 Harada (1939), 75. Gray (1959), 51,

observes that the "phoenix" of the "Sino-Sāsānian style" does not occur in Sāsānian art, though eagles and pheasants, and the winged dog, the mythical Senmurv, do. What are these phoenixes then? Perhaps they are Chinese adaptations of Iranian pheasants.

15 CTS, 5, 3074d.

16 See Barthold (1958), 235–236, for a translation of Maqdisī's detailed account of the textiles of Turkestan in the tenth century. There was also a considerable wool industry in Serindia, as Stein's discoveries have shown. See Priest and Simmons (1931), 8.

17 TS, 216b, 4139a; THY, 97, 1739.

18 YYTT, 5, 42; cf. Sarton (1944), 178.

19 TS, 41, 3728d; KSP, c, 20a.

20 TS, 37, 3720d–3721a.

21 Here "carpet" is *g'įu-g'įəu.* Compare the *g'įu-sįu* of other texts. The latter is equated with Sanskrit *varṇakambala,* "colored woolen blanket"; see Pelliot (1959), 484.

22 Here both "rug" and "carpet" are *g'įu-g'įəu,* but the former is qualified by *t'śįa-p'iek,* which Laufer takes to be akin to Persian *tāftan,* "to spin," and our "taffeta." See Laufer (1919), 493. Among the gifts from Turgāch, Chāch, and other places, to be mentioned presently, we find *t'âp-təng,* which is plainly from the Persian root. All these forms refer to woolen carpets.

23 TS, 221b, 4153d; TFYK, 999, 15b–16a.

24 TS, 221b, 4154a; TFYK, 971, 3a, 14b, and 15b. The texts which report these missions sometimes say simply "dance mats," but in other cases these ambiguous Chinese words are connected with the Iranian terms for woven woolens, and therefore we consider them all to have been woolen carpets.

25 TS, 221b, 4155b; CTS, 198, 3614b; THY, 100, 1784; TFYK, 971, 18a.

26 Li Ho, "Kan tiao," LCCKS, wai chi, 4b (first of six). Wang Ch'i's commentary says that this was a felt mat, but that is mere conjecture.

27 Li Ho, "Kung wa ko," LCCKS, 2, 22b–24a.

28 As quoted by Laufer (1915), 303–304. Pliny also tells of asbestos tablecloths, cleaned by fire.

29 Laufer (1915), 311.

30 Laufer (1915), 307–319 and ff., 339. Cf. Hirth (1885), 249–252.

CHAPTER XII (*Continued*)

31 TS, 221b, 4155b; CTS, 198, 3614b; THY, 100, 1784; Laufer (1919), 499–502.

32 Li Ch'i, "Hsing lu nan," ChTS, han 2, ts'e 9, ch. 2, 1a.

33 Yüan Chen, "Sung Ling-nan Ts'ui Shih-lang," ChTS, han 6, ts'e 9, ch. 17, 7a. My "for padding" is loose for "floss" (the noun used as a verb, "to put floss into.")

34 "Tree floss" is sometimes confused with cotton; see below for Chinese names for cotton in T'ang times.

35 Laufer (1937), 7–9 and 14–15.

36 Laufer (1937), 11. But the peoples of eastern Tibet preferred square tents of yak-hair cloth.

37 Laufer (1937), 10–11.

38 CTS, 196a, 3604b.

39 TS, 217b, 4143b.

40 YYTT, 4, 36.

41 TS, 37, 3719c.

42 TLT, 3, 17b.

43 TLT, 3, 17b.

44 TS, 34, 3713a. The text calls them "*$\gamma u\partial n$-$t'u\hat{a}t$*, felt hats." *$\gamma u\partial n$-$t'u\hat{a}t$* is an unidentified foreign word applied in China to objects made of sheep's wool.

45 YYTT, 1, 3.

46 See local tribute lists in TS, 37 and 39.

47 TFYK, 970, 14a; 971, 10b and 16b; THY, 95, 1713. This linen was called "*tsung* linen," the *tsung* meaning "comprehensive," and is said to have been linen taken regularly from the total stored in godowns for payment as tax. But the lexicographers are uncertain about the sense in which *tsung* is used here.

48 Chinese *$ji^w at$-$n\hat{a}k$*. Laufer (1919), 493–496, evolved a fanciful and unconvincing Iranian etymology for this expression. Pelliot (1928), 151, derived it more reasonably from the name of a nation in Sogdiana. But Pelliot (1959), 483–484, certainly has it right as transcribing some Prakrit form cognate to Sanskrit *varṇakā*, from *varṇā*, "color."

49 MS, 10, 46.

50 TFYK, 971, 3a; THY, 99, 1775.

51 Hirth and Rockhill (1911), 100. I follow their "Rūm," identifying Chinese *Lu-mei*.

52 Chinese *chüan*.

53 CTS, 17b, 3125d; TFYK, 972, 10a.

54 The Chinese word *ch'ou* is here translated "tussah" or "bombycine" in accordance with medieval usage. Nowadays *ch'ou* is a term for silks in general.

55 TFYK, 972, 5b. The cloth is called "Tibetan *$\cdot i\breve{e}n$-$p^w at$* bombycine."

56 Chinese *shih*. TS, 43a, 3733a; TFYK, 971, 10a.

57 CTS, 199a, 3617b; TFYK, 971, 5a; 972, 2b; THY, 95, 1712–1713.

58 TFYK, 971, 16b.

59 Laufer (1913), 341, and especially Laufer (1916), 355.

60 TFYK, 971, 7b; 971, 14b. Cf. Laufer (1919), 488–492.

61 TFYK, 971, 2a. The first syllable of the Chinese transcription *$\chi\partial k$-$mi\breve{e}t$-$mi\partial u$-nji suo-lji-muân* is puzzling, but the rest is excellent, if somewhat shortened.

62 A. Stein (1928), pl. LXXX [Ast. vii.1.06].

63 TFYK, 971, 2b.

64 Laufer (1915d), 104–107. Hirth (1885), 260–262, had already suggested that the wool of the "water sheep" was *pinikón,* an idea he had gotten from Emil Bretschneider. See Pelliot (1959), 507–531, for the most recent status of the problem; see also Yamada (1957), 488–489.

65 Laufer (1915d), 114.

66 TCWC (TTTS, 13), 72b.

67 TYTP (TTTS), 46b.

68 ShIC, 10, 5a. Laufer (1919), 499, thought that the material underlying these stories was Malayan bark cloth.

69 *Ping wan.*

70 HHS, 3, 0656a, with commentary.

71 Chang Liang-ch'i, "Hai jen hsien ping ts'an fu," CTW, 762, 15b–16b.

72 Wei Chih-chung, "Hai jen hsien ping wan fu," CTS, 524, 13b–14b.

73 P'i Jih-hsiu, "Ku yüan szu," ChTS, han 9, ts'e 9, ch. 3, 8a.

74 Chang Chi, "K'un-lun erh," ChTS, han 6, ts'e 6, ch. 4, 9a. Here I take "furs" to mean a cape of a substance other than animal fur, as frequently in T'ang literature.

75 Po Chü-i, "Mao yin," PSCCC, 36, 18a. In his poem on his famous tent, he uses "blue felt" by metonymy for "tent"; see Po Chü-i, "Ch'ing chan chang," PSCCC, 31, 9b–10a. So also here.

76 Same as *Eriodendron* sp. See Pelliot (1959), 429–430, for the cottons; Burkill (1935), 345–346, for simal; and Burkill (1935), 501–505, for kapok.

[77] Private communication of Prof. Paul Wheatley.

[78] Pelliot (1959), 433.

[79] Ch'en Tsu-kuei (1957), 4; Pelliot (1959), 447 and 449. Ch'en thinks that the perennial tree cotton came first from the South, but went out of use after the introduction of herbaceous cotton.

[80] Ch'en Tsu-kuei (1957), 3–4. This source has it growing in the Canton region in Sung, and in the Yangtze Valley at the end of that dynasty. As will appear presently, I believe it was planted in Lingnan in late T'ang. For the early history of the use of cotton cloth in south China, see TCTC, 159, 5b; Ch'en (1957), 22 ff.

[81] TS, 221a, 4151b; CTS, 198, 3612a; both tell of the industry. TS, 40, 3727a, tells of its import.

[82] CTS, 197, 3609d; cf. TS, 222b, 4159b.

[83] CTS, 197, 3609d; cf. TS, 222c, 4159d.

[84] TTHYC, 2 (not paginated).

[85] TTHYC, 12.

[86] TS, 222a, 4157a.

[87] TFYK, 971, 17a; THY, 98, 1751.

[88] TS, 221b, 4155b; TFYK, 971, 15a; THY, 100, 1793.

[89] For instance, *Pǝk-ịǝp. TFYK, 971, 17b.

[90] CTS, 197, 3610a.

[91] Ch'en Tsu-kuei (1957), 2 and 20; Pelliot (1959), 474–476. See the definition of *t'ung* in KY: "a flower which can be made into a 'linen.'"

[92] Pelliot (1959), 433; cf. Hirth and Rockhill (1911), 218. The common Chinese forms are *kiĕt-puâi, *kuo-puâi, and kịvp-puâi, all corresponding to a hypothetical Indo-Malayan form like *kappāi; Pelliot (1959), 435–442. The same original produced Greek kárpasos, Hebrew karpas, Persian kārbās, and others.

[93] Chinese *b'vk-d'iep. *B'vk means "white" in Chinese; Pelliot (1959), 447, thinks that this syllable in the transcription was chosen for its meaning; he does not know the original sense of *d'iep. The Iranian etymology for the binom is to be found in Fujita (1943), 548–549; Fujita shows how the -p of *d'iep can be interchanged with -k.

[94] Wang Chien, "Sung Cheng Ch'üan shang shu chih Nan-hai," ChTS, han 5, ts'e 5, ch. 3, 9a. *Nan hai*, "South Seas," here is the old name for the city of Canton and its environs; the poem celebrates the departure of an official (Cheng Ch'üan) to take up his post as imperial commissioner in the province of Lingnan, and the verses quoted describe the things he may expect to encounter there.

[95] Sun Kuang-hsien, "Ho Nan Yüeh," ChTS, han 11, ts'e 6, 10b. The translated fragment is all that survives of the poem.

[96] Li Ho, "Nan yüan," LCCKS, 1, 36b–37a (the twelfth of thirteen); the commentary of Wang Ch'i makes clear that the epithet, as applied to this light silk, but also to the "linens" (that is, cotton fabric) of the South, means that ". . . their color is red-yellow, like the sunrise clouds of morning." Hirth and Rockhill (1911), 218, supplied the ludicrous translation "blush of the Court," but also thought that the Chinese expression might be a transcription of Sanskrit *kausheya*, "silken stuff," an hypothesis rightly rejected in Pelliot (1912a), 480. Pelliot (1904), 390, notes that the phrase, which he renders "rose d'aurore," goes back to the *Ch'u tz'u*.

[97] Wang Po, "Lin t'ang huai yu," WTAC, 3, 11a.

[98] TS, 43a, 3733b.

[99] THY, 97, 1739.

[100] Coedès (1948), 132–133.

[101] CTS, 197, 3611c; cf. TS, 222c, 4160a.

[102] CTS, 197, 3609d; cf. TS, 222b, 4159b.

[103] *[Nǝu-]d'â-γuân, an island southwest of Champa, is another place where they wore the pink cotton. TS, 222c, 4159d; CTS, 197, 3610a.

[104] TuT, 146, 762c.

CHAPTER XIII (Pages 208–214)

[1] TLT, 22, 21a.

[2] *Polygonum tinctorium* (not *Indigofera tinctoria*, the Western indigo).

[3] *Po mu. Phellodendron amurense*, also called "Amur velvet tree."

[4] *Huang lu. Cotinus coggygria.*

[5] *Hsiao po*, "little phellodendron," *Berberis* sp. For this and the preceding two dyestuffs, see Ch'en Ts'ang-ch'i, in PTKM, 35a, 32b, and 33a; he has also useful information on other dye plants.

[6] YHTC, 7, 50, quoting HTS.

[7] P'ei Yen, Preface to "Hsing-hsing ming," CTW, 168, 1a–2b.

[8] PTKM, 51, 36b.

CHAPTER XIII *(Continued)*

[9] CYCT (TTTS, 1), 54b.

[10] The story of the *hsing-hsing* is at least confused with the story of another ape, called *fei-fei* (*$*b'j^w\rho i-b'j^w\rho i$*), also a native of the far Southwest, which could understand human speech, and whose blood made a red dye, used to color boots. In addition, if a man drinks the blood of a *fei-fei,* he will be able to see ghosts. YYTT, 16, 135; Ch'en Ts'ang-ch'i, in PTKM, 51b, 36b. Li Shih-chen believes that they are the same animal.

[11] Tate (1947), 138–139. *Hylobates concolor, H. lar,* and *H. hoolock.* Li Shih-chen's description of the *hsing-hsing* (PTKM, 51b, 36b) emphasizes the upright hair on the head, a feature of the "crested gibbon." But the hoolock is commoner in modern China. No doubt the two races once intermingled there.

[12] Chang Chi, "Sung Shu k'o," ChTS, han 6, ts'e 6, ch. 5, 3a. Cf. his "Ku k'o yüeh," ChTS, han 6, ts'e 6, ch. 1, 9b, which puts the gibbons at Chin-ling in the Central Yangtze region.

[13] McDermott (1938), 43.

[14] McDermott (1938), 83 and 86.

[15] McDermott (1938), 77–78, 82–83, and 108.

[16] Janson (1952), 115 and 125. So the ape was the image of man as a degenerate sinner, an emblem of folly and vanity, a symbol of the devil. Janson (1952), 13–22, 29–56, 199–225. It lacks these attributes in China.

[17] Kuan-hsiu, "Shan ch'a hua," ChTS, han 12, ts'e 3, ch. 2, 6a.

[18] Han Wo, "I liang," ChTS, han 10, ts'e 7, ch. 4, 3a.

[19] CTC (SF, han 77), 4a–4b. This purports to be a T'ang work, but it contains Sung dates, and, in the form it has in this edition, seems to date from the thirteenth century. Some of the cosmetic colors listed in this work appear also in the fragment of CCL (SF, han 77), 1a, which would appear to be an authentic T'ang book, and may be the source of CTC. The "gibbon nimbus" does not appear in the CCL. I assume that it would appear if the list survived in its entirety. Li Shih-chen, PTKM, 9, 39b, gives "gibbon red" as a name for vermilion made from quicksilver, but I do not know how old the name is.

[20] Various species of genus *Laccifer* (= *Tachardia*); taxonomists disagree on their arrangement. Burkill (1935), 1290–1294.

[21] Su Kung and Li Hsün in PTKM, 39, 7a.

[22] Burkill (1935), 1293.

[23] Schafer (1957), 135.

[24] TS, 43a, 3733b, has it as local tribute from two towns of Tongking. Cf. TLT, 22, 14b–15a.

[25] Schafer (1957), 135.

[26] Schafer (1957), 135. See especially Li Hsün, in PTKM, 39, 7a.

[27] Schafer (1957), 133.

[28] Various species of *Daemonorops.* The taxonomic status of *D. draco* seems doubtful; Burkill (1935), 747. Cf. Shih Lu (1954), 56.

[29] *Dracaena* sp.

[30] *Pterocarpus* sp.

[31] Su Kung, in PTKM, 34, 30b.

[32] Burkill (1935), 747.

[33] In our own time, a new use has been found for the dragon's blood of the rattan palm *Daemonorops,* ". . . as a facing for lithographic plates." *London Times* (Annual Financial and Commercial Review), October 24, 1960.

[34] "Brazil," from a Romance root meaning "glowing coals," was applied to a Malayan species of *Caesalpinia* because of the color of the dyewood obtained from it; later it was extended to a *Caesalpinia* of Pernambuco in South America, and hence to the nation Brazil. Yule (1903), 113.

[35] Burkill (1935), 390–393; Pelliot (1959), 104.

[36] Described in both KCC and NFTMC.

[37] Su Kung, in PTKM, 35b, 41a; Ku K'uang, "Su-fang i chang," ChTS, han 4, ts'e 9, ch. 1, 3b.

[38] Laufer (1919), 193; Takakusu (1928), 462.

[39] Su Kung, in PTKM, 35b, 41a.

[40] Mosaku Ishida and Wada (1954). The pigment *brasilin* in a specimen of *Caesalpinia* heartwood in the Shōsōin has now completely decomposed. Asahina (1955), 498. Yamada (1959), 139–140, observes that in later times one kind of sapanwood used in India was called "Chinese" because it came from the region of Siam in Chinese vessels.

[41] NPYHC (TTTS, 8), 72a.

[42] *Lan* (*Polygonum tinctorium*), which yielded the dye called *tien.*

[43] *Ch'ing tai,* made from *Indigofera tinctoria.* See PTKM, 16, 21b; Laufer (1919), 370–371; Christensen (1936), 123.

[44] Burkill (1935), 1232–1233.

[45] TS, quoted in TPYL, 982, 1b.

[46] CHC, 1a.

[47] TFYK, 971, 2b.

[48] Li Po, "Tui chiu," LTPWC, 24, 4b.

[49] CTC (SF, 77), 3b.

[50] Po Chü-i, "Ta k'o wen Hang-chou," PSCCC, 24, 4b–5a.

[51] Yüan Chen, "Ch'un," ChTS, han 6, ts'e 9, ch. 13, 4a.

[52] *Semecarpus anacardium,* Chinese **b'uâ-lâ-tək.* There is an alternate form with *-lək.* Laufer (1919), 482–483.

[53] Li Hsün and Ch'en Ts'ang-ch'i, in PTKM, 35b, 39a.

[54] Burkill (1935), 1991–1992.

[55] *Quercus infectoria* (= *Q. lusitania*).

[56] Laufer (1919), 367–369. Cf. Burkill (1935), 1043. The usual Chinese name was "**miu-dź'iək* seeds," but YYTT, 18, 150 (which has a careful account of the tree) also gives **muâ-dz'ək.*

[57] Su Kung, in PTKM, 35b, 39a.

[58] *Garcinia hanburyi* produces the gambodge of Siam and Cambodia. *G. morella* of western India also produces it, but it was not, it seems, exploited before the sixteenth century. The mangosteen is the product of *G. mangostana.* Burkill (1935), 1050–1051.

[59] Burkill (1935), 1050–1051.

[60] *T'eng huang.*

[61] Li Hsün, quoted in PTKM, 18b, 52a. He quotes KC, which claims that the plant grew in central China, but later authorities doubt that this was the same tree. Li Shih-chen refers to Chou Ta-kuan's account of it in Cambodia; he calls it "painter's yellow."

[62] YYTT, 2, 12.

[63] *Pien ch'ing.*

[64] See quotations from TPT in CLPT, 3, 35a, and PTKM, 10, 3a.

[65] Su Kung, in PTKM, 10, 3a. Li Shih-chen himself thought that Su Kung was wrong. Acker (1954), 187, makes it a green malachite, however; Read and Pak (1928), 58, call it a cobalt ore or smalt (though they say that it is sometimes azurite). I go along with Yü Fei-an (1955), 4, who identifies *pien ch'ing* with a "great blue" from Yünnan and

Burma, that is, a coarse azurite. Cobalt provided no Chinese painter's pigment; cobalt salts were just beginning to be used to color ceramic glazes in T'ang.

[66] Ho and Needham (1959), 182.

[67] *Tz'u huang.*

[68] *Hsiung huang.*

[69] Schafer (1955), 76.

[70] TFCY, quoted in CLPT, 4, 10b.

[71] Schafer (1955), 75.

[72] T'ao Hung-ching, quoted in PTKM, 9, 40b.

[73] Schafer (1955), 77.

[74] TS, 221b, 4154b. "Mastūj" is for T'ang *Shang-mi.*

[75] Harada (1944), 5–6.

[76] Burkill (1935), 242.

[77] Waley (1927), 3. Contemporary pictures illustrating the eyebrows here referred to, and other T'ang styles in fashions will be found in Liu Ling-tsang (1958); see especially pl. 10.

CHAPTER XIV (Pages 215–221)

[1] Yamada (1959), 147, n. 6, quoting Hsüan-tsang.

[2] Yamada (1959), 132.

[3] TPT, quoted in CLPT, 4, 19a. Calcite was called "stone which divides in squares," from its well-known cleavage. Gypsum (including alabaster) was "stone lard," from its whitish appearance.

[4] Ch'en Ts'ang-ch'i, quoted in PTKM, 11, 6a.

[5] Needham (1954), 93.

[6] Needham (1954), 244.

[7] CTS, 48, 3273b.

[8] Su Kung, in PTKM, 11, 7a, and in CLPT, 5, 20a. Sources specifically mentioned are Sha-*chou* (Tun-huang) and K'uo-*chou.* Su Kung states that this mixture is also called "*Hu* [Westerner] salt," and is called **t'uk-təng* at Tun-huang and "shaded earth salt" at K'uo-*chou,* since ". . . it grows on the banks of the river, and the shady side of hills and slopes." An apparently Taoist name is "divine bones which go upside down" (YYTT, 2, 12). The components of this mixture were identified by analysis of a sample in an unglazed pot in the Shōsōin. The scientists who did this call it a soil from

CHAPTER XIV (*Continued*)
a "salt lake in China." Asahina (1955), 496–497; Masutomi (1957), 46 and 58.

[9] Masutomi (1957), 46.

[10] Shih Sheng-han (1958), 75. The process of making this variety had been described in CMYS. Sen (1945), 88, wants to make this name (*yin yen*) mean "Indian salt," and he writes, "It is the rock salt of Sind which is known as Saindhava, best kind of salt according to the Āyurveda." An attractive but unlikely hypothesis.

[11] TS, 37, 3720c.

[12] TFYK, 971, 15b.

[13] TS, 221b, 4154b; TFYK, 971, 19a.

[14] Chao (1926), 958. Acker (1954), 247, n. 1, interprets *shu chih,* "matured paper," of T'ang as "paper hammered smooth and surfaced with alum." Artisans who "matured" papers were employed by the revisers and collators of texts in the imperial palace (TS, 47, 3742b) and by the imperial libraries (TS, 47, 3742c). TLT, 20, 18a–18b–19a, lists alum along with the yellow dyes, hemp, and other materials used in the palace paper factory.

[15] TLT, 20, 18a–18b–19a. The process of obtaining alum by roasting alunite was perhaps known in Asia Minor by the tenth century, but apparently came later to China. Needham (1959), 653.

[16] Li Hsün, in PTKM, 11, 11b.

[17] Masutomi (1957), 181.

[18] TS, 40, 3726d and 3727a.

[19] Su Kung, in PTKM, 11, 11b, and 13a.

[20] TS, 40, 3737a; Su Kung, in PTKM, 11, 12b.

[21] Masutomi (1957), 199.

[22] Su Kung, quoted in PTKM, 11b and 12b. "Green alum" was confused with a malachite or some other green mineral which was imported from Indochina. See CLPT, 3, 40a, comment on article in TPT.

[23] Li Hsün, in PTKM, 11, 11b. Laufer (1919), 475, attributes this to his imaginary "Malayan Po-se," but remarks that it is nowadays produced in India and Burma.

[24] Su Kung, in PTKM, 11, 10a. Cf. Needham (1959), 654–655.

[25] TS, 40, 3727b. Barthold (1958), 169, notes important sal ammoniac workings in the Buttam mountains near Farghāna. It also occurs in Kirmān; Laufer (1919), 507.

[26] Laufer (1919), 506.

[27] Su Kung, in PTKM, 11, 10a.

[28] Laufer (1919), 504.

[29] Chen Ch'üan, Ch'en Ts'ang-ch'i, and Su Kung, in PTKM, 11, 10a.

[30] Read and Pak (1928).

[31] Listed among the needs of the court jewelers in TLT, 22, 14b–15a. Su Kung, in PTKM, 11, 10b, explains why.

[32] See Laufer (1914), 89, and Laufer (1919), 503. Borax was called "great *B'əng granules" (*ta p'eng sha*). Laufer thought that *p'eng* was cognate to Tibetan *bul,* "soda," and therefore meant "natron," not "borax."

[33] Ch'en Ts'ang-ch'i, in PTKM, 11, 9a.

[34] Schafer (1955), 85. Cf. Chang Hung-chao (1921), 208–210.

[35] Wang Ling (1947), 164.

[36] Laufer (1919), 555–556.

[37] *P'u hsiao. Hsiao,* "niter," is cognate to *hsiao,* "melt," and presumably connotes "fluxstone."

[38] *Mang hsiao.*

[39] Su Kung, in PTKM, 11, 9a.

[40] Kimura (1954), 2. Until recently it was thought that "spiky niter" was a synonym of "crude niter." Study of the Shōsōin specimen, in the light of the T'ang texts, shows that this view was mistaken.

[41] Chen Ch'üan, in PTKM, 11, 9b; Su Kung, in PTKM, 11, 9a.

[42] Schafer (1956), 65.

[43] Chen Ch'üan, in PTKM, 11, 10b.

[44] YHTC, 1, 2. See PTKM, 11, 11a, for old recipes using sulphur cups.

[45] KSP, b, 17a.

[46] Li Hsün, in PTKM, 11, 10b. In the eleventh century (according to Su Sung) sulphur was imported *only* from the South Seas.

[47] Or "stony fluid yellow" (*shih liu huang*).

[48] Wen T'ing-yün, "Hsi chou tz'u," ChTS, han 9, ts'e 5, ch. 3, 1b.

[49] See meanings of *liu huang* given in the dictionary *Tz'u yüan,* especially the one citing "Ku yüeh fu."

[50] Chen Ch'üan, in PTKM, 9, 40a.

[51] Schafer (1955), 82.

[52] Schafer (1955), 82.

[53] YYTT, 2, 12.

[54] Schafer (1955), 83–85. From the eleventh century, at least, realgar was added to incendiary bombs; and, since Ming, small objects such as "hand-warmers" and medici-

nal cups were carved from it. See Schafer (1955), 87. I have no evidence of these applications of the mineral in T'ang times.

[55] Schafer (1955), 82; Chen Ch'üan, in PTKM, 9, 40a.

[56] Schafer (1955), 76 and 83, based on MS.

[57] Laufer (1919), 508; Schafer (1956a), 418.

[58] Su Kung, in PTKM, 8, 32b.

[59] Schafer (1956a), 418 n. The presence of these oil paints with litharge driers has been scientifically determined on objects in the Shōsōin.

[60] YYTT, 1, 3.

[61] Su Kung and Su Sung, in PTKM, 8, 32b.

[62] Ch'en Ts'ang-ch'i, in PTKM, 7, 28a; YYTT, 11, 85.

[63] NCIWC, quoted in TPYL, 808, 4b; Needham (1962), 107.

[64] Ch'en Ts'ang-ch'i, in PTKM, 7, 28a.

[65] Maenchen-Helfen (1950), 187–188.

[66] Schafer (1959a), 276.

[67] TS, 221a, 4153b.

[68] TS, 222b, 4159c.

[69] Pelliot (1903), 274.

[70] Ch'en Ts'ang-ch'i, in PTKM, 46, 37a.

[71] "From Persia to Liang-*chou,*" says the ambiguous source; TLT, 22, 14b–15a. Cf. Laufer (1919), 521.

[72] They did so in the tenth century at any rate; WTS, 73, 4480a.

[73] Laufer (1915c), 36–38.

[74] Soothill and Hodous (1937), 280–282.

CHAPTER XV (Pages 222–249)

[1] TS, 221b, 4154d. I take *Ḳịvp-tśịa* to signify Kapiśa.

[2] CTS, 194b, 3599c.

[3] THY, 97, 1730.

[4] TS, 221b, 4155d; CTS, 198, 3614d.

[5] TFYK, 971, 14b.

[6] TS, 221b, 4155b; TFYK, 971, 14a; THY, 100, 1793; Lévi (1900), 417; Chou (1945a), 292.

[7] CTS, 15, 3111b; TFYK, 972, 7a.

[8] CTS, 194b, 3599c; cf. THY, 94, 1693.

[9] ISTT (TTTS, 7), 1a.

[10] Yeh Te-lu (1947), 95 and 98–99. Cf. Schafer (1951), *passim.* See Eberhard (1937), 220–224, for modern versions of this theme,

mostly with a Muslim as seeker of the magical object.

[11] "Ts'en shih," CSL (TPKC, 404, 7b–8a).

[12] This poem is translated in Waley (1954), 5, though the rock crystal has there become a sapphire.

[13] Actually identical with the amphiboles tremolite and actinolite.

[14] Sitwell (1936), 147.

[15] Na (1953), 363–364, who discusses this famous problem, adds nothing to our understanding of it.

[16] KTCHC (TTTS, 3), 76b.

[17] SHC, "Hsi shan ching."

[18] TS, 221a, 4153a–4153c; Bailey (1961), 1.

[19] Other localities may have existed in antiquity; if so, they have vanished. In later times, the jade quarries of Yarkand were to become more important than the Khotan deposits. Dr. Cheng Te-k'un has drawn my attention to the exploitation of jade (nephrite?) in Liao-ning in southern Manchuria (reported in *Chung-kuo hsin-wen* for March 23, 1961). A huge piece, found in 1960, was partly yellow-green, partly turquoise green.

[20] TLT, 22, 14b–15a; TLT, 20, 18a–18b–19a.

[21] TS, 221a, 4153a–4153c.

[22] Grousset (1932), 233.

[23] See Laufer (1946), *passim.* P. 102 has "We see that all these jade objects of sovereign power are imitations of implements and derive their shapes from hammers and knives, possibly also from lance and spearheads." Laufer thought this might be a relic of solar worship.

[24] Compare *lung,* "rain dragon," with *lung,* "manipulate; play with," whose graph shows two hands and the jade symbol. The idea comes from P. A. Boodberg.

[25] See LC, "P'ing i," and KTCY.

[26] Laufer (1946), 116–117. Laufer here follows Chavannes' study of the *feng-shan* sacrifice.

[27] [C]TS, quoted in TPYL, 805, 1a; cf. the similar passage in TS, 14, 3663d; see also TS, 3, 3639c.

[28] Feng (1944), 6.

[29] [C]TS, in TPYL, 805, 1b.

[30] Trubner (1959), nos. 280–297.

[31] Wang Ch'i, commentary on Li Ho, "Hsü kung tzu Cheng chi ko," LCCKS, 4, 40b.

[32] YHTC, 5, 35.

CHAPTER XV (*Continued*)

33 [C]TS, quoted in TPYL, 805, 1b.

34 Trubner, (1959), nos. 280–297.

35 Laufer (1946), 219–220.

36 TFYK, 971, 13a.

37 TFYK, 970, 7b; Laufer (1946), 291–292.

38 TFYK, 972, 7b and 8b; THY, 97, 1737 and 1739.

39 Feng (1944), 6.

40 Trubner (1959), 280–297.

41 Laufer (1946), 245–246.

42 KYTPIS (TTTS, 3), 66a.

43 MHTL, quoted in TPYL, 805, 9b.

44 *Hsing shan szu,* in the *Ching-shan* quarter of Ch'ang-an.

45 YYTT, hsü chi, 5, 214. I wish that I knew whether a "Brahmanling" (*P'o-lo-men-tzu*), several inches high, delicately wrought in transparent jade, which was said to have once been in the royal treasury of Khotan, was a human figure, or something else entirely. See PKLT, 7, 27b. This information comes from K'ung Chuan's part of the encyclopedia.

46 Su Kung, in PTKM, 8, 35a. On crystal in China, see Needham (1961), 99–101 and 114.

47 Bromehead (1945), 116; Ball (1950), 221.

48 Reischauer (1955a), 82.

49 TS, 221b, 4153d; TFYK, 971, 3a and 13a; THY, 99, 1775.

50 TS, 221b, 4154d. See Needham (1961), 115, for these matters.

51 See p. 38.

52 Szu-k'ung T'u, "Yu hsien," ChTS, han 10, ts'e 1, ch. 3, 2b.

53 Ou-yang Chan, "Chih-ta shang jen shui ching nien chu ko," ChTS, han 6, ts'e 1, 7a.

54 Wu Chi-yu (1959), 358, who quotes a poem of Kuan-hsiu found at Tun-huang.

55 Wang Chien, "Shui ching," ChTS, han 5, ts'e 5, ch. 5, 2a.

56 Wei Ying-wu, "Yung shui ching," ChTS, han 3, ts'e 7, ch. 8, 1a.

57 Li Po, "Po hu t'ao," LTPWC, 23, 4a.

58 Smith (1940), 49.

59 Laufer (1913a), 10, n. 3.

60 PKLT, 13, 23a–23b.

61 CSC (TTTS, 6), 71a. The anecdote may be fictional, but that is irrelevant.

62 YYTT, 11, 85.

63 Ch'en Ts'ang-ch'i, in PTKM, 8, 36a.

64 In 718 and 740. TS, 221b, 4153d; TFYK, 971, 3a; TFYK, 971, 13a.

65 In 730 and 741. THY, 99, 1773; TFYK, 971, 13b.

66 TS, 221b, 4155b; CTS, 198, 3614b; TFYK, 971, 16a; THY, 100, 1784.

67 TFYK, 971, 8b.

68 CTS, 4, 307c; TFYK, 970, 14b.

69 Ch'en Ts'ang-ch'i (quoted in CLPT, 4, 40b) writes: "Carnelian comes from the country of Japan. If you use the burnishing wood on it, and it does not mature, it is the best; when it matures under the burnishing wood it is not genuine." This seems to mean that false carnelian is much softer than the true.

70 Mosaku Ishida and Wada (1954), fig. 62.

71 A. Stein (1921), 101.

72 TS, 39, 3723b.

73 TS, 41, 3729a.

74 Su Sung, in PTKM, 10, 2b; YLSP, for which see Schafer (1961), 86.

75 TS, 41, 3728d.

76 YHTC, 6, 47.

77 TS, 221b, 4155c; CTS, 198, 3614c; TFYK, 970, 12; THY, 99, 1778.

78 *P'en shan.*

79 Hao Hsü-chou, "P'en ch'ih fu," CTW, 624, 5a–6a; R. Stein (1942), 35–36; cf. Schafer (1961), 31 and 36. We read of "false mountains" or "simulated mountains" (*chia shan*), that is, "artificial mountains," in T'ang, but many of these seem to have been largish mounds built in private gardens, not dwarf constructions to sit on a table. See Stein (1942), 33.

80 ChIL, b, 20b. Cf. Stein (1942), 31. Sun Ch'eng-yu was a brother-in-law of Ch'ien Ch'u, ruler of Wu-yüeh.

81 ChIL, b, 23b.

82 ChIL, a, 3b. P'o-hai, conquered by the Khitans, became Tung-tan in 925, and this prince was placed over it.

83 SS, 488, 5714a.

84 TPT, in CLPT, 5, 26a; Hirth and Rockhill (1911), 226; Schafer (1961), 95. The stone could well have been translucent serpentine, mottled with colored veins like verd antique, or a lustrous white or green variety like bowenite.

85 TPT, in CLPT, 5, 26a. This text refers to *ch'ing lang-kan,* which I take to be a synonym of *pi kan.*

86 The word *ch'ing,* found in descriptions of the stone, must be treated with caution, but I am convinced that in medieval China it represented the blue rather than the green hue. Thus, LiHC (Ming), p. 14: "It might be asked why, when the color of the trees is ultimately blue (*ch'ing*), all herbs and trees are green. Surely this is because green is a color between blue and yellow, and since trees will not be brought to maturity except for Earth [conceived as yellow], the blue becomes green because of its dependence on this yellow." In short, *ch'ing,* "blue," was the traditional color of vegetation, of literary and symbolic worth, whereas *lü,* "green," was its true color, due to the admixture of the nurturing yellow earth. Note also that in artist's pigments *ch'ing* normally stands for "blue." So *shih ch'ing,* "stone blue," for azurite (blue verditer), and *shih lü,* "stone green," for malachite (green verditer).

87 Sodalite resembles lapis lazuli so closely that it is readily confused with it even today. But indeed lapis lazuli is an impure "mineral," and may contain sodalite as well as lazurite; Merrill (1922), 70. As for sapphire, the *sappir* of the Bible and the *sapphiros* of Theophrastus and Pliny were lapis lazuli; the name was transferred to blue corundum (our "sapphire") much later; Merrill (1922), 148–149; Lucas (1934), 347. Most sapphires come from clay (decomposed basalt) near Bangkok, and from steam gravels in Ceylon. I know of no T'ang sapphires, but there is a mirror in the Shōsōin whose back is inlaid with sodalite, amber, and turquoise.

88 Hirth and Chavannes thought that *se-se* meant "turquoise." Laufer (1913a), 25 and 45, showed how doubtful this was; and, for what it is worth, "in China the turquoise is not valued"; Boyer (1952), 173. But Laufer made the problem even more perplexing with his triple identification of *se-se* with ruby spinel, onyx, and emerald. Some years later Chang Hung-chao (1921), 69–71, proposed the identity of "sapphire." I have already suggested that the name was occasionally applied to this mineral, but it could not have been the common *se-se* of medieval China. Here, summarized, are the points on which *se-se* and lapis lazuli agree (documentary references accompany the main text, below): both are deep blue or indigo. *Se-se* is sometimes translucent; so is some lapis lazuli,

though most is opaque (but the deep color of the best opaque lapis lazuli gives it an icy appearance), while sapphire and sodalite are translucent or transparent. *Se-se* was a characteristic gem of Chāch (Tashkent), and mined in a great mine southeast of that city-state; this was certainly the famous lapis lazuli mine of Badakhshan, southeast of Tashkent, which had supplied the East, even Chaldea and Assyria, with the mineral since antiquity (Gettens [1950], 352 and 355), and is still an important source. Both were characteristic of Persia. *Se-se* could be purchased in Khotan during T'ang; lapis lazuli, under the new name "gold star stone" (*chin hsing shih*) because of the golden flecks of pyrite which typically occur in the mineral, like golden stars in the deep blue sky, was imported from the gem markets of Khotan in Sung times; this variety is described in the YLSP, b, 19 (cf. Schafer [1961], 90–91) of the twelfth century as one kind of "stone of Khotan"; another kind of "stone of Khotan" is greenish blue, not as much valued as the purer blue (the greenish variety also occurs at Badakhshan), but also imported into Sung under the name "kingfisher feather" (a name reapplied to Burmese jadeite in the eighteenth century); moreover, as is the case in medieval Persia, blue gems found in archaeological deposits of Khotan are lapis lazuli (not turquoise, for instance; Laufer [1913a], 38). Tibetans were fond of wearing *se-se* on their persons; lapis lazuli appears in ancient Tibetan enumerations of their gems, while turquoise, so much favored by them in recent times, does not; the old Tibetan kings sent lapis lazuli, not turquoise, to the emperors of China (Laufer [1913a], 12); even modern lapis lazuli ornaments among the Mongols ". . . have an unmistakably Tibetan character." Boyer (1952), 173.

89 One indigenous name of Khotan is *Gostana,* "Earth Breast"; its eponymous founder, the son of Aśoka it is said, was suckled by the goddess. A. Stein (1907), 153 ff.; Brough (1948), 334.

90 TS, 221a, 4153a. The man, overcome with avarice, pretended that he had been robbed by foreigners, and kept these things for himself when he returned to China, but he was discovered and banished.

91 YLSP, b, 19; and see n. 85, above.

92 There is a lapis lazuli cicada of late

CHAPTER XV (*Continued*)
Chou in the British Museum (from the Eumorfopoulos Collection); if the raw material came all the way from Badakhshan, it is a remarkable instance of the extent of ancient trade relations, before the opening of the "silk routes" through Serindia.

93 Dana (1892), 433; Barthold (1958), 66. But spinels are not yet identified in the language of medieval China.

94 TS, 221b, 4154a.

95 CTS, 104, 3391a.

96 TLT, 22, 14b–15a, gives the source of such minerals as lapis lazuli, amber, jade, diamond drills, and brass as "from Persia to Liang-*chou.*" I take this to mean that all were imported through Central Asia, the stretch between Persia and China. Cf. Laufer (1913a), 38. Chang Hung-chao (1921), 56, reveals a supposed *se-se* mine at P'ing-lu in T'ang times, but what blue stone was found there remains conjectural.

97 Horn and Steindorff (1891), *passim;* Osborne (1912), 149. No turquoise was found. The Sāsānids also favored blue "sapphirine" chalcedony, maybe sometimes confused with lapis lazuli. Osborne (1912), 149.

98 Christensen (1936), 461.

99 TS, 221b, 4155c.

100 Bk. 37, ch. 39.

101 MHTL (TTTS, 4), 3a.

102 TS, 76, 3869b.

103 Mosaku Ishida and Wada (1954), 117; *Shōsōin* (1960), no. 84 in the South Building.

104 TS, 216a, 4135a.

105 Laufer (1913a), 10.

106 TuT, 190, 1022c.

107 WTS, 74, 4480b.

108 Not faceted, as is the modern custom. Laufer thought that these were emeralds.

109 TS, 222a, 4156b–4157a. There is a specimen of lazurite from Mogok, upper Burma, in the Geological Museum, London. Not all lapis need have come from Badakhshan.

110 WFCSC, 8, 16b. Of course, the poet may describe some translucent pseudo-lapis—dark sapphire, sodalite, or an artificial stone—here.

111 YS, 181, 4061b. Chang Hung-chao (1921), 57, gives examples of beaded curtains of lapis lazuli, and banners decorated with lapis lazuli, pearls, and amber, from the fanciful text of TYLP.

112 TS, 177, 4053c. We may have paste jewelry here.

113 Sitwell (1941), 15 and 30–31.

114 MHTL (TTTS, 4), 2a; Schafer (1956), 76; and see the poem of Lu Kuei-meng, "T'ang chüan," in ChTS, han 9, ts'e 10, ch. 13, 12a.

115 Schafer (1961), 5–7.

116 Laufer (1913a), 32, citing WL.

117 Chang Hung-chao (1921), 59.

118 Lucas (1934), 348.

119 R. Campbell Thompson (1936), 194–195. In medieval Europe there were artificial carbuncles, diamonds, sapphires, emeralds, topazes, and others. Holmes (1934), 196.

120 Ultramarine is powdered lapis lazuli. It is rare in China, but has been detected in the Wei paintings at the Tun-huang caves. Gray (1959).

121 Stewart (1930), 72. Chaucer was also first to use "ruddy" (except as applied to the complexion), "sunnish," "citron," and "rosy" as color words.

122 "Hsi chai hsing ma," LCWTC, 2, 41a.

123 Yang Shen, SAWC, quoted in Dai Kan-wa Jiten, 7, 953b. Chang Hung-chao (1921), 64–65, gives other examples of this imagery.

124 "T'i Wu chung Lu Kuei-meng shan chai," ChTS, han 11, ts'e 1, 2a.

125 Kuan-hsiu (832–912), "Meng yu hsien," ChTS, han 12, ts'e 3, ch. 1, 4a.

126 His name is given as *Puâ-tâ-ljąk.* Hirth thought that this might represent an Oriental form of "Patriarch," as Needham, too, in (1962), 106. Constans II was actually ruling at Constantinople.

127 TS, 221b, 4155c; CTS, 198, 3614c; TFYK, 970, 10a; THY, 99, 1778. The versions in the two T'ang histories have dropped the "stone" from "stone green" (malachite), and accordingly read "green metal germ" instead of "stone green, metal germ." This accounts for Chavannes' view that this was lapis lazuli (Chavannes [1903], 159), an idea adopted by Laufer (Laufer [1919], 520) and accepted by Pelliot (1959), 59–60. This textual error is the only foundation of the lapis lazuli theory.

128 TFYK, 971, 13b. THY, 99, 1773, gives an identical statement, but has the year as 730. I take TFYK to be the more reliable source.

[129] TFYK, 971, 5b.

[130] TS, 221b, 4154d.

[131] CS, 87, 1308d.

[132] LIC (CTPS, ser. 11, ts'e 4).

[133] P'i Jih-hsiu, "I Mao kung ch'üan i p'ing hsien shang chien i yin chi," ChTS, han 9, ts'e 9, ch. 3, 5b.

[134] Chang Chiu-ling, in his "Preface to an Ode to the Lion," on the qualities of a lion sent as tribute from the Western regions, speaks of its bones as having the "hardness of metal germ," from which we might conclude that exceptional hardness was another quality of the stone; but this text really refers to "hardness of metal," the standard Chinese term for the diamond, whose "adamantine" hardness was world-famous; Chang Chiu-ling, "Shih-tzu tsan hsü," CTW, 290, 19a. Pliny tells of *auri nodus,* "germ of gold" (already known to Plato, Timaeus, 59), thought to be diamond; the story of that mineral is somehow involved with that of "germ of metal." See Ball (1950), 245. The T'ang pharmacopoeia, however, uses the term *chin ching* in the sense of "germ of gold," stating that orpiment is the germ of gold just as azurite is the germ of copper. HHPT, 4, 44.

[135] Ball (1950), 171. Some albite, another feldspar, has these qualities too, and is also named "moonstone." Ceylon is the source of the best moonstone, but the T'ang history, although it says that that country "abounds in singular jewels," does not enumerate them; TS, 221b, 4155b.

[136] For ancient Chinese glass, see Needham (1962), 101–104.

[137] The Chinese word *liu-li* apparently transcribes Pali *veḷuriyam* (Sanskrit *vaiḍūrya*) and in Buddhist literature continues to have the same referent, that is, "beryl" or some other green gem. For this reason, Laufer (1946), 111–112, did not accept the meaning "glass" for it, and, though he admitted that certain colored glazes were sometimes called *liu-li,* he considered *po-li* the only usual word for glass in China. *Po-li* transcribes a form close to Sanskrit *sphaṭika,* "crystal." Cf. Needham (1962), 105–106.

[138] Gray (1959), 53.

[139] As with the joint mission from Turgäch, Kish, *et al.,* of 746. TFYK, 971, 15b.

[140] TS, 222c, 4160a.

[141] TS, 34, 3713b.

[142] Hu San-hsing's commentary on reference to a *liu-li* bowl, under the date 778, in TCTC, 225, 14b. He seems to rely on a twelfth-century source; see Needham (1962), 110.

[143] Ou-yang Chiung, "T'i Ching huan hua ying t'ien szu pi t'ien wang ko," ChTS, han 11, ts'e 6, 3a.

[144] Ch'en Ts'ang-ch'i, in PTKM, 8, 36a.

[145] YYTT, 11, 85.

[146] TS, 221b, 4154d.

[147] CTS, 5, 3074a (for 675); TFYK, 970, 16b (for 761).

[148] TS, 221b, 4154d; TFYK, 971, 13b (for 741); THY, 99, 1773 (for 730).

[149] TS, 221b, 4155c; CTS, 198, 3614c; TFYK, 970, 10a; THY, 99, 1778.

[150] Harada (1939), 61–62; Mosaku Ishida and Wada (1954), figs. 59 and 60.

[151] Needham (1962), 103.

[152] Ishida and Wada (1954), fig. 69.

[153] Ishida and Wada (1954), fig. 58.

[154] Ishida and Wada (1954), fig. 63.

[155] *Shōsōin* (1928–), I, 32.

[156] Trubner (1957), no. 364.

[157] Trubner (1957), nos. 366 and 367.

[158] CTS, 197, 3609d; THY, 98, 1751.

[159] TFYK, 970, 6b; STCH (TTTS, 1), 13a. These sources seem to refer to the same event, but place it in 631. The identification of Rākshasa is from Laufer (1915e), 211.

[160] TS, 222c, 4159b.

[161] CTS, 197, 3610a; TFYK, 970, 13a.

[162] TS, 221b, 4155a.

[163] Laufer (1915e), 212.

[164] Reischauer (1955), 117.

[165] Laufer (1915e), 170, 174, 217, 225, and 228. Cf. Laufer (1915f), 563, where Tibetan *me šel,* "fire crystal," is equated with Sanskrit *Sūryakānta.*

[166] Needham (1962), 111–113.

[167] Laufer (1915e), 182 and 188.

[168] Needham (1959), 252; Needham (1960), 135, n. 3. Later this lunar image became a fiery sphere, apparently through confusion of the Dragon constellation with the invisible monsters of Indian astronomy, Rāhu and Ketu, who lie at the nodes of the moon's orbit and devour the sun (hence solar eclipses). In this way, the dragon's toy became again an image of the sun, or better, of the sun and moon together; Needham (1959), 252.

[169] Lessing (1935), 30.

CHAPTER XV (*Continued*)

170 Laufer (1915c), 58; Demiéville (1924), 289–292; Schafer (1952), 155, n. 8.

171 Laufer (1915c), 69.

172 TS, 219, 4146d; TFYK, 971, 4a; Laufer (1915c), 69.

173 Compare the *"piuk* of Indigo Field" (actually a green marble), used, along with pearls and kingfisher feathers, as a decoration on gold (HS, 97b, 0615a); the "nightshining *piuk"* of Rome (HHS, 118, 0905a); and *"piuk*-colored silks" (IL, P'in li, comm. on *shu chin*, "tied silks").

174 Hirth (1885), 243; E. Newton Harvey (1957), 19, 33–34, 372. Cf. Needham (1962), 76.

175 Berthelot (1938), 271–274.

176 *Ming t'ang.* I use Soothill's translation.

177 CTS, 22, 3157b–3157c.

178 CTS, 22, 3158a; TCTC, 205, 15a–15b; Needham (1958), 21.

179 TCTC, 205, 14a; Needham (1958), 21.

180 Ts'ui Shu, "Feng shih ming t'ang huo chu," ChTS, han 3, ts'e 2, 2b.

181 TCTC, 205, 15a–15b.

182 "Ts'ui Wei," in CC (TPKC, 34, 5b–6a).

183 Chen Ch'üan, in PTKM, 51a, 26a.

184 TLT, 22, 14b–15a.

185 TS, 43a, 3733a; from Huan-*chou*.

186 TS, 222a, 4157a.

187 TFYK, 971, 17a. As "tribute" in 748.

188 TFYK, 971, 17b; CTS, 197, 3610a.

189 TFYK, 971, 17b.

190 Laufer (1925), 67–68.

191 Mosaku Ishida and Wada (1954), pl. 76.

192 *Shōsōin* (1928–), I, 44.

193 TLT, 22, 14a–14b.

194 Ishida and Wada (1954), pl. 18.

195 Called *hu*.

196 PKLT, 12, 25a–25b.

197 TS, 24, 3682a.

198 TuT, 126, 659c.

199 TS, 24, 3681b.

200 Trubner (1957), 128.

201 Jenyns (1954), 49.

202 TS, 222a, 4157a.

203 TS, 43a, 3733a.

204 Jenyns (1957), 35 and 43. During Sung, the Chinese began to think the horn of the African rhinoceros superior to the Asian, and it appears that most horn objects of Ming and Ch'ing come from the former.

205 YYTT, 16, 134.

206 Ettinghausen (1950), 53. Po (1937), quotes a medieval source which lists "pat-terned rhinoceros" with "singular pearls, tortoise shell, and strange aromatics" as the rich products brought by sea to Canton.

207 Jenyns (1957), 40–41.

208 Li Hsün, in PTKM, 51a, 26b.

209 Meng Shen, in PTKM, 51a, 27a.

210 Jenyns (1957), 40–41.

211 *Shōsōin* (1928–), I, 31, shows one from the Shōsōin; cf. Ettinghausen (1950), 102; Jenyns (1957), pl. 20.

212 Jenyns (1954), 49.

213 Ettinghausen (1950), 102; Mosaku Ishida and Wada (1954), pl. 67 (a knife); Tu Fu, "Li jen hsing," CCCCTS, p. 25, tells of horn chopsticks used by elegant court ladies.

214 YHTC, 5, 34; cf. Jenyns (1957), 45.

215 Jenyns (1957), 44 ff., quotes Li Shang-yin; he has other T'ang sources on this subject.

216 Ettinghausen (1950), 54; Jenyns (1957), 47.

217 Chou (1945), 16; Sauvaget (1948), 16.

218 *Shōsōin* (1928–), VII, 33; cf. Jenyns (1957), 47.

219 TYTP, 2, 10a.

220 The modern form of the *ju-i* appears to have originated in early Sung times, when archaic belt hooks were misunderstood as primitive wands. Le Roy Davidson, quoted in Gray (1959), 49.

221 Mosaku Ishida and Wada (1954), pl. 117.

222 *Shōsōin* (1928–), XI, 55.

223 THY, 95, 1712–1713.

224 *Kuət-tuət.* Li Shih-chen has confused this with the sea animal, the source of a tonic drug to which I have given the Korean name *olnul;* see chap. xi on "Drugs," and see Laufer (1916), 373–374. But Laufer thought that *kuttut* might represent the beaver, and *olnul* the seal, though elsewhere (Laufer [1913], *passim*) he took the *kuttut* to be fossil narwhal ivory. Hirth and Rockhill (1911), 234, follow Li Shih-chen in confounding the two transcriptions.

225 Laufer (1925), 32–33. Maqdisī lists "fish teeth" among the products distributed from Khwārizm (Barthold [1958], 235), and Laufer thought that though these were normally walrus tusks, they might sometimes be mammoth ivory, and might even have reached China.

226 TS, 39, 3725a; Laufer (1913), *passim;* Laufer (1916), 369.

227 YHTC, 9, 71. The same story appears in more detail in YYTT, 10, 81.

228 "Ching ts'un chu," KIC (TPKC, 402, 3b–4a).

229 TS, 115, 3941b.

230 Soothill and Hodous (1937), 435.

231 Demiéville (1924), 291–292.

232 Schafer (1952), 155.

233 Schafer (1952), 156–157.

234 TS, 3, 3638d; Schafer (1952), 161.

235 Schafer (1952), 161.

236 Li Hsün, in PTKM, 46, 37a.

237 Li Hsün, in PTKM, 46, 37a.

238 Waley (1961), 105.

239 Lü Ying, "Hsi yü hsien ching ts'un chu fu," CTW, 740, 16b–17b.

240 TFYK, 970, 9a–9b.

241 THY, 98, 1751; TFYK, 971, 17a. Champa sent more in 750; TFYK, 971, 17b.

242 CTS, 198, 3614b; TFYK, 971, 18a and 972, 2a; THY, 100, 1784.

243 TFYK, 971, 17b.

244 CTS, 17b, 3125d; TFYK, 972, 10a.

245 Schafer (1952), 160.

246 Li Hsün, in PTKM, 46, 37a.

247 From the "hawk-billed turtle" (*Chelonia imbricata*), Chinese *tai-mei*.

248 TS, 43a, 3733a. From the same place came the "skin" of the *kəu-piek,* apparently the edible green turtle, from whose shell succulent soup was made.

249 CTS, 197, 3610a; TFYK, 972, 7b; THY, 100, 1782.

250 Harada (1939), 73.

251 Shen Ch'üan-ch'i, "Ch'un kuei," ChTS, han 2, ts'e 5, ch. 2, 3b. "Berylline" translates *liu-li,* i.e., "beryl paste"; see above, under "Glass."

252 *Tridacna gigas.* Chinese *kiᵂo-gʻiᵂo.* See Wheatley (1961), 91–92.

253 TS, 221b, 4155c.

254 Li Hsün, in PTKM, 46, 38a. Its Indian name was *musāragalva,* but the lexicographers disagree as to the meaning of this word; some say "coral"; some say "mother-of-pearl."

255 TS, 221b, 4155c.

256 Su Kung, in PTKM, 8, 35b; Chmielewski (1961), 85–86.

257 His dates are *ca.* 735–835. Biographical notes are in ChTS, han 3, ts'e 7, ch. 1, 1a.

258 Wei Ying-wu, "Yung shan-hu," ChTS, han 3, ts'e 7, ch. 8, 1a.

259 Tuan Ch'eng-shih (YYTT, 10, 73) reports a coral tree twelve feet tall in a lake in a Han garden, the gift of Chao T'o, overlord of Vietnam. If true, this was a prototype of all later miniature coral gardens.

260 Quotations from SHC, EY, and HNT, in TPYL, 809, 1a.

261 The "Raven-Black *Man*" and the "White *Man.*"

262 Su Kung, in PTKM, 8, 35b.

263 Su Kung, in PTKM, 8, 35b.

264 So Ch'en Ts'ang-ch'i, in PTKM, 8, 35b.

265 Hsüeh Feng (fl. 853), "Tsui ch'un feng," ChTS, han 8, ts'e 10, 3b.

266 Lo Yin (833–909), "Hsia jih . . . chün chung pin liao," ChTS, han 10, ts'e 4, ch. 1, 4b.

267 YYTT, 11, 88. Cf. Laufer (1905), 235. For the Greek and Latin lore, see Ball (1950), 234.

268 Boodberg (1937), 359, n. 60; Ball (1950), 130 and 236.

269 SPT, in CLPT, 12, 22a.

270 Wei Ying-wu, "Yung hu-p'o," ChTS, han 3, ts'e 7, ch. 8, 1b.

271 Su Kung, in PTKM, 37, 53a. A final stage in the series was jet.

272 TS, 221b, 4155c. Cf. Laufer (1905), 231–232; Laufer (1919), 521–523.

273 TLT, 22, 14b–15a; TFYK, 972, 2a.

274 TS, 222a, 4157a; Laufer (1905), 233–234 and 237; Needham (1961), 237–238.

275 THY, 98, 1751.

276 TFYK, 970, 14b.

277 Li Hsün, in PTKM, 37, 53a.

278 *Shōsōin* (1928–), I, 32; VII, 56; XII, 61; III, 59; II, 22, 24, 25 and 27.

279 Wolters (1960), 326.

280 Ch'en Ts'ang-ch'i and Li Hsün, in PTKM, 37, 53a–53b.

281 Chang Yüeh (667–730), "Ch'eng nan t'ing tso," ChTS, han 2, ts'e 4, ch. 2, 16b.

282 Arai (1955), 71, 82, and 84.

283 Li Ho, "Chiang chin chiu," LCCKS, 4, 37b.

284 Also called *i.* Cf. Schafer (1961), 93.

285 Ch'en Ts'ang-ch'i, in PTKM, 37, 53b.

286 Su Kung, in PTKM, 37, 53b.

CHAPTER XVI (Pages 250–257)

1 Eberhard (1950), 193.

2 Chang, Hsing-lang (1930), III, 2, 183.

3 TS, 42, 3729d–3731a.

4 Hsü T'ang (fl. 862), "Sung Lung-chou Fan shih chün," ChTS, han 9, ts'e 8, ch. 1, 3b.

CHAPTER XVI (*Continued*)

[5] TS, 43a, 3731–3733, gives many places in those regions which sent gold as "tribute."

[6] Ch'en Ts'ang-ch'i, in PTKM, 8, 30a.

[7] LPLI, a, 2.

[8] LPLI, a, 2. There was also placer gold in Yünnan, under Nan-chao control; TS, 222a, 4156b. A new gold-producing area appeared on the north coast of Shantung late in the tenth century. Large-scale production there began in the middle of the eleventh century, when there was a gold rush from all parts of the nation. Nuggets weighing more than twenty ounces were found. See NKCML, 15, 397.

[9] YCYI (TTTS, 4), 49a.

[10] Needham (1959), 676.

[11] TFCY, in CLPT, 4, 18a.

[12] Strachwitz (1940), 12–21; Garner (1955), 66; Trubner (1957), 24; Gyllenswärd (1958), 5.

[13] Examples from the Shōsōin. *Shōsōin* (1928–), III, 9, and VI, 20.

[14] Japanese *kirikane*. It was once believed that the use of this material was a peculiarity of Japanese art. However, despite the refinements developed in its use by Japanese craftsmen, there can be no doubt that the technique came to Japan from China, presumably in the Nara period. See Seckel (1954), 87.

[15] Waley (1931), xlvi.

[16] *Shōsōin* (1928–), I, 55.

[17] TS, 43a, 3733a.

[18] Chinese *p'ing t'o*.

[19] *Shōsōin* (1928–), VIII, 35–39.

[20] YYTT, 1, 3.

[21] Discovered by M. Rosenberg, in *Geschichte der Goldschmiedekunst auf technischer Grundlage* [Abtg. Granulation] (Frankfurt Am Main, 1918). See Griessmaier (1933), 32, n. 6. In Britain, Blackband approximated Etruscan granulation by dripping gold on charcoal dust, using a copper-gold solder, and removing evidence of the copper with sal ammoniac. See Blackband (1934).

[22] Griessmaier (1933), 31–37.

[23] Trubner (1957), 25, and nos. 298 and 309.

[24] Trubner (1957), nos. 310–323.

[25] Waley (1931), xlvi.

[26] *Shōsōin* (1928–), VI, 17.

[27] *Shōsōin* (1928–), IV, 20.

[28] Chang Tzu-kao (1958), 73, and see quotations involving *tu*, "metal plate," in PWYF. But metal plating, especially tin on bronze, goes back to Shang.

[29] Gyllenswärd (1958), 6.

[30] Wang Ch'i, commentary on Li Ho, "Hsü kung tzu Chen chi ko," LCCKS, 4, 40b.

[31] *Shōsōin* (1928–), IV, 37.

[32] Gyllenswärd (1958), 6: Trubner (1957), nos. 299–308.

[33] Trubner (1957), nos. 298 and 299. The latter has the bird mounted on a box cover. Cf. YHTC, 1, 7, which tells of golden phoenixes as expensive gifts to courtesans.

[34] Trubner (1957), nos. 300, 303, and 308.

[35] Ch'en Ts'ang-ch'i and Chen Ch'üan, in PTKM, 8, 30a.

[36] TS, 196, 4086b.

[37] Soothill and Hodous (1937), 280–283.

[38] CTS, 71, 3320d.

[39] Liu Tsung-yüan, "P'i sha chien chin fu," CTW, 569, 11b.

[40] CTS, 3, 3069c; THY, 97, 1730; Demiéville (1952), 187–188.

[41] LTMHC, 9, 269. This was the famous Wen-ch'eng Kung-chu.

[42] TS, 216a, 4135b; THY, 97, 1730; Bushell (1880), 445; Demiéville (1952), 203. The last-named source lists other such handsome examples of the goldsmith's art from Tibet, which I have not mentioned here. See also Bushell (1880), 446. There were gifts of precious metal in Tibet in 734 (TFYK, 971, 10b); 735 (TFYK, 971, 10b); 805 (THY, 97, 1737); 817 (TFYK, 972, 7b; THY, 97, 1737); 827 (TFYK, 972, 8b); 837 (THY, 97, 1739).

[43] TFYK, 970, 15a; Demiéville (1952), 203.

[44] TS, 216b, 4138d; Demiéville (1952), 202–203.

[45] Demiéville (1952), 202–203.

[46] TS, 221b, 4155c. Rome was said to abound in gold and silver.

[47] In 650 (TFYK, 970, 14a); 723 (TFYK, 971, 5a); 724 (THY, 95, 1712); 734 (TFYK, 971, 10b); 749 (CTS, 199a, 3617b); 773 (TFYK, 972, 2b).

[48] TFYK, 971, 16b.

[49] TS, 222a, 4157a.

[50] TFYK, 971, 16a. See also TFYK, 970, 12a, and THY, 100, 1796, for a confused account of the gift of golden eggs by a Western Khan.

[51] TFYK, 971, 16b.

[52] Braddell (1956), 17.

[53] MHTLCKC, 7b and 8b.

[54] Tu Mu, "Shao nien hsing," ChTS, han 8, ts'e 11, ch. 4, 12a–12b.

[55] CWTS, 2, 4202a.

[56] TS, 221b, 4154b.

[57] *Dai Kanwa jiten,* explaining the occurrence of the term in a verse by Liang Wu Ti ("The dragon horse's purple-gold saddle"), gives it as a synonym of "red metal," that is, copper. This is hardly likely. KKYL (fourteenth century with later Ming revisions) states that "purple gold" is now an alloy of copper and gold, but that no one of modern times has seen the true medieval purple gold. *Tzu,* like our "purple," ranges into crimson; this may rule out my Egyptian analogue.

[58] Wood (1934), 62; Lucas (1934), 190–191.

[59] Wood (1934), 63–64.

[60] Forbes (1955), 125–127.

[61] TS, 43a, 3731–3733. There was also a little produced in the central Yangtze region; see Schafer and Wallacker (1961), pl. 6, map 12. Su Kung, however (in PTKM, 8, 30a), states that the purest silver, with the least admixture of lead, comes from Kuo-chou in Honan, a place not otherwise notable as a source.

[62] Li Hsün, in PTKM, 8, 30a.

[63] TS, 54, 3757c.

[64] Gyllensgård (1958), 6.

[65] Trubner (1957), 24.

[66] Trubner (1957), 24; see nos. 326–354. I have relied heavily on Trubner in this section. Cf. *Shōsōin* (1928–), VII, 18; XII, 1 ff. Gyllensgård (1958), 6, notes "a silver bowl and a wine cup with ring handle which were found in Chinese soil but executed in Persia, and have characteristic T'ang forms."

[67] Trubner (1957), no. 326.

[68] Trubner (1957), 25.

[69] Trubner (1957), 26 and no. 362. Cf. *Shōsōin* (1928–), II, 34, for a lacquered ewer with silver *heidatsu.* For other objects in this technique see YYTT, 1, 3.

[70] Gyllensgård (1958), 6.

[71] Su Kung, in PTKM, 8, 30b.

[72] Su Kung and Ch'en Ts'ang-ch'i, in PTKM, 8, 30b. Cf. the comments of Li Shih-chen on these texts; he says the art was practiced in Szechwan. See also NKCML, 15, 381; its author concludes that "yellow silver" was no true silver, but made from arsenic minerals.

[73] Ch'en Ts'ang-ch'i, in PTKM, 8, 30b.

[74] Yüan Chen, "Ch'ien huo i chuang," CTW, 651, 25a.

[75] Han Yü, "Ch'ien chung wu ch'ing chuang," CTW, 549, 7b.

[76] CTS, 48, 3272b.

[77] TFYK, 971, 16a (for Turgäch, Chäch, et al.).

[78] TFYK, 971, 16b. (for Black Water Mo-ho and tribes of the Shih-wei).

[79] All the records are for the eighth century: 723 (TFYK, 971, 52); 724 (THY, 95, 1712); 734 (TFYK, 971, 10b); 748 (THY, 95, 1713); 749 (CTS, 199a, 3617b); 763 (THY, 95, 1713); 773 (TFYK, 972, 2b).

[80] In the eighth and ninth centuries: 734 and 735 (TFYK, 971, 10b–11a); 817 (THY, 97, 1737); 824 (TFYK, 972, 8a); 827 (TFYK, 972, 8b); 837 (THY, 97, 1739).

[81] *P'uâ-lâ.*

[82] TS, 221a, 4152d; TFYK, 970, 16b.

[83] TS, 221b, 4154a; THY, 98, 1754.

[84] Laufer (1919), 511–515.

[85] TLT, 22, 14b–15a.

[86] Laufer (1919), 511–515.

[87] Ho and Needham (1959), 182.

[88] TFYK, 971, 3a.

[89] YYTT, hsü chi, 5, 216.

[90] Chang Tzu-kao (1958), 74. Laufer (1919), 555, says copper, zinc, and nickel, but perhaps it is dangerous to assume that "white copper" always has the same content.

[91] *Shōsōin* (1928–), XI, 35.

[92] *Shōsōin* (1928–), XI, 32.

[93] Laufer (1919), 555; Ho and Needham (1959b), 74.

[94] Reischauer (1955a), 82.

[95] Yang (1955), 150–151. See also the coin lists in A. Stein (1921), 1340–1348, and Stein (1928), 648 and pl. CXX, nos. 17, 18, 19, for Byzantine and Sāsānian coins from Serindia.

[96] Hsia (1958), 67–68.

[97] Hsia (1957), 54. TuT, 193, 1042b, reports (it must be with some surprise) that the Persians paid their land taxes in silver coin. Persian silver currency of the fifth century has also been discovered in Ch'ing-hai, in northwestern Tibet, once on an important East-West trade route. See Hsia (1958), 105–108.

[98] Hsia (1958), 71.

CHAPTER XVI (*Continued*)
[99] Hsia (1957), 55.
[100] KCC, quoted by Li Hsün, in PTKM, 8, 30a. KCC must be a T'ang book, since it mentions the Arabs (Tadjik), and is quoted by Li Hsün. The late seventh or early eighth century is a likely date for it.

CHAPTER XVII (Pages 258–264)

[1] Reischauer (1955a), 82.
[2] TFYK, 972, 10b.
[3] From Feng-*chou*. TS, 43a, 3733a. This was also a product of Kwangsi.
[4] TLT, 22, 14b–15a; Torii (1946), 51–61. Torii also describes a carved green placque of green stone excavated at Liaoyang, which purports to show a man of the P'o-hai nation on a Persian-style ewer with a bird's head lid. There are analogues in the Shōsōin and in the Hermitage Museum in Leningrad.
[5] TFYK, 971, 13a; TFYK, 971, 3a. Actually, for Samarkand the text says only "egg," not "egg cup," but it is listed with other cups and vases.
[6] Laufer (1926), 2–4.
[7] TFYK, 971, 2a. I take the *ch'ih*, "pool," of the text to be an error for *ti*, "ground."
[8] ChIL (TTTS, 17), 8b–9a. This eighth-century book lists a number of exotic objects, said actually to exist, and appears to be reliable.
[9] ChIC (TTTS, 17), 8b–9a.
[10] TFYK, 971, 13a.
[11] TFYK, 971, 5a; THY, 95, 1712.
[12] TFYK, 972, 6a.
[13] TFYK, 971, 13a.
[14] PMSY, 1, 3. This passage from a tenth-century book seems to be based on YYTT.
[15] TS, 221b, 4154d; THY, 99, 1773.
[16] Harada (1944), 13.
[17] Ishida Mikinosuke (1948), 2–19. Harada (1944), 13–20, thinks that this festival derived from a Han holiday for the god T'ai-i, and later acquired a Buddhist character; perhaps the wheels of branches symbolized the wheel of the law. Ishida, on the other hand, regards it as primarily of Western origin.
[18] Harada (1944), 2–19; Hsüeh Sheng, "Tai Ts'ui ta fu chien tsao t'ung teng shu piao," CTW, 959, 4a–5a.
[19] Ishida (1948), 11.

[20] Reischauer (1955), 71; Reischauer (1955a), 128.
[21] Sui Yang Ti, "Cheng yüeh shih wu jih yü t'ung ch'ü chien teng yeh sheng nan lou," CHSKCNPCS, ts'e 20, 1, 5b.
[22] Wang Ling (1947), 164, suggests that the "flower flames" were a kind of fireworks display. Cf. section on niter in chap. xiv, "Industrial Minerals."
[23] Balazs (1932), 52.
[24] TLSI, 8, 69.
[25] TLT, 16, 6a.
[26] TS, 146, 3997d.
[27] Laufer (1914a), 189–190.
[28] TLT, 16, 13a.
[29] See, for instance, the poem of Lu Kuei-meng, quoted in PWYF, p. 1453c, with reference to *chiao han*.
[30] TLT, 16, 13a.
[31] Laufer (1914a), 292.
[32] TFYK, 971, 3b.
[33] Mahler (1959), 111–112, pls. 37c and 38.
[34] Laufer (1914a), 294–300.
[35] TLT, 16, 13a; Laufer (1914a), 190.
[36] *Ming kuang chia.* Listed with iron armor in TLT, 16, 13a.
[37] TS, 220, 4149a–4149b; CTS, 199a, 3616b; TFYK, 970, 5b and 8b.
[38] TS, 220, 4148b.
[39] CTS, 2, 3069b, says in 638; TFYK, 970, 9a, says in 639.
[40] "Dark" (*hsüan*) may have another meaning here. TLT, 16, 13a, lists "mountain pattern" among the iron armors of the imperial armory.
[41] TS, 220, 4148a.
[42] THY, 26, 503.
[43] Tu Fu, "Lan Po Chung-yün . . . szu lun," CCCCTS, p. 179.
[44] It had been adopted in Ch'in or Han from the Hsiung-nu. Demiéville (1952), 180–181, 373–376. Laufer (1914a), 277, calls this "plate-mail." See also Mahler (1959), 112 and pls. 37a–37b, for illustrations. In TLT, 16, 13a, it is called "fine scale armor" (*hsi lin chia*).
[45] Rock (1955), 5.
[46] A. Stein (1921), 463–465; Demiéville (1952), 180–181, 373–376.
[47] Laufer (1914a), 301–305, thought "lion armor" (using an archaic, not a contemporary, word for "lion") was a kind of iron scale armor. But this is uncertain.
[48] *So-tzu chia.*

340

[49] TS, 221b, 4153d; CTS, 198, 3614a; TFYK, 971, 3a; THY, 99, 1775. See Laufer (1914a), 247.

[50] Demiéville (1952), 180–181 and 373–376.

[51] YYTT, 10, 79.

[52] Demiéville (1952), 180–181 and 373–376.

[53] Waley (1931), 107.

[54] TLT, 16, 13a.

[55] Tu Fu, "Chung kuo Ho shih" (third of five), CCCCTS, p. 283.

[56] Li Ho, "Kuei chu cheng hsing yüeh," LCCKS, 2, 18b.

[57] Li She (fl. 806), "Yü ti Po Hsin-lo chien ko," ChTS, han 7, ts'e 10, 3a.

[58] YYTT, 10, 79.

[59] Chapin (1940), xv, 88, 95, 141, and 201.

[60] For example, Li Chiao (644–713), "Chien," ChTS, han 2, ts'e 1, ch. 3, 6b, beginning with "Treasure sabers come from K'un-wu." Cf. Chapin (1940), 2.

[61] Tu Fu, "Fan chien," CCCCYS, p. 329.

[62] *I tao.*

[63] *Heng tao.*

[64] *Mo tao.*

[65] TLT, 16, 11b–12a.

[66] *Ch'i ch'iang.*

[67] *Mu ch'iang.*

[68] TLT, 16, 12a.

[69] *Shōsōin* (1928–), IV, contains many examples. The one described is shown in pl. 3.

[70] TS, 40, 3725b. Made at Chung-*chou* and Fu-*chou*.

[71] TS, 222a, 4157a; TFYK, 972, 5b.

[72] TS, 219, 4146d.

[73] Laufer (1919), 515–516.

[74] Needham (1958), 44–46.

[75] Pelliot (1959), 42. Pelliot thinks this is the same as the *andanique* of Marco Polo.

[76] Chapin (1940), 186.

[77] TLT, 16, 10b. Other types are also listed here.

[78] TS, 37, 3720d; 39, 3724a and 3724c.

[79] *Shōsōin* (1928–), X, 1–7.

[80] Barthold (1958), 235–236.

[81] TS, 219, 4146c.

[82] TS, 41, 3729b; from Yung-*chou* (Hunan) and Fu-*chou* (Kiangsi); TLT, 16, 11a.

[83] TLT, 16, 11a–11b.

[84] TS, 39, 3724d.

[85] TS, 219, 4146d.

[86] TS, 222c, 4162a.

[87] *Shōsōin* (1928–), X, 13–24.

[88] TS, 39, 3724d.

CHAPTER XVIII (Pages 265–268)

[1] Gernet (1956), 162.

[2] Gernet (1956), 163–164.

[3] TFYK, 970, 14b.

[4] Bagchi (1950), 157.

[5] Chou (1945a), 301.

[6] Reischauer (1955), 248.

[7] SKSC (TSDZK, 50, 710b). Compare the holy loot brought back by Hsüan-tsang; see Waley (1952), 81.

[8] YYTT, hsü chi, 5, 220.

[9] Grousset (1932), 265.

[10] TTKSC (TSDZK, 51, 3c).

[11] Reischauer (1955a), 221–224; Wright (1957), 38.

[12] Lévi and Chavannes (1895), 359–360.

[13] Reischauer (1955), 300–301; Reischauer (1955a), 190. We have the record of the formal presentation of a sacred relic to T'ai Tsung by Kapiśa in 637, but its character is not described; TFYK, 970, 8a.

[14] Reischauer (1955), 235.

[15] YYTT, hsü chi, 6, 221.

[16] Reischauer (1955a), 157–158.

[17] KIC (TPKC, 402, 3a–3b). A Pratyeka-Buddha was a being of hermitic tastes, devoted to seeking his own enlightenment, a sort of anti-Boddhisattva.

[18] Gernet (1956), 23–24.

[19] HHHP, 1, 55.

[20] Twitchett and Christie (1959), 177–178.

[21] TS, 46, 3741b.

[22] Acker (1954), 250–251. Sandalwood, aside from its fine appearance and pleasant odor, has the virtue of keeping out insects.

[23] Grousset (1932), 334.

[24] *Ling hua szu.*

[25] YYTT, hsü chi, 5, 217.

[26] TFYK, 972, 6a; THY, 49, 859.

[27] Waley (1931), 81–82.

[28] LTMHC, 9, 298.

[29] Gray (1959), 35–36.

[30] Eberhard (1948), 52; Soper (1951), 79.

[31] LTMHC, 3, 135; Pelliot (1923), 270; Bagchi (1950), 157–158; Waley (1952), 129.

[32] CHC, 5a. This report was part of that made by Tu Huan, taken prisoner at the Talas disaster by the Arabs, and published by his relative Tu Yu in his *T'ung tien*

CHAPTER XVIII (*Continued*)

(chs. 191–193) after returning to China. The artists mentioned were probably made prisoner in the same battle. See Pelliot (1928a), 110–112.

[33] THY, 49, 861.

[34] Reischauer (1955), 268.

CHAPTER XIX (Pages 269–277)

[1] YYTT, 11, 85.

[2] YYTT, 11, 86. Some of these strange names undoubtedly reflect the many scripts of Central Asia known through archaeology. See, for instance, v. Gabain (1961), 65–68, on the variety of scripts used by the Turks of Qočo.

[3] Ishida Mikinosuke (1948), 117–125; Lionel Giles (1957), x–xii; and especially Carter (1955), *passim*. Most papers used at the palace were made in the towns of Chekiang, though there were some exceptions, as a white hemp paper made at Ch'ang-tu. See TLT, 20, 18a–18b–19a.

[4] FHTL (HFLSF, cf. 18 = ts'e 10), p. 9a. A Sung book reporting on T'ang.

[5] SC, 123, 0267b.

[6] A. Stein (1907), 347.

[7] *Borassus flabellifera* (or *B. flabelliformis*).

[8] Transcribed as *puâi-tâ*. There was an erroneous etymology current in China, interpreting the first syllable alone as *pattra*, and the second as *tāra* "palm." Demiéville (1929), 90.

[9] CTS, 198, 3613d.

[10] YYTT, 18, 150.

[11] *Hsing shan szu.*

[12] TLCCFK, 2, 5b; CAC, 7, 8a–8b, both in Hiraoka (1956).

[13] Chang Ch'iao, "Hsing shan szu pei-to shu," ChTS, han 10, ts'e 1, ch. 2, 1a.

[14] *Fan chia. Fan* might perhaps be translated "Brahman" or even "Sanskrit." The word was used especially of the language, script, and books of Buddhism.

[15] See Wang Ch'i, commentary on Li Ho, "Sung Shen Ya-chih ko," LCCKS, 1, 8b–19a. In our own times the books are prepared as follows: the midrib of the leaf is removed, a pile of the halves so obtained is pressed, and the edges trimmed; the pages so made are smoothed by sanding; the text is scratched on with a stylus, and soot rubbed in to make it

visible. Schuyler (1908), 281–283. Presumably this was the ancient method, too. For "ollah," see Yule and Burnell (1903), 485.

[16] Reischauer (1955), 235.

[17] TCTC, 250, 10a.

[18] TFYK, 971, 15a; THY, 100, 1793; Lévi (1900), 417.

[19] TS, 221b, 4154d.

[20] Li Shang-yin, "T'i seng pi," ChTS, han 8, ts'e 9, ch. 1, 2b.

[21] P'i Jih-hsiu, "Ku yüan szu," ChTS, han 9, ts'e 9, ch. 3, 8b.

[22] Ishida Mikinosuke (1948), 102–103.

[23] Ishida (1948), 102–103; *Dragon King's Daughter* (1954), 68. There are references to book buying in the poems of Yüan Chen and Po Chü-i.

[24] Ishida (1948), 103–104; Needham (1959), 167.

[25] First named *Ch'ung hsien kuan* in 639, renamed *Ch'ung wen kuan* in 712.

[26] Called *Chi hsien yüan*.

[27] In the *Li cheng tien*.

[28] K. T. Wu (1937), 256–259; Ishida Mikinosuke (1948), 107–110; these derive in turn from TS, 57, 3761c; CTS, 47, 3270a.

[29] K. T. Wu (1937), 258.

[30] Bagchi (1950), 125.

[31] YYTT, hsü chi, 6, 226.

[32] YHTC, 3, 22.

[33] KSP (HCTY), c, 7a.

[34] TS, 89, 3896a; CTS, 167, 3515a.

[35] K. T. Wu (1937), 259–260; Ishida Mikinosuke (1948), 105.

[36] Lü Wen, "Shang-kuan Chao-jung shu lou ko," ChTS (1960 edition), 371, 4171–4172.

[37] The Chinese name for Champa, *Liəm-ʽiəp*, has been ingeniously interpreted by R. Stein (1947), 233, as Prum Irap, "Prome of the Elephant."

[38] All of the titles (and others) may be found in TS, 57 and 58.

[39] Lévi (1900), 297–298.

[40] Bagchi (1950), 72. Hsüan-tsang's journey was familiar to almost everyone in T'ang; it is mentioned in many T'ang books, as in YYTT, 3, 31, and in TTHY (TTTS, 3), 95b.

[41] CTS, 198, 3613d.

[42] Translation from Bagchi (1950), 83, based on the French of Chavannes.

[43] Chavannes (1894), 39–40.

[44] Chavannes (1894), 27.

[45] Lionel Giles (1935), 1.

[46] Lionel Giles (1937), 1–2.

[47] The authoritative text of the school called Kegon in Japan. The Chinese translation of 700 was also called *T'ang Sutra* or *New Sutra*.

[48] SKSC (TSDZK, 50), 2, 718c–719a.

[49] Chou (1945a), 264; Bagchi (1950), 53.

[50] TFYK, 971, 12a.

[51] Bagchi (1950), 52–53. The mission was referred to a few pages back.

[52] Bagchi (1950), 54; Wright (1957), 32.

[53] TFYK, 972, 6a.

[54] THY, 49, 864. In 745, the "Persian" temples, that is, Nestorian temples, of the two capitals were renamed "Great Ch'in" (Roman) temples to clarify the origin of the religion.

[55] THY, 49, 864.

[56] TS, 217b, 4142a.

[57] Bagchi (1950), 68.

[58] TS, 221a, 4153c; TFYK, 971, 4a; THY, 99, 1776.

[59] Needham (1959), 202.

[60] *Kịu-d'âm Sịĕt-d'ât.*

[61] The *nāvagrāha,* "Nine Upholders" (Needham's English; translated into Chinese as *chiu chih*), are the nine planets, that is, the five inner planets, the sun, the moon, and Rāhu and Ketu, invisible planets at the nodes of the moon's orbit to account for eclipses.

[62] Yabuuti (1954), 586–589. Guatama Siddhārtha was the author of a book (*K'ai yüan chan ching*), published in 729, which em-

bodied these novelties; Needham (1959), 202–203. The calculations in the *navagrāha* calendar as translated are based on observations from Ch'ang-an, and it cannot therefore be an exact translation of the Indian original. It contains the zero, trigonometric functions, and so on.

[63] The "Seven Luminaries" (*ch'i yao*) are the sun, moon, and five planets.

[64] Yeh Te-lu (1942), 157.

[65] TLSI, 2 (ch. 9), 82.

[66] Needham (1959), 202. Title here as translated by Bagchi.

[67] Huber (1906), 40–41. The Iranian forms I have quoted are not actually Sogdian, but are more familiar than the Sogdian, which are as follows (Bagchi [1950], 171): *mir, max, wnxan, ṭir, wrmzt, maxid* (sic), and *ḳewan*. It is curious that Mars' name is transcribed with Chinese characters meaning "Cloudy Han," the name of the Milky Way in Chinese.

[68] Chuang (1960), 271–301 and plate.

[69] Needham (1959), 360.

[70] Huber (1906), 41.

[71] SuS, 34, 2452c. A list of books based on this source also appears in TC, 69, 812b.

[72] THY, 95, 1712.

[73] YYTT, 12, 92.

[74] P'an (1958), 97.

[75] TLT, 5, 20b.

[76] CTS, 198, 3613d. Cf. Lévi (1900), 308; Waley (1952), 91.

Bibliography

PRIMARY SOURCES

*Parenthetical abbreviations stand for books listed
under "Collectanea and Encyclopedias" in the bibliography.*

CAC	Sung Min-ch'iu 宋敏求, *Ch'ang-an chih* 長安志, (Hiraoka, 1956)
CC	P'ei Hsing 裴鉶, *Ch'uan ch'i* 傳奇
CCCCTS	Tu Fu 杜甫, *Chiu chia chi chu Tu shih* 九家集注杜詩 (*Concordance*, 1940)
CCF	Sun Szu-miao 孫思邈, *Ch'ien chin fang* 千金方
CCL	Wen T'ing-yün 溫庭筠, *Ching chuang lu* 觀粧錄 (SF)
CFC	Ts'ui Ling-ch'in 崔令欽, *Chiao fang chi* 教坊記 (TSCC)
CHC	Tu Huan 杜環, *Ching hsing chi* 經行記 (CCTSKTS)
ChIC	Li Chün 李睿, *Chih i chi* 摭異集 (TTTS)
ChIL	T'ao Ku 陶穀, *Ch'ing i lu* 清異錄 (HYHTS)
CHL	Wei Hsüan 韋絢, *Liu Pin-k'o chia hua lu* 劉賓客嘉話錄 (TTTS)
CHP	Tuan Ch'eng-shih 段成式, *Chi huan p'in* 髻鬟品 (SF)
ChS	*Chou shu* 周書
CIC	Hsüeh Chou-jo 薛周弱, *Chi i chi* 集異記 (TTTS)
CIL	Ch'in Tsai-szu 秦再思, *Chi i lu* 紀異錄 (HFLSF)
CL	*Chou li* 周禮
CLC	Chang Mi 張泌, *Chuang lou chi* 牧樓記 (TTTS)
CLCC	Chiang Tsung 江總, *Chiang Ling chün chi* 江令君集 (HWLC)
CLHC	Chou Tun-i 周敦頤, *Chou Lien-hsi chi* 周濂溪集 (TSCC)
CLPT	*Ch'ung hsiu Cheng ho cheng lei pen ts'ao* 重修政和證類本草 (SPTK)
CLWKC	*Ching lung wen kuan chi* 景龍文館記
CMYS	Chia Szu-hsieh 賈思勰, *Ch'i min yao shu* 齊民要書
CS	*Chin shu* 晉書 (KM)
CSC	Feng Chih 馮贄, *Chi shih chu* 記事珠 (TTTS)
CSL	Hsü Hsüan 徐鉉, *Chi shen lu* 稽神錄 (SF)
CSS	Kuo T'o-t'o 郭橐駝, *Chung shu shu* 種樹書 (SF)
CSYSC	Chang Chi 張籍, *Chang Szu-yeh shih chi* 張司業詩集 (SPTK)
CTC	Yü-wen—— 宇文氏, *Chuang t'ai chi* 粧臺記 (SF)
CTS	*Chiu T'ang shu* 舊唐書 (KM)

CW   Niu Su 牛肅, *Chi wen* 紀聞

CWTS   *Chiu Wu Tai shih* 舊五代史 (KM)

CYCT   Chang Cho 張鷟, *Ch'ao yeh ch'ien tsai* 朝野僉載 (TTTS)

EY   *Erh ya* 爾雅

EYI   Lo Yüan 羅願, *Erh ya i* 爾雅翼 (TSCC)

FCWC   Tu Mu 杜牧, *Fan ch'uan wen chi* 樊川文集 (SPTK)

FHTL   Ku Wen-chien 顧文薦, *Fu hsüan tsa lu* 負暄雜錄 (HFLSF)

FLHSWC   Lu Kuei-meng 陸龜蒙, *Fu-li hsien sheng wen chi* 甫里先生文集 (SPTK)

FSYL   Chang Yen-yüan 張彥遠, *Fa shu yao lu* 法書要錄 (TSCC)

HC   Chang Fan 張璠, *Han chi* 漢紀

HCLC   Han Yü 韓愈, *Han Ch'ang-li chi* 韓昌黎集 (KHCPTS)

HHHP   *Hsüan ho hua p'u* 宣和畫譜 (TSCC)

HHPT   *Hsin hsiu pen ts'ao* 新修本草 (facsimile, Shanghai, 1959)

HHS   *Hou Han shu* 後漢書 (KM)

HKI   Ying Shao 應劭, *Han kuan i* 漢官儀

HKSC   Tao-hsüan 道宣, *Hsü Kao seng chuan* 續高僧傳

HNT   *Huai nan tzu* 淮南子

HP   Hung Ch'u 洪芻, *Hsiang p'u* 香譜 (TSCC)

HS   *Han shu* 漢書 (KM)

HsHS   *Hsü Han shu* 續漢書

HTC   Ch'ang Feng-chen 常奉真, *Hsiang t'an chi* 湘潭記

ICCYI   Hui-lin 慧琳, *I ch'ieh ching yin i* 一切經音義 (TSDZK)

IL   *I Li* 儀禮

ISTC   Li Shang-yin 李商隱, *I shan tsa chi* 義山雜纂 (TTTS)

JCSP   Hung Mai 洪邁, *Jung chai sui pi* 容齋隨筆 (TSCC)

KC   Kuo I-kung 郭義恭, *Kuang chih* 廣志

KCC   Ts'ui Pao 崔豹, *Ku chin chu* 古今注

KHTS   Chou Mi 周密, *Kuei hsin tsa shih (hsü chi)* 癸辛雜識 (續集) (HCTY)

KHYHC   Fan Ch'eng-ta 范成大, *Kuei hai yü heng chih* 桂海虞衡志 (PSNIC)

KIC   Tai Fu 戴孚, *Kuang i chi* 廣異記

KKYL   Ts'ao Chao 曹昭, *Ko ku yao lun* 格古要論 (TSCC)

KSP   Li Chao 李肇, [*T'ang*] *Kuo shih pu* 國史補 (HCTY)

KSTI   *Kuo shih tsuan i* 國史纂異

KTCHC   Cheng Ch'i 鄭綮, *K'ai t'ien ch'uan hsin chi* 開天傳信記 (TTTS)

KTCY   Wang Su 王肅, *K'ung tzu chia yü* 孔子家語

KuCC   *Kuang chou chi* 廣州記

KY   Lu Fa-yen 陸法言, *Kuang yün* 廣韻 (rev. by Ch'en P'eng-nien 陳彭年)

KYTPIS   Wang Jen-yü 王仁裕, *K'ai yüan T'ien pao i shih* 開元天寶遺事 (TTTS)

LC   *Li chi* 禮記

LCC   Chang Chün-fang 張君房, *Li ch'ing chi* 麗情集 (SF)

LCCKS   Li Ho 李賀, *Li Ch'ang-chi ko shih* 李長吉歌詩 (1760)

LCCWH   *Liu ch'en chu Wen hsüan* 六臣註文選

LCWTC   *Liang Chien wen ti chi* 梁簡文帝集 (HWLC)

LHC   *Lin hai chih* 臨海志

LHSC	Liu Tsung-yüan 柳宗元, *Tseng kuang chu shih yin pien T'ang Liu hsien sheng chi* 增廣註釋音辯唐柳先生集 (SPTK)
LIC	Tu Kuang-t'ing 杜光庭, *Lu i chi* 錄異記
LiHC	Wang K'uei 王逵, *Li hai chi* 蠡海集 (TSCC)
LMCTC	Yang Chü-yüan 楊巨源, *Li Mo ch'ui ti chi* 李謩吹笛記 (TTTS)
LMTWC	Liu Yü-hsi 劉禹錫, *Liu Meng-te wen chi* 劉夢得文集 (SPTK)
LPLI	Liu Hsün, 劉恂, *Ling piao lu i* 嶺表錄異 (TSCC)
LS	*Liao shih* 遼史 (KM)
LTMHC	Chang Yen-yüan 張彥遠, *Li tai ming hua chi* 歷代名畫記 (TSCC)
LTPWC	Li Po 李白, *Li T'ai-po wen chi* 李太白文集 (Hiraoka, 1958)
LYC	*Leng yen ching* 楞嚴經
LYMTC	Ou-yang Hsiu 歐陽修, *Lo-yang mu-tan chi* 洛陽牡丹記 (PCHH)
MCML	Chang Pang-chi 張邦基, *Mo chuang man lu* 墨莊漫錄 (TSCC)
MCPT	Shen Kua 沈括, *Meng ch'i pi t'an* 夢溪筆談 (TSCC)
MHTL	Cheng Ch'u-hui 鄭處誨, *Ming huang tsa lu* 明皇雜錄 (TTTS)
MHTLCKC	Ch'ien Hsi-tso 錢熙祚, *Ming huang tsa lu chiao k'an chi* 明皇雜錄校勘記 (SSKTS)
MS	Fan Ch'o 樊綽, *Man shu* 蠻書 (TSCC)
MTTC	*Mu t'ien tzu chuan* 穆天子傳 (TSCC)
NCS	*Nan Ch'i shu* 南齊書 (KM)
NFIWC	Fang Ch'ien-li 房千里, *Nan fang i wu chih* 南方異物志
NFTMC	Chi Han 嵇含, *Nan fang ts'ao mu chuang* 南方草木狀
NHCSC	Wu Lan-hsiu 吳蘭修, *Nan Han chin shih chi* 南漢金石記 (TSCC)
NKCML	Wu Tseng 吳曾, *Neng kai chai man lu* 能改齋漫錄 (TSCC)
NPYHC	Feng Chih 馮贄, *Nan pu yen hua chi* 南部烟花記 (TTTS)
NS	*Nan shih* 南史
NYC	Shen Huai-yüan 沈懷遠, *Nan Yüeh chih* 南越志
PCS	*Pei Ch'i shu* 北齊書 (KM)
PHL	Tuan Kung-lu 段公路, *Pei hu lu* 北戶錄 (TTTS; HHLP)
PKLT	Po Chü-i 白居易 and K'ung Chuan 孔傳, *Po K'ung liu t'ieh* 白孔六帖 (Ming *Chia ching* edition)
PLC	Sun Ch'i 孫棨, *Pei li chih* 北里志 (TTTS)
PMSY	Sun Kuang-hsien 孫光憲, *Pei meng so yen* 北夢瑣言 (TSCC)
PS	*Pei shih* 北史 (KM)
PSCCC	Po Chü-i 白居易, *Po shih Ch'ang-ch'ing chi* 白氏長慶集 (SPTK)
PSMC	Lu Yu 陸游, *P'i shu man ch'ao* 避暑漫抄 (TSCC)
PTKM	Li Shih-chen 李時珍, *Pen ts'ao kang mu* 本草綱目 (*Hung pao chai* edition)
PTSI	Ch'en Ts'ang-ch'i 陳藏器, *Pen ts'ao shih i* 本草拾遺
SAWC	Yang Shen 楊慎, *Sheng an wai chi* 升菴外集
SC	*Shih chi* 史記 (KM)
SCC	Wang Shao-chih 王韶之, *Shen ching chi* 神境記 (SF)
SHC	*Shan hai ching* 山海經
ShIC	Wang Hsi 王嘉, *Shih i chi* 拾遺記 (PSNIC)
SIC	Jen Fang 任昉, *Shu i chi* 述異記 (HWTS)
SKC	*San kuo chih* 三國志 (KM)
SKSC	Tsan-ning 贊寧, *Sung kao seng chuan* 宋高僧傳 (TSDZK)
SLPT	Meng Shen 孟詵, *Shih liao pen ts'ao* 食療本草

SP	Wei Chü-yüan 韋巨源, *Shih p'u* 食譜 (TTTS)
SPT	Han Pao-sheng 韓保昇, *Shu pen ts'ao* 蜀本草
SS	*Sung shih* 宋史 (KM)
STCH	Liu Su 劉餗, *Sui T'ang chia hua* 隋唐嘉話 (TTTS)
SuS	*Sui shu* 隋書 (KM)
SWCY	Kao Ch'eng 高承, *Shih wu chi yüan* 事物紀原 (TSCC)
TC	Cheng Ch'iao 鄭樵, *T'ung chih* 通志 (KM)
TCTC	Szu-ma Kuang 司馬光, *Tzu chih t'ung chien* 資治通鑑 (Tokyo, 1892)
TCWC	*T'ai chen wai chuan* 太真外傳 (TTTS)
TFCY	Tu-ku T'ao 獨孤滔, *Tan fang ching yüan* 丹房鏡源
TFYK	*Ts'e fu yüan kuei* 冊府元龜 (1642 edition)
THPL	Wei T'ai 魏泰, *Tung hsüan pi lu* 東軒筆錄 (TSCC)
THY	*T'ang hui yao* 唐會要 (TSCC)
TLCCFK	Hsü Sung 徐松, *T'ang liang ching ch'eng fang k'ao* 唐兩京城坊考 (Hiraoka, 1956)
TLSI	Chang-sun Wu-chi 長孫無忌, *T'ang lü shu i* 唐律疏義 (KHCTPS)
TLT	*T'ang liu tien* 唐六典 (Kyoto, 1935)
TMC	[*Pieh kuo*] *tung ming chi* [別國] 洞冥記 (Tseng ting HWTS)
TMJHPT	*Ta ming jih hua pen ts'ao* 大明日華本草
TPHYC	*T'ai p'ing huan yü chi* 太平寰宇記 (1803 edition)
TPKC	*T'ai p'ing kuang chi* 太平廣記 (1846 edition)
TPT	Su Kung 蘇恭, *T'ang pen ts'ao chu* 唐本草注
TPYL	*T'ai p'ing yü lan* 太平御覽 (1892 edition)
TS	*T'ang shu* 唐書 (KM)
TTCLC	Chao Hsi-hu 趙希鵠, *Tung t'ien ch'ing lu chi* 洞天清錄集 (TSCC)
TTHY	Liu Su 劉肅, *Ta T'ang hsin yü* 大唐新語 (TTTS)
TTHYC	Hsüan-tsang 玄奘, *Ta T'ang hsi yü chi* 大唐西域記 (SPTK)
TTKSC	I-ching 義淨, *Ta T'ang hsi yü ch'iu fa kao seng chuan* 大唐西域求法高僧傳
TTSL	[*T'ang*] *T'ai Tsung shih lu* [唐] 太宗實錄
TuT	Tu Yu 杜佑, *T'ung tien* 通典 (KM)
TYF	Ts'ui Hsing-kung 崔行功, *Tsuan yao fang* 纂要方
TYTP	Su O 蘇鶚, *Tu yang tsa pien* 杜陽雜編 (TTTS)
WFCSC	Wen T'ing-yün 溫庭筠, *Wen Fei-ch'ing shih chi chien chu* 溫飛卿詩集箋注 (1920 edition)
WHTK	Ma Tuan-lin 馬端臨, *Wen hsien t'ung k'ao* 文獻通考 (KM)
WL	Kao Szu-sun 高似孫, *Wei lüeh* 緯略
WS	*Wei shu* 魏書 (KM)
WTAC	Wang Po 王勃, *Wang Tzu-an chi* 王子安集 (1922 edition)
WTS	*Wu Tai shih* 五代史 (KM)
YCYI	Fan Shu 范攄, *Yün ch'i yu i* 雲溪友議
YFL	Ch'eng Ta-ch'ang 程大昌, *Yen fan lu* 演繁露 (HCTY)
YFTL	Tuan An-chieh 段安節, *Yüeh fu tsa lu* 樂府雜錄 (TTTS)
YHCC	*Yeh hou chia chuan* 鄴侯家傳
YHTC	Feng Chih 馮贄, *Yün hsien tsa chi* 雲仙雜記 (TSCC)
YLSP	Tu Wan 杜綰, *Yün lin shih p'u* 雲林石譜 (TSCC)
YP	Hou Ning-chi 侯寧極, *Yüeh p'u* 樂譜 (ed. by T'ao Ku 陶穀) (TTTS)

Bibliography

YS	*Yüan shih* 元 史 (KM)
YSCCC	Yüan Chen 元 稹, *Yüan shih Ch'ang-ch'ing chi* 元 氏 長 慶 集 (1929 edition)
YTCC	Yü Chien-wu 庾 肩 吾, *Yü Tu-chih chi* 庾 度 支 集 (HWLC)
YTCWC	see TCWC
YYKYL	Chou Mi 周 密, *Yün yen kuo yen lu* 雲 烟 過 眼 錄 (TSCC)
YYTT	Tuan Ch'eng-shih 段 成 式, *Yu yang tsa tsu* 酉 陽 雜 俎 (TSCC)

Collectanea and Encyclopaedias

CCTSKTS	*Che-chiang t'u-shu-kuan ts'ung shu* 浙 江 圖 書 館 叢 書
CHSKCNPCS	*Ch'üan Han San kuo Chin Nan pei ch'ao shih* 全 漢 三 國 晉 南 北 朝 詩
ChTS	*Ch'üan T'ang shih* 全 唐 詩
CTPS	*Chin tai pi shu* 津 逮 秘 書
CTW	*Ch'üan T'ang wen* 全 唐 文
HCTY	*Hsüeh chin t'ao yüan* 學 津 討 原
HFLSF	Han fen lou *Shuo fu* 函 芬 樓 說 郛
HHLP	*Hsüeh hai lei pien* 學 海 類 編
HWLC	*Han Wei Liu ch'ao san po chia chi* 漢 魏 六 朝 三 百 家 集
HWTS	*Han Wei ts'ung shu* 漢 魏 叢 書
HYHTS	*Hsi yin hsüan ts'ung shu* 惜 陰 軒 叢 書
KCSH	*Ku chin shuo hai* 古 今 說 海
KHCPTS	*Kuo-hsüeh chi-pen ts'ung shu* 國 學 基 本 叢 書
KM	*K'ai ming* edition 開 明
PCHH	*Po ch'uan hsüeh hai* 百 川 學 海
PSNIC	*Pi shu nien i chung* 秘 書 廿 一 種
PWYF	*P'ei wen yün fu* 佩 文 韻 府
SF	*Shuo fu* (1647 edition) 說 郛
SPTK	*Szu pu ts'ung k'an* 四 部 叢 刊
SSKTS	*Shou shan ko ts'ung shu* 守 山 閣 叢 書
TSCC	*Ts'ung shu chi ch'eng* 叢 書 集 成
TSDZK	*Taishō Daizōkyō* 大 正 大 藏 經
TSPMCCC	*T'ang shih po ming chia ch'üan chi* 唐 詩 百 名 家 全 集
TuSCC	*T'u shu chi ch'eng* 圖 書 集 成
TT	Chu Ch'i-feng 朱 起 鳳, *Tz'u t'ung* 辭 通 (Shanghai, 1934)
TTTS	*T'ang tai ts'ung shu* 唐 代 叢 書 (1864 edition)
YSH	*Yüan shih hsüan* 元 詩 選

SECONDARY SOURCES

ACKER, W. R. B.
1954   *Some T'ang and Pre-T'ang Texts on Chinese Painting* (Leiden, 1954).
ANDERSON, J. K.
1961   *Ancient Greek Horsemanship* (Berkeley and Los Angeles, 1961).

ANDERSSON, J. G.

1943 "Researches into the Prehistory of the Chinese," *Bulletin of the Museum of Far Eastern Antiquities,* Vol. 15 (Stockholm, 1943), 1–304.

ARAI KEN

1955 "Ri Ga no shi—toku ni sono shikisai ni tsuite," *Chūgoku bungaku hō,* Vol. 3 (Kyoto, 1955), 61–90.

1959 *Ri Ga* (Tokyo, 1959).

ASAHINA YASUHIKO, ed.

1955 *Shōsōin yakubutsu* (Osaka, 1955).

AYMONIER, E.

1891 "Les Tchames et leurs religions," *Revue de l'histoire des religions,* Vol. 24 (1891), 187–237, 261–315.

AYSCOUGH, FLORENCE

1929 *Tu Fu: The Autobiography of a Chinese Poet, A.D. 712–770,* Vol. I (Boston, New York, London, 1929).

BAGCHI, PRABODH CHANDRA

1929 *Deux lexiques Sanskrit-chinois,* Vol. I (Paris, 1929).

1950 *India and China: A Thousand Years of Cultural Relations,* 2nd edition (Bombay, 1950).

BAILEY, H. W.

1937 "Ttaugara," *Bulletin of the School of Oriental and African Studies,* Vol. 8 (London, 1937), 883–921.

1961 *Indo-Scythian Studies, Being Khotanese Texts Volume IV (Saka Texts from Khotan in the Hedin Collection)* (Cambridge, England, 1961).

BALAZS, ETIENNE [Stefan Balázs]

1931 "Beiträge zur Wirtschaftsgeschichte der T'ang-Zeit," *Mitteilungen des Seminars für orientalische Sprachen,* Vol. 34 (1931), 1–92.

1932 "Beiträge zur Wirtschaftsgeschichte der T'ang-Zeit," *Mitteilungen des Seminars für orientalische Sprachen,* Vol. 35 (1932), 1–73.

1960 "The birth of capitalism in China," *Journal of the Economic and Social History of the Orient,* Vol. 3 (1960), 196–216.

BALL, SYDNEY H.

1950 *A Roman Book on Precious Stones, Including an English Modernization of the 37th Booke of the Historie of the World by E. Plinius Secundus* (Los Angeles, 1950).

BALTRUŠAITIS, JURGIS

1955 *Le moyen âge fantastique: antiquités et exotismes dans l'art gothique* (Paris, 1955).

BANG, W., and G. R. RACHMATI

1932 "Die Legende von Oγuz Qaγan," *Sitzungsberichte der preussischen Akademie der Wissenschaften* (Philosophisch-historische Klasse, 1932), 683–724.

BARTHOLD, W.

1958 *Turkestan Down to the Mongol Invasion,* 2nd edition (London, 1958).

BAXTER, G. W.

1953 "Metrical Origins of the Tz'u," *Harvard Journal of Asiatic Studies,* Vol. 16 (1953), 108–145.

BEAL, SAMUEL

1885 *Si-yu-ki: Buddhist Records of the Western World Translated from the Chinese of Hiuen Tsiang (A.D. 629),* 2 vols. (Boston, 1885).

BERGMAN, FOLKE
  1939 *Archaeological Researches in Sinkiang,* Publication 7 (Stockholm: Sino-Swedish Expedition, 1939).
BERTHELOT, M.
  1938 *Introduction a l'étude de la chimie des anciens et du moyen-âge* (Paris, 1938).
BLACKBAND, W. T.
  1934 "My Rediscovery of the Etruscan Art of Granulation," *Illustrated London News* (April 28, 1934), p. 659.
BLAIR, DOROTHY
  1960 "The Cloisonné-Backed Mirror in the Shosoin," *Journal of Glass Studies,* Vol. 2 (1960), 83–93.
BOODBERG, P. A.
  1935 "Some Early 'Turco-Mongol' Toponyms," *Hu T'ien Han Yüeh Fang Chu,* Vol. 9 (May, 1935), 11–13.
  1937 "Some Proleptical Remarks on the Evolution of Archaic Chinese," *Harvard Journal of Asiatic Studies,* Vol. 2 (1937), 329–372.
BOSTOCK, JOHN, and H. T. RILEY, trans.
  1855 *The Natural History of Pliny,* Vol. III (London, 1855).
  1856 *The Natural History of Pliny,* Vol. IV (London, 1856).
BOYER, MARTHA
  1952 *Mongol Jewellery: Researches on the Silver Jewellery Collected by the First and Second Danish Central Asian Expeditions Under the Leadership of Henning Haslund-Christensen 1936–37 and 1938–39* (København: National museets skrifter, Ethnografisk Raekke, 1952), V.
BRADDELL, DATO SIR ROLAND
  1956 "Malayadvipa: A Study in Early Indianization," *Malayan Journal of Tropical Geography,* Vol. 9 (December, 1956), 1–20.
BRIDGES, WILLIAM
  1948 *Wild Animals of the World* (Garden City, 1948).
BROCKELMANN, C.
  1928 *Mitteltürkischer Wortschatz nach Maḥmūd al-Kāšgarīs Dīvān Lugāt at-Turk* (Leipzig, 1928).
BROMEHEAD, C. E. N.
  1945 "Geology in Embryo (up to 1600 A.D.)," *Proceedings of the Geologists' Association,* Vol. 56 (1945), 89–134.
BROUGH, JOHN
  1948 "Legends of Khotan and Nepal," *Bulletin of the School of Oriental and African Studies,* Vol. 12 (London, 1948), 333–339.
BRYANT, P. L.
  1925 "Chinese Camphor and Camphor Oil," *China Journal,* Vol. 3 (1925), 228–234.
BURKILL, I. H.
  1935 *A Dictionary of the Economic Products of the Malay Peninsula* (London, 1935).
BURTON, RICHARD F.
  1934 *The Book of the Thousand Nights and a Night: A Plain and Literal Translation of the Arabian Nights Entertainments,* 3 vols. (New York, 1934).
BUSHELL, S. W.
  1880 "The Early History of Tibet. From Chinese Sources," *Journal of the Royal Asiatic Society,* n.s., Vol 12 (1880), 435–541.

CARTER, THOMAS F.

1955   *The Invention of Printing in China and Its Spread Westward*, 2nd edition, rev. by L. C. Goodrich (New York, 1955).

CHANG CH'ANG-KUNG

1951   *T'ang Sung ch'uan-ch'i tso-che chi ch'i shih-tai* (Peking, 1951).

CHANG, H. T.

1926   "On the Question of the Existence of Elephants and the Rhinoceros in Northern China in Historical Times," *Bulletin of the Geological Society of China*, Vol. 5 (1926), 99–106.

CHANG HSING-LANG

1929   "T'ang-shih Fei-chou hei-nu shu Chung-kuo k'ao," *Fu-jen hsüeh-chih*, Vol. 1 (1929), 93–112.

1930   *Chung-hsi chiao-t'ung shih-liao hui-p'ien* (Pei-p'ing, 1930).

1930a   "The Importation of Negro Slaves to China Under the T'ang Dynasty," *Bulletin of the Catholic University of Peking*, Vol. 7 (December, 1930), 37–59.

CHANG HUNG-CHAO

1921   "Shih ya (Lapidarium Sinicum)," *Ti-chih chuan-pao*, ser. B, no. 2 (Peking, 1921).

CHANG TZU-KAO

1958   "Ts'ung tu-hsi t'ung-ch'i t'an-tao wu-tzu pen-i," *K'ao-ku hsüeh-pao*, Vol. 3 (1958), 73–74.

CHANG WAN

1960   "P'u-sa-man chi ch'i hsiang-kuan chih chu-wen-t'i," *Ta-lu tsa-chih*, Vol. 20 (1960), 19–24, 47–49, 93–98.

CHAO WEN-JUI

1926   "T'ang-tai shang-yeh chih t'e-tien," *Ch'ing-hua hsüeh-pao*, Vol. 3 (1926), 951–966.

CHAPIN, HELEN B.

1940   "Toward the Study of the Sword as Dynastic Talisman: The Fêng-ch'êng Pair and the Sword of Han Kao Tsu," unpublished Ph.D. dissertation, University of California, Berkeley, June, 1940.

CHAVANNES, EDOUARD

1894   *Mémoire composé a l'époque de la grande dynastie T'ang sur les religieux éminents qui allèrent chercher la loi dans les pays d'occident par I-tsing* (Paris, 1894).

1903   *Documents sur les Tou-kiue (Turcs) Occidentaux* (St. Pétersbourg, 1903).

1905   "Le pays d'Occident d'après de *Wei lio*," *T'oung pao*, Vol. 6 (1905), 519–571.

CH'EN PANG-HSIEN

1957   *Chung-kuo i-hsüeh shih* (Shanghai, 1957).

CH'EN TSU-KUEI, ed.

1957   *Chung-kuo nung-hsüeh i-ch'an hsüan-chi*, A, 5, "Mien" (*shang pien*) (Shanghai, 1957).

CH'EN YÜAN

1928   "Manichaeism in China," *Bulletin of the Catholic University of Peking*, Vol. 4 (May, 1928), 59–68.

CHENG CHEN-TO

1958   Preface, *Shan-hsi-sheng ch'u-t'u T'ang-yung hsüan-chi* (Peking, 1958).

CHENG TSO-HSIN

1955   *Chung-kuo niao-lei fen-pu mu-lu*, Vol. I (Peking, 1955).

CHMIELEWSKI, JANUSZ

1958 "The Problem of Early Loan-Words in Chinese as Illustrated by the Word *p'u-t'ao*," *Rocznik orientalistyczny*, Vol. 22, no. 2 (1958), 7–45.

1961 "Two Early Loan-Words in Chinese," *Rocznik orientalistyczny*, Vol. 24, no. 2 (1961), 65–86.

CHOU YI-LIANG

1945 "Notes on Marvazī's Account of China," *Harvard Journal of Asiatic Studies*, Vol. 9 (1945), 13–23.

1945a "Tantrism in China," *Harvard Journal of Asiatic Studies*, Vol. 8 (1945), 241–332.

CHRISTENSEN, ARTHUR

1936 "L'Iran sous les Sassanides," *Annales du Musée Guimet, Bibliothèques d'Etudes*, Vol. 48 (1936).

CHRISTIE, ANTHONY

1957 "Ta-ch'in P'o-lo-men," *Bulletin of the School of Oriental and African Studies*, Vol. 20 (London, 1957), 159–166.

1957a "An Obscure Passage from the *Periplus*: κολανδιοφωντα τὰ μέγιστα," *Bulletin of the School of Oriental and African Studies*, Vol. 19 (London, 1957), 345–353.

CHU HSIU-HSIA

1957 *T'ang-tai ch'uan-ch'i yen-chiu* (Taipei, 1957).

CH'ÜAN HAN-SHENG

1947 "T'ang-tai wu-chia-ti pien-tung," *Kuo-li chung-yang yen-chiu-yüan, li-shih yü-yen yen-chiu-so chi-k'an*, Vol. 11 (Shanghai, 1947), 101–148.

1947a "T'ang-Sung shih-tai Yang-chou ching-chi ching-k'uang-ti fan-jung yü shuai-lo," *Kuo-li chung-yang yen-chiu-yüan, li-shih yü-yen yen-chiu-so chi-k'an*, Vol. 11 (Shanghai, 1947), 149–176.

1948 "Chung-ku tzu-jan ching-chi," *Kuo-li chung-yang yen-chiu-yüan, li-shih yü-yen yen-chiu-so chi-k'an*, Vol. 10 (1948), 73–173.

CHUANG SHEN

1960 "Mi jih k'ao" [An investigation of "Mihr" as Sunday in a Week Introduced into China During the T'ang Dynasty], *Bulletin of the Institute of History and Philology, Academia Sinica*, Vol. 31 (1960), 271–301.

COEDÉS, G.

1948 *Les états hindouisés d'Indochine et d'Indonesie* (Paris, 1948).

COLLIER, V. W. F.

1921 *Dogs of China and Japan in Nature and Art* (London, 1921).

Concordance

1940 "A Concordance to the Poems of Tu Fu," *Harvard-Yenching Institute Sinological Index Series*, Vol. II, Suppl. 14 (Cambridge, 1940).

Cox, E. H. M.

1945 *Plant-Hunting in China: A History of Botanical Exploration in China and the Tibetan Marches* (London, 1945).

CREVOST, CH.

1925 "Catalogue des produits de l'Indochine," *Bulletin Economique de l'Indochine* (n.s., 1925), 26–30.

DANA, E. S.

1892 *The System of Mineralogy of James Dwight Dana: Descriptive Mineralogy* (New York, 1892).

DAVID, A., and E. OUSTALET
  1877 *Les Oiseaux de la Chine* (Paris, 1877).

DAVIDSON, J. LEROY
  1954 *The Lotus Sutra in Chinese Art: A Study in Buddhist Art to the Year 1000* (New Haven, 1954).

DAVIS, FRANK
  1960 "A Ming Winecup and Cloisonné" (A Page for Collectors), *Illustrated London News* (October 15, 1960), p. 650.

DELACOUR, JEAN
  1947 *Birds of Malaysia* (New York, 1947).
  1951 *The Pheasants of the World* (London and New York, 1951).

DELACOUR, J., and P. JABOUILLE
  1931 *Les Oiseaux de l'Indochine Française,* Vol. IV (Paris, 1931).

DEMIÉVILLE, P.
  1924 "Review of Tchang Hong-tchao, *Che ya* (*Lapidarium sinicum*)," *Bulletin de l'Ecole Française d'Extrême-Orient,* Vol. 24 (1924), 276–301.
  1925 "La musique čame au Japon," *Etudes asiatiques publieés a l'occasion du vingt-cinquième anniversaire de l'Ecole Française d'Extrême-Orient,* Vol. 1 (1925), 199–226.
  1952 *Le concile de Lhasa: une controverse sur le quiétisme entre bouddhistes de l'Inde et de la Chine au viiie siècle de l'ère chrétienne* (Paris, 1952).

DEMIÉVILLE, P., ed.
  1929 *Hôbôgirin* (Tokyo, 1929).

Derniers Refuges
  1956 *Derniers Refuges:* Atlas commenté des réserves naturelles dans le monde, préparé par l'Union Internationale pour la Conservation de la Nature et de ses Resources (Brussels, 1956).

Dragon King's Daughter
  1954 *The Dragon King's Daughter: Ten Tang Dynasty Stories* (Peking, 1954).

DRAKE, F. S.
  1940 "Foreign Religions of the T'ang Dynasty," *Chinese Recorder,* Vol. 71 (1940), 343–354, 643–649, 675–688.
  1943 "Mohammedanism in the T'ang Dynasty," *Monumenta Serica,* Vol. 8 (1943), 1–40.

DUBS, H. H.
  1944 *The History of the Former Han Dynasty by Pan Ku,* Vol. II (Baltimore, 1944, reprinted 1954).

DUYVENDAK, J. J. L.
  1939 "The True Dates of the Chinese Maritime Expeditions in the Early Fifteenth Century," *T'oung Pao,* Vol. 34 (1939), 341–412.
  1949 *China's Discovery of Africa* (London, 1949).

EBERHARD, W.
  1937 *Typen chinesischer Volksmärchen* (FF Communications, no. 120, Helsinki, 1937).
  1942 "Kultur und Siedlung der Randvölker Chinas," *T'oung Pao,* Suppl. to Vol. 36 (1942).
  1942a "Lokalkulturen im alten China," I, *T'oung Pao,* Suppl. to Vol. 37 (1942); II, *Monumenta Serica,* Monograph 3 (1942).
  1948 "Some Cultural Traits of the Sha-t'o Turks," *Oriental Art,* Vol. 1 (1948), 50–55.
  1950 *A History of China* (Berkeley and Los Angeles, 1950).

ECKE, G., and P. DEMIÉVILLE
1935 *The Twin Pagodas of Zayton: A Study of Later Buddhist Sculpture in China* (Cambridge, Mass., 1935).

EDWARDS, E. D.
1937 *Chinese Prose Literature of the T'ang Period, A.D. 618–906*, Vol. I (London, 1937).

EGAMI, NAMIO
1951 "The k'uai-t'i, the t'ao-yu, and the tan-hsi, the strange domestic animals of the Hsiung-nu," *Memoirs of the Research Department of the Toyo Bunko*, Vol. 13 (Tokyo, 1951), 87–123.

Encyclopaedia Britannica
1956 *Encyclopaedia Britannica* (Chicago, 1956).

ERKES, EDUARD
1940 "Das Pferd im alten China," *T'oung Pao*, Vol. 36 (1940), 26–63.
1942 "Vogelzucht im alten China," *T'oung Pao*, Vol. 37 (1942), 15–34.

ETTINGHAUSEN, RICHARD
1950 *Studies in Muslim Iconography: I. The Unicorn*, Freer Gallery of Art, Occasional Papers, Vol. 1, no. 3 (Washington, 1950).

FARQUHAR, DAVID M.
1957 "Oirat-Chinese Tribute Relations, 1408–1446," *Festschrift für Nikolaus Poppe* (Wiesbaden, 1957), pp. 60–68.

FENG, HAN-YI
1944 "The Discovery and Excavation of the Royal Tomb of Wang Chien," *Szechwan Museum Occasional Papers*, no. 1 (reprinted from *Quarterly Bulletin of Chinese Bibliography*, n.s., Vol. 4, nos. 1–2 [Chengtu, 1944], 1–11).

FERNALD, HELEN E.
1935 "The Horses of T'ang T'ai Tsung and the Stele of Yu," *Journal of the American Oriental Society*, Vol. 55 (1935), 420–428.
1942 "In Defense of the Horses of T'ang T'ai Tsung," *Bulletin of the University Museum*, Vol. 9, no. 4 (Philadelphia, 1942), 18–28.
1959 "Chinese Art and the Wu-sun Horse," *1959 Annual*, Art and Archaeology Division, Royal Ontario Museum (Toronto), pp. 24–31.

FITZGERALD, C. P.
1933 *Son of Heaven: A Biography of Li Shih-min, Founder of the T'ang Dynasty* (Cambridge, England, 1933).
1938 *China: A Short Cultural History* (New York and London, 1938).
1947 "The Consequences of the Rebellion of An Lu-shan upon the Population of the T'ang Dynasty," *Philobiblon*, Vol. 2, no. 1 (September, 1947), 4–11.

FLETCHER, T. B., and C. M. INGLIS
1924 *Birds of an Indian Garden* (Calcutta and Simla, 1924).

FORBES, R. J.
1955 *Studies in Ancient Technology*, Vol. I (Leiden, 1955).

FRANKE, H.
1955 "Some Remarks on Yang Yü and His Shan-chü hsin-hua," *Journal of Oriental Studies*, Vol. II, no. 2 (Hongkong, July, 1955), 302–308.

FRIEDERICHS, HEINZ F.
1933 "Zur Kenntnis der frühgeschichtlichen Tierwelt Südwestasiens; unter besonderer Berüchtsichtigung der neuen Funde von Monhenjo-daro, Ur, Tell Halaf und Maikop," *Der Alte Orient*, Vol. 32 (1933), 45 pp.

FUJITA TOYOHACHI
1943 "Menka mempu ni kan-suru kodai Shinajin no chishiki," *Tōzai kōsha-shi no kenkyū, Nan-kai hen* (1943), 533–584.

VON GABAIN, ANNEMARIE
1961 "Das uigurische Königsreich von Chotscho, 850–1250," *Sitzungsberichte* der Deutschen Akademie der Wissenschaften zu Berlin, Klasse für Sprachen, Literatur und Kunst (1961, nr. 5).

GARNER, SIR HARRY
1955 "Chinese Art, Venice, 1954," *Oriental Art,* n.s., Vol. I, no. 2 (Summer, 1955), 66–70.

GERNET, JACQUES
1956 "Les aspects économiques du bouddhisme dans la société chinoise du ve au xe siècle," *Publications de l'Ecole Française d'Extrême-Orient,* Vol. 39 (Saigon, 1956).

GERSHEVITCH, ILYA
1957 "Sissoo at Susa (O Pers. *yakā-* = *Dalbergia sissoo* Roxb.)," *Bulletin of the School of Oriental and African Studies,* Vol. 19 (1957), 317–320.

GETTENS, R. J.
1950 "Lapis lazuli and ultramarine in ancient times," *Alumni: Revue du cercle des Alumni des Fondations Scientifiques,* Vol. 19 (Brussels, 1950), 342–357.

GILES, H. A.
1923 *Gems of Chinese Literature,* Vol. I (Shanghai, 1923).

GILES, LIONEL
1932 "A Chinese Geographical Text of the Ninth Century," *Bulletin of the School of Oriental and African Studies,* Vol. 6 (1932), 825–846.

1935 "Dated Chinese Manuscripts in the Stein Collection: II, Seventh Century A.D.," *Bulletin of the School of Oriental and African Studies,* Vol. 8 (1935), 1–26.

1937 "Dated Chinese Manuscripts in the Stein Collection: III, Eighth Century A.D.," *Bulletin of the School of Oriental and African Studies,* Vol. 9 (1937), 1–25.

1957 *Descriptive Catalogue of the Chinese Manuscripts from Tunhuang in the British Museum* (London, 1957).

GLAESSER, GUSTAV
1957 "Painting in Ancient Pjandžikent," *East and West,* Vol. 8 (1957), 199–215.

GODE, P. K.
1949 "History of Ambergris in India Between About A.D. 700 and 1900," *Chymia,* Vol. 2 (1949), 51–56.

GOODRICH, L. C.
1931 "Negroes in China," *Bulletin of the Catholic University of Peking,* Vol. 8 (December, 1931), 137–139.

1959 *A Short History of the Chinese People,* 3rd edition (New York, 1959).

GRAY, BASIL
1959 *Buddhist Cave Paintings at Tun-huang,* with photographs by J. B. Vincent (London, 1959).

GRIESSMAIER, VIKTOR
1933 "Die granulierte Goldschnalle," *Wiener Beiträge zur Kunst- und Kulturgeschichte Asiens,* Vol. 7 (Studien zur Kunst der Han-Zeit, Die Ausgrabungen von Lo-lang in Korea, 1933), 31–38.

GRIGSON, GEOFFREY
1947 *The Harp of Aeolus and Other Essays on Art, Literature, and Nature* (London, 1947).

GROUSSET, RÉNÉ

1932 *In the Footsteps of the Buddha,* transl. by Mariette Leon (London, 1932).

1948 *De la Grèce a la Chine* (Monaco, 1948).

VAN GULIK, R. H.

1954 "The 'Mango' Trick in China: An Essay on Taoist Magic," *Transactions of the Asiatic Society of Japan,* ser. 3, Vol. III (December, 1954), 117–175.

GYLLENSWÄRD, BO

1958 "Ekolsund: An Historic Swedish Country House with World-Famous Chinese Collections," *Connoisseur,* American edition (March, 1959), pp. 2–7.

HACKMANN, HEINRICH

1951–1954 *Erklärendes Wörterbuch zum Chinesischen Buddhismus: Chinesisch-Sanskrit-Deutch* (Leiden, 1951–1954).

HAN CHÜEH

1953 "Tiao p'i k'ao," *Ta-lu tsa-chih,* Vol. 6 (1953), 390–393.

HAN WAI-TOON

1941 "Lung nao hsiang k'ao," *Journal of the South Seas Society,* Vol. II, no. 1/3 (1941), 3–17.

HANSFORD, S. HOWARD

1957 *The Seligman Collection of Oriental Art: I. Chinese, Central Asian and Luristān Bronzes and Chinese Jades and Sculptures* (London, 1957).

HARADA YOSHITO

1939 "The Interchange of Eastern and Western Culture as Evidenced in the Shô-sô-in Treasures," *Memoirs of the Research Department of the Toyo Bunko,* Vol. 11 (Tokyo, 1939), 55–78.

1944 *Tōa ko-bunka kenkyū,* 3rd edition (Tokyo, 1944).

HARICH-SCHNEIDER, ETA

1954 "The Rhythmical Patterns in Gagaku and Bugaku," *Ethno-musicologica,* Vol. 3 (Leiden, 1954).

HARVEY, E. NEWTON

1957 *A History of Luminescence from the Earliest Times Until 1900* (Philadelphia, 1957).

HARVEY, G. E.

1925 *History of Burma, from the Earliest Times to 10 March, 1824, the Beginning of the English Conquest* (London, 1925).

ḤASAN, ḤĀDĪ

1928 *A History of Persian Navigation* (London, 1928).

HASTINGS, J., ed.

1927 *Encyclopaedia of Religion and Ethics* (New York, 1917–1927).

HAYASHI KENZŌ

1925 "Hō-kin kō," *Shinagaku,* Vol. 8 (1925), 447–456.

HIRAOKA TAKEO, ed.

1956 *Chōan to Rakuyō* (Kyoto, 1956).

1958 *Rihaku no sakuhin* (Kyoto, 1958).

HIRTH, F.

1885 *China and the Roman Orient: Researches into Their Ancient and Mediaeval Relations as Represented in Old Chinese Records* (Leipsic, Munich, Shanghai, Hongkong, 1885).

HIRTH, F., and ROCKHILL, W. W.

1911 *Chau Ju-kua: His Work on the Chinese and Arab Trade in the Twelfth and Thirteenth Centuries, Entitled Chu-fan-chï* (St. Petersburg, Russia, 1911).

Ho Ping-Yü and Joseph Needham

1959 "Theories of Categories in Early Mediaeval Chinese Alchemy," *Journal of the Warburg and Courtauld Institutes,* Vol. 22 (1959), 173–210.

1959a "Elixir Poisoning in Mediaeval China," *Janus,* Vol. 48 (1959), 221–251.

1959b "The Laboratory Equipment of the Early Mediaeval Chinese Alchemists," *Ambix,* Vol. 7 (1959), 57–115.

Holmes, Urban T.

1934 "Mediaeval Gem Stones," *Speculum,* Vol. 9 (1934), 195–204.

Horn, Paul, and Georg Steindorff, eds.

1891 "Sassanidische Siegelsteine," *Mitteilungen aus den Orientalischen Sammlungen, Königliche Museen zu Berlin,* Vol. 4 (1891), 1–49.

Hornell, James

1946 "The Role of Birds in Early Navigation," *Antiquity,* Vol. 20 (1946), 142–149.

Hou K'uan-chao

1957 *Kuang-chou chih-wu chien-so-piao* (Shanghai, 1957).

Hourani, G. F.

1951 *Arab Seafaring in the Indian Ocean in Ancient and Early Medieval Times* (Princeton, 1951).

Hsia Nai

1957 "Chung-kuo tsui-chin fa-hsien-ti Po-szu Sa-shan-ch'ao yin-pi," *K'ao-ku hsüeh-pao,* Vol. 16 (1957), 49–60.

1958 "Ch'ing-hai Hsi-ning ch'u-t'u-ti Po-szu Sa-shan-ch'ao yin-pi," *K'ao-ku hsüeh-pao,* Vol. 19 (1958), 105–110.

Hsiang Ta

1933 *T'ang-tai Ch'ang-an yü Hsi-yü wen-ming* (*Yen-ching hsüeh-pao chuan-hao* chih 2; Peking, 1933).

1957 *T'ang-tai Ch'ang-an yü Hsi-yü wen-ming,* enlarged edition (Peking, 1957).

Hsü Sung

1902 *T'ang liang ching ch'eng fang k'ao* (edition of 1902 reproduced in Hiraoka [1956]).

Huard, Pierre, and Wong, M.

1957 "Structure de la Médicine chinoise," *Bulletin de la Société des Etudes Indochinoises* (Saigon, 1957).

1958 *Evolution de la matière médicale chinoise* (Leiden, 1958).

Huber, E.

1906 "Termes Persans dans l'astrologie bouddhique chinoise" ("Etudes de littérature bouddhique," VII), *Bulletin de l'Ecole Française d'Extrême-Orient,* Vol. 6 (1906), 39–43.

Hung, William

1952 *Tu Fu, China's Greatest Poet* (Cambridge, Mass., 1952).

Ishibashi Gorō

1901 "Tō-Sō jidai no Shina enkai bōeki narabi ni bōekikō ni tsuite," *Shigaku zasshi,* Vol. 12 (1901), 952–975, 1051–1077, 1298–1314.

Ishida Mikinosuke

1932 "Etudes sino-iraniennes, I. A propos du *Hou-siuan-wou,*" *Memoirs of the Research Department of the Toyo Bunko,* Vol. 6 (Tokyo, 1932), 61–76.

1942 *Chōan no haru,* 3rd edition (Tokyo, 1942).

1948 *Tō-shi sōshō* (Tokyo, 1948).

ISHIDA, MOSAKU, and GUNICHI WADA
1954 *The Shosoin: An Eighth-Century Treasure-House,* English résumé by Jiro Harada (Tokyo, Osaka, and Moji, 1954).

JANSON, H. W.
1952 *Apes and Ape Lore in the Middle Ages and the Renaissance* (London, 1952).

JAYNE, H. H. F.
1941 "Maitreya and Guardians," *Bulletin of the University Museum,* Vol. 9 no. 4 (Philadelphia, 1941), 7.

JENYNS, R. SOAME
1954 "Chinese Carvings in Elephant Ivory," *Transactions of the Oriental Ceramic Society, 1951–1952, 1952–1953* (London, 1954), 37–59.
1957 "The Chinese Rhinoceros and Chinese Carvings in Rhinoceros Horn," *Transactions of the Oriental Ceramic Society, 1954–1955* (London, 1957), 31–62.

KATÔ, SHIGESHI
1936 "On the Hang or the Association of Merchants in China, with Especial Reference to the Institution in the T'ang and Sung Periods," *Memoirs of the Research Department of the Toyo Bunko,* Vol. 8 (Tokyo, 1936), 45–83.

KELLER, CONRAD
1902 *Die Abstammung der ältesten Haustiere* (Zürich, 1902).

KELLER, OTTO
1909 *Die Antike Tierwelt,* Vol. I (Leipzig, 1909).
1913 *Die Antike Tierwelt,* Vol. II (Leipzig, 1913).

KIANG CHAO-YUAN
1937 *Le voyage dans la Chine ancienne considéré principalement sous son aspect magique et religeux,* Vol. I, transl. by Fan Jen (Shanghai, 1937).

KIMURA KŌICHI
1942 "Honzō," *Shina chiri rekishi daikei,* Vol. 8 (Tokyo, 1942), 187–217.
1946 *Kan-wa yakumei mokuroku* (Tokyo, 1946).
1954 "Ancient Drugs Preserved in the Shōsōin," *Occasional Papers of the Kansai Asiatic Society,* no. 1 (Kyoto, 1954).

KISHIBE SHIGEO
1948 *Tōyō no gakki to sono rekishi* (Tokyo, 1948).
1952 "Seiiki-gaku tōryū ni okeru kogaku raichō no igi, " *Rekishi to bunka: Rekishi-gaku kenkyū hōkoku,* Vol. I (Tōkyō Daigaku kyōikugakubu jimbun-kagaku-ka kiyō; Tokyo, 1952), 67–90.
1954 "The Origin of the K'ung-hou (Chinese Harp): A Companion Study to 'The Origin of the P'i-p'a,' " *Tōyō Ongaku Kenkyū,* transl. by Leo M. Traynor (Tokyo, 1954).
1955 "Tō-dai gikan no soshiki," *Kodai kenkyū 2: Rekishigaku kenkyū hōkoku,* Vol. III, no 5 (Tōkyō Daigaku kyōikugakubu jimbun-kagaku-ka kiyō; Tokyo, 1955), 133–186.
1956 "Zen-Shoku Shiso Ō Ken kanza sekichō no nijūshi gakugi ni tsuite," *Kokusai tōhō gakusha kaigi kiyō,* Vol. 1 (1956), 9–21.

K'UNG TE
1934 *Wai-tsu yin-yüeh liu-ch'uan Chung-kuo shih* (Shanghai, 1934).

KUWABARA JITSUZŌ
1930 *T'ang Sung shih-tai chung-hsi t'ung-shang shih,* transl. by Feng Yu (Shanghai, 1930).

LAUFER, BERTHOLD

1905   "Historical Jottings on Amber in Asia," *Memoirs of the American Anthropological Association,* Vol. 1 (1905–1907), 211–244.

1909   *Chinese Pottery of the Han Dynasty* (Leiden, 1909).

1913   "Arabic and Chinese Trade in Walrus and Narwhal Ivory," *T'oung Pao,* Vol. 14 (1913), 315–364.

1913a   *Notes on Turquoise in the East,* Field Museum of Natural History, Publication 169, Anthropological Series, Vol. 13, no. 1 (Chicago, 1913).

1914   "Bird Divination Among the Tibetans," *T'oung Pao,* Vol. 15 (1914), 1–110.

1914a   *Chinese Clay Figures: Part I. Prolegomena on the History of Defensive Armor,* Field Museum of Natural History, Publication 177, Anthropological Series, Vol. 13, no. 2 (Chicago, 1914).

1915   "Asbestos and Salamander: An Essay in Chinese and Hellenistic Folk-Lore," *T'oung Pao,* Vol. 16 (1915), 299–373.

1915a   "Three Tokharian Bagatelles," *T'oung Pao,* Vol. 16 (1915), 272–281.

1915b   "Viḍaṅga and Cubebs," *T'oung Pao,* Vol. 16 (1915), 282–288.

1915c   *The Diamond: A Study in Chinese and Hellenistic Folklore,* Field Museum of Natural History, Anthropological Series, Vol. 15, no. 1 (Chicago, 1915).

1915d   "The Story of the Pinna and the Syrian Lamb," *Journal of American Folk-Lore,* Vol. 28 (1915), 103–128.

1915e   "Optical Lenses," *T'oung Pao,* Vol. 16 (1915), 169–228.

1915f   "Burning-Lenses in India," *T'oung Pao,* Vol. 16 (1915), 562–563.

1916   "Supplementary Notes on Walrus and Narwhal Ivory," *T'oung Pao,* Vol. 17 (1916), 348–389.

1918   "Malabathron," *Journal Asiatique,* 11th ser., Vol. 12 (1918), 5–49.

1919   *Sino-Iranica: Chinese Contributions to the History of Civilization in Ancient Iran, with Special Reference to the History of Cultivated Plants and Products,* Field Museum of Natural History, Publication 201, Anthropological Series, Vol. 15, no. 3 (Chicago, 1919).

1923   *Oriental Theatricals,* Field Museum of Natural History, Department of Anthropology Guide, Pt. 1 (Chicago, 1923).

1923a   "Review of V. W. F. Collier, *Dogs of China and Japan in Nature and Art,*" *Isis,* Vol. 5 (1923), 444–445.

1925   *Ivory in China,* Field Museum of Natural History, Anthropology Leaflet 21 (Chicago, 1925).

1926   *Ostrich Egg-Shell Cups of Mesopotamia and the Ostrich in Ancient and Modern Times,* Field Museum of Natural History, Anthropology Leaflet 23 (Chicago, 1926).

1937   *Felt: How It Was Made and Used in Ancient Times and a Brief Description of Modern Methods of Manufacture and Uses,* 5th printing (Chicago, 1937).

1946   *Jade: A Study in Chinese Archaeology and Religion,* 2nd edition (South Pasadena, 1946).

VON LE COQ, ALBERT

1925   *Bilderatlas zur Kunst und Kulturgeschichte Mittelasiens* (Berlin, 1925).

LESSING, F.

1935   *Über die Symbolsprache in der chinesischen Kunst* (Frankfurt am Main, n.d. [1935?]).

LÉVI, SYLVAIN
1900 "Les missions de Wang Hiuen-ts'e dans l'Inde," *Journal Asiatique*, Vol. 15 (1900), 297–341, 401–468.
1913 "Le 'tokharien B,' langue de Koutcha," *Journal Asiatique*, 11th ser., Vol. 2 (1913), 351–352.

LÉVI, S., and ED. CHAVANNES
1895 "L'Itinéraire d'*Ou-k'ong* (751–790)," *Journal Asiatique*, 9th ser., Vol. 6 (1895), 341–384.

LEVY, HOWARD S.
1951 "An Historical Introduction of the Events Which Culminated in the Huang Ch'ao Rebellion," *Phi Theta Annual*, Vol. 2 (1951), 79–103.
1955 *Biography of Huang Ch'ao*, Chinese Dynastic Histories Translations, no. 5 (Berkeley and Los Angeles, 1955).

LEWICKI, TADEUSZ
1935 "Les premiers commerçants Arabes en Chine," *Rocznik Orientalistyczny*, Vol. 11 (1935), 173–186.

LI, H. L.
1959 *The Garden Flowers of China* (New York, 1959).

LI LIN-TS'AN
1956 "Yen Li-pen chih-kung t'u," *Ta-lu tsa-chih*, Vol. 12 (1956), 33–50

LING CH'UN-SHENG
1958 "Chung-kuo chiu chih ch'i-yüan," *Chung-yang yen-chiu-yüan, Li-shih yü-yen yen-chiu-so chi-k'an*, Vol. 29, Ch'ing-chu Chao Yüan-jen Hsien-sheng liu-shih-wu sui lun-wen-chi, B (Taipei, 1958), 883–907.

LIU LING-TS'ANG
1958 *T'ang-tai jen-wu hua* (Peking, 1958).

LIU MAU-TSAI
1957 "Kulturelle Beziehungen zwischen den Ost-Türken (= T'u-küe) und China," *Central Asiatic Journal*, Vol. 3, no. 3 (1957–1958), 190–205.

LOEHR, MAX
1959 "A Propos of Two Paintings Attributed to Mi Yu-jen," *Ars Orientalis*, Vol. 3 (1959), 167–173.

LU GWEI-DJEN and JOSEPH NEEDHAM
1951 "A Contribution to the History of Chinese Dietetics," *Isis*, Vol. 42 (1951), 13–20.

LUCAS, A.
1934 *Ancient Egyptian Materials and Industries*, 2nd edition (London, 1934).

LUCE, G. H.
1924 "Countries Neighbouring Burma," *Journal of the Burma Research Society*, Vol. 14 (1924), 138–205.

LYDEKKER, R.
1898 *Wild Oxen, Sheep and Goats of All Lands: Living and Extinct* (London, 1898).
1912 *The Horse and Its Relatives* (New York, 1912).
1912a *The Ox and Its Kindred* (London, 1912).
1912b *The Sheep and Its Cousins* (London, 1912).

McDERMOTT, W. C.
1938 *The Ape in Antiquity* (Baltimore, 1938).

MACGOWAN, D. J.

 1854 "Chinese and Aztec Plumagery," *American Journal of Science and Arts,* 2nd ser., Vol. 18 (1854), 57–61.

MAENCHEN-HELFEN, OTTO

 1950 "Two Notes on the Diamond in China," *Journal of the American Oriental Society,* Vol. 70 (1950), 187–188.

 1957 "Crenelated Mane and Scabbard Slide," *Central Asiatic Journal,* Vol. 3. no. 2 (1957), 85–138.

MAHLER, JANE GASTON

 1959 *The Westerners Among the Figurines of the T'ang Dynasty of China* (Rome, 1959).

MAJUMDAR, R. C.

 1927 *Ancient Indian Colonies in the Far East: I. Champa* (Lahore, 1927).

MASPERO, H.

 1953 *Les documents chinois de la troisième expédition de Sir Aurel Stein en Asie Centrale* (London, 1953).

MASUTOMI JUNOSUKE

 1957 *Shōsōin yakubutsu wo chūshin to suru kodai sekiyaku no kenkyū, Shōsōin no kōbutsu,* Vol. I (Kyoto, 1957).

MATHEW, GERVASE

 1956 "Chinese Porcelain in East Africa and on the Coast of South Arabia," *Oriental Art,* n.s., Vol. 2 (Summer, 1956), 50–55.

MATSUI SHŪICHI

 1959 "Ro-ryū hanchin kō," *Shigaku zasshi,* Vol. 68 (1959), 1397–1432.

MEDLEY, MARGARET

 1955 "The T'ang Dynasty: A Chinese Renaissance, A.D. 618–906," *History Today,* Vol. 5, no. 4 (April, 1955), 263–271.

MERRILL, GEORGE P.

 1922 *Handbook and Descriptive Catalogue of the Collections of Gems and Precious Stones in the United States National Museum,* United States National Museum Bulletin 118 (Washington, 1922).

MILLER, ROY A.

 1959 *Accounts of Western Nations in the History of the Northern Chou Dynasty,* Chinese Dynastic History Translations, no. 6 (Berkeley and Los Angeles, 1959).

MOOKERJI, RADHA KUMUD

 1957 *Indian Shipping: A History of the Sea-Borne Trade and Maritime Activity of the Indians from the Earliest Times,* 2nd edition (Calcutta, 1957).

MURAKAMI YOSHIMI

 1955 "Tō-dai kizoku teien," *Tōhōgaku,* Vol. 11 (1955), 71–80.

NA CHIH-LIANG

 1953 "Lan-t'ien yü," *Ta-lu tsa-chih,* Vol. 7 (1953), 363–364.

NAGAHIRO, T.

 1955 "On Wei-ch'ih I-seng, a Painter of the Early T'ang Dynasty," *Oriental Art,* n.s., Vol. 1, no. 2 (Summer, 1955), 70–74.

NAKAMURA KUSHIRŌ

 1917 "Tō-jidai no Kanton," *Shigaku zasshi,* Vol. 28 (1917), 242–258, 348–368, 487–495, 552–576.

 1920 "Kanton no shōko oyobi Kanton Chōan wo renketsu suru suiro shūun no kōtsū," *Tōyōgakuhō,* Vol. 10 (1920), 244–266.

NAKANO KŌKAN
1924   *Shina no uma* (Peking, 1924).

NANJIO, BUNYIU
1883   *A Catalogue of the Chinese Translation of the Buddhist Tripiṭaka: The Sacred Canon of the Buddhists in China and Japan* (Oxford, 1883).

NEEDHAM, JOSEPH
1954   *Science and Civilisation in China,* Vol. I (Cambridge, England, 1954).
1958   *The Development of Iron and Steel Technology in China* (London, 1958).
1959   *Science and Civilisation in China,* Vol. III (Cambridge, England, 1959).
1959a "The Missing Link in Horological History: A Chinese Contribution," *Proceedings of the Royal Society,* A, 250 (1959), 147–179.

NEEDHAM, JOSEPH, WANG LING, and DEREK J. PRICE
1960   *Heavenly Clockwork: The Great Astronomical Clocks of Medieval China* (Cambridge, England, 1960).

NEEDHAM, JOSEPH, WANG LING, and K. G. ROBINSON
1962   *Science and Civilisation in China,* Vol. IV, no. 1 (Cambridge, England, 1962).

NYBERG, H. S.
1931   *Hilfsbuch des Pehlevi: II. Glossar* (Upsala, 1931).

OGAWA SHŌICHI
1957   "Ban-Tō-shi no ichimen—sono shakaisei—," *Tōkyō Shinagakuhō,* Vol. 3 (June, 1957), 97–114.

OGAWA TAMAKI
1959   "Chokuroku no uta—sono gengo to bungakushi-teki igi," *Tōhōgaku,* Vol. 18 (June, 1959), 34–44.

OSBORNE, D.
1912   *Engraved Gems, Signets, Talismans and Ornamental Intaglios* (New York, 1912).

P'AN HUAI-SU
1958   "Ts'ung ku-chin tzu-p'u lun Ch'iu-tzu-yüeh ying-hsiang-hsia-ti min-tsu yin-yüeh," *K'ao-ku hsüeh-pao,* Vol. 21 (1958), 95–124.

PARIS, PIERRE
1952   "Quelques dates pour une histoire de la jonque chinoise," *Bulletin de l'Ecole Française d'Extrême-Orient,* 46/1 (1952), 267–278, Vol. 46, no. 2 (1954), 653–655.

PELLIOT, PAUL
1903   "Le Fou-nan," *Bulletin de l'Ecole Française d'Extrême-Orient,* Vol. 3 (1903), 248–303.
1904   "Deux itinéraires de Chine en Inde à la fin du viiie siècle," *Bulletin de l'Ecole Française d'Extrême-Orient,* Vol. 4 (1904), 131–413.
1912   "Autour d'une traduction Sanskrit du *Tao-tö-king* [Tao Tê Ching]," *T'oung Pao,* Vol. 13 (1912), 350–430.
1912a "Review of Hirth and Rockhill, *Chau Ju-kua: His Work on the Chinese and Arab Trade in the Twelfth and Thirteenth Centuries, Entitled Chu-fan-chï,*" *T'oung Pao,* Vol. 13 (1912), 446–481.
1912b "Les influences iraniennes en Asie Centrale et en Extrême-Orient," *Revue d'histoire et de littérature religieuse,* n.s., Vol. 3 (1912), 97–119.
1923   "Quelques artistes des Six Dynasties et des T'ang," *T'oung Pao,* Vol. 22 (1923), 215–291.

1928 "L'édition collective des oeuvres de Wang Kouo-wei," *T'oung Pao*, Vol. 26 (1928), 113–182.

1928a "Des artisans chinois à la capitale abbasside en 751–762," *T'oung Pao*, Vol. 26 (1928), 110–112.

1959 *Notes on Marco Polo*, Vol. I (Paris, 1959).

PENZER, N. M.

1952 *Poison-Damsels and Other Essays in Folklore and Anthropology* (London, 1952).

PHILLIPS, RALPH W.

1958 "Cattle," *Scientific American* (June, 1958), pp. 51–59.

PHILLIPS, RALPH W., RAY G. JOHNSON, and RAYMOND T. MAYER

1945 *The Livestock of China* (Washington, 1945).

PO SHOU-I

1937 "Sung shih I-szu-lan chiao-t'u-ti hsiang-liao mao-i," *Yü kung*, Vol. 7, no. 4 (April, 1937), 47–77.

PRIEST, ALAN, and PAULINE SIMMONS

1931 *Chinese Textiles: An Introduction to the Study of Their History, Sources, Technique, Symbolism, and Use, Occasioned by the Exhibition of Chinese Court Robes and Accessories* (Metropolitan Museum of Art, New York, 1931).

PRŮŠEK, JAROSLAV

1939 "Researches into the Beginnings of the Chinese Popular Novel," *Archiv Orientální*, Vol. 11 (1939), 91–132.

PULLEYBLANK, E. G.

1955 *The Background of the Rebellion of An Lu-shan* (London, New York, and Toronto, 1955).

1958 "The Origins and Nature of Chattel Slavery in China," *Journal of the Economic and Social History of the Orient*, Vol. 1 (1958), 185–220.

1960 "Neo-Confucianism and Neo-Legalism in T'ang Intellectual Life, 755–805," *The Confucian Persuasion* (Stanford, 1960).

1962 "The Consonantal System of Old Chinese," *Asia Major*, Vol. 9 (1962), 58–144.

QUENNELL, PETER, transl.

1928 [Buzurg ibn Shahriyar], *The Book of the Marvels of India*, from the Arabic by L. Marcel Devic (London, 1928).

RABINOWITZ, L.

1946 "Eldad ha-Dani and China," *Jewish Quarterly Review*, Vol. 36 (1946), 231–238.

RAMSTEDT, G. J.

1949 *Studies in Korean Etymology* (Helsinki, 1949).

READ, B. E.

1932 "Chinese Materia Medica, Avian Drugs," *Peking Society of Natural History Bulletin*, Vol. VI, no. 4 (June, 1932).

1936 *Chinese Medicinal Plants from the Pen Ts'ao Kang Mu A.D. 1596*, 3rd edition (Peking, 1936).

1937 "Chinese Materia Medica, Turtle and Shellfish Drugs," *Peking Natural History Bulletin*, Vol. 12, no. 2 (December, 1937).

1943 "Influence des régions méridionales sur les médicines chinoises," *Bulletin de l'Université l'Aurore*, 3rd ser., Vol. 4 (1943), 475–483.

READ, B. E., and C. PAK

1928 "A Compendium of Minerals and Stones Used in Chinese Medicine from the Pen T'sao [sic] Kang Mu; Li Shih Chen, 1597 A.D.," *Peking Society of Natural History Bulletin*, Vol. III, no. 2 (December, 1928).

REINAUD, M.

1845   *Relations des voyages faits par les Arabes et les Persans dans l'Inde et la Chine dans le ixe s. de l'ère chrétienne,* Arab text and French transl. by M. Reinaud (Paris, 1845).

REISCHAUER, E. O.

1940   "Notes on T'ang Dynasty Sea Routes," *Harvard Journal of Asiatic Studies,* Vol. 5, no. 2 (June, 1940), 142–164.

1955   *Ennin's Diary: The Record of a Pilgrimage to China in Search of the Law* (New York, 1955).

1955a *Ennin's Travels in T'ang China* (New York, 1955).

ROCK, J. F.

1955   "The D'a Nv Funeral Ceremony with Special Reference to the Origin of Na-khi Weapons," *Anthropos,* Vol. 50 (1955), 1–31.

DES ROTOURS, R.

1947   *Traité des fonctionnaires et traité de l'armée; traduits de la nouvelle histoire des T'ang,* Vol. I, *chaps. xlvi-l* (Leyden, 1947).

1948   *Traité des fonctionnaires et traité de l'armée,* Vol. II (Leyden, 1948).

1952   "Les insignes en deux parties (*fou*) sous la dynastie des T'ang (618–907)," *T'oung Pao,* Vol. 41 (1952), 1–148.

ROUX, JEAN-PAUL

1959   "Le chameau en Asie Centrale: son nom—son élévage—sa place dans la mythologie," *Central Asiatic Journal,* Vol. 5 (1959), 27–76.

ROWLAND, BENJAMIN, JR.

1947   "Chinoiseries in T'ang Art," *Artibus Asiae,* Vol. 10 (1947), 265–282.

RUDOLPH, R. C.

1959   "Chinese Medical Stelae," *Bulletin of the Institute of History and Philology, Academia Sinica,* Vol. 30 (1959), 681–688.

SAMPSON, THEOS.

1869   "The Song of the Grape," *Notes and Queries on China and Japan,* Vol. 3 (1869), 52.

SARTON, GEORGE

1944   "Fishing with Otters (Query and Answer)," *Isis,* Vol. 35 (1944), 178.

SAUVAGET, JEAN

1948   *'Ahbār aṣ-Ṣin wa'l-Hind: Relations de la Chine et de l'Inde rédigée en 851* (Paris, 1948).

SCHAFER, E. H.

1948   "Notes on a Chinese Word for Jasmine," *Journal of the American Oriental Society,* Vol. 68 (1948), 60–65.

1950   "The Camel in China Down to the Mongol Dynasty," *Sinologica,* Vol. 2 (1950), 165–194, 263–290.

1951   "Iranian Merchants in T'ang Dynasty Tales," *Semitic and Oriental Studies Presented to William Popper,* University of California Publications in Semitic Philology, Vol. XI (1951), 403–422.

1951a "Ritual Exposure in Ancient China," *Harvard Journal of Asiatic Studies,* Vol. 14 (1951), 130–184.

1952   "The Pearl Fisheries of Ho-p'u," *Journal of the American Oriental Society,* Vol. 72 (1952), 155–168.

1954   *The Empire of Min* (Rutland, Vt., and Tokyo, 1954).

1955 "Orpiment and Realgar in Chinese Technology and Tradition," *Journal of the American Oriental Society,* Vol. 75 (1955), 73–89.

1956 'The Development of Bathing Customs in Ancient and Medieval China and the History of the Floriate Clear Palace," *Journal of the American Oriental Society,* Vol. 76 (1956), 57–82.

1956a "The Early History of Lead Pigments and Cosmetics in China," *T'oung Pao,* Vol. 44 (1956), 413–438.

1956b "Cultural History of the Elaphure," *Sinologica,* Vol. 4 (1956), 250–274.

1957 "Rosewood, Dragon's Blood, and Lac," *Journal of the American Oriental Society,* Vol. 77 (1957), 129–136.

1957a "War Elephants in Ancient and Medieval China," *Oriens,* Vol. 10 (1957), 289–291.

1959 "Falconry in T'ang Times," *T'oung Pao,* Vol. 46 (1959), 293–338.

1959a "Parrots in Medieval China," *Studia Serica Bernhard Karlgren Dedicata* (Copenhagen, 1959), pp. 271–282.

1961 *Tu Wan's Stone Catalogue of Cloudy Forest: A Commentary and Synopsis* (Berkeley and Los Angeles, 1961).

SCHAFER, E. H., and B. E. WALLACKER

1961 "Local Tribute Products of the T'ang Dynasty," *Journal of Oriental Studies,* Vol. 4 (1957–1958), 213–248.

SCHEFFER, VICTOR B.

1958 *Seals, Sea Lions and Walruses: A Review of the Pinnipedia* (Stanford, 1958).

SCHLEGEL, G.

1898 "Geographical Notes," *T'oung Pao,* Vol. 9 (1898), 50–51, 278.

SCHUYLER, MONTGOMERY

1908 "Notes on the Making of Palm-Leaf Manuscripts in Siam," *Journal of the American Oriental Society,* Vol. 29 (1908), 281–283.

SCLATER, P. L., and O. THOMAS

1897–1898 *The Book of Antelopes,* Vol. III (London, 1897–1898).

SECKEL, DIETRICH

1954 "Kirikane: Die Schnittgold-Decoration in der japanischen Kunst, ihre Technik und ihre Geschichte," *Oriens Extremus,* Vol. 1 (1954), 71–88.

SEN, SATIRANJAN

1945 "Two Medical Texts in Chinese Translation," *Visva-Bharati Annals,* Vol. I (1945), 70–95.

SHIDA FUDOMARO

1957 "Chūgoku ni okeru satō no fukyū," *Takigawa hakase kanreki kinen rombunshū,* Vol. I. *Tōyōshi* (Ueda, 1957), 125–139.

SHIH LU

1954 "Ch'i-lin chieh," *Ta-lu tsa-chih,* Vol. 9 (1954), 44, 56.

SHIH SHENG-HAN

1958 *A Preliminary Survey of the Book Ch'i Min Yao Shu: An Agricultural Encyclopaedia of the 6th Century* (Peking, 1958).

SHIRATORI KURAKICHI

1939 "The Mu-nan-chu of Ta-Ch'in and the Cintāmani of India," *Memoirs of the Research Department of the Toyo Bunko,* Vol. 11 (Tokyo, 1939), 1–54.

1956 "An New Attempt at a Solution of the Fu-lin Problem," *Memoirs of the Research Department of the Toyo Bunko,* Vol. 15 (Tokyo, 1956), 156–329.

Shōsōin
1928   *Shōsōin gyobutsu zuroku* (Tokyo, 1928–   ).
1960   *Shōsōin hōbutsu* (Tokyo, 1960–   ).

SIMMONS, PAULINE
1948   *Chinese Patterned Silks* (New York, 1948).
1956   "Some Recent Developments in Chinese Textiles Studies," *Bulletin of the Museum of Far Eastern Antiquities,* Vol. 28 (1956), 19–44.

SIRÉN, O.
1927   "Tch'ang-ngan au temps des Souei et des T'ang," *Revue des Arts Asiatiques,* Vol. 4 (1927), 40–46, 98–104.
1928   *Chinese Paintings in American Collections* (Paris and Brussels, 1928).

SITWELL, SACHEVERELL
1936   *Dance of the Quick and the Dead: An Entertainment of the Imagination* (London, 1936).
1941   *Valse des Fleurs: A Day in St. Petersburg and a Ball at the Winter Palace in 1868* (London, 1941).
1947   *The Hunters and the Hunted* (London, 1947).
1953   *Truffle Hunt* (London, 1953).

SMITH, MARION B.
1940   *Marlowe's Imagery and the Marlowe Canon* (Philadelphia, 1940).

SOOTHILL, W. E., and L. HODOUS
1937   *A Dictionary of Chinese Buddhist Terms, with Sanskrit and English Equivalents and a Sanskrit-Pali Index* (London, 1937).

SOPER, A. C.
1947   "The 'Dome of Heaven' in Asia," *Art Bulletin,* Vol. 29 (1947), 225–248.
1950   "T'ang Ch'ao Ming Hua Lu (The Famous Painters of the T'ang Dynasty) by Chu Ching-hsüan of Wu-chün Translated," *Archives of the Chinese Art Society of America,* Vol. 4 (1950), 5–28.
1951   *Kuo Jo-hsü's Experiences in Painting (T'u-hua chien-wên chih): An Eleventh-Century History of Chinese Painting Together with the Chinese Text in Facsimile* (Washington, D.C., 1951).
1958   "T'ang ch'ao ming hua lu: Celebrated Painters of the T'ang Dynasty, by Chu Ching-hsüan of T'ang," *Artibus Asiae,* Vol. 21 (1958), 204–230.

SOWERBY, A. DE C.
1937   "The Horse and Other Beasts of Burden in China," *China Journal,* Vol. 26 (1937), 282–287.
1940   *Nature in Chinese Art* (New York, 1940).

STEIN, A.
1907   *Ancient Khotan: Detailed Report of Archaeological Explorations in Chinese Turkestan* (Oxford, 1907).
1921   *Serindia: A Detailed Report of Explorations in Central Asia and Westernmost China* (Oxford, 1921).
1925   "Innermost Asia: Its Geography as a Factor in History," *Geographical Journal,* Vol. 65 (1925), 377–403, 473–501.
1928   *Innermost Asia: Detailed Report of Explorations in Central Asia, Kan-su and Eastern Īrān* (Oxford, 1928).
1933   *On Ancient Central-Asian Tracks: Brief Narrative of Three Expeditions in Innermost Asia and North-western China* (London, 1933).

STEIN, R.

1942 "Jardins en miniature d'Extrême-Orient," *Bulletin de l'Ecole Française d'Extrême-Orient,* Vol. 42 (1942), 1–104.

1947 "Le Lin-yi: sa localisation, sa contribution à la formation du Champa et ses liens avec la Chine," *Han-hiue,* Bulletin 2 du Centre d'Etudes Sinologiques de Pekin, (Pekin, 1947).

STEPHENSON, J.

1928 *The Zoological Section of the Nuzhatu-l-qulūb of Ḥamdullah al-Mustaufī al-Qazwīnī* (London, 1928).

STEWART, G. R., JR.

1930 "Color in Science and Poetry," *Scientific Monthly,* Vol. 30 (1930), 71–78.

STRACHWITZ, A. GRAF

1940 "Chinesisches T'ang-Silber und ost-westliche Kunstbeziehungen," *Ostasiatische Zeitschrift,* n.f., Vol. 15–16 (1940), 12–21.

STUART, G. A.

1911 *Chinese Materia Medica: Vegetable Kingdom* (Shanghai, 1911).

TAKAKUSU, J.

1896 *A Record of the Buddhist Religion as Practised in India and the Malay Archipelago (A.D. 671–695) by I-Tsing* (Oxford, 1896).

1928 "Aomi-no Mabito Genkai (779), *Le Voyage de Kanshin en Orient (742–754),*" *Bulletin de l'Ecole Française d'Extrême-Orient,* Vol. 28 (1928), 1–41, 441–472; Vol. 29 (1929), 47–62.

T'ANG HAO

1957 "Shih-k'ao wo-kuo Sui-T'ang i-ch'ien-ti ma-ch'iu," *Chung-kuo t'i-yü-shih ts'an-k'ao tzu-liao,* Vol. 2 (1957), 1–9.

TATE, G. H. H.

1947 *Mammals of Eastern Asia* (New York, 1947).

THOMPSON, A. P. D.

1951 "A History of the Ferret," *Journal of the History of Medicine and Allied Sciences,* Vol. 6 (1951), 471–480.

THOMPSON, R. CAMPBELL

1936 *A Dictionary of Assyrian Chemistry and Geology* (Oxford, 1936).

TORII RYŪZŌ

1946 "Shih-mien tiao-k'o chih P'o-hai-jen feng-su yü Sa-shan-shih hu-p'ing," *Yenching hsüeh-pao,* Vol. 30 (1946), 51–61.

TRUBNER, HENRY

1957 *The Arts of the T'ang Dynasty: A Loan Exhibition Organized by the Los Angeles County Museum from Collections in America, the Orient and Europe, January 8–February 17, 1957* (Los Angeles, 1957).

1959 "The Arts of the T'ang Dynasty," *Ars Orientalis,* Vol. 3 (1959), 147–152.

TWITCHETT, D. C., and A. H. CHRISTIE

1959 "A Medieval Burmese Orchestra," *Asia Major,* n.s., Vol. 7 (1959), 176–195.

VILLIERS, ALAN

1952 *Monsoon Seas: The Story of the Indian Ocean* (New York, 1952).

DE VISSER, M. W.

1920 "Die Pfauenkönigin in China und Japan," *Festschrift für Friedrich Hirth zu seinem 75. Geburtstag* (Berlin, 1920), 370–387.

WADA SEI

1947 "Shuju-kō," *Tōyōgakuhō,* Vol. 31 (1947), 345–354.

1955   "Kotsu-jaku-kō," *Tōyōgakuhō,* Vol. 38 (1955), 1–18.

WALEY, ARTHUR

1922   *The Nō Plays of Japan* (New York, 1922).

1923   "T'ai Tsung's Six Chargers," *Burlington Magazine,* Vol. 43 (September, 1923), 117–118.

1927   "Foreign Fashions: Po Chü-I (772–846)," *Forum,* Vol. 78 (July, 1927), 3.

1931   *A Catalogue of Paintings, Recovered from Tun-huang by Sir Aurel Stein, K.C.I.E., Preserved in the Sub-Department of Oriental Prints and Drawings in the British Museum, and in the Museum of Central Asian Antiquities, Delhi* (London, 1931).

1941   *Translations from the Chinese* (New York, 1941).

1952   *The Real Tripitaka, and Other Pieces* (London, 1952).

1954   "27 Poems by Han-shan," *Encounter,* Vol. 3 (1954), 3–8.

1955   "The Heavenly Horses of Ferghana: A New View," *History Today,* Vol. 5 (1955), 95–103.

1956   "Some References to Iranian Temples in the Tun-huang Region," *Bulletin of the Institute of History and Philology, Academia Sinica,* Vol. 28 (1956), 123–128.

1960   *Ballads and Stories from Tun-huang: An Anthology* (London, 1960).

1961   *Chinese Poems,* new edition (London, 1961).

WANG GUNGWU

1958   "The Nanhai Trade: A Study of the Early History of Chinese Trade in the South China Sea," *Journal of the Malayan Branch of the Royal Asiatic Society,* Vol. 31, no. 2 (June, 1958), 1–135.

WANG LING

1947   "On the Invention and Use of Gunpowder and Firearms in China," *Isis,* Vol. 37 (1947), 160–178.

WANG T'UNG-LING

1930   "T'ang Sung shih-tai chi k'ao," *Shih-hsüeh nien-pao,* Vol. 1 (1930), 21–32.

WANG YI-T'UNG

1953   "Slaves and Other Comparable Social Groups During the Northern Dynasties," *Harvard Journal of Asiatic Studies,* Vol. 16 (1953), 293–364.

WAYMAN, ALEX

1954   "Notes on the Three Myrobalans," *Phi Theta Annual,* Vol. 5 (1954–1955), 63–77.

WENLEY, A. G.

1948   "The Question of the Po-shan Hsiang-lu," *Archives of the Chinese Art Society of America,* Vol. 3 (1948–1949), 5–12.

WERTH, EMIL

1954   *Grabstock Hacke und Pflug* (Ludwigsburg, 1954).

WHEATLEY, PAUL

1961   "Geographical Notes on Some Commodities Involved in Sung Maritime Trade," *Journal of the Malayan Branch of the Royal Asiatic Society,* Vol. 32, no. 2 (1961), 1–140.

1961a   *The Golden Khersonese: Studies in the Historical Geography of the Malay Peninsula before A.D. 1500* (Kuala Lumpur, 1961).

WHITE, W. C.

1942   *Chinese Jews: A Compilation of Matters Relating to the Jews of K'aifeng Fu,* Pt. I. *Historical* (Toronto, 1942).

WILBUR, C. M.
1943 *Slavery in China During the Former Han Dynasty, 206 B.C.–A.D. 25*, Field Museum of Natural History, Anthropological Series, Vol. 34 (Chicago, 1943).

WILDER, G. D., and H. W. HUBBARD
1924 "List of the Birds of Chihli Province," *Journal of the North China Branch of the Royal Asiatic Society*, Vol. 55 (1924), 156–239.

WOLTERS, O. W.
1960 "The *Po-ssŭ* Pine Trees," *Bulletin of the School of Oriental and African Studies*, Vol. 23 (1960), 323–350.

WOOD, R. W.
1934 "The Purple Gold of Tut'ankhamūn," *Journal of Egyptian Archaeology*, Vol. 20 (1934), 62–65.

WRIGHT, A. F.
1951 "Fu I and the Rejection of Buddhism," *Journal of the History of Ideas*, Vol. 12 (1951), 33–47.
1957 "Buddhism and Chinese Culture: Phases of Interaction," *Journal of Asian Studies*, Vol. 17 (1957), 17–42.

WU CHI-YU
1959 "Trois poèmes inédits de Kouan-hieou," *Journal Asiatique*, Vol. 247 (1959), 349–379.

WU, JOHN C. H.
1939 "The Four Seasons of T'ang Poetry," Pt. X, *T'ien Hsia Monthly*, Vol. 8, no. 2 (February, 1939), 155–176.

WU, K. T.
1937 "Libraries and Book-Collecting in China Before the Invention of Printing," *T'ien Hsia Monthly*, Vol. 5, no. 3 (October, 1937), 237–260.

WU LIEN-TEH
1933 "Early Chinese Travellers and Their Successors," *Journal of the North China Branch of the Royal Asiatic Society*, Vol. 64 (1933), 1–23.

WU T'ING-HSIEH
1937 "T'ang fang chen nien piao," *Erh shih wu shih pu pien*, Vol. 6 (Shanghai, 1937), 186–192.

WYLIE, A.
1867 *Notes on Chinese Literature with Introductory Remarks on the Progressive Advancement of the Art* (Shanghai and London, 1867).

YABUUTI, KIYOSI
1954 "Indian and Arabian Astronomy in China" (transl. by L. Hurvitz), *Silver Jubilee Volume of the Zinbun-Kagaku-Kenkyusyo Kyoto University* (Kyoto, 1954), 585–603.

YAMADA, KENTARO
1954 "A Study on the Introduction of An-hsi-hsiang in China and that of Gum Benzoin in Europe," I, *Kinki daigaku Sekai keizai kenkyūjo hōkoku*, Vol. 5 (1954); II, *ibid.*, Vol. 7 (1955).
1955 "A Short History of Ambergris by the Arabs and Chinese in the Indian Ocean," I, *Report of the Institute of World Economics, the Kinki University*, Vol. 8 (1955).
1956 "Nyūkō motsuyō shi josetsu," *Shōgaku kensan* (Fukuda Yoshitarō Sensei kanreki shukuga kinen) (Kobe, 1956), pp. 201–236.
1956a "A Short History of Ambergris by the Arabs and Chinese in the Indian Ocean,"

II, *Report of the Institute of World Economics, the Kinki University*, Vol. 11 (1956).

1957 *Tōzai kōyaku shi*, 2nd edition (Tokyo, 1957).

1958 "Yashitsumei, matsuri, sokei (Jasminum) *kō*," *Oriental Studies in Honour of Juntaro Ishihama on the Occasion of His Seventieth Birthday* (Osaka, 1958), pp. 589–602 (reprint).

1959 "Perusya-Arabya-jin no daru-chini (dār-čīnī, shina-no-ki, sunawachi nikkei) to iū shōhinmei ni tsuite," *Momoyama gakuin daigaku keizaigaku ronshū*, Vol. 1 (1959), 131–150.

YANG, LIEN-SHENG

1952 "Hostages in Chinese History," *Harvard Journal of Asiatic Studies*, Vol. 15 (December, 1952), 507–521.

1955 "Notes on Maspero's *Les documents chinois de la troisième expédition de Sir Aurel Stein en Asie centrale*," *Harvard Journal of Asiatic Studies*, Vol. 18 (1955), 142–158.

1955a "Review of J. Needham, *Science and Civilisation in China*, I," *Harvard Journal of Asiatic Studies*, Vol. 18 (1955), 269–283.

YEH CHING-YÜAN

1958 "Chung-kuo wen-hsien-shang-ti kan-chü tsai-p'ei," *Nung-hsüeh i-ch'an yen-chiu chi-k'an*, Vol. 1 (1958), 109–163.

YEH TE-LU

1942 "Ch'i-yao-li ju Chung-kuo piao," *Fu-jen hsüeh-chih*, Vol. 11 (1942), 137–157.

1947 "T'ang-tai hu-shang yü chu-pao," *Fu-jen hsüeh-pao*, Vol. 15 (1947), 101–103.

YEN KENG-WANG

1954 "T'ang-tai kuo-nei chiao-t'ung yü tu-shih," *Ta-lu tsa-chih*, Vol. 8 (1954), 99–101.

YETTS, W. PERCIVAL

1934 "The Horse: A Factor in Early Chinese History," *Eurasia Septentrionalis Antiqua*, Vol. 9 (Minns Volume, 1934), 231–255.

YULE, HENRY, and A. C. BURNELL

1903 *Hobson-Jobson; A Glossary of Colloquial Anglo-Indian Words and Phrases, and of Kindred Terms, Etymological, Historical, Geographical and Discursive* (London, 1903).

YÜ CHING-JANG

1954 "Po-szu tsao," *Ta-lu tsa-chih*, Vol. 8 (1954), 193–195.

1955 "Yü-chin yü Yü-chin-hsiang," *Ta-lu tsa-chih*, Vol. 11 (1955), 33–37.

YÜ FEI-AN

1955 *Chung-kuo-hua yen-se-ti yen-chiu* (Peking, 1955).

YÜ KUNG-KU

1934 "Chia Tan yü Mo-ni-chiao," *Yü kung*, Vol. 2, no. 4 (October, 1934), 8–9.

VON ZACH, ERWIN

1952 *Tu Fu's Gedichte*, Harvard-Yenching Institute Series, Vol. I (Cambridge, 1952).

Glossary A

NAMES AND TITLES

*·A-lâ-puən 阿羅本
*B'iwăd-lək 吠勒
Bnam 扶南
Chāch 拓支, 拓折, 赭時, 拓羯, 者古, 石
Chang Chi 張籍
Chang Chiao 張晈
Chang Chih-ho 張志和
Chang Chou 張舟
Chang Hsüan 張萱
Chang I-ch'ao 張義潮
Chang Kao 張杲
Chang Nan-pen 張南本
Chang Ting 張鼎
Chang Ts'an 張參
Chang Yen 張垔
Chang Yen-yüan 張彥遠
Che-chih chi 拓技妓
Chen (River) 溱
Chen-chou 真州
Chen Ch'üan 甄權
Ch'en-liu 陳留
Cheng Ch'ien 鄭虔
Cheng Yin 鄭絪
Ch'eng-chou 澄州
Ch'eng Shih-chang 程士章
Chi-chou 冀州

Chi hsien yüan 集賢院
Ch'i Chiao 齊皎
Ch'i-chou 岐州
Ch'i-lien (Mt.) 祁連
Ch'i Min 齊賈
Chia Tan 鑑
Chien-chen 劍
Chien-chou 智
Chih-meng 金
Chin-chou 涇州
Ching-chou 靖
Ching-shan (Quarter) 周
Chou-ch'eng 周
Chou Fang 周
Chou Huang 珠
Chu Ju-yü 朱
Chu Mong 朱
Chu Tz'u 朱
Chu Ying 滁州
Ch'u-chou (chap. i) 楚州
Ch'u-chou (chap. xii) 處窐
Chumul 春鶯囀
Ch'un ying chuan 忠州
Chung-chou 崇賢館
Ch'ung hsien kuan 崇文館
Ch'ung wen kuan 隆婆登
*Dabatang

The characters for the names of the authors of most books and poems quoted or referred to in this book are not listed in the Glossary. Authors of books are listed in the Bibliography and in the Index, but poets are listed only in the Index.

373

Dvāravati 墮和羅

Deva 提婆

Fan Shu 樊淑

Fang Ch'ien-li 房千里

Fang Kan 方干

Farghāna 拔汗那

Feng-*chou* (Ordos) 豐州

Feng-*chou* (Annam) 峯州

Feng Jo-fang 憑若芳

Fu-*chou* (Kiangsi) 撫州

Fu-*chou* (Kwangsi) 富州

Fu-*chou* (Szechwan) 涪州

Fu-lu-*chou* 福祿州

*G'ja-b'ji-jäp 伽毗葉

*G'ja-śjĕt-pjĕt 伽失畢

Han-shan 寒山

Heng-*chou* 恒州

Ho ch'ao huan 賀朝歡

Hsi (tribe) 奚

Hsiao Ping 蕭炳

Hsien shao yüan 仙詔院

Hsin-*chou* 信州

Hsing shan szu 興善寺

Hsü Ching-tsung 許敬宗

Hsü Shen 徐申

Hsüan-chao 玄照

Hsüan-*chou* 宣州

Hsüeh-hsi 學喜

Hu Ch'ien 胡度

Hu-*chou* 湖州

Hu Kuei 胡瓌

Hua-*chou* 華州

Hua tu szu 化度寺

Huan-*chou* 驩州

Hui-*chou* 會州

Hui-yüan 慧遠

Jāguda 謝颶

Jambi 占卑

Jao-le 饒樂

Kabūdhān 曹

*Kaga 訶伽

Kalaviṅka (Karyōbin) 迦陵頻迦

Kalinga 訶陵

Kan-*chou* 甘州

Kao-liang 高涼

*Kapi 伽昆

*Kâp-miet 閣蔑

Kashmir 箇失蜜

Kat-kat Zāngī 葛葛僧祇

Khuttal 胃

*Kjɒp-t́śja 朅

Kirghiz 黠戛斯

*Kju-d'âm Sjĕt-d'ât 瞿曇悉達

*Kju-ləu-mjĕt 拘汗彌

K'o-han-na 可汗那

Ku Yin 顧愔

Kua-*chou* 瓜州

Kuan-hsiu 貫休

Kuang yün t'an 廣運潭

Kuei-*chou* 嬀州

Kumādh 俱密

K'un-lun 崑崙

K'un-wu 昆吾

K'ung K'uei 孔戣

Kuo-*chou* 虢州

K'uo-*chou* 廓州

Kurrung (Kut-lun) 胃論

Kurung (Ku-lung) 古龍

Kushaniyah 何

*Xâ-b'ji-śię 訶慈伽

*Xuo-dz'i 呼楞灘

Lankāvatāra-sūtra 伽經己乾

Li (River) 灕

Li Cheng-chi 李正己

Li cheng tien 正殿

Li Ch'eng-ch'ien 承勳

Li Chi 李漸

Li Chien 漸州

Li-*chou* 利州

Li Chung-ho 李仲和玉

Li Ch'ün-yü 李華昉

Li Fang 李昉

Li Han 李漢

Li Heng 李衡

Li Hsüan 李珙

Li Hsün 李珣

Li Kao 李皋

Li Mien 李勉

Li Pi 李沁伯時

Li Po-shih 李伯蘇沙

Li Su-sha 李蘇端昌

Li Tuan 李端

Li Yüan-ch'ang 李邑元

*Ljəm-jəp 林邑氏

*Ljəm-źię 林氏水

Lien-shui 漣水

Ling-*chou* 靈州

Ling hua szu	靈華寺	
Liu Po-ch'u	劉伯芻	
Liu Tz'u	劉泚	
Liu Yen-shih	劉言史	
Lo-chiang	羅江	
Lu-*chou* (Annam)	陸州	
Lu-*chou* (Shansi)	潞州	
Lu Chün	盧均	
Lu lung	盧龍	
Lu-mei	盧眉	
Lu Szu-tao	盧思道	
Lu Yü	陸羽	
Lu Yüan-jui	路元叡	
Lung (River)	瀧	
Lung-*chou*	龍州	
Lung-pien	龍編	
Lü Li	呂禮	
Lü Shu	呂述	
Ma Chou	馬周	
Mabito Makumon	真人莫門	
Māimargh	米	
Meng Shen	孟詵	
Merv (?Mu)	穆	
Ming-yüan	明遠	
*Mi̯uən-tân	文單	
Mo-ho	靺鞨	
Nandī	那提	
*Nəu-d'â-ɣuân (Dagon)	搙陀洹水	
Ni Jo-shui	倪若水	
*Niei-niet-ṣi	泥涅師	
Ning-*chou*	寧州	
Niu Shang-shih	牛上士	
Pa-tou	拔豆	
Pao Chi	包佶	
Pao-*chou*	保州	
Pao ying szu	寶應寺	
P'ei Chü	裴矩	
P'ei Hsing	裴鉶	
P'ei Shu-t'ung	裴叔通	
*Pək-i̯əp	北邑	
Pi Shih-to	畢師鐸	
Pien Luan	邊鸞	
Pin-*chou* (Kwangtung)	賓州	
Pin-*chou* (Shensi)	豳州	
P'ing-k'ang (Quarter)	平康	
P'ing-lu	平陸	
*P'i̯uət-niet	拂涅	
Po-lü	勃律	
Po Ming-ta	白明達	

Po [or Pa]-t'ou	撥 [鉢,拔] 頭	
P'o hu ch'i han	潑胡乞寒	
P'o-li (Bali)	婆利	
P'o-lü (Baros)	婆律	
Po ma kuo	駮馬國	
P'u-an	普安	
*Puâ-tâ-li̯ək	波多力	
Pyū	驃	
Qaqola	伽古羅,迦拘勒	
Qurïqan	骨利幹	
*Sâm-b'âk	三泊	
*Sâm-b'i̯uət-dz'iei (Serboza, Zabedj, etc. Cf. Śrībhoja)	三佛齊	
Sha-*chou*	沙州	
Shang-mi	商彌	
Shighnān	識匿	
Shih-wei (*Siet-jʷei)	室韋	
Shindu	申屠	
Sir-tardush	薛延陀	
Śrībhoja	尸利佛誓	
Su-hsieh-li-fa-wu-lan	蘇頡利發屋蘭	
Su O	蘇鶚	
Su Pien	蘇弁	
Su Ting-fang	蘇定方	
Sui-*chou*	嶲州	
Sui-yang	睢陽	
Sun Ch'eng-yu	孫承祐	
Sun Ju	孫儒	
Sun Szu-miao	孫思邈	
Ta yü ling	大庾嶺	
Tabaristan	陀拔斯單	
Tai	代	
Tai-*chou*	代州	
Tan-*chou*	丹州	
Tan-tan	丹丹	
Tao-hsüan	道璿	
Tao-sheng	道生	
Teng-*chou*	登州	
Tiao Kuang	刁光	
Tölös	鐵勒	
Toquz-Oghuz (Chiu hsing)	九姓	
Ts'ai-*chou*	蔡州	
Tsang-ko	牂柯	
Ts'ao Mu-kuang	曹務光	
Tseng-ch'i	鄫期	
Tsou (a monk)	鄒	
Ts'ui Jen-liang	崔仁亮	
Tsung Ch'u-k'o	宗楚客	

375

Tu Hsün-ch'üeh	鶴		
*T'uət-mjię	荀 施 渾		
Tuman	彌		
Tung-tan	受 丹 策 仲		
Turgäch	騎 州 羅 許		
Tzu-*chou*	梓		
*Ulaghun	烏 玄		
Wakhsh	烏 彎		
Wan			
Wang Hsüan-ts'e	王 玄		
Wang Mao-chung	王 毛 錺		
Wang O	王 勃		
Wang Po	王 熹		
Wang T'ao	王 定		
Wang Ting	王 延		
Wang Yen-pin	王 濵 彬		
Wei (Korea)	魏 微		
Wei Cheng	章 堅		
Wei Chien	維 州		
Wei-*chou*	章 莊		
Wei Chuang	章 巨 源		
Wei Chü-yüan	章		
Wei Kao			

Wei Shan-fu	甫 亦 玄 風		
Wei Shu	山 述 無 城 言 古		
Wei Wu-t'ien	章 章 無 道 景 瑀 長 師		
Wu Tao-hsüan	章 章 吳 陽 揚 閭 顏 瑩 渝		
Yang Ch'eng	陽 揚		
Yang Ching-feng	南		
Yang Yü	世		
Yen Ch'ang-yen	鎮 遠 載 滋		
Yen Shih-ku	元 元 元 袁		
Ying-*chou*	陽 州 陽 府 博		
Yü			
Yü Shih-nan			
Yüan Chen			
Yüan-ta			
Yüan Tsai			
Yüan Tzu			
Yü-ch'ih I-seng	尉 乙 僧		
Yüeh-*chou*	越		
Yüeh Huan	樂		
Yung-*chou*	永		
Yung-*fu*	驍		
*Ẓiäm-pâk			

Glossary B

WORDS

*â-dzʻi-bʻuət-tʻâ-ni	阿慈勒他你	chiao hsü	椒糈 (醑)
*â-lək-bʻuət	阿勒勃	chiao-liao	僬僚 = 鷦鷯
*â-ma-lək	阿麻勒	chiao-nao	鵁魗
*â-muât	阿末	chiao-yao	僬僥
*â-ngjʷɕi	阿魏	chieh-ku	羯鼓
*âm-lâ	菴羅	chien	監
*âm-muâ-lək	菴摩勒	chin ("brocade")	錦
An-hsi hsiang	安息香	chin ("spittle")	津
aṅkwa	阿魏	chʻin	琴
apursāmā	阿勃參	chʻin huo	笒簩
*bʻɒk-dʻiep	白氎	ching	京
*bʻieng (an aromatic)	瓶	ching tʻien	敬田
bīrzai	齊	chʻing	青
*bʻji-gʻjəp	鵯鶋	chʻing lang-kan	青琅玕
*bʻji-lji-lək	毗梨勒	chʻing tai	青黛
*bʻuâ-lâ-tək	婆羅得	chiu	九
*bʻuân-dʻᶻâ-kʻja	咩荼佉	chiu chih	九執
*bʻwât-lân	拔蘭	chiu hu-tzu	酒胡子
champa(ka)	薝蔔	chʻiung-chʻiung	芎藭
cheng	笙	chʻou	紬
cherpādh	撥攋	chu	柱
chi chʻü	枳朐	chu-lai	朱來
chi niu	楬牛	chü-hsü	駏驉
chʻi chʻiang	漆搶	chʻü-shu	氍毹
chʻi yao	七曜	chüan	絹
chia	夹	chüeh-tʻi	駃騠
chia chien	甲煎	chün	駿
chia hsiang	甲香	chʻün	群橦
chia shan	假山	*dʻân	特
chiao chiu	椒酒	*dʻək	特樓
chiao han	鮫函	*dzʻan (an aromatic)	檀

377

*dʑ'i̯uĕt	逄荃	ju hsiang	乳香
fan	梵	(kala)viṅka	頻迦
fan chia	梵夾	kan-lang	橄欖
fang	坊	*kân-dʻâ	乾陀
fei-fei	狒狒	*kɒng (an aromatic)	耕薑
*gharnoudja (*γuât-nəu-dʑ'ia) 活稽蛇		*kəu-piek	結
*g'i̯əu	釳	khār-burra	敦羅
*g'i̯u-g'i̯əu	氍毹	khelbānita	頓勃梨他
*g'i̯u-si̯u	氍氀	*ki̯ɒp-puâi	刧貝
han hsiao	含笑	*ki̯ĕt-puâi	吉貝
hang	行	*kiet-sat	結殺
hang t'ou	行頭	*k'i̯ĕt-tâ	詰多
heng tao	橫刀	*ki̯uən-li̯uk	薰陸渠
hiṅgu	形虞, 薰渠	*ki̯ʷo-g'i̯ʷo	車渠
ho ("woolen")	褐	k'o szu	刻絲
ho shih	鶴虱	k'u	窟
hsi lin chia	細鱗甲	kua	騙
hsia ting shui	下碇稅	kuan chün	蕾菌
hsiang li	香貍	kuang-lang	桄榔
hsiao ("syrinx")	簫	*kuət-nʷat	骨貀
hsiao ("melt")	消閑	*kuət-tuət	骨鶻
hsien	仙	kumuda	俱物頭
hsien mao	仙茅	k'un-pu (kompo)	昆布
hsien shu	仙樹	*kuo-puâi	古貝
hsing-hsing	猩猩	*kuttut (see *kuət-tuət)	
hsiung huang	雄黃	*χâ-liei-lək	訶黎勒
hsüan	玄	*χâ-lji-lək	呵黎勒
hsün lung	薰籠	*χək-mi̯ĕt-mi̯əu-nji	黑密牟尼
hu ("tablet")	笏	*χuo-pɒk	琥珀
hu chi	胡姬	la	膃肭
hu hsüan nü	胡旋女	lan	蘭
hu huang lien	胡黃連	lang-kan	琅玕
hu shih	胡市	liang	麖
hu t'eng wu	胡騰舞	Ling-ling hsiang	零陵香
hua lü	花釳	liu-li	琉璃
huan	黃	lo	駱
huang hsieh	黃屑	lo-le	羅勒
huang lu	黃蘆	lou	驢
huo hsiang	藿香, 鷖	lung hsien	龍涎
i ("jet")	翳	*luo-ʼuâi	蘆檔
i chih tzu	益智子	lü	璐
i tao	儀刀	ma-nao	瑪碯
*i̯a-sâi-muân	耶漫	mang hsiao	芒茅
*i̯a-si̯ĕt-mi̯ʷeng	耶悉茗	mao	茅
*i̯än-γuo-sâk	延胡索	mei ("decoy")	媒
*i̯ĕn-pʷat	印八	mi-li	薯羅
jan she	蚺蛇	ming kuang chia	明光甲
jila	薔蘿	ming t'ang	明堂
*i̯i̯ʷat-nâk	越諾	mirdāsang	密佗僧

*mi̯u-d'ź'i̯ək	無　食刀
mo tao	陌刀
mu ch'iang	木槍
mu hsiang	木香
*muâ-dz'ək	摩澤
*muât-lji	茉莉
*muət	沕
*nai-gi	柰　柢　勒
*ngi̯wɒn-dz'i-lək	元　慈　勒
*ngi̯wok	玉
nīla-utpala	泥　攮　鉢　羅
*njau-ṣa	硇砂
*noudyi (*neu-d'i̯ĕ)	耨　池　菁時
*nuo-ɬuâi	奴　禄
*ńźi̯wok-źi	褥
pa ("snake")	巴
p'ai ts'ao hsiang	排草香
*palinga	波稜　田
pei t'ien	悲盆　山
p'en shan	盆
pi(*pi̯äk)	碧
pi kan	碧玕　麻
pi ma	蓖麻
pi-li	篳篥
p'i ("cattle")	羆
p'i ("bear")	羆
*piɒk	駸
p'iao	扁　青
pien ch'ing	篳　撥　鶏
*pi̯ĕt-puât-lji	批　鶏　製
*p'iei-kap	批　頬
*p'iei-kiep	鐴
pin	釟
ping wan	萍　蓬　草
p'ing p'eng ts'ao	平　脱　鶏
p'ing t'o	鶏　附　子
*pjie-kap	白　合　香
po fu tzu	百　璃　木
po ho hsiang	破　藥
po-li	舶
po mu	舶　腳　子
p'o	婆　羅　仙
p'o chüeh	補　醉　多
p'o-lo-men-tzu	貝　硝　葜
pu tsui hsien	朴　蒲　羅
*puâi-tâ	顧
p'u hsiao	
p'u-k'uei	
*p'uâ-lâ	

*p'uân-d''a	般　茶
*-rāḵ	勒　寶
*sât-pâu	薩　瑟
*ṣɒt-ṣɒt	瑟　瑟
se	瑟
se-se (see *ṣɒt-ṣɒt)	
*səng-g'ji	僧　祇　都
*seng-g'jie	僧　祇　都
shad	殺
shen tu	神
shih	純　十
shih chi	十　石　驥　箸
shih ch'un	石　流渠　黄
shih liu huang	石　鮮
*si̯än-g'i̯wo	鮮　子　砂
śiśäk	獅　子　蜜
*si̯uk-ṣa-mi̯ĕt	縮　砂　甲
so-tzu chia	鎮　子
su-ho	蘇　合　牝
*suân-ngiei	狻　兒
szu	兒
szu chüeh	四　絕　毯
ta ch'iu	打　鵬　砂
ta p'eng sha	大　瑁　羅
tai-mei	玳　除　黄
*tâm-lâ	搗　駒　鈍
t'ao-t'u	駒　氍
*t'âp-teng	藤　邸
t'eng huang	郎　笛
ti ("godown")	邸　笛
ti ("flute")	跳　鯉　迦
t'iao t'ing	底　野　靛
*tiei-ia-ka	澱　店
tien ("indigo")	驛　豆　驕　寇
tien ("shop")	店
t'o-hsi	鍮
tou-k'ou	柘　碎
t'ou	摩　煎
*tśi̯a-p'iek	賀　汗　虜
*tśi̯äm (trâm)	驅　驄　釀
*tsi̯än (an aromatic)	鍍　醾
*tśi̯ĕt-ɣân	秃
*tṣi̯ə-ngi̯u	檀
ts'ung	塵
tu	
t'u-mi	
*t'uk-təng	
t'ung ("deer")	
t'ung ("cotton")	

t'ung (tree)	桐	wu chi yüeh yen	吳起越殷 艶
tzu	緇	yang ping fang	越坊
tzu ts'ai	紫菜	yang sui	姓病
tz'u huang	雌黃	yin yen	陽卯 煡壂
*ˑuət-ni̯uk (*or* -nʷat)	膃肭	ying yü	莫莫
varṇakā (*see* *ji̯ʷat-nâk)		yü	鍮魚 袋
viḍaṅga	畢澄茄	yü tai	
vilenga	毗陵茄	yüeh yen ching shu	越 艶 荆嵊
wei-mao	帷帽	*źi̯ang-tsi̯ʷo	上 沮
wo	猧, 矮, *cf.* 倭	*źi̯əp-bˑi̯ʷɒt	什 伐

Index

Abbāsid, 9, 12, 26. *See also* Arab, Islam

Aborigines, 45

Abrasive, 109

Abū Hasan, 173

Abū Zayd, 164, 176

Aconite, 180

Acorn, 208

Aelian, 209, 210

Africa (African), 46, 47, 48, 171, 191

Agate, 220, 228, 231, 259. *See also* Carnelian, Chalcedony

agnimaṇi, 237

Agnus scythicus. See Earth-born sheep

Ahura-Mazda, 53, 158, 257. *See also* Mazdean

Ala-yondlu, 62

Aladdin, 246

Alchemist (alchemy), 120, 170, 177, 181, 182, 190, 213, 217, 218, 219, 220, 227, 238, 255, 256, 257

Alexandria, 144

Alfalfa, 143

Almond, 141, 142

Aloeswood, 38, 125, 138, 158-165 *passim,* 173, 175, 180, 252, 253

Alum, 20, 217

Alunogen, 217

Amber, 14, 39, 135, 161, 232, 233, 247-249, 267

Ambergris, 166, 174-175

Amboina, 101

Amoghavajra, 99, 222, 265, 270, 275, 276

Amulet, 167. *See also* Apotropaion, Talisman

Amur cork tree, 208. *See also* Phellodendron

An Lu-shan. *See* Rokhshan

Andaman, 135

Angkor, 80

Anhwei, 140, 180

Animals, 32; as omens, 235

Annam (Annamese), 5, 11, 80, 81, 110, 111, 115, 134, 136, 141, 146, 152, 164, 166, 171, 175, 186, 191, 192, 201, 206, 209, 210, 221, 240, 241, 245, 251, 252, 255, 258. *See also* Vietnam

Antimony, 162, 257

Ape, 209, 210

Aphrodisiac, 157-158, 181, 192, 212

Apotropaion, 109, 165, 170, 181, 220, 225, 249. *See also* Demon, Talisman

Appliqué, 240, 252

Apricot, 181

Aquilaria. See Aloeswood

Arab (Arabian, Arabic), 9, 13-26 *passim,* 31, 38, 46, 49, 60, 62, 64, 85, 101, 136, 142, 147, 151, 166, 169-174 *passim,* 185-189 *passim,* 198, 199, 218, 234, 237, 242, 251, 257, 258, 268. *See also* Abbāsid

Arab horse, 61, 62

Archaism, 168, 199. *See also* Imagery

Architecture, 160, 164, 165, 232

Arhat, 32

Aristotle, 209

Armillary sphere, 276

Armor, 32, 107, 109, 134, 225, 230, 260-262

Aromatics, 18, 124, 136, 138, 149, 155-175, 226. *See also* Incense, Perfume

Arrow, 80, 167, 181, 264; head of, 257; shaft of, 153

Arsenic, 180, 220. *See also* Orpiment, Realgar

Art, 103, 111, 132, 267. *See also* Painting

Asafetida, 188

Asbestos, 44, 199-200. *See also* Salamander

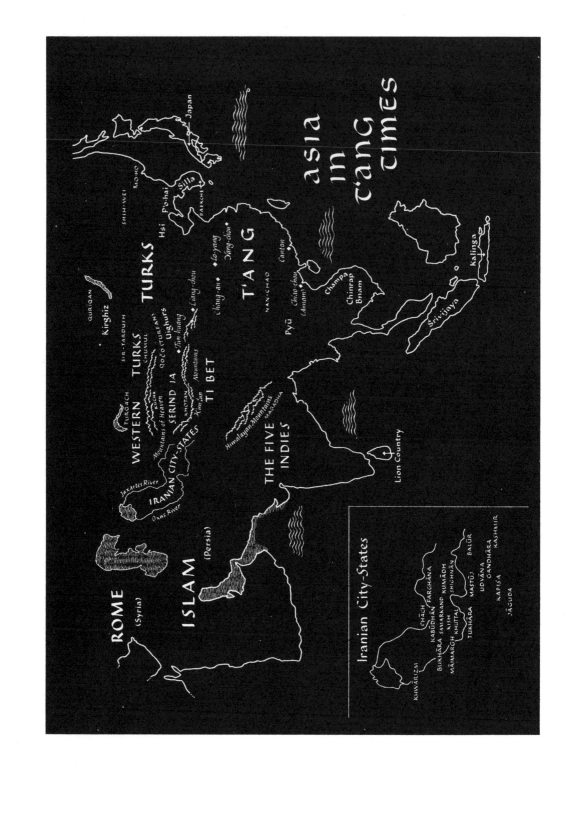

asia in t'ang times

ROME
(Syria)

ISLAM
(Persia)

TURKS

WESTERN TURKS

TURGACH

QURIQAN

Kirghiz

SIR-TARDUSH

CHUMUL

Uighurs

QOČO (TURFAN)

KUCHA

Mountains of Heaven

KHOTAN

Kun-lun Mountains

SERINDIA

IRANIAN CITY-STATES

Jaxartes River

Oxus River

TIBET

Tun-huang

Liang-chou

Chang-an

Lo-yang

Yang-chou

T'ANG

NAN-CHAO

Pyū

Chiao-chou
(Annam)

Champa

Chinrap
Bnam

Srivijaya

Canton

Kalinga

Himalayan Mountains

MAGADHA

THE FIVE INDIES

Lion Country

SHIH-WEI

KO-HO

Hsi Po-hai

Silla

PAEKCHE

Japan

Iranian City-States

KHWĀRIZM

CHĀCH

FARGHĀNA

BUKHĀRA

SAMARKAND

KUMĀDH

MĀIMARGH

KISH

SHIGHNĀN

KHUTTAL

TUKHĀRA

MASTŪJ

BALŪR

UDYĀNA

GANDHĀRA

KASHMIR

KAPIŚA

JĀGUDA

KABŪDHĀN